TYR

Myth—Culture—Tradition

TYR

Myth—Culture—Tradition

Edited by
Joshua Buckley and
Michael Moynihan

3

ULTRA
Atlanta, Georgia
2007–2008

TYR: Myth—Culture—Tradition
Volume 3, 2007
Editors: Joshua Buckley and Michael Moynihan.

Typeset by Joshua Buckley.

Contributors: Alain de Benoist, Jónína K. Berg, Collin Cleary, Marco Deplano, Andreas Diesel, Vilius Rudra Dundzila, Stephen Edred Flowers, Andrea Gál, Joscelyn Godwin, Jon Graham, Elizabeth Griffin, Carlos F. W. B. Hagen-Lautrup III, Róbert Horváth, Thierry Jolif, Gordon Kennedy, Annie Le Brun, Annabel Lee, Pentti Linkola, Christopher McIntosh, Thomas Naylor, Géza von Neményi, Michael O'Meara, Nigel Pennick, Ian Read, James Reagan, Ike Vil, Markus Wolff.

Special thanks to Jon Aaron, Liberty Buckley, Collin Cleary, Madeline von Foerster, Randall Hyman, Greg Johnson, Andrew King, Sol Kjøk, Kate Kretz, Roland Kroell, Annabel Lee, Stephen O'Malley, Random House Children's Books, Jim Silva, Turid Spildo, Dominik Tischleder, and Jerry Uelsmann.

Note: The reader may notice occasional stylistic inconsistencies between articles, as we have retained conventional British spellings and punctuation at the request of some contributors.

©2007, Ultra Publishing. All rights reserved. Copyrights for individual articles rest with the respective contributors. No part of this journal may be reproduced, transmitted, or utilized in any form or by any means without the express written permission of the publishers and/or authors, with the exception of brief quotations embodied in literary articles or reviews. To contact the publishers or authors, write to the address below.

Additional copies of this volume are available for $25.00 postpaid in the USA or $35.00 airmail postpaid elsewhere from:

Ultra
Post Office Box 11736
Atlanta, GA 30355
USA

Email: <elecampane@bellsouth.net>

ISSN: 1538-9413
ISBN: 0-9720292-3-0
ISBN-13: 978-0-9720292-3-0

Contents

Editorial Preface..9

Cipherspace..13
by Thomas Naylor

Catastrophe Pending..45
by Annie Le Brun

Survival Theory...51
by Pentti Linkola

The Primordial and the Perennial: Tradition in the
Thought of Martin Heidegger and Julius Evola.......................67
by Michael O'Meara

Spiritual Authority and Temporal Power................................89
by Alain de Benoist

Weaving the Web of Wyrd..111
by Nigel Pennick

The Abode of the Gods and the Great Beyond:
On the Imaginal and *Post Mortem* States in Celtic Tradition...127
by Thierry Jolif

Code of Blood: Counterfeits of Tradition from
The Spear of Destiny to *The DaVinci Code*............................147
by Stephen Edred Flowers

Esotericism Without Religion:
Philip Pullman's *His Dark Materials*...................................155
by Joscelyn Godwin

Humour in the Icelandic Sagas...173
by Ian Read

Rune Song or Magic Charms?
An Investigation of the *Hávamál*..183
by Geza von Neményi

Children of the *Sonne*: *Wandervögel*, Reformers,
Hippies, Greens, *Naturmenschen*, and Ferals............................193
by Gordon Kennedy

Carl Larsson's Greatest Sacrifice:
The Saga of *Midvinterblot*..215
by Michael Moynihan

Iceland's Pagan Renaissance..249
by Christopher McIntosh

Sveinbjörn Beinteinsson: A Personal Reminiscence..................263
by Jónína K. Berg

Selected Poems..273
by Sveinbjörn Beinteinsson

Baltic Lithuanian Religion and Romuva.....................................279
by Vilius Rudra Dundzila

The End Times According to the Indo-European Worldview:
Textual Selections From Four Traditions with Commentary..361
by James Reagan

A Modern *Minnesänger*: An Interview with Roland Kroell........369
by Michael Moynihan

Bitter Troubadour: An Interview with Andrew King................387
by Andreas Diesel and Marco Deplano

Reviews: Music..409

Review Essay: Paganism Without Gods....................................429
by Collin Cleary

Review Essay: A Critique of *Against the Modern
World* by Mark Sedgwick...449
by Róbert Horváth

Reviews: Books..463

About the Editors..517

About the Contributors...518

About the Cover Artist..526

Dedication..529

Editorial Preface

This issue of *TYR* has been a long time in the making. In the interval, many readers have undoubtedly questioned our claim that this is an "annual" journal, and for that we apologize. Mostly, we ask the forgiveness of our contributors, who have waited so patiently to see their work in print. While on hiatus, we have pursued other projects, honored educational and work commitments, and expanded our families. Hopefully, the extraordinary size and scope of this issue have been worth the wait. *TYR* will continue to appear on a regular basis, with each issue being published as time and resources allow. Rumors of our deaths have been greatly exaggerated.

Regarding the controversies generated by our last issue, and those that will inevitably follow from this one: we embrace them. The only thing we ask of our critics, and of our readers, is that they approach the journal on its own terms. Do not criticize us because *TYR* is not the publication *you* want it to be. As we have tried to emphasize in the past, we make no pretense of speaking for *anyone's* political, religious, or cultural movement—although many such movements are represented in *TYR*. We see the radical traditionalism articulated on the back cover of this and previous volumes as a nexus where any number of different ideas might intersect. Taken as a whole, it is our hope that this collection should be regarded as a self-contained milieu, at least as long as the reader is immersed in it.

One unifying theme that runs throughout these pages is the contrast (and often conflict) between *culture* and *civilization*. Our obvious antipathy for the civilization of the modern West has chafed more than a few readers, just as our considerable reservations about the technological apparatus of modern society are unsettling for those whose lives are closely intertwined with technology—and this now includes just about all of us. Of course, critiques of civilization are as old as the West itself. One early example is the Roman senator and historian Cornelius Tacitus's pioneering work of ethnography, the *Germania*. In its original sense, the word "civilization" (from *civis*—the status of citizenship) was used to describe the urban, sophisticated (and, after Constantine, *Christian*) society at the heart of the Empire. This was distinguished from the largely rural world of the *pagani*, or pagans, who lived on the outskirts of the city. But unlike most Romans, who looked on these unassimilated outsiders with contempt, Tacitus recognized in the ancient Germans certain virtues long lost to his civilized fellow countrymen. The eighteenth-century exaltation of the noble savage was a continuation of this tradition. Though even more fanciful in terms of any actual underlying historical basis, it was a useful attempt to dismantle the idea that the creation of civilization represented the apex of historical progress.

For many philosophers of history, culture and civilization are hardly synonymous. Culture is dynamic, organic, and rooted, while civilization is stilting, regimented, and cosmopolitan. The German philosopher Johann Gottfried von Herder contrasted the *Volk* stage of history, in which human cultures were self-contained, holistic, and bounded by tradition, with the "historical" stage of history, characterized by the spread of urban civilization. This was surely an influence on Oswald Spengler who, writing over a hundred years later, described civilization (which he equated with the *megalopolis*) as the final, terminal stage of culture. For Spengler, culture is the unified spiritual expression of a *people*, while civilization is the soulless, mechanized expression of a *mass*.

This pessimistic assessment is now more true than ever, when—with a few notable exceptions that merely prove the rule—civilization has become a genuinely global phenomenon. No longer bounded by the *limes* of the Empire, it spans its reach wherever there are cell-phone towers and fiber-optic networks, satellite dishes and Internet connections.

Consider that paramount symbol of global mobility, the international airport. Most of us have had the experience of being stuck in an airport for hours, or even days, with little else to do but watch the airport people go by. The first thing one notices is how much they look alike. Despite coming and going from every corner of the globe, and accounting for the odd Hare Krishna or Sikh, they are wearing the same t-shirts, sneakers, and baseball caps. They are listening to the same music on their portable media devices, and looking at the same websites on their laptop computers. (How many people do you know, for example, whose sense of self is circumscribed by a profile on MySpace or Facebook?) Their overstuffed bellies are filled with the same processed foods. No matter where they are going, it will be very much like the places they have left. The airport people are eminently civilized (just look how well they stand in line!), yet they have very little culture.

Editorial Preface

The preceding might be read as a measure of our misanthropy, but this is not the intent. We will be the first to admit that there are exceptions to these rather unfortunate generalizations and yet—once again—these merely reinforce the rule. In this issue of *TYR*, a number of essays directly address some of the issues surrounding modern civilization. Thomas Naylor dissects the sorry state of twenty-first-century America in "Cipherspace," and the French critic Annie Le Brun examines the Unabomber's radical response to the technological society in "Catastrophe Pending." Perhaps the most incendiary text featured here is "Survival Theory" by the infamous Finnish eco-philosopher Pentti Linkola. There is little doubt as to Linkola's misanthropy, and even *we* find his bold prescription for saving the planet a bitter pill to swallow. However, we challenge our readers to refute the grim reality of his analysis.

When we invoke the "myths, culture, and social institutions of pre-Christian, pre-modern Europe," we do so not out of mere antiquarian interest or a need to escape into historical fantasy. On a fundamental level, this is still the stuff of life, though it may be well submerged beneath the veneer of the modern world. We are deeply intrigued by the worldview that informed the minds of our ancestors, and the religious and magical practices that were part of their lives, but we have no desire to deck ourselves out in anachronistic costumes or re-enact ancient battles. By looking to the origins of our culture, what we hope to find is an alternative to the asphalt wasteland of our data-drenched civilization. This is a revolution in the most radical sense of the word: a turning back to the roots to reclaim a new beginning.

—The Editors, fall 2007

Dominion Press Is Proud to
Announce the Publication of

Confessions of a Radical Traditionalist
by John Michell

Confessions of a Radical Traditionalist is a wide-ranging collection of colourful essays by English author and philosopher John Michell. For those readers only familiar with his better-known writings on Earth Mysteries, unusual phenomena, and eccentric figures, much of the material here will be a pleasant surprise.

Since its inception, Michell has regularly contributed to the monthly magazine *The Oldie*, one of Britain's best-kept publishing secrets. Michell's column, "An Orthodox Voice," is a perpetual font of erudite insights, charming commentaries, wittily scathing pronouncements, and divine revelations. Writing in clear, exquisite language, he deftly applies traditional wisdom to various aspects of the modern conundrum. In author Patrick Harpur's words, "If Socrates had ever written a column, this would be it."

Divided into nine sections, *Confessions of a Radical Traditionalist* presents Michell's thoughts on a wealth of heretical topics, from ancient echoes of a Golden Age to the madness of modernity and the unfolding apocalypse. Undergirding these ruminations is the rarely heard perspective of an enlightened, idealistic Platonist. Even when slaying sacred cows or lancing contemporary buffoons, he never forgets that the elusive "paradise of the philosophers" is within reach for those with the strength of vision to see it. In our inverted modern world, these disarming orthodox writings have the delicious flavor of forbidden fruit.

The 108 essays in this volume have been carefully selected and introduced by Joscelyn Godwin, a long-time admirer of John Michell's work and himself an acknowledged authority in matters esoteric and metaphysical.

The book itself is beautifully typeset and produced, making use of traditional design and sacred measurements. The cover features a stunning tempera portrait of John Michell painted in 1972 by Maxwell Armfield (1881–1972), as well as artwork by Michell himself.

John Michell was born in London in 1933 and educated at Eton and Trinity College, Cambridge. His early books *The Flying Saucer Vision* (1967) and *The View Over Atlantis* (1969) exposed new generations to the lost wisdom and sacred sciences of the ancient world. His voluminous subsequent writings have chronicled forgotten eccentrics and illuminated the mysterious worlds of crop circles, ley lines, simulacra in nature, Stonehenge, and sacred geometry. Some of his recent works include *At the Center of the World* (1994), *The Temple at Jerusalem: A Revelation* (2000), and *The Measure of Albion* (with Robin Heath, 2004). An exhibit of his geometrical and other watercolour paintings was held in London in 2003 at the Christopher Gibbs Gallery. He lives in Notting Hill, London.

Clothbound, with full-color dustjacket, 5¾" x 9¼",
352 + xxi pages, Dominion, 2005, ISBN 0-9712044-4-6

"Refreshingly original, yet genuinely grounded in tradition. John Michell is wise, amusing and mischievous. He has expanded the frontiers of British sanity, and enriches the lives of those who know him and his works."
—*Rupert Sheldrake*

"A delightful read. Maybe there's some hope for the world after all!"
—*Thomas H. Naylor*, The Vermont Review of Books

As a special offer for readers of *TYR*, *Confessions of a Radical Traditionalist* is available for $25 postpaid in the U.S.A. and $40 airmail postpaid to the rest of the world. Please send check or money order payable to:

Dominion
P.O. Box 129
Waterbury Center, VT
05677

Inquiries and Paypal payments may be directed to our email address:
dominion@pshift.com

Cipherspace

Thomas Naylor

What are the people of Germany doing? Sleeping. Their sleep is filled with nightmares and anxiety, but they are sleeping. We have awaited their awakening for so long, yet they continue to remain stolid, stubborn, and silent as to the crimes committed in their names, as if the entire world and its own destiny had become alien to them. All agree: the German people slumber on amid the twilight of their gods. They do not love liberty, because they hate criticism. That is why they are sleeping today.
—Albert Camus, 17 September 1944[1]

Albert Camus's insightful description of life in Nazi Germany, which appeared in the clandestine Resistance newspaper *Combat* a few weeks after the Liberation of Paris, could just as well have been written about life in the United States during the so-called war on terrorism. Not unlike the people of Nazi Germany, the American people are also sleeping.

We slept through the annihilation of Afghanistan and Iraq, a war against Islam, the rendition of terrorist suspects, prisoner abuse and torture, the suppression of civil liberties, citizen surveillance, corporate greed, pandering to the rich and powerful, environmental degradation, pseudo-religious drivel, a foreign policy based on full-spectrum dominance and imperial overstretch, and a culture of deceit. Since we have been asleep, our massive military spending, huge budget deficits, and mounting trade deficit have gone virtually unnoticed. Our government is owned, operated, and controlled by Corporate America.

We call this global system of dominance and deceit *cipherspace*. Others call it *technofascism*. It is defined by:

1. Affluenza
2. Technomania
3. E-Mania
4. Megalomania
5. Robotism
6. Globalization
7. Imperialism

Affluenza: The All-American Bug

Like most Americans, are you spending more and enjoying it less? Do your kids still say, "We're bored. What can we do?" even though their playthings include lots of sports equipment, expensive mountain bikes, a laptop computer, a cell phone, the latest video games, and a room full of high-tech musical and video toys? Not content with your new Honda, don't you have your eye on a BMW or possibly a gas-guzzling Hummer? After skiing at Stowe, will your family accept anything less than Aspen or Whistler? And aren't you planning a vacation in Europe next summer? And maybe a second home?

How many times have your credit cards maxed out lately? What draws you to the mall, even though you hate crowds, and you complain about the schmaltzy piped-in music, the insipid smells, the fake glitter, and the plastic yuck? Do you enjoy working so hard to pay for all of the stuff your family buys—stuff which, more often than not, just sits around being used by no one?

Without realizing it, you may be suffering from a highly contagious malady, *affluenza*, popularized by the PBS television documentary bearing that title and described in the book by John deGraaf, David Wann, and Thomas H. Naylor, *Affluenza: The All-Consuming Epidemic*.[2] Millions have been infected with this virus, which originated in the United States but has spread throughout the world. Affluenza is an obsession with materialism—consumer goods and services—ranging from beer, cosmetics, clothes, cigarettes, soft drinks, junk food, recreational drugs, video games, and rock music to automobiles, computers, electronic gadgets, expensive homes, priceless art objects, high-tech health care, and international travel. In addition to viral overconsumption, those infected with this disease often suffer from overwork, stress, consumer fatigue syndrome, information overload, and stock market delirium. It affects both the rich and poor alike. The more you have, the more you want. *Enough never seems to be quite enough.*

In response to their insatiable psychological and sensory needs, those who are are obsessed with "having" often exhibit behavior patterns which are aggressive, competitive, and antagonistic. To have something is to take charge of it or to conquer it. Robbing, destroying, overpowering, and consuming are all forms of having. Those in the having mode are afraid of losing what they have either to someone else, or to the government, or possibly through death.

As a nation we are so obsessed with having that we have lost our ability to be human beings. Our happiness depends mostly on our superiority over others, our power, and our ability to manipulate others. Capitalist America may be the most efficient and productive nation in the world, but it extracts a high human cost. Conspicuous consumption is no longer a sign of our success, but rather of our spiritual vacuum.

To cope with powerlessness and our fear of nothingness, many of us spend our entire lives pretending we are invincible. One of the ways in which we try to convince ourselves that we will live forever is through conspicuous consumption. Illusory though it may be, consumption seduces us into believing we can find security and certainty in an otherwise uncertain, meaningless world. We think we can spend our way into a state of never-ending self-actualization without paying any psychological dues for our life of unrestrained pleasure. We live by the slogan, "I've got mine, Jack."

For capitalism to work effectively, those who do the work must believe that the path to happiness involves accumulating enough money and credit so that we can purchase a nicely furnished home, a couple of cars, a computer, a boat, and a college education for our kids. To be able to afford all these things, we must work hard until we retire or die. The harder we work, the more money we will have, the more we can buy, and the happier we will be—so the story goes.

But if that were really true, why are so many people in the United States so anxious, so angry, so unhappy, so cynical, and so stressed out? Why are the rates of divorce, suicide, depression, abortion, substance abuse, and incarceration so high, if the American dream is working the way it is supposed to work? Although real per capita personal consumption expenditures nearly tripled over the last half century, the percentage of people claiming to be "very happy" actually declined by 5 percent. The Index of Social Health decreased by nearly 50 percent during the past quarter century.

Even though we live in a period of unprecedented prosperity, it is also the time of the *living dead*. Many affluent Americans who deny themselves virtually nothing in the way of material satisfaction seem to be more dead than alive. As novelist Walker Percy once said, "There is something worse than being deprived of life; it is being deprived of life and not knowing it."[3]

Many of us who are infected with affluenza behave as though

we were spiritually, emotionally, and intellectually dead. The living dead can be found everywhere—surfing the Internet, checking their e-mail messages, frequenting Internet chat rooms, day trading, glued to Fox News or CNN hoping for an event in an otherwise uneventful life, driving alone across town to Wal-Mart in search of more low-priced plastic yuck, stopping at McDonald's for a quick taste-free meal, feigning interest in a mindless bureaucratic job and watching *The Bachelorette* on TV. Our government, our politicians, and the high priests of Corporate America pull our strings.

Our entire economy is driven by our intense psychological need to fill our spiritual and emotional vacuum with more and more stuff, and our illusion that the accumulation of wealth and material possessions can provide meaning to life. If we feel down and need a lift, we buy a new dress, have dinner in a nice restaurant, or rent a video. The less meaning we have in our life the easier it is to be seduced by the materialistic work hard, play hard, be happy syndrome—a syndrome that is based on a lie.

Although drug addiction is illegal, addiction to consumer goods, merchandise catalogs, shopping malls, cybershopping, and credit cards is encouraged by every form of advertising. From Washington and Corporate America the message is always the same, "Buy now and save for retirement later." If we don't play the game, the whole house of cards may come tumbling down. We have a patriotic duty to consume. To be a good American is to be a big consumer. Whoever dies with the most toys, wins the game.

The global economy is the altar at which consumers and investors alike worship. The market is our God. So important is meaninglessness to our economy that Chicago business economist David Hale once said, "The only way to prevent the global economy from going into recession is through profligate American consumerism."

During World War II, President Franklin D. Roosevelt challenged young Americans to enlist in the military and risk their lives fighting in Europe or the Pacific. To help fight terrorism President George W. Bush admonished us to shop or fly—either go to the mall and buy something or fly to Disney World. His multitrillion-dollar tax cuts were further evidence that the promotion of affluenza is official U.S. government policy.

Federal Reserve Board Chairman Alan Greenspan once congratulated the American people on the performance of the economy. And what precisely had we done to deserve such an accolade? Spend money like it was going out of style. Greenspan's

"The market is our God."
Hollywood actress Angelina Jolie as Virgin Mother.

"Blessed Art Thou," by Kate Kretz, 2006,
acrylic and oil on linen, 88" x 60".

worst nightmare was that through some medical, spiritual, or psychological miracle, an elixir might emerge which would significantly reduce the incidence of affluenza and render monetary policies impotent.

Is there enough meaninglessness in America to keep the global economy afloat? Most probably, there is. Meaninglessness breeds affluenza, and affluenza breeds more meaninglessness. Since there are no easy cures for either meaninglessness or overconsumption, there is absolutely nothing—other than ourselves—to prevent us from spending ourselves into oblivion.

Technomania: The Silent Hum of a Perfectly Running Machine

On the evening of 2 September 1998, the first-class and business-class passengers of Swissair Flight 111 bound for Zurich from New York's Kennedy International Airport had settled into their comfortable seats looking forward to a night of gourmet food, fine wines, and high-tech video entertainment aboard their McDonnell-Douglas MD-11 jumbo jet. Some were already enjoying Swissair's highly acclaimed, new $70 million state-of-the-art computer entertainment system which featured video games, music, a dozen movies, on-screen slot machines, and bingo. Bored travelers could painlessly pass the time away gambling—using their credit cards to bankroll their losses. To promote the system, Swissair ads proudly proclaimed that it provided passengers with "an unprecedented degree of freedom and choice."

Two hours out of Kennedy, Flight 111 filled with smoke, caught on fire, and plunged into the Atlantic near Peggy's Cove, Nova Scotia, killing all 229 aboard. Some Canadian and American crash investigators have speculated that the in-flight entertainment system may have sparked the fire which brought the MD-11 down—an eerie reminder of a similar crash two years earlier of TWA Flight 800, thought to have been triggered by a spark of unknown origin in the center fuel tank causing the Boeing 747 to explode off Long Island killing 230 people. A year later a third jumbo jet mysteriously crashed into the Atlantic after taking off from Kennedy Airport. For no apparent reason, one of the Egypt Air Flight 990's pilots appears deliberately to have flown the plane into the sea.

Flying across the Atlantic in a giant jumbo jet engenders feelings of freedom, power, and control—not unlike the feelings experienced by Apollo astronauts, B-2 bomber pilots, high-speed race car drivers, physicians conducting high-tech medical procedures, and genetic engineers creating designer plants, farm animals, and even babies. High-precision automobiles, high-tech musical instruments, telecommunication satellites, home computers, cell phones, and the Internet all make us feel like we are in charge. Although technology may increase efficiency, reduce drudgery, and improve the quality of life, it is also one of the most powerful metaphors for the illusion of control.

For some, technology provides more freedom, more time, and an increased sense of community. For others, it sucks up time, reduces freedom, and destroys community. Technology makes some of us faster, smarter, and richer. It makes others more materialistic and contributes to our alienation. Is technology our personal slave, or are we slaves to technology?

First-class passengers on Swissair 111 thought they were in control of their own destiny on that ill-fated night over the Atlantic even though the pilot and the co-pilot spent the final minutes of the doomed flight arguing over whether to fly the smoke-filled plane by the book or by instinct. John F. Kennedy, Jr. may have thought he was in control of his high-tech Piper Saratoga when he dove it into the sea off Martha's Vineyard. In reality, they were in control of nothing—nothing at all. Swissair filed for bankruptcy three years later.

Who could have ever imagined that a handful of terrorists armed only with box cutters and small knives could commandeer four wide-bodied jets, destroy the World Trade Center, and severely damage the Pentagon?

We place infinite faith in high-tech global communication systems, megacomputer networks, communication satellites, international electric power grids, high-speed planes and trains, and high-precision automobiles. They are our gods!

To assuage their existential pain caused by the human condition, many are easily seduced by technology—particularly big technology. Still others use technology such as the electronic media, computers, computer software, and the Internet to manipulate millions of adults and children alike. "Freedom's just another word for nothin' left to lose," sang Kris Kristofferson in "Me and Bobby McGee."

We don't just embrace new technologies, we place them on a pedestal and worship them—always in the name of progress. The automobile, television, nuclear power, the space program, high-tech weapon systems, the personal computer, and the Internet have all been viewed with God-like awe—the next panacea. It is as though the frontier spirit of the Old West has been reincarnated in the form of high-tech euphoria.

Historian David F. Noble argues in his book *The Religion of Technology* that our enchantment with technology, "the very measure of modern enlightenment," is rooted in "religious myths and ancient imaginings." He goes on to say that,

> Although today's technologists, in their sober pursuit of utility, power, and profit, seem to set society's standard for rationality, they are driven also by distant dreams, spiritual yearnings for supernatural redemption. However dazzling and daunting their display of worldly wisdom, their true inspiration lies elsewhere, in an enduring, other-worldly quest for transcendence and salvation.[4]

Since the early 1970s we have witnessed the arrival of a plethora of new high-tech gadgets ranging from voice mail, fax machines, cell phones, VCRs, camcorders, and CD players to personal computers, modems, laptop computers, video games, e-mail, and virtual-reality devices. Once they were accepted, they soon became indispensable to modern living.

Prior to the 1979 Three Mile Island nuclear accident and the meltdown of the Chernobyl nuclear power plant near Kiev, Ukraine in 1986, few technologies had been promoted as vigorously as nuclear power. Nuclear power plants were hyped by the industry as clean, quiet, cost-effective, and free of chemical or solid air pollutants. Billions of dollars were spent by the U.S. government on failed nuclear energy projects in the 1980s.

In his 1986 State of the Union address, President Ronald Reagan called for a security shield which one day could "render nuclear weapons obsolete and free mankind from the prison of nuclear terror." That Reagan was so attracted to the Strategic Defense Initiative (Star Wars) came as a surprise to no one, given his penchant for large-scale, high-tech ventures such as the B-1 bomber, the MX missile, the stealth bomber, the Trident II submarine, the Clinch River Breeder Reactor, the Space Shuttle, the space station, and the Super Collider. Reagan never encountered a high-tech weapon system he did not wish to buy—and the more expensive the better. Just as the Egyptian pharaohs had their pyramids and the Turkish sultans their mosques, so too did Reagan have his SDI.

As originally envisaged, SDI would consist of a complex network of systems including X-ray laser beams; particle beams; electromagnetic "sling-shots," which would hurl nonexplosive projectiles called "brilliant pebbles" through space at great speed; and sensing, tracking, and aiming devices. All these systems require the extraordinary coordination of advanced computers and other technologies to detect missiles, compute their trajectories, and direct intercepting weapons over great distances. There was only one hitch. Many of those who have worked on SDI have admitted that it is pure fantasy. During one nine-month period in 1999 there were six significant rocket failures related to our antimissile system resulting in losses of over $3.5 billion. In spite of the continuation of these failures, President George W. Bush, most members of Congress, and two-thirds of the American people enthusiastically support a scaled-down antimissile system similar to Reagan's dream. Whether or not it works seems to be completely irrelevant.

One Pentagon-inspired high-tech venture which never saw the light of day was the so-called Policy Analysis Market. The Defense Advanced Research Projects Agency (DARPA) proposed to launch a small-stakes Internet betting parlor to allow invited experts from government, industry, and academia to speculate on geopolitical events such as acts of terrorism, political assassinations, and guerrilla warfare. The idea was to use market forces to produce expert consensus forecasts of global political and military events which might impact national security. The public outcry against DARPA's high-tech, casino death game was so intense and so fast that the proposal was withdrawn a day later.

Through genetic enhancements and gene splicing, parents of the future will be able to design their own children, choosing whatever qualities they desire in the way of beauty, strength, intelligence, or artistic ability. The future will be just like Garrison Keillor's mythical Lake Wobegon, "where all the women are strong, the men are good-looking, and all the children are above average."

In spite of state-of-the-art nuclear power plants, sophisticated international electric power grids connecting the United States and Canada, computer controlled electronic switching networks, and modern high-tech communications equipment, tens of thousands of people in New England were powerless for over a week and nearly two million Canadians for over two weeks during the Great

Ice Storm of 1998. With four of the five major power transmission lines serving Montreal out of service, the city came perilously close to a complete power blackout. Much of New England and Quebec looked like a cross between a war zone and a frozen winter wonderland.

Then on 15 August 2003, over fifty million people in eight states and part of Canada lost power, some for as long as two days. About the Northeast power blackout Governor Bill Richardson of New Mexico and former Secretary of Energy said, "We are a major superpower with a third-world electric grid." As federal, state, and power-industry officials tried to sort out the cause of this fiasco and assign blame, no one raised the following question: "Why would any sane human being ever propose an electric power system in which fifty million people were dependent on a single interconnected grid for their power?" No one suggested subdividing the grid into smaller completely independent units. Indeed, some members of Congress called for a national grid so that the entire country could be at risk simultaneously.

Millions of Californians have also experienced repeated temporary power blackouts as a result of unencumbered corporate greed.

Size, entangling economic relationships, standardized mass production and distribution, and technological complexity are not risk-free in the electric power industry or any other industry. We are much more vulnerable than our politicians and Corporate America would have us believe.

Yet we remain mesmerized by the Internet, antimissile systems, video games, space travel, and computer-controlled financial markets. To account for the powerful influence of our irresistible attraction to computers and other high-technology there must be a psychological explanation. Have we been seduced by what English economist Joan Robinson once called, "the silent hum of a perfectly running machine; the apparent stillness of the exact balance of counteracting pressures; the automatic smooth recovery from a chance disturbance?"[5] Robinson questioned whether there was something Freudian about it. "Does it connect with a longing to return to the womb?"

But not everyone has benefited from all this technology, says David F. Noble in his book *Progress Without People*:

> In the wake of five decades of information revolution, people are now working longer hours, under worsening

conditions, with greater anxiety and stress, less skills, less security, less power, less benefits, and less pay. Information technology has clearly been developed and used during these years to deskill, discipline, and displace human labour in a global speed-up of unprecedented proportions. Those still working are the lucky ones. For the technology has been designed and deployed as well to tighten the corporate stranglehold on the world's resources, with the obvious and intended results: increasing dislocation and marginalization of a large proportion of the world's population—within as well as without the industrial countries; growing structural unemployment and the attendant emergence of a nomadic army of temporary and part-time workers; a swelling of the ranks of the perpetually impoverished; and a dramatic widening of the gap between rich and poor to nineteenth-century dimensions.[6]

Before embracing every new technology which comes our way—computerization, digitization, miniaturization, robotics, satellite communications, nanotechnology, fiber optics, the Internet, genetic engineering, and precision bombing—we need to ask the right questions. What will the technology do for people? What will it do to them? What will be the unintended side effects? How will people participate in its use? Will the technology serve us, or will we serve it?

E-Mania: Downloading the Human Mind

Before the e-bubble burst, millions had turned to cyberspace for everything from information, employment, business, shopping, entertainment, and low-cost telecommunications to more transcendental benefits such as spirituality, worship, meaning, and community. College graduates saw the Internet as a ticket to fame, fortune, financial security, self-actualization, and grassroots democracy. The Net was their virtual God—a God perceived to be much more responsive than the Biblical one. It provided an altar where the human mind could be downloaded and sacrificed for speed, greed, power, and instant gratification.

The intense frenzy with which the ubiquitous Internet was embraced was reminiscent of the nineteenth-century gold rush and Texas and California oil booms. Americans were mesmerized by the techno-hype and cant dished out by Silicon Valley, Wall Street, and the Ivory Tower.

Some saw it as our common global postal system, shopping mall, library, and university—an essential tool of life. It was also a place where you could unsuspectingly be placed under homepage arrest and detained endlessly against your will—particularly if you were easily seduced by advertising images, rock music, cool sounds, or video games.

Not since the advent of the automobile has any technology proven to be more seductive, more revered, or more mystifying than the Internet. One has the illusion of freedom, power, independence, and control as well as participation in a political system in which the individual user is in fact one of its powerless victims.

Pundits claimed that e-business, the use of PCs and the Internet within a firm, would radically transform the way megacompanies do business by extending without limit their ability to reduce average costs as output increases. However, the number of megamergers such as Enron, Global Crossing, Tyco International, and WorldCom which have gone sour casts doubt on such thinking.

Claims that information technology, the communication revolution, deregulation, and globalization would so alter the New Economy that inflation, deflation, business cycles, stock market crashes, and unemployment would vanish have proven to be premature.

With the Internet, large companies respond instantaneously to signs of softness in consumer demand by announcing plant closings and layoffs of tens of thousands. But when dozens of such companies do exactly the same thing, we soon have *recession at the speed of thought*.

To stay on top of our busy schedules we carry a cell phone, a laptop computer, and a handheld organizer as we dart from one meeting to another. Our problem is not too little information, but information overload. We are bombarded with so much information at such high rates of speed from so many computers, radios, television sets, VCRs, cell phones, fax machines, newspapers, periodicals, books, billboards, and pieces of advertising junk mail that we haven't a clue as to what to do with it all. What we need is not faster, more powerful computer chips, but more effective tools to help us make sense of all of this information.

A Stanford University survey concluded that the more time people spend online, the less time they spend with real people. For example, those who are online for over five hours per week spend less time with their family and friends; attend fewer social events; spend less time reading newspapers, watching TV, and shopping; and work more at home after hours.

A Carnegie Mellon University research study by Robert Kraut and others published in the *American Psychologist* found that the Internet may actually be bad for our psychological well being. The more time subjects in the study spent at their keyboards, the more depressed and lonely they became. "Greater use of the Internet was associated with declines in participants' communication with family members in the household, declines in the size of their social circle, and increases in their depression and loneliness."[7]

The "affordability, accessibility, and anonymity" of the Internet have spawned a new psychological disorder among men and women who seek sexual stimulation from their computers—*cybersex addiction*—according to Jane Brody in *The New York Times*.[8] Some of these addicts spend hours each day masturbating to online pornographic images or having online sex with someone they have never seen, heard, touched, felt, or smelled. Occasionally these online relationships have precipitated offline relationships and the breakup of marriages and families.

Is the Internet a new town square or a cruel hoax designed to perpetuate our separation, isolation, loneliness, and lack of community? Is it any more than a poor substitute for community in our high-speed chase to nowhere? Is it possible to experience community with someone with whom you are connected only by electronic impulses transmitted between two black boxes? We need more town squares and village greens where people can sit and talk, have a coffee, pass the time away, and experience real community. The Internet is *not* such a place.

Because e-mail messages are low-cost, fast, private, and accountable to no one, correspondents take liberties with their writing style, grammar, and the civility of their messages. Spelling errors, sentence fragments, and four-letter words are the rule with school kids and college students alike. They behave as though they are free to express any uncivil thought they ever had on e-mail—things they would never say to a person face-to-face. Is it any wonder that the intellectual content of so many e-messages is near zero, or that the Internet has contributed to the trivialization of the world?

To convince parents and teachers alike that our low-tech public schools must be computerized and every classroom connected to the Internet, IBM, Microsoft, and others have embarked on a public relations blitz. Just as Herbert Hoover once promised "a chicken in every pot," so too did President Bill Clinton promise to connect every classroom to the Internet. Virtually every public school in America is now online.

Connecting every classroom to the Net is a public relations gimmick aimed at conning Americans into believing there are high-tech, quick-fix solutions to America's public education problems—problems which are deeply rooted in excessive centralization, over regulation, and the absence of local community involvement.

At a time when many of our nation's students can't read a full-length book, write a coherent essay, or solve simple math problems, some educators are questioning the educational value of the Internet—once accepted as a virtual article of faith. There is increasing evidence that computers are not the educational panacea we have been led to believe.

Kids have access to a plethora of Web sites promoting violence, Satanic cults, drugs, alcohol, pornography, gambling, and suicide. The dehumanizing effects of kids glued to their PCs playing video games, chatting with strangers, and surfing the Net rather than playing outside, doing their homework, participating in sports, or helping around the house are immeasurable. Any kid can operate a PC, but fewer and fewer can write a poem, create an original story, compose a song, or play a musical instrument.

To see firsthand how PCs are impacting public schools, pay a visit to your local school's library. If your school is typical of most, many of the books are out-of-date and often in tatters. Yet the school's computer lab is stocked with state-of-the-art PCs and computer software—nothing but the best!

No institution has contributed more to downloading the minds of our youth than our universities with their frantic rush to the Web. The electronic God teaches that learning must be fun, fast, and facile. It encourages instant gratification, superficial research, poor writing, sloppy analysis, uncritical thinking, and unrelenting conformity. With the click of the mouse, the right answer always appears on the screen.

Many college students spend hours each day playing interactive computer games, searching the Web for visual images to be used as backgrounds for their computer screens, and illegally downloading their favorite CDs. It is not uncommon for college students to spend an evening chatting on the computer with friends who live a few feet down the hall.

An Israeli firm with the quaint name Schoolsucks.com offers college students essays, book reports, term papers, and even Ph.D. dissertations for easy downloading.

Have we not traded our own separation, alienation, meaninglessness, powerlessness, and fear of mortality—our very soul—for virtual reality?

Megalomania: Bigger Than Life

As I watched the two flaming, 110-story towers of the World Trade Center crashing down to earth on live television, I had the eerie feeling that I was witnessing the collapse of the American equivalent of the Tower of Babel.

The Biblical account of the Tower of Babel is the story of a group of Israelites in ancient Babylon who, in defiance of God's will, built for themselves a city and a pyramid-shaped tower "with its top in the sky," so that they might make a name for themselves. The tower was grounded in hubris and the belief of its builders that they were bigger than life, truly invincible. They all spoke the same language and mistakenly thought there was no limit to what they might accomplish.

God was unamused by the tower and the Israelites' sense of unity and arrogance. By confusing their language, God effectively shut down their project and scattered them over the face of the earth.

Surely there were no more important icons of America's obsession with bigness, globalization, and imperialism than the World Trade Center and the Pentagon, the other terrorist target. The unmistakable phallic message of the twin towers could have hardly gone unnoticed—particularly by Third World nations, many of whom were innocent victims of globalization and American imperialism.

Why would anyone in their right mind ever build two 110-story office buildings next to each other and then try to cram fifty thousand people into them? Why would anyone consider rebuilding them?

In the words of William H. Willimon, Dean of the Duke University Chapel, "In the process of perverted human attempts to unify and secure ourselves, we end up destroying ourselves, fracturing into a thousand different voices, falling to earth in disaster. Meltdown."[9]

Novelist Philip Roth described America's response to September 11 as "an orgy of national narcissism and a gratuitous victim mentality."[10]

Our sense of outrage at the perpetrators of these heinous crimes stems not just from the human casualties and property losses, but from the deep psychological wounds inflicted upon all of us by the terrorists who managed to pierce the heart and soul of the home of the free and the brave. The wide-bodied jets which destroyed the World Trade Center towers and deeply penetrated the Pentagon were not only a challenge to American freedom and democracy, but also to our arrogance, omnipotence, and sense of invincibility.

Neither our economic, political, technological, nor military might could protect us from a handful of terrorists. After the crushing attack, all that remained of two once-proud New York edifices was a smoldering ash heap of glass, concrete, and steel. At least symbolically, we had been rendered impotent. There could be no doubt that we were indeed vulnerable.

The terrorists exposed the fact that big buildings, big businesses, big cities, big government, and big military provide little solace to relieve the existential pain of our own separation, meaninglessness, powerlessness, and fear of death.

Robotism: Learned Helplessness

While claiming to be world-class individualists, millions of Americans behave as though they were robots—remote controlled, automatic devices which perform repetitive tasks in a seemingly human way. We pretend to be "the captain of our ship and the master of our soul," even though we all march to the beat of the same drummer. Not only do we appear to be content with our plight, but we consistently try to convince others that they should be just like us.

The cloning of Dolly, the Scottish sheep, through genetic engineering precipitated a national debate over the moral implications of human cloning. But what's the big deal about human cloning? Millions have effectively been cloned by our government, our politicians, our large corporations, our universities, and our public schools without altering a single DNA molecule.

Furthermore, no one seems to care.

Even though we all have different genetic maps, most of us think the same, vote the same, watch the same TV programs, visit the same Web sites, and buy the same consumer goods. While subscribing to an ideology that raises individualism to godlike status, most Americans are conformists.

It matters not which of the two major political parties elects the president of the United States. The results are always the same. We have a single political party, the Republican Party, disguised as a two-party system. The Democratic Party is effectively brain-dead, having had no new ideas since the 1960s. Our government is owned, operated, and controlled by Corporate America. National and Congressional elections are bought and sold to the highest bidder.

Not unlike the former Communist Party in Moscow, large American companies are among the least-democratic institutions in the world. They do everything possible to silence dissent and quell behavior which differs from the corporate norm. There are no rights to freedom of speech, freedom of assembly, freedom of the press, or due process. One can be fired on the spot at the whim of one's supervisor.

Most influential American newspapers and the five major television networks are owned by huge conglomerates. Nothing better illustrates the enormous influence of television than the overwhelming political support which American TV networks afforded Presidents Bush I and Bush II in their respective high-tech invasions of Iraq in 1991 and 2003. It was the Middle East equivalent of "cowboys and Indians." Americans were mesmerized by the one-sided patriotic hype and the apparent precision of the bloodless missile strikes. Iraqi casualties were treated as a non-event by the media.

The dumbing-down of our overcentralized, overregulated, values-free public schools is nothing new. Above all, what one learns at school is what it means to be "cool." What is cool determines how you dress, how you behave, how you speak, whether you have sex and whether you take drugs and abuse alcohol. Our schools are among our nation's more effective cloning agents. Most colleges haven't a clue as how to undo the damage wrought by four years of high school.

Nowhere is the pressure for conformity greater than in our colleges and universities. Too many students take too few courses, spend too much time grubbing for grades, drink too much, party too much, think too little and learn too little from faculties concerned more with political correctness rather than creativity, originality, morality or truth. If an undergraduate degree has any meaning anymore, it is to certify that the recipients are no different from thousands of like-minded graduates. Thus it was hardly surprising to see the cover-page article of the April 2002 issue of *Harper's* by Thomas de Zengotita entitled "The Numbing of the American Mind."

Although there is overwhelming evidence to the contrary, Microsoft's Bill Gates claims that the Internet leads to empowerment and enhanced democracy. But who is being empowered by whom? As e-mania has exploded, voter turnout has declined, as well as every other form of civic participation including involvement in religious groups, town meetings, local school activities, civic clubs, union meetings, and political organizations. People transfixed by PCs have little time to participate in anything and are a threat to no one.

Consider the case of former Vermont Governor Howard Dean's unsuccessful bid for the Democratic nomination in 2004. Before his campaign imploded in Iowa, pundits had proclaimed that Dean's use of the Internet to raise money and muster political support had redefined the political process in America. As it turned out nothing could have been further from the truth.

While Dean did indeed raise a lot of money, $50 million, some of which was generated by the Internet, he failed to translate his six hundred thousand Internet supporters into victory in a single state.

Many of Dean's on-line fans resonated to his mean-spirited, tough-talking, shoot-from-the-hip rhetoric and his attacks on the war in Iraq. Both his message and his style were clearly in sync with those who spend endless hours on the Net railing against the government, Corporate America, and the war in Iraq. On-line politicians trade heavily on the anonymity afforded them and their freedom to say anything that comes to mind, no matter how ridiculous it may appear. They are accountable to no one.

But very few of those who expound their political views in the form of blogs on the Internet know how to make a face-to-face pitch, run a political meeting, or solicit major campaign contributions. There were hundreds of Deaniacs in New Hampshire and Iowa but to little avail. They were clueless as to the social, political, and psychological skills required to win an election. These are not skills easily acquired while sitting alone in one's cubicle pretending to be involved in the political process. Elections are won and lost by real people interacting with each other face-to-face and not through an electronic black box.

Dean really didn't get it. It takes a lot more than six hundred thousand alienated desktop cowboys to be elected president of the United States. The Internet is no substitute for effective planning, organization, motivation, and execution.

Not only did Dean not reinvent American politics, but he may have lost the election because he believed his own rhetoric about on-line political campaigning. In the end, the Net could not deliver.

If one surfs the Internet one can find hundreds, if not thousands, of Web sites espousing every conceivable political philosophy. There are endless chat rooms devoted to the discussion of politics. But is anyone really listening to all of this electronic chatter? Above all, what the Net does extremely well is keep us busy—distracted from noticing what the cipherpriests are doing to us in the name of freedom and democracy.

While individual Internet junkies pretend to be doing their own thing, in reality they are insignificant pawns in a vast global experiment in commercially *controlled anarchy*. They are, in fact, doing precisely what the high priests would have them do.

Americans are bombarded with so much information at such high rates of speed that we are clueless as to how to process it all—information from cell phones, satellite TV, Palm Pilots, VCRs, DVDs, the Ethernet, and conventional radio to mention only a few sources. And now we have to deal with genetic engineering, cloning, robotics, artificial intelligence, and nanotechnology.

Through national television, the results of every conceivable international tragedy are brought into our living rooms including hurricanes, typhoons, tornadoes, earthquakes, droughts, famines, plagues, floods, plane crashes, riots, mass murders, and acts of genocide. Each evening on the local television news we are treated to a menu of homicides, mayhem, rapes, accidents, fires, and other acts of violence. The television coverage of the death of Princess Diana, the Columbine High massacre, the plight of six-year-old Cuban Elian Gonzalez, the death of Anna Nicole Smith, and the September 11 tragedy went on endlessly. What do we make of all of these tragedies over which we have no control and whose results we are powerless to affect?

Through Fox News or CNN we can witness the comings and

goings of every military dictator, every guerrilla movement, and every terrorist group in Africa, Asia, Latin America, and the Middle East. But the more we watch, the more confusing it gets. The differences between the good guys and bad guys have become increasingly blurred—particularly in the former Yugoslavia and in the Arab-Israeli conflict.

In his commencement address at Harvard University nearly three decades ago, Alexander Solzhenitsyn lamented the fact that we have forfeited the "right of the people not to know."[11] Ignorance may not be bliss, but it may be better than being overwhelmed by far more information than we can ever comprehend, process, or act upon.

Is it any wonder that so many college students are disillusioned with politics? Like experimental rats on an electric floor after experiencing learned helplessness from repeated shocks, some sit silently and motionless on the sidelines as though frozen in time. Others retreat from the world of politics to the world of hedonism, anti-establishment rock music, and substance abuse. Why should it be otherwise?

Globalization: Just Be Like Us

Globalization refers to the integrated international system of mass production, mass marketing, mass distribution, mass consumption, mega financial institutions, and global telecommunications. This global network of markets, transnational companies, and information technologies effectively eliminates the need for national political boundaries, since money, capital, goods, services, and people flow freely across national borders. Political and economic power are transferred from nation-states to transnational megacompanies accountable only to their shareholders.

Since globalization is often achieved through coercion, intimidation, exploitation, collectivism, monopoly, and American military might, local cultures, local values, local communities, and local environmental concerns often receive short shrift.

Transnational megacompanies not only tell so-called emerging market countries (most of the world) what they will produce, how it will be produced, when it will be sold, and at what price, but they also influence local working conditions, wages, benefits, and labor laws. They often dictate local government monetary, fiscal, trade, and banking policies. International money managers decide which foreign currencies are overvalued and which are not, as well as which countries should be punished for not playing by their arbitrary, self-serving rules. This is truly a one-size-fits-all game.

No photograph was ever more prophetic in portraying the future of unfettered capitalism than a picture of Ronald Reagan and Mikhail Gorbachev each wearing cowboy hats taken near the end of their political careers. So effective were Ronald Reagan and Margaret Thatcher in convincing governments everywhere to decentralize, to deregulate, to rein in organized labor, and to privatize public enterprises that transnational megacompanies like General Electric and IBM have virtually a free hand to operate globally with little or no interference from government or labor—just like the American West. They play off one country against the other in pursuit of low-wage, tax-free, regulation-free manufacturing environments.

The U.S. government, Federal Reserve Bank, International Monetary Fund, World Bank, and World Trade Organization are all committed to transforming the world economy into a giant global growth machine regulated by an international gambling casino in which resource allocation decisions are driven by a high-speed, multinational, high-tech crap shoot. Satellite communications, fiber optics, and the Internet make it possible to transform small, manageable local problems into unmanageable global problems overnight.

President Bill Clinton called for a New Global Financial Architecture. But what he proposed was nothing new at all—more trade, more budget cuts, more privatization, more foreign investment, more megamergers, more computer networks, less government control, lower interest rates, more IMF bailouts, and, as always, more economic growth. He wanted everything to be bigger, more complex, more high-tech, and more interdependent—bigger markets, bigger trade agreements, bigger loans, bigger bailouts, bigger banks and financial institutions, and bigger telecommunication networks. Our government's not-so-cryptic message to the rest of the world is: "Just be like us."

Economists justify globalization on the basis of the so-called trickle-down effect, in which the benefits of global trade to the superwealthy eventually trickle down to the poor. But half of the world's population lives on less than $2 per day, and many of these people have no access to clean water, electricity, or sanitation. World Bank figures suggest that the trickle-down effect may not be working so well. In 1987, 1.2 billion people in the world were trying to survive on one dollar a day. Now over 1.5 billion are trying to do so.

Nothing better illustrates the extent of corporate colonialism than the global empire of McDonald's. How many kids have been drawn to McDonald's worldwide by the attraction of a free plastic toy or a Michael Jordan slam-dunk? With over 30,000 restaurants operating in 120 countries, the McDonaldization of the world continues unabated. And every hamburger purchased at McDonald's drives one more nail in the coffin of each nearby neighborhood restaurant. McDonald's is no longer just a fast-food megachain but rather the defining metaphor for American economic imperialism.

McDonald's has become the subject of an increasing number of attacks by nutritionists, farmers, environmentalists, animal rights advocates, child advocacy groups, labor unions, and globalization opponents. They accuse the hamburger behemoth of promoting unhealthy food, exploiting workers, manipulating kids, harming the poor, damaging the environment, abusing animals, driving local restaurants out of business, and promoting a monocultural world.

In his broadside criticism of the fast food industry, *Fast Food Nation*, Eric Schlosser accuses McDonald's, Burger King, Wendy's, and others of "hastening the malling of our landscape, widening the chasm between the rich and poor, fueling an epidemic of obesity, and propelling the juggernaut of American cultural imperialism."[12]

McDonald's is the world's largest owner of retail property and the nation's largest buyer of beef, pork, and potatoes—and the second largest buyer of chicken behind KFC (Kentucky Fried Chicken). Schlosser makes a convincing case that the fast food industry has played a major role in transforming the American beef, pork, chicken, and potato industries into a handful of megacorporations which have almost total market control over the small farmers and producers which supply them.

According to Schlosser, the top four meatpacking firms—ConAgra, IBP, Excel, and National Beef—slaughter 84 percent of the nation's cattle. Eight chicken processors control two-thirds of the American market.

Schlosser claims that meatpacking is the most dangerous job in the United States. Working conditions in the vehemently antiunion industry are among the worst anywhere in the world. He further points out that a single fast food hamburger now contains meat from dozens or even hundreds of different cattle. The effects of tainted beef could literally reverberate around the world.

But in 2003 McDonald's got its brief comeuppance. When some of the aforementioned problems began to take their toll on sales, the company was forced to close old restaurants faster than it was opening new ones for awhile.

However, the real behemoth of Corporate America is Wal-Mart, the largest company in the world. With annual sales of over $350 billion, the Bentonville, Arkansas mega-retailer is three times the size of its nearest competitor, France's Carrefour. Every week, 138 million shoppers visit Wal-Mart's five thousand stores. In an October 2003 cover-page article entitled "Is Wal-Mart Too Powerful?" *Business Week* said, "Low prices are great. But Wal-Mart's dominance creates problems—for suppliers, workers, communities, and even American culture."[13]

Although there are no more gold rushes, railroad bonanzas, cattle booms, oil and gas windfalls, or Western land grabs, the frontier spirit of the Wild West lives on in the hearts, minds, and behavior of Wall Street high rollers and many who inhabit the executive suites of Corporate America. To assuage their narcissism, their greed, and their never-ending lust for money, power, and control, these high-tech, desktop cowboys trade heavily on megamergers and acquisitions, lucrative stock options, government subsidies, and political favors to conquer one country after another.

Just as the American frontier rewarded resourcefulness and ingenuity, encouraged individualism, and offered land and the chance for a better life, so too do corporate takeovers and megamergers offer global cowboys the possibility of fame, fortune, and enormous political power—always in the name of progress.

During the eight-year Clinton administration there were nearly seventy-five thousand mergers and acquisitions in the United States valued at over $7 trillion. This was in contrast to the twelve years of the Reagan and Bush administrations, known for their free-market oratory, in which there were fewer than forty-five thousand mergers valued at only $2 trillion.

At the apex of Soviet political influence, it's hard to imagine communist propaganda ever being as effective as our government, our media, and our academic experts in promulgating the lies, myths, and half-truths perpetrated by Wall Street and Corporate America about the benefits of global economic interdependence and technology. Many Americans were convinced by our government,

New Age swamis, crystal-ball-gazing economists, and financial gurus that this was truly the Age of Aquarius. Record-high profits, levitating stock market prices, strong economic growth and job creation, low unemployment, and scant inflation would surely last forever. Since there had been a paradigm shift in the American economy, business cycles, stock market crashes, and economic depressions were said to be anachronisms of the past. Unfortunately, such claims have proven to be spurious.

Federal Reserve Chairman Alan Greenspan described the Clinton boom at various times as a "once-in-a-generation frenzy of speculation" driven by "irrational exuberance" and "infectious greed."

The collapse of energy trading company giant Enron and telecommunications megacompany WorldCom provided at least a temporary wake-up call for Wall Street, Corporate America, the accounting profession, and the U.S. government. One of the greatest financial scandals of all time, Enron was a deceptive mixture of off-shore businesses, off-the-books loans, fake data, and creative accounting covered up by the firm's auditor Arthur Andersen. The $107 billion collapse of WorldCom resulted in the largest bankruptcy filing in American history. Unfortunately, Enron and WorldCom have proven to be the tip of the iceberg as one major company after another has been accused of shady bookkeeping or other misdeeds. Some of them include Adelphia, Computer Associates, Dynergy, ImClone, Qwest, Rite Aid, Martha Stewart, and Xerox.

When the Securities and Exchange Commission, state prosecutors, and market regulators announced a settlement with a dozen of the biggest Wall Street firms for conflicts of interest by their stock analysts, it amounted to little more than a slap on the wrist. These same firms are now pressing Congress to prevent the states from pursuing further charges against those, such as themselves, who violate security laws.

Finally, two particularly serious side effects of globalization are political and environmental instability. If by globalization one means the spread of free markets and democracy, Amy Chua has shown in her book *World on Fire* that this combination has proven to be "a recipe for instability, upheaval, and ethnic conflagration" in countries such as Indonesia, Venezuela, Zimbabwe, and the Philippines which have a market-dominant minority.[14]

The environmental consequences of globalization have proven

to be disastrous, taking the form of overmined resources, overlogged forests, overcropped farm lands, overgrazed grasslands, overdrained wetlands, overtapped groundwaters, overfished seas, and overpolluted air and water. And according to the Worldwatch Institute, these results have in turn given rise to climate changes form greenhouse gas emissions, ozone depletion, toxic build-up and dispersion, extinction and loss of biodiversity, forest loss, decline in fisheries, and scarcity of fresh water.

But in a provocative article in the March 2004 issue of *Harper's Magazine* entitled "The Collapse of Globalism," John Ralston Saul argues convincingly that globalization may soon be dead in the water. According to Saul, "Latin America no longer believes in globalization. Nor does Africa or a good part of Asia. Globalization is no longer global."[15]

Imperialism: The American Empire

As one of the most violent nations in the world, our attraction to war and military solutions to problems is nothing new. Our penchant for intergroup violence—ethnic, racial, agrarian, frontier, religious, and industrial—is without equal. Americans have always turned to violence when provoked by either domestic or foreign enemies.

Although our nation was founded on the principles of life, liberty, and the pursuit of happiness, the story of how Native Americans were relentlessly forced to abandon their homes and lands and move into Indian territories to make room for American states is a story of arrogance, greed, and raw military power. Our barbaric conquest of the Native Americans continued for several hundred years and involved many of our most cherished national heroes, including George Washington, Thomas Jefferson, James Monroe, and Andrew Jackson, to mention only a few. To add insult to injury, we have violated over three hundred treaties which we signed protecting the rights of American Indians.

With the exception of Hawaii, all of our states were pieced together from territory originally occupied by Native Americans. Some, like Louisiana and Alaska, were acquired through direct purchase from France and Russia, respectively. The military defeat of England, Mexico, and Spain paved the way for the annexation of others. The annexation of Texas, Oregon, New Mexico, and California was rationalized by the American equivalent of "Manifest

Destiny" or "God's will," as was our intervention in Cuba, Puerto Rico, Hawaii, and the Philippines.

In over two hundred years, the North American continent has never been attacked—nor even seriously threatened with invasion by Japan, Germany, the Soviet Union, or anyone else. But over a million Americans have been killed in wars and trillions of dollars have been spent by the military—$13 trillion on the Cold War alone.

Far from defending our population, our government has drafted Americans and sent them to die in the battlefields of Europe (twice), on tropical Pacific islands, and in the jungles of Southeast Asia. On dozens of occasions our political leaders have used minor incidents as provocation to justify sending troops to such far-flung places as China, Russia, Egypt, Greenland, Uruguay, the Samoa Islands, Cuba, Mexico, Haiti, Nicaragua, Panama, Grenada, Lebanon, and Iraq. Today the United States has a military presence in no less than 136 countries.

While accusing the Soviet Union of excessive military aggression, the Reagan administration was participating in nine known wars—in Afghanistan, Angola, Cambodia, Chad, El Salvador, Ethiopia, Lebanon, Morocco, and Nicaragua—not to mention our bombing of Libya, invasion of Grenada, and repeated attempts to bring down Panamanian dictator Manuel Antonio Noriega. President Bush I deployed over a half million American troops, fifty warships, and over one thousand warplanes to the Persian Gulf in 1991 at the "invitation of King Fahd of Saudi Arabia to teach Saddam Hussein a lesson." Most Americans were beside themselves over this little war. President Clinton's repeated bombing of Iraq invoked a similar response, even though the Iraqi people have never inflicted any harm on the United States. It matters not whether we send troops to Haiti, Somalia, Bosnia, or Kosovo, or bomb Afghanistan or Sudan; few Americans raise any objections whatsoever. Indeed, they seem to like it.

Although global corporate cowboys like Warren Buffet, Bill Gates, Rupert Murdoch, George Soros, and S. Robson Walton have no personal need for military weapons, the global markets, financial institutions, and communications networks on which they are dependent require political, economic, and financial stability. In a world in which the gap between the haves and have-nots continues to widen, it is not easy to maintain such stability—particularly in emerging economies in Africa, Asia, and Latin America. To ensure political stability, the United States acts as self-appointed policeman to the world. The Federal Reserve Bank, IMF, and World Bank play a similar role in preserving economic and financial stability.

Even though the U.S. government has actively promoted and subsidized the McDonaldization of the world and the paving of the earth with Wal-Marts, can it realistically protect thirty thousand McDonald's restaurants in 120 countries and nearly five thousand Wal-Marts worldwide? McDonald's restaurants have been the targets of terrorist attacks in England, France, Serbia, Turkey, and Indonesia. How safe is it for Americans to travel abroad—particularly to Third World countries?

There is no more effective way for an American president to boost his ratings in the polls than to demonize some tinhorn dictator. For example, every president since Eisenhower has used Fidel Castro as a political whipping boy. Taking his cue from British Prime Minister Margaret Thatcher, whose popularity soared after Britain's 1982 invasion of the Falkland Islands, Ronald Reagan's favorite targets—in addition to the Evil Empire—were Grenada's Maurice Bishop, Libya's Muammar Qadhafi, and Nicaragua's Daniel Ortega.

Reagan's 1983 invasion of Grenada was aimed at diverting public attention from the 241 U.S. servicemen who were killed in the bombing of the Beirut Marine headquarters. To justify this intervention, Reagan concocted a tale suggesting that the tiny island was about to come under Fidel Castro's influence. Each of these military forays resulted in dramatic increases in his popularity ratings.

The made-for-television Persian Gulf drama precipitated by Saddam Hussein's 1990 invasion of Kuwait contained all of the elements one might expect in a Tom Clancy post-cold war spy thriller—a demonic enemy, suspense, political intrigue, military heroics and Middle East oil. The bloodless, high-tech, action-packed TV series featuring surgically precise missile strikes with no visible civilian casualties was an instantaneous success with American viewers in need of a new demon to replace the Soviet Union. Ninety-five percent of the American people supported President George Herbert Walker Bush's Persian Gulf policy. Little did they know that such high-tech military adventures would become routine in the 1990s.

Without any sense of irony, Bush I condemned Saddam Hussein for replicating in Kuwait precisely what he himself had done in Panama a few months earlier; namely invading a tiny country with a huge military force and setting up a puppet government. Within a few days after Hussein invaded Kuwait, Bush I convinced most of the non-Islamic world that our former ally, whom he helped create, had become the moral equivalent of Adolf Hitler.

However, by 1998, the Iraqi dictator seemed to be losing his touch and was no longer able to sustain his image as a demonic enemy in spite of repeated military strikes on Iraq by the Clinton administration. With the simultaneous bombings of the American embassies in Kenya and Tanzania as well as frequent threats to other embassies throughout the world, the United States urgently needed a new bigger-than-life enemy to replace Saddam Hussein, who had lost some of his demonic luster. Neither Muammar Qadhafi, Fidel Castro, nor Yasser Arafat appeared to be up to the challenge.

Conveniently, during the midst of the Monica Lewinsky scandal, a promising new demon emerged—Muslim fundamentalist Osama bin Laden, a wealthy Saudi exile living in Afghanistan and thought to have been trained by the C.I.A.

Prior to Clinton's preemptive strikes against alleged international terrorist training bases in Afghanistan and a chemical plant in Sudan, few Americans had ever heard of bin Laden. Yet within a few days his name had become a household word synonymous with global terrorism. Almost overnight, bin Laden was transformed into Global Enemy Number One.

However, Saddam Hussein re-emerged as a credible threat in late 1998. The day before he was to be impeached by the U.S. House of Representatives, President Clinton ordered the U.S. military to attack Iraq again, the fourth such attack since 1993. Only the British saw fit to join the United States in this lopsided assault on Iraq. There were no American or British casualties and no Iraqi dead were ever shown on American television. The objective of the short war was to "degrade Saddam's weapons of mass destruction." It was declared a success and Clinton's popularity soared.

In March 1999, NATO was in need of a new mission to justify its post-cold war existence. With that thought in mind President Clinton bypassed the U.S. Constitution, the United Nations, and international law and led a seventy-eight day NATO attack against Yugoslavia. The nineteen-nation alliance flew thirty-five thousand missions and dropped twenty-thee thousand bombs and missiles on tiny Yugoslavia. This action was justified by the claim that Slobodan Milosevic was responsible for the deaths of two thousand Kosovars. Clinton portrayed Milosevic as the new Adolf Hitler. Yet when one hundred thousand people lost their lives in Chechnya at the hands of the Russians and eight hundred thousand were massacred in Rwanda, Clinton blinked. It was as though these were nonevents.

Unlike his father and Bill Clinton, Bush II turned up his nose at all forms of multilateralism except in the war on terrorism which at least initially attracted broad-based global support. During his first year in office he unilaterally abandoned a global warming treaty, rejected protocols enforcing a ban on germ warfare, demanded amendments to an accord on illegal sales of small arms, threatened to boycott an international conference on racism, and walked away from the 1972 Antiballistic Missile Treaty with the former Soviet Union—the bedrock on which all subsequent arms control treaties with Russia rest.

According to Thomas R. Stauffer in *The Washington Report on Middle East Affairs* (June 2003), since the end of World War II the cost to American taxpayers of support for Israel comes to $1.8 trillion.[16] Some Americans find our one-sided support of Israel and our cozy relationship with Saudi Arabia and other undemocratic Arab oil-producing states to be utterly reprehensible.

While Bush II denied any interest in a holy war with Islam, did he not inadvertently launch World War III—a global war between the haves and the have-nots? Although the invasion of Afghanistan may have been successful in silencing hundreds of Osama bin Laden's followers, whether dead or alive, bin Laden was transformed into the new Che Guevara of the poor, the powerless, and the disenfranchised worldwide. For every Muslim fundamentalist killed in Afghanistan, Iran, or Iraq or the FBI arrests in the U.S., Germany, or England, another hundred Arab, African, Asian, or Latin American dissidents may be radicalized.

Having failed in his bid to take out Osama bin Laden, eliminate the threat of terrorism, dismantle the Al Qaeda network, spin away the effects of corporate greed, and turn the ailing economy around, Bush II, like his father and Bill Clinton, decided to play the Saddam Hussein card.

Unlike bin Laden, who has always been a moving target, Hussein was much less elusive, since he rarely left Iraq. Other than the brief period when he was temporarily upstaged by bin Laden, Saddam was America's favorite demon for twelve years. He had the ability to deflect American public opinion away from virtually any serious economic, political, or social problem. This is why he was such a popular political whipping boy for our last three presidents. As we previously noted, every time Bill Clinton needed a boost in the polls, which was often, we bombed Iraq.

Because Iraq was said to have weapons of mass destruction, which could have been used against Israel or the United States, Bush II was obliged to finish the job begun by his father in 1991. So we were told. Never mind that the United States has the largest stockpile of weapons of mass destruction in history and is the only country to have ever used nuclear weapons during warfare—to kill civilians.

Did it make sense to try to pin all of the blame for global terrorism on Osama bin Laden, Saddam Hussein, and the so-called Axis of Evil? There was plenty of blame to go around. Pogo may have gotten it right on the money back in 1970, when he said, "We have met the enemy and he is us."

Notes:

1. Jacqueline Lévi-Valensi, ed., *Camus at Combat* (Princeton: Princeton University Press, 2006), p. 40.
2. San Francisco: Berrett-Koehler, 2001.
3. Walker Percy, *Signposts in a Strange Land* (New York: Strauss and Giroux, 1991), p. 163.
4. David F. Noble, *The Religion of Technology: The Divinity of Man and the Spirit of Invention* (New York: Knopf, 1997), p. 3.
5. Joan Robinson, *Economic Philosophy* (Chicago: Aldine, 1963), p. 81.
6. David F. Noble, *Progress Without People: New Technology, Unemployment, and the Message of Resistance* (Toronto: Between the Lines, 1995), p. xi.
7. Robert Kraut et al., "Internet Paradox: A Social Technology That Reduces Social Involvement and Psychological Well-Being?" *American Psychologist*, vol. 53, no. 9 (September 1998), p. 1017.
8. "Cybersex Gives Birth to a Psychological Disorder," 16 May 2000.
9. Thomas H. Naylor and William H. Willimon, *Downsizing the U.S.A.* (Grand Rapids: Eerdemans, 1997), p. 7.
10. Sam Leith, "Philip Roth attacks 'orgy of narcissism' post Sept 11," *The Telegraph*, 4 October 2002.
11. Speaking about "The Direction of the Press," he stated: "The press can both simulate public opinion and miseducate it. Thus we may see terrorists heroized, or secret matters, pertaining to one's nation's defense, publicly revealed, or we may witness shameless intrusion on the privacy of well-known people under the slogan: 'everyone is entitled to know everything.' But this is a false slogan, characteristic of a false era: people also have the right not to know, and it is a much more valuable one." <www.columbia.edu/cu/augustine/arch/solzhenitsyn/harvard1978.html>
12. See Eric Schlosser, *Fast Food Nation: The Dark Side of the All-American Meal* (Boston: Houghton Mifflin, 2001).
13. "Is Wal-Mart Too Powerful?", *Business Week*, 6 October 2003, p. 100.
14. See Amy Chua, *World on Fire: How Exporting Free Market Democracy Breeds Ethnic Hatred and Global Instability* (New York: Doubleday, 2003).
15. *Harper's*, vol. 308, no. 1846 (March 2004), p. 40.
16. See Thomas R. Stauffer, "The Costs to American Taxpayers of

the Israeli-Palestinian Conflict: $3 Trillion," p. 20.

Catastrophe Pending[1]

Annie Le Brun

What reason could there be to freely republish something that the *New York Times* and the *Washington Post* previously printed in September 1995—a text that both papers printed under threat? I am speaking of the murderous threat by an individual who defied American authority over an eighteen-year period with his booby-trapped packages mailed to various representatives of our technocratic civilization: academics, engineers, computer programmers, and so on.

What reason could there be to publish this text that specialists from every field—psychiatrists, psychologists, sociologists, and philosophers (all of whom were initially consulted by the FBI), and then the official commentators, professors, and journalists who followed on their heels—viewed unanimously as nothing but clichés directed against industrial civilization? This judgement was furthermore immediately echoed in the French press after the arrest on 3 April 1996 of the individual believed to be the author of this manifesto: in the 9 April issue of *Libération* it was described as a "muddled indictment against the alienation of industrial society," and in the 11 April issue of *L'Express* as "prose oozing with clichés from 1968 and petrified in the neo-hippie delirium of zero growth and rejection of the Information-Age Big Brother."

A consensus like this couldn't help but set off warning bells for certain people, such as myself, especially when our world so ardently defended here by so many experts has just provided us—in a span of less than two weeks' time—every possible scenario to reinforce the propositions of such a discredited text. First we have the "mad cow" crisis as an embodiment of the disdain for natural balances; then the playacting ten years after the Chernobyl catastrophe by those who caused it or did so little to fight it as proof of the collusion between physicists and those in authority. Finally, the total amnesia concerning the Tiananmen Square massacre, in order to sell our technology, can be viewed as a sign of the most serious deterioration in the state of human relations.

Moreover, because things have gone this route, none of these experts are in any position to note that the notion of criminality has become quite blurred—so why not consider the ideas of someone who wanted to have done with this situation? An individual who, while still active, had to his credit: the death in 1985 of a computer salesman, the death in 1994 of an upper-level adman of an agency associated with the oil company whose Exxon Valdez was responsible for the 1989 oil spill in Alaska, and finally the blowing to pieces of the president of the Forestry Association of California, in addition to the twenty-three victims maimed by his package bombs.

To boot, there is something fishy in the unanimity elicited by the *Unabomber* (a word coined by the FBI in regard to his first targets, university academics and airline companies). In fact, we find here groups of people who allegedly oppose one another making common cause: police and protesters, businessmen and intellectuals, and lastly the state and individuals, all joined as one in identical rejection of the "twisted genius" (as he was labeled by the 15 April edition of *U.S. News and World Report*). For the Unabomber is more than just the public enemy number one about whom we have been told. He is the Enemy.

He has, contrary to common-law criminals who are all more or less accidents of fate, chosen to reject this world. In this sense he "incarnates the greatest negativity in a society that denies any negativity," as noted by Jean-Marie Apostolides, to whom I owe my quick acquaintance with this affair. Moreover, outside of this friend whose sharp and unbiased eye I have known for a long time, not a single American academic at present has taken the Unabomber's propositions into serious consideration. If certain very rare intellectuals have accepted the interesting nature of one or another of his views, it is only to immediately insist on the aberrant nature of their entirety. This is not the case, however, for a part of the anarchist movement where discussions have multiplied in regard to this subject. This is proof that the Unabomber is undoubtedly correct in designating the academics as the most willing servants of a system from which he has broken all ties. And that is his major crime.

Since the arrest of the one-time brilliant mathematician Theodore Kaczynski, no one would doubt that there has been a clear sense of an intimate collaboration between the press and the police to impose upon this man the image of a "serial killer," one no different from all the rest. At best it is granted that he is the most educated serial killer, though it is not acknowledged that his ideas have any merit—especially ideas that have logically led him, not to contest this world, but to utterly refuse it in its organization as well as in its finality.

Hence the interest of this text, however criminal its author may be. It is without a doubt constructed from theoretical bric-a-brac. Nonetheless, it contains some impressive views on the life that we consent to lead—views whose oddity is connected to the extremely asocial nature of the life led by their author for more than eighteen years. Although distorted and distorting, these views however make us see what we will not accept, for example that "industrial-technological society cannot be reformed,"[2] by virtue of the fact that "restriction of freedom is unavoidable in industrial society."[3]

This is where the novelty of this phenomenon resides, even if one is tempted to attach it to the nihilist tradition of all or nothing. But since the Unabomber comes *after* the October Revolution, Stalinism, the fall of the Berlin Wall, as well as after the protests of the sixties, the hippiefests, ecological initiatives, and other alternative movements, the perspective is completely different. It is precisely this history against which the *Freedom Club* protests. *Freedom Club*—the entity with which the author of this manifesto, signed with the initials "FC," wished himself to be mistaken for—is, if it is to be taken at its word, one that is strictly anti-communist, anti-socialist, anti-leftist, but especially anti-science and anti-technology on the basis of natural anarchism.

After all, the Unabomber is *revolutionarily incorrect*. This is his real significance for us.

First of all, as a relentless defender of the individual, he doesn't trouble himself about anything he hasn't personally experienced. He says what he feels without any concern for appearing objective or not. It is in this manner that he proceeds with regard to the leftists of the American universities. Much has been said about his settling old scores with his former milieu. But the Unabomber developed reasons to see the latter as a fishpond of the best promoters of industrial society, to the extent that the activity of almost all of them can be summed up as envisioning this world in order to construct it, that is, ensuring its perpetuation in conformance to the system. This is what the dangerous buffoonery of "politically correct" demagoguery has no other objective than to conceal. On this point the Unabomber's judgment is final: "the goals of today's leftists are NOT in conflict with the accepted morality,"[4] even if he provides the proof for it much later, by demonstrating that "Leftism is in the long run inconsistent with ... the elimination of modern technology."[5]

Of course, by not taking the ideas he advances into account, it is easy to object to the weaknesses in his reasoning, even though he concedes at the end of his text: "Lack of sufficient information and the need for brevity made it impossible for us to formulate our assertions more precisely or add all the necessary qualifications. And of course in a discussion of this kind one must rely heavily on intuitive judgment, and that can sometimes be wrong. So we don't claim that this article expresses more than a crude approximation to the truth."[6] But is it because of the "need for brevity" that he has come to make use of "intuitive judgment," or is it not, rather, to escape "revolutionary" thought, to which he implicitly objects throughout the whole text for its abstract and dogmatic nature that has so little connection to reality?

In fact, if there is no time to lose, it is because he must transmit all the impressions of which he is certain, free to be pasted together pell-mell with whatever theoretical considerations came to mind. Thus, in the same manner he threw together his bombs, with as little elements of industrial civilization as possible, he threw together his proclamation, deliberately ignoring revolutionary rhetoric. It could even be said that his thought is apolitical just as his behavior is asocial. He has paid no heed whatsoever to everything that everyone else has felt forced to sacrifice to radical logic. He posits his ideas as acts because he formerly used acts as ideas.

With no pretensions, contrary to what has been said—"Unabomber Betrayed by His Own Pride" reads the headline of the 13 April issue of *Le Point*—this frustrated thought has the merit of revealing, by contrast, a kind of theoretical decorum which has perhaps affected revolutionary reflection, that concerns itself more with its consistency than reality. This point is far from unimportant at a time where we witness the frantic aestheticization of theories claiming to be radical, but which are not so radical as to have rendered such a process impossible. This is a danger that does not wait in ambush for the Unabomber, who pushes bad taste—in other words, honesty—so far as to announce the dangers inherent in what he proposes. Of all the world's would-be transformers, I believe he is the only one to place the terrible contract in our hands: catastrophe in payment for catastrophe. Isn't the one we design ourselves better than the one that is being prepared for us?

Is this not also the echo of another cry in the night that, for want of being understood in its time, returns here tragically deformed? At the time I became aware of this text I immediately thought once more of the revolt of André Breton, who, when confronted by the scope of the nuclear peril shortly after Hiroshima, explained: "This end of the world is not one of our choosing." But this led him to immediately conclude: "the transformation of the world, unquestionably more necessary and incomparably more urgent [...] by reason of the common threat hanging over all humanity, demands to be rethought out from top to bottom."

This was said in 1948 and no one responded to it—the leaders of the Left even less than the others. Four years later, Breton came back to the atomic question and the changes that it required: "Against his habitual laziness he [...] will have to shatter the old frameworks and so proceed to an overall recasting of ideas that today have become cut-and-dried, not one of which can be relied upon."[8] Then on 18 February 1958, facing the aggravation of this situation, together with his Surrealist friends he signed the tract entitled EXPOSE THE PHYSICISTS, EMPTY THE LABORATORIES.

No observation could have more clear and less understood: "Nothing, today, nothing distinguishes Science any longer from a universalized and permanent threat of death; the quarrel over whether it will assure the happiness or unhappiness of humanity is over, as it has become quite evident that it has ceased to be a means and become an end in itself. Modern physics has nevertheless promised, has maintained, and promises still more tangible results, in the form of heaps of corpses."[9] The immediate implication in consequence of this, according to the signatories of these lines, is that "revolutionary thought sees the elementary conditions of its activities made so marginal that it must reinvigorate itself at its sources of revolt, and, on this side of a world that no longer knows anything but how to feed its own cancer, and rediscover the unknown fortunes of rage."[10]

This rage has, incontestably, accompanied the entire journey of the Unabomber. Unfortunately, having been deliberately ignored by those who, in the course of the last fifty years, have each in their turn proposed to change the world, this fury reappears here, prisoner of an absolute solitude, for want of never having been capable of engendering that *other* way of thinking hoped for by Breton.

There is no doubt that over the last dozen years or so a certain number of people haven't failed to criticize this or that aspect of technology. Ecologists have transformed themselves into specialists who are consulted by those in power just like other specialists, since the current situation has become so alarming that they are henceforth obliged to act as if they were concerned with the crimes of their technology. But who else has proposed that everything be rethought in the light of this catastrophic illumination? Who has gone back, as Breton did fifty years ago, to this *mutinous sentiment* that, taken as a whole, has been shackled by the limitations of a theory that thought itself revolutionary?

To be, first of all, of the sensible order, this revolt is a weapon that doesn't kill, so long as we are fit to make use of it. But are we still fit? This is one of the serious questions the Unabomber has raised for us. Especially when, in view of the recent ravages caused by the bioengineering of food, nobody—in France, at least—has recognized that it already was a question of the *same* future of the *same* industrialized society, accurately depicted by someone it is most convenient to portray with the image of a "mad bomber."

Watch out! This blindness is a dangerous time bomb.

(*Translated by Jon Graham*)

Notes:

1. Originally published as the preface to the French edition of the so-called Unabomber Manifesto "Industrial Society and Its Future" (*Manifeste: l'avenir de la société industrielle d'Unabomber* [Paris: Éditions du Rocher, 1996]).
2. "Industrial Society and Its Future," Section 111. All quotes from the copy of this text posted at the *Sacramento Bee* newspaper site: http://www.unabombertrial.com/manifesto/
3. Ibid., Section 114.
4. Ibid., Section 28.
5. Ibid., Section 214.
6. Ibid., Section 231.
7. André Breton, *La Lampe dans l'Horloge* (Paris: Robert Marin, 1948), then republished in *La Clé des Champs* (Paris: Saggitaire, 1953), p. 117.
8. André Breton, *Entretiens* (Paris: Gallimard, 1952), p. 240.
9. "Démasquez les physiciens, videz les laboratories!" *Tracts Surréalistes et Déclarations Collectives*, Vol. II 1940–1969, (Paris: Eric Losfeld, 1982), p. 172.
10. Ibid.

Survival Theory

Pentti Linkola

A Refresher Course in the State of the World

An eco-catastrophe is taking place on Earth. Local eco-catastrophes are everywhere. Increasingly, large green and dynamic areas are being covered with concrete, crushed under buildings and roads. Vast spaces turn to desert or are poisoned, unproductive, and unfit for life. The topsoil of the great granaries of the world is flushed into the sea by wind and water erosion. There is an "everything-must-go sale" on finite natural resources, while renewable resources such as forests are rapidly diminishing. The gas balance in the atmosphere has been thrown off and oceans are becoming laden with oil, their food chains impoverished. The rapid warming of the climate poses insurmountable problems for natural as well as cultured vegetation. Trash and pollution are skyrocketing.

The above is a quick refresher course for us, a synopsis of everyday information. More or less unknown to the greater majority of mankind, these environmental megatrends and their incalculable connotations should be all the more familiar to the so-called enlightened nations of the cooler part of the Northern Hemisphere. These phenomena and their causal relationships are accepted as scientific fact; it is just specific calculations and timetables which vary in their uncertainty. I am ignoring all belief-based ideologies here, including the thoughts of private thinkers who—even with sensible-sounding arguments—deny the crisis affecting the circle of life. After all, until the world ends there will be people who insist that the sun rises from the west and sets in the east, that the female begets and that the male gives birth.

The amount and availability of information concerning the issue really isn't a problem here, nor even the basic understanding of it. *How* it is understood is what's interesting. How deeply does it hit home? What kind of connection is the informed person capable of making between the state of the world, his own community, and his personal life? Ultimately, the essential question is whether the realization of the crisis of all life affects the individual's practical choices as a decision-maker and a citizen.

Man—An Irresponsible Thief

This interim report really doesn't offer much hope. In fact, there is no perceptible difference whatsoever between the behavior of the conscious minority and the ignorant majority of the individuals and peoples of this world. All around the planet, man is still an irresponsible lout, the pest and bane of life. Among the conscious minority there just happens to be more idle talk and paper shuffling. There is activity like the work of the UN-appointed Brundtland commission and its recommendations. As we recall, the minimum requirement set by this commission—after all the compromises—was the reduction of energy consumption by half in all industrialized countries over the course of a few decades. Are we to believe, then, that in Finland we are well on our way to cutting back on construction, the industrial manufacture of goods, traffic, road network maintenance and expansion, lighting and domestic machinery? Are half of the power plants ready to be shut down?

In reality, the Finnish producers and consumers—the student and the pensioner, the farmer, metal worker, and doctor—are all similarly fighting tooth and nail for a material standard of living that exceeded all reasonable limits decades ago. They are still demanding increases in their annual purchasing power. And on and on they whine, 'till the end of the world! The current economic recession is seen as a shocking setback by these people, something that must be battled with religious fervor. As conscious people, they should actually *pray* for the depression to deepen tenfold. This medical conference itself is characterized by unnecessary excess, with tons of white chlorine-bleached paper, first-class conference rooms, fancy flights, and five-star hotel accommodations.

Preventing the Population Explosion—Or Rejecting the Notion?

Let's get back to the issue. Sorry—the bitter ecologist just got a bit carried away again. I was supposed to talk about the issues of overpopulation, value philosophy, and medical ethics. We'll get to them, too.

To repeat one more time: the primary reason—perfectly sufficient in itself—for the impending doom is the swollen number of human beings on this planet. The worst enemy of life is too much life, too much *human* life. The secondary cause for the acceleration of the catastrophe is the per-capita strain these masses put on nature. Today I am primarily concerned about the first reason.

Experience has shown that the extreme seriousness of a population explosion is very quickly blurred even among the conscious minority. Logical thought fades and the mind begins to seek distractions when faced with the conflict between optimism and one's sense of reality. Optimism, the most unfortunate human characteristic, successfully obscures the gravity of the overpopulation problem, first temporally into a distant future, then spatially, to distant lands, far away from home.

For as long as I have actively followed demographic trends, say forty-five years, global population growth has been seen as a serious problem. Through all these years, the population at any given time has been considered the maximum limit of what the planet can support, and any future expansion has been deemed unbearable. The rhetoric is always identical. But what does the voice of reality say? Already, millennia ago, irreparable damage had been done on a small scale. The green productivity of the Earth was replaced with deserts or semi-deserts. Where the population density got too high, the circle of life shrank. The frequency of animal and organism extinction represents one of the most shocking and irreplaceable losses. It exceeded any natural pace centuries ago, even before escalating into the all-out annihilation of the past few decades.

Essentially, the serious disruption of the natural systems of the air, sea, and soil seems to have begun during the two to three billion population mark, during a time of markedly lower standards of living, that is, strain on nature. It has therefore been stated that the sole reason why we still exist on this planet is because the Earth's massive chemistry is slow to react—just as it will later be slow to recover or stabilize. The notion that the planet could support the current global population of five billion without a dramatic drop in the burden each individual human being places upon the Earth's resources—that is to say, without completely abandoning the current Western culture and way of life—is simply insane. It is the blind faith of a child or an animal.

Just like all pollution is always said to originate from neighboring countries, overpopulation is also seen as someone else's problem. There are, however, two exceptions: China and India. They dare to admit that they have excess demographic density. These are the exceptions that prove the rule, being two ancient civilizations, culturally superior to the surrounding barbarians.

The Reality of Population Explosion

Just recently, the head of the National Statistics Bureau came to talk to me. He wanted to know how a person is supposed to bear the knowledge—the ultimate, internalized knowledge—of the world's downfall. In an effort to maintain his mental balance, he had tried to avoid facing the final conclusions. But now on the verge of retirement, and without work and meetings to distract him, he realized he would soon have too much time on his hands to think. Amid the surrounding din of the festive reception, we had a very private and serious discussion about the nature of depression, the treatments available, and the possibility of self-treatment. We agreed that the symptoms of destruction—the topics discussed here—are really not the domain of subjective opinions and worldviews, but of cold statistics, facts, and arithmetic.

So what does reality tell us about how the population explosion will be divided geographically? For the next few decades—in other words, the time humanity might have left—it will be centered on the industrialized countries of Europe, Japan, and the United States, where a high overall demographic density is combined with an enormous individual strain upon natural resources. Measured according to the best indicator, consumption of energy per capita, the average citizen of these countries already uses twenty-five times more energy than in most parts of the non-industrialized world. Not all important indicators are as uneven, however—for example, the consumption of food or the usage of forests.

With a more rapidly growing population, the relative danger posed by the non-industrialized countries is of course bound to escalate. But if the difference in living standards remains, it will be far off in the future before these nations steal the lead in destroying natural systems.

With these calculations one should always keep in mind that most of the natural resources of the non-industrialized countries are used by the industrialized North, which is also responsible for most of the environmental damage. This should always be remembered when discussing the world economy or the Third World. However, it is seldom noted that the strain caused by the industrialized countries is exponentially increased by immigrants arriving from poorer countries, who maintain the birthrate of their native culture, or—thanks to better welfare—even exceed it. As Matti Kuusi once put it, there is no use counting the immigrants at the border—one should wait a while, and look in their nurseries.

Bridgehead of the Bullies

The industrial countries are by no means all identical. As a marginal example, Finland boasts top scores in all indicators regarding consumption and environmental strain. The five million inhabitants of our country represent the elite in excessive population and natural resource depletion: Finland is the northern bridgehead of man's theft-based economy. Poor in natural resources, Finland's food production is limited by harsh climatic conditions, and the growth of forests is extremely slow. Elsewhere on the planet, only small populations inhabit the northern side of the 60° parallel, even in regions with comparable or even better conditions—as on both the eastern and western sides of our border. Supporting the population is possible only with an energy-based economy, oversized production costs, and a foreign trade requiring enormous amounts of energy, equipment, and the maintenance of trade routes. The recreational activities of the Finns are particularly wasteful and resource-depleting, even by European standards. During the aforementioned conversation with National Statistics Bureau manager Niitamo, he brought up a statistical figure which I wasn't aware of that vividly illustrates the Finnish population explosion. According to calculations made by Mauri Nieminen, the total number of Finns throughout the ages is 16.5 million. This means that almost a third of all Finns who have ever existed are alive today. What kinds of images does this number evoke? I thought about graveyards myself, how the parishes moan about the costs of grave-keeping, dragging away gravestones not older than a few decades to be piled in dusty oblivion in a distant corner of the stone wall. And yet—taking into account that the number also includes all Finnish-born emigrants buried elsewhere—each living Finn would have no more than two graves to tend, had we somehow managed to find out the names and burial sites of our ancestors since the Stone Age. Honoring our forefathers in this fashion would surely be no more peculiar than many of the odd rituals of our contemporary culture. When I passed my university entrance examinations in 1950—it still seems like yesterday—Finland's population had reached the four million mark. A year ago, in January, we hit five million. At my request, Mauri Nieminen calculated the net emigration during these forty years, adding 240,000 more Finns to that million. We're not concerned about the reproduction rate of those emigrants here, but it apparently exceeds that of the population that stayed home, as emigrants tend to belong to the fertile age groups.

During these past forty years, the editorials of Finnish newspapers throughout the political spectrum have constantly expressed their concern about the stagnation in population growth. The false start has been breathtaking: until recent years, the net population growth has been between twelve thousand and twenty thousand and growing steadily, though, it must be said, the net reproduction rate has dropped under one child per fertile female since 1969, indicating a cessation of growth during the next decade. Based on these numbers, Nieminen sees himself burying the last Finn in 3072—although whether or not mankind will reach the year in question is obviously an open question. In any case, we agree with Nieminen about one thing: the birthrate can easily be manipulated. If some lunatic government decided to multiply child-benefit payments, the birthrate would surely skyrocket. The glimmer of hope is thus quickly killed by the knowledge that during the last few years, there has been a sharp jump upward in the birthrate. We are apparently witnessing the same phenomenon that has increased—once again to the great amazement of demographers—the number of children in the welfare society of Sweden for the last twenty years.

Such news about increased natality belongs to the sorry batch of examples that demonstrate the hopeless mulishness of this animal called man. It's not easy to try and talk sense to an audience that, even in the midst of an eco-catastrophe, only seems to be truly moved by frivolities. As I scan over newspaper photos depicting the landscape that once became so familiar on my bicycle treks—the desolately uniform, rat-infested, ramshackle villages on the northern plains of Yugoslavia, where run-over dog carcasses litter the streets—I couldn't care less if it's a Serb shooting a Croat now, or vice-versa. And what about Estonia, Latvia, and Lithuania? Those thousand wars of independence in the history of mankind, all following the same pattern: the heroes and oppressors, oppressors and heroes, taking turns! I only see but one war underneath the ripples on the surface: the one war that counts, the never-ending war that man wages against nature, against the foundation of his own existence.

The Value-Basis of Protecting Life

From a philosophical viewpoint, the idea of protecting life—and the core message I've represented for years—really isn't that ingenious or new. Basically, it is concerned with the survival of life, enabling the options to stay open. As such, it doesn't say anything about the *quality* of life. Still, it is the most important of all messages and declarations in the world. Everything else is secondary and stands lower on the hierarchy of aims and goals. Even the most beautiful of mankind's ambitions become meaningless if there is no life and no mankind. Saving life is justified, at any cost.

Still, one who protects life doesn't derive his strength and confidence from reason and logic alone. For him, the basic principle of protecting life, preserving the diverse and rich life on our planet is a sacred thing, above all ridicule, infinitely more holy than the holiest of truths or goals among the society of men—though one might, of course, ask what's holy or serious at all in this age of despair worn as a cynical grin.

The diversity and richness of life is contingent on both a maximum number of species and of specimens—meaning that the greatest number of ecological niches are inhabited as fully as possible. The number of species is, however, definitely more important than the number of specimens. This is especially true when the two clash, for example when one species displaces or even destroys another. The latest calculations estimate that man annually causes the extinction of 525,000 different animals, plants, and fungi—or, one species per minute. From the viewpoint of a protector of life, this is something that man has no special right to do. Man sows unspeakable death, and so weighs down the scales with his horror, that even the greatest achievements of the human race become light as a feather in comparison.

In any case, we don't necessarily have to work out our relationship to nature or justify the rights of man or other life forms to life. In the end, eco-catastrophes are the death of man, too. Although these catastrophes swallow up a huge number of animals, plants, and fungi before they destroy him, man will be crushed in the end. Man will consume himself along with everything else. Even the most narrow-minded humanist must logically agree with the conclusions of a protector of life.

The Doctors' Burden of Sin

A clichéd statement places the blame of the approaching doom primarily on the engineer and the doctor, together responsible for the human deluge. But what does closer scrutiny reveal about the doctor's work and its justification? It is very clearly ambivalent. Keeping people physically and mentally as healthy as possible is surely a goal that is beyond reproach. And if mankind—the thief of life which treads down on other species—was itself sick, miserable, and plagued with suffering, there really would be no sense in protecting life, would there?

The most magnificent of all the achievements of the medical profession must be the extension of human life. In the current state of the world, it is clear that everything which even hints at development or progress is negative, accelerating destruction. In a world where the key to salvation lies in stopping, returning, and regressing, the value and meaning of old people is enormous. Man is so constituted that the scarce wisdom shown by a few slowly accumulates with age. One of the fateful insanities of this rampant, hectic age is the trivialization and marginalization of the elderly. Illnesses causing dementia are found only in a small percentage of old people, and most of us are surely wiser at the age of ninety than we were at eighty-nine. A young person is always a greenhorn and a bungler, and it is not until old age—if ever—that the meaningless trivialities of life give way to both wisdom and a sense of responsibility. If all of the decision-makers throughout the world had been at least eighty years of age, much would have been won. The world would have been saved from many a dangerous delusion and much noxious foam. The pace of destruction would surely have been slower.

Much of the positive work of medicine has thus been diverted by the youth-worshipping Zeitgeist. It has ultimately been ruined, however, by the stance of doctors to population growth, birthrates, and infant mortality; the fetus and the child. I am now talking about the medical profession as a whole, as it is gathered here at this conference—as it should always be, sharing responsibility as a whole. Not just any old mules of society, doctors have always enjoyed extra prestige and influence due to their important position. Had they wanted to, it would have been possible for the medical profession to keep the population issue largely under their control.

With no internal self-control evident, the medical profession can be loosely divided into the "good" and the "bad." With his surgical equipment and heart and blood-pressure medication, one doctor prolongs the lives of wise old people. At the same time, another doctor applies his skills towards senseless and destructive research, in order to rescue five-month-old fetuses at any cost, that is, regardless of the cost in natural resources. The cost of medical care, by the way, is something that touches the conscience of all doctors alike.

Surely, all the pills, diaphragms, and condoms deserve our exalted praise. Yet for some gynecologists and pediatricians, the burden of sin is as black as it is heavy, and it should fall on each doctor as a collegial responsibility. The deep drop that has been achieved in infant mortality alone should be deeply distressing to a biologist. After each new wonder-medicine and improvement in public health care, an uncompromisingly thorough campaign of contraception should follow. Only by serving as the engineer of strict population policy and family planning could the medical profession earn its place as the true benefactor of mankind.

Tabula Rasa

Western culture has brought mankind to a state that has been described in different ways. We're living in the eleventh hour, at the edge of the abyss, on the verge of extinction, two minutes to midnight. One phrase may be more eloquent than another, yet all are unfortunately equally true. Most people pay no mind; they either keep up the kind of revelry they're accustomed to, or, just to play it safe, try to grab as much as they possibly can, drowning themselves in material possessions while this is still possible. Even a part of the thinking, conscious minority gives up: "To hell with it, there is nothing we can do about it anymore." It is a very logical appraisal of the situation and most likely a correct one, too.

Then we have the tinkering activists, people whose watchwords are *recycling, filters, unleaded fuel, solar panels,* and *electric cars*—their actions as hopeless as they are ineffectual. Just like in a leaking old boat, one hole is being patched while two others appear somewhere else. These people revert to almost complete idiocy when discussing the birthrate of the Third World. We're told that we must raise the standard of living, and the level of education, and do something for the position of women, so that after five generations—when mankind is already extinct—we will have managed to cut the Third World birthrate in half and—thanks to Western living standards—increased the per-capita strain on nature twentyfold.

These "environmentalists" seem to strive for the same goal as the protector of life, but fail to understand what is grasped even by those who give up: the very depth of the hole into which Western culture has fallen. The entire system, all its social structures and legislation, is oriented solely toward economic growth and world downfall, and it is all beyond repair. The most stubborn still think that they can fix this leaking boat and make it seaworthy by, say, covering it in fiberglass. But the whole design of the boat was completely unsuitable in the first place; it was built so that it sinks when it hits the first small waves. Actually, it was already doomed before it ever left shore, overloaded with ballast as it was. If one seriously wants to sketch a blueprint for a world that could survive, one needs a clean canvas, a blank page. We would have to rewind almost all the way back to Adam and Eve.

Life-Protection and Humanism

I am most interested in humanist thinkers who have arrived at a biologically based theory of survival similar to my own. The most remarkable of Finnish thinkers, along with Matti Kuusi, must be Georg Henrik von Wright—a philosopher at home with cautious scholarly argumentation, yet seriously pondering the possibility of man's extinction among his scenarios. Along with Kuusi, he is remarkable for risking his reputation with his opinions. It is, however, from a personal letter that I now cite, one that he wrote to me two years ago, thanking me for my book *Johdatus 1990-luvun ajatteluun* (Introduction to the Thinking of the 1990s). In the book's prologue, I used the following allegory, referred to by von Wright in his letter:

> What to do, when a ship carrying a hundred passengers suddenly capsizes and only one lifeboat, with room for just ten people, has been launched? When the lifeboat is full, those who hate life will try to load it down with more people, inevitably sinking everyone. Those who love and respect life will take the ship's axe and sever the extra hands clinging to the gunwales.

I remind you that a personal letter might be the product of a passing thought, and not intended to be seen as a public opinion. In any case, the honest confusion of such lines should have a heuristic value. Von Wright writes:

> As you might know, I value you greatly as a thinker. It seems that in this country you are one of the few persons who sees the truth most clearly and deeply. Drawing conclusions from this truth is another thing. I might chop off the extra hands myself. Not from love of life, however, but from fear, and the will to save my own life. Maybe it would be better if we all drowned together, a final proof of the inability of mankind to live on this planet.

The letter shows how hard it is for a great humanist to let go of the overemphasis on the value of human life. Between those lines I think I read the same fears that often come up when discussing overpopulation, fears that could be called those of breaking loose, and of disgrace. It is feared that once begun, the act of reducing the world's population will spiral out of control, get out of hand, and that the value of human life will be permanently lost. It is also thought that mankind will forever lose its sense of self worth by sullying its ethical values, and will be unable to restore any norms and conventions after such an action. This fear endures, despite the methodological finesse with which the action could be carried out. Being even more dispassionate and discreet than the German gas chambers of WWII, modern tactical nuclear, bacteriological, or chemical strikes could be simultaneously launched on the great population centers of the world by an international organization (like the UN), or some smaller group that possesses hi-tech equipment and a responsibility to the world.

In the light of history, I see those fears as a clear misunderstanding. After wars and deliberate annihilations are over, societies have always returned to business as usual after a short, transitional period. Neither the massive decimations of Stalin or Hitler, nor the most nauseating torture tales of latter-day secret police—related to the world with every gory detail—have destroyed ethical norms. In fact, right on the street next to the offices of the secret police, people are writing poems and talking philosophy, and neighbors are helping a sick old person.

After all, we are now living in the age after gas chambers and various other atrocities. On a global scale, the main problem isn't the inflation of human life, but its ever-increasing, mindless overvaluation. Clinging to the idea that fetuses, the unborn, and the braindead have human rights is already like a collective form of insanity. One must also question the strange history of the death penalty. When there were only five million people on the planet, the death penalty seemed like a logically self-evident punishment for the terminally twisted deviants of society. Now, with a global population of over five billion, an increasing number of societies have decided to abandon the execution of even the most satanic arch-villains—with Amnesty International screaming "Murder!" at the last few nonconformists. Equally mindlessly, huge rescue organizations are deployed so that even the most insane fisherman might have a helicopter circling overhead when he decides to venture into a ten-beaufort storm in a rowboat, ready to save this unique and priceless human being from the waves. The mind boggles.

Legalizing euthanasia, re-instating the death penalty, and reducing overzealous rescue services are by no means enough to significantly impact the population-growth statistics. It is their principal, symbolic value that is important. As long as they continue to mirror the twisted mores and practices of the mindless glorification of human life, we have no means to solve the population explosion—and all the lifeboats will sink.

Unless Man Grows Humble...

The number of thinkers who have been able to question the basic philosophical foundation on which our culture lies is actually surprisingly small. Holding values such as "human rights," "allegiance to one's own species," "individual freedom," and "democracy" to be unassailable, most people will go only halfway in their attempt to understand the situation. They refuse to see that the world is crumbling not in spite of these ideals, but because of them. The old truth that thinking is to a great extent bound to one's values and is seldom really free holds frighteningly true here. After all, it's only logical that it is precisely the core values that should be examined when a culture is seen approaching its doom.

In this fundamental sense, I find myself to be an anomaly among thinkers. I have no problem in returning man to his place in a balanced hierarchy of life. I wonder if the difference arises from my basic conception of man? For me, mankind is a marvelous species, fighting tooth and nail for survival—but his greatness is manifested only in fleeting glimpses, and only in a small number of individuals. On the other hand, I have more than sufficient evidence of mankind's collective capacity for enormous destruction. He created the machinery of annihilation that is Western civilization, and he let its plague wash over the world.

I find it completely incomprehensible how an intelligent individual can still believe in man, in the majority, and keep banging his head against the wall despite all the clear evidence. How is it possible, given no less than the current state of the world, that man is unable to agree that his continuing existence is possible only through the discipline, prohibition, and oppression of another, far-seeing man, one who limits the first one's freedom—because nature is no longer capable of doing so—to fulfill his disastrous impulses and to commit suicide? How can he justify democracy? Is it so hard to understand that unless man, unless all of Western culture, grows humble and takes a deep, deep bow of submission, it will gnaw the world down to the bone, no matter how many chemicals and sources of energy are replaced by others? How is he so blind that he fails to see that if we cling to the idea of man's superiority over nature, and maintain the current valuation of human life, then all that we have ahead of us is the straight, black road to extinction? How can anybody be so mad as to try and maintain the same morals and the same valuation of human life regardless of the number of people on the planet? I find it self-evident that with the birth of each new child, the value of every other human being is slightly diminished. I find it self-evident that the morals we espouse during a population explosion should be wholly different from those of our beginnings, when man was an elite species, far fewer in numbers.

A Protector of Life Is Forced to Compromise

The harsh reality is that neither the minds of Western decision-makers nor the great majority of people are even remotely concerned about these issues; not about reducing the existing population, not even about restricting its rights. What little discussion occurs lags light-years behind, and revolves around controlling the birthrate.

In the furthest outposts of ignorance, people are still mired in discussing the rights of a newly fertilized ovum or a fetus. I am at a loss for words here. I simply won't retreat all the way back to the last defensive trench—I'd rather surrender. Maybe, at gunpoint, I could be persuaded to discuss restrictions on childbearing. "If I can't get a life-jacket, then maybe a life-vest, and if not a vest, then maybe at least a cap." Clutching at the last straws, the protector of life lessens his demands for avoiding extinction and examines the possibilities of delaying it. I guess I must agree that there is some kind of value in the temporary continuation of life. Everything is contingent upon time, after all, although the predicted, inevitable death of our sun, the source of all life, in ten billion years is, in this context, nothing short of eternity.

When it comes to controlling the birthrate, the guidelines for protecting life should be clear and simple. In no part of the world should reproduction be a matter of family decision-making, left to parents and individuals. Of all the human actions, it is the one most clearly in need of regulation by the state (and, ultimately, by an international council). Giving birth should require permission. National family, social, and educational policy might distribute the child quotas among families and mothers. It could be that even large families would have their place—anything as long as the principle of equality is forgotten, for it leads to nothing but misfortune. The average number must in any case be—universally and unambiguously, and at least for the coming decades—one child per fertile woman. If a population load that the planet can sustain is ever achieved, the population would then be stabilized by returning to a quota of approximately two children.

Other seemingly self-evident policies would include free and universally available contraceptives, and a universal right to free abortion. The fine-tuning of the system would decide whether the child quota would be controlled by forced abortions—which would still enable the conception of new children in case of the first one's death—or forced sterilization of either or both sexes. The better the control, the fewer living babies that would need to be eliminated. After all, it's not as if infanticide has been an uncommon human practice, even in recent centuries.

But I guess this is all just speculation. I would like to apologize to the listeners for the second time and confess that I forgot something else: man is neither capable of limiting the birthrate nor of getting rid of the surplus population—and eco-catastrophe won't wait. Though gifted with technical genius, man is in all other respects a thickheaded animal, driftwood in the cruel and capricious stream of evolution. The few who see are trampled down by their fellow men. Do you understand that we are actually dying of extinction? We are *really, definitely*, dying of extinction, as one species in a series of millions.

Or are we? Do we still have one chance in a million? Are there still some hidden reserves of the farsighted few available? Will enough individuals stand up and prove that man really does have a free will? Individuals with both insight and a will to wager everything they've got, against the gray majority—for the survival of that gray majority? Individuals with a brave heart, controlled by crystalline logic?

(*Translated by Ike Vil*)

This article consists of an invited lecture entitled "Survival Theory and Medical Ethics" delivered by the author on 7 January 1992 at Lääketieteen päivät, a major medical conference in Finland.

Editors' Note: In the fifteen years since the author delivered the above lecture, the world's population has increased by more than 1.6 billion human beings.

Crusade Against the Grail

The Struggle between the Cathars, the Templars, and the Church of Rome

OTTO RAHN

This is the daring book that popularized the legend of the Cathars and the Holy Grail. Author Otto Rahn believed that the medieval epic *Parzival* held the keys to the mysteries of the Cathars and the secret location of the Holy Grail. The 1933 first edition drew upon Rahn's account of his explorations of the Pyrenean caves where the heretical Cathars sect sought refuge during their suppression by the Vatican in the 13th century. *Crusade Against the Grail* has never appeared in English until now.

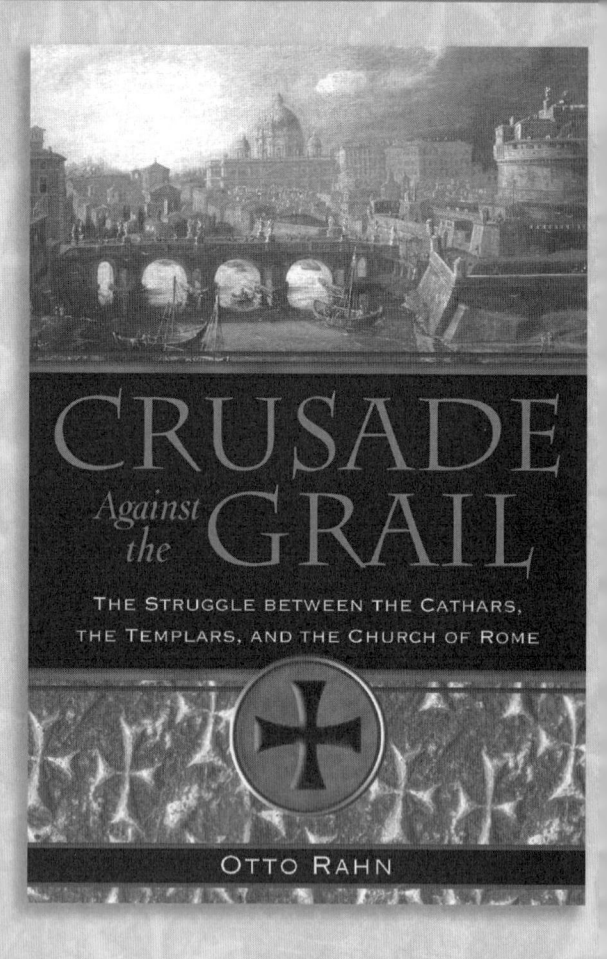

Otto Rahn was born in Michelstadt, Germany, in 1904. After earning his degree in philology in 1924, he traveled extensively to the caves and castles of southern France, researching his belief that the Cathars were the last custodians of the Grail. Induced by Himmler to become a member of the SS as a civilian archaeologist and historian, Rahn quickly grew disillusioned with the direction his country was taking and resigned in 1939. He died, an alleged suicide, on March 13, 1939, in the snows of the Tyrolean Mountains.

$16.95, paper, 256 pages, 6 x 9, ISBN-13: 978-1-59477-135-4

INNER TRADITIONS
BEAR & COMPANY

For these and other great titles visit us at www.InnerTraditions.com
800-246-8648

The Primordial and the Perennial: Tradition in the Thought of Martin Heidegger and Julius Evola

Michael O'Meara

The opposite of tradition, the historian Dominique Venner argues, is not modernity, an illusive notion, but nihilism.[1] According to Nietzsche, who developed the concept, nihilism comes with the death of the gods and "the radical repudiation of [all] value, meaning, and desirability."[2] A nihilistic world—like our own, in which the uppermost values have been devalued—is a world incapable of channeling life's entropic currents into a purposeful flow, which is why traditionalists associated with Guénonian perennialism, radical traditionalism, neo-paganism, revolutionary conservatism, anti-modernism, and ethnonationalism array themselves against it.

The tradition whose meaning-creating truths these traditionalists uphold against modernity's nihilistic onslaught is not the prevailing anthropological/sociological concept, defined as "a set of social practices inculcating certain behavioral norms implying continuity with a real or imagined past." It is also not G. K. Chesterton's "democracy of the dead" or Edmund Burke's "general bank and capital of nations and of ages." Tradition for them has little to do with the past per se, formalized cultural practices, or even traditionalism. Venner, for example, likens it to a musical motif, a guiding theme, that imparts coherence and direction to life's varied movements.

If most traditionalists concur in seeing tradition as both orienting and transcending a people's collective existence, representing something immutable that is perpetually reborn in its experience of time, in other respects they tend to disagree. As a case in point, the radical traditionalists associated with *TYR* oppose the "abstract but absolute principles" which the Guénonian school associates with "Tradition" and instead privilege the European heritage.[3] The implication here (other than what it implies for biopolitics) is that there is no Perennial Tradition or Universal Truth, whose timeless verities apply to all peoples everywhere—only different traditions, linked to different peoples in different cultural epochs and regions. The traditions specific to these histories and cultures embody, as such, the collective meanings that define, situate, and orient a people, enabling it to overcome the endless challenges specific to it. As M. Raphael Johnson writes, tradition is "something similar to the concept of ethnicity, that is, [it is] a set of basically unspoken norms and meanings that have developed out of a people's struggle for survival." Outside the specific context of this struggle, there is no tradition.[4]

But however cogent, this "culturalist" stance nevertheless deprives radical traditionalists of the elegant philosophical postulates and monist tenets underpinning the Guénonian school. Their project for an integral culture rooted in the European heritage loses thus not only the Guénonians' intellectual cohesion, it risks becoming a potpourri of disparate elements, lacking those knowing philosophical "vistas" that might order and illuminate the tradition they claim. This is not to say that tradition's revolt against the modern world needs to be waged philosophically, or that tradition's rebirth depends on a specific philosophical formulation. Nothing so utilitarian or utopian is implied, for philosophy never—at least never directly—creates "the mechanisms and opportunities that bring about a historical state of affairs."[5] Rather, such "vistas" provide an opening to the world—in this case, the lost world of tradition—pointing the way to those perspectives which radical traditionalists hope to regain.

I believe the thought of Martin Heidegger offers one such vista. In the following pages, the case will be made for a traditionalist appropriation of Heideggerian thought. The Guénonians are here taken as a foil to Heidegger not just because their metaphysical approach opposes the European historical one associated with *TYR*, but also because their discourse possesses something of Heidegger's rigor and profundity. René Guénon, however, is something of a problem, for he was a Muslim apostate of the European tradition, intent on "orientalizing" the Occident. This makes him an inappropriate interlocutor for radical traditionalists, especially in comparison with his fellow Traditionalist, Julius Evola, who was one of the great contemporary champions of the "Aryan" heritage. Of the perennialists, then, it is Evola rather than Guénon who offers the more appropriate foil to Heidegger.[6]

The Natural and Supernatural

Given the Guénonians' metaphysical foundations, Evola's Traditionalism focused not on "the fleeting alternation of things given to the senses," but on "the eternal order of things" situated "above" them. Tradition is his term for the "timeless wisdom, the *philosophia perennis*, the Primal Truth" inscribed in this suprahuman realm, whose eternal, immutable, and universal principles were known, allegedly, to the earliest men and whose patrimony (however neglected) is today that of all humanity.[7]

Evola's "Traditionalist method" thus aims at recovering the unity lost in the multiplicity of worldly things. This makes him less concerned with empirical, historical, or existential reality (understood as a deformed reflection of something higher) than with spirit—as found, for example, in symbol, myth, and ritual. Man's world, by contrast, possesses only a secondary order of significance for him. Like Plato, he sees its visible realm as an imperfect reflection of a higher invisible one. "Nothing exists down here," he writes, "...that doesn't have its roots in a more profound, numinous reality. Every visible cause is only apparent."[8] He thus refuses all historical or naturalist explanations of man's contingent world.

Seeing Tradition as a "presence" transmitting the transcendent truths obscured by the fleeting swirl of worldly appearances, Evola identifies Being with its immutable truths. Being in this conception is both outside of and beyond the course of history (that is, suprahistorical), while man's world of Becoming is associated with an ever-changing and ultimately meaningless flux of mundane sensate life. The "supreme value and the foundational principles of every healthy and normal institution are consequently unchanging, based, as they are, on Being."[9] From this principle comes Evola's doctrine of the "two natures" (the natural and the supernatural), which designates a physical order associated with the world of Becoming known to man, and another which depicts the unconditioned metaphysical realm of Being known to the gods.

Traditional civilizations, Evola claims, reflected the transcendent principles transmitted in Tradition, while the "abnormal and regressive" realm of modern man is only a decayed remnant of its celestial order. The temporal/historical world of Becoming, for this reason, is relegated to a lesser order of significance, while the timeless unity of Being is privileged. Like his "other master," Joseph de Maistre, Evola sees Tradition as anterior to history, unconditioned by time or circumstance, and thus unrelated to human origins.[10] The primacy he attributes to the metaphysical realm is indeed what leads him to argue that without the perennial law of Being transmitted in Tradition, "every authority is fraudulent, every law is unjust and barbarous, every institution is vain and ephemeral."[11]

Tradition as *Überlieferung*

Heidegger takes the opposite track. Educated for a vocation in the Catholic Church and dedicated to the rooted, provincial ways of his native Swabia, he too oriented himself to "the old transcendence and not modern worldliness." But his anti-modernism opposed the tradition of Western metaphysical thought and, by implication, the Guénonian philosophy of Tradition (with which he was apparently unfamiliar).

Metaphysics is that branch of philosophy that addresses the major ontological questions, the most fundamental of which is the question: What is Being? Yet starting with Aristotle, metaphysics tended to orient to the non-physical, non-worldly facet of Being, attempting to grasp the transcendence of different beings as spirit, force, or substance.[12] In resorting to such generalized categories, this tendency postulates a transcendental realm of permanent forms and unconditioned truths that understands Being in ways that, according to Heidegger, limit man's understanding of its truth, preventing a simultaneously concealed, opened, and elusive presence from disclosing itself. In an opaque but nevertheless key formulation, Heidegger writes: "When truth [becomes an indisputable] certainty, then everything which is truly real must present itself as real to the real being that it [supposedly] is"—that is, when metaphysics posits its truths, truth for it must present itself not only in a self-referential way, but in a way that conforms to a preconceived idea of itself.[13] The difference here between metaphysical truth, as proposition, and Heidegger's notion of an ongoing disclosure is somewhat analogous to that differentiating the truth claims of the Christian God from those of the Greek gods, with the former presupposing the total objectivity of a timeless, unconditioned universal truth preconceived in the mind of God, and the latter accepting that "concealment" is as inherent to truth's polymorphous nature as disclosure is.[14]

Given its ahistorical assertion of immutable truths ensconced in pure reason, Heidegger claims that metaphysics' prefiguring and decontextualizing impetus alienates beings from Being, freezing them in their momentary representations and hence preventing them from unfolding in accord with the possibilities posed by their specific world. The oblivion of being culminates in modern technological civilization, in which being is defined merely as availability for scientific investigation, technological manipulation, and human consumption. The metaphysical tradition has obscured Being by defining it essentially in anthropocentric and even subjectivist terms.

But more than rejecting the unconditioned postulates of metaphysics,[15] Heidegger associates the word "tradition"—or, at least, its Latinate form (*die Tradition*)—with the Western philosophical heritage and its intensifying oblivion of being. Similarly, he uses the adjective *"traditionell"* pejoratively, linking it to metaphysics' generalizing impetus and to the thoughtless quotidian conventions contributing to the forgetfulness of Being.

But after noting this semantic peculiarity and its anti-metaphysical intent, we must stress that Heidegger was no enemy of tradition, for his philosophy privileges those originary "breakouts of being" in which the great traditional truths come to be. As such, tradition for him is not a body of bloodless postulates, not something passively inherited, but a facet of Being that opens man to a future wholly his own. In this spirit, he links *Überlieferung* (also meaning tradition) with the transmission of those transcendent principles informing every "great beginning."

Tradition in this primordial sense enables man, he believes, "to come back to himself," to discover his unique historically situated possibilities, and to realize himself in the fullness of his essence and truth. As a destining heritage, Heidegger's *Überlieferung* is the opposite of the Traditionalists' decontextualized ideal. In *Being and Time*, he says *die Tradition* "takes what has come down to us and delivers it over to self-evidence; it blocks our access to those primordial 'wellsprings' from which the categories and concepts handed down to us have been in part quite genuinely drawn. Indeed, it makes us forget that they had such an origin, and makes us suppose that the necessity of going back to these sources is something which we need not even understand."[17] *Die Tradition* in this sense forgets the formative possibilities bequeathed by its destining origin, while *Überlieferung*, as transmission, reclaims them. Heidegger's thought is about uncovering the heritage of these ancient wellsprings.

His critique of modernity (and, contrary to what Evola writes, he is one of its great critics) rests on the notion that the loss or corruption of Europe's tradition accounts for "the flight of the gods, the destruction of the earth, the reduction of human beings to a mass, [and] the preeminence of the mediocre."[18] Emptied now of its primordial truths, the European life-world, he argues, is in danger of dying: Only by "grasping its traditions creatively," and reappropriating their original impetus, will the West avoid the "path of annihilation" down which modernity's rationalist, bourgeois, and nihilistic civilization seems headed.[19]

The tradition (*Überlieferung*) the anti-metaphysical Heidegger defends is not, then, the universal, suprasensual realm the Guénonians refer to when they speak of Tradition. Rather, it is those primordial truths which Being makes present "in the beginning"—truths whose deep, historical sources and abiding certainties tend to be forgotten in quotidian concerns or disparaged in modernist discourse, but whose possibilities nevertheless remain the only ones meaningfully accessible to us. Against the metaphysicians, Heidegger argues that there is no *prima philosophia* to provide a foundation for life or Being, only truths rooted in specific historical origins and in the hermeneutical conventions situating a people in their larger narrative.

He thus refuses to reduce tradition to a reflexive analysis independent of time and place. Instead, his phenomenological approach to man's world sees it as stemming from a past in which Being and truth reflect one another and, however imperfectly, affect the present and the way the future is approached. Being, truth, and tradition cannot as such be grasped outside of temporality (i.e., the way humans experience time). This makes Being, truth, and tradition preeminently historical in nature (though not in the progressive, evolutionary, and developmental sense favored by modernists). Only in posing the question of Being, the *Seinsfrage*, is the Being of human being opened to "the condition of the possibility of [its] truth."

It is through temporality, then, that man uncovers the enduring presence which is Being.[20] Indeed, if man's Being were not temporally situated, its transcendence, the principal concern of Guénonian metaphysics, would be inconceivable. There is, accordingly, no truth (about the world or the heavens above it) that is not anchored in our Being-in-the-world—no ultimate truth or Universal Tradition, only truths and traditions born of who we were ... and can be still. This is not to say that the Being of human being lacks transcendence, only that its possibility stems from its imminence—that Being and beings, the world and its objects, are a unitary phenomenon and can't be grasped one without the other.

Because Heidegger's conception of tradition is linked to the question of Being and because Being is inseparable from Becoming, Being and the tradition faithful to its truth cannot be dissociated from their emergence and realization in time. *Sein und Zeit*, immutable Being and historical change, are inseparable in his thought. Being, he writes, "is Becoming and Becoming is Being."[21] Only through the process of becoming in time is it possible, he argues, for beings to unfold in the essence of their Being. The constant presence that metaphysics takes as the essence of Being is itself a character of time and can only be addressed in time—for time and Being share a primordial co-belongingness.

The Guénonians' Platonic world of imperishable forms and timeless ideals is here dismissed for a Heraclitian one of flux and appearance, in which man, true to himself, endeavors to realize himself in time—in terms that speak to his age and his place, doing so in relation to his destining heritage. Given that time implies space, being's relation to Being is not simply an individualized aspect of Being, but a specific "being there" (Dasein)—situated, thrown, and hence temporally grounded in that place where Being is not only "presenced," but "enowned." "Without being there," there is no Being, no existence. Human engagement in the world for him is not simply a situated facet of Being, it is its basis.

To discard a being's relation with its time and space (as the atemporal metaphysics of the Guénonians does) is "just as hopeless as if someone wanted to explain the cause and ground of a fire [by declaring] that he need not bother with the course of the fire or the investigation of its scene."[22] Only in "facticity" (the nexus of practices, assumptions, traditions, and histories situating its Becoming), and not in some putative supra-reality, does the full weight of Being—and the "fundamental condition for ... everything great"—make itself felt.

When perennialists interpret "beings without asking about [the way] man's essence belongs to the truth of Being," they could not be more opposed to Heidegger. Indeed, Being for them is manifested as Cosmic Soul (the master plan of the universe, the indefinable Unity, the Eternal Being), which is detached from the originary and worldly presence distinct to Heidegger's Being-in-the-world.[23] Against the metaphysicians' decontextualized, otherworldly notion, Heidegger stresses that Being's presence is disclosed only in its mundane, temporal, and never fully revealed states. Different worlds give us different possibilities, different ways to be or to live. These historically situated worlds dictate the specific possibilities of human being, imposing an order and a meaning on it. Heidegger does not deny the possibility of human transcendence here, but seeks it in the one place in which it is accessible to man—that is, in his *da* ("there"), his specific situation. This makes Becoming both the existential backdrop and the "transcendental horizon" of Being, for even when transcending its situation, human existence is necessarily time-bound and place-bound.

By posing the *Seinsfrage* in this way, it follows that one cannot start from scratch, isolating an abstract, atomized being from all that situates it in a specific time and space, for to do so ignores that man's being is something finite, rooted in a historically conditioned and culturally defined context—it ignores, in effect, that it is a Being-there (Dasein). For if human existence is caught up in the flux of Becoming—if it is something culturally, linguistically, racially, and, above all, historically situated—it cannot be understood as a purely unconditioned Being.

The open character of human temporality means, moreover, that man is responsible for his being. He is the being whose "being is itself an issue," for, however situated, his existence is never fixed or complete, never determined in advance whether it will be lived authentically or inauthentically.[24] It is experienced as an ongoing possibility that projects itself toward a "not yet actual" future, as man endeavors to "make something of himself" from the possibilities bequeathed by his specific origin. This causes man to "care" about his Dasein, individuating its possibilities in terms of the world in which he dwells.

Time here serves not just as the horizon against which man is thrown, it serves as the ground (the predetermined facticity) upon which his possibility is realized. The possibility man seeks in the future (his project) is inevitably affected by the present situating him and the past shaping his sense of possibility. Dasein's projection comes thus "toward itself in such a way that it comes back," anticipating its possibility as something that "has been" and is still ready-at-hand.[25] For it is only in terms of its Being-there, its "thrownness," that it can be fully enowned—and transcended.[26]

In rejecting abstract, unconditioned, and timeless concepts of metaphysics, Heidegger treats truth, especially the primordial truths that tradition hands down, as historical/temporal in nature, linked with distinct (though often obscure) manifestations of Being, and imbued with a past whose destiny-creating origin informs man's sense of possibility. Indeed, it is the distinct configuration formed by temporal situationality, the openness of Being, and the facticity situating this encounter that shape the great issues facing man, as he seeks to realize (or avoid) his possibility on a ground not of his own choosing. "The history of Being," Heidegger writes, "is never past but stands ever before us; it sustains and defines every *condition et situation humaine*."[27]

Man confronts the choices defining his Dasein not, then, in the existentialist sense of being "condemned" to making endless, seemingly arbitrary decisions about it. Rather, the openness he faces is informed by the possibilities specific to his historically situated existence, while the "decisions" he makes are about being authentic (i.e., about being true to his historically-destined possibilities, his fate). Since there are no timeless metaphysical truths inscribed in tradition, only ones posed by a world "always already," to live in light of Being's truths requires that man know his place in history, know where and in what way he originated, and confront his history as the unfolding (or, negatively, the distorting) of the promises posed by an original predestination.[28] An authentic human existence, Heidegger claims, is "a process of taking over who we have been in the service of who we are."[29]

The Primordial

Man's "first beginning"—the "unprecedented and monumental" beginning (*Anfangen*) in which his ancestors were "caught" (*gefangen*) as a specific form of Being—brings other beginnings into play, becoming the ground of all his subsequent groundings.[30] By setting history in a certain direction, the beginning—the primordial—"does not reside back in the past but lies in advance of what is to come."[31] It is "the distant decree that orders us to recapture its greatness."[32] Without this "reconquest," there can never be another commencement: for it is in reappropriating a heritage, whose beginning is already a completion, that man comes back to himself, inscribing himself in the world of his own time. "In coming to grips with the first beginning heritage ... becomes heritage; and only those who belong to the future ... become [its] heirs."[33] Heidegger's student Hans-Georg Gadamer says all questions about beginnings "are always [questions] about ourselves and our future."[34]

In transmitting the truth of man's origin, tradition for

Heidegger challenges man to realize himself in the face of all that conspires to distort his being. Just as Evola believed history was an involution from an earlier Golden Age, hence a process of decadence, Heidegger saw origins—the inexplicable outbreak of Being which brings what is "ownmost," not universal, to Dasein into existence—as posing not merely the possible trajectories of man's life, but the obstacles inherent to its realization. Unfolding on the basis of its primordial foundation, history tends as such to be a flattening out, a decline, a forgetting or concealment of the possibilities bequeathed by its "beginning," as the idle chatter, the exaltation of the common, and the quotidian, or the reign of the mediocre triumph over the destiny, decisiveness, and authenticity of earlier epochs, whose closeness to Being was immediate, unconcealed, and full of evident possibility.

Where Evola sees history in cyclical terms, with each cycle remaining essentially homogenous, representing a segment of a recurring succession governed by certain immutable principles, Heidegger sees history in terms of the possibilities posed by their enownment. Only from the possibilities intrinsic to the originary genesis of his "sphere of meaning"—not from the Guénonians' suprahistorical realm—is it possible, he argues, for man to discover the historically situated tasks "demanded" of him and open himself to their possibility.[35] Relatedly, the words "oldest," "beginning," and "primordial" are associated in Heidegger's thought with the essence or truth of Being, just as the remembrance of origin becomes a "thinking ahead to what is coming."[36]

Because the primordial lies in front of, not behind, man, the initial revelation of Being comes in each new beginning, as each new beginning draws on its source for its posterity. Like Mnemosyne, the goddess of memory who was the chief muse of the Greek poets, what is prior prefigures what is posterior, for the "truth of Being" found in origins causes Dasein's project to "come back to itself." It is, then, as "the innermost enowning of Being" that origins are all important. They are not antecedent or *causa prima*, as modernity's inorganic logic holds, but "that from which and by which something is what it is and as it is … [They are] the source of its essence" and the way truth "comes into being … [and] becomes historical."[37] As the French New Rightist Alain de Benoist puts it, the "original" (unlike modernity's *novum*) is not that which comes once and for all, but that which comes and is repeated every time a being unfolds in the authenticity of its origin.[38] Origins in this sense represent the primordial unity of existence and essence affirmed in tradition. And because both the original and subsequent "enowning" of Being denotes possibility, not the purely "factual" or "momentary" environment affecting it, Dasein achieves self-constancy only when projected on the basis of its authentic inheritance.[39]

Heideggerianism Is Not an Existentialism

Evola devoted several chapters of *Ride the Tiger* (Cavalcare la Tigre) to a critique of the postwar "existentialism" popularized by Jean-Paul Sartre and derived, allegedly, from Heidegger's thought.[40] Though acknowledging certain differences between Sartre and Heidegger, Evola treated them as basically kindred spirits. His Sartre is thus depicted as a petty-bourgeois non-conformist and his Heidegger as a pettifogging academic, both of whom see man as stranded in a meaningless world, condemned to make endless choices without any transcendent recourse. The existentialists' dreary concept of freedom, Evola holds, sees the universe as a void, against which man must forge his own meaning (Sartre's "essence"). Their notion of freedom (and by implication, Heidegger's notion) is thus deemed a nihilistic one, entirely individualistic and arbitrary.

In conflating Sartrian existentialism and Heideggerian thought, Evola was apparently unaware of Heidegger's "Letter on Humanism" (1946–47), in which he—eloquently and unambivalently—repudiated the existentialist appropriation of his work. Evola also seems to have known only Heidegger's monumental *Sein und Zeit*, which he, like Sartre, read as a philosophical anthropology on the problems of human existence (i.e., as a humanism), rather than as a preliminary part of an early attempt to develop a "fundamental ontology" investigating the meaning of Being. He thus tarred Sartre and Heidegger with the same brush, depicting them as "modern men," severed from the world of Tradition and imbued with modernity's "profane, abstract, and rootless categories" of thought. Referring to Sartre's nihilistic contention that "existence precedes essence" (which he wrongly attributed to Heidegger, who equated rather than opposed the two), Guénon's Italian disciple concluded that by situating man in a world, where essence is self-engendered, Heidegger made the concrete present ontologically primary, with situationality a requisite, rather than the context, of Being.[41] Heideggerian Being is seen, then, as lying beyond man, pursued as an unrealizable possibility.[42] This supposedly binds Being to the here and now, unmooring it from Tradition—and hence from the transcendence which alone illuminates the great existential tasks.

Evola's critique of Heidegger, as already suggested, is an impertinent one, targeting a caricature of his thought. History and temporality may be central to Heidegger's philosophical project and he may accept Sartre's contention that there are no absolute, unchanging ways of being human, but it is not because he believes it is necessary "to abandon the plane of Being" for the sake of situationality. Situationality for him is simply the context in which beings encounter their Being.

Heidegger insists on Dasein's "temporal event structure" because he sees beings as rooted in time and enmeshed in a world not of their own creation (however much the Being of these beings might transcend the "now" or series of "nows" situating them). At the same time, he emphasizes that Dasein is experienced "ecstatically," for thoughts of the past, present, and future are interrelated facets of man's consciousness. Indeed, only by recognizing its ecstatical dimension (which both existentialists and metaphysicians ignore) is Dasein able to "heed the opening of Being," live in its light, and transcend its ephemeral *da* (its situationality). Heidegger thus writes that Dasein is "the being that emerges from itself"—it is the unconcealment of a historical-cultural-existential essence whose unfolding is alien to the objectifying impetus of Platonic forms.[43]

By rethinking Being in terms of human temporality, restoring it to historical Becoming, and establishing time as its transcendent horizon, Heidegger endeavors to free the existential from the inorganic properties of space and matter, from the senseless busyness of modern life, with its instrumentalist evasion of Being and its "exhausted pseudo-culture"—as well as free it from the timeless ideals the Guénonians privilege. For if Being is inseparable from Becoming and occurs in a world-with-others, then beings, he insists, inhere in a "context of significance" saturated with history and culture. Pursuing his project in these terms, man's various existential modes, along with his world, are not just shaped by interpretations stemming from a history of previous interpretations. Interpretation itself (i.e., "the working out of possibilities projected in the understanding") puts the present in question, affecting the

The Primordial and the Perennial

unfolding of one's essence. In fact, the meaning-laden matrix spun by interpretation constitutes much of what makes up the "there" (*da*) in Dasein.[44]

Given that there is no *Sein* without a *da*, no existence without a ground, man, in his ownmost nature, is inseparable from the matrix that "makes possible what has been projected."[45] Within this matrix, Being inheres in "the enowning of the grounding of the there."[46] Contrary to the argument of *Ride the Tiger*, this historically conscious hermeneutics neither deprives man of Being, negates Being's primacy, nor leaves man at the mercy of situationality. It also has nothing to do with Sartre's radical "indeterminism"—which makes meaning contextually contingent and essence effervescent.

Man for Heidegger exists not in any one of his given moments, but in all of them, for his situated being (the project he realizes in time) lies in no single instance of its unfolding (or in what Guénon called "the indefinitude of possibilities in each state"). Rather, it exists in the whole temporal structure stretching between man's birth and death, as he realizes his project in the world. Without a past and an as-yet-unrealized future, human existence would not be Dasein, with a future bequeathed by a past that is at the same time an incitement to a future. Unlike the Sartrian individual (whose being is an uncertain and limitless possibility) and unlike the perennialist (who sees his soul in terms abstracted from worldly references), Heideggerian man finds himself only in a return to (a "heeding of") the essence posited by his origin.

This heeding of essence, the self-discovery requisite to an authentic existence, is not pure possibility, subject to individual "planning, designing, scheming, and plotting," but the heir to a specific origin which determines its fate. Indeed, being only comes from Being.[47] Heidegger's notion of tradition consequently privileges *Andenken* (the recollection that recovers and renews tradition) and *Verwindung* (which is a going beyond, an overcoming)—a notion of tradition which implies the inseparability of Being and Becoming, as well as Becoming's role in the unfolding, rather than the negation, of Being.[48]

"The original repose of Being" that has the power to save man from the "din of inauthentic, anodyne, exterior life" is not, though, easily gained. To "recapture the beginning of historical-spiritual existence in order to transform it into a new beginning" (which, in my view, defines the radical traditionalist project) requires "an anticipatory resoluteness" that resists the mindless routines oblivious to human temporality.[49] Such an anticipatory resoluteness inevitably comes only when questioning the "rootless and self-seeking freedoms" that keep us from Being's unfolding truths and thus from realizing who we are—a questioning whose necessity stems from the farthest reaches of man's history and whose answers are integral to the tradition they form.[50]

History for Heidegger is accordingly a "choice for heroes," demanding the firmest resolve and the greatest risk, as man, in anxious confrontation with his origin, realizes an indwelling possibility in the face of an amnesic, complacent, or fearful conventionality.[51] The historical choices he makes have, of course, nothing to do with individualism or subjectivism (with what is arbitrary or willful), but arise from what is true and "original" in tradition. A man's fate (*Geschick*), like a people's destiny (*Schicksal*), is not about "choice," but about something "sent" (*geschickt*) from a distant past which has the power to determine a future possibility. Being, Heidegger writes, "proclaims destiny, and hence control of tradition."[52]

As the enowning embrace of the heritage man inherits at birth, his fate is never forced or compelled. It takes over the unchosen circumstances of his community and generation, as he pursues the possibility bequeathed by his heritage, grounding his existence in his "ownmost particular historical facticity"—even if this enownment entails opposition to "the peculiar dictatorship of the public realm."[53] This makes individual identity inseparable from its collective identity, as Being-in-the-world recognizes its Being-with-others (*Mitsein*). Heideggerian man realizes who he is only through his mindful involvement in the time and space of his own destined existence, as he keeps himself at "the disposal of the gods," whose present "withdrawal remains most near."[54]

The community of one's people, *Mitsein*, is the necessary context of one's Dasein. As such, it is "the in which, out of which, and for which history happens."[55] As Gadamer writes, *Mitsein* "is a primordial mode of 'Being-we'—a mode in which I is not supplanted by a you [but...] encompasses a primal commonality."[56] For even when opposing the prevailing conventions for the sake of individual authenticity, Dasein's pursuit of possibility is a "co-historizing" with a community—a co-historizing in which a past legacy becomes the basis of a meaningful future.[57] The destiny it shares with its people is, indeed, what grounds Dasein in historicity, linking it to the heritage (the tradition) that determines and is determined by it.⁵⁸

As the horizon of Heideggerian transcendence, history and tradition are consequently never universal, but plural and multiple, product and producer of different histories and traditions, each with its specific origin and quality of being. There may be certain abstract truths pertaining to peoples and civilizations everywhere, but for Heidegger there is no abstract history or tradition informing them, only the pure transcendence of Being. Every great people, as a distinct expression of Being, possesses its own history, its own tradition, its own transcendence, which are *sui generis*. This very specificity is what lends form, purpose, and meaning to its experience of a perpetually changing world. The Being of Dasein's history and tradition may be universal, but Being is manifested only in beings, ontology is manifested only in the ontic. In Heidegger's terms, "only as long as Dasein is ... is there Being."⁵⁹

When Guénonian metaphysics depicts the Perennial Truth as the transcendent unity that embraces all the "archaic religions" and most of the "world religions," it offers modern man a commanding height from which to appraise the failings of his age. But the broad compass of this view comes at the expense of reducing the history and tradition of different peoples and civilizations (whose singular trajectories it effectively dismisses) to variations on a single universal theme. ("Modern, Enlightenment, Masonic thought," it might be added, similarly denies the significance of specific histories and traditions.)

By contrast, a radical traditionalist in the Heideggerian sense defines himself in reference not to the Perennial, but to the Primordial in his history and tradition, even when he finds things in the history and tradition of non-Europeans to admire. For it is Europe that calls him to his future possibility. Like truth, tradition in Heidegger's thought is never an abstraction, never a suprahuman formulation of timeless principles pertinent to peoples everywhere (though its formative effects and futural possibility may assume a certain timelessness for those to whom it speaks). Rather, it is a force whose presence illuminates the distant reaches of a people's ancestral soul, bringing its being in accord with the heritage, order, and destiny distinct to it.

Heraclitus and Parmenides

Whoever takes history seriously, refusing to dismiss millennia of European temporality, is not likely to follow the perennialists in their metaphysical quest. This seems especially so in our contemporary world, where the regressive forces of globalization, multiculturalism, and technoscience seek to destroy all that distinguishes Europe's peoples and civilization from non-European ones. The radical traditionalist faithful to the incomparable tradition of *Magna Europa* (and faithful not in the egoistic sense of petty nationalism, but in the spirit of "belonging to the destiny of the West") cannot, as a consequence, but feel a certain reserve toward the Guénonians—though, and here my argument turns, not toward Evola himself. For after rejecting the Perennial Philosophy and its Evolian distillation, it is important, I want to conclude, to "reconcile" Evola with the radical traditionalist imperatives of Heideggerian thought—for the mountain-climbing Evola was not just a great European, an indefatigable defender of his people's heritage, but an extraordinary Kshatriya, whose heroic Way of Action inspires all who identify with his "Revolt against the Modern World."

Though it would take another article to properly argue the point, Evola, even where metaphysically off target, offers the radical traditionalist a body of work whose Borean motifs demand the deepest study and discussion. But given the argument above: how can the radical incompatibilities between Heidegger and Evola be reconciled?

The answer lies, perhaps, in that "strange" unity linking the two earliest thinkers of the European tradition, Heraclitus and Parmenides, whose philosophies were as antipodal as those of Heidegger and Evola. Heraclitus saw the world as a "great fire," in which everything was always in the process of being consumed, as Being perpetually gave way to Becoming. Parmenides, on the other hand, emphasized the world's unity, seeing it as a single seamless entity, in which all its apparent movements (Becoming) were part of a single universality (Being), the ripples and waves on the great body of the sea. But while one saw the world in terms of flux and the other in terms of stasis, they each nevertheless recognized a common unifying logos, an underlying structure, a "gathered harmony," that lent unity and form to the whole—whether that whole was to be found in the apparently meaningless swirl of worldly events or in the interrelatedness of its endless parts. This unity is Being, whose world-ordering dominion underlies the kindred sensibility animating the original distillations of European thought.

Heidegger's and Evola's competing projects might be viewed in a similar light. In a metaphysics stressing the universal and timeless, the opposition of Being and Becoming, and the primacy of the unconditioned, Evola opposes Heidegger's emphasis on Dasein's thrown and temporal character. Evola nevertheless grasps something akin to the higher reaches of Heidegger's thought. For when Heidegger probes the primordial ground of different beings, seeking the transcendent (Being) in time's imminence (Becoming), he too grasps Being in its imperishable presence, for the primordial at this point becomes perennial—not for all peoples (given that a people's origin and destiny are inevitably singular), but still for those collective forms of Dasein whose differences are of the same essence (insofar as they stem from the same Indo-European heritage).

Heidegger's emphasis on primordialism is, I think, more convincing than Evola's perennialism, but the latter need not be rejected in toto. (Indeed, the argument can be made that in *Being and Time* Heidegger himself failed to reconcile these two fundamental facets of ontology). Heidegger and Evola may therefore approach Being from opposing points of departure and arrive at different (often radically different) conclusions, but their thought, like that of Heraclitus and Parmenides, converges not just in the primacy they attribute to Being, but in the way their understanding of Being, especially in its relation to tradition, becomes an antidote to the crisis of European nihilism.

Notes:

1. Dominique Venner, *Histoire et tradition des Européennes: 30,000 ans d'identité* (Paris: Rocher, 2002), p. 18. Cf. Michael O'Meara, "From Nihilism to Tradition," *The Occidental Quarterly* 3:2 (Summer 2004).
2. Friedrich Nietzsche, *The Will to Power*, trans. by W. Kaufmann and R. J. Hollingdale (New York: Vintage, 1967), pp. 9-39; Friedrich Nietzsche, *The Gay Science*, trans. by W. Kaufmann (New York: Vintage, 1975), §125. Cf. Martin Heidegger, *Nietzsche: 4. Nihilism*, trans. by F. A. Capuzzi (San Francisco: Harper, 1982).
3. "Editorial Prefaces," *TYR: Myth—Culture—Tradition* 1 and 2 (2002 and 2004).
4. M. Raphael Johnson, "The State as the Enemy of the Ethnos," at http://es.geocities.com/sucellus23/807.htm. In *Human, All Too Human* (§96), Nietzsche writes: Tradition emerges "without regard for good or evil or any categorical imperative, but ... above all for the purpose of maintaining a community, a people."
5. Martin Heidegger, *Introduction to Metaphysics*, trans. by G. Fried and R. Polt (New Haven: Yale University Press, 2000), p. 11.
6. Although Guénon had a formative effect on Evola, who considered him his "master," the Italian was not only independent enough to differ with Guénon on several important issues, especially in emphasizing the "Borean" or Indo-European origins of Tradition, but also in giving the Traditionalist project a distinctly militant and Europeanist slant. (I suspect it is this tendency in Evola's thought, combined with what he takes from Bachofen, Nietzsche, and De Giorgio, that put him—at least latently—at odds with his own appropriation of Guénonian metaphysics). As a result, some Guénonians refuse to recognize him as one of their own. For example, Kenneth Oldmeadow's *Traditionalism: Religion in Light of the Perennial Philosophy* (Colombo: The Sri Lankan Institute of Traditional Studies, 2000), now the principal work in English on the Traditionalists, makes no reference at all to him. My view is that Evola's work is not just as important as Guénon's for Perennialism but, for the European "radical," it is its most interesting and pertinent distillation. Cf. Mark Sedgwick, *Against the Modern World: Traditionalism and the Secret History of the Twentieth Century* (New York: Oxford University Press, 2004); Piero Di Vona, *Evola y Guénon: Tradition e civiltà* (Naples: S.E.N., 1985); Roger Parisot, "L'ours et le sanglier ou le conflit Evola-Guénon,"

L'age d'or 11 (Fall 1995).

7. Both the attraction and mystification of Evola's concept is perhaps best captured in the following excerpt from Gottfried Benn's famous review of *Revolt against the Modern World:* "What, then, is this World of Tradition? First off, its novel evocation does not represent a naturalist or historical concept, but a vision, an incantation, a magical intuition. It evokes the world as a universal, something both celestial and suprahuman, something that occurs and has effect only where the universal still exists, where it is sensed, and is already exception, rank, aristocracy. Through such an evocation, culture is freed from its human, historical elements, freed to assume that metaphysical dimension in which man again takes on the great, primordial, and transcendent features of Traditional Man, bearer of a heritage." "Julius Evola, Erhebung wider die moderne Welt" (1935), http://www.regin-verlag.de.

8. Julius Evola, "La vision romain du sacrée" (1934), in *Symbols et mythes de la Tradition occidentale*, trans. by H. J. Maxwell (Milan: Arché, 1980).

9. Julius Evola, *Men Among the Ruins*, trans. by G. Stucco (Rochester, Vermont: Inner Traditions, 2002), p. 116; Julius Evola, "Che cosa è la tradizione" in *L'arco e la clava* (Milan: V. Scheiwiller, 1968).

10. Luc Saint-Etienne, "Julius Evola et la Contre-Révolution," in A. Guyot-Jeannin, ed., *Julius Evola* (Lausanne: L'Age d'Homme, 1997).

11. Julius Evola, *Revolt against the Modern World*, trans. by G. Stucco (Rochester, Vermont: Inner Traditions International, 1995), p. 6.

12. Following an earlier convention of English-language Heideggerian studies, "Being" is used here to designate *das Sein* and "being" *das Seiende*, with the latter referring to an entity or a presence, physical or spiritual, real or imaginary, that partakes in the "beingness" of Being (*das Sein*). Though different in intent and ramification, the perennialists retain something of this distinction. Cf. René Guénon, *The Multiple States of Being*, trans. by J. Godwin (Burkett, N.Y.: Larson, 1984).

13. Martin Heidegger, *The End of Philosophy*, trans. by J. Stambaugh (Chicago: University of Chicago Press, 1973), p. 32.

14. Cf. Alain de Benoist, *On Being a Pagan*, trans. by J. Graham (Atlanta: Ultra, 2004).

15. Admittedly, Guénonian metaphysics is closer to Plato's

identification of truth and Being than to the post-Aristotelian tradition, whose distinction between idea and reality (Being and being, essence and appearance) emphasizes the latter at the former's expense. Heidegger, *The End of Philosophy*, pp. 9–19.

16. Martin Heidegger, *Being and Time*, trans. by J. Macquarrie and E. Robinson (New York: Harper & Row, 1962), §6; also Martin Heidegger, "The Age of the World Picture," in *The Question Concerning Technology and Other Essays*, trans. by W. Lovitt (New York: Harper and Row, 1977).

17. Heidegger, *Being and Time*, §6.

18. Heidegger, *Introduction to Metaphysics*, p. 47.

19. Heidegger, *Introduction to Metaphysics*, p. 41.

20. Heidegger, *Being and Time*, §69b.

21. Martin Heidegger, *Nietzsche: 1. The Will to Power as Art*, trans. by D. F. Krell (San Francisco: Harper, 1979), p. 22

22. Heidegger, *Introduction to Metaphysics*, p. 35.

23. Martin Heidegger, "Letter on Humanism," in *Pathmarks*, ed. by W. McNeill (Cambridge: Cambridge University Press, 1998).

24. Heidegger, *Being and Time*, §79.

25. Heidegger, *Being and Time*, §65.

26. Parts of this paragraph and several below are taken from my *New Culture, New Right: Anti-Liberalism in Postmodern Europe* (Bloomington: 1stBooks, 2004), pp. 123ff.

27. Heidegger, "Letter on Humanism."

28. Martin Heidegger, *Plato's Sophist*, trans. by R. Rojcewicz and A. Schuwer (Bloomington: Indiana University Press, 1976), p. 158.

29. Heidegger, *Being and Time*, §76.

30. Martin Heidegger, *Contributions to Philosophy (From Enowning)*, trans. by P. Emad and K. Mahy (Bloomington: Indiana University Press, 1999), §3 and §20.

31. Martin Heidegger, *Parmenides*, trans. by A. Schuwer and R. Rojcewicz (Bloomington: Indiana University Press, 1992), p. 1.

32. Martin Heidegger, "The Self-Assertion of the German University," in *The Heidegger Controversy*, ed. by Richard Wolin (Cambridge, Mass.: MIT Press, 1993). Also: "Only what is unique is retrievable and repeatable ... Beginning can never be comprehended as the same, because it reaches ahead and thus each time reaches beyond what is begun through it and determines accordingly its own retrieval." Heidegger, *Contributions to Philosophy*, §20.

33. Heidegger, *Contributions to Philosophy*, §101.

34. Hans-Georg Gadamer, *Heidegger's Ways*, trans. by J. W. Stanley (Albany: State University of New York Press, 1994), p. 64.
35. Gadamer, *Heidegger's Ways*, p. 33.
36. Martin Heidegger, *Hölderlin's Hymn "The Ister,"* trans. by W. McNeill and J. Davis (Bloomington: Indiana University Press, 1996), p. 151.
37. Martin Heidegger, "The Origin of the Work of Art," in *Basic Writings*, ed. by D. F. Krell (New York: Harper & Row, 1977).
38. Alain de Benoist, *L'empire intérieur* (Paris: Fata Morgana, 1995), p. 18.
39. Heidegger, *Being and Time*, §65.
40. Julius Evola, *Ride the Tiger*, trans. by J. Godwin and C. Fontana (Rochester, Vermont: Inner Traditions, 2003), pp. 78–103.
41. Cf. Martin Heidegger, *The Basic Problems of Phenomenology*, trans. by A. Hofstadter (Bloomington: Indiana University Press, 1982), pt. 1, ch. 2.
42. When Evola writes in *Ride the Tiger* that Heidegger views man "as an entity that does not include being within itself ... but rather before it, as if being were something to be pursued or captured" (p. 95), he completely misreads Heidegger, suggesting that the latter erects a wall between Being and being, whereas in fact Heidegger sees human Dasein as an expression of Being—though given man's nature, an expression that may not be recognized as such or authentically realized.
43. Heidegger, *Parmenides*, p. 68.
44. Heidegger, *Being and Time*, §29; *Contributions to Philosophy*, §120 and §255.
45. Heidegger, *Being and Time*, §65.
46. Heidegger, *Contributions to Philosophy*, §92.
47. Heidegger, *Being and Time*, §37.
48. Gianni Vattimo, *The End of Modernity*, trans. by J. R. Synder (Baltimore: The John Hopkins University Press, 1985), pp. 51-64.
49. Heidegger, *Introduction to Metaphysics*, pp. 6-7.
50. Heidegger, *Contributions to Philosophy*, §117 and §184; cf. Carl Schmitt, *Political Theology*, trans. by G. Schwab (Cambridge, Mass.: MIT Press, 1985).
51. Heidegger, *Being and Time*, §74.
52. Martin Heidegger, "The Onto-theo-logical Nature of Metaphysics," in *Essays in Metaphysics*, trans. by K. F. Leidecker (New York: Philosophical Library, 1960).

53. Heidegger, *Contributions to Philosophy*, §5.
54. Heidegger, *Contributions to Philosophy*, §5.
55. Heidegger, *Introduction to Metaphysics*, p. 162.
56. Gadamer, *Heidegger's Ways*, p. 12.
57. Heidegger, *Being and Time*, §74.
58. Heidegger, *Being and Time*, §74.
59. Heidegger, *Being and Time*, §43c.

Spiritual Authority and Temporal Power

Alain de Benoist

In the first half of the twentieth century, three authors considered as outstanding representatives of "traditionalist thought" turned their attention to the same doctrinal question. In 1929 René Guénon released a work entitled *Autorité spirituelle et pouvoir temporal* published by J. Vrin.[1] That same year, Julius Evola responded with an article bearing the same title that appeared in the Italian journal *Krur*.[2] Finally, in 1942, Ananda K. Coomaraswamy published an essay that took up the same issue, although he confined his remarks to its Indian context. This was entitled *Spiritual Power and Temporal Authority in the Indian Theory of Government*.[3] It is worth comparing the three views because, although all of them boast an identical source of inspiration, they come to tangibly different conclusions.

Guénon, in the footsteps of many others, observes that history, like myth, constantly stages an opposition or rivalry between temporal and spiritual powers. In ancient India, this opposition placed the Brahmans and Kshatriyas—the priests and warriors—at odds. This opposition appears again in Celtic society with the symbolic rivalry of the boar and the bear (Merlin and Arthur in the tales of the Round Table). In medieval Europe, it forms the framework for the struggle between the Priesthood and the Empire. This struggle, Guénon writes, "invariably takes place in the same fashion: we see the warriors, the holders of temporal power, after initially submitting to spiritual authority, rise up against it and declare themselves independent of any higher power, or even seek to subordinate this authority which it had originally recognized as the legitimate keeper of power and convert it into a tool that serves their domination."

By the term "spiritual authority," Guénon does not mean simple religious authority. With respect to the royal function, symbolized by the scales and the sword, which includes martial and military activity but also administrative, judicial, and governmental activity, spiritual authority can be defined as what appears first and foremost as "knowledge of principles, free of any contingent application." This gives the priesthood the essential function of "the preservation and transmission of the traditional doctrine, in which all regular social organization finds its fundamental principles"—and it is this doctrine that possesses a literally sacred character. Between spiritual and temporal there is thus the same distance that separates *authority* and *power*; whereas the latter manifests externally, with recourse to external means, the former is by essence internal and only asserts itself on its own.

A similar distance separates knowledge and potency, or even thought and action. The Brahman represents the contemplative path (*jñânamârga*). In the order of the *gunas*—the constitutive qualities of beings apprehended in their manifestations—he primarily possesses *sattva*, which is wisdom, intellectualism, and sovereignty coming from conformity to the pure essence. So the king represents the active path (*karmamârga*) and is characterized by *rajas*, which is the impulse of expansion and excess energies. The result of this distinction is that the royal-warrior function needs to be subordinate to the sacerdotal function, just as potency should be subordinate to knowledge and action to thought.

Like the Pole Star, knowledge represents a fixed point in the midst of movement. It corresponds to Aristotle's "unmoved mover." It is transcendence opposed not so much to immanence as to contingency and change. "Change," Guénon underscores, "would be impossible were there no principle from which it proceeds and which, by virtue of the fact that it is its principle, can not be under its control." Knowledge therefore has no need of action to attain possession of the *principles*, in other words, the truth, whereas action would be meaningless unless it is deployed as a result of principles that are necessarily external to it (if they were not and thus subject to contingencies, they would vary ceaselessly and no longer be principles). In other words, knowledge dominates action, because it provides action its *law*. And by the same token, temporal power, being completely subject to the vicissitudes of the contingent, can only be subordinate to spiritual authority—founded on the knowledge of the principles—which in return confers upon it a *legitimacy* stemming from its conformity to the principles that reflect the "order of things."

The dependence of temporal power upon the priesthood is revealed, for example, in the coronation of kings. Kings are not fully legitimate until they have received sacerdotal investiture, which even confers supernatural powers upon them (such as the thaumaturgic powers of the French kings, which Guénon claims are conferred upon them not by inheriting the office but clearly from coronation).

The reversal of the relationship between knowledge and action, as is expressed mainly in all forms of activist volunteerism or "Prometheanism," or even in the belief that ideas are the reflection of socio-historical practices and not the other way around, is thus regarded by traditionalist thought as a complete aberration. This aberration is similar to "the usurpation of supremacy by temporal power," when it claims to emancipate itself from spiritual authority by declaring that there is no domain higher than its own. In so doing, temporal power unwittingly saps the foundations of its own potency. As it is incapable of finding a legitimizing principle in itself, it merely provides the example of an attitude of revolt that by contagion will inevitably lead, step by step, to its own downfall. Guénon cites here the case of the French kings, who, starting with Philip the Fair, ceaselessly sought to make themselves independent of spiritual authority, which led them to rely for support on the bourgeoisie and the newborn economic power, which in turn would eventually dethrone them. As Guénon explains:

> It could be said that the Kshatriyas, once they have entered a state of revolt, degrade in some way and lose their specific character to take on that of a lower caste. It could even be added that this degradation must inevitably be accompanied by the loss of legitimacy ... If the king is no longer satisfied with being the first of the Kshatriyas, in other words the leader of the nobles, and to play the role of "regulator" that this title entails, he loses his reason to exist and, at the same time, he places himself in a position of opposition to that nobility of which he was only the emanation and the most complete expression. This is how we can see the monarchy, in order to "centralize" and absorb into itself the powers that belong collectively to the entire nobility, enter battle with the noble class and relentlessly toil to destroy feudalism, from which, however, it emerged. Furthermore, it can only do this by relying on the third estate, which corresponds to the Vaishyas; and this is why we also see, starting with precisely Philip the Fair, the French kings almost constantly surrounding themselves with members of the bourgeoisie, especially those who, like Louis XI and Louis XIV, pushed the work of "centralization" furthest, from which the bourgeoisie would necessarily harvest the

benefits later when it assumed power with the Revolution.[4]

Guénon later goes on to say, "The revolution that toppled the monarchy is both its logical consequence and its punishment, meaning its reward for the revolt of this same monarchy against spiritual authority."[5]

In the following stage, the temporal does not even claim to impose itself on the spiritual, but radically separates from it and even denies its very existence. The systematic dispossession of the higher by the lower, triggers a process that will lead increasingly downward. The lower castes get the upper hand over the Kshatriyas; economic activity trumps political authority; and personal advantages and profits prevail over the common good. The reign of bourgeois capitalism therefore corresponds to the era of the Vaishyas and that of Bolshevism to the era of the Shudras. In parallel to this, the initial usurpation brings about the process of social atomization that leads into modern individualism.[6] Of course, for Guénon, this involution is part of a traditional vision of cyclical history characterized by waning spirituality and waxing "materialization," in which the darkest age (the Kali Yuga), which corresponds to the present era, is headed both toward the nihilism of chaos and the inevitable final regeneration—inevitable because every tendency pushed to its extreme will lead to its own reversal: "Like all that has only a negative existence, disorder destroys itself."[7]

Therefore Guénon absolutely refused the idea of a complementary relationship between the spiritual and the temporal within one sovereign function. This point of view, which he called "insufficient," masks the necessary *subordination* that should exist between the two domains. For example, he saw the fact that the Roman emperor was both *imperator* and *pontifex romanus* as an "anomaly" that smelled to him like an "usurpation." This led him to finally acquire the conviction of a radical superiority of the East (which has always maintained the primacy of knowledge over action) over the West (which has held the opposite belief, at least since the time of the Renaissance).

Evola's opinion is completely different. Evola in fact reacted strongly against Guénon's argument, saying that it only expressed "the Brahmanical-sacerdotal point of view of an Oriental" and that, for that very reason, needed "to be rejected in whole." This argument, Evola asserted, was mistaken when applied to the Western tradition. Furthermore it amounted to justification of the

Guelph faction with respect to the Ghibellines, a theme on which Evola specifically declared himself the "avowed adversary" of Guénon.

Evola's fundamental thesis is that action has a sacred nature and that there is "a *spiritual* meaning of royalty," which Guénon intentionally fails to take into account, although the very notion of "king of the world" that he has studied on its own demonstrates that royal symbolism can be directly connected to the highest form of spiritual authority. The antagonism that has been visibly displayed since prehistoric times between a royal or warrior tradition and a sacerdotal tradition should therefore not be viewed as "a struggle between the spiritual authority and a rebellious temporal power," but rather as "a struggle between two distinct forms of authority that are equally spiritual and yet insurmountable."[8]

Evola further feels that Guénon falls into rationalism when he insists on the absolute value of the "principles" (the *letter*) more than the "spiritual states to attain" (the *spirit*), and that the opposition he draws between knowledge and action is to a large extent artificial, since tradition (especially the Eastern tradition) has always taught that knowledge is a form of action and higher realization, and that an action, when it is just, *goes beyond the action* that manifests it. Additionally, wouldn't the idea that thought is an "unmoved mover" make it a modality of action through the very notion of a "mover"? And wouldn't this be the reason for which the Roman Emperor, just like the Chinese Emperor or Egyptian Pharaoh, was invested with a "religious" as well as a "royal" responsibility? In fact, Evola believes Guénon confuses spiritual authority and sacerdotal authority. This is the reason why he refuses to accept that "the consecration of the king or chief does not have the sense of a subordination to the priestly caste" but that "through the consecration, the king assumes rather than receives power—a power of a higher kind that invests him with a spiritual influence." Finally, Evola, who was strongly influenced by the theories of Bachofen on the "primitive matriarchy," did not shy from seeing in the "Indian" opposition of king and Brahman the trace of an ancient antagonism between the "Nordic-Iranian" male principle and a "Southern-Demetrico" female or gynecratic principle. This strengthens his idea that, in some way, the king should always have the last word:

> The domination of the sacerdotal castes by a warrior tradition, the primacy of action over contemplation, do not on their own constitute any kind of lowering of the level; to the

contrary it is the loss of contact with the metaphysical reality that constitutes this—whether it is manifested in the form of a materialization of the sacred concept of royalty, which has become simply "temporal power," or whether it is manifested in the form of the decadence of the sacerdotal function that has degenerated into ecclesiastical survivals, dogmatic oversimplifications, and into simple "religion."

Evola goes on to conclude: "It is not in the sacerdotal vision but in the imperial and warrior vision—and by reclaiming the occult sapience that, in the form of *Ars Regia*, is tied to it and is perpetuated within the very heart of the West—where it is appropriate to seek out the symbols of our affirmation and our liberation."

Based on a remarkable knowledge of ancient India, Coomaraswamy's[9] point of view finds accord, in a more academic and perhaps more erudite way, with that of Guénon on a number of essential points. Coomaraswamy, in particular, emphasizes the blatant superiority of the Brahman over the king that exists in India. Symbolically, the Brahman is the womb that gives birth to the Kshatriya. The Kshatriya can offer sacrifice, but only the Brahman can both offer and perform sacrifice. Indian texts also stress that monarchy has no principle in and of itself, but is governed by the eternal law of *dharma*, which is action conforming to the norm as opposed to *artha*, action conforming to vested or contingent interests. In passing, Coomaraswamy also criticized the position of Evola, in which he sees a concession to that same "modern world" that the Italian author so often attacked.[10]

But at the same time, Coomaraswamy stressed, from the beginning of his book to the end, the importance of the "marriage" between monarchy and the priesthood. The entire Indian political doctrine can be summed up, he claimed, in the "nuptial" speech addressed by the Brahman to the king in the *Aitareya Brâhmana* (VIII, 27). "I am That, you are This, I am the Heavens, you are the Earth." This phrase is in fact an essential one. On the one hand, it confirms that the king, who is "male" in relation to his kingdom (for the prosperity of his people and the fertility of the earth depend upon him), is with respect to his "priest," his *purohita*,[11] "on the side of the earth," which symbolically means on the "natural" and "female" side. On the other hand it indicates that the relationship between the priesthood (Brahma) and the royalty is as strict as a marriage, it makes this hierarchy relative by placing it in the perspective of a "hierogamy." The union of the Brahman and the king in fact takes place in the celebration of the sacrifice in the same way Earth and Heaven unite on the Cosmic plane,[12] or, in a traditional society, the man and woman on the sexual plane. Their relationship is therefore based on a reciprocal asymmetrical dependency, symbolized by the fact that the *purohita* sometimes walks in front of the king, to clearly show he is not his subject, and sometimes behind him to indicate that he nonetheless is dependent upon him. "Whereas, spiritually or absolutely, the priest is superior," writes Louis Dumont on this subject, "at the same time from the temporal or material point of view he is subjugated and dependent. Conversely the spiritually subordinate figure of the king is the master on the material plane."[13]

The *Satapatha Brâhmana* (IV, 1.4) specifies on the other hand that the *purohita* is to the king what thought is to action, and Mitra to Varuna. In the Vedic religion, Mitra (but also Krishna, Agni, and Brihaspati) in fact represents the archetype of spiritual authority just as Varuna (but also Arjuna and Indra) represents temporal power. For example, in the *Satapatha Brâhmana* (IV, 1.4), it is said that Varuna (the Monarchy) could not subsist apart from Mitra (the Priesthood): "Turn thou unto me that we may unite; I assign to you the precedence; quickened by thee, I shall do deeds." The same text (II, 4.4.19) also indicates that Mitra and Varuna are like male and female: "Mitra ejaculated his semen into Varuna." This explains the apparent paradox that views the "masculine" element as being on the side of the Brahman, despite his "passive" character, and the feminine element on the side of the king, despite his warrior nature. Mitra's "passivity" is that of the unmoved mover that is the dominant law of all action. Hence the eloquent Sanskrit two-in-one Mitrâvaruna, "Mitra and Varuna combined as a couple," as if one was in the presence of a "joint" person here.

The analogical correspondence is therefore complete between Mitra and Varuna, the Brahman and the king, the day and the night, consciousness and action, Truth and the Word, the "knower" (*abhigantr*) and the "doer" (*kartr*), and so on.[14] In each case, there is a clear hierarchy between two principles, but this hierarchy is inseparable from the "nuptial" union that reveals a transcendental unity and produces its own surpassing. Here, of course, we find another example of the theme of the identity of opposites (*coincidentia oppositorum*). In the ancient texts, the relationship of the Brahman and the king is frequently depicted by the image of twins of the opposite sex or even spouses called upon to unite (*Aitareya Brâhmana* VIII, 27). Equally revealing is the episode of the marriage of "Indragni" recorded in the *Satapatha Brâhmana* (X, 4.1.5), in which Agni (the Priest) and Indra (the King) tell one another: "So long as we are thus, we shall be unable to bring forth offspring. Let us twain become a single form."[15] "That the Spiritual Authority, Plato's *hieron*, etc," Coomaraswamy concludes, "is also the Ruler, Plato's *arkhon* just as the *brahma* 'is both the *brahma* and *kshatra*,' means indeed that the Supreme Power is a royal as well as a priestly power." Necessary for the formation of the Perfect Sovereign, the union of the two principles is also the model for every human being of the conquest of his *autonomy*. It is in fact the equivalent of the merger of opposing complementarities, which corresponds to the surpassing of the human condition and the instauration of a new *regnum*.

With respect to Mitra and Varuna, Georges Dumézil writes, "There is never a conflict between these two authentic beings, but, to the contrary, constant collaboration."[16] Elsewhere he stipulates that "the Mitra and Varuna opposition is never nor can it ever be hostile or competitive; it can only be complimentary. […] From the perspective of man as well as that of the cosmos, it is the common works of the god that matter first and foremost, the specificity of each one being of less interest than their complicity."[17] Mircea Eliade meanwhile shows that the two Indian figures of sovereignty illustrate a duality "that is not at all static, but rather is expressed in the rhythmic alternation of the contrary principles," so that their "alternating rituals" primarily express the "obscure desire of reintegrating the two opposing principles and thereby winning back the primordial unity."[18] All of these opinions are in agreement.[19]

As the traditional world was founded on the idea of an analogy between human society and the cosmic order, which was mediated by the society of the gods, in order to grasp the idea that the ancient Europeans had of political and social sovereignty, we should now study the way this sovereign role was articulated in the religious ideology of the Indo-Europeans. We are quite familiar with this ideology today, mainly thanks to the works of Georges Dumézil (who Guénon, Evola, and Coomaraswamy all seem to overlook, incidentally). Now Dumézil, who devoted particular attention to the first function, meaning the function of sovereignty,[20] shows that it is clearly distinguished from the warrior or second function, despite the privileged ties that connect these two by comparison to the third function. The king and the warrior, at least in theory, do not belong to the same functional level. Furthermore Dumézil, with respect to the first function, emphasizes, its Janus Bifrons–like, ambivalent nature, by indicating that it "is organized around the combination of a more cosmic god with a god displaying a greater concern for humanity's welfare; a sovereign magician god, who is disturbing and creative with one rather a jurist, a pacifist, and an organizer."[21] The first function therefore combines a king and a priest, a temporal power and a spiritual authority. This brings us to the very heart of our discussion.

In India, as we have seen, Mitra and Varuna represent the first function viewed in its two aspects. Mitra is the sovereign under his benevolent, clear, luminous, calm, orderly, male, and sacerdotal aspect; he is the patron god of oaths and contracts (the etymology of his name confirms that he is the Contract personified), and legal and religious activity. Varuna is the sovereign in its terrible, dark, nocturnal, disturbing, strict, violent, female, and bellicose aspect. In this aspect this god is the patron of martial activities; he often punishes, and intervenes in human affairs through the use of "bonds" and "knots" that are characteristic of magic. Mitra is the god closest to man. He embodies this world and is therefore the god of the diurnal sky, day, life, and the Sun (with which he is frequently incorporated). Varuna is intimately connected to cosmic forces. He incarnates the "other world"; thus he is on the side of the nocturnal sky, shadows, death, and the Moon. Mitra is a god oriented toward reflection and wisdom. This is why he is incorporated into the Brahman, the keeper of spiritual power. Varuna is an active god, incorporated into the kshatriya and temporal power, and sponsors the king in the ceremony of his consecration (*râjasûya*).

"Mitra and Varuna," states Dumézil, "are the two terms for a large number of conceptual and antithetical couples, whose juxtaposition defines two planes. Each point of one of these planes, one could say, calls up another similar point on the other plane, and these couples, diverse as they may be, possess a certain kinship that is so clear that for every new couple added to the files, it is easy to safely foresee which would be given the term "mitrian" and which the term "varunian."[22] As can be seen, both Mitra and Varuna are in fact equally necessary for the establishment of *ṛta*, the harmonious order of both human societies and the cosmos.

In Rome, Jupiter is first and foremost a king (*rex*). He controls lightning like Zeus for the Greeks (and like the gods of the second function, Indra and Thor among the Indians and Germans respectively). He is thus a counterpart of Varuna. The correspondence of Mitra would be Dius Fidius, a deity who was quickly supplanted by a personified abstraction, Fides. In the mythic history of the Roman people, this bipartition can also be found in the couple formed by the first two kings: Romulus (= Varuna) and Numa (= Mitra). For the Germans, Odin-Wotan is like Varuna the patron of war and the master of magic: it is he who welcomes to Valhalla the fighters he has chosen. Tyr, a "Mitrian" deity who is the counterpart of the Vedic Dyaus and the Greek Zeus, is the god of contracts and the patron of the assembly, the *thing*. Taking into consideration the slipping of the first function toward the martial function, characteristic of the Germanic religion, he was distorted within the relatively recent past to the point of sometimes being incorporated into Mars, whereas the true "Germanic Mars," Thor, has "slipped" into the third function.

In each great sector of the area covered by the Indo-European expansion, we thus find a clear bipartition of the sovereign function. This is represented by two distinct deities who, by way of a certain number of symbolic analogies, respectively reflect spiritual authority and temporal power. These two deities form a couple, and Dumézil is perfectly correct when describing the first function to speak of "two faces, two halves that are antithetical but complementary and equally necessary."[23]

"Equally necessary" but not equal. The "Mitrian" deity is in fact normally perceived as relatively superior to the "Varunian" deity. On the other hand—and this is where we find again the trace of an opposition between spiritual authority and temporal power—one can detect, at a stage that seems later chronologically speaking and more or less marked in a way according to the Indo-European "provinces," a kind of obliteration of the "Mitra side." Just as among the Germans, Tyr was finally made subordinate to Odin-Wotan,[24] among the Romans, Dius Fidius suffered from the theological reform of Jupiter (which coincided with the promotion of this god and the creation of his Capitoline cult), to the point where he was entirely absorbed by Jupiter. In India Mitra ultimately attracted less attention from the poets than Varuna. This suppression needs to be understood in context of the "inevitabilities of the martial function" (as Dumézil describes it), which is naturally driven to contest the primacy of the sovereign function. The hymns in which Indra defies Varuna and boasts of abolishing his potency—similar to the *Hárbarðsljóð* of the *Poetic Edda* which depicts Thor insulting Odin—bear testimony to this in their particular way, not to mention the Roman example concerning the impiety of the overly martial king Tullus Hostilius against whom Jupiter exacted his just revenge.

It is in light of these clues that we need to study the problem of royalty as conceived by the Indo-Europeans. The antiquity of this institution is confirmed by the linguistic concordance of the Vedic *raj- (rajah), the Celtic *rig (-rix), and the Latin *-reg (rex).[25] From the onset however, the "royal question" (the relationship of the three functions and the king) proves to be one of great complexity. Dumézil expressed it this way:

> The king is sometimes superior, at least externally, to the trifunctional structure, in which the first function is then centered on the purest possible administration of the sacred by the priest, rather than on the power of the sovereign and his agents; sometimes the king—and the priest-king to the same or to a greater extent than the governing king—is, to the contrary, the most eminent representative of this function; sometime he displays a varying blend of elements borrowed from the three functions, most notably the second, and it is from this function and eventually the martial class from which he most often emerges."[26]

That for "practical" reasons the king is most often a product of the military class should be in no way surprising. In India, the word *râjanya*—derived from *râjan*, meaning "king"—is a synonym for *kshatriya*. The first Indo-European kings were "elected," that is to say chosen, from among the royal family or the great feudal lords by an assembly of free men. In the case of incompetence such that they lost their legitimacy, which is to say they were not striving to realize "here below" the harmony that rules "on high," they could be deposed (as the last Merovingian king was in 751) or even killed. This should not be taken to imply that the royal function was purely and simply military in essence. The *rex* is not equivalent to the *dux*, and this is why Dumézil, in another passage in his work, writes that the king most often is "qualitatively extracted" from the second function, which amounts to saying that by acceding to the royal position he has passed into another function, that of sovereignty. Now, as we have already seen, this function is ideally perceived as one that includes two antithetical but complementary aspects: a temporal one and a spiritual one. Thus there is every reason to think that, among the Indo-Europeans, royalty originally had a sacral character, with the king (as was the case in Sumer, Egypt, or even the Chinese Empire) being invested with "magical" or religious prerogatives in addition to those of a political nature.

Finally, we still need to take into consideration the fact that social distinctions in the ancient societies of Indo-European origin attested to historically do not always correspond to the ideal tripartition proposed by their religious ideology. Trifunctionality, we must remember, is first and foremost an idea. It is only potentially and secondarily a human social reality.[27] And its transposition into the social sphere, when it occurs, is always subject to being distorted. Among the Germans, for example, the first function corresponds to the nobility, whereas among the Celts and Indo-Iranians, it corresponds exclusively to the priests (here the nobles occupy the second class). This obviously raises a question, as the choice of the king from the warrior class will change meaning depending on whether or not this class occupies the first function. But this then also raises the question of whether the separation of the royal function and the sacerdotal function was originally Indo-European or whether, as Louis Dumont hypothesized about India, it resulted from a "process that would have transpired during the Vedic Era," a process during which the king "would have lost in India his religious prerogatives." It is difficult to take any kind of firm position on this point. The apparent absence of the priest class from the "central" Indo-European peoples like the Germans, which stands in contrast to the Brahman institution of India, the *flamines* of Rome, and the druids of the Celts, as it does to the incontestably "magical" nature of the political royalty of most of these peoples, seems nonetheless to argue in favor of Dumont's hypothesis.[28] According to other authors, however, the sacerdotal class would only have appeared as a distinct class in tandem with the necessity of maintaining or preserving the tradition and the collective identity with a force that has increased in strength within a human environment grown increasingly heterogeneous (Jean Haudry).[29]

Among the Germans, where the priest class seems non-existent, the royal institution took on a sacral character once the "Wotanic" royalty definitively prevailed over the ancient "Vanic" institution (which persisted however in Scandinavia until the seventh century C.E.).[30] The royal function then became that of the "magician" and "warrior"; the god Wotan was installed as the ancestor of the dynastic line while the new name of the Germanic king, *kuningaz, was substituted for the former name.[31] This phenomenon seems to have taken place during the start of our historical era in connection with the rise and spread of warrior bands and the Germanic expression of the *Völkerwanderung*, which would successively give birth to the Franks, Lombards, Visigoths, Vandals, Ostrogoths, Burgundians, Saxons, and other peoples.[32] From this point on the Germanic king was the first among warriors and lords (*jarls*), as well as a "magician" who acted as the intermediary between his people and the gods from whom he descended. He possessed the knowledge of the runes and guaranteed the prosperity of all his people. "A religious and institutional revolution," writes Jean-Paul Allard, "the emergence of 'Wotanic' royalty definitively exalted the king, raising him above the contingencies of the second function, but not detaching him from that class. It conferred upon him a sacred nature he had not held formerly. He henceforth possessed an essentially magical charisma of divine origin through which the royalty reinforced its Indo-European nature."[33]

The monarchical institution of Western Europe was directly inherited from these Germanic migrations of the fifth century C.E. "Royalty," writes Georges Dumézil, "comes out of the Germanic past, carried by people that Rome, for good or ill, had welcomed into its midst, without detracting from the power of their leaders."[34] Behind the superficial coloring that Christian tradition had adopted from the "kings" of the Old Testament, in many respects medieval royalty continues—whether through symbolic insignia (torques, scepters, spears, cloak, and so on), or the thaumaturgic powers attributed to "healing" kings (the scrofula)—the ancient sacral royalty whose titleholder's powers were conferred by his possession of uncommon abilities.[35]

The problem of the relationship between spiritual authority and temporal power is posed in a parallel and acute way with the famous quarrel between the Priesthood and Empire that has left its imprint on centuries of the history of Western Europe. We have an extremely interesting text in this regard at our disposal. It is a letter addressed to the Emperor by Pope Gelasius I, in which the sovereign pontiff—who ruled during the final years of the fifth century, the era of Theodoric—set out a fairly remarkable theory of the relations between the papacy and the emperor. Gelasius wrote: "There are two powers, august Emperor, by which this world is chiefly ruled, namely, the sacred authority of the priests and the royal power. [...] Yet in things divine you [must] bow your head humbly before the leaders of the clergy and await from their hands the means of your salvation. [...] The ministers of religion, recognizing the supremacy granted you from heaven in matters affecting the public order, obey your laws."[36]

Louis Dumont, who included a copy of the text of this letter in his book, analyzed it as follows: "The priest is therefore subordinate to the king in worldly affairs that concern public order. [...] The priests are superior, for it is only at a lower level that they are inferior. We are not dealing with a mere 'correlation' (Morrison) or the simple submission of kings to priests (Ullmann), but with a *hierarchical complementarity*." Dumont then goes on to say, "It so happens that I found the same configuration in ancient Vedic India. There, the priests viewed themselves as religiously or absolutely superior to the king, but materially subject to him. While the phrasing is different, the arrangement exactly mirrors the arrangement described by Gelasius."[37] In fact what we find here is the outline mentioned earlier: higher than the king in spiritual matters, the priest is beneath him when it comes to public affairs, which themselves are of lesser importance than the first. "We should understand Gelasius," adds Dumont, "as saying that, while the Church is in the Empire for the affairs of the world, the Empire is in the Church when it comes to divine matters."[38] In certain respects, this orientation is a kind of Ghibelline position before the fact. If it had in fact been instituted, Europe would have been spared the Investiture Controversy born out of the rivalry between the Priesthood and the Empire.

This was not the case. Starting in the middle of the eighth century, the papacy adopted an attitude that was radically different from the one suggested by Gelasius. It strove to gain control of imperial authority, including that over worldly matters. The hierarchical diarchy was replaced by a "spiritual monarchy" in which the spiritual was viewed as superior to the temporal *even for temporal matters*. The Pope, from that point on, holds all powers, which raises the question of the limits of imperial authority. The quarrel of the Guelphs and Ghibellines that took place four centuries later, would allow this question to be raised publicly.

Alluding to the partisans of the Empire (the twelfth-century Ghibellines, William of Occam, and Marsilius of Padua in the fourteenth century), Louis Dumont observes: "The partisans of the

Empire did not deny the essential superiority of the Church, nor its independence or right to sovereignty within its domain, but they extolled the doctrine from the early days of the Church and its recognition of the *sacerdotium* and *imperium* as two independent spheres instituted by God himself, two powers to coordinate [...]. They sometimes proposed a relationship suggestive of that in Hinduism: the State must be subordinate to the Church in spiritual matters, the Church to the State in temporal matters."[39] In a more general manner, the Ghibellines asserted the sacral character of temporal authority in continuity with the heritage of ancient Rome and the purest European tradition.[40] But in the final analysis neither the Pope or the Ghibellines prevailed. In the wake of the birth of secularization, the Investiture Controversy would lead to the *separation* of temporal and spiritual powers, a modality that is far removed from the unidimensional hierarchy advocated by some and the hierarchical complementarity and reciprocity sought by others.

The light shed by the preceding material makes it easier to see how we should evaluate the respective positions of Evola, Coomaraswamy, and Guénon. Guénon is correct to emphasize the superiority of spiritual authority, but he is incorrect when assigning it an absolute primacy, which leads him to interpret the Brahman/Kshatriya opposition from the angle of a fight for the top rank, in other words a power struggle.[41] He does not see that spiritual authority is only superior when in its own domain, whereas it is inferior in those "inferior things" known as public affairs. Nor does he see that temporal power in traditional societies also possesses an intrinsically sacred nature. Finally, he does not appear to realize that the Brahman and the king form an inseparable couple, characteristic of the two complementary aspects that are a feature of sovereignty. Similarly, his linear, non-dialectical interpretation of the relationship of thought and action, contemplation and realization, knowledge and power, beyond the fact it is insufficient to exhaust the analysis of the sovereign function in ancient European societies, leads him to adopt an overly one-dimensional, hierarchical perspective, which does not give enough weight to the principle of the conciliation of opposites.[42] Although he only brings up the case of India, with respect to the subject at hand, Coomaraswamy sees things more clearly when he emphasizes the fact that the primacy of the Priesthood is not exclusive of its structural complementarity with Royalty, and stresses the importance of the "marriage" of the two principles.

For his part, Evola rightly underscores the intrinsically sacred character of royal or imperial power. On the other hand, he is wrong, falling into the opposite error of Guénon, when he claims spiritual authority was entirely submissive to temporal power. Concerning his interpretation of sacerdotal power as being essentially "feminine," right spiritual authority being in some way a kind of relic of "gynecocratic" influence, there is no way this can be given any serious consideration both because of the dubious nature of the hypothesis of a primitive matriarchy as well as the clearly "masculine" symbolism constantly attributed to the Brahman by Indian texts. For Guénon, the king is nothing but the highest individual among nobles and warriors; he is characterized by strength alone, just as wisdom is the chief characteristic of the priest function. Now, while it is true as we have seen that the king often is a product of the military class and maintains privileged relations with this class, his function also gives him access to a qualitatively different level. So it is not possible to simply reduce the royal function to that of the warrior.

It is also easy to see that Guénon and Evola both tend to systematically confuse the royal function and the martial function, one proclaiming it intrinsically inferior to the sacerdotal function, the other proclaiming it superior or at least equal.

Temporal power should not be imposed over spiritual authority, but spiritual authority does not hold absolute primacy either. The two principles are inseparably bound up in the same sovereign function, without this bond serving to form any kind of theocracy. The couple formed this way should be interpreted from the angle of reciprocal dependency and the conflict of opposites. Spiritual authority and temporal power correspond to differential orientations inside a hierarchical complementarity of a unideminsional tendency.

(*Translated by Jon Graham*)

Notes:

1. René Guénon, *Autorité spirituelle et pouvoir temporal* (Paris: Vrin, 1929). The most recent edition of this work was published by Guy Trédaniel, 1984.

2. The French translation of this appears as "Autorité spirituelle et pouvoir" in *"Ur" & "Krur," Introduction à la magie*, vol. 3 (Milano: Arché, 1985), pp. 171–89, trans. Gérard Boulanger. This text was reprinted in the revue *Totalité*, 27 (Winter 1986–87). A revised Italian version appears in Julius Evola, ed., *Introduzione alla magia. A cura del "Gruppo di Ur"* (Rome: Edizioni Mediterranee), vol. 3, pp. 354–63.

3. Ananda K. Coomaraswamy, *Spiritual Authority and Temporal Power in the Indian Theory of Government* (New Haven: American Oriental Society, 1942).

4. Guénon, *Autorité spirituelle*, pp. 85f.

5. Ibid., p. 113.

6. Guénon states in passing that individualism and "naturalism" are closely aligned. This statement appears debatable to me, to say the least.

7. For Guénon, unity corresponds to spiritual harmony, whereas "matter is multiplicity and division." Hence his condemnation of the principle of nationalities: the formation of the modern nations accelerated the subjugation of spiritual authority by temporal national powers.

8. See also Julius Evola, *The Mystery of the Grail: Initiation and Magic in the Quest for the Spirit* (Rochester: Inner Traditions, 1996). In his review of *Revolt Against the Modern World*, Guénon himself confirmed his disagreement on this point. "So, when it concerns the unique original source of the two sacerdotal and royal powers, the author has a very marked tendency to emphasize the royal aspect at the expense of the sacerdotal aspect" (*Comptes-rendus*, Paris: Ed. Traditionnelles, p. 13). The Guénonian point of view is restated by Bruno Hapel in "Affrontements dantesques," in *Vers la Tradition* (September–November 1995), pp. 29-34.

9. Ananda K. Coomaraswamy, born in Colombo, Ceylon on 22 August 1877, was the son of an English woman and an Indian lawyer of Tamil descent. He pursued his education in Great Britain and was given charge of mineral exploration on Ceylon in 1904, where he took part in the founding of the Society for the Social Reform of Ceylon, of which he was named president. Summoned

to Boston in 1917 to head the Indian Art section of the Museum of Fine Arts, he spent the rest of his life in the United States. He died in 1947. See also Roger Lipsey, *Coomaraswamy: His Life and Work* (Princeton: Princeton University Press, 1977), and Giovanni Monastra, "Ananda K. Coomaraswamy, de l'idéalism à la tradition," *Nouvelle École*, 47 (1995), pp. 25–42. Starting in 1936, Coomaraswamy became a regular contributor to the review *Études traditionnelles*, then directed by Guénon. His work, written in English, focuses primarily on the sacred art and traditional thought of ancient India. Some of his additional works are: *What Is Civilization? and Other Essays* (Lindisfarne Books, 1989), *Buddha and the Gospel of Buddhism* (Kessinger Publications, 2003), *Dance of Shiva* (South-East Asia Books, 1997), and *The Door in the Sky* (Princeton: Princeton University Press, 1997).

10. Coomaraswamy, *Spiritual Authority and Temporal Power in the Indian Theory of Government*, p. 10.

11. This literally means "[he who is] placed in front." Its translation with the word "priest," although traditional, is simply an approximation.

12. The analogical Christian expression: "Thy Will be done, on Earth as it is in Heaven," probably retains the trace of much older formulations.

13. Louis Dumont, *Homo hierarchicus. Le système des castes et ses implications*, 2nd ed. (Paris: Gallimard, 1977), p. 354.

14. Subsequently Indian literature will interpret even the opposition between the Self (*purusha*) and the Nature (*prakriti*) as an illustration of the Mitra-Varuna antithesis.

15. The *Hieros gamos* is again realized in the *Taittirîya Samhitâ* (V, 2.4) with the union of the two Agni. The *Rig Veda* (V, 3.1) states explicitly in this regard that Agni is born as the chthonian figure of Varuna and is set ablaze in the celestial form of Mitra. Further one, one can read again that "Agni is both Mitra and Varuna" (*Rig Veda*, VII, 12.3).

16. Georges Dumézil, *L'idéologie tripartite des Indo-Européens* (Brussels: Latmous, 1958), p. 64.

17. Georges Dumézil, *Les dieux souverains des Indo-Européens* (Paris: Gallimard, 1977), pp. 59-60.

18. Mircea Eliade, *Briser le toit de la maison. La créativité et ses symbols* (Paris: Gallimard, 1986), pp. 303f.

19. René Prévost also describes the couple formed by the Brahman and the king as a unit for which neither half forms a

complete entity by itself, and which consists of two inseparable elements, complementary but unequal. "None of the elements is complete without the other. Their connection is that of the part to the whole where the whole is the source of the part and its fertilizing element" ("Le brâhmane et le roi," in *Georges Dumézil, In memoriam*, vol. 2, special issue of *Études indo-européenes* (1988), p. 61f). A complete theology can be seen outlined here, in which man's relationship to God is comparable to that of the king and the Brahman. Man is incomplete without God, but God is also incomplete without man, although he is superior to him.

20. See notably his book, *Mitra-Varuna. Essai sur les deux représentations indo-européenes de la souveraineté* (Paris: Gallimard, 1948); and *Les dieux souverains des Indo-Européens*, op. cit.

21. "Le messager des dieux," interview with Françoise Ewald in *Le Magazine littéraire* (April 1986).

22. Dumézil, *L'idéologie tripartite*, p. 63.

23. In many respects the origin of this bipartition remains a mystery. A particularly interesting hypothesis advanced by Jean Haudry connects it with the Indo-European concept of the three heavens ("The heavens are three in number," *Rig Veda*, I, 35.6). The dual nature of the first function would stem from an older opposition that combined the heavens and the colors of the cosmos. Tyr and Mitra in fact seem first to have been gods of the day sky and Varuna and Odin, gods of the night sky. "Mitra is the day and Varuna the night," the *Brâhmana* says. The former name of Tyr, **Tiwaz*, is moreover a derivative of Proto-Indo-European **deywos*, "one of the daytime sky" (a term that is also the source of the French word for god, *"Dieu"*). The "marriage" of these gods would give us the "third heaven" personified by the goddesses of the daily or annual Dawn: Athena, Aphrodite, Ourania, *Austro, Mater Matuta, the Minerva of the Capitoline triad, Helen in the Trojan cycle, and so forth. For more see Jean Haudry, "La tradition indo-européen au regard de la linguistique," in *L'Information grammaticale* (March 1986), pp. 3–11 (reprinted in *Nouvelle École*, 45 [Winter 1988–89], pp. 116–29); and *La religion cosmique des Indo-Européens* (Milan: Arché and Belles lettres, 1987).

24. Hence the idea maintained by some authors, which is almost certainly wrong, that Odin would be a more "recent" god.

25. This same root became **rik-* in the ancient Germanic language, which gives us the modern German word for Realm or Empire (*Reich*).

26. Dumézil, *L'idéologie tripartite*, pp. 32f.

27. Dumézil, who for a time believed that he had detected traces of an ancient social tripartion conforming to the ideological model in all Indo-European societies, later backed away from this point of view.

28. For his part, Christophe Levalois writes that "in the entirely traditional societies, there was no distinction […] thus separation made between spiritual authority and temporal power" (*Principes immémoriaux de la royauté* [Paris: Léopard d'or, 1989], p. 54), but this formulation appears flawed to me. Distinction and separation are not in fact synonyms. Temporal power and spiritual authority can be distinguished within a traditional society even if they are not separate. The sacred, likewise, can only be truly expressed and grasped if it is accompanied by a profane zone that is simultaneously distinct from it and connected with it.

29. For his part, Guénon feels that "the two powers originally did not exist with the status of separate duties exercised by different individuals," and that, "to the contrary, they should both have been held within the common principle that gave them birth and of which they merely represented two indivisible aspects." These remarks make his subsequent reasoning somewhat paradoxical.

30. For more see Jean-Paul Allard, "La royauté wotanique des Germains," in *Études indo-européenes* (January 1982), pp. 66–83, and (April 1982), pp. 31–57. Also see Otto Höfler, *Germanisches Sakralkönigtum I: Der Runenstein von Rök und die germanische Individualweihe* (Tübingen: Niemeyer, 1952).

31. The oldest name for king among the German peoples, corroborated by the old Anglo-Saxon *thiodan*, contains the same root as the word defining the "people" (*thiot-*, *thiud-*). This term was subsequently replaced by **kuningaz*, which gave birth to the modern Germanic and English words (*König, king, koning, konge*, and so forth). The Germanic root **kun-* is connected to the Indo-Eurpoean root **gen-*, that can be seen in the Latin genus and the Greek γενοσ. Etymologically speaking, **kuningaz* therefore means "one belonging to the lineage" (**kunja-* meaning "race" or "lineage").

32. "Wotanic" royalty therefore seems to be directly connected to the migrations typical of the *Völkerwanderungen*. The Saxons, as long as they remained inhabitants of the continent, did not have a king.

33. Allard, "La royauté wotanique," p. 77.

34. Duménzil, *Le temps des cathédrals. L'art et la société, 980-1420* (Paris: Gallimard, 1976), pp. 21f.

35. I should also mention here the famous doctrine of "the king's two bodies," to which Ernst Kantoriwicz devoted a large book translated into French thirty years later (*Les deux corps du roi* [Paris: Gallimard, 1989]). First set forth in Elizabethan England, then in that of the Stuarts, during the sixteenth century by the legists of the Crown, this doctrine makes the sovereign a "Gemini" individual. "The king consists of two bodies, that is to say a natural body and a political body. His natural body, considered by itself, is a mortal body subject to all the infirmities it is heir to by nature or by accident. [...] But his political body is a body that cannot be seen or touched, consisting of one political society and one government, and formed for the guidance of the people and the administration of the public body, and this body is entirely free of childhood and old age, and all other natural defects and weaknesses to which the natural body is exposed, and for this reason, what the king does in his political body cannot be made invalid or annulled by any failing of his natural body." The two bodies, one temporal, the other spiritual, are indivisibly united and can only be parted by death, which only affects one of them. Here can be seen a new formulation of the old dual formula: one whole comprised of two unequal halves. Kantorowicz shows that this doctrine is the culmination of an entire line of thought, first formulated in a purely theological manner (the duality of the royal body reflects the duality of Christ's nature, who was both a real man and a real God, the sovereign being then considered as the "vicar of God"), and then introduced into law in the twelfth century. The law itself became increasingly sacralized with the king no longer a sacred figure because of his similarity to Christ, but because he represented "living justice" and the "animation of the law." In its final stage, the political and moral body of the sovereign—the "corporation" that he forms with his kingdom, of which he is the leader and his subjects the members—becomes the equivalent of the spiritual and mystical body of the Church, thereby transforming itself into a secular *corpus mysticum*. The doctrine of the "two bodies of the king" denotes in this sense the beginning of the secularization of the political theology of the Middle Ages.

36. Gelasius, Epistle 12, translated in J. H. Robinson, *Readings in European History* (Boston: Ginn, 1905), p. 72f.

37. Louis Dumont, *Essais sur l'individualisme. Une perspective*

anthropologique sur l'idéologie moderne (Paris: Le Seuil, 1983), pp. 52f.

38. Ibid., p. 54.

39. Ibid., p. 76f.

40. Or as it is now commonly stated: "What God is to Heaven, the Emperor is to the Earth." Through his mystical union with God, the emperor is creator (and not merely the preserver) of law on the earth, which makes him both the father and son of justice. Frederich II of Hohenstaufen resorted to the doctrine known as that of the "two luminaries," which incorporates respectively the papacy and the Empire to the moon and sun, planetary bodies which being created by God, are not totally independent of each other but whose orbits do not interfere with one another.

41. In the majority of Indian tales recounting the struggles of Brahmans versus Kshatriyas, the motive of the fight is never to gain possession of the other's function. For example, in the famous legend that depicts the extermination of the Kshatriya by the Brahman Paracurâma, the victor makes no attempt to replace his adversaries or to rule in their stead.

42. The triad "thought-word-action" is constantly mentioned in the *Vedas* as well as in the *Avesta*, which confirms that this enumeration comes from times of the greatest antiquity. It is expressed in a hierarchical perspective with no break in continuity.

Weaving the Web of Wyrd

Nigel Pennick

The three states of being—commonly perceived as the past, present and future—are personified in European traditional spirituality in the form of three female human figures. More precisely, these personifications describe the states or processes of formation, becoming, and dissolution. Their earliest literary manifestation was in ancient Greece, where they appear as the Moirai, the avenging daughters of Night. In his *Theogony* (ca. 850 B.C.E.), Hesiod writes: "And Night bore hateful Doom and black Fate and Death ... she bore the Destinies and ruthless avenging Fates, Clotho and Lachesis and Atropos, who give men at their birth both evil and good to have, and they pursue the transgressions of men and of gods: and these goddesses never cease from their dread anger until they punish the sinner with a sore penalty."[1] The English word *fate* is derived from a past participle form of Latin *fari*, "to speak." The Fates are thus involved with "what has been spoken," decreeing what shall become of individuals.

Orpheus, the prophet of the religion of Dionysos, referred to them as "the Moirai in white raiment." His followers, the Orphics, experienced these three daughters of Night as the Moon's phases, ever transient and ever regenerating. Clotho is the waxing First Quarter; Lachesis, the Full Moon; and Atropos, the waning Last Quarter. The most widespread perception of the Fates, however, is that of craftswomen, spinning and weaving. Clotho spins the thread of existence, Lachesis measures it out, and Atropos cuts it. Clotho is the bringer into being; Lachesis, "the disposer of lots," decides which way the thread shall be used, and Atropos, "she who cannot be turned" or "the Fury with abhorred shears," cuts it. The locus of their actions is in a cave by a pool of water.

According to the Romans, the three Fates are the Parcae. Their name comes from the Latin verb *parcere*, "to bring forth." They have a close relationship with human pregnancy and parturition, bearing the names or epithets Nona (Ninth), Decima (Tenth), and Morta (Death). The Germanic tradition has its own parallel with the Fates in the shape of the Weird Sisters and the Norns. Sadly, the names of the Old English Weird Sisters have not survived, though Brian Branston (1957) has reconstructed them speculatively as Wyrd, Weorthend (or Metod), and Sculd.² They are associated with a cave and cauldron, and appear most famously in Renaissance English literature as the Three Witches of Shakespeare's *Macbeth*. In England they are best known as the Weird Sisters. In the Old Norse world, they are the Norns, described by Snorri Sturluson (ca. 1220). The Norns' names are Urðr, Verðandi, and Skuld, which may best be seen as representing that which has become, that which is becoming, and that which is to become. The Norns are thus the general agents of eternal becoming, not exclusively the foretellers of human individuals' lots in life.

Their residence is at the well of Urðr by one of the roots of the World Tree, Yggdrasil. German tradition tells of the *Kinderbrunnen*, subterranean waters and holy wells like that of Urðr, that contain the souls of the unborn. The Quickbrunnen at Dresden, with its image of a stork, bird guardian of the souls, is one of these. Local lore in both Cologne and Strasbourg tells that beneath the cathedrals there are also lakes of souls. The Germanic Elder Faith teaches that souls live in the form of frogs or fishes before being born as humans.

Urðr is thus the overseer of the emergence of human souls into the world at birth. There is some evidence that this belief also involves a return to the waters at death. Julius von Negelein (1906) quotes a German source of 1456 that states: "when a person dies, then the soul goes into the waters."³ Thus, Urðr's well symbolizes the source of the souls that she chooses to bring into the world of humans.

Spinning and Weaving Flax and Lives

The craft of spinning is a real human handicraft, and it is through examining its techniques that we can best understand the cosmic symbolism of the Norns. Frequently, the three are shown as handling a thread or cord. In such depictions, there is no particular act shown of the first Fate, Clotho, Nona, or Urðr making the thread from the raw material. In the Northern Tradition, the fibre that Urðr spins is linen, extracted from the flax plant, a gift to humanity from the goddess Frigg.

In the Old Icelandic poem *Lokasenna*, Freyja remarks how the goddess Frigg "knows all *ørlög*," spinning flax.⁴ *Ørlög* being the "primal law" laid down by the Norns, this links her with Urðr. Her icon as Queen of Heaven or Cosmocratrix portrays her with a distaff and spindle, or riding on a distaff like a witch's broomstick (such as the twelfth-century mural in Schleswig Cathedral, north Germany). In Nordic astronomy, Frigg's cloak is the starry heavens. Her spindle is the Nowl, the North Star, Polaris, whilst her distaff is formed from the three stars called the Belt of Orion in Graeco-Arabic astronomy.

The image of the spinner who enables new human life to come into the world is reflected in Christian images of the Annunciation. Some of these show Our Lady spinning with a spindle and, beside her, a woven wickerwork basket containing wool (e.g., a fifth-century mosaic at Ravenna, ivories at Metz and Brussels, and a ninth-century stone panel at Hoveningham, North Yorkshire). The spinning woman denotes the conception of Jesus, a beginning fitting the symbolism of the first Fate.

In addition to its symbolic meaning as the fount of unborn souls, the water from Urðr's well has a practical function, for in spinning flax, the spinner must continually wet the fibres to enable them to adhere to one another and form a thread. In the craft of spinning, the thread must be spun at least twice. Firstly, a single strand is spun from the raw fibres onto a rotating spindle: through this rotation, a coherent thread is created from disconnected fibres. Linear order is brought out of chaos, the character of the thread depending on how the spinner selects the fibres. Then the original thread is re-spun on itself, being twined for strength. Only then is it strong enough to undergo another winding process, being wound into a skein. It can then be woven into a fabric. Neither the spinning and twining of a thread and then its measuring and cutting, nor spinning, twining, and weaving on a loom, are continuous processes. They are repetitive, cyclical actions. At the end of each cycle, the accumulation of new thread can be appreciated. This is literally progress—step by step, as the work moves forwards.

Certain words in the old Germanic languages afford us a functional understanding of the ancient religious concepts of Fate, spinning and weaving existence. The OHG word *wurt* (cognate with the ON name of the first Fate, Urðr, and the OS *uuurð*), is related to the verb *werdan*, "to become" or "to come to pass." This is cognate with the Latin verb *vertere*, "to turn." It also relates to the OHG *wirtel*, "spindle." OHG *Wurt* is closely related to the OE word *wyrd*. This word is derived from the OE verb *weorþan*, "to become." The notion of Fate as being "woven" by Wyrd is evident in the OE saying *"me þæt wyrd gewæf"* ("Wyrd wove me that," i.e., "that is my lot in life"). The OE word *gewæf* or *gewif* also means "fortune" or "destiny." Wyrd cannot be altered: *wêwurt*, "woeful Wyrd," (a compound appearing in the OHG fragment the *Hildebrandslied*) is invincible. Even the gods are subject to Wyrd. As the OE gnomic verse in the Cotton manuscript tells us: "the glories of Christ are great: Wyrd is strongest of all."

Lachesis, Decima, or Verðandi, the middle of the three Fates, is depicted in one of two ways. Often she is shown measuring the thread, symbolic of measuring the duration of a single life. The middle Fate is also depicted as interweaving many threads into a fabric. English tradition calls this the Web of Wyrd, Wyrd meaning an individual's "fate," "lot in the world" or "destiny," but without the inference of predestination inherent in the modern understanding of "destiny." The warp of the weaving is seen as time and events, whilst the weft is human individual acts. Thus, as the web is woven, the pattern of interactions of the threads, which are lives and events, irreversibly come together. So it was that in Anglo-Saxon England a historian was called *wyrdwritere*. The pattern thereby formed is the history of all events (*ørlög*) that have taken place at any given time. In this way, the middle Fate signifies eternal becoming—the present. Weaving is alluded to obliquely in the poem *VafÞruðnismál*, in which Odin has a battle of wits against the giant VafÞruðnir, whose name means "the mighty weaver." The poem's content is a series of prophetic riddles concerning the fate of the gods, an exposition of the nature of the Web of Wyrd in which humans, giants, and gods play their part.

The final Fate is Atropos or Skuld, the destroyer, called by the Romans Morta, "death." She wields her shears to cut the thread of life, or rip apart the weft and warp of the Web of Wyrd. She denotes that which is to become, the future. In *Gylfagynning*, Skuld is described as the chief of the three *walkurjas* (OE *wælcyrge*; modern English valkyries), "choosers of the slain," who hovered above ancient battlefields, carrying the souls of dead heroes to Valhalla. It appears that they were thought to choose those who were about to die, and hence fit in very well with the idea of Skuld as a conscious cutter of the thread of life. Hesiod tells how the shield of Herakles (Hercules) has an image of the ancient Greek Fates fighting one another to decide who should take the selected dead from the battlefield.

"VAFÞRUÐNISMÁL," 1908, BY W. G. COLLINGWOOD.

The Interweavings of Being

The Roman emperor and Stoic philosopher Marcus Aurelius Antoninus (121–180 C.E.) wrote *Meditations*, a book of philosophy expounding the pagan virtues that has been translated into all of the Western languages and has remained in print continuously in English since 1634. His philosophy emphasises the interconnectedness of all things, symbolized as the weavings of Fate. "Always imagine the Cosmos as a living organism," wrote Marcus, "possessing one substance and one soul: see how everything is related to the nature of the whole, how all things are moved by its energy, and how all play their part in the chain of cause and effect in everything that happens. Note the intricacy of the threads; the complexity of the weaving."[5]

Marcus's *Meditations* include this advice for having a happy life: "Offer yourself wholeheartedly to Clotho. Let her spin your thread to serve whatever purpose she wills."[6] Also, he warns us not to complain about our bad luck: "Everything that happens to one was from the beginning destined and spun for you as a share of the Whole."[7] But Marcus's advice is not fatalistic. On the contrary, it expounds the creative acceptance of life that is the pagan way. It offers us a positive way to live in an unpredictable world, for within the conditions that our Wyrd has given us, we are free. As Beowulf tells us, "Wyrd often spares the man who is not doomed, as long as his courage holds."[8]

Interlacing Matters: Spiritual Arts and Crafts

In the European traditional arts and crafts, the interweaving of materials is not restricted to the fibres used in textiles. Hair has doubtless been plaited since time immemorial. Ancient corpses with the hair done in the Swabian Knot have been found preserved in peat bogs. Interweavings and interlace are omnipresent in ancient northern artefacts that include jewelry; weapons and armour; carvings on wood; leatherwork; stone-sculpture, belt-, rope-, basket-, and hurdle-making. Interlaced patterns were used by the Roman mosaic masters, both as borders and as "carpet panels." As many surviving Roman mosaics have spiritual themes, it is not unlikely that these interweavings refer to the composition of the cosmos.

Predating Roman mosaics are the Iron Age British torcs, made from twisted and plaited gold wire. In the best surviving ancient Celtic metalwork, such as the Hunterston and Tara brooches, interlaced patterns are made in filigree metalwork, assembled from twisted wires of various cross-sections. The wires themselves, masterfully hand-drawn in an age without machine tools, are metallic examples of the symbolic thread of existence. Much has been written about the origin and meaning of these patterns, but they are rarely related to the underlying spiritual ethos that is present in the Web of Wyrd. It is inconceivable that our ancestors, with their holistic and symbolic view of existence, made patterns without meaning, for European traditional philosophy tells us: "Nothing exists apart: everything has a share of everything else" (Anaxagoras).[9]

The Shapers of Becoming

That which is becoming is the only state of being. It is ever changing, and cannot be grasped. This present state is the result of everything that has gone before. Although modernity calls this the past, the Northern Tradition speaks of *ørlög*, "primal laws" and "primal layers." *Ørlög* refers both to the structural ways that the cosmos works (the so-called Laws of Nature), and to the events and things that have existed in the past. *Ørlög* is the source of the present, and although it is past, it has not disappeared. In accordance with nature, all things that come to individuals are neither rewards or punishments sent by the gods—they are the inevitable consequences of actions or chance.

Those who shape our actions are described by the OS *giscapu*, "fates," and the OHG *sceffarin*, "creatresses." In ON *sköp* is one's fate, the scope that we have to do anything within our own *ørlög*. These shapers mete out our fate, the OS and OE *metod* (destiny, doom, death) that is brought about through *metodogiscapu* (OS), the "decree of Fate" or "the shaping of destiny." The Norns have a name that is interpreted as "the whisperers," or "to snarl" (related to the ME *nurnen*, "to say"). Their utterances or decrees are couched in the language of runic writing, the ON and OE *stafir* and *stafas*, "staves." Staves can mean both runic characters and the wooden staves upon which they are cut, runestaves cut on a runestaff.

The idea that the Fates write destinies in a book is mentioned by the Roman author Martianus. The *Fatal Book* appears to be related to the actual ancient Roman books of the Sybilline Oracles, a small fragment of which survives in Florence. Similarly, in Northern Europe, the Eddic poem *Völuspá* tells us that the Norns "staves did cut, laws did they make, lives did they choose: for the children of men they marked their fates."[10] The OE word *wyrdstafas* refers to the decrees of Fate, and *endestafas* is death.

Though perceived as a giver of destinies, the Roman goddess Fortuna (the Lady Luck of modern gamblers) is somewhat different from the Three Fates. She presides over truly random events, as evidenced by her symbol, the Wheel of Fortune, giving and taking by blind chance. In antiquity, Fortuna was associated with the Etruscan oracle of Praeneste, traditionally founded by an Egyptian priestess. The oracle operated by drawing dice made of olive wood at random from a box or bowl of silver—the *arcana* (a word much later given to the trumps of the occult Tarot).

Fortuna is related to the Fates and the Idises in that she was invoked for the wellbeing of newborn babies. An *idis* (Anglo-Saxon) or *dís* (Norse) is a female ancestral spirit, the revered guardian of a clan, family, or individual. Each part of life has its guardian *dís*; for example, the *ættardís* protects the family, the *barnadís* the children, and *hjördís*, fighting men. The *idises* are responsible for giving newborn babies their individual destinies, and also function as bringers of death. In Lithuania, the goddess Laima, as "the goddess above the gods" expressing Wyrd, performs the same function. She oversees the birth of babies and gives them their physical, mental, and spiritual qualities. Her name comes from the Lithuanian *leist*, "to let be."

There are many ancient Celto-Roman and Germano-Roman sacred images and altars that depict three women together similar to the Fates. Although they often bear woven wickerwork baskets, they are not shown spinning. Collectively, they are known as the "Mothers" (*matres* or *matronae*). Some images have inscriptions that express their tribal connections, such as the Swabian Mothers or the Frisian Mothers. Although little is really known, these inscriptions infer that they were tribal ancestresses, or *idises*. Norse texts tell us that the *dísir* came to take their kinsmen and women back at death. This is the function of Skuld as chief of the *walkurjas*.

We ignore the Fates at our peril, so it has always been customary to offer them respect. In the Viking era, images of the *dísir* were set up in *hofs* and temples. There were even *dísasálr*, chapels dedicated exclusively to particular *dísir*. Ironically, the proper rites and ceremonies for the Fates are recorded in the writings of the Christian priests who attempted to suppress them. Because they were incompatible with the Christian doctrine of infallible godly omnipotence, those who continued to acknowledge the Weird Sisters suffered heavy penalties if caught. In his *Corrector* (ca. 1010), Burchard set out punishments for those who acknowledged the Fates. Around 1190, Bartholomew of Exeter prescribed two years' penance for "she who lays a table with three knives for the service of the Fates (Parcarum) that they may predestinate good things to those who are born there."[11] Despite the suffering that Burchard and his followers inflicted upon those whom they caught honouring the reality of the Fates, people have never forgotten them, and they are honoured to this day.

There is a religious painting, dating from around 1600, in the church of St. Peter am Perlach in Augsburg, Bavaria, Germany. This church is probably built upon the site of a temple of the goddess Zisa. The painting depicts Our Lady as Maria Knotenlöserin, "Mary Undoer-of-knots." She is dressed in un-Marian red, the traditional colour of Zisa's raiment. She undoes the knots in a thread handed to her by an angel on her left, passing on the undone thread to another on her right. Maria Knotenlöserin between the two angels appears to be a Christian version of the three Fates, where the role of Lachesis/Verðandi as weaver is reversed. If we read her image in the opposite way, ignoring her literary name, then she performs the Verðandian function.

The Sisterhood of Wyrd

The activities of the Fates in overseeing the birth, life, and death of human individuals have sometimes been considered to involve foresight. But the Northern Tradition concept of *ørlög* does not claim the possibility of precise foresight, for the future does not yet exist and therefore is not predetermined. Events take place because of the conditions and actions that lead up to them, no more than that. There is no predestined event other than that which is unavoidable because of natural processes, such as the inevitable death of those who are born, or actions where it is too late to avoid the consequences. When the human race finally dies out, having laid waste the planet that sustains us, our extinction will not be a punishment sent by a judgmental deity, but merely the impersonal consequence of human *örlog*. By knowing all *ørlög*, as does Frigg in *Lokasenna*, the Fates or human seeresses are able to best determine what will happen next as the result of what has gone before, and this is a most useful ability. But sometimes, the seeress is like Cassandra, unheeded, and her veracity is only recognized retrospectively.

In heathen times, the old Germanic tribal rulers were accompanied by seeresses who served them as advisers. In the mainstream European tradition of the sybils of the Mediterranean region, these Germanic sybils performed divinations and gave oracles to assist the workings of statecraft and warfare. Sybils also appear to have personated the Norns. Saxo Grammaticus (ca. 1200) notes that in former times, Swedish mothers went to a certain sacred place to consult three priestesses, "three maidens sitting on three seats," regarding the future of their children.[12]

History records the names of some of these awesome sybils. The most celebrated is Weleda of the Bructerians in Westphalia. She was taken to Rome in 78 C.E. After her death, she was apotheosised, and worshiped. In the years 91–92 C.E., a seeress called Ganna accompanied the king of the Semnonians to Rome. In the second century C.E., the Semnonian seeress Waluburg accompanied Germanic mercenaries in Egypt. She carried an ostracon from the holy island of Elephantine in the River Nile. The Vinnilish seeress Gambara prayed for the victory of her tribe over the Vandals. In the mid-ninth century C.E., we know of an Alamannic-Frankish seeress called Thiota.

Seeresses' names were often epithets, such as Gambara, from OHG *gambrî*, "astuteness." Waluburg refers to the *walus* (Gothic for a "staff") that she carried. St. Walpurga, the eighth-century English nun who in Germany gave her name to Walpurgisnacht (May Eve), on which the witches ride, may have borne the name of a pagan seeress. The witch's broomstick, traditionally ridden on Walpurgisnacht, is certainly a form of magic stave. The *völva* of Viking times was literally a "staff carrier," whose magic runestaff was also her badge of office.

The runes, too, appear among the ancient Germanic wise women. The seeresses called Haliarunos were expelled from the lands of the Goths by King Filimer. Many Germanic wise women had personal names containing the OHG element *rûn* (rune), such as Alarûn, Ortrûn, Fridurûn, Kundrûn, Hiltirûn, Paturûn, Sigirûn, and Rûnhilt.

"The Birth of St. George," an English ballad dating from around 1600, tells how the Weïrd Lady of the Woods foresees the birth of the English hero (for here George is born of a knightly family in Coventry).[13] After his birth, during which his mother dies, the baby George is taken away by the Weïrd Lady to be brought up and trained in the martial arts. Here, the Weïrd Lady is reminiscent of the old Germanic Alahgunt, a priestess who oversaw the practise of the martial arts.

Like the Fates, seeresses frequented particular places in the landscape for their divinations. This is recalled by the OE word *bleóðorstede*, an oracle-place. Water is a significant feature in the Northern Tradition, where the well of Urðr provides life-giving waters for the world tree, Yggdrasil, and is the receptacle of souls. The name for one of the kinds of priestesses who took care of and administered holy washing and bathing places was *wihlaug*. The seeresses who accompanied Ariovistus observed the upwelling patterns in flowing streams and the sound that the waters made. In Ireland is the parallel tradition of the wise women called *banfathi*, who read meaning into the swirling patterns of running water.

The Unbroken Recognition of the Fates

Recognition of the Fates has never died. Wyrde is equated with the Parcae in the Anglo-Saxon *Corpus Gloss* (ca. 725 C.E.). In medieval England, William of Waddington (thirteenth century), Robert

Mannyng of Brunne (ca. 1330), Geoffrey Chaucer (1385), and Bishop Reginald Pecock (ca. 1450) all acknowledged the Three Weirds as sisters who shape human destiny at birth. Geoffrey Chaucer wrote in his *Legend of Good Women* of "the Werdys that we clepen Destiné" (the Wyrds that we call destiny)[14] and in *The Court of Love* (ca. 1450) he tells of "the susters waried and misseid ... the thre of fatall destyné, That be our wordes" (the sisters cursed and slandered ... the three of fatal destiny, that be our weirds).[15]

In his *Chronicles* (1577), Raphael Holinshed, recounting the history of Mac Beth, High King of Scotland from 1040 to 1057, refers to "three women in wild apparel resembling creatures from an eldritch world." These he equates with the "Weird Sisters, that is (as ye would say) the goddesses of destinie..."[16] Around 1606, William Shakespeare refashioned them into the unforgettable Three Witches who foretell the future of Macbeth. They describe themselves in lines 33–34 of Shakespeare's play of the same name as "The weird sisters, hand in hand, Posters of the sea and land." And in 1648, Robert Herrick published a poem called *The Parcæ, or, Three Dainty Destinies:*

> Three lovely Sisters working were
> (As they were closely set)
> Of soft and dainty Maiden-haire,
> A curious Armelet.
> I smiling, ask'd them what they did?
> (Faire Destinies all three)
> Who told me, they had drawn a thread
> Of Life, and 'twas for me.
> They shew'd me then, how fine 'twas spun:
> And I reply'd thereto,
> I care not now how soone 'tis done,
> Or cut, if cut by you.[17]

In his music dramas that retell Germanic mythology, Richard Wagner acknowledged the place of the Fates. In the first part of the "Ring Cycle," *Das Rheingold* (The Rhine Gold), Wagner saw Erda, Mother Earth, in the same light as Frigg in *Lokasenna*:

> All that was I know,
> All that is I know,
> All that ever shall be done,

"THE THREE NORNS," 1897, BY HANS THOMA.

This as well I know.
Erda the name I bear,
The Fates my daughters are...[18]

Illustrating Wagner, both in texts and operatic costume design, various artists have created imaginative images of the Norns. They appear in a short foreboding scene at the very beginning of the last opera in Wagner's cycle, *Götterdämmerung* (Twilight of the Gods), for even the gods are subject to Wyrd. Among the most notable "Nornic" artists are Hans Thoma (1839–1924), Carl Emil Döpler (1824–1905), and Franz Stassen (1869–1949).

Allegories of Clotho

When he advises us to let her spin our threads to serve whatever purpose she wills, Marcus Aurelius directly acknowledges Clotho (Urðr). In addition to deciding the colour and texture of the life-thread of a newborn baby, Clotho also rules beginnings and foundations of human institutions. Although modernity has abolished true symbolism in contemporary national festivities, in former times it was an essential component of them. In 1603, the unification of England and Scotland as the United Kingdom was marked with a reference to her. In The King's Entertainment, performed on Thursday, 15 March of that year, at the coronation of King James VI of Scotland as King James I of the United Kingdom, Ben Jonson introduced the character of the Genius Urbis. This genius, the spirit of the city of London, was personated as a man "attired rich, reverend and antique: his hair long and white, crowned with a wreath of plane-tree, said to be *arbor genialis* ..."[19] In his speech, the genius refers to the founding of London and celebrates the final unification of Great Britain on that day:

> Time, Fate and Fortune have at length conspired,
> To give our age the day so much desired ...
> When Brutus' plough first gave thee infant bounds,
> And I, thy Genius, walk'd auspicious rounds
> In every furrow; then did I forelook,
> And saw this day mark'd white in Clotho's book.[20]

The *arbor genialis* still flourishes today in the London parks and squares in the shape of the local variety of plane tree, the London Plane (*Platanus hybrida*).

Just as the *arbor genialis* flourishes as a living witness to symbolic tradition in London, so the traditional teachings of Wyrd are relevant today. In 1994 the Odinist writer Ingvar brought back from the edge of obscurity an important Northern English and Lowland Scots adage, "Let us dree our weird."[21] Loosely translated into Standard English, this maxim means "Let us accept our lot in life" (without complaint). Offering ourselves wholeheartedly to Clotho is still part of the British spiritual tradition, in direct continuity of the Elder Faith.

Abbreviations:

ME: Middle English
OE: Old English
OHG: Old High German
ON: Old Norse
OS: Old Saxon

Notes:

1. Hesiod, *Theogony, in The Homeric Hymns and Homerica*, trans. by Hugh G. Evelyn-White. (Cambridge, Mass.: Harvard University Press, 1914). <www.perseus.tufts.edu>
2. Brian Branston, *The Lost Gods of England*. (London: Thames and Hudson, 1957) p. 71.
3. Julius Von Negelein, *Germanische Mythologie* (Leipzig: B. G. Teubner, 1906), p. 75.
4. The comment appears in stanza 21 and refers to Gefjon, but this seems to be a confusion for Frigg.
5. Marcus Aurelius, *Meditations*, Bk. 4, 40 (see also: Bk. 6, 38).
6. Ibid., Bk. 4, 34.
7. Ibid., Bk. 4, 426.
8. *Beowulf*, 573–74.
9. Fragment six. Cf. Arthur Fairbanks, ed. and trans., *The First Philosophers of Greece* (London: K. Paul, Trench, Trubner, 1898), pp. 235–62.
10. *Poetic Edda*, "Völuspá" 20.
11. Cf. the "German Church Corrector's Penitential" which states "Did you do as certain women do during a certain time of the year? Did you set two tables and fix two meals in your house? Did you put a drink on the table along with three knives in case the 'three sisters' arrive? Previous generations called them the 'fates' (*parcae*) out of ignorance. Did you do these things so that the fates could be refreshed? Did you take away the power of divine piety and give it to the devil so that he and the sisters could help you now or in the future?" in James Chisholm, *Grove and Gallows: Greek and Latin Sources for Germanic Heathenism* (Smithville, Texas: Rûna-

Raven, 2001), pp. 75–76.

12. *History of the Danes*, Book Six.

13. Anonymous, *The Birth of St George* (Bar Hill, England: Old England House, 2001).

14. Cf. Albert H. Tolman, "Notes on Macbeth," *PMLA*, vol. II, no. 2 (1896), pp. 200–219.

15. Geoffrey Chaucer, "The Court of Love," in Kathleen Forni, ed., *The Chaucerian Apocrypha: A Selection* (Kalamazoo, Michigan: Medieval Institute Publications for TEAMS, 2005), p. 38.

16. Raphael Holinshed, *Holinshed's Chronicles of England, Scotland, and Ireland* (London: J. Johnson et al., 1808), pp. 268–69.

17. Robert Herrick, *The Poems of Robert Harrick* (London: Grant Richards, 1902), p. 16.

18. Cf. the original German libretto text in Richard Wagner, *Das Rheingold* (Boston: Oliver Ditson, 1904), p. 53.

19. Ben Jonson, *The Works of Ben Jonson* (9 vols.) (London: W. Bulmer & Co., 1816), vol. 6, pp. 437–439.

20. Ibid.

21. Ingvar, "Let Us Dree Our Weird" *Odinism Today* 13 (February 1994), pp. 2–6.

Works Not Specifically Cited:

Green, D. H. *Language and History in the Early Germanic World.* Cambridge: Cambridge University Press, 1998.

Haseloff, Günther. *Kunststile des Frühen Mittelalters.* Stuttgart: Württembergisches Landesmuseum, 1979.

Herrmann, Paul. *Nordische Heldensagen nach Saxo Grammaticus.* Jena: Diederichs, 1925.

Jones, Prudence and Nigel Pennick. *A History of Pagan Europe.* London: Routledge, 1995.

Pennick, Nigel. *Practical Magic in the Northern Tradition.* Wellingborough: Aquarian Press, 1989.

Reuter, Otto Sigfrid. *Skylore of the North.* Trans. Michael Behrend. Bar Hill, England: Rune Staff, 1999.

Thoma, Hans. *Hans Thomas Kostümentwürfe zu Richard Wagners Ring des Nibelungen.* Leipzig: Breitkoph & Haertel, 1897.

CAMDEN HOUSE HISTORY OF GERMAN LITERATURE
VOLUME ONE

Early Germanic Literature *and* Culture

Edited by Brian Murdoch and Malcolm Read

"An excellent introduction to the world before circa 800. ... [A]n exciting reading experience, even for nonexperts in this field. ... The editors and authors deserve praise for an insightful, concise, and highly readable collection."
—*German Studies Review*

Early Germanic Literature and Culture views the development of writing in German with respect to broad aspects of the early Germanic past, drawing on a range of disciplines including archaeology, anthropology, and philology in addition to literary history. The first part considers the whole concept of Germanic antiquity and the way in which it has been approached, examines classical writings about Germanic origins and the earliest Germanic tribes, and looks at the two great influences on the early Germanic world: the confrontation with the Roman Empire and the displacement of Germanic religion by Christianity. A chapter on orality—the earliest stage of all literature—provides a bridge to the earliest Germanic writings. The second part of the book is devoted to written Germanic—rather than German—materials, with a series of chapters looking first at the Runic inscriptions, then at Gothic, the first Germanic language to find its way onto parchment (in Ulfilas's Bible translation). The topic turns finally to what we now understand as literature, with general surveys of the three great areas of early Germanic literature: Old Norse, Old English, and Old High and Low German. A final chapter is devoted to the Old Saxon *Heliand*.

List price $85 (discount price $63.75); 344 pp.; 6 b&w, 4 line illus.; hardcover
ISBN-10: *1-57113-199-X*; ISBN-13: *978-1-57113-199-7*

―――――――― CONTACT US AT ――――――――

Camden House • 668 Mt. Hope Ave., Rochester, NY 14620 • www.camden-house.com
(ph) 585-275-0419 • (fax) 585-271-8778 • boydell@boydellusa.net
Please quote the reference code $07109 when ordering to recieve your discount.

The Abode of the Gods and the Great Beyond: On The Imaginal and Post Mortem States in Celtic Tradition

Thierry Jolif

We have only limited information on what the Celts believed about the *post mortem* state of the soul, although it widely known that the Druids taught that the soul was immortal. We are also vaguely familiar with the Other World of Irish mythology, a place that Celtic studies experts know as *Síd*. Much has been written on the wondrous islands, especially those described in the renowned *Immrama*, the odysseys of the Irish saints. But how were these beliefs actually structured? What was the doctrine behind the scant data we have available today? In particular, what is the basis for the three circles of existence—as they are perceived by some modern Celto-maniacal groups, whose ideas are unfortunately often taken too seriously? This last question is easy to answer: although the Druids' conception was that there were several "worlds," the names the neo-Druids give them do not appear anywhere at all. According to this more or less transmigrationist theory, the three major circles are: *Keugant* [Ceugant], which is God's residence, no second-in-command, no complement; *Gwenved* [Gwynfyd], a world of spiritual happiness but with room for improvement; and *Abred*, the circle of necessity, which is much like Midgard in the Scandinavian tradition. The terms are given their Breton spellings here, but these are sometimes just improper transliterations of Gallic terms.[1] Surprisingly, there is no mention of the Gallic name for the Other World, *Annwvyn*, among these terms, although it is present in the Mabinogi *Pwyll, Prince of Dyved*.[2] Moreover, none of these terms correspond to the usual traditional designations in Irish mythological texts and epics, where mention is often made of the Other World, although it would have been simple to name this region after the Gallic *heddwch*, "peace", the equivalent of the Irish *Síd*. It is obvious that the matter is fairly open-and-shut, and not really worthy of further consideration.

As for the rest, we should start by seeing what we can discover from the etymology of the Irish term *Síd*. To do this, we will use the commentary by C. J. Guyonvarc'h on this topic.[3] The Irish word *sid*, therefore, has two primary accepted meanings, including several variations of the ones we will discuss. On the one hand, it refers to the Other World, and on the other hand, it means peace. In Gaulish, there are a certain number of anthroponyms, topnonyms, and ethnonyms formed with the prefix *sed* or *sid* (the variation no doubt a result of e/i ablaut). So *sed* would be equivalent to **sedo-*[4] "seat," while *sid-* still has no precise meaning,[5] perhaps because we have no written trace of Gaulish thought on the Other World. Some light could no doubt be shed on the problem were we to allow that among the Irish and Gaulish Druids there would probably have existed very few major differences with regard to doctrine.[6] The relationship between *sed* and *sid* would surely be the same as that between *sid* "peace" and *síd* "Other World." In all cases, the terms designated a place as well as a "state." In Irish mythological and epic texts, therefore, the word *síd* refers to different realities, and in 1962 Professor Guyonvarc'h proposed the following semantic distinctions:

> 1. the world of the Great Beyond in general;
> 2. collectively and by extension, the ordinary inhabitants or possibly protean emanations of this Great Beyond;
> 3. conveying the same general sense, but with restriction of place (in this case the word is generally used in the dative plural *sídaib* or *sídhaibh*), the hills, mounds or other locations serving as a point of contact or passage;
> 4. shifting the meaning still further, finally, the "magic" of the great beyond in a generalized sense.[7]

As for the second meaning, or second word, the dictionary of the Royal Irish Academy yields the following:

> a. peace, goodwill, peaceableness; a state of peace; a period of peace, a truce; peacemaking, pacification, conciliation;
> b. peace-offering, compensation, atonement, indemnity, compact of peace; pl. peace-conditions;
> c. pardon, forgiveness;
> d. peace, quietness, stillness.[8]

Obviously, there are multiple meanings, but they all refer back to a particular state, and we believe that for the men who disseminated these concepts, it was a state of being. This is why we feel confident asserting that the Other World, as a place, was the same thing as peace, understood as a state of being. Both terms also call to mind the idea of stability, for example, state, status, and so forth, but we will discuss this in more detail later.

First, we should more closely probe the Celtic vision of the Other World. We mentioned earlier that most people know that the Druids taught that the soul was immortal. But who has informed us of this, and in what context? In fact, several classical authors mention this belief:

Caesar, *De Bello Gallico*, VI, 14:

> They wish to inculcate this as one of their leading tenets, that souls do not become extinct, but pass after death from one body to another, and they think that men by this tenet are in a great degree excited to valor, the fear of death being disregarded.[9]

Caesar, *De Bello Gallico*, VI, 19:

> Their funerals, considering the state of civilization among the Gauls, are magnificent and costly; and they cast into the fire all things, including living creatures, which they suppose to have been dear to them when alive; and, a little before this period, slaves and dependents, who were ascertained to have been beloved by them, were, after the regular funeral rites were completed, burnt together with them.[10]

Marcus Annaeus Lucanus, *Pharsalia*, Book I, 511–20:

> If what ye sing be true, the shades of men
> Seek not the dismal homes of Erebus
> Or death's pale kingdoms; but the breath of life
> Still rules these bodies in another age—
> Life on this hand and that, and death between.
> Happy the peoples 'neath the Northern Star
> In this their false belief; for them no fear
> Of that which frights all others: they with hands
> And hearts undaunted rush upon the foe
> And scorn to spare the life that shall return.[11]

Pomponius Mela, *De Chorographia* III, 2, 18–19:

> One of their dogmas has come to common knowledge, namely that souls are eternal and that there is another life in the infernal regions, and this has been permitted manifestly because it makes the multitude readier for war. And it is for this reason too that they burn or bury with their dead things appropriate to them in life, and that in times past they even used to defer the completion of business and the payment of the debts until their arrival in another world. Indeed there were some of them who flung themselves willingly on the funeral piles of their relatives in order to share the new life with them.[12]

Strabo, *Geographica* IV, 4:

> However, not only the Druids, but others as well, say that men's souls, and also the universe, are indestructible, although both fire and water at some time or other prevail over them.[13]

In a previous work[14] we compared these different texts with the *Bhagavad-Gîtâ* (II, 12, 18, 19, 20), and the authors we mentioned emphasized that this point of Druidic doctrine had a connection to war fervor. We think that Mela's remarks on the subject are also of interest, when he states that "one of their dogmas has come to common knowledge," which leads us to assume that other teachings remained secret. However, in our opinion this specific teaching was addressed not so much to "society" as a whole but rather to the class of aristocrats and warriors.[15] "Among the ancient Europeans—Greeks, Romans, Celts, Germans—only the initiates went to Heaven, possibly also the heroes, who would therefore have been likened to them; the others remained in the shadows, in some underground Hades, which combined the state of perishable psychic elements with that great unknown that is transmigration through non-human and extraterrestrial states."[16] Here, we are getting back to the Celtic concepts of *post mortem* states, because very few were those who actually managed to enter the *Síd*, and it is very apparent that this Other World was not attainable by common mortals, that the only ones having access were magnificent kings, the king's sons, exceptional heroes, and doubtless the Druids themselves. The most remarkable thing is that these exceptional beings often entered the kingdom of the *Síd* while they were still alive, almost always at the invitation of astonishingly beautiful messengers. But wasn't the *Síd* also called *Tir na mBan*, the "land of the women," or sometimes *Tir na mBeo*, "the Land of the Living," or *Tir na nOg*, "Land of the Young"?[17] Journeys to this land took place frequently in dreams, and this is not insignificant. But we are straying from the point here, which is the *post mortem* state in a strict sense.

In Ireland, following the written collection of the *scéala* (that is, mythological accounts transmitted orally by the *filid*) and due to the effect of Christianization, confusion developed in regard to certain places (hills, mounds, cairns, megaliths) symbolically considered to be in contact with the Other World, and the location of the Great Beyond, which—being a "bad, infernal world"—was situated under these same hills or mounds. You can imagine how this confusion would have occurred by observing, for example, the beginning of the account entitled *The Intoxication of the Ultonians*. Here, it says that when the sons of Mil or Goidels [Gaels] arrived, the gods of Ireland sought refuge underground:

Do-chuata Túath Dé Danann i cnoccaib & sídbrugib cu ra accallset sída fo thalmain dóib.

The Túatha Dé Dánann went into the hills and mounds, the *sidhe* underground were taken over by them.[18]

This does not, as some thought, make the Túatha Dé Dánann earth-gods, nor does it make them demons. This event occurred during the fifth invasion of Ireland, an invasion of humans, ancestors of the Irish, called the Sons of Mil. It is within this mythological context that the episode should be interpreted. We have already mentioned elsewhere[19] that the name "Sons of Mil" is related to the mythic origin of the Gauls, who according to Caesar called themselves descendants of Dispater, due to the origin of the name Mil, which comes from the root **miletu*, meaning "death, destruction." This mythological fact surely refers to the doctrine of cycles and the progressive unveiling of spiritual centers, as well as to the means by which men are offered contact with the Other World. Therein too lies the symbolic expression of a 'hardening' effect, linked to the conditions prevalent in the Dark Age. This is an age characterized by confusion, leading in particular to a blurring of the Great Beyond with the Other World, a confusion that would have had significant consequences. Observe that, among the authors cited above, confusion already reigns. Thus Caesar, on the one hand, states that "souls do not become extinct, but pass after death from one body to another" and, on the other hand, that the property and beings dear to the deceased were burned with him. But if the soul returns to enter another body, how could the deceased and their loved ones expect to find themselves in another world? It seems that Lucan was closer to the truth when he stated that, according to the Gauls, "the same spirit controls the body in another world." Still, one might ask why he then hurries on to say that a life must return. Of course, in Mela no trace can be found of this "belief" in a form of transmigration, because if according to the Druids the soul was eternal, then how could it come back? Unless we consider there again that there were two very different posthumous destinies: that of the initiates "resuscitated" in the Other World, whose conditions of existence allow them to come back, sometimes, and that of common mortals leaving for a Great Beyond from which they did not come back, unless metempsychosis could be considered as a return. Strabo's allusion had previously led us to speculate on the possible existence of a doctrine of Self within the body of Druidic thought, and to compare the *Bhagavad-Gîta* to the texts cited above. It is highly probable that this interpretation is the more correct one, given the links between the Celtic warrior and the Celtic god of war, who was also a guide for the deceased. As far as resurrection in the Other World, this was not in any way a literary device, but rather exactly what the texts specify on the subject of Dagda, the Irish Druid-God, master of the living and the dead. Dagda's club (*lorg*)[20] kills with one end in this world and resuscitates with the other in the Other World, as clearly indicated in the texts of the *Yellow Book of Lecan* (fifteenth century): "this great club that you see has one soft end and one hard end. One of the ends kills the living and the other end brings the dead back to life."[21]

Therefore it seems that for the Celts there was only one way out from the human and infra-human world, the one leading to the Other World, a place that could be reached via maritime voyage or by the contact points we mentioned earlier. Since the subterranean location of the Great Beyond, for its part, corresponded to posthumous "destinies" of various sorts but never led to higher states of Being, it represented the aforementioned combination of "the state of perishable psychic elements with the great unknown that is transmigration through non-human, extraterrestrial states."[22] This exit, this "door," could be compared to the one in Hindu tradition that gives access to *dêva-yâna*.[23] In this connection, it should be pointed out that the common Celtic **Litavia* (that is, Armorican Brittany, actually considered as a "pier" for departing souls) would have to be comparable to the Sanskrit *Prithvi*, meaning the Portal to the Other World. Moreover, it is worth pointing out that the contacts between the *Síd* and our world occur not only as a function of precise places, but also of a precise time, that of the feast of Samhain,[24] just as access to the *dêva-yâna* corresponds to "the period when the sun traveled to the north (*uttarâyana*), going from the winter solstice to the summer solstice."[25] This is doubtless related to the special time for the *Síd*, which could be defined as a non-time, a time entirely other than that of this world. It is also significant that the Irish word *bith* serves to designate both the world and the time. Henry Corbin has mentioned specifically that liturgical time is very much the same as "time become space,"[26] and in the Celtic context, human time is sacralized by the influence of the *Síd*, for whom time and space are not only commingled, but in some way also eternally unified.

The *Síd* is most certainly not a heaven, nor, as F. Le Roux convincingly stated, is it a Great Beyond which is just the reflection of the Other World.[27] This is very much a different world, with dimensions which cannot be measured in the same way we know, but still a real world, eminently real, resembling our own but having a more exemplary reality because it is closer to the divine source. The Other World is the divine world which in Celtic tradition, as opposed to certain beliefs, is contiguous to our own, and the "Celtic heaven"—as some still call it—is, to repeat P. Geay's felicitous expression, "one of the abodes of the *mundus imaginalis*"[28] or more exactly *the* Imaginal World with multiple abodes. This can be verified with a glance at the Trudeau translation of the *Immram Brain, Mac Febal* (The Voyage of Bran, Son of Febal)[29] by Professor Guyonvarc'h, which, when placed alongside the translation of the *Aislinge Oenguso*,[30] sheds light on the proximity of the Other World and its links to the dream state.

The *Immram Brain* begins with Bran, son of Febal, meeting a splendid young woman, a messenger from the Other World, who describes the wonders of her "country" to him in an outstanding twenty-eight quatrain poem:

> There is a distant isle,
> Around which sea-horses glisten:
> A fair course against the white-swelling surge,
> Four feet uphold it.
>
> A delight of the eyes, a glorious range,
> Is the plain on which the hosts hold games:
> Coracle contends against chariot
> In southern Mag Findargat.
>
> Feet of white bronze under it
> Glittering through beautiful ages.
> Lovely land throughout the world's age,
> On which the many blossoms drop.[31]

From the beginning we can see the characteristic traits of the *Síd*: its similarity to a marvelous island, held up in this case by four pillars of white bronze, as well as its supremacy over "the worlds."[32] This refers directly to the traditional concept of the Supreme Center, unique in its principle, multiple in its manifestations, and very clearly expressing the fact that the Primordial Center was, for the Irish Celts, identified with four islands which were different but obviously part of the strict unity of the Spiritual Authority.[33] This apparent paradox is expressed further in the following quatrains:

> There are a hundred and fifty faraway isles,
> in the ocean to the west.
> Each of them is twice
> or even three times as large as Ireland[34]

Here we witness the multiple locations of this Other World, the various islands of which could be (in our view)[35] regarded as symbols of different, higher states of being. These states, at least according to this poem, seem to govern a solar principle incarnated by the God Mananánn,[36] comparable to the God of the ocean but above all the name of the supreme god Lug in his "King of the Other World" aspect:

> There will come with the sunrise
> a white man lighting up the plains.
> He travels the white plain that abuts the sea

and stirs up the waters into blood.[37]

The link between Mananánn, called "son of the Ocean", and the Other World should not be surprising because, in Celtic doctrine, passage to the "Land of the Living" was often by water. It is worth making the effort to tease out the symbolism in this concept. Water is a mythic element that encompasses one of the principles of manifestation, along with fire.[38] The tangible reality of the substance as reflection of the principle serves as a symbol for the latter, and so water—and also fog (the Celtic equivalent of the Hindu *akasha*)—becomes the primary frontier of the Other World. Moreover, the informal nature of these two elements corresponds perfectly to the very nature of the *Síd* as a genuine intermediary world. The passage through one of the two mythical elements also symbolizes a return to a state predating the dyad, predating opposition, any dualism being thereafter abolished:

> "We play with yellow gold pawns on golden chessboards; we drink clear mead in the company of a proud and armed warrior"[39]

The game of chess is the quintessential royal game, and not insignificantly is it chosen in this text describing the pleasures of the Other World, to symbolize the absence of dualism or—more exactly—proximity to the principle of Unity. If in the *Síd*, as has been frequently and brilliantly demonstrated by F. Le Roux and C. J. Guyonvarc'h, a peace reigns which is characterized by the attributes of the Dumézilian third function, that is, beauty, fertility, satiation, and drunkenness, it is precisely because the social categorization so meaningful in our own world is abolished there. However, we should take a closer look at this—for lack of a better word—"abolition" or even "leveling" from above. The peace, stability, fertility, and abundance which reign in the kingdoms of the *Síd* would tend to mislead us into thinking that perfection was attributed to the reigns of legendary kings in Irish texts. This cannot fail to evoke the close links existing between royalty and the Other World.

If we want to start at the beginning, we should mention an essential Irish text, that is, the *Serglege Con Culaind* or more exactly a passage from this text relating the royal election ritual, the "Tarb fes," or "Festival of the bull."

The festival of the bull was held as follows: a white bull would be killed and a single man would eat as much as he wished of the meat and the broth, then fall asleep sated, and a word of truth would be chanted over him by four Druids; he saw, in his dreams, the appearance of the man who should be elected to royalty: his looks, his character, his style, and the work he was doing.[40]

We can see very clearly that the choice of the king originates directly in a vision obtained during sleep. Now, a number of other texts cite the "oneiric" nature of encounters between men and the inhabitants of the *Síd*. In the same text, it is during a nap that Cuchulainn will "meet" two messengers of the *Síd*, and during another respite that he is healed by Lug in person, in the *Tain Bó Cúailnge*. It is also in his sleep that Oengus makes the acquaintance of the very beautiful and divine Caer; in the same way, Brian is slumbering when the elegant poetess invites him to depart for the Land of the Women (*Tir na mBan*). Although this allows us to establish a relationship between the dream state and the Other World, we cannot see in it further proof of the links between the *Síd* and earthly royalty. However, the connection between the dream state and the realm of the soul per se confirms the fundamental relationship we are establishing between the royal and warrior function and the *Síd*, this realm being traditionally recognized as especially linked to this function. Let us refer to another text, the *Baile in Scáil*, which describes how the legendary Conn becomes sovereign. After having passed over a stone that cried out under him, Conn asks his Druids about the stone and the meaning of this cry. They tell them that it was the stone of Fal, which identified the future kings of Tara with its cries. That is where they are when a cloud envelops them and a horseman comes to meet them. They follow him:

> Entering the house, they saw before them a lovely young woman with a golden diadem on her head. A silver vessel with golden ornaments was at her side, full of brown ale, and next to it a golden vase. The young woman was holding a golden cup to her lips. They saw the hero himself in the house, before them, on the royal throne. No man in Tara could be found taller or more charming than he, for the beauty of his figure and the exotic cast of his face.

He spoke to them and told them: "I am not actually a hero, and I will reveal to you something of my mystery and glory: it was after death that I came, and I am of the race of Adam. This is my name: Lug son of Ethlenn, son of Tigernmas. I came to reveal to you the destiny of your own sovereignty and of each ruler Tara will know." The young woman who was in the house with them represented the eternal sovereignty of Ireland.

It is the young woman who gives the two items to Conn, a cut of beef and a cut of pork. The cut of beef was eighty feet wide and eight feet tall. As the young woman is about to distribute the meat, she asks them, "To whom shall this cut be given?" The hero answers that each sovereign would be named, from Conn into eternity. They left the hero's shadow and never again saw the royal fortress, nor the house. Conn had been given the golden vase and the meat. And it was from this that the Hero's Dream, the adventures and voyage of Conn originated ...[41]

The text itself says that this is in fact a dream, but a dream giving access to a higher world. Moreover, note that this form of dream does not exactly allow humans to enter the *Síd* at their own wish but rather authorizes the *áes síde* to make contact with mortals. That is to say, even though this is a door it would not necessarily be open in the same way on both sides.

It is also in a dream that the Gallic hero Rhonabwy[42] meets the fantastical warrior troops of King Arthur in the Other World. His sleep lasts three days and three nights, which for the Celts expressed the "time taken away" for an encounter with the Other World. These visions are very much reserved for heroes and warriors, as they almost always relate to combats, battles, or the exquisite delights of a timeless peace, but are always sent specifically to individuals belonging to the same function. The link is indissoluble and even comes down through an actual genetic line. Thus Ireland illustrates this link over three generations of kings: Grandfather Con of the Hundred Battles, his son Art, his grandson Cormac. These three rulers see the beginning and the end of their reigns subject to the determinations of the *Síd*. Moreover, we find the motif of the cup in The Adventures of Cormac in the Promised Land. This "cup of truth" belonging to Manannán Mac Lir, king of the Promised Land, breaks if three lies are spoken over it, but all it needs to come back together is for three truths to be spoken over it. The divine king will give it as a gift to Cormac.

This close link between the king and the *Síd* can be found not only during election of the king or during his reign; it also exerts an influence on his decline and death in an almost cyclic manner. The triple sacrificial death[43] of the Irish king is played out entirely within a paradoxical relationship with the Other World, and in particular with one of its princesses. This relationship happens to be situated in a given time, a time one could refer to as liturgical time, a ritual time in which the death of the king will occur at the appointed hour:

> —killed by the enemy's sword or lance (occasionally the magic of the *áes síd* has had something to do with this);
> —burned in a palace conflagration;
> —drowned in a vat of beer or wine.

This of course entails not the end of royalty and of the kingdom, but quite the contrary, its rebirth by the renewed energies of the sovereign, having no other possible intermediary to our world than the *Síd*.

Thus, as we have seen, the *Síd* does not appear to be a uniform world, but rather is composed of multiple abodes, various and sundry islands which doubtless had both precise and broad signification. Its links to the actual realm of the soul, which give rise to its special relations with the feminine aspect of the divine, the king, the warriors, and the dream state are clearly evident in the extracts we have briefly examined. All of its elements can once again be found in the *Aislinge Oenguso* [The Dream of Angus].

We summarize:

> One Samhain night, Oengus, son of the Dagda, had a dream in which a young woman came to him. He could not touch her, he could not speak to her, and she was playing beautiful music to him. The young woman reappeared every night for a year. Oengus fell head over heels in love, became heartsick with longing and remained that way for a year, because he knew nothing of the young woman. The physician Fingen was then called, because he could guess the nature of an illness from a patient's appearance. Fingen

then divined the cause of Oengus' suffering and asked that Boann, the latter's mother, seek information about the young woman. After a year was up, Boann still knew nothing of this mysterious unknown person. Fingen then requested that the Dagda be called to intervene with King Bodb, who was renowned for his knowledge. The Dagda complied and Bodb agreed as long as he was given a year to do it. Once a year had passed, Bodb stated that the young woman was Caer Ibormaeth, daughter of Ethal Anbual, of the Uaman *Síd* in Connaught. Oengus was led to the place where she could be found, and there she was, surrounded by a hundred and fifty young women, all joined two by two with a silver chain. However, he had to obtain the consent of her father and none of those present had any authority over him. He therefore had to request the assistance of Aillil and Medb, the rulers of Connaught. The Dagda approached them and asked their help, and they sent a messenger to King Ethal Anbual, who refused their request even before the messenger asked the question. Aillil, Medb and the Dagda then decided to attack the *Síd* of Uaman. They killed sixty men, took their heads and seized Ethal as their prisoner. The latter was threatened into revealing the whereabouts of his daughter. He told them that for the time being she was at Loch Bel Dracon, in the shape of a swan, and that she spent one year in the form of a bird and another as a human being. The Mac Oc then went to Loch Bel Dracon and called Caer. The pair stayed there three days as swans, then Oengus took her to Brug Na Boinne, where they remained together.

Here again, we can see the importance assigned to the dream state, but we should point out one other thing; the motif of music:

Boi and do aidchi dano aithirriuch. Co n-accae timpán inna laím as bindam boíe. Sennid céol(n)dó. Con-tuil friss.

He was there one more night and he saw a "cymbal" in his hand, the loveliest ever. It played music to him, and he fell asleep.[44]

This motif is also present at the beginning of the *Immram Brain*.

And the music here appears to play, concomitantly with sleep, the role of a means of access to the realm of immortality. Although this music causes you to fall asleep, it is with a view to an awakening to the vision of the intermediary world, and therefore to participation in this world's reality. Moreover, the Other World is frequently characterized by its music, which is a means of awakening, forgetfulness, pleasure or a magical bond. In this account, it is a little of all four, but particularly the bond, which extends over a year, that is, from one Samhain to another. We have already mentioned that this ritual time is actually the same as that of the meeting: "Tlachtga, daughter of Mog Ruith. It is there that the men of Ireland came to light the fire with the young people of the Tuatha Dé Dánann every Samhain."[45]

It is also from this place that a number of symbols appear to originate; this is the case for not only the cup, but also the apple branch (offered to Cormac as proof of his contact with the *Síd*) and even birds (swans in particular). We could say then that the Celtic Other World has "in abundance, all the qualitative wealth of the world of the senses but in an incorruptible state."[46]

Although, admittedly, we have not covered all aspects of the matter, it can be safely asserted that the *Síd* for the Celts was indeed the intermediary or imaginal world, a paradise for warriors and initiated kings having attained "salvation," the abode of the gods, goddesses, and symbols. In sum, it is fairly logical that the myths and epic accounts handed down to us should inform us only about the posthumous fate of representatives of the second class, that of the warriors (and possibly initiated artisans from the third), conquering the immortality of heaven, residing in the sphere of individual states. It is also quite logical that the Druids did not play a direct role in this, and that there is no explicit mention of them in the texts. This is because the so-called purpose of priestly initiation is Deliverance, not salvation, which obviously could not have been described and is not even mentioned in the texts, which the monks committed to paper much later.[47] On the other hand, what the monks *could* allow with no qualms would be that "heavenly" afterlife that the Christian priest himself wanted to offer the people.

(*Translated by Elizabeth Griffin*)

The Abode of the Gods

Notes:

1. The reader will find as an appendix in Ph. Le Stum's book *Neo-druidisme en Bretagne*, (Rennes: Ouest-France, 1998), pp. 292–93, a text by Yves Berthou offering a summary of this "doctrine." In this regard see also Morganwg Iolo, *An Triadoù, Triads of Bardism, Les Triades* (Brasparts: Beltan, 1987) and Paul Ladmirault, *Abrégé du Barddas ou Libre du Bardisme* (Paris: bibliothèque Chacornac, 1931), as well as Michel Raoult, *Les Druides, les sociétés initiatiques celtiques contemporaines* (Monaco: Le Rocher, 1983). Concerning the specific names of the neo-druidic "worlds," the reader would do well to read C.-J. Guyonvarc'h, "Notes d'étymologie et de lexicographie gauloises et celtiques. XXV. 110. Gallois *ceugant*, vieux-breton *(int) coucant*, moyen-breton *cougant*, celtique *Kovio-Cantos.," *Ogam* XVIII, nos. 107–108 (1966), and "XXXII. 158. Gallois *abred* 'relâchement, délivrance'," *Ogam* XXI, nos. 121–26 (1969).

2. In *Les Quatre Branches du Mabinogi et autres contes du Moyen Age*, translated and annotated by Pierre-Yves Lambert (Paris: Gallimard, 1993), a volume in the series *L'Aube des peuples*. See also Philippe Jouet, *L'Aurore celtique* (Paris: Editions du Porte-Glaive), 1993. P. Jouet translates Annwvyn (pronounced "Ane-ou-ine") as: "not-world," "anti-earth."

3. "Notes d'étymologie et de lexicographie gauloises et celtiques. XIII. 47. "Irlandais *Sid*, gaulois *Sedos 'siège, demeure des dieux'," *Ogam* XIV (1962), p. 329. Also useful are his other two essays "Notes d'étymologie et de lexicographie gauloises et celtiques. XXVIII. 133. Celtique commun *Letavia, gaulois *Letavis*, irlandais *Letha*; la porte de l'Autre Monde" in *Ogam* XIX, nos. 113–14 (1967), pp. 490–94 and XX, nos. 115–16 (1968), p. 165, and "MEDIOLANVM BITVRIGVM. Deux éléments de vocabulaires religieux et de géographie sacrée," in *Ogam* XIII, no. 73 (1961), pp. 137–58. See Françoise Le Roux, "Introduction générale à l'étude de la Tradition Celtique," *Ogam* XIX, nos. 111–12 (1967).

4. The asterisk placed in front of some words means that these words are reconstructed common or proto-Celtic forms.

5. In his note XIII, p. 335, Guyonvarc'h proposes the following translation for the ethnonym Sidones mentioned by Strabo: "the folk of the Great Beyond, [or] those well versed in the science of the Great Beyond."

6. In *Les Druides* (Rennes: Ouest-France Université, 1986), p.

281, note 36, C.-J. Guyonvarc'h and F. Le Roux point out on that Salomon Reinach has demonstrated how in the expression *orbe alio* in Lucan's *Civil War*, I, 453–458 ("...*nemora alta remotis incolitis lucis; vobis auctoribus umbrae non tacticas Erebi sedes Ditisque profundi pallida regna petunt: regit idem spiritus artus orbe alio; longae, canitis si cognita, vitae mors media est.*"), *orbis* did not mean the Great Beyond in a lunar or stellar universe, but actually another region of the terrestrial world. This led S. Reinach to say: "So it is not a question in Lucan, an interpreter of Druidism, that there was another life in another world, but rather a prolonging of terrestrial and sublunar life in another part of the world," to which the authors added: "Salomon Reinach demonstrates, without even having to come out and say it, that the Gauls' conception of the Other World was the same as that of the Irish *síd*."

7. C.-J. Guyonvarc'h, op. cit., p. 334.

8. E. G. Quin, ed. *Dictionary of the Irish Language* (Dublin: Royal Irish Academy, 1990) under letter S, col. 215–18.

9. Julius Caesar, *Commentaries on the Gallic and Civil Wars*, trans. W. A. McDevitte and W. S. Bohn (New York: Harper & Bros., 1869). <www.perseus.tufts.edu>

10. Ibid.

11. Marcus Annaeus Lucanus, *Pharsalia or the Civil War*, Bk. I, trans. by Sir Edward Ridley (London: Longmans, Green, and Co., 1905). <www.perseus.tufts.edu>

12. Pomponius Mela, *Chorographia*, from the French translation of A. Silbermann (Paris: Les Belles Lettres, 1988).

13. Strabo, *Geographica*, trans. H. L. Jones, Loeb Classical Library, 8 vols., (Cambridge, Mass.: Harvard University Press, 1917–32), p. 245f.

14. T. Jolif, *B.A.-BA Tradition celtique*, (Puiseaux: Pardès, 2001), pp. 36–37.

15. In Ireland, the theme of the woman from the Other World coming into contact with a warrior or king for the purposes of either love or prophecy, or even destruction, is very common. The Druids needed no such mediation to contact the *Síd*, while heroes (and maybe even some artisans) did. See, for example, the account "Ces Noinden Ulad" (The Nine Days' Pangs [or Debility] of the Ulstermen) in C.-J. Guyonvarc'h and F. Le Roux, *La Souveraineté guerrière de l'Irlande* (Rennes: *Ogam*-Celticum, 1971), pp. 50–52. The fact that the "mediators" of these contacts were women is understandable if we realize that "woman—understood as a crea-

ture of craft, passion and power (*çakti*), following the example of the warrior for whom she is a 'sin' and eternal 'temptation'—represents the 'left' part of Celtic tradition, and this is the necessary, sufficient and normal justification for according her a rather 'Varuna-like' place in the religious hierarchy: poetess, prophetess, magician, warrior woman, 'Druidess' (*bandrui*) by generalization of terminology, she never has a speculative function." F. Le Roux, "Le rêve d'Oengus, commentaire du texte," in *Ogam* XVIII (1966), p. 139.

16. Frithjof Schuon, "Ambiguïté de l'exotérisme," in *Approche du phénomène religieux* (Paris: Le Courrier du Livre, 1984), p. 27.

17. The latter term might also be rendered "Land of the Everliving." (Translator's note)

18. Cf. *Mesca Ulad*, ed. J. Carmichael Watson, Mediaeval and Modern Irish Series, Vol. XIII (Dublin: The Stationery Office, 1941), p. 1. This passage is taken from a translation we have begun but not yet completed. For the text in its entirety, refer to the translation by C.-J. Guyonvarc'h in *Ogam* XII (1961), p. 409.

19. See "La doctrine des cycles dans la tradition celtique," *La Règle d'Abraham*, no. 14 (2002). See also *B.A.-BA Tradition celtique*, op. cit. p. 31–32.

20. It should be mentioned that in *Cath Maige Turedh* (The Second Battle of Mag Tuired) it is written that the Dagda "trailed behind him a wheeled fork which was the work of eight men to move, and its track was enough for the boundary ditch of a province." Cf. C.-J. Guyonvarc'h, *Textes mythologiques irlandais* I, vol. I, Celticum 11 (Rennes: *Ogam*–Tradition Celtique, 1980), pp. 53–54, §93. There is a morphological analogy to be drawn between *lorg*, "club" (and there is no doubt that the club mentioned here is not literally Dagda's club but something else), and *lerg*, "track." Although here the track plays the symbolic role of a boundary, its link with the club, whose relationship with death and the Other World we have already noted, would tend to make us think that the boundary drawn by the "track of the Dagda's club" could obviously be interpreted as being the one "separating" our world and the *Síd*.

21. See J. Chevalier and A. Gheerbrant, eds., *Dictionnaire des Symboles* (Paris: Robert Laffont, 1999), p. 618, under the entry "Massue."

22. F. Schuon, op. cit, above. In order to clarify our position, let us point out again that in Christian Celtic tradition, hell is cold, which would most certainly refer to this particular conception

of the Other World as a place of non-being, which makes it a negative mirror-image of the Other World, a kingdom with multiple abodes where Being could exult in its splendor. The Celtic monks' poetic visions of nature, bathed in divine light, are highly suggestive of the descriptions of the Other World as it reflected in our own world.

23. See C.-J. Guyonvarc'h, "Celtique commun *Letavia, gaulois Letavis, irlandais Letha; la porte de l'Autre Monde," op. cit.

24. See F. Le Roux and C.-J. Guyonvarc'h, *Les Fêtes Celtiques* (Rennes: Ouest-France Université, 1995), and by the same authors, *Les Druides*, op. cit., pp. 231, 259, 280. Also see T. Jolif, op. cit., p. 61.

25. See René Guénon, "Les Portes solsticiales," in *Symboles de la Science sacrée* (Paris: Gallimard, 1998), pp. 217–21.

26. Henry Corbin, *Le Paradoxe du monothéisme* (Paris: L'Herne, 2003), p. 158.

27. "Le rêve d'Oengus, commentaire du texte," op. cit., p. 141.

28. P. Geay, *Hermès trahi, impostures philosophiques et néo-spiritualisme d'après l'oeuvre de René Guénon* (Paris: Dervy, 1996), p. 201.

29. *Ogam* IX (1957), pp. 305–307, and also *Les Druides*, op. cit. pp. 282–84.

30. In *Textes mythologiques irlandais*, op. cit., pp. 233–35.

31. Cf. *Les Druides*, op. cit. p. 282. Version here from Kuno Meyer's 1895 translation.

32. The author uses the word *monde*, or "world," here, although Meyer translated the Irish as "age." (Translator's note)

33. "The North and the West are interchangeable in the Celtic folk tradition and these are the two cardinal points indicating the direction to the Other World, to the world of the gods or the primordial 'spiritual center.'" F. Le Roux, "La mythologie irlandaise du Livre des Conquêtes," *Ogam* XX (1968), nos. 117–20.

34. *Les Druides*, op. cit., p. 283.

35. Because for those who find themselves there, these islands are both the localization of a particular state and this state itself. "In fact, the heavenly realms, like those—every bit as real—of hell, are the formal manifestation of the internal state of those who inhabit it and therefore the imaginal externalization of a world corresponding to their essential predisposition." P. Geay, *Hermès trahi*, op. cit., p. 200.

36. In this regard we should briefly mention a striking simi-

larity, which, although it does not seem closely related to our subject matter upon first examination, could still provoke some thought on the critical importance of taking only a very rigorously traditional approach to Celtic tradition. Manawyddan (Gaulish equivalent of Manánann) is led to practice the art of cobbler in a Gaulish tale, while in another text of the same origin, it is Llew Llaw Giffes (that is, the Gaulish equivalent of Lug) who pursues this profession for awhile, and even Enoch, whose role as Center of the imaginal world linking Earth and Sky is well known, is said to have been a cobbler. Moreover, in one ancient Hebrew tradition it is through his profession that he discovers the powerful link which "joins the above and below." P. Geay, *Hermès Trahi*, op. cit., p. 200.

37. *Les Druides*, op. cit., p. 283.

38. It should also be mentioned that there is a significant association in Celtic tradition, as in many others, between woman and water. In the Irish texts, with rare exceptions it is always women who invite mortals to follow them into the *Síd*, and of course this is done by getting on a boat. Regarding the links between the goddess, water, and sovereignty among the Celts refer to: *Les Druides*, op. cit., "Le passage de l'eau," p. 315; and T. Jolif, "Dana, Etain, Macha, l'Eternel féminin dans la tradition celtique," in *Aux sources de l'Eternel féminin*, ed. Arnaud Guyot-Jeannin (Lausanne: L'Age d'Homme, 2001), pp. 85–106.

39. *Echtrae Loegairi*, cited in Myles Dillon et al., *Les Royaumes celtiques* (Crozon Armeline, 2001), p. 283.

40. Cf. the translation by C.-J. Guyonvarc'h in *Ogam* X, nos. 58–59 (1958), §23, p. 294.

41. According to the fragment of the MS Harleian 5280, fol. 119, published by O'Curry in *Lectures on the MS Materials of Ancient Irish History*. Cf. the translation in F. Le Roux, "Etude sur le festiaire celtique : IV. Lugnasad ou la fête du roi," *Ogam* XIV (1962), nos. 80–81, pp. 365–66.

42. The dream of Rhonabwy, in *The Four Branches of the Mabinogi*, op. cit., pp. 186–205.

43. Regarding the death of King Muirchertach (see "Aided Muichertaig Maic Erca, The Death of Muirchertach Mac Erca," ed. and trans. by Wh. Stokes, in *Revue Celtique* XXIII (1902), pp. 395–437. A French translation of this account by F. Le Roux and C.-J. Guyonvarc'h can be found in *La Légende de la ville d'Is*, (Rennes: Ouest-France Université, 2000, pp. 22–46. The following verse can be found in the *Lebor Gaballa Erenn*, IX, CXIX (ed. R. A.

S. Macalister, Irish Texts Society, Dublin, 1938–56), evoking the triple death with a very traditional conciseness:

Oididh Muircertaigh na modh
guin is bátadh is loscad.

"The tragic death of Muichertach of the armies, wounded, drowned, burned." (Translation of the quoted text by T. Jolif.)

44. *Aislinge Oenguso*, British Museum, Egerton, 1782, folios 70r, 1–71v, ed. Edward Müller, in *Revue Celtique* III, 1876–78, pp. 334–50. Translation of the quoted text by T. Jolif.

45. "Tract on the chief places of Meath," MS H.3 17 of Trinity College, col. 732/800, published by T. P. McLaughey in *Celtica* V (1960), p. 173, cited in F. LeRoux, "Le Celticum d'Ambigatus et l'Omphalos gaulois," *Ogam* XII (1961), p. 174.

46. H. Corbin, op. cit., p. 250.

47. In this respect, two elements are worth mentioning: first, in relation to the "conversion" of Irish Druids who, as we know, largely populated the ranks of the first Christian monks, it should be understood that Druidic initiation completed during a human life led to a surpassing of all individual traditional forms, and consequently it is not correct to say that the Druids converted when all they did was obey the cyclic laws and adapt, as their initiation permitted them to do, to a new traditional form for the purpose of transmitting the material with which they were entrusted. It would be of interest therefore to further study the link between the idea of *epectasis* (etymology from the Greek word meaning "stretching"), dear to the Eastern commentators of the Exodus, and which consists in a vision of the abundance of the Kingdom as a dynamic migration "from glory to glory," an infinite exodus of the soul to God, and the theme of the *Immramas*, which also relates to a genuine initiation conception of the soul's destiny.

Code of Blood:
Counterfeits of Tradition from
The Spear of Destiny *to* The Da Vinci Code

Stephen Edred Flowers

Propagandists for various medieval and modern trends have continually twisted and exploited traditional mythic paradigms to serve their own ideological and financial interests. Here I will focus on two related examples of this phenomenon: the twentieth-century motifs of the "spear of destiny" and the "holy blood/holy grail." The latter in particular has been utilized in Dan Brown's popular recent novel *The Da Vinci Code*,[1] which has given rise to all manner of misconceptions. These misconceptions are necessarily fueled by what I call *conventional mysteries*. Such "mysteries" depend upon preexisting support in the popular imagination. If the popular imagination alights on the notion that whatever the hidden truth is, it must be clothed in Judeo-Christian, or Egyptian, or Chinese imagery, or, failing that, it would *have to* emerge from a UFO, then the would-be propagandist tends to dress up his message in precisely this way. However, it is our position that real mysteries are *primordial*, and thus ultimately free from considerations of external or visual imagery. Nevertheless, such mysteries are often best understood when illuminated by the cultural traditions from which they first emerged. Here we seek the deep—if unconventional—mysteries underlying the two aforementioned popular modern myths. What emerges will lead us back to authentic mysteries.

Holy Blood

The "holy blood" motif concerns the idea of a sacred or godly descent or "bloodline." In short, *divine DNA* as symbolically, yet perfectly, understood in ancient tradition. In the bestseller *Holy Blood, Holy Grail* by Michael Baigent, Richard Leigh, and Henry Lincoln,[2] it was argued that Jesus of Nazareth did not die on the cross, but escaped to southern Gaul (now France), and there with his wife, Mary Magdalene, sired a bloodline (the House of Sion = Zion) which appears in Frankish legendary history with Merovech or Merovingus or Merovée (died 456). The "fact" that this bloodline, the family of Jesus, existed at all appears to have been a secret which had to be preserved at all costs. This myth serves as a backstory for the fictionalized events in *The Da Vinci Code*.

First of all, it should be pointed out that this myth has origins in Gnosticism. Furthermore, it has already enjoyed a revival of sorts, thanks to Hugh Schonfield's book *The Passover Plot*.[3] I would further point out that the idea of Jesus' survival entirely negates the *raison d'être* of mainline Christianity by denying the essential meaning of Jesus' life, which is revealed by his death (sacrifice), whereby humanity's sins are washed away. Most Gnostic and pagan sects had no need of this belief, holding instead that the individual must achieve his own salvation or enlightenment through arduous spiritual discipline.

If it is therefore the case that the very notion of a holy bloodline left behind by Jesus—whether true or not—is entirely antithetical to Christian belief, we might then ask ourselves: are the indicators so voluminously pointed out by Lincoln and his ilk entirely groundless and insubstantial? Not necessarily. Is there a more plausible, much deeper traditional explanation for many of the historical phenomena observed in these speculative works? It seems likely.

If we wish to explain the idea that the bloodline of kings is imbued with the sacred, we need look no further than the native traditions of the Franks and other neighboring Germanic tribes. Among these Germanic peoples, kings and other members of the aristocracy were believed to be genetically descended from divinities. Many Germanic royal houses traced their ancestry back to a god, for example, the Anglo-Saxons to Woden, the Swedish Ynglings to Yngvi (Freyr), and the Völsungs to Óðinn (according to the *Völsunga Saga*). Jordanes reports in his *History of the Goths* that the Gothic leaders were descended from Ansis, which he defines as "demigods."[4] These Ansis are the ancestral sovereign gods known in North Germanic as Æsir.

Etymologically the very word "king" really indicates a "descendant of good kin." Originally, most kings were elected, not by the "people," but by a council made up of representatives of the same aristocratic body that was itself connected to the "holy blood." Two things stand out here: 1) the "possession" of the holy blood is not unique to one individual, or even exclusive to one bloodline alone; and 2) the link between the gods and humanity was one of substance—not, as in the case of the Judeo-Christian or Muslim god, one involving a legal contract.

Regarding the founder of the Merovingian dynasty, the authors of *Holy Blood, Holy Grail* report:

> Merovée ... was a semi-supernatural figure worthy of classical myth. Even his name bears witness to his miraculous origin and character. It echoes the French word for "mother" as well as the French and Latin words for "sea."
> According to the leading Frankish chronicler and subsequent tradition, Merovée was born of two fathers. When already pregnant by her husband, King Clodio, Merovée's mother supposedly went swimming in the ocean. In the water she is said to have been seduced and/or raped by an unidentified marine creature from beyond the sea...[5]

The first comment to be made here is that this quote, typically, misses all the basic truths. The name Merovech is, of course, a Frankish (i.e., Germanic) name. Merovech and all the Frankish kings spoke only Frankish and had only Frankish-Germanic names. The element *mer-* is cognate to the Latin *mare*, but it is a Germanic, not a Romance form. The name may mean "sea-creature." Lincoln and the "Priory of Zion" interpreters want to see in this reference to a sea-creature either their aforementioned idea of something "from beyond the sea" (i.e., from a foreign source), or more particularly a reference to the "fish" as an early Christian icon. In other words, this legend is supposed to represent the coming of the seed of Jesus to the Merovingian line. The "leading Frankish chronicler" is not explicitly named by Lincoln, but in fact the legend is only found in the *Chronicle of Fredegar*, which was produced in the middle of the seventh century, in the time of the Carolingians. It is most likely that Fredegar is reporting on a pagan, court-based myth, which in fact was meant to point away from, not toward, a Christian origin for the dynasty. Gregory of Tours (539–594) simply states: "Some say that Merovech, the father of Childeric, was descended from Clodio."[6] Fredegar was apparently freer to report on the non-Christian, pagan origins of the Merovingians, whereas Gregory, writing a hundred years earlier, preferred to keep quiet about it, if he was privy to the inner mythology at all.

Few have commented on the improbability of the first and best evidence the "Priory of Zion" group has, as it seems to hinge on this legend about Merovech, which dates from about four centuries after the time of Jesus himself, and originates with tribes who were still practicing paganism. The Franks would not become Christian until the conversion of Chlodvig (Clovis) to Roman Catholicism in 497, several decades after the death of Merovech. All of this does not make a very strong case for the Christian interpretation of the mysteries these authors are purportedly investigating. It is more probable that whatever traditions seem to relate the bloodline in question to the "grail" and to the "secrets" of the church at Rennes-le-Château can be traced to surviving pagan Frankish and Gothic traditions. But in order for these mysteries to survive they had to be rendered in conventional forms—in other words, they had to be Christianized and provided with an at least superficially acceptable and intelligible symbolic pedigree. This conventional veneer, however, only masks the real mystery.

Spears of Destiny

The historical process of masking ancient myths with newer and more acceptable forms is not unique to one time or place, or one set of symbols. The same thing was done with the so-called holy lance, now recognized as part of the Hapsburg imperial regalia and popularly referred to as the "spear of destiny." This object was the focus of an occult fantasy of Dr. Walter Johannes Stein (1891–1957), whose student Trevor Ravenscroft used it as the basis for his occult potboiler *The Spear of Destiny*.[7] According to Stein's theory, this spear was allegedly that of the Roman soldier who pierced the side of Jesus as he hung on the cross. This proved that Christ was already dead, and so did not have to have his legs broken—the usual way victims of crucifixion were "finished off" by the Romans. According to Stein, this is important because it allowed a biblical prophesy to be fulfilled. In the *The Spear of Destiny*, Ravenscroft says: "Isaiah had prophesied of the Messiah, 'A bone of Him shall not be broken.'"[8] The supposed importance of all this is that the Roman spearman, whom later Catholic tradition identifies as Longinus, is thought to have held the fate of mankind in his hands at that moment. If he had not stabbed Jesus, his legs would have been broken and he would have been disqualified from being the messiah. Longinus held the destiny of humanity in his hands, and the spear, his fateful instrument, continues to possess this magical power. Thus, according to this line of thought, whoever holds the spear holds the destiny of mankind in his hands! As a talisman of power, the spear was ultimately lusted after by that arch-villain of the twentieth century, Adolf Hitler.

Code of Blood

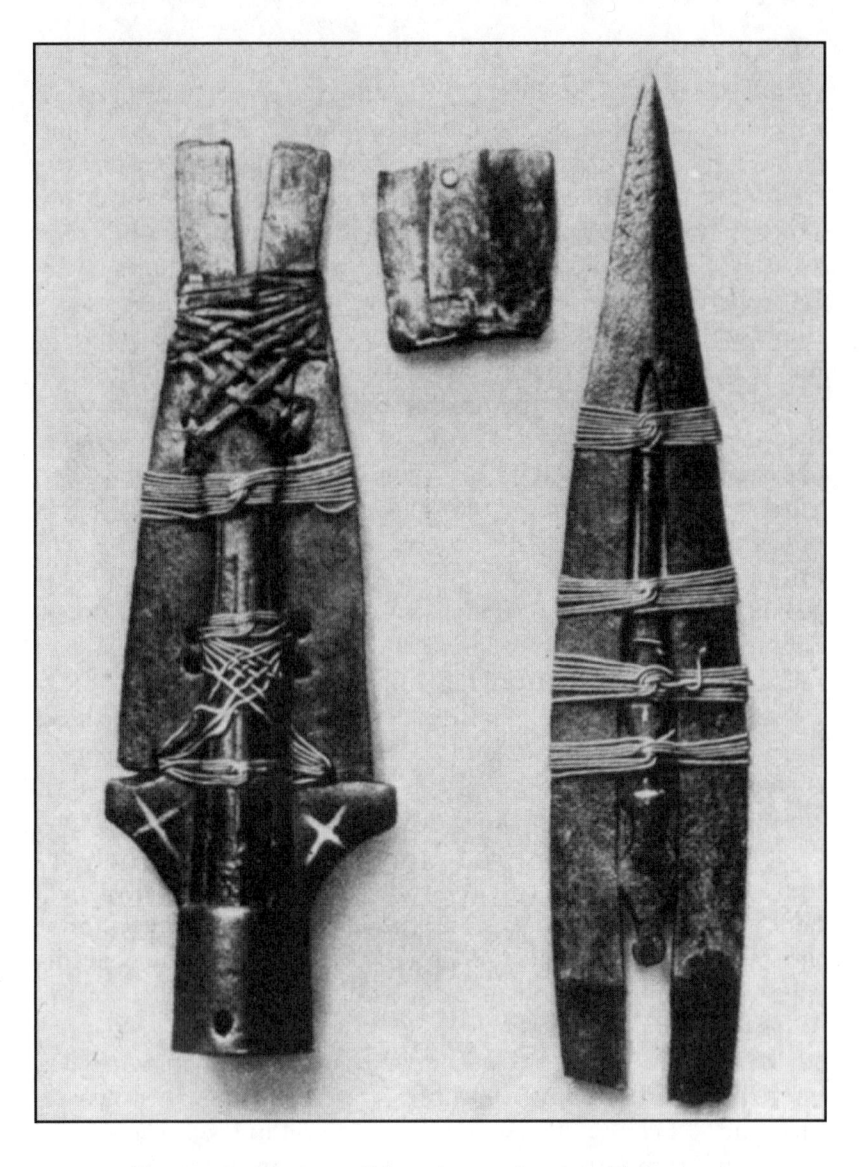

THE PIECES OF THE "HOLY LANCE" IN THE TREASURE
CHAMBER OF THE HOFBURG PALACE, VIENNA.
(IMAGE FROM "THE SPEAR OF DESTINY" BY TREVOR RAVENSCROFT)

In all of this we are again confronted by a set of conventional—albeit sensationalistic and even propagandistic—myths that conceal deeper and more authentic mysteries.

To begin with, the very idea that the piercing of the side of Jesus in some way fulfilled Isaiah's Old Testament prophecy is a fraud and a forgery. No such passage exists in the Book of Isaiah.

The quote, "not a bone of him shall be broken," is really from the New Testament (John 19:36), and simply and erroneously purports to refer to a fulfillment of scriptural prophecy. Secondly, the "holy lance," or "spear of destiny," has been scientifically analyzed and has been shown to be of eighth- to tenth-century Germanic (probably Langobardic) manufacture. Historically, it is possible that Charlemagne (768–804) took it with him from his conquest of the Langobards. These facts do not, therefore, support the conventional mystification of occult propaganda. The same facts do, however, point us in the direction of a deeper truth.

In order to discover that truth, we have to ask the question: is it more likely that the spear has a significance that predates Christian influence, and if so, what could that significance be?

Among the Germanic tribes, spears were symbols of royal power and of the political power (enfranchisement) of free men. Often it was the practice to "shake the spear" to vote in legal assemblies (hence the personal names Shakespeare and Notker, which derives from the older Germanic roots *[H]not-, "shake, swing" + *gar, "spear"). In mythic iconography, of course, the spear is a symbol of the sovereign power of the Germanic god Woðanaz, known in Scandinavia as Óðinn, or Woden/Wodan in the south. Interesting spearheads have been found—especially in eastern Europe—engraved with runic inscriptions and other holy signs (including Sarmatian *tamgas*). It is most likely that such spears were used as scepters of royal power by Germanic kings and chieftains and that the actual spear was seen as an earthly reflection of the spear of the ancestral sovereign god, Wodan. He who held this spear—sanctified to Woden—would indeed have held the destiny of his people in his hands.

Here again we see an ancient traditional paradigm which has been obscured by a later counterfeit that profoundly alters its meaning. Of course, this was quite common in the early Middle Ages during the progressive Christianization of the Germanic peoples. In modern times, the process expanded beyond the boundaries of ecclesiastical polemics into the world of the occult.

What I am proposing here is that we look at such symbols *traditionally*, that is, in their original mythic context. If and when this is done, the manifold obfuscations bound up with the conventionally "mysterious" will fall away and something of actual spiritual benefit can be reclaimed. This method tends to use historically and objectively verifiable data as a basis for symbolic or mythic investigation, and when utilized properly can illuminate even the "ooga-booga" world of popular occultism.

When considering both the *sang real* ("royal, holy blood") and the spear of destiny, it appears most likely that there was an early medieval syncretism which occurred between pagan tradition and Christian mythology. Old, established pre–Christian paradigms were co-opted into marginally plausible Christian frameworks: pagan sacral kingship is linked to the royal lineage of "King" Jesus, and the spear of Wodan is linked to the spear of Longinus. These syncretisms are then obviously and naturally later misinterpreted in such a way that the new and secondary myths come to be seen as the primary origins, and the true origins are forgotten by all but the vigilant.

Vigilantibus!

Notes:

1. New York: Doubleday, 2003.
2. New York: Dell, 1983.
3. New York: Bantam, 1967; new edition New York: Disinformation, 2005.
4. *The Gothic History of Jordanes*, trans. Charles Christopher Mierow (Princeton: Princeton University Press, 1915), XIII: 78 (p. 73).
5. Baigent et al., *Holy Blood, Holy Grail*, p. 235.
6. Gregory of Tours, *History of the Franks*, trans. Lewis Thorpe (Harmondsworth: Penguin, 1974), section II: 9 (p. 125).
7. New York: G. P. Putnam's Sons, 1973.
8. Ravenscroft, *The Spear of Destiny*, pp. xi–xii.

This article is based on research and findings contained in an as-yet-unpublished manuscript entitled Mysteries of the Goths, *in which the world of the pagan Goths is delineated and mysterious elements in their later culture—Gothic Christianity, hidden treasures, and secrets of heritage—are explored and explained.*

The Woodharrow Institute is proud to introduce our flagship publication:
Symbel: A Journal of Early Germanic Studies

Issue 1 (Fall 2006) is now available and contains the following articles: "Elf-Quern and Elf-Shot: Language of Healing and Harming in Germanic Ritual Practice" by Stephen C. Wehmeyer; "On Magical Runes" by Magnus Olsen (originally published in 1916, translated by Stephen E. Flowers); "The Germanization of Christianity in the Theologia Germanica" by Glenn Alexander Magee; and "The State of Traditional Germanic and Scandinavian Studies in the Universities of the United States" by Michael Moynihan. A book review section discusses recent publications of interest.

A subscription to *Symbel* is included as a benefit of membership in the Woodharrow Institute. The journal is also available to the general public.

To receive a copy of Issue 1 (Fall 2006), please send $15.00 postage paid in the USA, or $20.00 elsewhere, payable to:

The Woodharrow Institute
P.O. Box 557
Smithville, TX 78957
U.S.A.
www.woodharrow.com

Esotericism Without Religion: Philip Pullman's His Dark Materials

Joscelyn Godwin

When in 1995 Philip Pullman's publishers offered a novel called *Northern Lights* to the market niche of "young adults," he had no great hopes for it.[1] Several years before, he had left the security of teaching to write full-time, and had had moderate success with that dwindling readership; he reckoned that his new book "would be read by about five hundred people at the most."[2] But the right people did read and review it, and the next year it was awarded the Carnegie Medal for the best children's book. A sequel, *The Subtle Knife* (1997), was an instant best-seller. Three years later, the trilogy was completed by *The Amber Spyglass*, and Pullman's fans, now exceeding his gloomy estimate by several orders of magnitude, argued over whether or not the final volume was a let-down. It did not matter: the book won the Whitbread Book of the Year award, given for the first time to a so-called children's book—though more than one reader exclaimed: "This is Harry Potter for grown-ups!" Translations into dozens of languages followed. In 2004, London's National Theatre staged *His Dark Materials* (the collective title) in two plays of three hours each. Now the first of three movies is reaching a vastly wider audience. After years of precarious survival in the home of lost causes,[3] Pullman has found himself showered with literary prizes, honorary degrees, and the plaudits of the great and the good.

Not everyone is pleased by his success, for reasons that will become obvious. For those who have not read *His Dark Materials*, the essentials can be summarized quite briefly. The heroine, twelve-year-old Lyra, lives in a parallel world somewhat resembling our own, in which history has taken a different course. In the sixteenth century of Lyra's world, the fanatical reformer John Calvin was elected Pope. After his death, the papacy was replaced with a theocratic "Magisterium" headquartered in Geneva, which succeeded in gaining control over every aspect of life. (31)[4] Science was classed as "experimental theology," and all speculation subjected to rigid censorship. By the present day, when the story happens, technology has advanced to the point of steam trains and majestic zeppelins.[5]

That is the modern history of Lyra's world. The ancient history, scattered in hints throughout *His Dark Materials*, embraces not only hers but all the myriad worlds, and it goes as follows.[6] The universe is uncreated and consists of material particles, the most subtle of which are known in the book as "Dust." At some point, these particles became self-conscious, and matter began to understand itself, and to love itself. As it did so, more Dust was formed, and the first conscious being emerged: an angel, known in the book as "The Authority." When other angels emerged from the evolving substance, the Authority told them that he had created them (which was a lie), and sought to exercise his power over all conscious beings. Later, one came who was wiser than the Authority (elsewhere identified as Sophia or wisdom), but she was banished. (622)

Before our present world was created, some of the angels, followers of wisdom, rebelled against the Authority and were cast down. (367) They continued to work for his downfall and for the opening of the minds he sought to close. (983) Led by Sophia, they gave to the evolving beings in each world a gift that would help them understand themselves and become wise. In some worlds, they gave them a dæmon.[7] In our world, these angels had dealings with humans, and interbred with them. (439) The awakening to fully human consciousness occurred here between 30,000 and 40,000 years ago, as part of the rebel angels' plan against the Authority. (530)

On rare occasions, humans on both sides of the conflict were able to rise to angelic status. Such was Baruch, one of the pair of angels who helps in the assault on the Authority. Another was Enoch, who graduated from the human state four thousand years ago (648) and was chosen as Regent of the Authority under the name of Metatron.[8] At the time of the story, this Regent, seeing conscious beings becoming dangerously independent, is planning to intervene much more in human affairs and to set up a permanent Inquisition in every world. (647) The Authority, for his part, has gradually withdrawn to his residence in the "Clouded Mountain." When we meet him near the end of the book, he is in the last stages of senility, and dies. (926)

One of the defining characteristics of epic literature is the presence of the divine and its interaction with humans. It figures largely in Homer's *Iliad* and *Odyssey*; Ovid's *Metamorphoses* and Virgil's *Aeneid*; Dante's *Divine Comedy*, Milton's *Paradise Lost*

PHILIP PULLMAN (PHOTO BY JERRY BAUER,
COURTESY OF RANDOM HOUSE CHILDREN'S BOOKS)

(together with Blake, the primary literary influence on Pullman and the source of the phrase *His Dark Materials*), Goethe's *Faust*, and Wagner's *Ring of the Nibelung*. If these do not always "justify the ways of God[s] to man," at least they represent them, with all their implications. Another characteristic of epic is that it usually contains a cosmogony or creation myth, and a cosmology or explanation of the world-system.

His Dark Materials satisfies epic tradition in these respects, as also in the heroic and tragic nature of its protagonists. This summary also reveals some of the things that irk the defenders of the faith. Pullman's depiction of the Church and its ministers makes them out to be sleazy, repressive, and cruel. The trilogy's dramatic mainspring is the reversal of the outcome of the last War in Heaven—the one described in *Paradise Lost*, in which God's angels conquered Satan's. In the process, Lyra and her boy companion Will Parry travel to the Land of the Dead (another requisite of epic literature) to find a drab Homeric Hades in which the Authority has imprisoned the spirits of all conscious beings. Will and Lyra's task is to let these ghosts out, so that their subtle atoms can return to nature: a process of dissolution experienced as ecstatic release. The children learn the lesson that there is no paradise but the here and now, and no prospect superior to the "republic of heaven" that we may build while we are alive. The promises and threats of the monotheistic religions, in short, are revealed as a pack of lies.

Catholics and Evangelicals alike have savaged *His Dark Materials* on the grounds that it denigrates religion and woos its young readers to atheism.[9] As we know from the examples of Salman Rushdie (author of *The Satanic Verses*) and, more recently, Mel Gibson (director of *The Passion of the Christ*), nothing generates more publicity than upsetting people's religious sensibilities and getting them to protest against one's work. But one has to be careful about whom to annoy. Although Mr. Pullman has rightly said that "every single religion that has a monotheistic god ends up by persecuting other people and killing them because they don't accept him,"[10] he has more sense than to attack Islam or Judaism directly. In secular Britain, Christianity is easier game, and less likely to hit back in unpleasant ways.[11] Instead of slinking around in fear of the Ayatollah's assassins, as Mr. Rushdie did for years, Pullman has the Archbishop of Canterbury eating out of his hand.[12] It remains to be seen how this will go down in the U.S.A., if the film-makers do not shirk Pullman's image of what many Americans still regard as God.

Seen from the other side, it is no wonder that many Christians of another stamp, Archbishop Williams included, feel no animus toward Pullman and his novel. For one thing, they can recognize fiction when they see it. For another, the Calvinist theocracy of Lyra's world is the last brand of Christianity they want to identify with. They share what Pullman describes as his "deep anger and yes, horror at the excesses of cruelty and infamy that've been carried out in the name of a supernatural power."[13] As to whether the books encourage atheism in their young (or even older) readers, that is a matter for reflection rather than hysteria. Dr. Williams says that it is healthy for anyone to ask themselves what sort of god they do *not* believe in.[14]

While its cosmogony is atheist, in the sense that the universe is uncreated, and its cosmology materialist, *His Dark Materials* lacks for nothing in wonder and magic. Spurning the drab, denatured universe of the existentialist novelists, Pullman has drawn on another current that has often run in opposition to the churches: the esoteric tradition. Magpie-like, he has picked up fragments from Hermeticism, from Kabbalah and Jewish legend, from Gnosticism, theosophy, and the occult sciences, and interwoven them with current notions of physics. His worlds proliferate with angels, witches, shamans, specters, talking beasts, and especially with dæmons.

Readers and critics agree that one of his happiest inventions is the dæmon: a part of the individual exteriorized in the form of a beast, bird, or insect of the opposite sex, which accompanies every person closely their life long. The dæmon speaks with a human voice, but has the senses and skills of the appropriate animal. It acts as playmate or companion, as an ever-present partner in conversation, and often as a wise counselor. The dæmons of children are unstable, changing from one animal to another according to whim or circumstance, until at puberty they settle into a permanent form. Lyra is distressed when she first comes into the world of her friend Will, which is our world, and sees people without their accompanying dæmons: it seems to her indecent, or tragic, until she persuades herself that people in our world have their dæmons inside themselves. Among the obvious forerunners of this brilliant notion is the *daimon* of Socrates, with its habit of warning him against imprudent actions or dangerous circumstances. Another is Carl Jung's anima or animus as a contra-sexual element in the unconscious, its instinctual wisdom sometimes represented in dreams or visions by an animal or bird. Then there is the idea of finding one's own "animal spirit," which has entered the imagery of the New Age by way of Native American and other shamanic cultures. These parallels show why Pullman's invention rings so true, especially to young readers who yearn for a close and faithful companion, and often find an invisible one, to the annoyance of rational parents and teachers.

Pullman, like any author in touch with the mysterious sources of the creative imagination,[15] is definitely on the irrational side here.

He skillfully avoids the reductionism to which the atheist world view is often prone, and the consequent one-dimensionality of the human being. Lyra, already familiar with her dæmon-soul, speculates that humans comprise three things: the body, the dæmon, and the "ghost." Mary Malone, a character from our world, remarks on how Saint Paul talks of body, soul, and spirit, so that Lyra's three-part view of human nature is not so strange to her. (949) As for the ultimate fate of these components, the body eventually decays and its atoms return to nature, as do those of the dæmon, which vanishes into thin air immediately upon death. That leaves the spirit or ghost, which as Lyra says is "the part that can think about the other two." (733) So long as the Authority ruled, the ghosts of all conscious beings have been kept captive in the Land of the Dead. After Lyra and Will have opened a way out, the ghosts, too, return to their natural elements, joyfully recombining with the wind and dew and earth, and perhaps with the very atoms of their own sweethearts and dæmons. (906)

Readers of the late-antique writings ascribed to Hermes Trismegistus will detect an echo of a famous passage describing what happens after death:

> First, in releasing the material body you give the body over to alteration, and the form that you used to have vanishes. To the demon you give over your temperament, now inactive. The body's senses rise up and flow back to their particular sources, becoming separate parts and mingling again with the energies. And feeling and longing go on toward irrational nature.[16]

In short, each human element and faculty returns to its appropriate cosmic reservoir. But in Hermetism this is not the end of the human being. The sage continues: "Thence the human being rushes up through the cosmic framework," surrendering its evil tendencies as it passes the sphere of each planet, "and then, stripped of the effects of the cosmic framework, the human enters the region of the *ogdoad* [the eight higher powers]; he has his own proper power, and along with the blessed he hymns the father." And beyond this stage, suggestive of the Christian Paradise, there is still more: "The final good for those who have received knowledge [is] to be made god."

The consensus among esotericists, at least the non-Christian ones, is that few humans attain personal immortality, much less the deification that Hermetism holds out as the highest possibility for man. It supposedly takes a heroic effort of preparation during one's lifetime in order to achieve this in the after-death state; the great majority of humans are simply recycled in soul as well as body. (There is a separate current, more occult than esoteric, that takes quite seriously the idea that human souls, after death, are imprisoned—whether by an Authority, by the Moon, or by their own incapacity—in some intermediate sphere.[17]) In Pullman's worlds, this recycling is welcomed as the normal course of nature. After body, dæmon, and ghost have all dispersed, nothing is left to rush up through the cosmic framework and eventually become a god. But in *His Dark Materials*, too, there are the exceptional instances of humans like Metatron and Baruch, who have become angels and are virtually immortal. Surprising as it may seem, the eschatology of *His Dark Materials* is quite Hermetic.

An aura of Hermeticism,[18] this time of the Renaissance rather than classical antiquity, surrounds the *alethiometer*, a golden compass-like instrument which Lyra learns to use for divination. It seems to have been invented in Prague (the Prague of Lyra's world), about three hundred years ago, and its function is to "tell the truth" (Greek *alètheuein*). The device displays thirty symbols on its dial, each of them like a ladder of meanings down which one must search for the right one. Farder Coram, the Gypsy sage, explains to Lyra that the first meaning of the anchor, for example, is hope, the second steadfastness, the third snag or prevention, the fourth the sea, and so on. (109) Under his guidance, Lyra finds that she can work the instrument by setting its three pointers to define a question, then entering a state of suspended awareness. The answer comes in symbolic form, which has to be interpreted either through intuition (as in Lyra's case) or, more laboriously, through consulting treatises.

One thinks immediately—and Pullman confirms the association[19]—of the order of ideas made familiar by Frances A. Yates: the emblem books of the Renaissance; the ranked images employed in the art of memory and in artificial languages like Kircher's Polygraphy; the rotating volvelles in the books of Ramon Llull and other cosmographers. Other associations are with the exquisite clockworks and dials of German workmanship; the questioning of angels by John Dee and Edward Kelley; and the use by occultists of child mediums whose innocence grants them privileged access to

> Into this wild abyss,
> The womb of nature and perhaps her grave,
> Of neither sea, nor shore, nor air, nor fire,
> But all these in their pregnant causes mixed
> Confusedly, and which thus must ever fight,
> Unless th' almighty maker them ordain
> His dark materials to create more worlds,
> Into this wild abyss the wary fiend
> Stood on the brink of hell and looked a while,
> Pondering his voyage...
>
> John Milton, *Paradise Lost*, Book II

IMAGE FROM THE NATIONAL THEATRE'S PROGRAM OF "HIS DARK MATERIALS," PART ONE, LONDON, 2003. BASED ON A COMPOSITE PHOTOGRAPH BY JERRY UELSMANN. (COURTESY OF JERRY UELSMANN) wisdom. I note parenthetically that if the alethiometer had been invented in *our* Prague, it would have had to be a century earlier, in the time of Michael Maier, Emperor Rudolf II, and the Rabbi Loew. But in Lyra's world, with a Calvinist theocracy in place by the mid-sixteenth century, there would have been no wars of religion, no Thirty Years War to extinguish the alchemical and Hermetic tendencies of central Europe, and no Scientific Revolution to impose a mechanistic view of nature.

Later we learn that it is Dust that makes the alethiometer work. Mary Malone discovers that Dust (which as a physicist she calls Shadow-particles, or dark matter) will respond intelligently to a certain state of mind, (401) a state she has cultivated through consulting the Chinese oracle *I Ching* (406). She uses a similar "trance-like open dreaming" to perceive her own dæmon. (1005) These are some of the many instances of altered states of consciousness in *His Dark Materials*. Will Parry also has to control his mind in order to wield the subtle knife that cuts through everything and makes windows between worlds. He first develops this control under excruciating pressure, after the knife has cut off two of his fingers; later, when he lets himself be distracted by thoughts of his mother, the knife breaks. During the reforging of it by the armored bear Iorek Byrnison, Will is ordered to "Hold it still in your mind! You have to forge it too!" (750), which demands another excruciating effort. This resembles the situation of the alchemists, whose work in the chemical laboratory was futile unless accompanied by prayer and mental effort, with due observance of astrological conditions—all in obedience to the law of correspondences.

No less dedication was required of Will's father, John Parry, whose curiosity compelled him to undergo the initiation of a shaman. In a ritual lasting two nights and a day, his skull was perforated by a trepanning drill. (423) As a result, he gained the power to control men, summon up storms, and travel out of the body, even to other worlds. This he did through "the faculty of what you call imagination. But that does not mean *making things up*. It is a form of seeing." (997) John Parry's definition of the imagination is precisely what one meets with in the school of Henry Corbin, the Sorbonne scholar who first brought the theosophy and Neoplatonism of Persia to the attention of the West.[20] For Corbin and his English admirer Kathleen Raine, the imagination is the organ through which one has access to the "imaginal world" that is without a material substratum, but absolutely real. However, for

Pullman, as for Raine, a readier source of such ideas lay to hand in William Blake—if a creative genius needs a source for anything so obvious.

As these pieces of evidence add up, it appears that *His Dark Materials* is esoteric through and through. From the academic point of view, it satisfies all four primary requirements through which Professor Antoine Faivre has defined the Western Esoteric Tradition.[21] There is the *principle of correspondences* in the alethiometer, whose multiple symbols that convey an infallible truth imply that their source, the cosmic Dust, is similarly structured. There is the principle of *living nature* in which everything receives being, consciousness, and even love from the same mysterious Dust. There is the *function of the imagination* and the presence of an imaginal world, which in many of Faivre's examples is coupled with an angelology—also present in the book. There is the *experience of transmutation* on Lyra's part as she meets her own death, her dæmon reaches its fixed form, and she fulfils her destiny as the new Eve. (In fact, the whole trilogy is about Lyra's transmutation.) Faivre defines two further components of esotericism that are often present, but not indispensable as the first four are. One is an *esoteric transmission or tradition*, which is found in the crucial episode of Will's initiation as bearer of the subtle knife. This object was created about three hundred years ago by a guild of philosopher-alchemists, the last of whom, Giacomo Paradisi, bestows it on Will, together with instructions as to its use and the rules that must be observed. (479-480) Faivre's final component is the *practice of concordance*, which reconciles the differences between exoterically conflicting religions and philosophies, but this is of little account when all religious beliefs are regarded with indifference.

Other critics have sensed in *His Dark Materials* "some form of à la carte Buddhism"[22]—a religion (or philosophy) that is never mentioned in the book but bears many points in common with it. No single, personal God is responsible for the creation of the Buddhist universe, summarized in the image of the Wheel of Existence to which all beings, except the enlightened ones, are bound. The "long-lived gods" do exist as an order of beings within the Wheel, but they do not deserve human attention, much less worship. Like the Authority, they are prone to inflate their own importance, but unlike him they have no power over us. Both the Buddhist system and that of *His Dark Materials* accord special importance to the human state, though Buddhism specifically excludes the existence of a personal, immortal soul. In Buddhism, it is only from the human state that liberation from the wheel of existence can be achieved; neither the gods, the animals, nor the dwellers in the other sectors of the wheel have the opportunity of this.

For Pullman, the special quality of the human state resides in our physical bodies: in the fact of our incarnation, which is lacking in other orders of beings, even ones that seem superior, such as angels. Like the gods of Buddhism, Pullman's angels live for aeons, but are eventually subject to decay (like the Authority) and death. They envy our physicality and the intensity of experience that is only achieved in the material world. (898) They also need us. In an episode of heartbreaking beauty, Pullman describes how the children, Lyra and Will, have come to the end of their endurance and are in an exhausted sleep, and angels come on pilgrimage to be near them: "She [the witch Serafina Pekkala] understood why these beings would wait for thousands of years and travel vast distances in order to be close to something important, and how they would feel differently for the rest of time, having been briefly in its presence." (550)

Commentators on *His Dark Materials* can hardly miss its strong flavor of Gnosticism. The theogonic episode briefly summarized above, in which the Authority lies to the other angels and is defied by one female spirit, later identified as Wisdom (Sophia), comes straight from the Gnostic myth of the First Father, Yaldabaoth:

> When the ruler saw his greatness—and he saw only himself; he did not see another one except water and darkness—then he thought that he alone existed ... And he rejoiced in his heart, and he boasted continually, saying to [the gods and their angels]: "I do not need anything." He said, "I am god and no other one exists except me." But when he said these things, he sinned against all the immortal ones, and they protected him. Moreover, when Pistis [=Sophia] saw the impiety of the chief ruler, she was angry. Without being seen, she said, "You err, Samael," i.e. "the blind god."[23]

In Valentinian Gnosticism, the true God is the *deus absconditus*, "inconceivable and invisible, eternal and uncreated, existing in great peace and stillness in unending spaces."[24] Yet in a sense he (or rather It) reaches out to mankind, extending the possibility of *gnosis*, saving knowledge, on which the whole religious philosophy depends (in Christian Gnosticism, Jesus Christ was the representative of this true God). Pullman's trilogy does not attempt to define a "true God"—which in any case can only be defined by negatives—but it includes the saving gnosis in the form of Dust, which likewise responds to its creatures and promotes conscious life, love, and freedom. In the same Gnostic school, "a deep contempt is now displayed towards the biblical God of creation and his government of the world."[25] *His Dark Materials* names this God unambiguously by the Hebraic terms of "Yahweh, El, Adonai, the King, the Father, the Almighty." (622) But when Lyra and Will actually see him, and watch him die, it is not contempt or triumph they feel, but compassion. At the same time, the value-system of *His Dark Materials* turns this "very powerful and persuasive system of thought" on its head, because as Pullman points out, "The essence of Gnosticism is its rejection of the physical universe and the whole tendency of my thinking and feeling and of the story I wrote is towards the celebration of the physical world."[26]

Although it is bad practice to identify the beliefs of fictional characters with those of their authors, Pullman has been forthcoming enough in interviews and autobiographical writings about the connections between his story-telling and his own thoughts and feelings. More than once, he has stated that he is an atheist. Asked to explain this, he has modified it by saying that he is an atheist in respect to his own experience, having no need or place for the hypothesis of what people call God; but in respect to the whole of reality, since he cannot know everything about it (and nor can anyone else), he is an agnostic.[27] As with any other mature and complex personality, there are different sides to his character, and they all contribute to his writing. There is something in him of the conventional left-wing intellectual, which emerged in his reproach of C. S. Lewis's Narnia books for racism and sexism.[28] Yet he shares the moral earnestness that, in Lewis's case, arose out of "mere Christianity." At the dénouement of *The Amber Spyglass*, an angel tells Lyra and Will how to collaborate in the work of Dust: "by helping [everyone else] to learn and understand about themselves and each other and the way everything works, and by showing them how to be kind instead of cruel, and patient instead of hasty, and cheerful instead of surly, and above all how to keep their minds open and free and curious…" (995-996) If I had met this quotation out of context, my best guess would have been that it came from somewhere in the Narnia books.

Pullman is often impatient with current pieties, as when he tells the Archbishop of Canterbury: "I'm temperamentally 'agin' the postmodernist position that there is no truth and it depends on where you are and it's all a result of the capitalist, imperialist hegemony of the bourgeois ... all this sort of stuff." Again, when asked a question about the spiritual education of children, he shows disdain for trendy and cliché-ridden thinking: "I don't use the word spiritual myself, because I don't have a clear sense of what it means. But I think it depends on your view of education: whether you think that the true end and purpose of education is to help children grow up, compete and face the economic challenges of a global environment that we're going to face in the twenty-first century, or whether you think it's to do with helping them see that they are the true heirs and inheritors of the riches—the philosophical, the artistic, the scientific, the literary riches—of the whole world. [...] I know which one I'd go for." As a parson's grandson, he knows how much the Church has contributed to civilization, and deplores the way that the Church of England has discarded the Elizabethan language, the music, and the rituals in which he was raised: "... if ever I go into a church and look at the dreadful, barren language that disfigures the forms of service they have now, I am very thankful that I grew up at a time when it was possible for me to go to Matins and sing the Psalms in the old versions." [29] Lyra's world, though gently comical in its old-fashioned ways, is a nostalgic vision of what the world might have been if untouched by modernism, infatuation with technology, and the proletarianization of culture.

The more one learns of Pullman's tastes and moral vision, the less he seems to share with the aggressively secular intellectuals who lord it over the British cultural scene and who, on a superficial understanding of his books and beliefs, acclaim him as one of their own; and the more rooted he seems to be in the traditional values of the humanist—using the term in the historical sense of a student and lover of the *litterae humaniores*. In the quotations gathered above, in his many other pronouncements, in his efforts to save the state educational system, and of course throughout his books, he has always taken the side that seeks to enrich the life of the imagination.

Can a sense of the sacred exist apart from, and even in defiance of, the revealed religions? Without a doubt, all peoples have had this sense, mediated as may be through ritual, philosophy, meditation, aesthetic or erotic experience. The dogmatic atheist alone shuts it out: if he begins to feel it, he immediately checks the feeling and substitutes scientific awe (or existential angst). The sense of the sacred announces the presence of something incomprehensible and greater than ourselves, with qualities akin to benevolence and intelligence. Dust, of course, has all these properties. It is not mindless matter or whatever modern physics has reduced matter to, but the source of all the mind, consciousness, and love in the universe. As soon as Lyra hears of it, she is attracted by it, and her quest to find the source of Dust is her spiritual quest.

Unfortunately it is religious people who have defined all the terms one would like to use in discussing these matters: spiritual, sacred, holy, divine, etc. As soon as one uses them, one seems to be on their ground. This is a problem for those outside religion but with a strong spiritual consciousness: they don't want to sound pious. No wonder Pullman shuns the word "spiritual." In the English intellectual world from which he comes, there is a marked division between the Christians and the non-believers. Christian intellectuals, second to none in their brain-power and erudition, dominate one side of the divide; their allies are the college chaplains of Oxford and Cambridge. Although the two sides treat each other with perfect decorum and often friendship, there is an uneasy feeling that the Christians would *like* to convert the others, and that they rejoice when someone enters their fold. The non-believers are usually uninterested in conversion, but Pullman is an exception, and it is his potential success in "de-evangelizing" the young that causes consternation.

What does he offer as an alternative? *His Dark Materials* adopts an esoteric world-view, but he can hardly expect people to live by that in the real world; there is no indication in his own interviews and other writings that he practices alchemy, Kabbalah, Buddhism, or whatever Gnostics are supposed to practice. Like William Blake, instead of the Authority he offers the Imagination.

The creative imagination is independent of belief, for it does not obey the structures and strictures of this world. It has the power to create new worlds for the outer and inner senses, and to transmute the experience of a world which we appear to share with other beings (though we can never be quite sure of that). In recent millennia, one of its sources of energy has been the biblical mythology and its believers. The irony of *His Dark Materials* is that, like *Paradise Lost*, it co-opts the Hebrew myth: within the rules of the story, the Authority is a real being, the angels did rebel against him, Eve was tempted, etc. Outside the story, the author has an agenda, as surely as Milton did, though in the contrary direction. But to those who value the imagination more than the certainties of believers (religious and atheistical alike), it is the stories that count.

Readers of *The Amber Spyglass* will recall the emphatic command to the dead: "Tell them stories!" and its context. Until Lyra's "harrowing of hell," the ghosts of all humanity have been trapped in the Authority's prison. Under the new covenant that Lyra makes with the Harpies who guard the Land of the Dead, the ghosts will henceforth tell their lives' stories, then, if they have told true, will return to the impersonal bosom of nature, their every atom rejoicing in its freedom. There are no posthumous rewards for good conduct, or punishments for evil; the story is literally the meaning of life. In our world, Philip Pullman may be something of a moralist, but in *His Dark Materials*, the ultimate value is aesthetic: the alchemical distillation of experience into art.

This article was first presented as a paper to the Association for the Study of Esotericism at Michigan State University, Lansing, in June, 2004.

Notes:

1. The title *Northern Lights* refers to the journey to the Arctic regions that occupies much of the book, and to the Aurora Borealis, which provide a spectacular backdrop to its climax. In the American edition, as in some foreign editions, the title was changed to *The Golden Compass*, to match those of the other two books of the trilogy; but this does not do justice to the theme and atmosphere that make *Northern Lights* one of the great Arctic novels.
2. Quoted from P. Pullman, "About the Writing." http://www.philip-pullman.com/about_the_writing.asp.
3. A common sobriquet for the university city of Oxford, Pullman's home.
4. Page references are to the one-volume edition of *His Dark Materials* (London: Scholastic Press, 2001).
5. Lyra's world somewhat resembles the theocratic Britain of Kingsley Amis's novel *The Alteration* (1976), in which it is supposed that Martin Luther became Pope. Pullman's little book *Lyra's Oxford* (London: Scholastic, 2004) fills in some further details

about Lyra's world and its ways of life.

6. In his conversation with Archbishop Rowan Williams, Pullman says that this creation myth is never fully explicit, but that he discovered it as he was writing it. "The Dark Materials debate: life, God, the universe...," chaired by Robert Butler, *Arts Telegraph*, March 17, 2004. http://www.telegraph.co.uk/arts/ain.jhtml?xml=/arts/2004/03/17/bodark17.xml.

7. This is not stated in *His Dark Materials*, but in the BBC's "Interview with Philip Pullman." http://www.bbc.co.uk/religion/programmes/beliefs/scripts/philip_pullman.html.

8. Pullman's theology and angelology are based, often quite faithfully, on apocryphal scriptures such as *I Enoch* and the collection of texts found at Nag Hammadi. See James C. VanderKam, *Enoch, a Man for All Generations* (Columbia: University of South Carolina Press, 1995); J. Edward Wright, *Baruch Ben Neriah, from Biblical Scribe to Apocalyptic Seer* (Columbia, University of South Carolina Press, 2003).

9. The Catholic writer Leonie Caldecott deplores that "Pullman is effectively removing, among a mass audience of a highly impressionable age, some of the building blocks for future evangelization." L. Caldecott, "The Stuff of Nightmares," *The Catholic Herald*, October 29, 1999. http://www.christendom-awake.org/pages/misc/reflections.htm.

10. "Heat and Dust," interview with Huw Spanner, *Third Way*, 2000. http://www.thirdway.org.uk/past/showpage/asp?page=3949. Pullman described this interview as "the best I've ever read."

11. Sarah Johnson puts it with brutal bluntness (and a total lack of appreciation of the novelist's art): "What if Pullman had replaced the Magisterium's crosses and churches with crescents and mosques? Not that he would have dared. Like any playground bully, Pullman knows which kids are least likely to kick him back." "A preachy rant against the Church," *The Catholic Herald*, January 16, 2004. http://www.christendom-awake.org/pages/misc/reflections.htm.

12. Rowan Williams, "A near-miraculous triumph," [review of the dramatization of *His Dark Materials*] *The Guardian*, March 10, 2004. http://www.guardian.co.uk/arts/features/story/0,11710,116 5873,00.html. See also "The Dark Materials debate."

13. BBC "Interview with Philip Pullman."

14. R. Williams, "A near-miraculous triumph."

15. "I am the servant of the story—the medium in a spiritualist

sense, if you like..." Pullman in "Heat and Dust."

16. *Corpus Hermeticum*, I, 24 (translated by Brian P. Copenhaver).

17. See J. Godwin, "The Survival of the Personality, According to Modern Esoteric Teachings," in R. Caron, J. Godwin, W. Hanegraaff, & R. VandenBroeck (eds.), *Mélanges Antoine Faivre* (Leeuven: Peeters, 2001), 403-414. Several of the esotericists mentioned there refuse to make a distinction between spirit and matter, or regard the whole of manifestation as to some degree material.

18. In the developing vocabulary of esoteric studies, "Hermetism" refers to the teachings of Hermes Trismegistus, while the broader term "Hermeticism" refers to later developments along Hermetic principles, especially alchemy.

19. "Philip Pullman Webchat," response to question by Graham King. http://www.bbc.co.uk/radio4/arts/hisdarkmaterials/pullman_webchat.shtml.

20. For example, in Henry Corbin's *Creative Imagination in the Sufism of Ibn 'Arabi* (Princeton: Princeton University Press, 1969), and more accessibly in his *Spiritual Body and Celestial Earth* (Ibid., 1977).

21. A. Faivre, *Access to Western Esotericism* (Albany: SUNY Press, 1994) is one of the many places in which Prof. Faivre defines esotericism through these 4+2 components.

22. Greg Krehbiel, "Philip Pullman's *His Dark Materials*," *Journeyman* I/1 (2001). http://www.crowhill.net/journeyman/Vol1No1/Darkmaterials.html.

23. "On the Origin of the World" II, 100, 103, in James M. Robinson, ed., *The Nag Hammadi Library in English* (San Francisco: Harper & Row, 1977), 163, 165.

24. Kurt Rudolph, *Gnosis: the Nature and History of an Ancient Religion*, tr. R. McL. Wilson (Edinburgh: T. & T. Clark, 1983), 62.

25. Rudolph, *op. cit.*, 79.

26. "Philip Pullman Webchat," reply to question by Russell: "Would you call yourself a Gnostic?"

27. This précis is based on the BBC's "Interview with Philip Pullman" and on "Heat and Dust."

28. Pullman made these remarks at the 2002 book festival in Hay-on-Wye; see *The Guardian*, June 4, 2002.

29. "Heat and Dust."

Dominion Press Is Proud to
Announce the Publication of

The Golden Thread: The Timeless Wisdom of the Western Mystery Traditions

by Joscelyn Godwin

Foreword by Richard Smoley

The Western Esoteric Tradition—which includes magic, Hermeticism, Gnosticism, alchemy, and theosophy—can be viewed as a continuous thread running beneath the surface of Western history. Those within the walls of traditional faith, and even more so those outside it, have all drawn upon its perennial wisdom throughout the ages.

The Golden Thread traces the interconnectedness of esoteric wisdom in the Western world, from classical antiquity to contemporary Europe and America. Every chapter makes reference to some aspect of contemporary life and issues of immediate concern. Educated readers who are curious about the esoteric and mystery traditions and interested in finding surprising new approaches that veer away from the trends of current thought will be particularly drawn to *The Golden Thread*.

NOW AVAILABLE AS A LIMITED CLOTHBOUND EDITION

A beautiful clothbound edition of this important book by a masterful modern scholar of esotericism is now exclusively available from Dominion Press. The edition is strictly limited to 200 copies, signed and numbered by the author and will never be available again in this form. Each book features sewn signatures, dark maroon cloth with gold stamping of a calligraphic design by Joscelyn Godwin, and a special translucent protective dust-wrapper.

5¾" x 9", 200 + xii pages. ISBN-13: 978-0-9712044-5-4

A trade paperback edition of *The Golden Thread* is published by Quest Books.

"Thoughtful and thought provoking, this is a delightful and erudite collection of gently subversive essays—a book to savor."
—Arthur Versluis, author of *Song of the Cosmos: An Introduction to Traditional Cosmology*

Price: $40.00 postpaid in the U.S.A., or $50.00 airmail postpaid to the rest of the world. Please send check or money order payable to:

Dominion
P.O. Box 129
Waterbury Center, VT
05677

Inquiries and Paypal payments may be directed to our email address:
dominion@pshift.com

Humour in the Icelandic Sagas

Ian Read

That the ancient Germanic peoples had a well-developed sense of humour is amply demonstrated in the sagas and in the *Eddas*. Humour has many uses, and in an often violent and brutal age, it could serve as a stick to beat an enemy, as well as stirring a man's spirit before the onset of fighting. Humour is a good indicator of a people's mood and character, although, as I will demonstrate, humour from another time and place may not always be easy for us to interpret.

A good example of how difficult it may be to interpret a society alien to one's own is illustrated by the following: an Englishman will instantly be aware of the class of any other Englishman he meets, even if only on a subliminal level. However, I have met Europeans who have been in England for a few years without ever being aware of how much this class-consciousness impinges on English society. Imagine, then, how fraught with difficulty it might be to understand a society that is hundreds of years old. We must attempt to empathize with the worldview of this society, an effort seldom made by many if not most contemporary academics. Fortunately, the humour recorded in the sagas and *Eddas* does not differ greatly from the humour one might hear expressed in the modern workplace, or during an evening at a local hostelry. Even the more rumbustious examples will be familiar to those of us who sat at the feet of our elders, who survived the Blitz by thumbing their noses at the German planes as they dropped their bomb-loads.

A modern example will serve to illustrate the difficulties encountered when trying to understand humour from a distance. The Jockey Club in Britain is the body responsible for regulating horse racing, and oversees the registration of racehorses. Since horse racing is considered the "sport of kings" by its followers, it amuses certain wits to give the horses names that the "toffs" would consider unsavoury, or downright rude. Recent examples have included Hoof-Hearted and Norfolk Enchants. The humour in the first case should be obvious. In the second instance, the joke becomes clear when one says the name "Norfolk Enchants" using an accent from the north of England, or a Scots-Irish brogue. Then the penny drops. The so-called upper class race followers would be expected to speak what used to be called the Queen's English, and might well miss the innuendo. This is precisely the point. The humour lies as much in making fools out of them, as it does in the name itself.

The Christian Church has long condemned laughter, mainly because Jesus is never shown laughing in the New Testament, but also because the Church Fathers saw laughter as somehow pagan. Nevertheless, the medieval world often ignored this stricture, so, for example, Wolfram von Eschenbach develops Parzival's naiveté to comic effect, and Walter von der Vogelweide created many humorous poems. The pagan view is illustrated by Aristotle, who said that "laughter is man's own" because it distinguishes men from the animals.[1] Fortunately, due to the nature of early Christianity in Iceland, the sagas were written by men with a more open-minded view than is often the case elsewhere in the Christendom of the period.

In ancient Iceland, humour could be used to attack a man's most important possession—his honour—to such great effect that the old Icelandic law book, *Grágás*, has a section "On Poetry" which opens with the following injunction: "No man is to versify either praise or blame about another."[2] Ostensibly innocent stanzas were known to conceal *níð* (contumely, often of a sexual nature) and the law was intended to prevent this.

Sagas can be an acquired taste, because their style is so distinct from most modern writing. Humour occurs in saga narrative, but it is mentioned only when it is essential to the story. *Bandamanna Saga* (Saga of the Confederates) is a family saga that uses comedy in the form of satire to critique the author's society, and particularly the chieftains who ruled over it. The sagas contain little descriptive prose, and many readers are taken aback by the cold and matter-of-fact way that the most gruesome and violent events are reported. The way humour is utilized and appreciated can tell us a great deal about the way people lived in the medieval period (when most of the sagas take place) or, at the least, they illustrate how people in the thirteenth century (when most of the sagas were composed) *thought* that their ancestors had lived.

In *Njal's Saga* there is a fight between Kol Egilsson and Kolskegg Hamundarson:

> Kolskegg whirled round and leapt at him, swung at his thigh with the short-sword, and cut off Kol's leg.

"Did that one land or not?" asked Kolskegg.

"That's my reward for not having my shield," said Kol. He stood for a moment on one leg, looking down at the stump.

"You don't need to look," said Kolskegg. "It's just as you think—the leg is off."[3]

To us it might seem strange that Kol does not seem shocked at having lost his leg, but merely expresses regret at being caught without his shield. Facing death with a smile and a joke was considered to show great *drengskapr* (courage). Another example from *Njal's Saga* illustrates this. Gunnar Hamundarson is attacked by a party of men when he is at home in the loft where he sleeps. One of the attackers, Thorgrim the Easterner, climbs up to the roof to find out if Gunnar is at home but Gunnar sees Thorgrim's red tunic and spears him in the stomach, causing Thorgrim to fall from the roof to the ground. He walks over to the others and Gizur the White looks up at him, asking: "Is Gunnar at home?" Thorgrim answers, "Find out for yourself, but this I know, his spear was at home."[4]

It is not at all unusual for the successful combatant to offer an amusing aside at the conclusion of battle. Sigurd Hlodvisson, Earl of Orkney, asks Flosi Thordarson, the leader of Njal's assassins, "What can you tell me about my retainer Helgi Njalsson?" To which Flosi replies, "Only this, that I cut off his head."[5] This amazing act of bravado nearly costs Flosi his life, but a relative is able to broker a settlement, and in the end Flosi becomes one of the Earl's retainers. It is quite possible that Flosi's flippancy might have demonstrated just the sort of courage a man as powerful as the Earl of Orkney would have sought in a member of his retinue. In this instance, things ended well. Nevertheless, Flosi's actions could just as easily have brought him to disaster.

Earlier in *Njal's Saga*, we see exactly what the women of Njal's time were made of. Glum Olafsson and Thjostolf, foster-father of Glum's wife, Hallgerd, who loves Glum dearly, are out on the hills when they fall to arguing over some escaped sheep. Glum hacks at Thjostolf with a short-sword, and Thjostolf defends with his axe. He succeeds in severing Glum's shoulder and collarbone in one sweep. Thjostolf takes a bracelet from Glum. When he returns, he tosses the bracelet to Hallgerd, who asks him why his axe is covered in blood.

"I don't know how you'll take this," replied Thjostolf. "Glum has been killed."

"Then you must have done it," said Hallgerd.

"Yes," he replied.

Hallgerd laughed. "There's nothing half-hearted about your way of doing things," she said.[6]

Hallgerd's laughter could mean many things, but it is most likely calculated to put Thjostolf at ease. When he asks Hallgerd's advice, she suggests that Thjostolf should go to her uncle Hrut—who promptly kills him. This is no doubt what Hallgerd expects. We are dealing with quite a different breed of woman here than the vapid type who has up until recently been portrayed in Western literature.

Derisive laughter calls for vengeance, and men might be prepared to forego laughter until certain stipulated or mutually accepted events have come to pass. One would not normally wish to laugh after friends have been killed, especially in medieval Iceland, where such actions demanded revenge:

Asgrim's men said, "That must be Thorgeir Skorar-Geir."

"I certainly do not think so," said Asgrim. "These men are laughing and joking, but Njal's kinsmen, men like Thorgeir, will never laugh until Njal has been avenged."[7]

Another source of humour is the nickname, a word whose very origins contain humorous elements. Just as "a norange" became "an orange," and "a nadder" became "an adder," so "an ekename" became "a nickname," due to the way it is spoken and heard. More than four thousand nicknames have been found in the corpus, and these are given more frequently to men than to women. Some names that must surely have been given in jest include:

Björn bunu (*Laxdaela Saga*): Bjorn Clumsyfoot
Ölvir barnakarl (*The Saga of Grettir*): Olvir the Babyman
Kolbjörn sneypr (*The Saga of Grettir*): Kolbjorn the Sneak
Björk inn digri (*The Saga of Gisli*): Bjork the Fat
Raza-Bersi (*The Saga of Kormak*): Buttocks Bersi
Eysteinn fretr (*The Saga of Hrafnkel*): Oystein Fart

It has even been suggested that the nickname *Geitar-*, meaning "goat," may have been given because someone "had an interesting adventure involving a goat."[8] The misadventures of lonely shepherds have of course been a cause of much mirth, even down to our own time. Intention had a bearing here too. For example, Njal is called *"skegglauss"* (beardless). This was simply a statement of fact, and was probably never intended as an insult. But as we see in the eponymous saga, the nickname is used maliciously. Njal has no choice but to take offence, and defends his honour with lethal consequences. We cannot always be certain whether or not a nickname was designed to give offence. In *The Saga of Grettir* we find a character called Geirmundr heljaskinn, "Hell-skin" or "Swarthy Skin," which may or may not have been an accurate description of his colouring. In this case one may well imagine that Geirmundr was dark skinned, but sometimes a man is referred to as "the White" or "the Black" because just the opposite is true.

Obviously, in an age when all men were armed, if only with a knife, laughing at a man or making fun of him could be dangerous. For this reason, *Grágás* stipulates that to award a nickname that gives offence is punishable by lesser outlawry. One suspects that this law was somewhat ineffectual, due to the difficulty in ascertaining exactly who coined a nickname in the first place.

In *Laxdaela Saga*, An the Black has a nightmare that makes him so restless that his comrades wake him up to find out what he has been dreaming:

> "A horrible woman came to me and dragged me to the edge of the bed," he replied. "She had a huge knife in one hand and a trough in the other. She plunged the knife into my breast and ripped my whole belly open, and pulled out all my entrails and stuffed brushwood in their place. Then she went away."
>
> Kjartan and the others laughed aloud at the dream and said he ought to be called An Brushwood-Belly [*hrísmagi*]. They caught hold of him and said they wanted to feel if there was any brushwood in his stomach.[9]

The joke is on An's comrades, however. Because they ignore his conviction that the dream is a premonition, Kjartan is attacked and killed. An Brushwood-Belly is stabbed and fights "for some time with his entrails coming out" before seeming to die.[10] Later, An sits up, having dreamt that the same horrible woman has returned, removed the brushwood, and replaced it with his intestines.

A good example of a misunderstanding leading to a darkly

humorous incident occurs in *The Saga of Grettir,* the tale of an ill-fated outlaw. Grettir volunteers to swim across a channel and fetch fire from a house on the other side:

> Grettir now made his way into the house, not knowing who was there. His cloak was all icy when he got ashore and he was absolutely huge to look at as if he were a troll. Those who were there were much taken aback at this and thought it must be a monster. They hit him with everything they could lay their hands on and there was now a great uproar among them, but Grettir beat them off with his arms.

Initially, the merchants Grettir has rescued are grateful, but later, when they discover the house reduced to a pile of ashes and human bones, they blame him for the deaths. Naturally, Grettir is not happy about this, having saved their lives (or at least made them much easier) by fetching the fire. He ascribes their ungratefulness to a lack of honour. This may well be a sideswipe at the merchant class, who, depending on how they conducted their business, were an obvious target for humour.

Men do not take well to having their manliness impugned, particularly when they are young. But in this following scene, reminiscent of how Nausikaa found Odysseus on the beach, Grettir acquits himself rather well when a serving-girl and the farmer's daughter discover him sleeping naked in the living room. The serving-girl speaks:

> "My goodness, sister, this is Grettir Asmundarson come here, and he looks really big about the ribs, lying there with nothing on. But it seems to me very strange how little he has developed between the legs, and it is not in keeping with his size elsewhere."
>
> The farmer's daughter answers, "Why do you chatter on so? And you are a more than average fool, and be quiet."
>
> "I cannot be quiet about this, dear sister," says the serving-girl, "because I wouldn't have believed if anyone had told me."
>
> She now went over to him and peered at him, and now and again ran up to the farmer's daughter and burst out laughing. Grettir heard what she was saying and when she ran back again across the floor he took hold of her and

uttered a verse:
"A caution is the scatterbrain's behaviour.
Arrow-wind desiring bushes [warriors]
Cannot usually see the sword in another one's hair properly.
This I bet, they do not have bigger balls than I
Even if the spear-storm trunks [warriors] have larger cocks."

Then he snatched her up onto the bench, and the farmer's daughter ran out. Then Grettir uttered a verse:
"Seam-prop spinster said I had got small in the sword.
The boastful balls-branch Hrist [serving-girl] is telling the truth.
My low maned-horse can grow quite long
In my young man's thigh forest,
Island-bone [jewel] Freyia [servant-girl]; wait a moment."

The maid shrieked at the top of her voice, but they parted with her no longer taunting Grettir by the time it was finished.[11]

It is worth noting here that the farmer's daughter is shown behaving in a more mature way than the serving-girl, which is not surprising given that the sagas were written for or even by the chieftain class. The reader is also reminded of a tradition in fairy tales where the sleeping hero is ridiculed.

The stylised battle of words called in Old Norse *senna* or *mannjafnaðr*, but which we most commonly refer to as flyting, often involves a humorous element, albeit a mostly insulting one. *Lokasenna* (The Flyting of Loki) from the *Poetic Edda* is a good and well-known example, but flyting also takes place in various other stories including *Njal's Saga, The Saga of the Confederates*, and *Beowulf*. The example I would like to consider is from Snorri Sturluson's *Heimskringla: History of the Kings of Norway, Saga of the Sons of Magnús* chapter 21, "The Kings Match Their Accomplishments."

In this story, King Eystein and King Sigurth are drinking ale in Eystein's hall. Eystein begins instigating, telling Sigurth "We two have the same title and equal possessions. There is no difference between our birth and upbringing." Sigurth replies with a series of comparisons, and each man then attempts to best the other by recounting various accomplishments. Needless to say, the competition grows ever more heated and insulting. Eystein claims that, when it comes to skating, Sigurth is "not better at that than a cow." A few turns later, Sigurth boasts of an expedition he has undertaken and says, "meanwhile you stayed at home as though you were the daughter of your father." This is equivalent to an Englishman standing at the bar in a public house and calling someone "a big girl's blouse." It is also likely to evoke a violent response. Eystein responds, "Now you come to the point. I would not have started this controversy if I did not have an answer to that. It seemed to me rather that I dowered you as though you were my sister before you were ready to go on that expedition." Eystein has the last word, which implies that he is the victor in the contest. Similar competitions lead inexorably to an outbreak of violence or war; luckily, Eystein and Sigurth never allow their subsequent enmity to escalate to this point.[12]

Senna, then, is a ritualised comparison between men, often leading to insults as each antagonist attempts to reduce the prestige of the other. Those who witnessed these exchanges must have found them amusing. One can imagine a king's retainers trying to maintain straight faces when their leader's opponent advanced a particularly scurrilous but funny point. After all, they would know whether or not the barb rang true (*senna* is related to *sanna*, "to prove, give evidence"). Loyalty is important, but a joke is a joke to a hardy warrior, well accustomed to the rough-and-tumble of the warband.

I shall end this paper with a section from the Eddic poem *Þrymskviða* (Lay of Thrym), which, although not from the saga corpus, does serve to illustrate an important point regarding the difficulty of interpreting the material: translations are only an approximation, and to fully understand a text it is often necessary to approach it in its original language.

The section begins when the giant Thrym steals Thor's hammer and demands the hand of the goddess Freya as the price for its return. Freya refuses this proposal and so Thor travels to Giantland dressed in the goddess's bridal wear.

> Then quoth Loki,   Laufey's offspring:
> "With thee I will,   to wait on thee;
> we twain shall wend   to the world of etins."[13]

In another translation, we find the final line rather less accurately rendered as, "We will journey together to Gianthome." However, the original reads: *"Vit skulum aka tvau í Jötunheima."* And as Prof. Richard Perkins pointed out to my Old Norse class at University College London, the first four cardinal numerals were declinable. *Tvau* here is the nominative neuter, and neuter was used when two different sexes were being discussed. In other words, Loki is saying that one of them is a woman. Because he has yet to change clothes and Thor has on a bridal veil, he is referring to Thor. Clearly this concept is not going to be easily conveyed in English and probably will not be apparent at all. Even modern German, which is inflected, does not have declinable numbers, and so would present the same problem.

This paper was first presented to the Seventh International Rune-Gild Moot in Austin, Texas, October 2004.

Notes:

1. Aristotle, *De Partibus Animalium*, William Ogle, trans., Book III, Ch. 10: "That man alone is affected by tickling is due firstly to the delicacy of his skin, and secondly to his being the only animal that laughs."(http://etext.library.adelaide.edu.au/a/aristotle/parts/book3.html)
2. Vilhjalmur Finsen, ed., *Grágás* (I–III), Copenhagen 1852–83.
3. Magnus Magnusson and Hermann Pálsson eds., *Njal's Saga* (London: Penguin, 1977), p. 149.
4. E. V. Gordon, *An Introduction to Old Norse* (Oxford: Clarendon Press, n.d.), pp. 88–89. Translated by Ian Read.
5. Magnusson and Pálsson, *Njal's Saga*, p. 340.
6. Ibid., pp. 69–71.
7. Ibid., p. 287.
8. Private communication with Prof. Richard Perkins.
9. Magnus Magnusson and Hermann Pálsson, eds., *Laxdaela Saga*, (London: Penguin, 1978), p. 171.
10. Ibid., p. 175.
11. Anthony Faulkes, trans., *Three Icelandic Sagas* (London: Everyman, 2001), p. 235.
12. Snorri Sturluson, *Heimskringla: History of the Kings of Norway*, Lee M. Hollander, trans. (Austin: University of Texas Press, 1991), pp. 702–03.
13. Lee M. Hollander, trans., *The Poetic Edda* (Austin: University of Texas Press, 1994), p. 107.

Rune Song or Magic Charms?
An Investigation of the Hávamál

Géza von Neményi

In German editions of the Old Icelandic *Poetic Edda*, the last two sections of the *Hávamál* are typically given the headings "Óðinns Runenlied" (Óðinn's Rune Poem) and "Die Zauberlieder" (The Magic Charms). The question thus arises whether the latter section is a set of stanzas that correspond to a runic Futhark, or a list of magical invocations that remain obscure to us. As I will demonstrate in this essay, there is much evidence that these so-called Magic Charms of the *Hávamál* do, in fact, refer to a traditional ordering of specific runes.

Let us first examine the context of the *Hávamál* as a whole. The very name of this Eddic poem makes it clear that it originates from the god Óðinn, since one of his names is Hárr ("the high one"). In the genitive case, this is "Hávi," and thus *Hávamál* means "The Mnemonic Song of the High One." This Eddic poem makes a disjointed impression on most academic researchers. The Swedish scholar Ivar Lindqvist, for example, concluded that a pious thirteenth-century Christian must have intentionally distorted the text, and even went so far as to call it a "devastated" poem.[1]

Karl Simrock has divided the *Hávamál* into the following sections:

Stanza
1–80 The Old Poem of Ethics
81–94 Fragments of Various Kinds
95–110 The First Example of Óðinn
104–110 The Second Example of Óðinn
111–137 The Lay of Loddfáfnir
138–145 Óðinn's Rune Poem
146–164 The Magic Charms

Of course, after many centuries of oral transmission, not all of the songs are preserved in the form first uttered by Óðinn. In spite of this, with a little good will one can discern an overall system. I only want to discuss this briefly, since this essay is first and foremost concerned with the stanzas comprising the Rune Poem and the

Magic Charms. The *Hávamál* forms an inner, secret, unified whole, and these stanzas function as its climax and conclusion.

Taken as a whole, the *Hávamál* deals with the initiation of an aspiring pupil (especially of the scholastic class) who acquires various teachings and ethical guidelines. Accordingly, stanzas 1–83 (or alternately, 1–94) encompass the rules of conduct for the first level of this pupil's initiation. Such an initiation was comparable to today's *Jugendweihe* [a secular German version of the confirmation], and would have been undergone by anyone who had come of age. These initial stanzas therefore comprise the universally valid basic precepts for the conduct of life: hospitality, table manners, friendship, wisdom, property relations, and proper conduct at folk assemblies (Things).

With stanzas 84 (or alternately, 95) to 102/3 there follows the First Example of Óðinn, called "Billings mær" (Billing's Maiden), in which Óðinn recounts his unsuccessful attempt to seduce Billing's daughter. Stanzas 103/104–10 encompasses the Second Example of Óðinn, "Suttungs mær" (Suttung's maiden). Here, Óðinn tells how he was able to seduce Gunnlöð. For the researcher, these are merely profane examples of misfortune and success in love. However, Gunnlöð is the guardian of the mead called Oðroerir, which has an important function in the mythos of runic initiation. The two examples therefore do not illustrate profane seduction, but recount Óðinn's attempts to gain both the mead of wisdom and initiation at the hands of the maiden. In the mythos, Billing's and Suttung's maidens are identical. Initiation often involved the loss of virginity; it was the time when the young person had his or her first amorous experiences. At first, Óðinn fails to complete the seduction/initiation, but with Gunnlöð he is successful. Incidentally, in the Eddic manuscripts, the Examples of Óðinn do not have their own headings. Stanza 111 marks the beginning of the "Loddfáfnismál," a heading that is found in the manuscripts of the *Edda*. "Loddfáfnir" means something like "buffoon," and describes the uninitiated simpleton. It contains precepts of a higher ethical quality, the knowledge of which is apparently a prerequisite for the second initiation, into the runic mysteries. And the text is unequivocally concerned with the *þulr*, the "Thule" or "cultic speaker." Stanza 111 begins with these words:

> It is time for the institution of the Thule on the Thule-chair,

At the well of Urth.

Unfortunately, in German translations of the *Edda*, the word *þulr* is mostly rendered as "speaker," thereby obscuring the meaning of the stanza. It concerns the "institution of the *þulr*," the education of a *þulr*-to-be. This is confirmed by stanza 134:

> Do not mock the gray-haired Thule:
> Often it is good what the old man speaks.
> Often beneficial wisdom comes out of a withered bag,
> That hangs among the skins,
> Hangs among the hides,
> And dangles with malicious men.

Thus it is stated here that the *þulr* is wise because he has ritually hanged himself as part of his initiation.

Stanza 137 concludes the "Loddfáfnismál," and now the Rune Poem begins. Here, too, we only find a separate heading in the somewhat younger written manuscripts of the *Edda*: "Rúnatalsþáttr Óðinns" (Óðinn's Rune Listing Section), or "Rúnaþáttr Óðinns" (Óðinn's Rune Section), and also "Rúnacapituli" (Rune Chapter). What now follows is the description of Óðinn's self-sacrifice and his runic initiation, the myth of his attainment of the runes. It is the second, higher initiation to become a *þulr* that the god undergoes here. What Óðinn experiences on the divine plane is imitated by men on earth, making this description an ideal model for all *þulr*-initiations. It should be stressed at this point that Óðinn is allowed to drink the mead Oðrœrir once his fast is over. According to the narrative in the *Younger* or *Prose Edda* (and in the First Example of Óðinn), Óðinn won this mead of wisdom and poetry from Gunnlöð, and brought it to the Æsir. Apparently, he was only able to drink it after undergoing the ordeal of runic initiation. In modern German editions of the *Edda*, we now find the heading "Lióðatal" (Listing of Magic Songs) or "Die Zaubersprüche" (The Magic Charms) above stanza 146. Hans Kuhn writes: "This last segment of the *Hávamál* recounts the content, application, and effect of eighteen magic spells, but unfortunately does not contain any of them verbatim."[2]

Here we must state clearly: such headings above stanza 146 are not found in the original Eddic manuscripts. The heading "Ljóðatal" first appears in the Karl Müllenhoff *Edda*, dating from

A PAGE OF THE CODEX REGIUS MANUSCRIPT,
WITH THE "HÁVAMÁL" 142–61 (RUNIC POEM).

1883–91. Since then, it has been adopted into other editions of the text. But since the stanzas 146–64 of the *Hávamál* do not have their own headings in the manuscripts, one may assume that the heading over stanza 138 still applies. And this heading definitely translates as "Óðinn's Rune Listing Section." Hence, runes are enumerated here, rather than any unknown magical spells. It is also especially obvious that these supposed magic stanzas always start with a count, making it easy to assign runes to them. The fact that runes are the subject of these passages is also explicitly proven by stanza 157, where it says: "thus I carve and the runes I color" (*sva ek ríst ok í rúnom fák*). A list of magical incantations that are never quoted would be senseless, and would only serve to emphasize the mighty power of Óðinn. In contrast to the desert demon Jehovah, the Germanic gods seldom make such ostentatious boasts simply to intimidate men.

It is thanks to the otherwise very unscientific work of Professor Friedrich Fischbach that runes were actually assigned to the final part (stanzas 146–64) of Óðinn's Rune Poem. In his book *Ursprung der Buchstaben Gutenbergs* (The Origin of Gutenberg's Letters), published in 1900, Fischbach assigned runes from the Younger Futhark to the first sixteen stanzas, and completed the picture with two runes from the Elder Futhark. Guido von List took up this association and disseminated this eighteen-rune row in his book *Das Geheimnis der Runen* (1908).[3] Fischbach's and List's specific interpretations were scientifically untenable, but they were nevertheless correct in their assumption that the Rune Poem is also an enumeration of runes.

If one assigns the runes of the Younger Futhark to the supposed magic stanzas without altering the sequence of either in any way, one will find astounding correspondences with the meanings known to us from the other extant rune poems. This is especially interesting, since the interpretations found in Óðinn's Rune Poem tend to have greater esoteric significance.

A few arbitrary examples will now follow. I am using the meanings that I have arrived at in my research, and that are in use in scientifically based heathen associations like the Germanische Glaubens-Gemeinschaft. They diverge from the interpretations of Edred Thorsson or Gerhard Heß, for example, even though both work with the Elder Futhark.

The rune ᚠ stands for "money, gold" according to the rune poems; its name **fehu* is interpreted as "livestock (i.e., property), movable goods = wealth." In the *Icelandic Rune Poem*, the disputes of relatives are mentioned in connection with *fé*, for these quarrels often revolve around money and property. At first, it might seem confusing how this rune relates to the first stanza (*Hávamál* 146):

'Help' one is called, for it may help

in disputes, and need, and with all worries.

The confusion quickly dissipates, however, when we remember that at Thing assemblies, disputes and feuds were often settled by the payment of money. The common folk argue about property, while Óðinn uses the rune—symbolic of property—to end such strife.

To give another example: the rune **hagalaz*, ᚼ or ᚷ respectively, means "hail" and therefore also "hailstorm," as well as figuratively "to destroy" (i.e., to ruin by hail). In the Rune Listing Section, Óðinn uses it to protect a hall from fire (*Hávamál* 152). The showers of hail extinguish the burning building. This correspondence is so unequivocal that one wonders why runologists still do not acknowledge the rune enumeration piece as such. Of course, the burning hall is also a reference to Valhöll (Valhalla) during the great cosmic battle, suggesting the presence of much deeper esoteric concepts. Nevertheless, the correspondence remains clear.

In the rune poems, the rune **tiwaz* ᛏ signifies the god Tyr or his symbol, the North Star (at that time not yet the Pole Star, but the star 32 Camelopardalis Hevelii). In the *Icelandic Rune Poem*, the name Mars has been added as an additional reference. Tyr is the god of war analogous to Mars and therefore he also embodies the energy that the astrologer knows as the "power of Mars" or "martial energy." This power signifies movement, activity, and vitality. By utilizing this power, Óðinn is able to resurrect the dead—the deceased regain movement and activity. As in our earlier example, the rune is used according to its traditional meaning, but its esoteric level of significance is addressed first and foremost. Admittedly, such lines of reasoning are a strain for researchers who possess no understanding of esotericism or astrology.

Let us examine one final example: the rune **mannaz*, ᛗ or ᛦ respectively, which signifies "man" and originally probably the god Mannus mentioned by Tacitus. He is the ancestor of the three classes of the Germanic peoples and therefore corresponds to the moon deity Heimdallr. Etymologically, the name Mannus is also related to Old Norse Máni (moon). In an old folk belief that has been especially well preserved in Latvia, the moon god (Ménuo, Ménulis, Menes) is the first scientist, for he has to count his children or descendents: the stars. The stars in turn are regarded as symbols of the departed (ON *einherjar*) or spirits (ON *dísir*) in the beyond, for the whole "folk of the Æsir." According to the tradi-

"Mars edur Tyr" (Mars or Tyr), illustration from an eighteenth—century Icelandic "Edda" manuscript.

tional sequence, the rune *mannaz* ᛘ or *maðr* ᛉ corresponds to stanza 159 of the *Hávamál*. In this stanza, Óðinn explains his ability to name all of the Æsir and elves, just as the Latvian moon god is able to name the stars.

According to both Fischbach and List, the rune *mannaz (maðr) corresponds to stanza 160 of the *Hávamál*, but this is an erroneous association. Until the middle of the ninth century, the final runes had the sequence *maðr, lögr, yr*. Only later did *maðr* and *lögr* change places, so that the visually similar runes *maðr* and *yr* were positioned next to each other. The fact that the *Hávamál* has the older rune sequence as its foundation also proves the age of this poem. A poem that exhibits the rune row of the ninth century cannot be dated to the tenth, or to the Christian thirteenth century.

Of course, the text itself is much older, and parallels with the parables of Cato, the fourth-century *disticha catonis*, further prove this. These should, however, be viewed as Christian modifications of originally pagan ethical precepts. Such collections of proverbs can also be found in the High Middle Ages, but these originate with the minnesingers, and not with the gods. One can surmise that before 650 C.E., at a time when the Younger Nordic Futhark was slowly emerging from the Elder Common Germanic Futhark in Scandinavia, this poem also featured stanzas for all twenty-four runes. However, these were gradually abandoned when the corresponding runes were no longer in use. Yet obviously single runes of the old rune row, and the corresponding stanzas of Óðinn's poem, were still known to those passing down the oral tradition—that is why they appended two stanzas for older runes to the sixteen rune stanzas of the Younger Nordic rune row.

Evidence exists that runes of the Elder Row were still occasionally used in inscriptions during the transitional period and the age of the Younger Futhark. One example is found on the Stentoften Stone, dating from the transitional period around 620 C.E., where the older rune **jeran* is used next to the *ar* rune in the line **hathuwolAfR gAf j**(ara) ("Haduwolf gave a good year"). In the Swedish inscription of Ingelstad, dating from the ninth century, the long out-of-use **dagaz* rune is found. The inscription reads: **:salsi: karþi sul I :d**(agR) **:skutli þina hiu** ("Salsi made the sun. Day. Carved these [symbols].") Older runes like **opala, *wunnjo*, or **gebo* also appear on the Rök Stone (ca. 820 C.E.).

Therefore, we must find the two runes from the additional eight that were present in the Elder Futhark that correspond to the remaining stanzas of Óðinn's Rune Song. Fischbach and List assigned the runes "*eh*" ᛡ and "*gibur*" ᚷ to these positions. The first is really the older form of the *ar* rune and not **ehwaz* ᛖ, and thus is already included in the row, while the last is an Anglo-Saxon scriptural variant of the rune *gebo X. Both runes are misplaced in terms of their meanings. The rune *oþala ᚸ fits much better with stanza 17 (*Hávamál* 162), because Óðinn prevents a woman from leaving him, and this rune also sometimes means "seclusion" or "(place of) security." To the eighteenth stanza (*Hávamál* 163) I assign the rune *ingwaz ◊ because here the subject is ostensibly fertility and sexuality—and thus the rune of the fertility god Yngvi-Freyr is appropriate. It should be noted that both of these assignments are based on my own interpretations, and are neither certain nor conclusive.

In conclusion, I hope that these expositions have helped to show that there is more to these stanzas of the *Hávamál* than some scholars believe, and it will now be possible to undertake a complete interpretation of the runes that takes into consideration all of the various Rune Poems.

(*Translated by Markus Wolff*)

The original German version of this essay first appeared in *Germanen=Glaube*, Nr. 4 (Autumn 2000).

Notes:

1. Ivar Lindqvist, *Die Urgestalt der Hávamál* (Lund: Gleerup, 1956).

2. *Die Götterlieder der Älteren Edda, Nach der Übersetzung von Karl Simrock neu bearbeitet und eingeleitet von Hans Kuhn* (Stuttgart: Reclam, 1991).

3. English edition: Guido von List, *The Secret of the Runes*, ed. and trans. Stephen E. Flowers (Rochester, Vermont: Destiny Books, 1988).

Die Wurzeln von Weihnacht und Ostern
Heidnische Feste und Bräuche

Unsere bekannten Feste wie Weihnachten, Fasnacht, Ostern usw. gehen auf die uralten Jahresfeste unserer heidnischen Vorfahren zurück und wurden durch das Christentum nur oberflächlich verändert und umgedeutet. In diesem Buche werden die Bräuche der Feste beschrieben und aus dem heidnischen Verständnis des Allsherjargoden Géza von Neményi heraus interpretiert. Wir erfahren, welche Inhalte, Mythen und Vorstellungen den acht großen heidnischen Jahresfesten zugrunde liegen und bekommen zahlreiche Anregungen, um diese Feste wieder in ihrem eigentlichen Sinne zu feiern. Das Buch erläutert die Feste unter Anfügung der alten Quellen und Überlieferungen, ist aber zugleich eine Anleitung für diejenigen, die diese Feiern auch selbst im traditionellen Sinne begehen möchten, um so in Einklang mit Natur, Göttern und Kosmos zu gelangen.

Neményi, Géza von
Die Wurzeln von Weihnacht und Ostern
Heidnische Feste und Bräuche
ca. 292 S., Paperback,
viele, teils farbige Abbildungen,
24,80 EUR
ISBN 9783894231323

Götter, Mythen, Jahresfeste - Heidnische Naturreligion

Die Glaubensvorstellungen unserer heidnischen Vorfahren werden in diesem Buche vorgestellt und für Menschen unserer Zeit entschlüsselt.
Es enthält eine Rekonstruktion des heidnischen Götterglaubens unter ausschließlicher Verwendung der alten Überlieferungen und bildet die Grundlage des traditionellen germanischen Heidentums, das sich eines stetig wachsenden Interesses erfreut. Außerdem eine Vorstellung der einzelnen Gottheiten, die Mythen von der Entstehung und dem Untergang der Welt, die nordischen Tierkreiszeichen mit ihren Götterzuordnungen, Geisterglaube mit Geisteranrufungen, Jenseitsvorstellungen, Priester und Hexen, die Jahresfeste und ihre Riten, Geburtstag, Einweihung, Hochzeit usw. In über 20 Jahren hat Allsherjargode Géza von Neményi aus den zahlreichen erhaltenen Bruchstücken ein Gesamtbild erarbeitet, das nun in vollkommen überarbeiteter Neuausgabe für alle am Alt-Heidentum interessierten vorliegt.

Neményi, Géza von
Götter, Mythen, Jahresfeste
Heidnische Naturreligion
ca. 288 S. Paperback
mit zahlreichen Abbildungen
23,90 EUR
ISBN 9783894231255

Demnächst als Neuerscheinung
Géza von Nemènyi
Kommentar zu den Götterliedern der Edda - Teil 1: Die Óðinslieder

Textausgabe nach der korrigierten Übersetzung von Karl Simrock mit ausführlicher Einleitung und Kommentierung zu den Liedstrophen aus heidnischer Sicht von Allsherjargode Géza von Neményi.
Inhalt: Völuspá, Grímnismál, Vafþrúðnismál, Hrafnagaldr Óðins, Vegtamsqviðu, Hávamál, Loddfafnismál, Rúnatalsþáttr Óðins

All books can be ordered online and paid conveniently with PayPal on our homepage at: http://www.kc-verlag.de
For countries outside of Europe add EUR 3,-/9,- (normal/airmail) for one of the above books and EUR 4,50/17,- for two of them.
KC-Verlag - Sigrid Kersken-Canbaz - Schloßstr. 3 - 29525 Holdenstedt - Germany
Phone +49 581 3891566 - Fax +49 581 3891567 - Mail mail@kc-verlag.de

Children of the Sonne: Wandervögel, *Reformers, Hippies, Greens,* Naturmenschen, *and Ferals*

Gordon Kennedy

As the rising sun burns over the south Pacific on another Australian morning, the light begins to illuminate the waves just enough to see some bodysurfers frolicking in the Byron Bay rollers. It's November and, as always, the water is warm in the subtropical springtime beach town. After thirty minutes the surfers emerge and walk back onto the sandy shore. They are all naked. The guys, longhaired and bearded, and the girls, with beads and no tan lines, greet their friends on the beach. This is a daily ritual for these kids, who are mostly from Australia, some from Europe, and a few from the U.S.A.

About twenty-five kilometers west, in the hills between Byron and the town of Nimbin, there are several thousand mostly young folks affectionately known as "Ferals." They live native-style in the bush—on hillsides, in canyons and in trees, inside primitive dwellings like small tipis and makeshift earth lodges. Although they borrow heavily from the indigenous cultures of the Australian aborigines, Native Americans, or Jamaican Rastafarians, most of these tribesmen are of European vintage. It almost seems to be programmed into their genes, like some biological impulse or inner calling that demands a replay of their Celtic and Germanic forebears on the modern stage of some primitive empty forest: white natives incarnate.

This is the latest chapter of a return-to-nature episode, or, as one American tourist proclaimed, "the last vestige of California's counterculture transplanted into the south Pacific." Indeed, rumor has it that a few West Coast 1960s veterans, like Owsley the LSD chemist and George Greenough the filmmaker, have taken up residence amongst the local populace.

Most locals will agree that Australia's "hippie" culture began after the 1973 Aquarius Festival in Nimbin, four years after America's Woodstock, and that California surfers were instrumental in introducing to Australia many of the elements that defined that era's lifestyles and attitudes. Surely many Californians did migrate to Australia at the end of the 1960s and early 1970s.

And today, more than anywhere else in the world, Byron is the place where the vegetarian restaurants, hostels, yoga studios, and surf shops fill the streets, and the shaggy set has taken up residence.

California, on the other hand, has become the most populous state in America, and anything that even echoes a flavor of Bohemia is usually displaced into towns like Arcata and Santa Cruz. The original 1960s hippies have now either merged into the dominant culture and become square—or graduated on to things like environmental activism, political and social concerns, yoga and fitness, natural healing, and so on.

But did this whole subculture really have its genesis in California, as most of us have been taught to believe by the media? Were "hippies" just a spontaneous phenomenon that began in the 1960s and had some cultural roots in the Beat era of the 1950s?

According to Webster's dictionary (2004) a "hippie" or "hippy" is: "a young person of the 1960s who rejected social mores, advocated spontaneity, free expression of love and the expansion of consciousness, often wore long hair and unconventional clothes, and used psychedelic drugs."

This mass-media definition of the 1960s dropouts has eclipsed all pre-1960s uses of the actual word, such as that mentioned by Malcolm X in his famous autobiography. As a seventeen-year-old hustler living in Harlem in 1939 Malcolm noticed, "A few of the white men around Harlem, younger ones whom we called 'hippies,' acted more Negro than Negroes. This particular one talked more 'hip' than we did. He would have fought anyone who suggested he felt any race difference."[1]

So clearly the actual word "hippie" was a form of Ebonics (black slang) from Harlem that made its way from the 1930s, through the Beat era of the fifties, then into the sixties ... until Herb Caen of the *San Francisco Chronicle* had used it enough times by late 1965 to describe the young arrivals in his city, that the national media soon swallowed it whole and patented it.

But apart from the slick, zoot-suit-clad "white Negroes" of 1930s Harlem there actually were longhaired, bearded individuals during the early part of the twentieth century who wore sandals or bare feet and often favored mild sub-tropical places like southern California where they could forage their meals from the fruit trees that were so plentiful then.

"Nature Boys," as they were later called, were without exception either German immigrants or American youths whose lives

SEVEN OF CALIFORNIA'S "NATURE BOYS" IN TOPANGA CANYON, AUGUST OF 1948. THEY WERE THE FIRST GENERATION OF AMERICANS TO ADOPT THE "NATURMENSCH" PHILOSOPHY AND IMAGE, LIVING IN THE MOUNTAINS AND SLEEPING IN CAVES AND TREES, SOMETIMES AS MANY AS FIFTEEN AT A TIME. BY 1968, GYPSY BOOTS HAD PASSED THE TORCH TO A NEW GENERATION OF FLOWER CHILDREN AND HIPPIES, AND WAS A PAID PERFORMER AT POP FESTIVALS LIKE MONTEREY AND NEWPORT, ALONG WITH ACTS LIKE JIMI HENDRIX, THE GRATEFUL DEAD, AND THE JEFFERSON AIRPLANE. (BACK ROW: GYPSY BOOTS, BOB WALLACE, EMILE ZIMMERMAN. FRONT ROW: FRED BUSHNOFF, EDEN AHBEZ, BUDDY ROSE, AND UNKNOWN.)
(PHOTO COURTESY OF GYPSY BOOTS)

"BACK TO THE EARTH." POSTCARD BY GUSTO GRÄSER, 1900.
NOTE AIR POLLUTION AND SMOKESTACKS IN THE BACKGROUND.

were influenced by transplanted Germans who had spread their *Lebensreform* (life-reform) message to anyone ready for a radical departure from the accepted boundaries of twentieth-century civilization.

Modern primitives, *Naturmenschen*, *Wandervögel*, bohemians, reformers, wayfarers, and vagabonds are all descriptive expressions that evoke a tone of something wholly apart from the orthodox.

So why Germany? Even if the later counterculture became thoroughly "Americanized," and characterized by excesses of drugs and sex, it had begun with the longhaired, bearded *Naturmenschen* as something innocent and organic, Germanic and romantic.

Germany had always made a virtue of its late submission to Latin civilization and had glorified the natural man and woman with all of their virtues and vices. In about the year 51 B.C.E. Julius Caesar noted of the Germans: "The only beings they recognize as gods are things that they can see, and by which they are obviously benefited, such as sun, moon and fire; the other gods they have never even heard of."[2] It is worth noting that the word "god" was originally neuter in gender in the Germanic languages, and was only made masculine after the arrival of Christianity.[3] The Romans were quite surprised at how much political and spiritual prominence the Germanic tribes gave to women. Tacitus (circa 98 C.E.) wrote:

> According to the German outlook, pronouncements of destiny seem to acquire a greater sacredness in the mouth of women. Prophecy and magic in a good as well as an evil sense is by choice the gift of women. If it is inherent in the nature of men to show the female sex a great consideration and respect, then this was particularly shaped on the German people from of old. Men earn deification through their deeds, women through their wisdom.[4]

Thus the religiosity of the Indo-Germanic peoples shares considerably more feminine input than most other creeds. Whenever their nature can unfold itself freely, their faith emerges in that form which religious scholarship has described as "nature religion" or "earth religion." To remove the German soul from the natural landscape is to kill it. The Romans knew this, and once Christianity had become the state religion of the Roman Empire, Christian missionaries were then eager to chop down the Germanic forests and set their temples on fire.

Whenever the church encountered pagan elements that it could not suppress it gave them a Christian dimension and assimilated them. These ancestral traditions were reinterpreted and revised, but the Church never succeeded in effacing the Germanic pagan heritage. Hermann the Cherusker's victory in the year 9 C.E. had forestalled Roman colonization, and Germania had thereby retained its ancient languages and avoided early Christianization.

More than a millennium later, another significant influence would be Meister Eckhart (1260–1328), who represented most strongly the development of mysticism as a result of the revolt of the Teutonic Indo-European spirit against Roman Christianity.

During the Middle Ages, a group called "Brothers and Sisters of the Free Spirit" existed in Germany and Holland. Also known as the Adamites, they were spiritual descendants of an earlier group, the Adamiani. They held nude gatherings in womb-like caverns to achieve rebirth into a state of paradisiacal innocence.

In 1796 Christoph Wilhelm Hufeland of Weimar published his landmark study of aging, *Die Kunst das menschliche Leben zu verlängern* (The Art of Prolonging Human Life). He used the term "macrobiotic" in the preface of the book, and the second edition

A YOUNG FIDUS (RIGHT) WITH HIS TEACHER KARL WILHELM DIEFENBACH AT HOLLRIEGELSKREUTH, GERMANY IN 1887.

incorporated the word into its title. His emphasis on exercise and fresh air, sunbathing, cleanliness, regular scheduling, temperate diet, stimulating travel, and meditation, was far ahead of its time.

Goethe's (1749–1832) perspective erased the boundary between man and nature altogether. The poet of nature religiosity believed that "God can be worshiped in no more beautiful way than by the spontaneous welling up from one's breast of mutual converse with nature."⁵

Another quote from Goethe from 1832 shows his prophetic nature:

> Man in his misguidance has powerfully interfered with nature. He has devastated the forests, and thereby even changed the atmospheric conditions and the climate. Some species of plants and animals have become entirely extinct through man, although they were essential in the economy of nature. Everywhere the purity of the air is affected by smoke and the like, and the rivers are defiled. These and other things are serious encroachments upon nature, which men nowadays entirely overlook but which are of the greatest importance, and at once show their evil effect not only upon plants but upon animals as well, the latter not having the endurance and power of resistance of man.[6]

In 1866 Ernst Haeckel of the University of Jena first employed the term "ecology," thereby establishing it as a permanent scientific discipline for all future generations. Ecology as a concept had more in common with Buddhism, and its recognition of the oneness of all life, than it did with Christianity.

It was also in the 1860s that an ex-Protestant minister named Eduard Baltzer published his four-volume book on *Die naturliche Lebensweise* or "natural lifestyle." He organized some vegetarians and founded a Free Religious Community, then later published a book on Pythagoras as the ancestor of his movement.

Baltzer's writings had a strong influence upon a young painter named Karl Wilhelm Diefenbach (1851–1913) who also went on to form several communities and workshops for religion, art, and science. Diefenbach spent the last portion of his life on the Mediterranean isle of Capri, which was a retreat for other life-reformers. Two of his pupils, Fidus (Hugo Höppener) and Gusto Gräser, were to make a tremendous impact with their art and reform messages.

Fidus (1868–1949) could be recognized as perhaps the greatest psychedelic artist ever, predating the multi-colored posters and album covers of the 1960s by over half a century. Gusto Gräser later went on to become a close friend and teacher of the writer

FIDUS, 1887. BORN IN LÜBECK, GERMANY IN 1868, HIS PROTO-PSYCHEDELIC ART WAS A PERSONAL FAVORITE OF HERMANN HESSE.

Hermann Hesse. Hesse's report written in 1908, "Among the Rocks—Notes of a Nature Man," described how he, along with Gräser, lived the lives of natural men and hermits, sleeping in caves in the Swiss Alps and fasting for days and weeks.[7] The guru–disciple relationship that appears in Hesse's 1922 novel *Siddhartha* was a mirror of his own association with Gräser, his teacher. Gräser's poetry appeared in some of the magazines of the emerging *Wandervögel* movement.

In 1870 the population of Germany was two-thirds rural, but by 1900 it had become two-thirds urban. Near the end of the nineteenth century, the German middle class had become superficial, coarse, complacent, gluttonous, materialistic, industrialized, technocratic, and pathetic. As a response to this phenomenon, many natural healing modalities came into existence, and many youth movements and fitness groups were organized.

The modern bodybuilding craze, too, has very strong roots in late nineteenth-century Germany, with Eugen Sandow reigning as the most important and recognizable strongman since Hercules.

In 1883 Louis Kuhne of Leipzig, Germany published a book titled *Die neue Heilwissenschaft* (The New Science of Healing) and this work laid the foundation for what was later to become known as Naturopathy. Translated into fifty languages, it was the inspiration for a whole generation of health practitioners and was also highly praised by Mahatma Gandhi in India.

In 1896 Adolf Just opened his Jungborn retreat in the Harz Mountains near Isenburg, Germany. This was a model institution for the true natural life, and was meant to show how the most intimate communion with nature could be re-established. In his best-selling 1896 book *Kehrt zur Natur zurück!* (Return To Nature), Mr. Just spoke out against air and water pollution, meat, vivisection, vaccination, coffee, alcohol, smoking, and so-called education in schools. Gandhi was so moved by Adolf Just's rebellion against scientific medical treatments that it helped him to formulate his ideology for the future. When he was released from prison in 1944, he opened a Nature Cure sanitarium in India based on Just's model.

In 1904 German author Richard Ungewitter wrote a book titled *Die Nacktheit* (Nakedness), wherein he advocated nudism and abstention from meat, tobacco, and alcohol. He had to publish it himself but it quickly became a bestseller. The vegetarian aspect focused on the purity of the body and soul, with adherence to a regular program of fitness.

The German attitude towards nudity has not changed too much in one hundred years because even now on a warm summer day people along lakes and rivers can be found enjoying themselves in the sunshine without clothing.

In the 1890s, hiking societies proliferated in Germany. One group, *Die Naturfreunde* or "Friends of Nature," advocated social hiking and adopted the slogan "free mountains, free world, free people." Another group called the *Wandervögel* was founded in 1895 by Hermann Hoffman and Karl Fischer in Steglitz, a suburb of Berlin. They began to take some high school students on nature walks, then later on longer hikes. Soon a huge youth movement arose, composed of mostly middle-class German children organized into autonomous bands, that was both anti-bourgeois and Teutonic pagan in character.

Wandervögel members were typically between fourteen and eighteen years old. They spread to all parts of Germany and eventually numbered fifty thousand. Part-hobo and part-medieval, they pooled their money, wore woolen capes, shorts, and Tyrolean hats, and took long hikes in the country where they sang their own versions of Goliardic songs and camped under primitive conditions. Both sexes swam nude together in the lakes and rivers. In their hometowns they established "nests" and "anti-homes," sometimes in ruined castles, where they met to plan trips and play mandolins and guitars.

Their short weekend trips became three- to four-week-long

"WANDERVÖGEL," 1926. STARTING IN 1895, AS MANY AS FIFTY THOUSAND GERMAN YOUTHS WERE HIKING IN GROUPS ALL OVER THE FORESTS AND MOUNTAINS, SOMETIMES FOR AS LONG AS SIX MONTHS AT A TIME. THE AMERICAN BOY SCOUTS AND GIRL SCOUTS WERE ALSO MODELED AFTER THE "WANDERVÖGEL."

journeys over hundreds of miles. Soon they were establishing permanent camps in the wild that were open to all. With no thought of pay, the bands worked at improving their campsites and building cabins for which they built the furniture, ultimately inspiring the youth hostel movement which began in 1907 when Richard Schirmann opened the first hostel in Altena, Germany.

Mostly the *Wandervögel* sought communion with nature, with the ancient folk spirit as embodied in traditional peasant culture, and with one another. They developed a harmonious mystic resonance with their environment. The spirit of *Wandervögel* music would again be embodied more than three-quarters of a century later in the folk songs of American singer John Denver, who frequently sang about nature and the environment.

The expression *Lebensreform* (life-reform) was first used in 1896, and comprised various German social trends of the nineteenth and the first half of the twentieth century. These included in particular:

—Vegetarianism
—Nudism
—Natural medicine
—Abstinence from alcohol
—Clothing reform

—Settlement movements
—Garden towns
—Soil reform
—Sexual reform
—Health food and economic reform
—Social reform
—Liberation for women, children, and animals
—Communitarianism
—Cultural and religious reform, that is, a religion or view of the world that gives weight to the feminine, maternal, and natural aspects of existence.

Further south in Switzerland, Ascona was a little fishing village on the shore of Lake Maggiore, which lies on the border with Italy. In the year 1900 a countercultural renaissance began and lasted until about 1920. Ascona became the focal point for many of Europe's spiritual rebels.

Life experiments were in vogue: Surrealism, modern dance, Dada, paganism, feminism, pacifism, psychoanalysis, and Nature Cure. A few of the participants were Hermann Hesse, Carl Jung, Isadora Duncan, D. H. Lawrence, Arnold Ehret, and Franz Kafka.

At the turn of the century Germany had a population of fifty-six million, and as many large cities as all of the rest of Europe combined. Industrialism, technology, pollution, and "affluenza" began a crisis amongst the over-privileged German-speaking people of that period. The disenchanted began to arrive in Ascona by the hundreds. The beautiful natural setting inspired urban people to sunbathe in the nude, sleep outdoors, hike, swim, and fast. This village quickly developed a universal reputation as a health center.

Hermann Hesse was excited when he saw four longhaired men with sandals walk through his village on their way to Ascona. He followed them, settled in, and then took a Nature Cure for his alcoholism. The year was 1907. The idea of the Nature Cure was powerful in the German mind, and was a widespread and profound rebellion against science and professionalism. Most of the *völkisch* neo-pagans tended to be apolitical and anarchistic, and did not fuse their spirituality with racial or political agendas.

On 20 August 1903, an anarchist newspaper in San Francisco, California published a large article about Ascona, describing the people and their philosophies. This was certainly one of the first times that detailed news of the European counterculture had

BEGINNING IN THE 1950S WITH THE BEAT GENERATION, HERMANN HESSE'S NOVELS BECAME IMMENSELY POPULAR IN THE ENGLISH-SPEAKING WORLD, WHERE THEIR CRITICISM OF BOURGEOIS VALUES AND INTEREST IN EASTERN SPIRITUALITY AND JUNGIAN PSYCHOLOGY ECHOED THE EMERGING REVOLT AGAINST THE UNREFLECTED LIFE. LEGITIMATE HISTORY WILL ALWAYS REMEMBER HESSE AS THE MOST IMPORTANT LINK BETWEEN THE EUROPEAN COUNTERCULTURE OF HIS YOUTH, AND THEIR LATTER-DAY DESCENDANTS IN AMERICA.

reached the California coast.

As the twentieth century dawned, many Germans began to feel the weight of oppressive political forces that would later lead their nation into two world wars and change the coarse of European history. Between 1895 and 1914, tens of thousands of Germans emigrated from their homes and families and settled in America. After all, America was the country of the future, and they saw themselves as pioneers helping to lead a new society by transplanting and nurturing the most valuable ideas from their homeland into their new dreams for the United States.

There were several key individuals who made a substantial contribution, but probably none more so than Dr. Benedict Lust. Born in Michelbach near Baden, Germany on 3 February 1872, Lust first came to America in 1892, became ill with tuberculosis, then returned to Germany and took a Nature Cure treatment from the renowned Father Sebastian Kneipp. He regained his health and found his true purpose in life, and then returned to America in 1896 to become a Kneipp representative in America.

Rightfully called the "Father Of Naturopathy" in America, Lust introduced all of the great naturist movements that were in vogue in Europe: hydrotherapy, herbal remedies, air and light baths, and various plant-based diets. He also translated and distributed the classic German health writings of Father Kneipp, Louis Kuhne, Adolf Just, Arnold Ehret, and August Englehardt. Near the turn of the century in New York City, he founded a school of

PROFESSOR ARNOLD EHRET, CIRCA 1905. BORN IN FREIBURG, GERMANY IN 1866, ARNOLD MIGRATED TO SOUTHERN CALIFORNIA IN 1914 AND HELPED TO SPAWN A NEW SUB-CULTURE IN AMERICA, BASED UPON HIS NATURAL PHILOSOPHY AND LIFESTYLE. HIS BOOKS HAVE NEVER GONE OUT OF PRINT SINCE THEIR ORIGINAL PUBLICATION SEVENTY-FIVE YEARS AGO.

massage and the Naturopathic Society, and in 1918 he published the *Universal Naturopathic Encyclopedia* for drugless therapy. *Nature's Path* magazine and a radio show devoted to natural healing were also some of his notable achievements.

Dr. Lust's school of Naturopathy was the starting point for hundreds of America's natural health practitioners, while his magazines introduced the English-speaking world not only to the German Nature Cure, but also ancient East Indian concepts like Ayurveda and Yoga. Paramahansa Yogananda was one of several Indians who wrote articles for *Nature's Path* magazine in the 1920s, gaining wide exposure to a large American audience.

Dr. Lust was "busted" repeatedly by American authorities and medical associations for promoting natural methods of healing, massage, and nude sunbathing at his Jungborn sanitarium. He was arrested sixteen times by New York authorities and three times by Federal agents. One news headline simply read: "They Have Lust Again."

As many as 30 to 40 percent of the graduates of Dr. Lust's school were women, and his magazines were full of enthusiastic letters and praise from practicing Naturopaths in India, Jamaica, and all over Latin America. No one was more devoted to introducing the Nature Cure to the Spanish-speaking world than Dr. Lust.

LEFT: BILL PESTER, 1917, AT HOME IN THE NATURAL OASIS OF PALM CANYON, SAN JACINTO MOUNTAINS OF SOUTHERN CALIFORNIA. WITH HIS "LEBENSREFORM" PHILOSOPHY AND RAW FOODS DIET, HE INTRODUCED A NEW HUMAN TYPE TO CALIFORNIA. (PHOTO COURTESY OF PALM SPRINGS DESERT MUSEUM) RIGHT: BILL PESTER IN 1917 WITH HIS WEISSENBORN SLIDE GUITAR. BILL WAS ONE OF MANY GERMAN IMMIGRANTS WHO IMPORTED THE HIPPIE LIFESTYLE TO CALIFORNIA. HE WAS FLUENT IN ENGLISH, SPANISH, HIS NATIVE GERMAN, AND WAS NEVER SHY ABOUT HAVING HIS PICTURE TAKEN. (PHOTO COURTESY OF PALMS SPRINGS HISTORICAL SOCIETY)

Another influential Nature Doctor, Dr. Carl Schultz, arrived in Los Angeles, California in 1885 and became the Benedict Lust of the West Coast. In 1905 he created the Naturopathic Institute and Sanitarium and also opened the Naturopathic College on Hope Street. Most of the practicing Nature Doctors in the western U.S.A. were graduates of this college.

In 1906 Bill Pester first set foot on American soil, having left Saxony, Germany that same year at age nineteen to avoid military service. With his long hair, beard, and *Lebensreform* background he wasted no time in heading to California to begin his new life. He settled in majestic Palm Canyon near Palm Springs, California and built himself a palm hut by a flowing stream and palm grove.

Bill spent his time exploring the desert canyons, caves, and waterfalls, but was also an avid reader and writer. He earned some of his living making walking sticks from palm blossom stalks, selling postcards with *Lebensreform* health tips, and charging people ten cents to look through his telescope while he gave lectures on astronomy. He made his own sandals, had a wonderful collection of Indian pottery and artifacts, played slide guitar, lived on raw fruits and vegetables, and managed to spend most of his time naked under the California sunshine.

During the time when Bill lived near Palm Springs he was on Cahuilla Indian land, with permission from the local tribe who had great admiration for him. His name even appeared on the 1920 census with the Indians, and in 1995 an American Indian woman, Millie Fischer, published a small booklet about Palm Canyon that included a chapter on Pester.

The many photos of Pester clearly reveal the strong link between the nineteenth-century German reformers and the flower children of the 1960s: long hair and beards, bare feet or sandals, guitars, love of nature, draft dodging, simple living, and an aversion to rigid political structure. Undoubtedly Bill Pester introduced a new human type to California and was a mentor for many of the American Nature Boys.

In 1914 another German immigrant, Professor Arnold Ehret, arrived in California. The philosophy he preached had a powerful influence on various aspects of American culture. Ehret advocated fasting, raw foods, nude sunbathing, and letting your hair and beard grow untrimmed. His *Rational Fasting* (1914) and *Mucusless Diet Healing System* (1922) were popular handbooks in hippie circles of the 1960s.

Maximilian Sikinger was born in Augsberg, Germany in 1913 and spent most of his childhood and youth living wild in the environs of various European cities. Through his wanderings, personal contacts, and outdoor living he developed a keen interest in various aspects of natural healing: nutrition, water cure, fasting, sitz baths, deep breathing, and sunshine.

Max left Europe in 1935 at age twenty-two, arrived in America, and then eventually made his way west to California where he traveled with the Nature Boys who valued his introspective and philosophical ideas very highly. Maximilian's world travels and rugged background had given him deep insight into many of life's puzzles. His influence in California was substantial and he not only inspired people in matters of natural healing, but he was part of a dance troupe that frequented the very early performances of an unsigned band called "The Doors" on Sunset Strip in 1966.

Thus it was through the influence of these and many other German immigrants that seeds were planted in the minds of many American kids, and people's lives began to shift toward a more European view of health and fitness.

In 1948 singer Nat King Cole recorded his massive hit song "Nature Boy," which was written by Brooklyn-born eden ahbez, a forty-year-old Jewish wanderer whose life had been transformed after meeting Bill Pester and Maximilian Sikinger. One of his close friends, Gypsy Boots from San Francisco, was also changed radically after meeting Max and some of the other Nature Boys. Boots, who was also Jewish, met Max on the beach at Kelly's Cove in the mid-1930s, and the two remained close friends for life, both passing on within three months of one another in 2004.

When Beat poet Jack Kerouac was traveling through Los Angeles in the summer of 1947 he saw "an occasional Nature Boy saint in beard and sandals," as noted in his 1955 bestseller *On The Road*.[8] Undoubtedly these were some of the young Americans who lived the radical lifestyle inspired by their association with people like Pester and Sikinger. During the 1950s many of the Beats read books by Hermann Hesse, who would posthumously become the novelist of the decade during the sixties. Most of the Beats, however, had little interest in Nature, health, or fitness, though some were quite enthralled with Nietzsche and Goethe.

The most popular musical group of all time, the Beatles, received their first big break playing in clubs in Hamburg in 1960. The four English lads from Liverpool with slicked-back 1950s-style hair radically changed their image and hairstyles after meeting Klaus Voorman and several of the other German art students who wore shaggy long hair with bangs. The Beatles' lead guitarist George Harrison said that German photographer Astrid Kirchherr "invented" the Beatles with her camera, giving them tips on dress and posing, and capturing their images in some priceless early photo shoots. As a deep, heartfelt thanks to their faithful German fans, the Beatles later recorded "Komm gib Mir Deine Hand" (I Want To Hold Your Hand) and "Sie Liebt Dich" (She Loves You), singing in German. Klaus Voorman later designed the cover and drew the artwork for the Beatles' landmark 1966 album *Revolver*. The Beatles' German period can be viewed in the video *Backbeat* (1994).[9]

Nobody knew what the sixties would bring. The decade started off innocently enough, but after President Kennedy was assassi-

EDEN AHBEZ WITH HIS WIFE ANNA JACOBSON AND THEIR BABY ZOMA IN 1948. TWENTY YEARS LATER THEIR LIFESTYLE AND BOHEMIAN APPEARANCE HAD BECOME MAINSTREAM, CO-OPTED BY MILLIONS OF BABY BOOMERS THE WORLD OVER. IN 1948 EDEN'S SONG "NATURE BOY," RECORDED BY NAT KING COLE, REACHED NUMBER ONE ON THE HIT PARADE AND STAYED THERE FOR FIFTEEN WEEKS. (PHOTO COURTESY OF PALM SPRINGS HISTORICAL SOCIETY)

nated in November of 1963, it left a massive void in the hearts and minds of folks all over America, particularly the young. The Beatles seemed to fill this emptiness in February of 1964 when they appeared on the *Ed Sullivan Show* to the largest viewing audience in television history.

Other changes worked their way into the youth culture. Scientific psychedelic research being conducted on both coasts later found its way onto the streets and into the hands of underground chemists and college students. There were probably more social and cultural changes during the last five years of the sixties, 1965–69, than during any other period in twentieth-century America. Anti-war movements, environmental concerns, equality for minorities, women's rights, voting age issues, birth control, organic foods, natural healing, global traveling, new types of music and artistic expression, and so on, all came to the fore.

BORN IN 1879, GUSTO GRÄSER WAS A CLOSE FRIEND AND TEACHER OF THE WRITER HERMANN HESSE. DURING THE SUMMER OF 1907 THEY LIVED THE LIVES OF NATURAL MEN AND HERMITS, SLEEPING IN CAVES IN THE SWISS ALPS, FASTING, AND STUDYING OLD SCRIPTURES. HESSE'S NOVEL "SIDDHARTHA" (1922) WAS A MIRROR OF HIS OWN ASSOCIATION WITH GRÄSER. GRÄSER ALSO WROTE POETRY THAT APPEARED IN SOME OF THE "WANDERVÖGEL" MAGAZINES. ABOVE: GUSTO AND ELISABETH WITH THEIR BABY IN 1910.

Not surprisingly, young people in America began to pay attention to concerns and values that had already been mapped out and experienced in Germany for over a half a century. Hermann Hesse's novel *Siddhartha*, written in 1922, was carried in the backpacks of a whole generation of baby boomers. Health foods and Naturopathy, once relegated to the quack fringe, became immensely popular and even entered the mainstream. Yoga and vegetarianism, promoted and lived by faithful subscribers to health magazines like *Herald of Health* and *Nature's Path*, which were founded by Germans, have now made the cover of *Time* magazine.

The 1950s American military crew cut was finally replaced by the longhaired and bearded "hippie" style, formerly worn by German-speaking *Naturmenschen* since the time of Tacitus. Weight lifting and bodybuilding, now practiced in gymnasiums all across America, had struggled to gain acceptance for decades. California governor and former Mr. Universe, Austrian-born Arnold Schwarzenegger, devoted several pages of his book *Pumping Iron* to

GUSTO AND ELIZABETH GRÄSER WITH
THEIR TRAVELLING WAGON, 1911.

the German fitness god Eugen Sandow.

The Green political Party began in Germany in the late 1970s as an outgrowth of the 1950s anti-nuclear movement in Europe, later spreading to other parts of the world including America.

Chiropractic, first introduced by Benedict Lust in 1900, is now practiced by college-trained physicians in every city in America. Dr. Lust also started the first massage schools in New York City, circa 1900.

Health food stores, now in nearly every city in America, had their European antecedents with the German *Reform Haus* stores or "Bio-Shops" still found everywhere in modern Germany.

Herbal medicine, though once a universal practice, was heavily promoted by Dr. Lust throughout his long career as a publisher, and has now gained mainstream acceptance in the States.

Nudity, a regular habit of the sun-loving Germans on any summer day, was popular in America in the 1960s and 1970s ... but has since reverted to a more secluded practice. Hosteling, also a German invention, was common in the 1960s when young Americans traveled with backpacks to Europe, Latin America, and India. More recently, however, Americans have become some of the least well-traveled people on earth, particularly when it comes to the budget type of traveling with backpacks.

For most of the young people who had an awakening during the massive cultural changes that had taken place, the spiritual focus was generally upon something Eastern or native. Book publishers catered to the flocks of spiritual seekers and more than a few dozen books relative to Native American, Buddhist, or Hindu philosophy reached the bestseller lists. But by the 1980s the focus began to shift to European roots. American-born citizens who were three to seven generations removed geographically from their Celtic and Germanic forebears began to hunger for their ancestral paths. After all, Christianity was really a foreign religion imposed upon the northern Europeans as a measure of control and subjugation. And the Eastern and native religions were traditions that the media decided were "innocent" enough to pass along to a disillusioned generation of recovering substance abusers and spiritual junkies. But somehow the Celtic traditions could be packaged and marketed more politically correctly than the Germanic ones. I found this out firsthand while trying to market my end-of-the-century tribute to Germany, *Children of the Sun*.[10] Published in 1998, it may be the only book issued to commemorate the two-thousandth anniversary of Tacitus's *Germania*, the ethnological bible of the Germanic peoples, from 98 C.E.

I've always been interested in the totality of things, so with the twentieth century coming to a close I felt the time was ripe for paying homage to those who came before us and were pioneers of health, social reform, and environmental consciousness. Essentially a pictorial anthology documenting the spiritual trajectory from Germany to California that occurred between 1883 and 1949, it includes short biographies of sixteen people and four social reform movements. But the 144 photos are what tell the story. Both black and white and in color, it took a few decades to collect many of these artifacts.

This was a counterculture without rock and roll, pot, or psychedelics, and partly for this reason the theme doesn't seem to fit into the same niche as most related works.

Up and down the West Coast, from San Diego to Vancouver, B.C., just about every bookstore has a section on Beat literature—and they falsely give the drugged-out beatniks full credit for inspiring the hippie generation. But it was especially the hippie bookstores in Arcata, Santa Cruz, and Eugene, Oregon that were frightened of *Children of the Sun*. This obviously irrefutable version of history was so controversial that they would not even consider carrying the book in their shops. Even the ones who read Hesse and drive old Volkswagen buses were shocked by the nudity and one-hundred-year-old German psychedelic art.

It seems that most of these neo-hippies are not as turned on, tuned in, or dropped out as they wish they were... because the American media has obviously convinced them of what it isn't politically correct for their hippie clientele to read. What a devastating blow to find out that it wasn't the Hopis, Hindus, Tibetans, or some universal "all-is-one" doctrine that inspired the hippies—it was Germany after all.

No matter. Truth always wins out in the end.

Notes:

1. Malcolm X, *The Autobiography of Malcolm X*, as told to Alex Haley (New York: Ballantine, 1965), p. 109.
2. Julius Caesar, *The Conquest of Gaul*, trans. S. A. Handford (New York: Penguin, 1983), p. 143.
3. See, for example, the brief discussion of this in Alain de Benoist's essay "Thoughts on God" in *TYR* 2 (2003), p. 65.
4. Tacitus, *The Agricola and the Germania*, trans. H. Mattingly (New York: Penguin, 1970), p. 108.
5. Quoted in Adolf Just, *Return To Nature*, trans. Benedict Lust (New York: Benedict Lust, 1904), p. 4.
6. Ibid.
7. Hesse's text appears in the booklet *Der Eremit Von Ascona: Hermann Hesse in Wald, Fels und Hohle*. (Freudenstein: Monte Verita Archiv, 1998).
8. (New York: Signet, 1957), p. 7.
9. PolyGram Video, 1994.
10. Gordon Kennedy, ed., *Children of the Sun: A Pictorial Anthology from Germany to California 1883–1949* (Ojai, Calif.: Nivaria Press, 1998).

The Source
The Untold Story of Father Yod, Ya Ho Wha 13, and The Source Family
By **Isis Aquarian** and **Electricity Aquarian**
Introduction by Erik Davis

At last, the legendary saga of Father Yod and his '70s Los Angeles cult/commune and psychedelic band is revealed by the Source Family members themselves.

200 photographs • Source recipes and rituals • Includes a CD with never-before-released recordings by Ya Ho Wa 13, including a live performance at Beverly Hills High School in 1973. 7 x 10 • 280 pages
ISBN 978-0-9760822-9-3 • $24.95

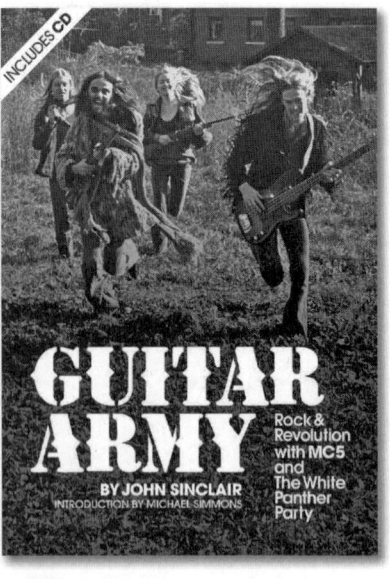

Guitar Army
Rock and Revolution with The MC5 and the White Panther Party
By **John Sinclair**, Introduction by Michael Simmons

"*Guitar Army* was our manual for revolt. It's a rainbow-colored *Howl*, still resonating today with the singular value of idealism."
—Michael Simmons

35th Anniversary Edition of a revolutionary classic • First time in print since 1972 • 40 additional photos • Includes 18-track CD with rare recordings by MC5, Black Panthers, White Panthers, Allen Ginsburg & more. 6 x 9 in • 360 pages, CD included
ISBN 978-1-934170-007 • $22.95

Moondog, the Viking of Sixth Avenue
The Authorized Biography
By **Robert Scotto**
Preface by Phillip Glass

"Moondog is one of America's great originals. He is an awesome figure whose horizons are vast."
—Alan Rich, *New York Magazine*

6 x 9 • 320 pages • photographs • CD included • 978-0-9760822-8-6 • $24.95
AVAILABLE IN OCTOBER/NOVEMBER

Eye Mind
The Saga of Roky Erickson and the 13th Floor Elevators, The Pioneers of Psychedelic Sound
By **Paul Drummond**
Foreword by Julian Cope

"One of the most exhilarating rock 'n' roll stories ever told."
—Julian Cope

6 x 9 • 450 pages • 120 photographs • ISBN: 978-0-9760822-6-2 • $19.95
AVAILABLE IN OCTOBER/NOVEMBER

processmediainc.com

Carl Larsson's Greatest Sacrifice:
The Saga of Midvinterblot

Michael Moynihan

The end of the nineteenth century and first decades of the twentieth mark a period of intensified social, political, and spiritual ferment in Scandinavian society, as was the case throughout much of Europe. Amid anguished conflicts—between tradition and modernity, religion and science, and even the sexes—there arose a golden age of creativity in the literature and arts of the Far North.[1] Since the turn of the preceding century, movements of National Romanticism had also established themselves in these countries, and many subsequent writers and painters gave voice to nationalist impulses in their work. The most dramatic—and in many ways uncharacteristic—example of such a project in the visual arts is the monumental 1915 painting *Midvinterblot* (Midwinter Sacrifice) by the Swedish artist Carl Olof Larsson (1853–1919). This has been described as the "most sensational and remarkable painting of an heroic Scandinavian subject of the twentieth century ... which has fascinated, frustrated and muddled the Swedish establishment from the moment the first studies for it were released in 1911."[2] Contentious debates surrounding the painting continue to the present day. By unraveling the background, sources, and history of *Midvinterblot*, this essay seeks to situate the work in its wider social, artistic, and cultural contexts—and in the tumultuous inner world of its creator.

Larsson's Entry into National Romanticism

Carl Larsson had already become a popular artist-illustrator in his homeland by the 1890s, and this recognition grew increasingly international in scope over subsequent decades. He is most famous for the numerous images of his family's domestic life, often collected into small books or reproduced as prints and postcards, which have come to represent a romantic ideal of rural Swedish life. In stark contrast to this apparently idyllic portrayal, his childhood and early years were rife with hardship and quite atypical of the fellow Swedish artists of his generation. Larsson was born on 28 May 1853 in a slum neighborhood of Stockholm, the son of extremely poor, working-class parents. Many of the squalid details of what he experienced did not become widely known until the posthumous publication of his autobiography *Jag* (I), in which he related these anecdotes with a palpable degree of embarrassment.[3]

Larsson's talent for art became apparent very early. He was accepted by the preparatory division of the Royal Academy of Fine Arts at age thirteen, and three years later by the academy proper. By the beginning of the 1870s he had found professional work as an illustrator before entering the academy's School of Painting in 1873. During the next few years Larsson traveled to Paris in order to learn new techniques and escape the stifling intellectual climate in the conservative capital of his homeland. Similar journeys were undertaken by many Scandinavian painters at this time, for identical reasons. Larsson made a second trip to France in 1882 when he joined the Scandinavian artists' colony in the village of Grèz-sur-Loing, along with Christian Krogh (1852–1925), Karl Nordström (1855–1923), and Richard Bergh (1858–1919), the latter of whom would later become the director of the Swedish National Museum in Stockholm. While many of the radical young Scandinavian self-exiles had been driven by an urge to relocate themselves "away from the land of barbarians. Away from ice and snow. Away from all coarse excesses,"[4] Larsson soon began to feel homesick and alienated in his French surroundings. He returned to Sweden the following year with his fiancé, the artist Karin Bergöö (1859–1928), whom he married in the summer. Larsson became deeply involved with the "Opponents Group" and the Swedish Artists' Union. These were both elements of a considerable protest movement against the conservatism of his former school, the Royal Academy, and its dominance over the Stockholm Art Association. As both an artist and organizer, Larsson played a large role in the successful 1885 secessionist exhibit in Stockholm, *From the Banks of the Seine*.[5] Although many of the participants absorbed profound influences from their time working in France, they also began to move in a distinctly nationalist direction. It is in this same period that Larsson's own increasing nationalist tendencies begin to find overt expression with a series of ambitious monumental works that would demand new techniques and approaches.

FACING PAGE: THE MAIN PANEL OF CARL LARSSON'S MONUMENTAL "MIDVINTERBLOT," 1915.
(PHOTO BY GEORG SESSLER AND PER MYREHED)

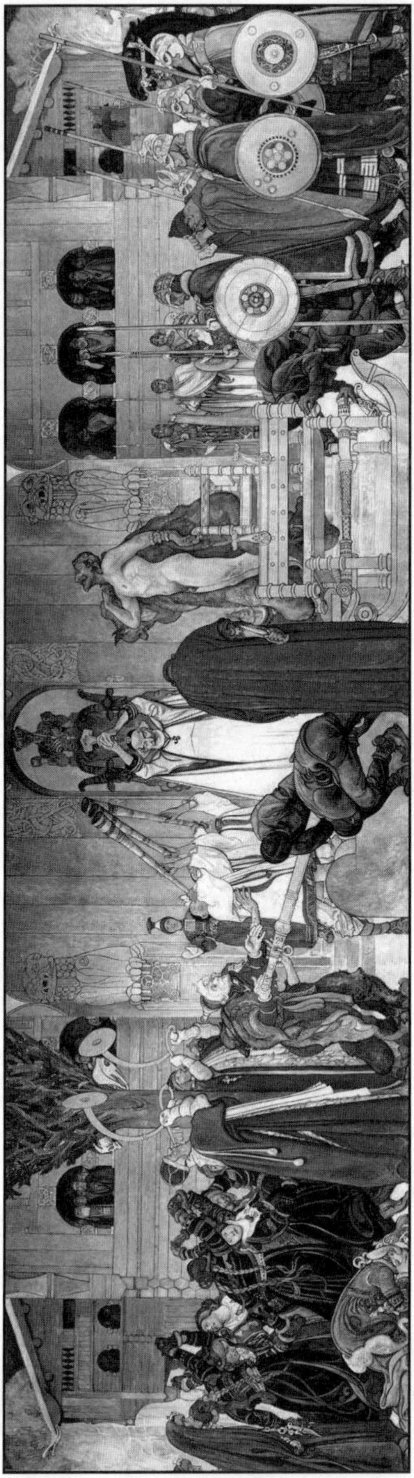

LARSSON (CENTER, ON LADDER) AND ASSISTANTS AT WORK ON THE MONUMENTAL SERIES "SWEDISH WOMANHOOD THROUGH THE CENTURIES," NEW ELEMENTARY GRAMMAR SCHOOL FOR GIRLS, GOTHENBURG, 1890. (DETAIL FROM A PHOTO BY J. JONASSON, FROM "CARL AND KARIN LARSSON: CREATORS OF THE SWEDISH STYLE" BY MICHAEL SNODIN AND ELISABET STAVENOW-HIDEMARK)

Larsson as a Monumental Artist

During the final decade of the nineteenth century a "veritable mania for monumental painting emerged" in Sweden.[6] This was largely inspired by grandiose works such as *Le Bois sacré cher aux Arts et aux Muses* (The Sacred Grove Cherished by Arts and Muses) by the French proto-Symbolist painter Pierre Puvis de Chavannes (1824–1898) and the German church frescoes of Peter von Cornelius (1783–1867). Larsson became a key exponent of this genre, beginning with wall-paintings in the New Elementary Grammar School for Girls (now the Engelbrekt School) in Gothenburg. Larsson received the commission, which was funded by Pontus Fürstenberg, at the invitation of one of the schoolteachers, Hedda Key.[7] Originally asked, in his words, to "put an ever-so-small dash of color somewhere on the downstairs hall so there would be a touch pleasing to the eye of whoever entered," Larsson was soon possessed by "megalomania to such a degree" that he proposed paintings which would stretch through the halls on a series of floors in the building.[8] The resulting work, *Svenska kvinnan genom seklen* (Swedish Womanhood through the Centuries), depicts a series of vignettes which ascend from the lower floor and include a Stone Age woman, Viking Age figures (a mother with children contemplating the memorial runestone for her husband; a weaver at work), Saint Bridget, women of later centuries, and contemporary girls. It represents a number of themes that would reappear in his monumental work and *Midvinterblot*: archaic ethno-nationalist subject matter, images relating to nobility and sacrifice (the fallen Viking hero, immortalized on a runestone), and a procession that is eclectically anachronistic and mystical: a symbol of the kinship-chain that extends across time.[9] In their depiction of socially significant ceremonial parades, many of Larsson's future wall-paintings would emphasize this processional quality in a literal, more historically accurate way as well.[10] Larsson later felt the New Elementary School series to be "hastily put together" and "a little too didactic," but it was well received by the public and resulted in further commissions for monumental work.[11]

The National Museum Frescoes

In his autobiography, Larsson recalls visiting the newly opened National Museum in Stockholm as a thirteen-year-old student to attend the Scandinavian Art and Industry Exhibit in 1886. His "attention was caught by the flat walls in the foyer, where there were signs saying: 'Space for fresco painting,'" and he claims to have felt "as if those walls had belonged to me from the beginning."[12] In 1888 the museum staged a competition to award an artist the opportunity to decorate the walls, and Larsson's National Romantic proposal entitled *Allt för fosterlandet* (All for the Fatherland) was awarded second place. This meant he could paint only a few vestibule panels, with the bulk of them being allotted to the first-place winner, Gustav Cederström (1845–1933). A series of arguments over the exact content of the paintings took place between the artists and the museum. Cederström later withdrew from the project as he ultimately favored Larsson's plan for a series of images depicting historical scenes of royal patronage for the arts during the seventeenth and eighteenth centuries. In 1894 Larsson traveled to Italy and other parts of Europe to study the demanding technique of painting *al fresco* on fresh plaster, considered to be the most permanent and colorfast method for executing large works of this nature. The actual frescoes were executed over two years, 1895–96, with a team of assistants that included the Italian fresco expert Antonio Bellio and the young National-Romantic painter Gustav Fjæstad (1868–1948).[13] Certain members of the museum's committee expressed misgivings about Larsson's works, and these debates were a source of stress for the artist. His eyesight was also affected by the time-consuming and intensive work of the *al fresco* technique.

In the final years of the decade a further significant project took place in Stockholm with regard to monumental art. This was the decoration of various atrium walls in the Northside Classical High School and involved Larsson and two other painters, Prince Eugen (1865–1947) and Bruno Liljefors (1860–1939). Each artist was allotted a specific wall panel to work upon. Larsson's image is entitled *Skolungdomens korum* (School Students at "Korum"), and depicts an annual outdoor springtime event called Korum in which the "all-male student body gathered to recite prayers, sing songs, and play music, a ritual meant to foster solidarity among students and to inspire allegiance to the nation."[14] In order for the artist to capture the image, a version of the ceremony was specially staged in the fall of 1898, during which Larsson experienced a vision of "angels and cherubs in the sky."[15] In the final mural an angelic, youthful female figure stands atop a hallucinatory central sun-altar bursting with brightly colored flowers, a tall sunflower stretching above them. Art historian Michelle Facos describes this as a "metaphor for the vital forces of nature."[16] In Larsson's choice of subject matter we see the importance of panorama, procession, social collectivity (adults and children, both male and female, are all participants), a somber "Nordic" bearing, and seasonal ceremonial tradition, all revolving around the central, mystical symbolism of the natural world's rejuvenating fertility. There are a few significant differences between the final version of the mural and the large 1899 color study for it on the east wall of Larsson's studio at Lilla Hyttnäs in Sundborn, Dalarna. In the sketch the female figure bears prominent wings, and clusters of cherubs float above and amid the crowd. In the final painting Larsson has eliminated all but an obscured single cherub who hovers behind the female figure's right shoulder. These alterations emphasize the mystical but *worldly* nature of the vision, removing any allusion to an overtly Christian transcendent heaven. The figure might also be viewed as a youthful, universalized precursor of the "house spirit" Larsson would depict in the 1909 watercolor *Hemmets god ängel* (Home's Good Angel).

By the time he was working on the Northside Classical High School mural, Larsson had already become a household name in Sweden. This was largely through the publication of a series of small, illustrated books that cheerfully documented his domestic life with Karin and his eight children. The images revolve around activities at Lilla Hyttnäs, the home which the family had inherited in 1888, and they were eagerly received by the public. The production of hundreds of watercolors and ink drawings of this type, many of them collected into various books or published in magazines, would dominate Larsson's work for the remainder of his life. While Larsson seemed to enjoy churning out these small images, which in their own way effused a folksy, National Romantic aura, he still relished the challenges and deeper drama of a monumental project. He turned his attention to the National Museum once more, and in 1906 proposed a painting for the upper foyer wall opposite the building's main entrance: this would depict *Gustav Vasas intåg i Stockholm midsommaraftonen 1523* (Gustav Vasa's March into Stockholm on Midsummer Evening, 1523).[27] Larsson experienced the now-predictable arguments with the museum commission, but also arranged that he would paint it in oil on canvas in his studio. This would force the committee to either accept or reject the final work; if accepted it would be mounted directly in place.[18] In a ritual for approval that would repeat itself with *Midvinterblot* some years later (and to a far more humiliating degree), Larsson relates: "The huge canvas was spread out on the floor, and next to it a high tower of Babel was erected, from which the commission scrutinized it. I had wanted to mount it, and I even offered to take it down again if it wasn't appreciated, and even to keep it and bear

"Gustav Vasa's March into Stockholm on Midsummer Evening, 1523." Monumental 1908 painting on canvas by Carl Larsson hanging in its place in the Swedish National Museum. (Courtesy of National Museum, Stockholm)

the costs myself."[19] Although King Oscar II also required a private screening of the painting and declared his dislike for it, permission to hang it permanently in the museum's foyer was granted by the commission in 1908.[20]

Larsson's Gustav Vasa painting has a precedent in the 1830 fresco by J. G. Sandberg in the Uppsala cathedral which depicts the exact same event.[21] Whereas Sandberg's portrayal has a dense, claustrophobic atmosphere, Larsson stretches out the processional nature of the scene, placing the king in the exact center, framed within the fixtures of the drawbridge at the city gates. The beams above him are draped with greenery and flowers, with a blue bouquet affixed to the head of his horse. The social classes of the other figures in the painting—burghers, foot soldiers, cavalry, priests—are evident through their stylized garments. The blue and yellow colors of the Swedish flag are diffused through the painting via the flags at the right side and the golden ships in the harbor, as well as the blue sky and bluish tone of the king's armor. Stylistically one can see influences of Italian Renaissance and Pre-Raphaelite painting, along with Art Nouveau and traditional folk art (present not only with the use of color, but also in the costumes of the young, garland-bearing girls at the left edge of the painting). Regal triumph emanates not only from the king's stately posture, but also atmospherically from the golden ships and upwardly illuminating horizon of light. All attention is focused reverently upon the king from both front and back; he is the symbol of the folk as a whole. The scene appears as if from a fairy tale, and Larsson himself "assumed the whole work was more of an allegory than accepted reality."[22]

Larsson's Final Monumental Works and *Midvinterblot*

Carl Larsson undertook two further monumental projects in the last fifteen years of his life. The first of them was a stunning 1907 ceiling panel in Stockholm's Royal Dramatic Theater entitled *Dramats skapelse* (The Creation of Drama). Painted in oil on canvas, the image shows a naked male figure with a wreath and sword floating upward in the night sky to meet an angelic, robed female figure. The edges of the painting are dense with wooded foliage and a series of smaller floating naked bodies which wrestle gymnastically (and violently—two figures wield knives, one of them already bloody) through the air while a pagan priestly figure looms over one end with outstretched arms, and a man in contemporary clothing points inward from the opposite side. The dreamlike scenario is, along with his 1888–94 painting *Evas dotter* (The Daughter of Eve), one of Larsson's most overtly Symbolist works.[23] Here again one finds the processional quality of his other monumental work, but in this case brilliantly transposed to a vertical axis. With a vantage point as if from the underworld, the viewer's attention is pulled upward to the center of the panel where a royal hierogamy or consecration seems to be on the verge of taking place. In terms of vertical perspective, the earthly vegetation is also in a central and prominent position, as it had been in a number of Larsson's previous murals.

Larsson's most personal project of his later years—and probably his entire life—was the last painting he felt was necessary to complete the wall decorations at the National Museum: *Midvinterblot*. Its theme is a pagan sacrifice at the famous royal temple of Gamla (Old) Uppsala, and like most of his monumental works, it is simultaneously rooted in both Swedish history and the realm of the mythic. Old Norse images had occasionally been present in Larsson's earlier work, such as the girls' school murals, but overt elements of pre-Christian religion were heretofore nonex-

"The White Temple," an early example of "Tempelkunst" (Temple Art) by Fidus, 1898.

istent.[24] His interests in this area were longstanding, however, and one of his close friends was the popular poet and author Viktor Rydberg (1828–95), whose idiosyncratic three-volume study *Undersökningar i germanisk mythologi* (Investigations in Germanic Mythology) appeared in 1886–89.[25] Larsson's book illustrations of scenes from Nordic mythology would also be included in popular editions of philologist Erik Brate's 1913 Swedish translation of the *Poetic Edda*.

In 1907, while still completing his monumental Gustav Vasa painting, Larsson was already thinking about the site of the heathen temple at Old Uppsala, although not yet in terms of a painting. Rather, in an essay published the following year in the journal *Ord och Bild* (Word and Image), he proposed the erection of a "Swedish Pantheon" at the site. This was undoubtedly inspired by the Walhalla memorial monument in Regensburg designed by Leo von Klenzes, and built in 1830–42. Judging from the small sketch that accompanied Larsson's essay, it also seems likely that Larsson was influenced by some of the nationalistic and romantic German temple designs created by the artists Karl Wilhelm Diefenbach (1851–1913) and his even more well known student Fidus (b. Hugo Höppener, 1868–1948).

LARSSON'S 1907 DRAWING OF HIS CONCEPTION FOR A NATIONAL ROMANTIC "SWEDISH PANTHEON" AT OLD UPPSALA INCORPORATING CHRISTIAN AND PAGAN SYMBOLISM.

While Fidus's temple designs are far more elaborate than Larsson's, they evince a similar sensibility in some key respects. Larsson may have been familiar with the earliest reproductions of these images, which appeared in various German publications from 1898 on.[26] Unlike German temple proposals such as Fidus's 1901 *Tempel der Erde* (Temple of the Earth), Larsson's sacred site was not an overtly neo-pagan conception by any means, but rather a combination of Christian and pagan elements in the overall service of a National Romantic vision.

In his essay, Larsson writes:

> Yes, on one of the mounds at Gamla Uppsala a Pantheon shall be built. In this vicinity existed the old temple which, according to Adam of Bremen, was entirely gilded and housed the images of Frey and Thor. Outside it stood the sacred grove. Here all of the North used to gather, here at this admired sacred site, mentioned in the last days of heathendom by a Norwegian king as the place

"where the Swedes lick their sacrificial stones." For me, and probably for you as well, this place is still sacred. Let us bury our dead here! During great national misfortunes we'll go there to pray, and for great national successes we'll go there to cheer. It will be called *The Temple of Memory*, and the grove, which we'll cultivate once more, will be called *The Grove of Life*. Bells will sound in the old church, and processions of youths will travel from the city, past Milles's genial and mighty Sten Sture monument, along the Appian Way which I am planning to extend there.

This road shall be called *The Road of Youth*, since it will be lined on both sides by the graves of the dead. ... *The road of youth?* Yes, because if we no longer believe in death, we will believe even less in old age: We Swedes will forever be young![27]

Larsson's Pantheon would house a strange assortment of treasures ranging from ancient Vendel-era archeological artifacts; earlier National Romantic art such as the trinity of classical-style sculptures of Odin, Thor, and Balder by Bengt Fogelberg (1786–1854); and even the heart of King Gustav Adolph.[28] He concludes his essay with these wistful lines:

Thoughts pour over me when I, with fantasy's divine eye, envision this Swedish Pantheon (i.e., the high holy place) shining out there at Gamla Uppsala, where surely the foundations of the old sacrificial temple still remain, though the centuries have shrouded them and hidden them from our view.

O, thou Swede, who readeth this, linger a while by this my thought...

We, who desire to become the noblest people of the earth.[29]

Larsson's plan for the Pantheon did not gain any real momentum but the imagery of the Uppsala cult site and its adjacent royal burial mounds, was now firmly planted in his fertile imagination. Larsson had always envisioned a final wall-painting in the upper stairwell foyer of the National Museum, facing opposite his Gustav Vasa procession. Originally he had planned this to be an image of Gustav II Adolf landing in Germany in 1630 when Sweden entered the Thirty Years' War.[30] Larsson subsequently lost his enthusiasm for the theme, and sought another subject. He writes in his memoir: "I searched my *'inneres Bewusstsein'* [inner consciousness] for something else and woke up one morning with the inspired thought that I should reawaken the feeling for our pagan forefathers and their culture. 'Midwinter solstice sacrifice at the temple in Uppsala.'"[31] This would serve as a dynamic ancient historical counterpoint to the "midsummer" painting of Gustav Vasa's triumphal march.

In 1910 he submitted a formal proposal with a rough sketch to the museum's mural commission, along with a brief description: "Here a king is being sacrificed for the weal of the people (to ensure a good harvest year). He was drowned in the sacred well at the root of the tree (according to Adam of Bremen there stood before the well a tree whose leaves were green all year)."[32]

The Sources for *Midvinterblot*

The two primary sources for Larsson's *Midvinterblot* image are clearly the aforementioned Adam of Bremen (birth/death dates uncertain) and Snorri Sturluson (1178/9–1241). In order to see how Larsson has interpreted this material, and altered it to fit his own vision, it is worth examining both of these texts. Adam of Bremen was an eleventh-century canon at the Catholic Church at Bremen who wrote his *Gesta Hammaburgensis Ecclesiae Pontificum* (History of the Archbishops of Hamburg-Bremen) circa 1074–85.[33] Beyond merely recounting the activities of the churches in northern Germany, Adam also provides significant geographic and ethnographic details, a number of them based on first-hand reports. Considerable parts of Scandinavia were not yet Christianized at the time, and Adam's book is a unique source of information regarding pre-Christian culture. While some of his descriptions are clearly paraphrasings from other sources such as Tacitus (writing almost a millennium earlier!), other accounts appear to be contemporary. He speaks of the Northmen, "a very ferocious folk," as well as of "the temple called Uppsala, which the Swedes consider the most eminent in the cult of their gods."[34] He also describes the Swedish countryside as being inhabited by "hordes of human monsters."[35] In the final Book Four of his text, he describes the goings-on at the temple of Uppsala:

DETAIL FROM THE CENTER OF "MIDVINTERBLOT" SHOWING, FROM LEFT TO RIGHT: RITUAL TRUMPETERS WITH BIRCH-BARK HORNS, THRALLS PULLING THE SACRIFICIAL WAGON, THE PAGAN PRIEST, THE EXECUTIONER, AND THE NAKED KING. AN IDOL OF THE GOD THOR WITH HIS CHARIOT DRAWN BY GOATS IS VISIBLE INSIDE THE TEMPLE'S MAIN ENTRANCE. (PHOTO BY GEORG SESSLER AND PER MYREHED)

In this temple, entirely decked out in gold, the people worship the statues of three gods in such wise that the mightiest of them, Thor, occupies a throne in the middle of the chamber; Wotan [i.e., Odin] and Frikko [i.e., Frey] have places on either side. The significance of these gods is as follows: Thor, they say, presides over the air, which governs the thunder and lightning, the winds and rains, fair weather and crops. The other, Wotan—that is, the Furious—carries on war and imparts to man strength against his enemies. The third is Frikko, who bestows peace and pleasure on mortals. His likeness, too, they fashion with an immense phallus. But Wotan they chisel armed, as our people are wont to represent Mars. Thor with his scepter apparently resembles Jove.[36]

Comments are appended to this which further describe the large evergreen tree near the temple, and "a spring at which the pagans are accustomed to make their sacrifices, and into it plunge a live man. And if he is not found, the people's wish will be granted."[37] As for the temple itself, it is draped with a "golden chain" that "hangs over the gable of the building and sends its glitter far off to those who approach, because the shrine stands on level ground with mountains all about it like a theater."[38] In the following section, Adam says of the religious ceremonies, "For all their gods there are appointed priests to offer sacrifices for the people. If plague and famine threaten, a libation is poured to the idol Thor; if war, to Wotan; if marriages are to be celebrated, to Frikko."[39] Adam then recounts the grisly sacrifices made at a prominent festival held every nine years, in which:

> Of every living thing that is male, they offer nine heads ... The bodies they hang in the sacred grove that adjoins the temple. Now this grove is so sacred in the eyes of the heathen that each and every tree in it is believed divine because of the death or putrefaction of the victims. Even dogs and horses hang there with men.[40]

To bolster the credibility for this description, which might otherwise sound like gruesome propaganda, Adam notes that a seventy-two-year-old Christian informed him personally of seeing these sacrificed bodies "suspended promiscuously" in the trees.[41] An additional note mentions that the grand sacrifice takes places at the vernal equinox, over a period of nine days.

While Adam's descriptions provide the backdrop for what Larsson wanted to depict in *Midvinterblot*, the specific example of a royal sacrifice comes from a different source: the Icelandic poet and chronicler Snorri Sturluson. In *Ynglinga saga*, the first book of Snorri's *Heimskringla* (History of the Kings of Norway) and a euhemeristic account of the Norse gods and their royal descendants, chapter 15 tells of how "King Dómaldi is Sacrificed for Better Seasons."[42] Snorri writes that during Dómaldi's reign there was blight and starvation, and great sacrifices were offered at Uppsala as an attempt to restore fertility to the land. Each sacrifice was held in the fall. First oxen were sacrificed to no avail, then human sacrifices were made the next year, but these also had no effect—if anything, the situation worsened. Snorri states:

> In the third fall the Swedes came in great numbers to Uppsala at the time for the sacrifices. Then the chieftains held a council, and they agreed that the famine was probably due to Dómaldi, their king, and that they should attack him and kill him and redden the altars with his blood; and so they did. As says Thjóthólf:

> ... Lifeless lay then
> Dómaldi,
> dead in his blood,
> when that him,
> harvest-eager,
> his folk gave
> as gift to gods.[43]

In conceiving his *Midvinterblot* painting, Larsson took as a starting point the accounts of these historical writers, Adam of Bremen and Snorri Sturluson, but then allowed his imagination relatively free play. To complete his vision he made use of numerous disparate ornamental details, material objects, and costumes. While these are all based on historical sources, they often anachronistically derive from much different eras than the one in which Dómaldi's sacrifice would have taken place.[44] Occasionally they seem to come from another cultural tradition altogether—the most disconcerting example being the Chinese-style dragons that sit atop two pedestals in front of the temple, in the center area of the painting. During the period when Larsson tried to gain support for his creation, it would not only be the grim subject matter, but these elements as well, which elicited harsh criticism from those who weighed in with their opinions.

The *Midvinterblot* Controversy

Larsson's initial proposal was accompanied by a very rough pencil sketch. This already reveals, however, how well formulated the overall composition was in his mind. Despite the fact that the image contains none of the violent or gruesome details from the literary sources that inspired it, the proposal was heavily criticized and rejected by the mural commission as inappropriate. This profoundly affected the artist: "The setback incapacitated him. He was bothered by exhibitions and orders for pictures of children and he was fed up with his pictures of home; he was neurotic for awhile."[45]

Larsson was by nature willful and determined. His obsession with *Midvinterblot* would have to reach some kind of fruition, and he pressed on in painting further studies, more elaborate and in color, in 1911–13, 1913, and 1914–15.[46] The debate over the appropriateness of the proposal spilled over to the newspapers and the public, and would haunt the fate of the work.[47] While he received some support, especially from fellow artists such as Anders Zorn (1860–1920), many of the reactions were highly critical. Larsson frequently wrote letters in response to what he perceived as attacks; this perpetually defensive position began to wear him down.

Although Larsson altered many details in the subsequent preliminary sketches, often significantly, it was rare that these changes made the work more palatable—if anything, they may have had the opposite effect. The changes do, however, reveal much about the artist's attitude toward his subject matter. In the first sketch Dómaldi appears to have his hands tied behind his back, indicating he may not be a willing sacrifice. This would seem to be in line with Snorri's account. Larsson's idea that the king was about to be drowned alive would also fit in with the lines from Adam of Bremen that certain victims were sacrificed this way in order to fulfill a wish on behalf of the people. In Larsson's painted color study from 1911–13, the king's bearing has changed considerably. As he is drawn up to the edge of the well on a sled, he stands proudly and magnanimously, a rope loosely draped around his neck, and throws aside his fur cloak in a gesture that indicates his willing readiness to die. The heathen priest officiates over the well, which—as in Adam's account—lies adjacent to the towering sacred tree. He appears to hold aloft a knife, pointing downward. It now appears that the king will be first stabbed and then drowned, a combination of details from both historical accounts.

Midvinterblot was primarily criticized from two directions: the unsuitability of the theme itself and the historical inaccuracies of how Larsson chose to depict it. With regard to the first accusation, the museum commission "could not approve of the king's voluntary sacrifice as a motif, since no such event was to be found in the historical sources. They therefore suggested he depict a midwinter festival without this savage touch."[48] Other commentators were more caustic: the painting's theme had "as much to do with modern Swedes as cannibals in darkest Africa."[49] A typical response attacking the solecism of the image is a letter to the editor of a daily paper from an anonymous "archeologist" which criticized the details in the 1911 sketch that spanned "three centuries"—but most offensive was the temple, which looked like "an airy summer restaurant adorned with motifs from the [recently built] biological museum."[50] Regardless of the accuracy of the preceding criticism, the carvings on the temple do have a flashy exuberance that is more Jugendstil than Old Norse. This should not be so surprising, however, since the building that Larsson depicts seems as much based on Nordic Revival–style architecture of the 1870s in Sweden as it does any ancient historical model. A resemblance in various architectural details can be seen, for example, with the famous Curman summer villa of Lysekil, Sweden, constructed in the mid-1870s. Although based on the prototype of medieval Norwegian farm storehouse buildings, the villa was constructed with factory milled wood from Stockholm and may also reflect Swiss chalet influences.[51] Larsson made use of some stylized old Nordic details on his own home Lilla Hyttnäs, and I think it quite possible that certain basic architectural outlines of the latter, particularly on the western side, may have also consciously or subconsciously influenced his depiction of the temple—especially considering how important *Midvinterblot* was to him personally.[52]

Although Larsson wrote a letter to the minister of religious affairs in the spring of 1914 stating that he was withdrawing his proposal for the *Midvinterblot* wall-painting, he privately could not abandon the idea and set about executing it to correct proportions of nearly seven-by-fourteen meters, on canvas, in his studio.[53] This he did with no outside patronage. The final painting was unveiled in 1915, and through persistence Larsson succeeded in having it hung provisionally on the intended wall of the museum that summer. One of Larsson's staunchest supporters was Anders Zorn, who publicly announced that he would personally finance the execution of both *Midvinterblot* and the Gustav Vasa image as frescoes. This proposal was turned down—as was the painting itself, which Larsson offered to sell to the museum for 35,000 Swedish

Kroner. The debates over it were too contentious, and although the museum committee hoped Larsson would contribute a final wall-painting for the space in question, the theme would have to be a different one. Even Larsson's old friend and fellow painter Richard Bergh, who had just been appointed the National Museum's director, could not bring himself to endorse the work. He had been favorable toward the previous sketches but voted against accepting the actual painting.[54] At this point the Minister for Ecclesiastical Affairs, K. G. Westman, who was considered to be sympathetic to Larsson, stepped in and proposed that opinions on the work be solicited from a committee, to include experts in art history and archeology, in order to make a final decision. In the meantime, with no end to the debate in sight, Larsson formally withdrew the painting in anger and disgust.

The Fate of *Midwinterblot*

Following the National Museum debacle, Larsson's epic painting was briefly exhibited again in Stockholm at the Liljevachs Gallery in 1916 in a group exhibit which also included works by Bruno Liljefors and Anders Zorn. Soon it would effectively go into cold storage for more than half a century. In the year before his death in 1919 Larsson wrote: "Right now it is rolled up ... in my garage attic, and I hope that my children and grandchildren will one day take it out and show it to a later generation of Swedes."[55]

After Larsson's death, *Midvinterblot* was exhibited again in its intended place in the National Museum from 1924–32. A decade later in 1942 it was deposited at the State Archive for Decorative Art in Lund. With the exception of a brief stretch in 1953 when it was included in an exhibit at the Liljevachs Gallery occasioned by the centenary of Larsson's birth, the painting remained on deposit for nearly forty years at the State Archive. The controversy surrounding the painting's fate surfaced again during the Liljevachs exhibit, and the series of rejections from various museum directors continued. The director at the time, Otte Sköld, stated: "Carl Larsson's reputation would suffer if the painting were hung up again."[56] During this period *Midvinterblot* would occasionally attract the interest of researchers, such as in 1965 when *Bilden på muren*, the journal for studies about the Archive's holdings, published a new analysis of the painting by the archeology professor Holger Arbman.[57] In 1974 the painting was publicly discussed in the news-

CARL LARSSON'S "MIDVINTERBLOT" HANGING IN ITS DESTINED PLACE IN THE THE UPPER MAIN ENTRANCE HALL OF THE SWEDISH NATIONAL MUSEUM. (PHOTO BY PER MYREHED)

papers as a result of another campaign to have it hung in the National Museum, but the director, Bengt Dahlbäck, rejected the idea. In late 1981 Larsson's family, who were the owners of the painting, offered to donate *Midvinterblot* for free to the museum, provided it hang where the artist had intended. The museum director at the time, Per Bjurström, once more vetoed the idea. His reasons seem to have been somewhat personal and political, for a decade later he would express views that the painting was "racist" and plead that the museum not provide it with a permanent home.[58]

At the beginning of the 1980s the fate of the work became uncertain and the possibility arose that it might be placed on the international art market. The title of a 1982 magazine article asked "Should *Midvinterblot* Really End Up in America?"[59] The painting underwent restoration before Larsson's family loaned it for display at the State Historical Museum in Stockholm for the year 1983–84, as part of a large exhibit entitled *Myths*.[60] A Swedish art dealer, Werner Åmell, together with a financier, Carl-Erik Björkegren, purchased the painting from Larsson's estate for four million Kronor. It was offered for sale once more to the National Museum, whose management again declined it. A sale was then proposed to the Historical Museum for twelve million Kronor. The museum was interested but felt the asking price to be too high. Public arguments again broke out as to whether the painting should be sold on the open market, to possibly disappear from Sweden altogether, and a nationwide campaign was even launched to raise the funds to purchase it.[61] Despite what was now a generally positive public feeling toward the work, the rescue campaign was unsuccessful and in the spring of 1987 *Midvinterblot* was put up for auction as part of a major Scandinavian art sale at Sotheby's in London.[62] The accurate assessment in the Sotheby's catalog reads: "With the passage of time *Midvinterblot* can now be recognised as one of the most important expressions of Scandinavian nationalism, as well as being a major work in the wider European tradition of Symbolism and Art Nouveau."[63] It was bought by a Japanese art collector, who later loaned it to the Swedish National Museum for a massive Larsson retrospective staged there in 1992 as part of the museum's bicentennial jubilee.[64] The painting was a major attraction of the exhibit and was viewed by more than 300,000 visitors. The collector offered to sell it to the museum for twelve million Kronor, and this set off more heated debates as to the cultural, artistic, and financial worth of the painting. While the museum did not end up buying it outright, the painting was allowed to remain there on extended loan. Controversy over the painting continued, but in 1997 the National Museum finally purchased the work for 14.7 million Kronor—the highest sum ever paid for a single work in their collection—with the help of various private donors, foundations, and the support organization Friends of the National Museum. The asking price was considered to be very reasonable and a generous gesture on the part of the Japanese owner, who was apparently happy that the painting might finally return to its intended place. After more than seventy-five years of often contentious diversions, *Midvinterblot* is now displayed exactly as Larsson had wished. Opinions about it today are certainly less divided than they were in 1911–15, although both old and new debates periodically flare up in the public sphere.[65]

Symbolism and Sacrifice

Midvinterblot is a fascinating blend of fact and fiction, of historical accuracy and Larssonian fantasy. The painting has been criticized for ahistoricity, mainly in its cavalier juxtaposition of objects (lur trumpets, weapons, folk costumes, the cart upon which the king is standing, etc.) that originate from disparate centuries and sundry locations in Scandinavia. This was, of course, conscious and deliberate on Larsson's part, and undoubtedly he saw it as reflecting the continuity of countless generations of ancestors. But it was also an outcome of allowing his intuitions to take precedence:

> For example, when I wanted to let the image of Thor be glimpsed through the gate of the temple, I seemed to rock myself into a kind of ecstasy, a kind of clairvoyance into the past, and I created a stately figure with a pointed headdress and a pointed, trimmed beard and turned up *es-ist-erreicht mustachios*, and soon thereafter, Sahlin, the national antiquarian, showed me a small, recently found bronze image of the god Frö [Frey], which has precisely these attributes.
> Isn't it quite mystical?
> Now, I do not for one moment doubt that I have also intuitively represented the sacrifice scene just as it was seen in reality at that time. Of course I have used all the suitable objects I could find in Scandinavia. I have not shied from selecting them all the way back to the early Iron Age and Bronze Age, and I do not consider myself guilty of any anachronisms, since these objects can still be seen, and since ritual objects increase in value and holiness with age.[66]

The description which Larsson had attached to the watercolor sketch of 1913 is just as fitting for the final painting: "a dream vision."[67] In this vision Larsson united various styles, colors, and contrasts. Along with Larsson's own distinctive artistic traits, there are elements of Art Nouveau and Jugendstil, as well as decorative elements that prefigure Art Deco. Not only the subject matter, but the flatness and de-emphasis of perspective, along with the stylized portrayals of the trees, share much in feeling with certain Symbolist paintings and in particular the Kalevala-inspired images by the Finnish painter Akseli Gallen-Kallela (1865–1931). The bright use of color, already a Larsson trademark in his domestic paintings, serves a didactic purpose, to make the past as vivid and alive as possible for a modern viewer: "In Scandinavian art ... [our Viking forefathers] have been represented as clumsy dogs with a simplicity devoid of all color and fantasy. This seems to me to be basically false. Surely they loved splendid clothes and shining jewelry. Surely, one will come closest to truth by making them highly dazzling."[68]

The painting brings together a series of contrastive images. The ecstatic dancing women on the left side are clad in black and red, while the stoic warriors marching in somberly from the right wear clothes of myriad colors. The heathen priest figure, the trumpet blowers, and the king himself are all gesturing in some way toward the sky, while the thralls dragging and pushing the cart look downward, as does the figure holding the knife behind his back who will ultimately dispatch the king. On a mythic level, this contrast is also present in the fact that the king, a vital earthly representative of the celestial gods, who stands elevated head-and-shoulders above everyone around him, will soon be stabbed and cast down below into the well that lies at the exact center of the painting. In death he will plunge into the water, the symbolic and literal source of life and fertility.[69] If the sacrifice is accepted, he will sink to the chthonic depths of the sacred well: sky and earth—king and queen, father and mother—will unite.

Many of the themes of Larsson's other monumental works reach their apex in *Midvinterblot*. The procession here is at its most dramatic and climactic; both sides push toward the center, as well as upwardly with their trumpet and spear points. These energies seem to be channeled into the heathen priest at the center who holds aloft his ritual hammer, an emblem of the heavenly weapon that causes thunderclaps and storms of rain. He is the representative of Thor, whose demonic likeness looms above him as an idol amid a fiery blaze of gold, visible through the open temple door. Blind in one eye, and overseeing sacrificial death, he also embodies the high god Odin. Conceptually, the regality and fertility that often figured into the center areas of Larsson's previous monumental paintings are here in their symbolic extreme, with one about to be sacrificed for the other.

While the sacrifice of a Norse pagan king is the theme of *Midvinterblot*, there appears to be more than simply this going on in the mind of the artist. In contrast to the unwilling sacrifice that was depicted in Larsson's earliest sketch, the king is now a fearless volunteer for his own death—as Larsson noted on the 1913 color sketch: "A king offers himself for his people."[70] There is something of a Christian sensibility here, as if the stoic Jesus of Luke's gospel has been transported to the heathen north. But there is also something of Larsson himself present in this figure. The painting clearly meant a great deal to him, and he considered it a gift—in other words, a sacrifice—for his own people, the Swedes.

Larsson had always felt messianic feelings about himself as an artist. He once wrote to his friend Viktor Rydberg that an artist's duty was to be a "priest of art ... going out and preaching the beautiful and joyful message of art to all the people."[71] Some commentators have gone further: "Carl confessed ... that he identified himself with the self-sacrificing king. Since the slit of the executioner's right-hand cuff is shaped like a heart, it seems probable that the artist felt himself being loved to death by his own people—the fatal knife is carried by a hand that loves. It has even been speculatively alleged that subconsciously Larsson may have identified the executioner with his wife Karin."[72] On one of the final pages of his memoirs, Larsson states: "all my life I have felt a knife at my throat."[73] He is speaking here figuratively of an "economic knife," and the need to provide support for his ample family, but this image is not far off from that of the tribal king who is symbolically responsible for the agricultural bounty that sustains his people. Georg Sessler has remarked, "Both as a narrative and as an object, *Midwinter Sacrifice* or the Story of Domald is an allegory of Carl Larsson's final battle. He felt denuded by his critics and 'banes' and the advocates of the new art. His long futile battle for *Midwinter Sacrifice*, which ended in rejection, poisoned the last years of his life."[74]

Larsson's final years were full of physical pain. Expressing a strange mixture of Buddhist and Christian guilt, he writes: "For two years, an unbearable headache tormented me day and night, but I told myself this was my Karma, something I had to suffer for my sins, in this existence or a previous one, and when I had done my penance, the pains would go away."[75] The excruciating headaches would never leave him, nor would his dismay over the fate of his greatest sacrifice, one which had been rejected by those who should have welcomed it most. Larsson did not entirely lose hope, however. He confesses in his final year: "The fate of *Midvinterblot* broke me! This I admit with dark anger. And still, it was probably the best thing that could happen, for now my intuition tells me—again—that with all its weaknesses, this painting will some day be honored with a far better placement after my death."[76]

With the passage of time, Larsson's wish has finally been granted, his sacrifice largely vindicated. It will also never be forgotten. Certainly no other modern Scandinavian artistic work was the subject of as much tumultuous debate in its day, nor does any retain the same kind of power to still inspire controversy today. Nearly a century after he created it, Carl Larsson's *Midvinterblot* has lost none of the epic grandeur, or monumental conflict, that its creator poured into it.

The author would like to dedicate this essay to Sherrill Harbison, an inspired teacher of medieval and modern Scandinavian literature, romanticism, and art who has shared many of her insights on these subjects in our exchanges over the past few years. Thanks are due to Ulwa Neergaard, the granddaughter of Carl Larsson, who kindly discussed certain details of the painting's history with me; to Carl Abrahamsson, Max Fredrikson, and Didrik Søderlind, who all assisted with researching Scandinavian press materials and reactions to Midvinterblot; *to Georg Sessler, for permission to reproduce his remarkable photography; and to Annabel Lee, who first suggested I investigate the strange saga of Larsson's* magnum opus.

Notes:

1. Kirk Varnedoe, *Northern Light: Nordic Art at the Turn of the Century* (New Haven: Yale University Press, 1988), p. 13; Michelle Facos, *Nationalism and the Nordic Imagination: Swedish Art of the 1890s* (Berkeley: University of California Press, 1998), p. 2.

2. David M. Wilson, *Vikings and Gods in European Art* (Højbjerg: Moesgård Museum, 1997), p. 68.

3. This was published posthumously in 1931. English edition translated by Ann B. Weissmann and retitled *Carl Larsson: The Autobiography of Sweden's Most Beloved Artist* (Iowa City: Penfield, 1992). Pages 1–61 concern Larsson's childhood; chapter titles such as "The Cholera" and "House of Thieves and Whores" give an idea of some of his experiences.

4. Anonymously quoted in Bo Lindwall, "Artistic Revolution in the Nordic Countries" in Varnedoe, *Northern Light*, p. 39.

5. These conflicts are detailed by Lindwall in Varnedoe, *Northern Light*, pp. 36–42.

6. Facos, *Nationalism and the Nordic Imagination*, pp. 167–69.

7. Ibid., p. 37; Larsson, *Autobiography*, p. 133. Hedda Key was the sister of the well-known feminist writer and educator Ellen Key.

8. Larsson, *Autobiography*, p. 133.

9. Larsson also designed a number of wall decorations with Old Norse and Nordic Bronze Age symbolism. See Michael Snodin and Elisabet Stavenow-Hidemark, eds., *Carl and Karin Larsson: Creators of the Swedish Style* (Boston: Little, Brown and Co., 1997), p. 105. For a survey of similar general tendencies in nationalist art (which often exhibit parallels to Larsson's approaches) see Athena S. Leoussi, "The Ethno-Cultural Roots of National Art," *Nations and Nationalism* 10 (1/2, 2004), pp. 143–59.

10. The idea of cultural continuity and evolution had already been present in an ambitious triptych of *Renässans*, *Rokoko*, and *Nutida konst* executed for the Fürstenbergs' gallery during 1888–89; this depicted the historical periods of Renaissance, Rococo, and Modern Art in a Symbolist style. The triptych won a Gold Medal at the 1889 Paris World's Fair. A diagram of the complete progression appears in *The World of Carl Larsson* (La Jolla: Green Tiger, 1982), p. 30. Literal processional imagery becomes apparent in *Ute blåser sommarvind...* (Outdoors Blow the Summer Winds...), Larsson's 1903 interior mural for the Classical High School in Gothenburg.

11. Larsson, *Autobiography*, p. 133.
12. Ibid., p. 135; Facos, *Nationalism and the Nordic Imagination*, p. 169. The walls had originally been envisioned as frescoes by the architect of the museum, Friedrich Stüler.
13. The saga of the first National Museum competition and Larsson's resulting paintings is detailed in *Nationalism and the Nordic Imagination*, pp. 168–74. A detailed history of all of Larsson's work for the National Museum can be found in Bo Lindwall, ed., *Carl Larsson och National Museum* (Stockholm: Rabén & Sjögren, 1969). For the frescoes in particular, see Karl Axel and Bo Lindwall, "Plats för freskomålning" in the same volume, pp. 7–109. A personal account of the fresco project appears in Larsson, *Autobiography*, pp. 135–42. A museum guide to the frescoes also provides the titles and a historical background for the works. Cf. *Lärarhandledning: Freskerna* (Stockholm: Nationalmuseum, n.d.).
14. Facos, *Nationalism and the Nordic Imagination*, p. 176.
15. Ibid.
16. Ibid.
17. The alternate wording of "Midsummer's Day" is sometimes used in connection with the painting.
18. Larsson, *Autobiography*, p. 150.
19. Ibid.
20. A detailed history of the Gustav Vasa painting is given in Karl Axel Arvidsson and Bo Lindwall, "Gustav Vasas intåg" in Lindwall, *Carl Larsson och National Museum*, pp. 110–134. The best photographic view of the painting is in Snodin and Stavenow-Hidemark, *Carl and Karin Larsson*, p. 43.
21. See reproduction in Lindwall, *Carl Larsson och National Museum*, p. 113.
22. Larsson, *Autobiography*, p. 150.
23. The 1888 painting was originally called *Sankt Antonii frestelse* (The Temptation of St. Anthony), but retitled after Larsson retouched it in 1894.
24. In 1873 Larsson began a painting entitled *Thor Unwittingly Slaying His Son Svade*, but he abandoned the project before it was finished. Significantly, Görel Cavalli-Björkman remarks of his work in the early 1870s: "Displaying the same fantastic quality found much later in his vast Midwinter Sacrifice, these paintings are indicative of the melancholy and despair that he hid so well from his friends but which drove him to the verge of suicide." From "Carl Larsson: A Brief Biography" in *Carl Larsson* (New York: Brooklyn

Museum, 1982), p. 27.

25. On Larsson's friendship with Rydberg, see Larsson, *Autobiography*, pp. 135–38. Larsson also illustrated Rydberg's romantic 1894 novel *Singoalla*. One of these pen-and-wash drawings, "Gypsy Dance in the Courtyard," may have served as a model for the dancing women on the left side of his *Midvinterblot* painting (cf. Karl Axel Arvidsson, "Midvinterblot," in *Carl Larsson och National Museum*, pp. 142–43.)

26. For a survey of such fantastical temple designs in the wider German context, see the material on "Tempel und Siedlung" in Janos Frecot, Johann Friedrich Geist, and Diethart Kerbs, *Fidus 1868–1948* (Frankfurt am Main: Zweitausendeins, 1997), pp. 232–52. Carl and Karin Larsson were avid readers of foreign art and design periodicals, including many from Germany; determining the extent to which Jugendstil publications and the temple ideas of Diefenbach and Fidus may have influenced Larsson's work would be a worthy subject for further investigation. Fidus's work sometimes appeared in the widely read Munich weekly *Jugend*; Larsson also had eleven illustrations published there in the years 1905–08.

27. The entire "Ett svenskt pantheon" (A Swedish Pantheon) essay is reprinted in Carl Larsson et al., *Midvinterblot* (Stockholm: Statens Historiska Museum, 1983), pp. 51–54; the quote appears on pp. 52–53. My thanks to Carl Abrahamsson for assistance with the translation of Larsson's text.

28. On Larsson's peculiar romantic ideas for the Swedish Pantheon, see his original essay (op. cit.); Holger Arbman, "En arkeolog ser på 'Midvinterblot'," *Bilder på muren: Studier i arkiv för dekorativ konst i Lund*, vol. 33–34, pp. 77–88; Arvidsson, "Midvinterblot," *Carl Larsson och National Museum*, pp. 135–6; and Jöran Mjöberg, "Romanticism and Revival" in David M. Wilson, ed., *The Northern World* (New York: Abrams, 1980), p. 234. Fogelberg's statues dated from the first half of the nineteenth century. They have long stood in the same multi-leveled grand stairhall of the National Museum, below where Larsson would plan to install his *Midvinterblot*.

29. Larsson, "Ett svenskt pantheon" in Carl Larsson et al., *Midvinterblot*, p. 54.

30. Larsson, *Autobiography*, pp. 174–5.

31. Ibid., p. 174.

32. *The World of Carl Larsson*, p. 40. Larsson's first study for the painting is this 1910 pencil sketch, 39 x 59 cm. Information from

Sotheby's auction catalog "Scandinavian Paintings and Drawings 1880–1930" (London: Sotheby's, 1987), p. 68. The sketch is in the collection of the museum at his former home, the Carl Larsson Garden, Sundborn.

33. For a discussion of the dating of the book, and the author's life, see the Introduction by Francis J. Tschan in his translation of Adam of Bremen, *History of the Archbishops of Hamburg-Bremen* (New York: Columbia University Press, 1959), pp. xiii–xvi.

34. Adam of Bremen, *History*, bk. 1 (v); bk. 2 (lviii). A recent scholarly study of the role of the sacrificial site at Uppsala is Olof Sundqvist, *Freyr's Offspring: Rulers and Religion in Ancient Svea Society* [Historia Religionum, 2] (Uppsala: Uppsala Universitet, 2002).

35. Ibid., bk. 4 (xxv).

36. Ibid., bk. 4, (xxvi).

37. Ibid., schol. 138.

38. Ibid., schol. 139.

39. Ibid., bk. 4, xxvii.

40. Ibid.

41. Ibid.

42. Snorri Sturluson, *Heimskringla: History of the Kings of Norway*, trans. Lee M. Hollander, (Austin: University of Texas Press, 1964), pp. 18f.

43. Ibid., ch. 15.

44. For a list of the some of the archeological sources and their dates and places of discovery, see Wilson, *Vikings and Gods*, p. 103. The most detailed and fascinating analysis, however, appears in Jan Peder Lamm's article "Kring Midvinterblots archeologiska rekvista" in Carl Larsson et al., *Midvinterblot*, pp. 77–95.

45. *The World of Carl Larsson*, p. 41.

46. The 1911–13 study is in oil, 205 x 304 cm, and now at the Dalarnas Museum in Falun; the 1913 study in pencil and watercolor, 44 x 78 cm, is in the National Museum's collection (NMH 64/1921); the final study of 1914–15 in oil, 123 x 199 cm, was most recently purchased at a 2002 auction for 3.2 million Kronor. A number of minor sketches of specific details in the work also exist. Information from Sotheby's, "Scandinavian Paintings and Drawings," p. 68.

47. This entire saga is delineated in detail with many excerpts from the opposing commentators in Arvidsson's essay "Midvinterblot" in *Carl Larsson och National Museum*, pp. 139–79.

48. *The World of Carl Larsson*, p. 41.
49. Quoted in Wilson, p. 68.
50. *Dagens Nyheter* 20 February 1911, quoted in Arvidsson, "Midvinterblot," *Carl Larsson och National Museum*, p. 144. See also Wilson, p. 68.
51. Cf. Snodin and Stavenow-Hidemark, *Carl and Karin Larsson*, p. 60. The Curman villa burnt down in 1878 but has since been rebuilt. Part of what is disconcerting about Larsson's temple is its almost pre-fab uniformity and unrustic appearance. Larsson was also certainly aware of genuine historical predecessors, and it is likely he viewed the remnants of an eleventh-century stave church from Gotland which were exhibited at the Swedish Historical Museum at this time. Georg Sessler, who points this out, calls the temple "a mixture of Dalecarlian log cabin and stave church." See his introduction to *Midwinter Sacrifice* (Stockholm: Nationalmuseum, 2007), pp. 10f.
52. Cf. various images of the house in ibid., pp. 98–101.
53. *The World of Carl Larsson*, p. 41. The work is in fact composed of two horizontally oriented canvases; the upper painting (which was actually executed by Gustaf Magnusson according to Larsson's instructions) measures 280 x 1360 cm and the lower painting 360 x 1360 cm. Details from Sotheby's, "Scandinavian Paintings and Drawings," p. 68, though this never mentions Magnusson's contribution.
54. Arvidsson, "Midvinterblot," *Carl Larsson och National Museum*, pp. 171–2.
55. Larsson, *Autobiography*, p. 175.
56. Quoted in Görel Cavalli-Björkman, "Carl Larsson and Midwinter Sacrifice," in *Midwinter Sacrifice*, p. 14.
57. Holger Arbman, "En arkeolog ser på 'Midvinterblot'," op. cit. note 28.
58. See note 65. Bjürstrom wrote a second article in 1995 entitled *"Midvinterblot* och tidsandan" (*Midvinterblot* and the Zeitgeist) that appeared in issue 29 of the journal *Res Publica*, pp. 146–58.
59. *Vi*, 2 (1982), referred to in Olov Isaksson, "En vida bättre plats..." in Carl Larsson et al., *Midvinterblot*, p. 5.
60. At this time the Historical Museum published a useful 96-page book in its "Historia I fickformat" series on the history of the painting's conception and subsequent controversy as related through articles by Larsson and various commentators. See Carl Larsson et al., *Midvinterblot* (op. cit. note 26).

61. This entire convoluted chain of events is detailed in the pamphlet "Midvinterblot: Sveriges mest omdiskuterade målning" (Stockholm: Nationalmuseum, n.d.), on which I have based some of my chronological account. Cavalli-Björkman's "Carl Larsson and Midwinter Sacrifice" in *Midwinter Sacrifice*, pp. 14–16, also fills in essential details, some of which were further clarified for me by Ulwa Neergaard.

62. See the catalog for the complete listing of the 25 March 1987 auction of "Scandinavian Paintings and Drawings 1880–1930" (op. cit.). *Midvinterblot* was Lot 72 with an estimated sale price of £700,000–£1,000,000 (see p. 68). The actual sale price was £800,000 (= $1,288,000 according to exchange rates at the time, or approx. 8.8 million Swedish Kroner), the highest price paid for any work in the 348-lot auction. My thanks to Olena Whipple of the Sotheby's Library in New York City for her kind assistance researching the sale of the painting.

63. Sotheby's, "Scandinavian Paintings and Drawings," p. 68.

64. There is a small touch of irony in that it was auctioned off to someone in Japan, as Larsson had once written in his 1895 book *De Mina* (My Loved Ones), "for me as an artist, Japan is my mother country" (cf. *The World of Carl Larsson*, p. 53). His own work was influenced by Japanese illustration, and various Japanese prints and objects were displayed in his home. Reciprocally, his art has been popular in Japan since the 1970s. The Japanese art collector is alleged to be Dr. Hiroshi Ishizuka, whose collection includes a number of European masterworks, although the Swedish press has kept his identity anonymous.

65. An example of a new debate—or an attempt to start one—would be Per Bjurström's article "Vad berättar Midvinterblot" (What Does *Midvinterblot* Narrate?) in *Konsthistorisk tidskrift*, Vol. LXIV, Issue 1 (1995), pp. 4–15. Bjurström argues that the painting should be removed from the National Museum because it is informed by a thinly veiled racist-political subtext that depicts primitive Lapps—à la Jews in the Nazi worldview—as a threat to the racial hygiene of noble Swedes. Bjurström's argument is questionable for numerous reasons, and he makes a poor case for Larsson being a racist propagandist. The article seems to reveal more about its author's own political views than those of Larsson, as becomes apparent in a rhapsody about the 1968 left-wing student rebellions on p. 12. A similarly political attack of sorts came from the artists' group the Vaners ("the Vanirs," referring to the myth-

ical tribe of Northern fertility gods and goddesses) who offered to donate their "Midsummer [1666 B.C.E.])" painting to the museum in 1998. This would replace *Midvinterblot* with a fanciful gynocratic vision of ancient northern society. They claimed their painting also beat out *Midvinterblot* by a few square feet for the Guinness World Record (since surpassed by other works) for the largest painting on canvas. See <www.vaners.com/midsummer-gig.html>. More importantly it would replace the "war, violence, and chaos" of Larsson's vision with "peace, love, and harmony." Apparently the museum was unimpressed by this elaborate gesture. An example of the painting's long-overdue recognition by the National Museum is the latter's recent publication of a large-format book featuring beautiful close-up color photographs of the work by Georg Sessler and Per Myrehed, and texts by Sessler and Görel Cavalli-Björkman. See *Midvinterblot* (Stockholm: Nationalmuseum, 2007). A simultaneous English-language edition has been issued under the title *Midwinter Sacrifice* (op. cit.).

66. Larsson, *Autobiography*, pp. 174–75.

67. Arvidsson, "Midvinterblot," *Carl Larsson och National Museum*, p. 149.

68. Larsson, *Autobiography*, p. 174. Translation slightly adapted.

69. In certain old Germanic traditions, water is also the source from which new souls arise or are formed. See Hans-Peter Hasenfratz, *Die Germanen: Religion, Magie, Kult, Mythus* (Erfstadt: HOHE-Verlag, 2007), p. 73.

70. Arvidsson, "Midvinterblot," *Carl Larsson och National Museum*, p. 149.

71. Quoted in Snodin and Stavenow-Hidemark, *Carl and Karin Larsson*, p. 45.

72. Madeleine von Heland, "Karin and Carl Larsson" in *Carl Larsson* (New York: Brooklyn Museum, 1982), p. 64. Von Heland also states (p. 61): "Carl was aware of his dependence on Karin and at least subconsciously often plagued by it. Over and over again he filled his portraits of her with scissors, knives, and needles, as if she wanted to cut, stab, or prick him to death."

73. Larsson, *Autobiography*, p. 189.

74. Georg Sessler, introduction to *Midwinter Sacrifice* (Stockholm: Nationalmuseum, 2007), p. 12.

75. Larsson, *Autobiography*, p. 189.

76. Larsson, *Autobiography*, p. 175, translation slightly amended.

Pagan Christmas

The Plants, Spirits, and Rituals at the Origins of Yuletide

CHRISTIAN RÄTSCH and CLAUDIA MÜLLER-EBELING

The history of Christmas provides a unique view of the religion that existed in Europe before the introduction of Christianity. This evolving feast has over the centuries absorbed elements from cultures all over the world—practices that give plants and plant spirits pride of place. The authors contend that the emphasis of Christmas on green plants, and the promise of the return of life in the dead of winter, is an adaptation of the pagan winter solstice celebration. In fact, the symbolic use of plants at Christmas effectively transforms the modern-day living room into a place of shamanic ritual.

$24.95, paper, 224 pages, 8 x 10, 156 color and 40 b&w illustrations, ISBN-13: 978-1-59477-092-0

INNER TRADITIONS
BEAR & COMPANY

For these and other great titles visit us at www.InnerTraditions.com
800-246-8648

The Little Wonder Series Presents
ON GNOMING
A Pocket Guide to the Successful Hunting and Cooking of Gnomes

If you like gnomes, then you'll love eating them! Foremost fairy authority Reginald Bakeley outlines the principles of hunting and cooking these small, malignant, and particularly tasty woodland creatures. The pamphlet is both informative and a little humorous.

Bakeley details the best tactics for gnome hunting whether you prefer to go it alone, with a partner, or with a hound, and covers bagging techniques using slingshots, bows, clubs, and rifles. You'll get prepared for the big hunt with useful notes on proper attire and the best way to camouflage yourself against the gnome's keen senses. There is also a helpful section on troll hunting. Of course, no one would willingly eat troll meat because it tastes awful. Bakeley includes this section in case you ever happen to meet a dangerous troll while out gnoming.

On Gnoming: 12 pp., 2 illustrations

Also Available: **Goblinproofing One's Chicken Coop** (An Instructional Pamphlet for Use in Successful Animal Husbandry), by Reginald Bakeley; **Lewis Carroll's Croquet Companion** (Rules for Arithmetical Croquet and Croquet Castles) by Lewis Carroll, with an introduction by Reginald Bakeley; **Murphy's Smear** (An Account of the Controversy Surrounding the World's First Specimen of Fairy Phlegm) by Percival Dwight; **Lanrick**, by Lewis Carroll; **Non Libri Sed Liberi**, by Kenneth Grahame. Little Wonder pamphlets are designed like single book signatures and are printed at 4½ by 6½ inches on 67 lb. Vellum Bristol paper. They are wonderful to hold and will appeal to antique and rare book collectors. Send $3 per copy, including $1 with each order to cover shipping costs. Please make checks payable to "Clint Marsh."

Two of Wonderella's other pamphlet series have been collected in handsome editions by Weiser Books. These hardcover books are available through Wonderella Printed. Inquire for price and availability:
The Museum of Lost Wonder (A Visual History of the Human Imagination) by Jeff Hoke
The Mentalist's Handbook (An Explorer's Guide to Astral, Spirit, and Psychic Worlds) by Clint Marsh, with a foreword and illustrations by Jeff Hoke

Wonderella Printed
PUBLISHERS OF PRACTICAL ESOTERICA
Post Office Box 10145
Berkeley, Calif. 94709

Complimentary catalog available via post

Visit us online at www.wonderella.org

Iceland's Pagan Renaissance

Christopher McIntosh

There is no place where you can feel the spirit of Iceland more strongly than at Thingvellir, the place of the Thing, the country's ancient parliamentary assembly. It is located in the middle of a long, narrow gorge that lies exactly on the rift between the great continental plates of Europe and North America. On either side loom cliffs that look in places like walls crudely built of great cyclopean blocks. A waterfall, dropping like a long silver ribbon from the rock face, feeds into a stream running down to the largest lake in Iceland, Thingvallavatn, which stretches away to the south. There are enormous elemental forces here, and one feels that the gods are close at hand. Thingvellir is also a place of great significance in the religious history of Iceland. It was here in the year 1000 that the decision was taken to accept Christianity, and today it is a place intimately connected with the renaissance of the old religion, called Ásatrú by its present-day followers. After many centuries the site is once again the meeting place of the Thing, as the Ásatrú community call their annual midsummer assembly.

At the Thingvellir in June 2003 I witnessed the installation of the present Allsherjargoði (chief *goði*, or priest, of Ásatrú), Hilmar Örn Hilmarsson, a friend of many years' standing. A crowd of over a hundred, including press and broadcast media, were assembled on the grassy slopes of the gorge. Many Viking Age costumes were in evidence, and a forest of flagpoles with colourful banners had been planted in the ground, some of the banners depicting the symbols of the assembled *goðar* (plural of *goði*), others showing the four guardian creatures of Iceland—bull, dragon, eagle, and giant—that protect the four compass points of the country. The newly elected Allsherjargoði, accompanied by a dozen or so leading *goðar*—all dressed in ceremonial costumes—ascended a natural podium of rock facing the spectators. Torches and a fire bowl blazed in the evening light. The *goðar* stepped up in turn to give speeches of welcome and to read from the *Edda* and the ancient Icelandic laws. Then the new Allsherjargoði took his oath, drank from a mead horn, and delivered his inaugural speech.

It was a deeply moving occasion and a demonstration of how far the pagan religion in Iceland has come since it was officially revived

INSTALLATION OF HILMAR ÖRN HILMARSSON AS ALLSHERJARGOÐI, 26 JUNE 2003. HAVING TAKEN HIS OATH, THE NEW ALLSHERJARGOÐI DRINKS FROM A MEAD HORN. (PHOTO COURTESY OF THE AUTHOR)

some three decades ago. A few other European countries, the latest being Denmark, have now recognised paganism as a legitimate religion. But Iceland is one of the few countries where one can one speak of a real spiritual continuity between pre-Christian paganism and that of the present day.

Until the forced conversion, Icelandic pagans and Christians lived together in relative harmony, but this peaceful coexistence was brought to an end by the Norwegian King Olaf Tryggvason, a zealous convert to Christianity who threatened to kill or maim all Icelandic men living in Norway unless the country declared itself Christian. Under this pressure the Thing was convened, and a much respected *goði* named Thorgeir was asked to reach a decision. Thorgeir went off to meditate, lying under a bull's hide, as the tradition was on such occasions, and came back with the decision that the country should accept Christianity. Certain concessions, however, were made to paganism, including permission to continue sacrificing to the old gods as long as it was done in private.

Even these small concessions, however, were too much for the more zealous Christians, and over the next few centuries the

Church tried repeatedly to exterminate the old beliefs. These attempts never succeeded, partly because Iceland was so far away from the heart of Europe, partly because the Icelanders were clever at prevaricating when orders came from Rome, and partly also because even certain of the clergy were prepared to compromise with paganism to a degree. Nevertheless, in the course of time the old beliefs went underground. They ceased to be part of any systematic religious practice, but they lived on in the hearts and minds of the Icelanders, waiting until the time was ripe for them to surface again.

I believe there are a number of factors that account for why paganism was able to survive in this way and why there is today such a strong pagan revival in Iceland. Probably the most important factor is the old Icelandic literature, notably the *Eddas* and the sagas. These writings have always had a sacred character for the Icelanders, and even when a family emigrated from Iceland they usually carried their copy of the *Edda* with them. The *Edda* (the name means "great-grandmother") is our main source for what we know today about the old gods. There are essentially two versions of it: one is the *Younger* or *Prose Edda*, often called Snorri's *Edda* after Snorri Sturluson who composed it in the thirteenth century. Snorri was a curious mixture of scholar, poet, politician, and libertine, who came to a violent end when he was murdered by his son-in-law in a complex family quarrel. Many accounts describe him as being corrupt, venal, and unscrupulous, but he wrote beautifully, and his *Edda* is one of the world's great books. It is essentially a handbook for poets in which he combines instructions of the art of poetry writing with accounts of the old myths and legends and with quotations from an earlier collection of poetry. This earlier source, which came to light later, is now called the *Poetic* or *Elder Edda*.

The most complete manuscript of the *Elder Edda*, the so-called *Codex Regius*, was kept for many centuries in Denmark along with other ancient Icelandic manuscripts such as the *Flateyjarbók*, which contains a collection of heroic sagas. After long negotiations, the Danes finally agreed in 1971 to give these two books back to Iceland, and their arrival by ship at Reykjavík was a major national event. When they were carried ashore a brass band played, there were jubilant speeches from leading politicians, and a crowd of many thousands lined the harbour cheering their heads off. It was a demonstration of how precious these writings are to the Icelanders. The two manuscripts, along with other historic documents, can now be seen in the Culture House, an exhibition centre in Reykjavík.

The importance of these writings for the survival of paganism has been confirmed by Sigurður Nordal (1886–1974), a writer in many different genres and one of the most influential scholars of the twentieth century in the field of Icelandic literature. Sigurður said that anyone who studies the *Edda* and the other old sources deeply cannot avoid becoming a pagan. For him the study of these sources was no mere academic exercise. It was a process akin to biblical exegesis, which uncovered certain profound truths belonging to the unbroken heritage of the Icelanders. Sigurður was one of a number of literary scholars who, through studying these texts, developed a profound sympathy for the old beliefs.

Another group of people who helped to keep the pre-Christian traditions alive were the poets—or *skalds* as they were called—traditional bards, who were and still are also seers and keepers of folk memory. A glance at Snorri's *Edda* reveals the rich and complex poetic tradition of Iceland, with its *kennings* (elaborate poetic circumlocutions), its store of imagery, its different metres and rhythms, and its ability to convey many levels of meaning at the same time. This tradition has been kept alive in certain families, handed down from one generation to the next, along with certain special techniques for chanting the verses, which can put the listener into a kind of trance. In a car journey across the Icelandic countryside, Hilmar Hilmarsson pointed out to me that places traditionally associated with the poets often have the prefix *saur-* (possibly an earlier word for "sow") as in Saurir (place of the sow) or Saurbær (sow farm). As one of the names of the goddess Freya is *sýr* (sow), these places appear to indicate that the poets were dedicated to Freya and the Vanir (one of the two groups of Nordic gods). Significantly, as we shall see, it was one of these traditional poets who officially revived the old religion.

The Icelandic language is a marvellous medium for poetry, and modern Icelandic is not very far removed from the language in which the *Eddas* were written, creating a further sense of continuity with the ancient times and beliefs. Keen to protect the integrity of the language, the Icelanders prefer to coin new Icelandic words when the need arises, rather than simply borrowing terms from English. Even with the endlessly expanding vocabulary of information technology they have been fairly successful in this regard. For example, instead of "computer" the Icelanders say *tölva*, from the word *tala* (genitive *tölu*), meaning "number."

WOMEN IN VIKING AGE COSTUMES AT THE RECONSTRUCTED WEST ICELAND HOUSE OF ERIK THE RED, WHO COLONISED GREENLAND IN 985 C.E. (PHOTO COURTESY OF THE AUTHOR)

Another factor contributing to the survival of paganism is the widespread belief in the elves. These are seen as a race of mysterious and elusive beings, who have certain supernatural powers but are in many ways similar to human beings—living in communities, working, marrying, and reproducing. This belief has a semi-official status in Iceland, and sometimes it is considered necessary to negotiate with the elves, such as when a building project is to be carried out on land traditionally inhabited by an elf community. On these occasions the Icelanders rely on an elderly woman called Erla Stefánsdottir, a legend in her lifetime, who is the country's *de facto* envoy to the elves. Not long ago, as a result of her negotiations, an oil company shifted the location of a projected filling station because the original site was on elf land. Highway plans have also been altered for the same reason, after bitter experience of roads mysteriously crumbling when they were built without elf permission.

To go against the elves is considered highly dangerous, as many stories confirm. One particularly tragic incident happened some years ago in a remote valley in the area known as the North-Western Fjords, where a young farmer wanted to build a house, against the advice of his father, who told him that there were elves

ÁSATRÚ CEREMONY. THE MAN IN THE CENTRE, WITH THE BOY, HAD REQUESTED A KIND OF ÁSATRÚ "BAR MITZVAH" OR CEREMONY OF PASSAGE FOR HIMSELF (NOT THE SON). HERE THE ALLSHERJARGOÐI (LEFT) CONDUCTS THE CEREMONY, WATCHED BY SOME LEADING GOÐAR (RIGHT). THIS TOOK PLACE JUST AFTER HILMAR'S INSTALLATION. (PHOTO COURTESY OF THE AUTHOR)

living at the spot. The story goes that when the young man insisted on going ahead, his father said: "Very well, as long as I live nothing untoward will happen, but when I die you will have to beware." The house was built, and the farmer and his family lived there in peace until one December when the father died. A few days later came a heavy snowfall, and in the night the house was struck by an avalanche that killed the farmer's wife and children. He himself survived but went mad shortly afterwards. In the light of such stories it is not surprising that even the local authorities take the elves seriously. In the same area, I visited a couple that had applied for permission to build an extension to their house. When two inspectors from the local building authority came to call, one of the first questions they asked was whether there were elves living there. As the answer was no, the permission was granted without hindrance. I came across a particularly amusing example of the belief in the elves while driving with Hilmar Hilmarsson through a wild, rocky part of the countryside. Near a small house by the roadside were several rocks, standing perhaps one or two metres high, each of which was painted with a front door and a house number. Evidently the elderly woman who lived in the house had painted the rocks in this way as homes for the elves.

There is also a strong survival of certain traditional beliefs concerning death. According to the ancient writings one of the places where the dead reside is under the earth in certain mountains. The most famous of these is Helgafell (Holy Mountain), and it is related in the sagas how dead heroes live there in a magnificent great hall, spending their time feasting, drinking, and singing. The *Landnámabók* (a record of the early settlement of Iceland) mentions a number of families who believed that after death they would enter some particular hill or mountain in their locality, and this belief is found in certain areas to this day. One farmer whom I met in the North-Western Fjords pointed out a sloping piece of ground near his house and said that this was a place where the spirits of the dead resided and therefore it could never be built on.

All of these traditions are evidence of how deeply the pagan worldview is rooted in Iceland. As Hilmar put it to me: "We have these things in our blood." So it was natural that, when the time was ripe, the old religion would be formally revived. A number of things helped to prepare the ground for this revival. One was the work of scholars like Sigurður Nordal, who began with a literary interest in the old writings and ended up as pagans. Another person who paved the way was Helgi Pjeturs, a distinguished geologist and writer, who lived from the late nineteenth to the early twentieth century. Helgi developed a belief system that he called "Nyall," and his followers (who are still active today) are known as the Nyallsinnar ("believers in the Nyall"). The system is a complex mixture of Nordic mythology, astronomy, evolutionary biology, and various other elements. Human beings, according to the Nyall, are images of the gods, who live in another part of the universe and attempt to push human evolution forward. At the same time a kind of Manichean contest is continually going on between two cosmic forces, that of *Lifstefna* (the force of life or creation) and *Helstefna* (the force of destruction). Our task is to assist the gods in promoting the former and thus raising our world to a higher level.

The real founder of modern Ásatrú, however, was a farmer and poet named Sveinbjörn Beinteinsson (1924–1993). He came from a family of many clairvoyants and poets, and learned from his father the art of *rímur*, the traditional way of chanting poetry, in due course becoming the most famous *rímur* chanter in Iceland. Various recordings exist of him chanting poems from the *Edda* in a strangely haunting, hypnotic tone. In the latter part of his life he found himself something of a cult figure in the Icelandic pop music scene and contributed to a number of albums by avant-garde groups. Sveinbjörn, an impressive looking man with an enormous white beard, believed firmly in the old gods and said that he had once met Odin himself when walking in the countryside. By the 1970s he felt the time was ripe for an official revival of the old religion. After initial resistance from the government, this was accomplished without any change in the country's constitution, which was found to contain a somewhat vaguely phrased clause allowing for the recognition of Ásatrú—a Danish term, probably of nineteenth-century coinage, which up to then had been seldom used and means roughly "loyalty to the Æsir" (one of the two groups of Nordic gods). Thus Ásatrú became the official name of the pagan religion in Iceland, and has of course since been adopted by many followers of the Nordic religion throughout the world.

So it was that in 1973 Ásatrú became one of Iceland's official religions, with initially only a handful of followers. Hilmar Hilmarsson joined in 1974 at the age of sixteen, when there were some thirty members. Today there are more than a thousand official members (plus many more sympathisers), and their number is steadily growing. They include many prominent people—university professors, journalists, artists, and at least one member of Parliament. The Allsherjargoði himself is well known as a musician and composer of film music, who has been widely honoured for his scores for films such as *Children of Nature, Cold Fever, In the Cut*, and more recently *Beowulf and Grendel*. His name is frequently coupled with that of the phenomenally successful Icelandic music group Sigur Rós (meaning "victory rose"), for whom he often writes and performs musical pieces with Nordic pagan themes. They have drawn huge audiences in London, Oslo, Reykjavík, and elsewhere with their rendering of an ancient Icelandic poem called *Odin's Raven Magic*. The performances feature an orchestra, a choir, and the soloist Steindór Andersen, a bearded giant of a man, by profession a fisherman, who could have stepped out of the pages of a saga. One of the instruments used is a huge stone *marimba*, made by the artist and sculptor Páll Gudmundsson from flat pieces of stone found in the vicinity of his home. This fusion of avant-garde Icelandic music with the poetry and mythology of the ancient religion is one of the most exciting features of the modern Ásatrú scene and a sign of its great vitality (see also Joshua Buckley's review of the Sigur Rós album *Rímur* in *TYR* 2, pp. 378–80).

ARTIST, SCULPTOR, AND MUSICIAN PÁLL GUDMUNDSSON AT HIS STONE "MARIMBA," WHICH HE SOMETIMES PLAYS AT SIGUR RÓS CONCERTS. (PHOTO COURTESY OF THE AUTHOR)

Ásatrú is today firmly established in Iceland. The Ásatrúarfélagið (Ásatrú Fellowship) has its own headquarters in Reykjavík, and there is now a project, supported by the city council, to build a proper Ásatrú temple in the city. On the organisational level, the Ásatrú community has a leading group of between five and eight *goðar*, called the Lögrétta (meaning roughly the "law-giving group"). In contrast to pagan communities in other countries, there have so far been no splinter groups. The title *goði* is very selectively conferred. In order to become a *goði* one has to fulfil certain strict criteria, such as being able to prove a detailed knowledge of the *Edda* and the other ancient sources.

The Ásatrúar celebrate four great annual festivals, coinciding approximately with the equinoxes and solstices, and a number of smaller ones. The most important festival, which is also the annual assembly of the community, is the one that takes place at the summer solstice and is known as the Thing. As already mentioned, this is held at Thingvellir. In between there are smaller rituals, such as weddings and funerals. Relations with the Christian churches are ambivalent and often tense. Many people in the churches do not want to accept the existence of Ásatrú as an official religion, and sometimes the Ásatrúar have to fight hard for their rights. On the other hand, among certain sections of the Christian community there is often a degree of tolerance towards Ásatrú. This is illustrated by a monument created by Páll Guðmundsson at Skálholt, site of the country's first Christian church, about sixty kilometres east of Reykjavík. The monument is in the form of two stone reliefs side by side, one showing the god Thor with his hammer, the other showing the first Icelandic bishop Ísleifur Gissurarson (installed 1052, died 1080). Furthermore, the borderline between Christianity and paganism is often blurred. A number of people told me that they had been brought up as Christians but that deep down they had always been pagan.

How much of a connection exists with the original paganism remains a matter of debate. Occasionally a relic of the earlier religion turns up, such as the ceremonial stone bowl known as a *hlautbolli*, found in the Western Fjords. This used to be filled with the blood of an ox and carried by the *goði*, who went around the circle of worshippers, flicking the blood at them with a twig. This practice is not part of present-day Ásatrú, but some people argue that the word *blót* (ritual) is related to *blóð* (blood). "Thirty years ago," Hilmar told me, "if you had asked people what the word *blót* meant they would have said it was something sacrilegious. Today they would probably see it as something positive. The word has been recaptured, resanctified." This is a measure of how far Ásatrú in Iceland has come since 1972 and an encouraging sign for other pagan communities in the world.

HILMAR ÖRN HILMARSSON HOLDING A STONE "HLAUTBOLLI,"
OR RITUAL BOWL, FOUND IN THE WESTERN FJORDS.
(PHOTO COURTESY OF THE AUTHOR)

Appendix: Hilmar Örn Hilmarsson in His Own Words

As the article above relates, Hilmar Örn Hilmarsson is not only the current leader of Ásatrú in Iceland, he is also a successful composer and popular musician. He has worked with performers like Sigur Rós, Björk, Psychic TV, The Hafler Trio, and Current 93, and recently composed the score for Sturla Gunnarsson's film *Beowulf and Grendel*. The comments below were excerpted from an interview by Dominik Tischleder for the German magazine *Zinnober*.

On becoming Allsherjargoði:

I became Allsherjargoði because there had been a leadership crisis, and I stepped in because I could be a uniting factor while things were sorted out. I joined the Ásatrúarfélagið on my sixteenth birthday, less than a year after it got official recognition. So I have been part of this for the better part of my life. I do not think I will remain in this position for long, but I am willing to do whatever it takes to help the Ásatrúarfélagið to thrive.

On Ásatrú outside Iceland:

We try not to get too involved with other movements abroad. And we do not want Iceland to become the "Rome" of the North. Stretching that analogy further, there are many people in this area who are "more Catholic than the Pope" and that sort of mindset is impossible to deal with. The *Eddas* are also a part of a vibrant and dynamic tradition of poetry that has been with us for over a thousand years, and those who rely on translations sometimes ignore this fact.

On early musical influences:

My greatest formative influence was the composer and organist Páll Ísólfsson, who was married to my grandmother's sister. We lived in the same house and I spent a lot of time with him. He was the first non-German to be hired as an organist at the St. Thomas Church in Leipzig and was considered one of the five best Bach interpreters in the world. He was a tremendous influence regarding music, literature, and philosophy, and he taught me to listen to the sea and the wind and to hear the symphonies played out in nature. So I guess it can all be traced back to him.

On Iceland's musical heritage:

Iceland is such a paradoxical place, where opposites meet and unite all the time, and I think that being surrounded by these extremes is bound to surface in your art—whether it be literature, painting, film, or music. Many Icelandic composers have been mining the tradition for the better part of the last century and there are also some sounds that seem to "be in the air" as it were.

Going into the highlands is a unique and wonderful experience, and if that does not make you break into song, nothing on earth ever will.

THE RETURN OF A CLASSIC

"The book's great strength is in the clarity of vision it offers. . ."
—Steve Pollington, *Wiðowinde*

"For those who are just starting to learn about Ásatrú, this book will provide a firm grounding in both lore and modern understanding; for those more experienced, the plurality of ideas presented should provide new ways of looking at and thinking about our theology."
—Ronald Rowand-White, *IDUNNA*

When first published in 1993, *Our Troth* was hailed as the definitive work on Heathenry, ancient and modern. Now, the Troth is proud to announce the publication of the revised second edition of *Our Troth*.

Updated with the latest scholarship on Germanic religion and culture, the second edition of *Our Troth* contains contributions from over fifty Heathen leaders, authors and thinkers, surveying the rich and vibrant spectrum of modern Heathen lore and practice.

Deeply rooted in the past, filled with solid advice for today, and presenting a bold vision for the future. . . *Our Troth* is the single most comprehensive book ever published on Heathenry.

Volume 1: ISBN 1-4196-3616-2 (hardcover)
1-4196-3598-0 (paperback). Published in April 2006.

Volume 2: ISBN 1-4196-3615-4 (hardcover)
1-4196-3614-6 (paperback). Coming in June 2007.

Available from Amazon.com. Or contact BookSurge at 1-866-308-6235, or customerservice@booksurge.com

For more information, contact the Troth at http://www.thetroth.org/

Sveinbjörn Beinteinsson:
A Personal Reminiscence

Jónína K. Berg

At this time, when more than eighty years have elapsed from when the first modern Allsherjargoði, or chief leader, of Icelandic Ásatrú heathenism was born (on 4 July 1924), I want to relate some vignettes and episodes from his life that are rather special.

Sveinbjörn (in Iceland we generally refer to people by their first names) was born on the family farm at Grafardalur in West Iceland. He was the youngest of eight brothers and sisters, all of whom became poets. A selection of the poems written by all the siblings came out in a book a few years ago entitled *Raddir Dalsins* (Voices of the Valley). Besides writing his own compositions, as he grew up Sveinbjörn also liked chanting the rhymes of the ancient, traditional Icelandic poetry.

The poetry of those brothers and sisters from Grafardalur differs from person to person, but something that consistently shines throughout is an intense love of nature and the land, combined with a respect for its *landvættir* (protective spirits) and *huldufólk* (hidden beings). Like those entities of a parallel and often invisible world, the poets also become the protectors of our pure Icelandic water, air, soil, and our nature in general. The folktales and experiences of so many people in Iceland—both today and through the ages past—speak to us not only of elves, *huldufólk*, and *landvættir*, but also ghosts and the spirits of humans and animals, as well as bad places and *álagablettir* ("spellbound places") toward which people should be respectful and aware. In the sagas, for example, we find stories dealing with humans coexisting in harmony with those other worlds and we read there that settlers in East Iceland and at Snæfellsnes in West Iceland gave specific orders stating that no living beings should he harmed in their areas of settlement. There we see a manifestation of pagan thinking: the immense respect for all nature.

When Sveinbjörn was five years old his family moved from Grafardalur to another farm close by and they lived there for five years. They then moved to a more permanent site, a place called Draghals. Those three farms are all fairly close, in a valley in between the same circle of mountains. Later on he always referred

"When he grew a beard he used to say that afterwards 'something' had happened which attracted women to him."
(Photo By Randall Hyman)

to himself as Sveinbjörn á Draghálsi.

Children at that time did not receive much education, just a few weeks in winter and then of course preparation for confirmation which everyone had to go through. Besides this, Sveinbjörn studied for half a winter, in 1940, at a high school in Hafnarfjörður. At age twenty Sveinbjörn started farming on his own at his farm in Draghals. He did not care much for the new farming machines. Therefore most of the work was done the old way, with only the help of a tractor—when he had someone else to drive it. Thus one could say that the farmer and the poet in the heath did the work of farming in his own way, very much like so many other things he liked to do differently. The other farmers in the neighborhood found this strange, and also a bit funny.

There were periods when the poet and the scholar readily grew stronger within himself, and this of course meant research and browsing through old materials, something that required time and traveling. On such occasions some very friendly neighbors would come to his assistance when he had to be away from his farming work. Sveinbjörn was largely self-taught. He was also a passionate collector, especially of old songs, music, and ancient rhymes (*rímur*), and he liked to read old manuscripts at libraries. Although Sveinbjörn had nothing against going to Christian ceremonies, he specifically visited all the churches he could in order to look at the places where they were situated and to measure their length and width. The reason was that in Iceland, in another effort to eradicate heathenism, many churches in the old times were built directly on the places where the ancient people used to hold *"hof,"* or heathen ceremonies.

In a way Sveinbjörn was a loner, but he also enjoyed the company of people. He got along well with children and had a very good rapport with young people. He was a strongly charismatic man and women found him quite attractive. When he grew a beard he used to say that afterwards "something" had happened which attracted women to him.

When Sveinbjörn was in town he liked to have conversations over a cup of coffee or a glass of *Brennivín* (the national liquor of Iceland, similar to aquavit). However, he always left the place before people started to get drunk. The same was true at heathen ceremonies or *"blóts."* He was always a very moderate person; in a way he followed the many examples for restrained conduct given in the Eddic *Hávamál*. Earthly wealth was of no interest to him, nor did he care about elite approval or the like. He lived very frugally. This is evident from the fact that he never owned a car and never installed electricity at his farm in Draghals.

Sveinbjörn was a prolific poet who published a number of books. Concerning his writings on his own poetry, old Icelandic poetry, and the poetry of West Iceland, there is one book in particular that should be mentioned. The winter of 1949–51 was a very bad one in Iceland, mainly due to a plague of *jagziekte*, a disease that decimated the sheep population. At Sveinbjörn's farm in Draghals all the sheep had to be killed. At that time, this farmer who had lost all his sheep wrote a famous and most extraordinary book. It is a book that I consider as one of the greatest works in Icelandic, and even superior to a similar book written by the renowned poet, historian, and political leader Snorri Sturluson (1179–1241). When Snorri wrote his book *Háttatal* in the Middle Ages he illustrated the various aspects of traditional poetic style and composition not with his own poems, but through those of other poets. Sveinbjörn, on the other hand, in his 1951 book *Bragfræði og Háttatal*, describes the many and varied ways of composing poems in Icelandic—an incredibly complex, subtle world, offering a multitude of stylistic potentials. He does this with twenty of his poems connected in context, and with each stanza illustrating different metrical applications, rules, and even rhyming letters suited for the different rhyme schemes: internal, middle, or end rhyme. The poems in the book offer a total of 450 stanzas, all demonstrating variations in poetic meter and style. This remarkable book is really a most comprehensive treatise describing all the complex approaches that can be used to compose poetry in Icelandic.

My earliest memory of Sveinbjörn is a day when I was seven years old and this strange yet friendly character visited my school, chanting the traditional *rímur* and other ancient poems, telling stories about the old times and from our ancient heathen past and history, as well as tales of the old gods and goddesses. Afterwards he approached me and asked my name, where I was from, and so on, and from that moment on we entered into a very good and friendly relationship. This was three years before the official foundation of the Ásatrúarfélagið (Ásatrú Fellowship). Like many other people in West Iceland, I naturally took notice when this organization was founded. Besides, my mother was a friend of Sveinbjörn and his family, and she had been doing some work with him regarding poetry and poetic chanting. So very early in life I was introduced to these ancient Icelandic arts and traditions. Two of my

"HE WAS ALSO A PASSIONATE COLLECTOR, ESPECIALLY OF OLD SONGS, MUSIC, AND ANCIENT RHYMES (RÍMUR), AND HE LIKED TO READ OLD MANUSCRIPTS AT LIBRARIES."
(PHOTO BY RANDALL HYMAN)

best friends were also close relatives of Sveinbjörn.

Sveinbjörn was often asked to perform at various gatherings and meetings. After the Ásatrúfélagið was officially established and received considerable attention worldwide, he was much in demand to give lectures, and often chanted ancient poems and spoke about Nordic mythology at various events. Sveinbjörn's tone and delivery, especially when reciting Icelandic poems, had a sort of enchanting power and energy that is difficult to explain to those who never heard him. Somehow he was able to convey the spirit of the sagas, the folklore and the rhythm and intonation of the Icelandic language, something that Sveinbjörn knew so well and loved so much. When he performed in such a way, the Eddic poems, the texts of the ancient manuscripts, and the words of old and new poems, easily and gently came alive to our ears. The vast knowledge Sveinbjörn had of the Icelandic language made it possible for him to faithfully revive the chanting of the Eddic poems, something that is quite extraordinary because for centuries music, dancing, acting, and singing were not allowed to be performed outside a Christian context. When Sveinbjörn "rediscovered" this way of chanting the Eddic poems some of the people at Iðunn (Idun), the traditional society for *rímur* chanting established in 1929, were very skeptical, partly because they thought that he was making it up, and partly because of Christian religious objections.

When I think of our many years of friendship, I feel that what I liked the best about Sveinbjörn was his mild temper, good humor, and his respect for other religious views of life, other practices and customs. For example, the priest who was one of his neighbors was his best friend. Sveinbjörn used to say that it should be very good to get to know different religions and philosophies. But on many occasions he also expressed his deep feelings about the contradiction of how we had been forced to adopt something foreign and distant, so alien to our ancient roots and background, when we already had something so beautiful, so ethical, as the ideas expressed in Ásatrú in our own culture!

Sveinbjörn was very much in favor of always seeking knowledge and always asking questions, because often raising questions is more important than knowing the answers. We frequently engaged in long conversations when I would take him by car from Reykjavík to various destinations, going to many *blóts* at places such as Þingvellir, or to spiritual festivals at Snæfellsjökull (by the glacier), a very powerful and sacred place in West Iceland.

Sveinbjörn took great notice of dreams. He told many people that he never felt alone because he always felt very close to our elves, spirits, and the *huldufólk*. He also had a great interest in the various herbs, berries, and native plants of Iceland. The tea blends that he used to make were very good and he liked to experiment with different herbs. For example, as one of his favorite ingredients he liked to use a little Reindeer Moss, *Cladonia rangiferina*, which he believed had especially beneficial properties. I recall that we tried to find more information about this moss but with no luck. Many years later I heard about research done with this moss that proved that it is strengthening for our immune system.

When he died suddenly of a heart condition on 23 December 1993, Sveinbjörn took lots of knowledge with him. He left much too soon, at a very symbolic time for us, that of the winter solstice. But having been able to establish Ásatrú as an officially recognized "religion" in Iceland—despite much opposition, especially by the large, well-established State Church—is one of his most important legacies, an example that now is being followed in other Scandinavian and North European countries. To this achievement can be added his remarkable work in the fields of Icelandic and Nordic arts and culture.

Sveinbjörn and the Founding of the Ásatrúarfélagið in Iceland

Three decades after the indefatigable efforts of Sveinbjörn and the other founding members of Ásatrúarfélagið finally succeeded, many stories, anecdotes, and descriptions of these events have accumulated that are told and retold—often with inaccuracies and incorrect facts. For this reason I decided to go through my records, memories, and the data of our long friendship, and to talk to some of the people and friends who were well acquainted with Sveinbjörn's efforts, so as to provide, once and for all, as factual an account as possible of the chain of events by which the Ásatrúarfélagið came to be officially recognized.

From his early childhood Sveinbjörn was interested in Nordic mythology, folklore, mysticism, and the sagas. Later on he wanted to form a religious society based on the ideas relating to all this—not merely a club to discuss things, but a genuine religious society with the same rights and obligations as other approved religious organizations.

Things got started in the late winter of 1971–72 when Sveinbjörn, the writer Dagur Þorleifsson, and Jörmundur Ingi Hansen (who would later become Allsherjargoði after Sveinbjörn's death), met each other and discovered that they all wanted to invigorate and renew heathenism in Iceland. They decided to form a society if they could succeed in finding a few more members.

On 20 April 1972, the first day of summer (a very old heathen festival day), twelve women and twelve men gathered in Reykjavík, in the tower-room of the Hotel Borg, to begin work on the foundation of the Ásatrúarfélagið. At a subsequent meeting a little later the establishment of the Ásatrúarfélagið was formally declared and Sveinbjörn was chosen to be the head, the so-called Allsherjargoði, of this new heathen society in Iceland.

The members of the Ásatrúarfélagið were excited, but many people thought that they were not serious or might be just doing this for fun. The Ásatrúarfélagið was not established as some anarchist group to start a revolution, but to show the value of heathen ideas and that it was possible to be a heathen without being in any conflict with the law and order of the society. They discussed legalization and Þorsteinn Guðjónsson, together with Sveinbjörn, started to gather information, run errands, compose writings, and hold discussions concerning this goal.

Two months later at summer solstice the Ásatrúarfélagið had a *blót* at Sveinbjörn's place in Draghals. The media, especially the

"HE TOLD MANY PEOPLE THAT HE NEVER FELT ALONE BECAUSE HE ALWAYS FELT VERY CLOSE TO OUR ELVES, SPIRITS, AND THE 'HULDUFÓLK.'" (PHOTO BY RANDALL HYMAN)

newspapers, took an interest and followed the steps of this new heathen group from the beginning.

Under a dark, misty sky in rough weather, on 18 December 1972, Sveinbjörn and Þorsteinn headed to a meeting with Ólafur Jóhannesson, the Minister of Justice and Church Affairs. Before this, they had sent a letter to the ministry asking for legalization. The minister was very courteous, but not so favorable, and they could tell by the look on his face that he thought they were not serious.

Sveinbjörn presented him with the application for legalization and Þorsteinn stated the reasons for their request, and then they discussed the issue. They did not reach a conclusion and the minister could not give them a direct answer. He referred to the Icelandic law on religious societies and asked them to provide documents such as identification papers, bylaws, and the number of members of the Ásatrúarfélagið. Ólafur walked them to the door, and, as they stepped out of the ministry, thunder and lightning struck, the electricity went out in the center of Reykjavík, and the minister was left in the darkness. A story quickly developed that a bolt of lightning had struck the ministry itself, but the truth is that it hit the adjacent building and caused some damage. Afterwards, people used to say both seriously and humorously that with this lightning the god Þór (Thor) was taking action because of the delay of the Ásatrúarfélagið in getting approved or legalized. It has also been said that without the lightning, it would have been more difficult to get it legally approved.

The bishop of Iceland, Sigurbjörn Einarsson, was against the legalization. According to the law of religious societies at that time, the bishop had a say regarding applications for legalization of different religious societies. Minister Ólafur knew better, though, and did not allow this to sway his decision.

On 3 May 1973 the Ásatrúarfélagið received a letter from the Ministry of Justice and Church Affairs stating that the decision of the members of Ásatrúarfélagið about Sveinbjörn being a *goði* was approved and that he was invited for a meeting with the state prosecutor, where the decisions would be given to Sveinbjörn.

He went there on 16 May and received a document stating that he was the head of Ásatrúarfélagið, now fully and legally approved with all due rights and obligations. By this time the number of members had increased to twenty-one.

The first weekend of August the same year, the Ásatúarfélagið held a *blót* at Sveinbjörn's place and, later in the autumn, another *blót* at the Sigtún dancehall in Reykjavík.

Sveinbjörn said that he was hardly ever aware of any real animosity toward paganism or its background and the legalization. He and the Ásatrúarfélagið have always tried to avoid extremists, never attacked other religions, never try to convert others, and never tried to tell others that Ásatrú is the only right faith.

Sveinbjörn's way of working was very much like how his friend and well-known poet Þorsteinn frá Hamri described it, that he never put pressure on things—not on time, nor his surroundings, nor on other people.

As my last thought, I can just say this: His form of art, and Sveinbjörn Beinteinsson himself, were and are more Icelandic than almost anything we consider as such.

Sources:

Beinteinsson, Sveinbjörn. *Bragfræði og háttatal.* Reykjavík: Leiftur, 1953.

Beinteinsson, Sveinbjörn and Gunnarsdóttir Berglind. *Allsherjargoðinn.* Akranes: Hörpuútgáfan, 1992.

Magnússon, Jón, ed. *Raddir Dalsins.* Akranes: Hörpuútgáfan, 1993.

Selected Poems

Sveinbjörn Beinteinsson

Draumur

Heimdallur kallar á hugarfund
hjálpi mér Freyr og Njörður,
ás hinn almáttki alla stund
ókvíðinn Miðgarðsvörður.

Alkyrra hálfbjarta óttustund
orð og myndsýnir birtust
komnir á nýjan fagnaðsfund
fornhelgir guðir virtust.

Upptök draums þessa einn ég veit
ekki má leyndum svifta
hér vill goðliðsins göfug sveit
gleymskutjaldinu lyfta.

Skyldist mér þá hvað skáldið kvað
skaphljóma dýrra laga
lyfti hug yfir lágan stað
ljóðmál úr stefi Braga.

Verði bjartara ljós um láð
lífgrös á jörðu dafni
styrkri hendi sé stöfum skráð
stefið í Óðins nafni.

Dream[1]

Heimdallur summons a meeting of minds
help me Freyr and Njörður,
the Almighty of all times,
the guardian of Miðgarð fears nothing.

Stillness, half-bright, half-dark,
words and visions appeared

the ancient sacred gods seemed to be
back to a meeting of celebration.

Only I know the origin of this dream
not allowed to unveil secrecy
noble flock of deities
shall lift the veil of forgetfulness.

I understand what the poet chanted
noble songs about fate
the lyric language of poet Bragi
lifted the mind high above.

Let brightness shine over the earth
healing herbs growing well,
strongly in the name of Óðin
let songs and poems be written.

Staka

Dularmögn frá eldri öldum
óspillt þögnin dró að sér,
rímuð sögn af römmum völdum
rökkurfögnuð veitti mér.

Staka[2]

Hidden magical powers from old ages
brought in by the stillness
rhymed stories of strong forces
have given me joy at dusk.

Dís

Hitinn af bálinu
birtan af grjótinu
ljóðið í nóttinni
ljósið í trénu
seiðurinn í augunum;
góðar eru gjafir þínar
geymi ég þær.

Líður dagur í ljóði
löngun dró mig að söngvum
fagurt kvað fugl í skógi
flest er skylt við það besta
verður mér enn að orðum
undur þessara stunda
þaðan af þú skalt ráða
þínum hug og mínum.

Dís[3]

Heat of fire
glow of rocks
poem of this night
light of this tree
magic of your eyes
your precious gifts to me
I shall keep within me.

The day goes in a poem
always I was drawn to songs
the bird sang so beautifully in the forest
most things were at their best
the wonder of those moments
still now brings me words
from that moment you are leading
your thoughts and mine

Vorkoma

Þó mig goð eða gyðjur dreymi
ein er sú dís að ég aldrei gleymi.
Loks kom vorið með ljóð frá henni
sem heilagur eldur í hug mér brenni.
Ylinn leggur frá orðum þínum
klakinn hverfur úr huga mínum.
Aldrei vermdi mig vorið betur.
Þetta gat skeð eftir þungan vetur.

Álfar vilja að orð mín geymi
Kveðju til þín frá huliðsheimi.

Spring Comes

Though I have dreams of gods and goddesses
there is one of the *dísir* I shall never forget.
Finally Spring came with a poem from her
as a sacred fire burning in my mind.
Warmth comes from your words
ice disappears from my mind.
Spring never gave me such warmth as now
and this happens after so heavy a winter.

The elves want me to convey this message to you:
Good wishes from the hidden world!

Kveðja

Heimsins vegur hulinn er
huga manns og vilja,
enginn þarf að ætla sér
örlög sín að skilja.

Trúin hrein og hugsun djörf
Hjálpa mest í raunum,
Þakkir fyrir fögur störf
Flyt ég þér að launum.

Farewell[4]

The road of the world is hidden
from one's mind and will,
no one needs
to understand fate.

Clear belief and brave thinking
are the best help in trouble,
Many thanks for your beautiful works
are the best rewards I bring you.

*(Translated with notes by
Carlos B. Hagen-Lautrup III and Jónína K. Berg)*

Notes:

1. In the first stanza of this poem, lines 1 and 4, Sveinbjörn describes, as a narrator, what he observes. Then in the same stanza, in lines 2 and 3, he quotes an almost sacred summons that even today in Iceland is solemnly pronounced on high and important occasions and celebrations, and especially at the seasonal *blóts*.

   Heimdallur is the name of the deity chosen by the gods of the Æsir pantheon to keep guard at the entrance of the rainbow bridge (Bifröst) that leads from Miðgarð (the realm of mankind) to Asgarð (the realm of the gods). Freyr is a joyful deity. He is the god of summer, agriculture, and the harvests of golden grain. He came to Asgarð with his father Njörður and his sister Freya, the goddess of beauty, love, and fertility. Njörður became the god of the ocean and especially the northern seas surrounding Iceland. The "Almighty" in this first stanza refers, of course, to Óðin. Also, with the phrase "the guardian of Miðgarð who fears nothing" Sveinbjörn refers to one of the most important deities for mankind, namely Þór.

2. *Staka* is a word that can be used to describe a short poem written in the style of a Japanese Haiku. Technically *staka* can also be translated as a stanza or more precisely as a quatrain, that is, a stanza of four lines. However, the word *staka*, like *dís*, has a much wider variety of meanings. It is a sort of artistic, unconscious communication between the artist and the reader or listener, and it is left to the latter to sense and feel the topic or message that the artist has given to each single piece. Typically these little creations need not have individual names or titles, similar to an untitled painting or other artwork. Generally, in a book the poems are simply grouped together under the title *stökur* (pl. of *staka*), or the name *staka* is given to each one. In such cases each short poem or artistic creation has its own message, but by placing them together they may present a somewhat different meaning. So the word *staka* has a sort of fluid meaning with a number of subtle variations. Like many Icelandic poets, Sveinbjörn wrote a great number of these short poems and often gave them that same "name": *Staka*.

3. *Dís* is a word that in Icelandic has a wide and profound variety of meanings. A *dís* is a sort of universal female spirit. She can be a goddess, a valkyrie, an *álfkona* (elfin woman), or a *huldukona* (a woman from the hidden world). She can also be a spirit of the land, a lake, the fire, or the wind and air. She is generally benevolent, but at times she can be malevolent. She can be a fairy godmother, or a flower spirit, or one of the three Norns; or she can be a real, living

woman, the love of our life, or a woman with such an intense and powerful soul, vision, intellect, beauty, sensitivity and passion that a man can never forget her. Generally the nature of that real woman or female spirit can only be described within the context of a poem and that is the case with this poem by Sveinbjörn. Another good example is the next poem, *Spring Comes*, where we see that the *dís* is, for the poet, the spring. But this *dís* could also be a very special woman. That simple word, *dís*, is very evocative of a most important and primeval force, a sort of eternal feminine spirit and power—one generally idealized and benevolent, but which can also suddenly shift from positive to negative, and back to positive again. One can thus understand why this word, as the second half of a compound, forms part of a number of personal names for women: Ásdís, Álfdís, Vigdís, and so forth.

In Icelandic phonology, the "accented" vowels (with the acute accent [´]) do not indicate vocal stress on that syllable, as virtually all words in Icelandic are stressed on the first syllable. What that accent indicates is a different sound quality of the vowel. In this case, an unaccented "i" has the sound in English of *pin* or *gift*. However, with the accent, the "i" sounds like the "ee" in English, like *feel* or *meet*, but a bit elongated and pronounced with more emphasis and the lips stretched. For children it is one of the first sounds they learn to pronounce clearly, as it is the initial sound for *ís* which means both "ice cream" and "ice." Take, for example, the name for Iceland, *Ísland*, "land of ice."

4. This deep yet simple poem of farewell is one that Sveinbjörn wrote for Bjarni M. Brekkmann, one of his dear friends, when he passed away on 24 March 1970.

Baltic Lithuanian Religion and Romuva

Vilius Rudra Dundzila

A white crown stands on the hill, on the tall one.
A grey little boulder lies underneath that white crown.
Father, dearest mother, sit on that grey little boulder.
Sitting there, they cried with grief as they prepared their son for war.[1]

The excerpt is from a *daina*, a folk song. In it, we find ourselves in the celestial heaven before the divine throne. The throne is a magnificent rock; on the earth, it would be a sign of godly power. The white crown and grey stone on the hill also can be a ritual stone crowned by the sun at daybreak or nightfall. Who is the deity we meet? An earthly father and beloved mother—probably our own—represent the god and goddess. They perform a sad, inevitable task, uniting human sorrow with divine providence and concern. This *daina* provides a typical example of the religious, spiritual, and mythological content of Lithuanian folklore that synchronizes the heavenly realm with the natural world and human life.

Lithuanians never thought of their way of life as a religion until the nineteenth and twentieth centuries when they realized their "world-feeling" (the Lithuanian concept for worldview) was, in fact, a religion. It is a religion because it provided and still provides communal religious expression to the spiritual practices inherent in traditional Lithuanian culture. The roots of the religion reach back to ancient times. The modern name "Baltic Lithuanian religion" specifically refers to the Lithuanian branch of a shared Baltic religious and spiritual heritage. Folklore would be its "scripture"—although no one calls it that—because it records the myths, beliefs, practices, and worldview of the religion. Although Lithuanians are now predominantly Christians, Lithuanian culture preserved and propagated its ethnic religious traditions in various ways, including under Christian guise. Romuva is the modern group that practices the religion. It is a late twentieth-century development with historical antecedents from the first half of the century. It takes its name from a famous Prussian pagan temple. This article will first outline the history of Baltic Lithuanian religion and of Romuva and then survey the belief system and religious practices. Most of the article will summarize scholarly research and findings.[2]

The History of Baltic Religion

Linguistically, culturally, and geographically, the Baltic peoples are situated on the southwestern shores of the Baltic Sea. They include the Lithuanian and Latvian nations today, and the Western (or Baltic) Byelorussians (descendents of the Yotvingians) who practice their variant of Baltic culture, but no longer speak a Baltic tongue. In the past, the Old Prussian nation and several other now extinct tribes belonged to the Balts.

Baltic religion does not have a founder or any single source, and it predates recorded history. It evolved from the natural and native beliefs of its indigenous people. Three prehistoric formative periods contributed to the development of Baltic religion before it declined due to the introduction of Christianity. First, the initial nomads entered the region of the present-day Baltic after the last Ice Age (circa 10,000–9000 B.C.E.) receded. They survived by hunting, gathering, and fishing. They focused their religion on these ends as well.[3] Second, the agrarian settlers (circa 3500–2500 B.C.E.) practiced a version of the earth-focused Old European religion.[4] The Lithuanian archeologist Marija Gimbutas (1921–2004) is the primary proponent of this controversial theory. Third, a wave of cultural changes spread across Europe and into the Baltic (circa 3000–2500 B.C.E.). The transformation developed a form of Indo-European religion.[5] The Indo-European character of modern Baltic religion has been studied at great length and is extremely well documented. Each wave of changes incorporated elements from its predecessors.

Reindeer hunters representing the Malden culture from the Germanic region populated the Baltic circa 10,000–9000 B.C.E. After the climate improved circa 7000 B.C.E., fishing became the secondary food source. The inhabitants sustained themselves by hunting primarily elk, aurochs, and boar, and by fishing. They worshiped a God (or Goddess) of the Beasts in the forms of a northern elk, moose, bear, water birds, snakes, and garter snakes, sometimes with clear female characteristics. They eventually anthropomorphized their deity, but with minimal human details and without gender. They built totems to the deity and wore amulets of it, often made of amber. The lack of sufficient details, general cultural context, and secondary background information make it very difficult to draw any clear sort of picture about the religion of this civilization. Evidence from the subsequent Mesolithic

PART OF A NINETEENTH-CENTURY
LITHUANIAN SPINNING WHEEL,
DECORATED WITH
COSMOLOGICAL SYMBOLS.
(COLLECTION OF THE AUTHOR)

period reveals a complex system of hunting magic that must have had its origins in this Paleolithic period.[6]

Baltic Kunda, Narva, and Nemunas cultures evolved with the advent of agriculture in the Baltic during the Mesolithic and early Neolithic periods. During the fifth millennium B.C.E., the inhabitants established permanent settlements, built houses, and made pottery that they decorated with biomorphic and geometric designs. Statues of deities with full human features set in poses of worship appear. The people made sacrifices to the deities by drowning model boats filled with gifts in water or swamps and by burning them. They also used ladles shaped like waterfowl, probably in water rituals.[7] Gimbutas, who developed the theory of Old Europe, believes the Mesolithic period in the Baltic region belonged to Old European culture.

Old Europe came into existence circa 7000 B.C.E., at the same time as agricultural societies spread across Europe.[8] The term "Old Europe" originally referred to some three thousand culturally similar settlements anchored on the southeastern shores of the European continent. This region comprised the Old European homeland. In general terms "Old Europe" includes all of Europe and parts of Western Asia because these areas developed cultures reminiscent of the Old European homeland. Old European civilization came to an end between circa 4300 B.C.E. to circa 2800 B.C.E. when the Indo-Europeans migrated throughout Europe.[9]

The Old Europeans built settlements, within which they achieved the highest possible level of cultural, technological, and agricultural success. Furthermore, Old Europe did not know warfare or domination in either their material or their artistic cultures. It continued the previously established traditions of sculpture and painting. The inhabitants successfully adapted to their environment.

Since agriculture completely replaced hunting and fishing as the basis for sustenance, a new, different worldview constituted the foundation for the Old European religion. It bonded to the earth, emphasized the cycles of nature, and focused on the regeneration of life after death. Old Europe worshiped goddesses as its principal deities. The Old European heartland produced around 30,000 divine figurines, of which only 2 to 3 percent depict male gods.[10]

On the shores of the Baltic Sea, the Kunda culture developed two Neolithic societies: the Nemunas culture on riverbanks, and the Narva culture on lake shores. Narva culture first developed Old European religious artifacts: ritual staffs, wooden and amber sculptures of elk heads and human heads, bears, birds, and snakes. An unnamed "goddess-as-bird" played a prominent role in the religion. The Narva and Nemunas cultures lasted until cultural transformations ascribed to Indo-European invasions began to take place around 2500 B.C.E.[11]

The Old European theory is in dispute. The variety of cultures attributed to Old Europe may be too vast and diverse to identify under a single umbrella label. Moreover, the differences between the cultures generally outweigh the similarities. Cynthia Eller, a scholar of women and religion, reasonably questions supporting the theory of Old Europe. She concludes that earlier feminists were too driven by ideology in searching for a prehistoric matrifocal culture like Old Europe. In another vein of critique, the dates of the Indo-European invasion that replaced the Old European culture are contested.[12] Archaeologist Colin Renfrew advocates that the Indo-European cultural transformation was synonymous with the spread of agriculture in Europe, although linguists contend that the archeological evidence predates the linguistic phenomenon by at least a millennium and a half.[13] Due to Gimbutas's influence, Lithuanian scholars entertain and some even support the Old European theory, although it may be inaccurate. It serves as a useful paradigm for interpreting Baltic goddesses and gods.

Whether or not an Old European culture existed, numerous slow, successive waves of Indo-Europeanization did transform Europe and some other parts of the world. Indo-European culture reached the Baltic region between 3000 B.C.E. and 2800 B.C.E.—in other words, relatively late. First, Finno-Ugric invaders coming from Eastern and Central Russia swept over the Narva culture, settling on the northeastern shores of the Baltic Sea. The nomads replaced the Narva culture, and evolved a culture which millennia later yielded the Estonians and Finns. Second, Indo-Europeans entered from the south and the west. They transformed the Nemunas culture, eventually creating the familiar modern Baltic Lithuanian and Latvian cultures.[14]

The Indo-European inhabitants generally settled in fortified yet remarkably small hilltop settlements that offered natural defensive protection. They built castles and fortifications in their territories, although this generally did not occur until the Dark Ages in Lithuania. Male hierarchical social structures formed the basis of Indo-European organization. Warriors appeared as a superior social class where one did not exist before. The Indo-European distinction between warriors and laborers relegated the latter to lower social status. Patriarchy also dictated the superiority of man over woman, which even the earliest recorded Indo-European myths already indicate. The culture also carried with it an ideology that conceptualized light as good and dark as evil, thereby denigrating all chthonic deities. It practiced animal husbandry and small-scale farming. It introduced private property, patrilinear kinship, and an organized priesthood. The simple style and decoration of Indo-European pottery completely replaced the previously existing, highly elaborate pottery.[15]

In physical stature, the Indo-Europeans were noticeably larger and more agile than the Old Europeans. They rode horses and horse-pulled wagons, which they introduced to Europe and included in their art and graves. These tall horse-riders must have seemed like giants to the indigenous populations. The appearance and strength of these giants left an unforgettable impact on the native peoples, recorded in the mythology and folklore of Europe.[16]

Indo-Europeans believed in an afterlife that resembles human existence. They did not believe in circular time and feared the prospect of endless, repetitive time. They buried relatives together in structures resembling houses, accompanied by tools needed for daily existence. Distinguished people, such as members of the higher classes (rulers, priests, warriors), received elaborate burials.

Sometimes the people also buried sacrificial animals alongside the humans, providing the dead with animals for labor or food. Images appear of anthropomorphic thunder gods with axes (presumably forerunners of Perkūnas) as well as burial slabs decorated with gigantic human feet (reminiscent of Velnias).[15]

The Indo-European religion centered on bulls, horses, fire, and the sun. Solar symbols such as solar disks, concentric wheels, and radiating suns accented the artistry of this culture. The male gods associated with these images represented super-beings capable of overcoming the destructive impersonal forces of nature, which the Indo-Europeans considered evil. The isolated symbols quickly became horse-drawn solar wagons, solar ships, or the world tree. Hunting continued to exert an influence on the religion. Gimbutas concludes that reindeer, elk, birds, reptiles, and the heavens represent male, sky-oriented elements of divinity, while water, rocks, and plants represent female, earth-oriented elements.[18] Nevertheless, the culture also displayed a few sexless images of divinity in human form.

Georges Dumézil has comparatively reconstructed the religion of the Indo-Europeans, based on common elements present in the mythologies of the various Indo-European successor peoples. The religion of the Indo-Europeans divided the universe into three parts: the heavens, the earth, and the underworld. A tripartite system also divided the Indo-European social classes of divinities and humans. The kings and priests, who possessed juridical and magical powers, belonged to the highest class; the warriors, who bore martial force, represented the second class; and stockbreeders and farmers, responsible for fecundity and economic prosperity, supported the upper two classes.[19] These divisions categorized both the divinities and the humans. Human society, therefore, reflected the divine order, legitimizing human social classes.

Two individuals—a ruler and a priest—equally compose the sovereign class. The two work in symbiosis: the ruler rules and the priest protects the ruler from the risks of royal power. This division reveals deeper structural differences. In Dumézil's Indo-European paradigm, the king effects magic that controls chaos and creates society, while the priest organizes and civilizes what the king has made. The application of this structure to Baltic material will prove to be difficult. The European concepts of divine kingship and priestly sovereignty likely stem from the Indo-Europeans.[20]

The residence of the royal sovereign on a mountaintop echoes the traditional hilltop location of Indo-European settlements.

Equating divinity with the sky, the Indo-Europeans called their principal god *deiwos,* which also means sky. He becomes the Lithuanian heavenly god Dievas (and Proto-Germanic Tîwaz as well as Old Norse Tyr, both gods of warfare and battle).[21] Celestial light and transcendence comprise the realm of the supreme, sovereign god. Thus, the cosmological order underpins the divine order.

The earth did not belong to the initial Indo-European pantheon, appearing later in a limited area that includes the Baltic. The earth, called *ghcem,* combined energy opposed to the sky with the concept of humans, also named from the same root as earth.[22] In Lithuanian, this becomes žemė "earth," žmogus "person" or literally "earthling," and the root of the name Žemyna, the earth goddess. Indo-European religion rationalized and metamorphosed the ties the goddess had to the natural world: earth and death took on new meanings. It incorporated the earth into its pantheon in a binary manner: the vital energy of the Mother Earth was in contrast to that of the Father Sky.

The agrarian class provided goddesses with the greatest possible expression of their powers. As nurturers, the goddesses provided for society, especially farmers, craftspeople, and mothers in childbirth. Almost all Indo-European goddesses had some nurturing functions, which often focused on childbirth. In this role, the goddesses best exemplified the "connectedness to the life force and a facilitation of the life force" that power-from-within provides.[23] Only in the third class did women serve as the actual protectors of the earth.

Critiques of Dumézil's theory tend to fall along two lines of thought. On the one hand, the presence of similar structures in cultures who speak related languages does not necessarily indicate a common proto-structure, since each of the cultures could develop the structures spontaneously and independently, as occurs in language. Likewise, the theoretical Indo-European structures do not readily appear in all Indo-European societies, as the forthcoming discussion of the Baltic demonstrates. Although cultures that adopted literacy relatively late may have lost certain structures over time, they may have also not possessed the structures in the first place. On the other hand, Dumézil's tripartite division of classes is not unique to the Indo-Europeans: a similar division occurs in both Hebrew Scriptures, which may have incorporated Indo-European influences, and in ancient Japan, which had no contact with ancient Europe.[24]

The transformation of Old European culture into an Indo-European one took a long time. An indigenous Baltic culture developed that further subdivided into the various cultures of the Baltic tribes. Few records exist from this long period. The Roman Historian Tacitus (circa 55 C.E.–117 C.E.) writes that Balts worshiped a goddess. At the end of the first millennium C.E., chronicles begin to record information about the Baltic, but without providing religious details (other than that the Balts were "pagans").

Probably sometime in the first millennium C.E., Baltic religion underwent several quasi-historical reforms recorded by mythology and legend. Sovijus (dates unknown) introduced cremated burials that eventually gained widespread acceptance.[25] In Lithuania, Duke Šventaragis (circa fifth–sixth centuries) relocated cremations to sacred grounds and extended them to the nobility.[26] In Prussia, the chief prophet Prutenis (or Brutenis) (?–573) and his younger brother King Vaidevutis (?–573) unified the Prussians into a theocratic state, reformed the pantheon, and built the Romuva temple at Nadruva with the Gods Patolas (Velnias), Perkūnas, and Patrimpas (Dievas) as the presiding trinity.[27] This Prussian sequence of the presiding deities is noteworthy because the chthonic god is the first god. The order changed during later periods of religious development. Each Baltic tribe eventually developed its own ethnic variant of Baltic religion.

Archeology provides limited information about the Baltic religion during the first millennium C.E. Several social developments are noteworthy: a differentiation between rich and poor individuals becomes evident, the first castles are built, and a professional warrior class develops where none had existed before. The latter two items respond to Germanic and Slavic migrations encroaching on Baltic territories, resulting in the eventual assimilation of some Baltic tribes. Graves offer important data about the religion. The dead are buried with ornamentation, with some weapons and tools, and sometimes with horses. Cremation spreads as a form of burial (the Balts had cremated in the first millennium B.C.E., but the practice had become unpopular in the first half of the first millennium C.E.[28]). Solar, lunar, and stellar symbols decorate ornaments and jewelry, especially bracelets, earrings, and neck rings. It is not clear if these decorations had magical associations, as there are no supplemental explanatory sources of information from the period. Amulets are shaped like stylized animal heads or maple tree seeds. They depict garter snakes. The people probably worshiped deities associated with the sky, earth, water, and underworld. Reverence for the ancestors was an important component of the religion. Temples did not exist; religious rites probably took place at home and in cemeteries. A social class of priests, žynys (singular), did not exist, but there probably were individuals endowed with special religious duties and abilities.[29]

Baltic religion freely thrived in the Baltic territories until the ninth century C.E., by which time many eastern Baltic groups had come under the influence of migrating Slavic tribes. These Balts eventually lost their linguistic and—in most cases—cultural identities. They were Christianized into Greek Christianity in 998, which came to be known as Orthodoxy after the culmination of the Great Schism in 1054.

The western Balts faced attacks from the Roman Catholic Church and its declared crusades starting in 1199. The invading knights were promised heavenly salvation. It soon became evident the Catholics were interested in land conquest and not propagation of the faith, because only minimal proselytization efforts were undertaken (until the Reformation and Counter-Reformation in the sixteenth century). The Baltic peoples spent the Middle Ages defending themselves from various orders of knights. The Balts succumbed to Christianity rather late: in fact, they were the very last Europeans to be Christianized (except for the Sámi, a.k.a. Lapps, who never formed their own state). Lithuanians tend to be very proud of this historical fact.

German crusader knights conquered the Baltic Prussian lands by 1280 and established a Germanic Prussia that lasted until World War I. Due to Germanization, the Baltic Prussians ceased to exist as a people by the start of the eighteenth century (circa 1710). Another group of knights subjugated the Latvian principalities (as well as parts of modern-day Estonia), officially Christianized them, and created a Germanic Livonian state in 1290. The knights attacked only the Lithuanian seashore territories and lowlands known as Samogitia, conquering and losing the region repeatedly.

Lithuania accepted Catholic Christianity as a political maneuver on two occasions, although Orthodox endeavors were also undertaken. First, Mindaugas (?–1263), his wife Morta (?–1262/3), and their court officially converted to Roman Catholicism in 1251 to end the crusades. Lithuania became a Christian kingdom two years later, with Mindaugas and his wife being crowned king and queen. The Samogitian duchies, under attack from the knights, rebelled against Mindaugas. Mindaugas allegedly continued to practice Lithuanian religion secretly, and formally renounced Christianity

FIRST WORLD CONGRESS OF ETHNIC RELIGIONS, VILNIUS, LITHUANIA, 1998. SPONSORED BY ROMUVA. THE PARTICIPANTS POSE IN FRONT OF THE STATUE OF GEDIMINAS, THE LAST PAGAN KING OF LITHUANIA. (PHOTO COURTESY OF THE AUTHOR)

in 1261, having failed to end the crusades. The second attempt at Catholic Christianity occurred several centuries later.

A few generations after Mindaugas, the penultimate pagan Grand Duke Gediminas (ca. 1275–1341) defended Lithuania from the onslaught of the knights. Although he was a lifelong pagan, he allowed all people to worship their own gods in Lithuania, explaining that the Lithuanians, Catholics, and Orthodox worship the same deity, each in their own way. One of his letters addressed to the Pope indicated a notion of Baltic Lithuanian monism, although some interpret the text as a forced syncretism: "we all worship the same God." In his letters, he repeatedly explained that Lithuania rejects Christianity because of "the heinous offenses and numerous treacheries undertaken by 'the knights.'"[30] He welcomed Christian clergy to Lithuania, but demanded that they do not behave like the Christian monks already there. They were acting immorally by selling the donations they received for personal profit.

Lithuanian mythology credits Gediminas with establishing the capital city of Vilnius, although the city predates his lifetime by

ANNOUNCING THE START OF THE FIRE RITUAL AT
GEDIMINAS HILL IN VILNIUS, LITHUANIA
(PHOTO COURTESY OF THE AUTHOR)

several centuries. Archeological excavations indicate that Vilnius was a settlement from the end of the last millennia B.C.E. In Gediminas's day, Vilnius already served as an important religious center with a sacred forest and numerous temples. Some of the temples stood on the seven hills at the confluence of the Neris and Vilnia rivers. Others stood on present-day church locations: the Cathedral replaced the Perkūnas (thunder god) temple, the Peter and Paul church replaced the Milda (love goddess) temple, and the Passion Church replaced the Ragutis (horned god) temple. Vilnius also served as a center of commercial trade. It had the prerequisite characteristics for the establishment of a "holy" city according to Indo-European mythology: a religious center, sacred forest, seven hills, and the confluence of rivers (a form of crossroads).

A summary of the legend about Gediminas founding Vilnius is as follows: One day, Gediminas was hunting near the confluence of the Vilnia and Neris rivers. He shot and killed a large taurus bull on what is now called Taurus Hill. In a dream that night, he saw an iron wolf on the Kreivasis, or "crooked," hill. The wolf howled with the force of a hundred wolves. Disturbed by the dream, Gediminas rode to the pagan priest Lizdeika. Lizdeika immediately understood the meaning of the dream: the iron wolf represented a city that Gediminas was to build. The howl of the wolf meant that the renown of the city would be heard around the entire world.[31]

The legend about Gediminas emphasizes his divine calling and divine right. Gediminas was hunting in a sacred forest, exercising his royal privilege. Religious and political rulers enjoy equal status in Indo-European religions. Gediminas shot a divine animal, according to Lithuanian and Indo-European mythology. In killing the taurus bull, Gediminas received the life force from the animal and in effect communed with the heavenly gods and goddesses. By allowing Gediminas to catch their sacred animal, the divinities bonded themselves with Gediminas. Via the dream, the gods gave Gediminas guidance and predicted the future. Another divine animal, the wolf, becomes Gediminas's vehicle of destiny as well as the new symbol for his rule. The association of the wolf with the city also makes Vilnius a city under the protection of the gods and goddesses. Gediminas did not understand his dream because he is a political leader, not a religious one. To discover the meaning of his dream, he went to a sage. The religious man understood and explained the dream. The dream focuses on the future greatness of the city. Vilnius will combine the raw power of nature—the wolf—with the forces of civilization—iron.

Two generations later, Gediminas's grandson Duke Jogaila (Jagello in Polish) became King of Poland through a very complicated political compact. The deal required the Lithuanian Grand Duke Vytautas, another grandson of Gediminas and first cousin to Jogaila, to accept Christianity for himself and his country. This happened in 1386–87. The Samogitian duchies accepted Christianity in 1410, after liberation from Germanic crusaders. Groups of Lithuanians received baptism *en masse*, but without any catechesis. Candidates for baptism received a free white shirt or blouse; many underwent baptism several times for additional garments.

Christianity advanced slowly as the Lithuanians continued to practice their Baltic Lithuanian religion. Protestants and Catholics began serious evangelization campaigns after the Protestant Reformation of 1517.[32] The Catholic and Protestant churches also at times banned various Lithuanian "pagan" holidays, such as Kūčios, Kalėdos, Vėlinės, and Rasa or Kupolinė, all of which survived until the present as cultural or semi-religious celebrations. Throughout the centuries, various Christian records frequently documented Lithuanian obstinacy to Christianity.[33]

According to legend, Grand Duke Stanislovas Augustas Poniatovskis (1732–1798; ruled 1764–95) cut down the last holy oak that was still worshiped in Vilnius.

By the mid–nineteenth century, most Lithuanians were nominally Christian. Elements of Baltic Lithuanian religion took on a Christian guise or survived as folk traditions in this period. The Lithuanian National Awakening in the second half of the century promoted an interest in Lithuanian ethnic culture, including the religion. People readily collected and published Lithuanian folklore, especially *dainos* (plural of *daina*) and folk tales. Simonas Daukantas (1793–1864) and Dr. Jonas Basanavičius (1851–1927) are the two leading individuals who propagated Baltic religious interests during the century.

Daukantas worked for fifteen years in the St. Petersburg archives, where he had the opportunity to study Lithuanian state documents dating from the fifteenth to eighteenth centuries. He wrote several Lithuanian and Samogitian histories, all of which included sections on Baltic religion. His most important book was *Būdas senovės lietuvių kalnėnų ir žemaičių* (The Character of Ancient Lithuanian Highlanders and Lowlanders). He underscored the Baltic religious elements in Lithuanian culture. Under the influence of Romanticism, he idealized the Lithuanian past, emphasizing the good and noble aspects of the peasantry, while attributing the bad to the nobility. He also collected and published folklore. Basanavičius was a medical doctor with a keen interest in Lithuanian history and folklore, in particular the ancient Baltic religion. His major publications form an important and influential series of *daina* and folk-tale anthologies. Most modern collections of folk tales come from his compendium. He also promoted the values of Baltic religion.

History of Romuva

Baltic Lithuanian religion became a somewhat popular phenomenon during Lithuania's period of inter-war independence (1918–1939/40). The most colorful individual had to be Jonas Beržanskis Klausutis (1862–1936) who began calling himself Duke Gediminas-Beržanskis-Klausutis. Under Czarist rule, he had himself declared a pagan on his passport. In independent Lithuania, he ardently propagated Lithuanian religion, but had little following. He "baptized" his son to the thunder god Perkūnas during a thunderstorm. He held the child naked in the rain, and named him after a thunderclap.[34]

The Lithuanian philosopher Vilius Storosta-Vydūnas (1868–1953) organized public celebrations of Lithuanian ethnic religious holidays and song festivals. He was the first to revive communal Rasa celebrations. These have become a mainstay of modern Lithuanian culture. He also wrote a number of very important and influential philosophical, historical, and literary works, many based on Lithuanian mythology. These emphasized the inherently noble values present in Lithuanian ethnic religion. He particularly favored the Lithuanian fire ritual.

In his writings, Vydūnas focused on the spiritual dimension that traditional Lithuanian culture saw in daily life. He lamented the loss of this vision in modern culture. He believed that Lithuanians lived in harmony with nature, expressing a deep reverence for the earth. He said that Christianity was a foreign religion for the Baltic peoples. The ancient Lithuanians worshiped God via fire. The belief is so deep that modern Lithuanians still hold fire sacred. Fire was the gateway to the spiritual and the basis of Lithuanian morality. The Balts saw the universe as a great mystery, an idea absent from modern culture. The whole world and every individual living being was a symbol of life. Because of this, the Balts respected every living being.

Domas Šidlauskas-Visuomis (1878–1944) reformed Baltic Lithuanian religion, calling it Visuomybė (Universalism). He established congregations in Lithuania and abroad, and founded a landed sanctuary called Romuva in 1929 in northwestern Lithuania. His followers combined Lithuanian ethnic religious practices with universalist ideals, while simultaneously hailing Visuomis as a messianic prophet.

In 1930, an academic fraternity called Romuva and, in 1932, a sorority called the Vestals of Romuva were founded at the Vytautas Magnus University of Kaunas. The groups included some notions about Baltic religion. They disseminated their ideas in Lithuanian society and at the university. National (and transnational) unity was an important psychological defense against the Nazi and Soviet threats on the Lithuanian borders. Unfortunately both groups ended up serving the political interests of the Lithuanian nationalist dictatorship.

The Soviet Occupation (1939) completely disbanded all associations of Lithuanian religion and executed or deported many participants to Siberia. In 1941 and again at the end of World War II, the Soviets deported several hundred thousand Lithuanians to Soviet labor camps. In the late 1940s, a handful of Lithuanians in Inta, Russia, gathered regularly to sing *dainos*, especially ones with a spiritual resonance. The group was seeking solace to cope with the harshness of political imprisonment. Another Lithuanian—probably seeking favor with the regime—disclosed the group to the authorities. Because the purpose of the camps was to indoctrinate so-called enemies of the people with Soviet ideology, including atheism, the regime prohibited any kind of religious activity in them. As punishment, the authorities exiled the folk singers once again, this time to the depths of Siberia. After Joseph Stalin's death in 1953, the Soviets commuted sentences of the surviving members and eventually allowed them to return to Lithuania in the late 1950s.[35]

After Stalin, the Soviet Union began to promote the ethnic cultures of its republics, including Lithuania, as stage showcases. This period saw the founding of folkloric and ethnographic groups that operated independently of the officially sanctioned, state-sponsored ensembles. Individuals interested in the inherent spiritual elements present in Lithuanian folklore practice found each other. This included a survivor or two of the Inta group. They formed the Vilnius City Folk Expedition Group Ramuva in 1967. The name Ramuva, spelled with the first vowel of "a," was intentionally altered to disassociate it from "Romuva," the name of the prehistoric Prussian pagan temple and its overt religious associations. The group celebrated ethnographic traditions with a covert religio-spiritual emphasis. One of its very early and famous successes was a national Rasa, or summer solstice celebration, in 1967 at the early Medieval Lithuanian capital of Kernavė. This ritual served as a symbolic anti-Soviet protest. It was a catalyst that inspired people interested in folklore to propagate an independent folklore movement.

The regime banned Ramuva in 1971 when it realized the underlying religious nature of its activities. The leaders were punished with expulsions from the university and terminations from employment, including denial of subsequent employment commensurate with their education and experience. Some were sent into internal exile, in other words, they were forced to live in remote locations without the right to travel. Ramuva's goals were not extinguished, however, since various ethnographic ensembles continued to propagate them. Ramuva and other independent groups from the period were collectively instrumental in beginning the national folkloric movement that opposed the Soviet occupation. In the 1980s, the collective singing of folklore became a primary act of anti-Soviet protest and civil disobedience.

The Soviet policies of *glasnost* and *perestroika* allowed Ramuva to be reestablished in 1988. Some of the same individuals from 1967 were involved. Ramuva quickly gained momentum and developed working groups in five cities. Overtly, Ramuva studied and taught Lithuanian folklore, sponsored folkloric expeditions, and organized annual summer camps (several had about a thousand attendees). Ramuva served as a locus of discussion about the religio-spiritual elements in Lithuanian folklore. Covertly, Ramuva sought the spiritual essence of the ethnographic traditions.

Lithuania declared its independence from the Soviet Union in 1990 and achieved it in 1991. Lithuania's rejection of Soviet rule was dubbed the "Singing Revolution" since civil disobedience took the form of mass demonstrations singing Lithuanian *dainos*. After independence, Romuva abandoned the altered pseudonym from the 1960s. It registered as a church, beginning with the second largest city of Kaunas in 1991–92.[36] Other cities, including the capital of Vilnius, and a national umbrella organization, soon followed. Difficulties encountered included fallacious government claims that Romuva was not compatible with Catholicism. Registration eventually succeeded. The existence of a pagan church became a small-scale national sensation. In comparison, the Latvians established their church, Dievturi, in 1926, while the Byelorussians formed Krywya in 1994. Incidentally, the university Romuva was also reestablished as a united fraternity and sorority promoting Baltic unity, folklore, and religion in 1990.[37] In 1997, Romuva installed Jonas Trinkūnas (b. 1939) as the first modern *krivis*, high priest, in six hundred years.

Romuva currently has eleven congregations in Lithuania, one in Canada, and two in the United States. The groups meet weekly to sing *dainos*, the mainstay of Baltic Lithuanian religious and spiritual practice. Each congregation elects its own leader, called *seniūnas*, "elder." The term is the title of a village elder from premodern Lithuania; that individual also served as the religious leader of the community.

Romuva has been very active in Lithuanian social and political life. In 1993, Romuva conducted the ritual to bless the first post-

KULGRINDA AND GERMAN PAGANS CONDUCTING A FIRE RITUAL AT CAPE ARKONA ON THE ISLAND OF RÜGEN, GERMANY, IN 2005. UNDER THE LEADERSHIP OF FRANK WILKE (CENTER) FROM THE UKRANENLAND MUSEUM, TURGLOWE, THE GERMANS ERECTED THE POLE-SCULPTURE HONORING THE SLAVIC GOD SVETOVIT. IT COMMEMORATES THE MEDIEVAL TEMPLE-FORTRESS AND STATUE THAT WERE DESTROYED IN 1168. (PHOTO COURTESY OF JONAS TRINKŪNAS)

independence presidential flag in a nationally televised, highly symbolic ceremony at Gediminas Castle. The Catholic blessing in the cathedral followed the Romuva rite. When the government was returning property that had been nationalized under the Nazi and Soviet occupations, Romuva unsuccessfully applied to have former temples and their grounds returned to it, some of which were lost centuries ago. It has also unsuccessfully advocated for a strict separation of church and state in the Lithuanian constitution. In 1995, Lithuania passed a new law regulating religious organizations. It recognizes nine "traditional" religions and requires all "non-traditional" groups, including Romuva, to wait twenty-five years before receiving rights as a church. Thus far, efforts have failed to amend this law. In contrast, the analogous Latvian law recognizes the

Latvian Dievturi.

Baltic Lithuanian Religion is a vibrant spiritual and religious tradition that has found accommodations to changing circumstances, both in historic and in modern times. Romuva serves as the self-avowed religious community for Baltic Lithuanian religion. Lithuanians who reject Christianity and want to follow the Lithuanian ethnic tradition join Romuva. Many others practice a syncretism of Baltic Lithuanian religion and Christianity, readily acknowledging the "pagan" elements of their Christianity. Essentially, they worship a Balto-Christian Dievas alongside the Baltic Lithuanian Perkūnas, Laima, and Žemyna. Most Lithuanians accept their ethnic holidays and gods as something natural and folkloric. They eagerly participate in them because they consider it part of their cultural heritage.

Sources of the Belief System

The next issue to address is the religious belief system with its vertical (or transcendental) dimension and horizontal plane. The latter includes myths and beliefs in a real world context. The interpretation of the ancient Baltic religion, as well as its Prussian, Latvian, and Lithuanian successors, presents several challenges. Most of the underlying research on Baltic mythology occurred in a folkloric perspective that generally interprets source materials from a twentieth- or twenty-first-century synchronic perspective. The Baltic mythological record is incomplete and contains discrepancies. The religion never established a canon and never wrote a ritual formulary. The oral tradition is still alive and resists codification, although there have been many published collections of the Lithuanian religious heritage. These various considerations make it nearly impossible to establish an accurate developmental history of Baltic religion.

There are several broad source categories for the study of Lithuanian mythology. The first one comprises records from chronicles and other historical sources. Most early authors were often inaccurate because they did not know what they were writing about and they did not speak the language. They frequently relied on second- and third-hand information. They also followed paradigms, expecting Baltic Lithuanian religion to have the same structures as, for example, Roman religion, or the Christian trinity. The spelling of Lithuanian terms is frequently unrecognizable, sometimes requiring linguistic interpretation to decipher the words. At face value, these sources are generally unreliable, but scholars have managed to glean trustworthy information from them.

The early chronicles describe the state religion of Lithuania, whereas the later materials record peasant versions of Baltic Lithuanian religion. The state and peasant religions are noticeably different, with different sets of emphases, primarily based on an axis separating heavenly, governmental, and military concerns versus earthly, familial, agrarian ones. The state religion apparently had an organized temple system with priest-like individuals, while the peasants focused on farming and community.

A second set of records with questionable contents comes from the Romantic period. Lithuanian authors composed a new national ideology and mythology based on fragmented Lithuanian antecedents and foreign-inspired models. For example, the Hindu Prajapati, the Vedic primordial lord of creatures, appears in Lithuania as Pradžiapatis, the god of creation. A folk etymology—which assumes that two words must be identical if they sound similar—Lithuanianizes the Hindu name into a Lithuanian one. The conflation reflects the fashionable belief that everything Lithuanian must somehow reflect Sanskrit and Hindu phenomena. This derives from a popular misinterpretation of the linguistic principle that Sanskrit and Lithuanian are related Indo-European languages. The linguist Suniti Chatterji documents the deities that Vedic Hinduism and Baltic religion share: the sky god Dievas, the father sky god Dievas Tėvas, the mother earth goddess Žemė Motina, the wind god Vėjas, the solar goddess Saulė, the fire goddess Ugnis, the lunar god Mėnulis, the dawn goddess Aušra, the thunder god Perkūnas, the blacksmith god Kalvaitis, the garter-snake god Žaltys, and the poisonous snake goddess Gyvatė.[38] Lithuanians (and Latvians) often claim the *dainos* are the Baltic Vedas. Actually, Chatterji relates the word *daina* to the Vedic Sanskrit *dhena*, meaning "to think, to ponder over, to give thought to."[39] Aspects of singing the *dainos* could be considered a meditative tradition.

The third and most important source is folklore, all of which was recorded in the last two and a half centuries. That is very late, compared to the long time span that the chronicles and historical sources cover. The folkloric record comes from the period when the Lithuanian populace was becoming Christian, syncretizing Baltic Lithuanian and Christian belief systems. *Dainos* were collected first, as early as the 1700s, followed by folktales at least a century later. There are several categories of folklore: sung folklore, narrated folklore (stories), minor folklore (aphorisms or proverbs, riddles, superstitions, and spells or magic formulas), folk art, and folk traditions. A small percentage of Lithuanian folklore contains mythology. A subgroup of *dainos* is designated "mythological folk songs"; to be placed in this category the *daina* must mention a deity by name. Few such Lithuanian *dainos* exist (the Latvians have substantially more). The rule excludes the many *dainos* with mythological content that do not name a divinity, such as the one that introduced this article. To supplement absent or vague information from the Lithuanian tradition, I have included relevant Latvian parallels that help form a more complete picture.[40]

A fundamental cultural practice for Lithuanians and spiritual-religious practice for Romuva is the singing of *dainos*. It is an uninterrupted living tradition in Lithuania. Every occasion and every event provides an opportunity for a *daina*. Lithuania's "Singing Revolution," mentioned earlier, is therefore not incidental.

The archives of the Lithuanian Folklore Institute in Vilnius literally contain in excess of 500,000 *daina* entries alone. It is a national treasure. This includes variants, as some *dainos* are very widespread throughout Lithuania, while most are localized in a specific region. There are even a few Lithuanian-Baltic Byelorussian *dainos* as well: these have survived over a millennium of cultural and linguistic separation. Expeditions to collect folklore are still undertaken annually, adding to the collection. Only a small fraction has been published.

An example of a *daina* will serve to demonstrate its mythological and cryptic nature. The most important *daina* that Romuva sings and the one that it has adopted as its own hymn is "Šalyj kelio" (Along the Road):

> A poplar stood on the side of the road, oh noble plant, beloved rye. *Kanklės* (zither-like instruments) resounded from below the roots. Bees buzzed in the middle. The children of the falcon were on the top. And a group of brothers comes riding on horseback. Please stop, young brothers. Listen to the resounding *kanklės*. Listen to the buzzing bees. We will look at the children of the falcon.[41]

This *daina* was traditionally sung at the conclusion of the rye harvest in the fall. Its place at the harvest signifies that the annual agrarian labor cycle is nearing the end, and that it is time to rest and contemplate. Nature is withering, fall is here, and the *daina* asks humans to take note. The black poplar is a sacred tree with special powers in Lithuanian folklore. In this *daina*, it is the world tree.[42] The *daina* invites reflection or meditation at the three levels of the tree. The three horizons depict the past, present, and future in the form of the dead, the living, and the newborns.

From below the roots come the uncanny sounds of the zither-like Lithuanian stringed instrument *kanklė*. Traditionally constructed in the coffin form of a hollowed-out tree trunk, *kanklės* commemorated a birth or a death. In case of a death, the *vėlė*, or spirit, of the deceased took residence in the *kanklė* and brought the family blessings through the music. The sound of such a *kanklė* was the voice of the *vėlė*. When a *kanklė* lost its acoustic ability—it could take many years and even decades—the *vėlė* had left the world of the living to go beyond. The *kanklė* is also the instrument of a Lithuanian bard. The bard played a quasi-religious role in Lithuanian society, mediating through music and *dainos* between the world underneath the Sun (*pasaulis*, the word for "world" in Lithuanian, literally means "place under the sun, Saulė") and the other worlds.

Bees buzz in the center of the tree. The bee is the best friend and closest spiritual companion to humans in Lithuanian culture. It is a sin to kill a bee. A friend of bees is called a *"bičiulis,"* and very close, life-long friends call each other *"bičiulis."* Lithuanians see very close parallels between human life and that of the bees: residential living, shared duties, collecting and storing food, rearing the young, dancing, singing, and so on. No other member of the natural world shares all these common traits with humans. The Lithuanian language is very expressive, and has different vocabularies to depict human, animal, bird, and fish life. Only bees are born, live, and die according to the same vocabulary as is reserved for humans. Beekeeping is the most noble of professions. When a beekeeper dies, his bees are the first to be told of his death. In the *daina*, the bees represent human society symbolized in its ideal and spiritual form.

The children of a falcon are seen at the top of the tree. The falcon is a powerful, noble bird that can be trained to assist humans. The key here is not the falcon, but the children. By fall, offspring of the falcon are mature and have left the nest. The new eggs and brood will come in the spring, in the future. The falcons represent the heavens and the future in the *daina*.

The group of young brothers represents everyone. First, the word *pulkas*, which means "group," can also denote a flock of birds in a certain context. Second, groups of men are often called brothers, just as groups of women are referred to as sisters in Lithuanian folklore. The notion that all people are brothers and sisters is very literal in Lithuanian culture, but its deep meaning is overlooked in common parlance.

Who does the talking in the *daina*? It is either an unnamed supernatural voice or perhaps the tree itself. This identity of the speaker is not important. Lithuanian folklore is filled with disembodied voices intervening in human life. In this *daina*, the voice invites the brothers to pause, and tells them to listen and to see. It is very important to note that the imperative tense is used to listen to the *kanklės* and bees: a command is given to the brothers. For the children of the falcon, the future tense first person plural is employed: "we will look." The speaker and the audience are united in the quest for the future.

The *daina* describes the world tree. The *koplytstulpis*, the "shrine pole," is the Lithuanian physical manifestation of the world tree. A simpler variant is the *stogastulpis*, or "roof pole." It is a folkloric shrine atop a tall pole. A miniature ethnographic roof decorated with cosmological symbols caps the pole. Statues of deities used to reside in the four sides of the shrine. Christianity introduced its own saints, but it is not unusual to find a shrine with a statue of Perkūnas. The accompanying symbols that decorate the shrines remained: solar, lunar, stellar, and ophidian signs. The *koplytstulpis* itself is a model of the world tree. Archaic poles had three levels, representing the three worlds of the past, present, and future. In 1975–76, twenty-six folk artists made a series of these shrines with modern and mythological themes. The shrines were erected on the road from Vilnius to Druskininkai, a resort town. UNESCO has included the *koplytstulpis* in its World Cultural Heritage list. People used to visit the numerous roadside shrines erected all over Lithuania. The tradition of building and visiting shrines continues today.

The Deities of Baltic Religion

The ancient Balts worshiped a large number of divinities who embodied abstract ideas, represented human characteristics, and anthropomorphized natural objects. Through the gods, the world became perceptible to humans. It is noteworthy that Baltic religion placed great importance on its goddesses, in other words, the feminine divine. Tacitus, who calls the Balts the Aestii, distinguishes them from their neighbors by their prominent worship of an unnamed Mother Goddess.[43] In modern times, the Lithuanian semiologist Algirdas J. Greimas confirms the emphasis on goddesses in searching for the canonical sovereign divinities of Baltic religion.[44]

The main gods begin with the historical Prussian pantheon: the heavenly god Dievas, the weather and justice god Perkūnas, and the chthonic and afterlife god Velnias. Other important sky deities include the sun goddess Saulė and the moon god Mėnulis. Two divine mothers complement the celestial pantheon, but do not truly belong to it: the life goddess Laima and the earth goddess Žemyna. There are many other minor deities, including Velnias's female counterpart Laumė, the snake god Žaltys, and the beer god Ragutis. Baltic religion also acknowledges many other animistic spirits, some beneficial and some malevolent, almost according them a semi-divine status.

Gimbutas divided the Baltic Lithuanian goddesses and gods into categories based on Old European and Indo-European origins. Old European divinities generally belong to the spheres of earth and water. They focus on agriculture and life. Their functions reflect natural phenomena. They commonly take multiple human as well as animal forms, and duplicate themselves, especially into threes and into groups. In contrast, the Indo-European deities represent the sky. They stress pastoralism and stockbreeding, especially in its symbolism. They control and organize, requiring human subordination. They maintain a single, attractive human form, repeat human patterns of coexistence, wear clothing made of precious metals and exquisite fibers, live in heaven, and ride horses or drive horse-drawn carriages.[45]

Dievas received his name directly from the Proto-Indo-European word *deiwos*, which apparently meant both god and heaven.[46] Christianity, Judaism, and Islam adopted his name to identify their godhead, although the name is a proper noun of an undeniably Baltic deity. Appellations such as Praamžius, Audrimpas, Prakurimas, Ukopirmas, Andojas, and others refer to Dievas.[47]

As a young man, Dievas dresses in lavish silver, felt, and silken clothing. Reflecting the wardrobe of the Baltic dukes, he carries a shining or green or copper sword. He sometimes appropriated veiled appearances for himself. He can dress in a white shirt and a grey coat, which do not distinguish him as a ruler. As an old man, he can visit people from house to house and from village to village. In this form, he acts completely human, except that he gives opulent gifts to those who treat him well.[48]

Dievas lives and works on his own heavenly farmstead located at the top of a high, steep, stony mountain. His farm repeats all the elements of a rich, typical, earthly farm, including surrounding fields, gardens, buildings, and sauna. His work on his farm accurately repeats the work undertaken by farmers on their land, indicating his personal commitment to agrarian success. However, he does not participate in most of the physical labor of the farm. Specifically, he tills, sows, and weeds. His work on the farm guarantees a bountiful harvest. In addition to the work of farmers, Dievas encircles the fields, which symbolizes blessing and protection.[49] He drives down from the heavenly mountain to bless the fields. The slow drive down the mountainside parallels the approach of spring and summer and prevents the disruption of dew, which is sacred water. His ride coincides with the seasons. The agrarian work of Dievas is unusual for an Indo-European god of the kingly class, because such work reflects the interests of the agrarian class.

Dievas drives a golden or silver wagon or sleigh drawn by magnificent, multicolored steeds. He also rides his steeds. He has a superb pair of twin steeds, the *ašvieniai*. All forms of twins are an especially auspicious double blessing.[50] Dievas also actively participates in stockbreeding, especially of horses. He presents horses as gifts, helps with their upkeep, and gives advice on the raising of horses. He also goes hunting.[51]

Dievas's cosmological functions depict him as the creator of the world, as the establisher of order, and as the god of light. However, Dievas is not the sole creator. He is paternal, but not absolute. He ensures cosmological-religious stability. This combination of traits indicates that Dievas assumes both functions of the first sovereign Indo-European class: royal and priestly (judicial) power. However, even though he determines law, he himself never executes the law, which makes him a highly atypical representative of the Indo-European priestly function.[52] In a related vein, he determines goodness and morality. According to Gimbutas, the independence of morality and goodness in Baltic religion reflects the unpredictable, non-judgmental cycles and powers of nature.[53]

Dievas represents the royal function of the Indo-European sovereign class. He incorporates many Indo-European mythological themes. He is in many ways an exemplary model of the Indo-European kingly function. As the successor to the Indo-European sky god, he creates and rules the world, but he cannot create alone. He also establishes order in the world, but does not enforce that order. The other heavenly gods and goddesses and the humans remain subservient to Dievas. In contrast to the Indo-European paradigm of Dumézil, he represents the royal function imperfectly: his creativity lacks the expected wild, chaotic impulsiveness that the royal sovereignty should embody. He embraces human-divine friendship *par excellence*, whereas he should be terrifying.

The following *daina*, "Ant kalnelio" (On the Small Hill), combines mythological images of Dievas with raising human children, breeding horses, preparing for marriage, and looking forward to the future:

> On the small hill, on the tall one, stands a multi-colored manor. In the manor, in the colored one, an old man is sitting. He is sitting, calmly sitting, rocking his baby boy. He is singing a lullaby to the dear one, the so very little one. When he has lulled him to sleep, [he tells him to] feed the little bay steed. When you have fed the bay, the dark-bay horse, put a pounded leather saddle on him. With the saddle on him, the leather one, lock the golden stirrups. When the stirrups are fastened, the golden ones, mount the horse, little young son. When you are mounted, beloved one, ride to the girl. On the small hill, on the tall one, there stands a green linden. On top of the linden tree, the green one, a falcon was still building and building his nest. I wish that my dear girl, my lily, would cover the bed in the same way. On the small hill, on the tall one, there stands a green linden. On top of the linden tree, the green one, the bees are droning. Those bees do not drone so sadly, as the girl was crying, as the bride-to-be was crying. Those bees, the droning ones, had written their pairs [selected their mates]. I wish that my girl, my lily, would sew her embroidery as the bees. [54]

As in many cultures, the Lithuanian mythological language

creates complex semantics. The images are not merely allegories, metaphors, or symbols, but mythologem, each containing powerful and deep multiple layers of expansive meanings. The units interact with each other, creating an expressive mythological system of constructs.

The hilltop location is the heavenly manor of the gods. The old man is Dievas caring for his son (or a human child) in a very tender way. At the same time, the man portrays a human father with his son. The divine and human layers constantly interact in this *daina*. Rocking a baby is typically woman's work, but the father is doing it, at least for his son. The voice of the *daina* abruptly shifts from narration to the man speaking with his sleeping son.

The dream that the father suggests to his son is about feeding and riding the steeds. It clearly reflects male equestrian interests. The steeds are of divine origin due to their golden stirrups. They are not mere plough horses, but magnificent stallions. They can also be a farmer's horses. In this image, the divine layer intersects with the human one.

The son will ride to his beloved, but the *daina* never directly introduces the girl. The linden tree—the sacred tree of the goddess Laima—substitutes for her, twice. The girl, like the boy, lives in the heavens. Both depictions of the linden refer to the top of the tree, envisioning the future. In this *daina*, the linden simultaneously represents the girl, the goddess Laima, and the world tree. The falcon in the treetop fortifies his nest, while the bees are busy at work. The falcon, analogous to the steeds, is the superior heavenly bird of Baltic religion. It frequently represents the future in myths. Because of their social structure and industriousness, bees enjoy a special relationship to humans, as discussed previously. They also serve as a model for people to follow. The bees are an example of perfect work and order in this *daina*.

The boy rides to the girl, called a fiancée once, acknowledging her preparation for marriage. The voice abruptly shifts again: the grown son is now speaking. He may still be dreaming, and his father may be speaking. Marriage plans invoke future hope. The marriage of a daughter is an apex moment. It culminates the raising of children, forms a new family, transforms the girl into a woman (puberty represents maturation), and transitions the couple from immaturity to adulthood. In both encounters with the girl, the boy is disappointed with perceived faults of the girl. She has not prepared her dowry according to his expectations. He is unhappy and judgmental. The girl cries. She may cry about this criticism, but her tears have another origin. Girls cry before they wed because they leave the protected world of their parents, home, and childhood behind. They venture into an unknown life with a strange man, moving to his family's homestead. Returning to the divine imagery once again, the goddess, like the girl, is imperfect, in comparison to the god. That is the male patriarchal view presented in this *daina*. In spite of its misogynistic tendencies, the language and melody of the *daina* are beautiful. It expresses deep human sentiments in the enigmatic language of mythology. The *daina* accurately reflects the cultural reality of men and women in Lithuanian society.

Laima, whose name means "fortune," determines fate. She is the goddess of human life. Human interaction with Laima involves a friendly dialogue between equal partners, or bitter lamentations directed at her. Her appellations include "mother," "mother fortune," and "mother of life."[55] She appears as a human woman, as a female animal, or a cuckoo, which also represented Laima in ancient statuary. In the form of a bird, she specifically warns people of misfortune and announces fate to people. Most often Laima makes her presence known as a disembodied voice that only few can hear.[56]

Laima remains in close contact with humans at all phases of life. She decides the prosperity of physical life when she appears at births, marriages, and deaths. At birth, she protects mothers, bestows human and animal life, and determines the fate and course of life. She determines fate independent of morality. She also insures that the fate she determines will fulfill itself. At weddings, she determines the marital life of the newlyweds. Wedding traditions to this day focus on Laima. Called a slaughterer, at the end of life she sets the exact hour of death.[57]

The Balts turned to Laima to overcome burdensome situations, especially difficult work or injustice. They placed offerings to her on rocks that bore impressions of human or animal feet, called "chairs of Laima." Flat rocks or rocks that resembled women served as physical signs of Laima. Thursday evenings were considered sacred to Laima. Women refrained from domestic chores, such as spinning, weaving, and washing clothing. The twelve to fourteen days of the solar standstill at the Winter Equinox are also sacred to Laima. These days precluded routine domestic chores for both men and women. It was a time of rest.[58]

Under Indo-European religion, a conflation between Laima

and Dievas occurred. Laima becomes Dievas's wife, even though she does not belong to the heavenly family or have one of her own. She also does not acquire any heavenly traits, but does assume (and sometimes surpasses) some of the functions of Dievas.[59] In contrast to the vague characteristics generally attributed to the wives of gods in Indo-European religion, Laima's role is extraordinarily well defined. Her responsibilities only reflect Indo-European child-bearing concerns, but in an unusually great variety of very specific ways. She quite specifically continues the Old European life-giving and life-affirming goddess tradition.

Laima and Dievas often discuss who will die. Although Dievas disagrees with her, Laima's determination of fate always transpires.[60] Reflecting the Indo-European paradigm, Dievas is solely interested in the absolute continuation of human life, regardless of the natural laws that expect death. Laima, on the other hand, executes the limits that nature imposes on life, which reiterates Laima's Old European heritage. Under Christianity, the figure of Mary incorporated many traits and characteristics of Laima.[61]

Laima has a double, Dalia, whose name means "fate" and comes from the noun *dalis*, meaning "share." She differs from Laima in that she determines the health and prosperity one experiences in life, but not the course and length of life itself.[62] In other words, she apportions the lot one has in life.

Laima also has a deadly sister, Giltinė. She patiently waits for the apportioned time of death to arrive, and then takes life away. This ancient, tall, meager woman dresses in a huge white shawl and has a blue face with grey-white hair, eyelashes, and brows. Her long, versatile tongue poisons people and literally draws their breath out of them. This nocturnal goddess also appears as a howling hound, or as an owl sharing her wisdom. She sneaks around the world unnoticed by anybody, except for dogs and the dying. Since the dying see her coming, some either turn themselves around in bed on turn their beds around. When the goddess approaches the wrong end of the bed, she cannot kill the person by their feet and has to come back another time. She figures out the ploy quickly enough and goes to the correct end of the bed the next time. Her inability to resolve the human trickery efficiently indicates a general problem that the supernatural experiences in the earthly realm: some divinities do not know how to manage the human world.[63]

Perkūnas is second to Dievas and his name means thunder.[64] He is the weather, thunder, mountain, and oak god. He clearly combines a variety of Indo-European traits. He receives special attention during the growing season as the guarantor of fertility because he provides rain. He controls the weather, his lightning ripens the grain, and he fertilizes the earth.[65] He is the most popular deity represented in statuary. The artisans who make religious statues are called *dievdirbiai*, "god makers."

Perkūnas, in human form, appears in several ways: as a middle-aged man, with a reddened, angered face, a curly black beard, and a crown of flames; as an old man with a brown beard dressed in hunting gear; as an old man with a long grey beard sitting on an amber throne; or as a strong, young man with an ax and a crown of lightning. He inevitably remains human, but is represented in different stages of life.

Perkūnas unquestionably equals the other heavenly gods who likewise live atop the heavenly mountain. Like them, he has a large family, owns majestic steeds, but does not have his own house. He drives a horse-drawn, two-wheeled wagon across the clouds. His life atop the heavenly mountain reflects human life in every detail, except that his ride across the sky causes thunder. People with the gift of prophetic ability interpret the will of Perkūnas from his thunderclaps. Thunder and lightning remain Perkūnas's weapons *par excellence*. His weapons also include balls, axes, and hammers.[66] In particular, Perkūnas persecutes chthonic beings, especially the earth- and water-bound chthonic god Velnias. Lithuanian mythologist Pranė Dundulienė views the conflict between Perkūnas and chthonic "demons" as an explanation for inexplicable natural phenomena, such as drought.[67]

In addition to seeking help with the harvest, the Balts invoked the remarkably impatient and just Perkūnas to punish evil injustice and to defend injured morality. In a similar vein, fear of Perkūnas exhibits itself in the attempt to avoid his wrath, indicating a widespread understanding of Perkūnas as a judge. Perkūnas protects truth and morality, and receives numerous requests to correct injustice, especially injustice stemming from the feudal order.[68]

A sanctuary to Perkūnas stood at the confluence of the Nemunas and Neris rivers in Kaunas. It became part of the castle and medieval city. According to legend, an official discovered a six-inch-tall bronze statue of the god Perkūnas in a wall of the Perkūnas house in 1818. The crown on the statue possibly indicated that Perkūnas served as the protector of the city. He held three fish in his hands, probably symbolizing the Neris, Nemunas, and nearby

Nevėžis rivers. The statue was turned over to the Hermitage Museum in St. Petersburg (the Grand Duchy of Lithuania was occupied by the Russian Empire at that time, and St. Petersburg was the capital). The museum lost it. In 1864 or 1865, a 500-year-old stone statue of Perkūnas was found in the Nemunas River. This may have served as the focal point of the Perkūnas sanctuary. The governor turned the statue over to the authorities in St. Petersburg, who sold it in an auction.[69] The current statue to Perkūnas is modern.

As the executor of justice, Perkūnas fulfills the priestly function of the Indo-European sovereign class, although he is not a priest and lacks magical abilities. Perkūnas nevertheless represents the priestly aspect of the Indo-European sovereign class. He maintains law and order in the heavens and on the earth, and always responds to violations with justice. He fails as the ideal representation of the priest because of his feared terribleness: he should be the friendly god. It appears that Dievas and Perkūnas exchanged the friendly/feared attributes.

Although historical records name Perkūnas as a war god, he never directly or indirectly participates in any type of war activity. Perkūnas merely serves as a helper and protector of warriors. Greimas insists with the strongest possible language that Perkūnas is not, and never was, a war god.[70]

Žemyna is "Mother Earth," the earth goddess.[71] Her name is used synonymously with the word for earth, *žemė*. Her name is of Indo-European origin, as noted previously. She is the grain mother and mother of nourishment, out of whom humans arise and to whom they return. She probably represents the most ancient form of divinity. As the mother of all, she gives birth to humans and animals, feeds them, and allows them to create new life. She also grants health and receives the dead. The life force of dead people returns to the earth, to be renewed in a new cycle of creativity. Žemyna does not bring death herself, but transforms the dead into new life. She is womb and tomb, birth and death. Her parthenogenetic ability gives life, creates the harvest, and ensures prosperity.[72]

A clear anthropomorphic image of Žemyna never evolved. A number of descriptions refer to Žemyna with metaphors of nature, while others emphasize her birth-giving abilities. Large boulders contain Žemyna's power. Amber statues with the "characteristics of a birth-giving mother"[73] remain vague iconic images, reminiscent of Old European statuary. The tree goddess Medeinė; rock, cliff, and cave goddess Ragainė; hazelnut goddess Lazdona; grove god Giraitis; blowing noise god Puškaitis; and forest god Miškinis repeat specific aspects of Žemyna's functions, but are limited to a particular part of nature. Several chroniclers listed the forest goddess Medeinė, the beast goddess Žvėrūnė, or a variant of these as one of the principal canonical Baltic divinities.[74]

Žemyna is the universal mother, treated like a human mother. People kiss her and give her gifts. No one dares hit her. Lithuanians are very attached to the earth. They call her holy, pray to her, kiss her, and fight for her. She is the most precious treasure for a Lithuanian. Burial customs include pouring a handful of soil on the corpse, so that the body could rest at peace under its own land. Abroad, the soil must come from Lithuania.

Under the influence of Indo-European religion, Žemyna becomes the wife of Praamžius, who is one of several specific versions of the heavenly god Dievas, or the wife of the weather and thunder god Perkūnas. Both guises complete the Father Sky/Mother Earth duality indigenous to Indo-European religion. Žemyna then requires the seed of Perkūnas, which comes in the form of the first spring thunder, for growth to start.[75] She also manifests Indo-European agrarian concerns, but with a plethora of detail that is highly unusual for Indo-European mythology.

Lithuanian folklorist Jonas Balys has compiled a series of prayers to Žemyna. Lithuanians often said these types of prayers while kissing the earth. The morning prayer reads, "I came from Žemelė, to Žemelė I will return." An extended version of the same supplication may also be used at memorials for the dead: "Žemė, my mother, I am from you, you feed me, you carry me, and you will also take me after death." When departing home for a long time, one prays, "Good bye, black Žemelė, my carrier! I ran around on you when I was small, I kissed you every morning and evening." The following prayer accompanies food offerings to the goddess: "Žemyna, raiser of blossoms, bloom with rye, wheat, barley, and all grains; be happy, Goddess, upon us."[76]

Velnias, in general, protects the wealth of the earth, which includes the poor and good people.[77] Specifically, he helps peasants, guides the dead, fights Perkūnas, and pursues sex. Velnias mostly reflects the lives of the Lithuanian peasants. He has a family, a black steed, but no farmstead and no elegant clothing. He can appear as a half-man and half-animal, with a cloven foot and tail (Christianity took his name for its anti-god Satan). These traits make him appear as an atypical Indo-European god. His industriousness links him to humans, whom he always helps. He mostly engages in men's work related to farming. When he helps people, he expects a reward for himself. However, people manage to gain his assistance without paying him back. In such cases, folklore labels him the "foolish Velnias." Kazys Boruta's novella *Baltaragio malūnas* (The Windmill of Baltaragis) tells the tale of one man's ill-fated deal with Velnias, wherein he loses his wife, daughter, her fiancée, and happiness. It was transformed into a modern ballet and a hit movie. Velnias's non-human, chthonic origins limit his understanding of humans, like the earlier-mentioned Giltinė. As a result, the modern Velnias lies hidden under a veneer of alien elements. The name "Velnias" denotes not only an individual deity, but also groups of Velniases.

Appearing mostly at twilight or at night, Velnias consorts with the dead, especially the drowned and the hanged. This illustrates his relation to the world of the dead, accessible through bodies of water, which also serve as his residence. He is the god of the dead. He devours the dead and herds them in great corrals. These images unmistakably reveal an Indo-European religious understanding. He also leads armies of the dead across the sky. Velnias clearly represents the Indo-European god of the dead.

Of all the Baltic divinities, Velnias regales in sexuality. In folklore, he shows his enormous phallus to women, who, in turn, expose their breasts, buttocks, or vagina to him. Although this may appear as an Indo-European trait, this is incorrect because the Indo-Europeans regulated sexuality to maintain patrilinear lines of progeny. Velnias likes to copulate with maidens. Appearing as a virile youth, he goes to weddings and other celebrations with young people. He seeks out women as dancing partners. He then beguiles them into sexual trysts with him.

Velnias engages in a constant struggle with Perkūnas. In these battles, the pursued Velnias always hides from Perkūnas who sometimes succeeds in killing him with his lightning, cannons, or bullets. Perkūnas needs Velnias's earthly waters to make it rain. The battles between heavenly and chthonic forces are common in Indo-European mythologies. Velnias represents the Old European earth-based world order; he becomes the enemy of Indo-European order and power. The following outlines a typical folk tale about the conflict between Velnias and Perkūnas: A drunk was coming home from a bar during a thunderstorm. When he got home, he hid

WOOD SCULPTURES WITH MYTHOLOGICAL MOTIFS ON THE CIURLIONIS ROAD, DRUSKININKAI-VILIUS, LITHUANIA. FROM A POSTCARD. (COLLECTION OF THE AUTHOR)

under the eaves of his house, where he found a Velnias. Due to the storm, the man warned him that Perkūnas was trying to kill him. The man lit a pipe. Velnias sat down on it, the man inhaled, Perkūnas hit the pipe with lightning, and the man died. Velnias was unscathed.[78]

The incident reveals Velnias's nerve as well as lack of human concern. He used the man as a lightning rod to protect himself from the lightning. In addition, the man got what he deserved because he dared lecture a Velnias: the man overstepped his human limits in the encounter. The folk tale also mentions Velnias's pastime of smoking pipes. He is often portrayed in folk art standing on a pipe or sitting on one.

The opposition between Velnias and Perkūnas reflects other Indo-European structures. The priestly sovereign encounters an unrestrained opponent, whom he fights, but must tolerate. The opponent is often an ithyphallic beast-man, who is sexually promiscuous and fertile. He can be one individual or a group of beings. This describes the Lithuanian Velnias very well. In this respect, Velnias exhibits many characteristics which indicate an Old European (or even older shamanistic) origin.

Velnias occasionally assumes the Indo-European magical sovereign function in mythology. For example, Dievas cannot create the world without Velnias's cooperation. Velnias partially fulfills this deficiency of Dievas: Velnias's creativity stems from uncontrollable, ferocious impulsiveness, but leads to worthless, useless, or imperfect creations. With Dievas, Velnias does not have these limits. In one myth, Dievas sends Velnias to the bottom of the sea to bring up dirt, from which Dievas creates the earth.[79] Although the two compete, Dievas cannot undertake the work of creation without Velnias. It is noteworthy that Dievas cannot enter the water, whereas Velnias can. This symbolically underscores the mythological understanding of Velnias as the god of chthonic waters.

Velnias's fecundity and productivity make him an agrarian deity of the third Indo-European class. He still has Old European traits and associations, such as his inability to manage the human world, frenzied work habits, and unbridled sexuality. Baltic religion quite successfully integrated Velnias into the Indo-European pantheon of gods. For example, he became the first member of the trinity in Baltic Prussian religion, mentioned earlier.

Laumė is a goddess of Old European or possibly even older origin.[80] She represents a multifaceted, unpredictable deity. She is very often simply called Deivė, meaning goddess. She helps with women's work quickly and effortlessly, often entering into a work frenzy, becoming destructive, and bringing death. Laumė's anthropomorphic forms also reflect her Old European association.[81] Capable of endless transformation, Laumė usually takes the human form of a huge, goat-like woman with enormous, sagging breasts, or of an ugly woman with a long tongue, long fingers, long breasts, and sharp, long nails and teeth. She can also appear as a beautiful, blond, naked, sexually irresistible woman. She can appear as a single Laumė or, most often, as a group of Laumės. During the period of Old European civilization, the bird goddesses established many fundamental traits of Laumė. To this day, the bird familiars and substitutes of Laumė include pigeons, hens, and roosters. Laumė also frequently has hen's feet in place of human feet, or lives in a house built on a single stilt, called a "hen's foot."

Laumė helps women—especially orphans and poor peasants—with traditional women's work. She assists with the care of children and in the production of clothing. She always protects lost or accidentally forgotten children, rewarding the mother upon her return. On the other hand, she kills the children and punishes the women who dishonestly deceive her to seek rewards from her. She replaces healthy children with her own sick or crippled ones, which serves as an etiological explanation for natural deformity. Her appearance alone results in overall enhanced fertility: plant, animal, and human. Laumė seeks unrestricted carnal relations with men. She then either rewards the man who succumbs to her or kills him.[82] She spins and weaves fine, thin thread of exceptional quality. However, she does not know her own limits. She enters a supernatural industrious frenzy that she cannot stop. She then spins or weaves anything she can find, including human hair and intestines.[83]

Water and earth define Laumė's existence. She lives and appears in the vicinity of water and many bodies of water bear her name. The rainbow, called the sash of Laumė, reiterates the latter's relationship to water. Particular rocks and earth formations, resembling a woman's body, embody Laumė,[84] although this may be a sign of a well-documented confusion with Laima in the later mythological record.

Laumė is dangerous. Controlling a supernatural being such as Laumė requires naming it. The following synopsis of a myth reveals the power of a name. A woman was weaving and took a break. Laumė took her place and proceeded to weave exceptionally beautiful fabric at a superhuman speed. The woman came back and realized what had happened. Laumė told her to guess her name if she wanted to get rid of her. The woman went out and listened to Laumė's song: "Weave, weave, Krauzelė." She came back in and thanked Laumė, by name, for the weaving. Laumė left furious because she was not paid for her work.[85] What the myth leaves unsaid is the woman's knowledge about Laumė. She would have to pay her for her work; moreover, it could become very costly and dangerous, possibly even life-threatening.

Under Indo-European religion, a small number of rare myths depicted Laumė as the wife of Perkūnas, but this may also be an example of the conflation between Laumė and the aforementioned Laima. This very odd combination promoted Laumė into the heavenly family, probably in order to control her unrestrained abilities.[86] It also instituted mythological hierarchical and patriarchal control of the potential chaos that Laumė represents. Her absolute disinterest in ships, horses, the heavens, and other aspects of Indo-European culture emphasizes her more ancient origins. Christianity demonized Laumė as a type of witch.

In spite of the connection to Perkūnas, Laumė's true mythological counterpart (not paramour) is Velnias. Both are chthonic deities related to earthly waters. Both perform complementary tasks: she does women's work, he does men's work. Both work equally well and fast. Both engage in human chores exceedingly well, but get into dangerous, all-consuming frenzies in their work. Both innately lack the ability to stop when they run out of material or when they complete their task. Both excel in complementary spheres: Velnias in the pastoral, and Laumė in the domestic. Both punish people, including killing them. Both live in or near bodies of water. Both help orphans and the poor. Both also maintain an animosity to Perkūnas, although Laumė's conflict lacks the prominence of Velnias's. Both names refer to an individual and to a group of similar individuals. Both exhibit unrestrained sexuality that readily violates social sexual norms. It is important to note that both also have a tenuous relationship with the Indo-European pantheon.

The sun goddess Saulė perfectly reflects the Indo-European solar deity.[87] She appears as a golden-haired woman or maiden in golden or white silk clothing, including a golden or silver woolen shawl. She wears a decorated golden crown and golden rings. The course of the sun across the sky determines the hours worked on the fields: sunrise and sunset, therefore, remain reserved for special activities.

As a country woman and female head of the heavenly family, Saulė lives in her own house on her own homestead on the heavenly mountain, where she cultivates her own gardens. Her domestic and agrarian duties encompass all of woman's work, as determined by Baltic definitions of gender. She also plays the zither-like instrument called *kanklės* in Lithuanian. Although she owns a great number of them, she never rides her steeds, instead driving a magnificent, multi-wheeled carriage. Like Dievas, she drives her wagon slowly up and down the heavenly mountain. The ride corresponds to the changing of the seasons.

A wonderful tree known as the "sun's tree" symbolizes Saulė. In addition to trees, Saulė maintains a close association with the sea, into which she sinks daily. She crosses the sea by boat at night, sometimes sleeping on an island in the sea. She often cries for a variety of reasons, or engages in prolonged arguments with her unfaithful husband Mėnulis, her own daughters, or with the sons of Dievas.

In the earthly realm, Saulė always helps humans, especially those in need or hard at work. She also heals the sick and the injured. She participates in the propagation of well-being and of earthly fecundity, especially at weddings and in the summer solstice celebration. Under Christianity, Saulė's traits were transferred to Mary, the Mother of God.

The following *daina*, "Kas tar teka" (Who is Flowing There?), greets Saulė on summer solstice morning and serves as the morning hymn to the sun.

> Who is flowing there, through the manner, dear sun? What is she carrying while flowing, dear sun? She is bringing presents, dear sun. Who will get the presents, dear sun? The first one whom I will meet in the morning, dear sun. I met my father-in-law, dear sun. I gave him the presents, dear sun. He is thankful for the presents, dear sun.[88]

This *daina* belongs to a specific sub-genre called a *sutartinė*. It is a polyphonic *daina* sung by women in an asynchronous, fourfold round.[89] The sun travels through the sky by flowing like a river of water. The presents that she brings are, at a minimum, sunlight and the new day. They are intended for the first person awake, that is, an industrious individual dedicated to his work. The father-in-law, the head of the household, happens to be that person this morning. This indicates his concern for his family and farm. He is thankful for the gifts.

Mėnulis is an ideal representation of the Indo-European moon god.[90] His name derives from a Proto-Indo-European word that means both moon and time measurement. He travels across the sky in a small boat, indicating the notion that the Balts understood the sky as a sea. His appellations recognize him as a traveler and giver of light, especially at night. Furthermore, the phases of the moon possess special healing powers and determine a variety of agrarian activities and prohibitions. As such, he becomes a helper in times of need, in particular for people living in difficult social situations, such as the oppressed, the poor, and the orphaned.

Mėnulis belongs to the heavenly family, and participates in all of the communal activities of the heavenly farmstead, including those in the sauna. He also has his own family. He maintains a give-and-take relationship with the sun goddess, his former wife, whom he left in favor of an affair with the morning star Aušrinė. As a handsome young man or sometimes old and wise, he wears a princely cloak of stars, other silken and silver clothing, a crown of stars, and boots. He has his own house on the heavenly mountain, and usually drives a wagon and only rarely rides his horses. He can also transform himself into a wondrous white steed.

In addition to lunar function, some of the mythology of Mėnulis represents him in the Indo-European warrior class. Mėnulis sometimes appears as a knight with his own troops, indicating he is a war god. His princely warrior garments emphasize his subjugation to the rule of Dievas. His garb makes him the only divinity indicating hierarchic rank in the Baltic. He and his massive company of troops participate in battles, ensuring victory. Relatives of warriors, especially sisters, call on him seeking his protection for their loved ones. His direct and active warrior engagement makes him a good representative of the Indo-European warrior class.

In Lithuania, Mėnulis's warrior traits, his troops, his lunar imagery, and his pursuit of Aušrinė were transferred to St. Casmir by the start of the sixteenth century, that is, very soon after the saint's death. His hagiography depicts him in deep devotion to St. Mary (Saulė), waiting at dawn (Aušrinė) for the church to open. During a battle with the Russians, St. Casmir appeared in the sky (the daytime moon) and led the Lithuanians to victory.

Saulė divorces Mėnulis for his affair with Aušrinė, the morning star. The following etiological *daina* tells the circumstances of their divorce:

> In the first spring, the moon married the dear sun. The dear sun rose early, the darling moon left her side. The moon walked around by himself. He fell in love with the morning star. Perkūnas, with great anger, split him in two with his sword. Why did you leave the dear sun? Fall in love with the morning star? Walk around alone at night?[91]

The *daina* reveals the primordial arrangement of the sun and the moon, according to Lithuanian understanding. It also accounts for the discrepancy between the lunar and solar calendars. Perkūnas demonstrates his role as divine judge according to the Indo-European paradigm. His sentence is harsh, but it accounts for the phases of the moon.

In the most ancient of times, the Balts used to worship a snake as a goddess.[92] According to Gimbutas, the Lithuanian Žaltys may have originated as a son of such a snake goddess, or may have developed as a male variant of her. Very few ancient Baltic sculptures depict garter snakes, and only historical sources provide any religious information about them.[93] Modern folklore is resplendent with garter-snake motifs and imagery. According to the extant remnants of Žaltys mythology, Žaltys brings domestic prosperity and dwells in a magical, underground world. Farmers keep a garter snake as a pet as well as a household god.

"Eglė, Queen of the Snakes" is the most famous myth about Žaltys. It has been adapted for Lithuanian literature, drama, ballet, art, and music many times. The Lithuanian Symbolist painter Mikalojus Konstantinas Čiurlionis included the Žaltys as a motif in his paintings. The most famous literary version is the poem by Salomėja Nėris. A summary of the myth follows. Eglė ("fir") and her sisters were bathing nude in a river when a Žaltys ("garter snake") in his natural earthly form of a garter snake crawled into Eglė's blouse. His name was Žilvinas. When she found him, he demanded her hand in marriage. She refused at first, but had to agree, because he would not leave otherwise. She thought she would be able to evade her promise. Her family decided to prevent the marriage by killing Žilvinas, but relented when a myriad of garter snakes descended upon their home. When the couple arrived in Žilvinas's underwater kingdom, Žilvinas transformed into a beautiful young prince, and all the other garter snakes became human beings as well.

Eglė and Žilvinas were married, spent many happy years together, and had three sons and a daughter, all named after trees, like their mother: Ąžuolas ("oak"), Uosis ("ash"), Beržas ("birch"), and Drebulė ("trembling poplar"). The children wanted to visit their grandparents. Realizing danger from his in-laws, Žilvinas tried to discourage and prevent Eglė, but finally reluctantly agreed to let his wife and children go. He stayed behind. He gave them a spell for their return, making them promise not to reveal it: "Žilvinas, dear Žilvinas, send a milky foam if you are alive. If you are not, send bloody foam."

Eglė and the children had a wonderful vacation at her parents' house. When it was time to leave, Eglė's brothers tried to persuade her to stay. They then interrogated each of the children individually, seeking to find out the secret of their return. The boys held fast, but the fearful Drebulė revealed the secret. The brothers quickly killed Žilvinas. When Eglė and her children called Žilvinas, bloody foam rose from the waters and Žilvinas's disembodied voice revealed the trickery, "Our little daughter did not keep her word." Everyone began to cry. Eglė wished for them to turn into trees, and they did, according to their names. The names were significant

THE KULGRINDA ENSEMBLE PERFORMING A WOMEN'S WEDDING DANCE. (PHOTO COURTESY OF JONAS TRINKŪNAS)

because they symbolized the human characteristics of the individual. The weak and fearful Drebulė became trembling poplar that shakes and weeps in the slightest breeze.

The myth addresses various themes. The concern of Eglė's family for her safety is genuine because she is being forced into a marriage with an unknown, supernatural husband. However, the marriage turns out well. Danger always lurks when the human and supernatural realms encounter each other: Eglė's family does not trust her married life. It wants to keep her squarely in the human realm. Eglė's brothers are also the children's uncles. They share responsibility for protecting their nephews and nieces according to Lithuanian custom. They use extraordinary means—force against their own—to protect Eglė and her children. The family is betrayed from within: the weak young female child becomes the object of both betrayal and blame. Mythologically, this reinforces an Indo-European stereotype about women. From the perspective of the paternal family, she has done no wrong. From Eglė's perspective, she has effectively destroyed her nuclear family and the happiness she had obtained. The myth ends with grief and metamorphosis of the character into non-human nature. After death, humans can return as plants or trees.

The Lithuanian god Ragutis protects beer, mead, and those who make beer and mead.[94] These drinks were ritually poured as libations to Ragutis and other deities at certain holidays. A Ragutis festival used to be held in February, during which a statue of Ragutis was borne about on a sleigh. People in animal and mythological costumes accompanied the procession, as well as cross-dressers. Ragutis's wife Ragutienė was honored at a special ritual for opening a keg. This was a family ritual led by the female and male heads of the household. Special women-only rituals for Ragutis called *ragutienės* were also held.

Ragutis's name stems from the word *ragas*, meaning "horn." Horns served as drinking vessels. Originally, they probably came from the taurus bulls that once populated the Lithuanian forests. Many richly decorated ritual horns depicted Ragutis and his wife. Several locations bear Ragutis's name. Houses called *"troba ragutiškė"* were used for beer rituals.

The Ragutis temple at Vilnius used to stand within the walled medieval city, on the periphery of the castle territory. The entire castle complex and inner city belonged to the sacred Vilnius forest that contained multiple sanctuaries. In 1345, a wooden Russian Orthodox Church replaced the temple.

Milda is the goddess of love and beauty. She had a sanctuary in the Aleksotas hills of Kaunas, at the confluence of the Nemunas and Neris rivers. Oak and linden trees grew on the hills. Ideal offerings to Milda are flowers. Her festival in May at the height of spring bloom attracted many young people: couples took rides around the winding hills, while women floated flower wreaths in the Nemunas. The goddess rode through the skies in a carriage pulled by pigeons, sprinkling the earth with spring flowers (May in Lithuanian means "pigeon"). A temple to Milda used to stand in Vilnius where it served as the northern border of the holy forest. The St. Peter and Paul Church replaced the sanctuary.[95]

Myth relates that Milda's son Kaunas founded Lithuania's second city Kaunas. Like Vilnius, it has a rich religious past, originally serving as a sanctuary, and later becoming a medieval castle and a merchant city. The confluence of the rivers attracted many black crows, an animal of death in Lithuanian mythology. Cremations probably took place at the confluence. The noble dead became black crows after cremation.[96]

How can the Lithuanian deities be summarized? Most of the

gods and goddesses share in the duties of the agrarian class, which encompasses farming and stockbreeding. Dievas and Saulė, through their seasonal journeys up and down the heavenly mountain, deliver agrarian vitality to the earth as well as retract it. They also work the fields with their families. Perkūnas impregnates the earth and imparts maturation upon the grains. Žemyna protects and propagates the earth while Laima watches over human life. Velnias and Laumė concern themselves with human work and sexuality.

The relationship between Lithuanians and their gods deserves some discussion. In its transcendental aspect, Baltic Lithuanian religion reveres divine and other supernatural beings. Some—but not all—of them are prayed to for blessing. For example, Dievas, Perkūnas, Žemyna, and Laima are beings of reverence and recipients of prayer, but Giltinė, Velnias, and Laumė are not. The deities and some other supernatural beings can help people, while most non-divine supernatural entities are dangerous or even hostile. An *aitvaras* (fiery dragon), *kaukas* (agricultural dwarf or elf), or *barstukas* (forest dwarf or elf), for example, possess mysterious and dangerous powers.

Traditional Lithuanian understandings of divinity reveal anthropomorphic, pantheistic, and animistic characteristics. The anthropomorphic or personified deities are forces of nature or sometimes animals that have taken on human forms. The anthropomorphic deities are not human or superhuman. They do not have the full range of human passions or drives, although they exhibit some human emotions and concerns. Saulė and Mėnulis serve as excellent examples. They are natural bodies or phenomena that have assumed human form, regalia, and functions. The deities can also be personified concepts. The prime examples would be the heavenly sky god Dievas and the weather and justice god Perkūnas. In myths, they appear as if they were human characters.

Lithuanians have conventionally categorized their pagan religion as pantheism, erroneously defining pantheism as a belief in many gods. Actually, pantheism denotes an all-inclusive immanent deity who is both synonymous with nature as well as personal, conscious, and omniscient. The earth goddess Žemyna is the prime Lithuanian example of normative pantheism. The earth and all growing things are this deity: she is a goddess and living nature. She does not take human form. A retinue of minor deities, representing the flora and fauna, are emanations of this all-important deity. Some of these sometimes take an anthropomorphic form, but they always revert to their natural state.

Animism is the belief that spirits inhabit and control ordinary objects. Lithuanian beliefs include various animistic elements, many of which reflect metempsychosis, the post-mortem transmigration of a human soul into a non-human object. Lithuanians often perceive their afterlife as a tree or even a flower, for example, as in the myth of Eglė. In addition, forests, groves, and bodies of water can be filled with various unpredictable and beneficial spirits.

Religious Practices

The practical expression of Baltic Lithuanian religion is a national living tradition, even more popular than singing the *dainos*. Most Lithuanians celebrate the major holidays according to ethnographic customs. Lithuanians refer to their holidays by name or as a *šventė*, "holiday." The word *apeiga*, meaning "ceremony," applies to the ritual portions of the holidays. The English words "rite" and "ritual" have very different connotations from their Lithuanian equivalents, especially in a Western pagan religious context: the Lithuanian ceremonies contain none of the content or structures that are commonplace in neopaganism, ceremonial magic, Wicca, and the like. In this article, I have used the words "rites" and "rituals" in the comparative religious sense to identify the communal religious practices of Baltic Lithuanian religion. Moreover, Lithuanians—not just Romuva—celebrate the practices described below. The customs relating to each celebration have a great variety of regional and local variations.

Rituals with prehistoric roots mark seasonal agrarian and lifecycle celebrations. The cycle of the solar calendar includes the following primary holidays (there are many more): Kūčios (winter solstice eve), Kalėdos (winter solstice day), Užgavėnės ("escort of winter"), Velykos (spring equinox), Rasa or Kupolinė (summer solstice), Rugių šventė (rye harvest), and Vėlinės (the commemoration of the dead). The primary human rites-of-passage focus on birth (name-giving), weddings, and funerals.[97] Christianity initially opposed the Lithuanian ethnic religious practices, but eventually incorporated many elements from them or Christianized them outright by replacing the Baltic Lithuanian content with a Christian one. Twentieth-century urbanization often combined regional varieties to form new national composite versions. Modernity also saw the secularization of some holidays. The discussion of the holidays will begin with the household shrine.

The *alka* is the home shrine.[98] The traditional Lithuanian home of a farmer stands on the ancestral land. It is the homestead and houses the hearth fire. Home shrines are erected in the sacred corner of the home, where the family or household gods and Žemyna would be worshiped. A *krikštas* chair stands in that corner: it is the chair of transition from one stage of life to the next. Relatives welcome all newborns and take leave of the dead at the shrine. Newlyweds first go to the home shrine after their wedding. The household gods are sometimes called the Numėjai. They live in the home and protect it. They are also called the Pagirniai or "gods under the millstone." They frequently take the guise of a garter snake. At most holidays, these gods are the first to be worshiped with libations and food offerings.[99]

Kūčios and Kalėdos, now celebrated on 24 and 25 December, mark the end and beginning of the solar year, respectively.[100] The two holidays celebrate the transition from light to darkness and back to light again. They also herald the return of the sun. In all of their aspects, both rites celebrate human solidarity, encompassing the nuclear and extended families, the local community, and all the living and the dead.

Adults begin to prepare for the winter solstice by placing a cherry twig in water on the day when bears start to hibernate. This is in early December. This is the first day of winter, according to folklore. The twigs sprout roots in time for the solstice. For their part, children play games by planting crops: they imitate sowing the floor with hemp seeds, for example. For girls, this magical game invites dreams about future husbands. Indo-European cultures traditionally greet the New Year with rituals that reenact and relate the creation of the world. In Lithuania, an elderly mendicant called Senelis Elgeta retells everything that has happened since the creation.

The solemn feast of Kūčios unites the living with the dead, as well as people and their animals.[101] Kūčios continues the commemoration of the dead that began with Vėlinės in mid-autumn. Houses require special preparation. Families hang up an iconic grove called a *sodas*: birds made of wood, straw, or eggshells surrounding a straw sun. These groves and many burning candles invite the *vėlės*, shades of the dead. The ancestral spirits sit at a small table with bread, salt, and the *kūčia* dish on it. The *kūčia* contains traditional grains and legumes that symbolize regeneration: cooked wheat, barley, peas, beans, rye, poppy seeds, hemp seeds, and so forth, mixed with nuts and honey water. It feeds the ancestors and the living. The living sit at another table, covered with hay and a tablecloth. In earlier days, hay also used to cover the floor. Symbols of the life force that sustain the human world decorate the main table. This includes a bundle of unthreshed rye that the family will use the next day to bind its apple trees.

Before gathering for the Kūčios meal, everybody bathes in the *pirtis* or sauna bath, makes up with their neighbors, and forgives their enemies. It is a ritual washing. As with most major holidays, the ritualized *pirtis* bath precedes the holiday. It is a wood-stoked steam sauna heated by hot rocks. The oven of the *pirtis* is heated for three to four hours, making the rocks inside red hot. Men precede women and children in the *pirtis*. Very hot water, also heated in the *pirtis*, is poured on the rocks, filling the room with boiling hot steam. Sitting in the *pirtis* alternates with dunking in a river or lake (or barrel of water) several times. While in the *pirtis*, people do not wear clothing. To stimulate circulation, they beat themselves with sapling birch tree twigs.

Kūčios is an exclusively nocturnal celebration. It begins when the evening star appears in the sky. In olden days, the head of the household, wearing high black boots, a large black woven sash, and a prominent black hat, used to circle the farmstead three times. This was a ritual blessing. He would approach the door of the home after everybody else had entered. He would knock. His wife would ask at the door, "Who is there?" He would answer, "Dearest Dievas with the *kūčia* begs admittance."

Once the family gathers, the eldest member (man or woman) says a traditional invocation and breaks the *Kūčia* rye bread, which everybody gives to each other. Every member of the family, placing bread on the floor, prays as follows: "Žemėpatis (god of the homestead), we thank you for the good bread you give us. Help us work the fields while blessing you, that dearest Žemyna would continue to give us your good gifts." Then everyone, raising the bread to the sky, concludes with: "Nourish us."[102] The Christian version uses unconsecrated communion wafers called *plotkeliai* in place of bread: the Polish name reveals the alien origins of this substitution. After the exchange of the *Kūčia* bread, each person sips some beer, pouring libations onto the floor for the *vėlės*, the souls of the dead.

Kūčios traditionally required seven, nine, twelve, or thirteen different foods, reflecting the seven days of the week, twelve solar months, or thirteen lunar months. Nine is the magical combination of 3 x 3, with 3 being the base magical number. The Christian version has twelve dishes, one for each of the apostles (including the traitor Judas). This, of course, is a specious explanation since no apostles attended Jesus' birth. The foods may not contain any meat or milk, although a few locations in Lithuania include a stewed pig's head. The meal consists of *kūčia* (mixed-grain dish described above), hot beet soup, mushroom dumplings, hazelnuts, cabbage, herring, pike, and other seasonal seafood. Sweets include *kisielius* (a sweet cranberry soup, thickened with starch), *prėskutis* (small sweet poppy seed biscuit), poppy seed milk, apples, and fruit compote. All the dishes are simple, rustic, country food, although modern additions include shrimp cocktail, salmon, and even sushi.

Animals partake of the solemnities by eating the same food as the people. On farms, families still feed their animals with the leftovers from Kūčios (as do pet owners in cities). They share the food with bees and fruit trees. In the depths of the night, people may not listen to the animals because humans can understand animal language during this night: the animals discuss the fate of their human masters. Whoever hears an animal talking is likely to die in the following year.

After dinner, the children and teenagers pull straws of hay out from underneath the tablecloth to predict their fate. For example, a long straw represents a long and prosperous life. The adults would also predict their own fortunes in a variety of ways, especially by reading melted wax or lead poured into a bowl of cold water. Participants exchange wishes and blessings for each other by pouring grains into the hearth fire. Each single grain "sown" in the fire grows and prospers in someone's life. Some families burn a birch wreath, stump, or log in the hearth, representing the destruction of the old year. Participants can destroy evil by burning splinters they infuse with meaning. Late-night dancing follows for the young.

The following day, the merry traditions of Kalėdos celebrate the return of the sun, called Mother Saulė. The word Kalėda symbolically means the sun, as in the following holiday *daina*: "Look, holy Kalėda returns, the great Kalėda, for it is the day of Kalėda. Iron wheels, silk lashes, the great Kalėda, for it is the day of Kalėda."[103] The solar carriage has iron wheels, instead of the wooden or ironclad wheels that farmers had. Saulė uses a silk lash to control her horses. Nine-horned reindeer can accompany the sun. They represent the unity of the three worlds: past, present, and future. The season lasts twelve to fourteen days, accompanying the weeklong solstice standstill of the sun in its travels through the sky.

People carry solar disks through the fields and the towns in an act of blessing. They wish prosperity for everyone they meet. They visit relatives, friends, and neighbors during this season and exchange good wishes with each other. Greetings and wishes expressed during Kalėdos possess a magical potency that guarantees their fulfillment. This represents the power of the word spoken during an auspicious time. Various characters called *kalėdotojai* wander about, including Senelis Elgeta, mentioned earlier. These are humans dressed as goats, cranes, bulls, steeds, bears, and other animals. The supernatural Juodas Kudlotas, "the black curly furry one," represents the power of harvest prosperity and richness. The traditional meal includes pork, meats, cakes, and ash berry juices.

During the day, wandering men and women drag a log called a Kalėda or a *blukis* ("log") from house to house and around the entire town. It symbolizes the old year. They sing, dance, play music, and enact tricks along the way. In the evening, they burn it. In Latvia, this tradition took place during Kūčios, which the Latvians call *Bluka vakars*, "log evening." Some Lithuanians practice a family version of this rite, mentioned earlier, during Kūčios.

Užgavėnės, or the "escort of winter," essentially anticipates spring and helps prepare for the new season.[104] Under Christian influence, this festival became the movable holiday of Fat Tuesday or Carnival (the day before Ash Wednesday). Earlier it was probably celebrated on the first day of spring, 1 March. Many varied traditions accompany this celebration. The holiday consists of processions, costumes, merrymaking, games, and skits. It is a community celebration: all families participate in the revelries of the village. The region of Samogitia has preserved many holiday traditions, most of which spread and became national in the twentieth century.

The main foods of the holiday are pancakes; jelly-filled, fried yeast dumplings called *spurgos*; and a hodgepodge stew of groats, peas, and meat. Contestants race in sleds trying to tip each other over so that everybody rolls around in the snow. The sleigh-riders also splash anyone they can with water. People visit their neighbors and nearby villages. The head of the household greets the strange guests as if he were a government bureaucrat by asking, "Who are you? Do you have your ID card?" The costumed revelers respond with, "We are poor people from a land that has been pinched away. This land lies on the other side of running water, two weeks away."[105] In each house, one of the guests steals something from the household and tries to sell it to the head of the household, who buys it with food and drink.

People dress in various extraordinary costumes. No one is who he or she seems to be. A crane hops about and tries to pinch people and peck at them. A goat walks around bleating. Children block its way, asking for milk. When someone tries to milk it, the goat kicks over the bucket. A horse tries to kick people. A Hungarian doctor tries to sell his medicine (bottled water), saying in an accented voice, "Whoever drinks my potion will regain health with the sweep of a hand." The goddess Giltinė, dressed in black with a white veil over her face, carries a sickle and tries to kill the doctor. A Gypsy carries a baby and a bottle. She asks for alms and predicts the future, while the baby cries ceaselessly and urinates (pours water) over everyone. Wandering mendicants sing songs, carry bags, and ask for alms. Soldiers wear straw ties as belts and carry straw swords. A cross-dressed wedding party consists of a small fat woman as the groom, a tall thin man as the bride, and other weird guests. Mythologically, the characters represent the inversion of the human and supernatural realms.

In addition to pouring water on people, the wanderers strew ashes all around, carrying them in a sock that they hit on people's backs. One person carries around a hen's bone and tries to hang people on it. Someone constantly shakes a rattle. A group of children buzzes like bees under a cloth, as if in a beehive. Others sprinkle them with water. Someone sells herring from a vat filled with water, but buyers merely get splashed. People go swinging on swings: the sympathetic magic encourages the grains to grow as high as the swings reach. The holiday ends with the burning of the straw doll of Morė, the winter witch. Symbolizing the old, she is made from the last grain sheaves of the previous year. Her burning accompanies the victory of the weak and meager Kanapinis ("hemp being")—who embodies spring—in his war against the fat and strong Lašininis ("bacon being")—winter.

Velykos, the spring equinox, begins the many springtime celebrations.[106] Christianity combined Velykos with Easter and made it a movable holiday. The week before Velykos is called the Velykos of *vėlės* ("souls"). It concludes the annual cycle of commemorations of the dead: Vėlinės, Kūčios, and Velykos. The cycle accompanies the *vėlės* as they come home in fall, visit their progeny in winter, and return to the fields in spring. There they protect and bless the harvest. In other words, *vėlės* continually visit the living. Families remember their dead and leave their dinners on the tables overnight for the *vėlės* to eat. The *vėlės* are asked out of the homes and invited to spend the growing season outdoors in the fields.

The main symbol of Velykos is the *verba*, principally made of juniper, birch, and willow twigs interwoven with colored papers and flowers. It symbolizes the force of life, the birth of new life, and the rebirth of nature. It also restores health. About a week before Velykos, people whip each other with *verbas*, wishing each other well and reminding each other that Velykos is coming soon. The region of Vilnius makes a special kind of *verba* that is a bouquet of dried flowers and herbs tied to a hand-held pole. This type of *verba* is preserved through the year.

On the morning of Velykos everyone tries to rise as early as possible in order to find the other family members sleeping and whip them awake with the *verba*. This insures completing work on time as well as good health. People respectfully whip the earth with *verbas*, awakening her life powers: plants, buds, and fruits. On no other occasion does anyone dare hit the earth. For the daring, Velykos includes swimming in rivers and lakes or—for those who fear the cold—in saunas. People place *verbas* by natural wells, thus blessing the spring water.

The traditional foods for Velykos include eggs, cheeses, cakes, ham, and oat sprouts. People give each other gifts of dyed multi-colored and decorated eggs called *margutis*. It is the other main symbol of Velykos. The meal starts with the exchange and hitting of *margutis* eggs. The eggs symbolize the rebirth of nature, the creation of life, the birth of plants, and rejuvenation in general. Decorations include solar and ophidian symbols. Everybody tests the durability of their eggs by participating in various egg-hitting contests. The winners—those with the strongest eggs—gain strength for the entire year. Cheaters use wooden eggs or hollowed eggs filled with wax. Breaking eggs reenacts the breakage of the cosmic egg, from which the snake comes to grant life and fertility. The *žaltys*, the zigzagged garter snake, also wakes from hibernation at this time.

In a tradition called *lalavimas*, the young men, women, and children of a village go from house to house, serenading young women and girls with their musical instruments. The visitors give *margutis*

CELEBRATION OF RASA (SUMMER SOLSTICE) AT LAKE SARTAI, 1988. FROM A POSTCARD. (COLLECTION OF THE AUTHOR)

eggs as presents, wishing the women and their households good fortune. Young people also wander outdoors, through the fields and forests, singing loudly and yelling *"skalsa!,"* which expresses wishes for life and for prosperity.

Swinging at Velykos and throughout the spring helps nature arouse out of its long winter's sleep. People hang swings from tree branches and sometimes even build tall swings for the occasion. The goal is to swing as high as possible. Special *dainos* accompany the frantic and often daredevil swinging. Families extinguish their winter hearth fires. Outdoors, the villagers kindle a new fire with flint, invoking the fire and hearth goddess Gabija. The spring fire symbolizes the light and warmth which new growth requires for maturation.

The summer solstice has two names: Rasa focuses on the dew, while Kupolinė emphasizes the blooming and blossoming herbs.[107] Nights are longest and nature is at the height of its growth. No other holiday is as joyous as Rasa. In parts of Lithuania, the holiday lasted for fourteen days, a tradition that continues in a few remote locations. Christianity converted Rasa into St. John's Day. In

Latvia, St. John's is a two-day state holiday celebrating the Baltic Latvian holiday and the Christian one.

Before Rasa night, everybody went to holy rivers and lakes to wash and bathe in hopes of staying young. People who completed all Rasa rituals were believed to become immensely wise, possessing the power to see evil people, charlatans, and witches. A gate demarcates the festival area from the outer world. Everyone who passes through the gate becomes a participant. The men dance a circle around one side of the gate, while the women do so around the other side: they greet each other where the circles meet.

The name Rasa, meaning "dew," reflects the deep chthonic origins of water and dew in folk belief. The amount of dew on Rasa morning predicts the abundance of that year's harvest. Before sunrise, Rasa dew possesses exceptional healing powers. Washing in the dew, especially in the rye fields, increases one's beauty. Girls washed in the dew before dawn, and returned to bed hoping to dream of their future husbands. People dragged sheets across the fields, collecting the dew, which was then used as healing water. Witches did the same and might drag their towels over cows, stealing their milk. In addition to dew, a light rain or drizzle is considered an auspicious Rasa blessing.

At midsummer, herbs, especially medicinal ones, possess the greatest possible healing ability. On the eve of Rasa, girls collect herbs into bundles that are tied to an herb pole, called the *kupolė*, hence the second name of the holiday, Kupolinė "festival of the herb pole." The flowers include daisies, St. John's wort, bilberries, and other yellow flowers. A *kupolė* is set up in the center of the grounds: the top of the *kupolė*, which represents the world tree, has a three-pronged branch. The *kupolė* is a magical tree whose one branch blossoms like the sun, the other branch like the moon, and the third branch like the stars. Lithuanians in Prussia crowned their *kupolės* with wreaths and multicolored, fluttering ribbons. They erected their *kupolės* at the edge of their homesteads, near the fields of rye.

Rasa is also the festival of woven wreaths, made from flowers and herbs; women wear them as headgear. They decorate houses, doors, and gates with the wreaths. Men wear wreaths of oak leaves. Girls predict their weddings by tossing their wreaths over their heads, backwards on to the *kupolė*. The number of throws indicates the years to wait before marriage. At night, the young people float their wreaths with candles on them. A girl's and a boy's wreath floating side by side indicates their impending marriage.

Hearth fires are extinguished with clean water and a new fire is ignited at the Rasa bonfire. People greet each other, wish each other well, greet the sun, and honor nature at this fire. Newlyweds bring embers from the fire into their homesteads, thereby inviting harmony and goodness into their homes and lives. In the early hours of the morning, couples jump over the bonfire embers holding hands: if they do not break their grip, they will remain together. Smaller bonfires are set up on platforms, illuminating the night sky. Burning wheels are sometimes rolled down hillsides.

For a blink of an eye at midnight, the fern blooms. The brave search for this magical blossom occurs alone and in silence, resisting nocturnal supernatural dangers, for giants, witches, Laumės, and other spirits also want the all-powerful fern blossom. Whoever finds the blossom gains eternal happiness.

During the night, people wander through the fields, visiting the grain. They carry burning sticks and sing Rasa *dainos*. This blesses the grain. Everybody eats a picnic meal together. The foods include beer, cheese, bread, and eggs. People stay awake all night to greet the morning sun. The short solstice night lasts only about six and one-quarter hours in Lithuania,[108] but it never really gets dark: the twilight of dusk lasts all night long. At dawn, the sun begins its magical dance through the sky, revealing all the colors of the rainbow. The goal is to stay awake through the night for strength and prosperity in the following year.

Rasa was not only a public communal celebration. Some Lithuanians individually sought a deep communion with nature at this time of year. They would leave their jobs and families to disappear for about two weeks. They could not survive the year without pausing to contemplate the halting of the sun.

Vydūnas revived the public celebration of Rasa in 1881 on the sacred hill of Rambynas. During the years of Lithuania's interwar independence (1918–1940), the popularity of the holiday grew steadily. Visuomis-Šidlauskas popularized the celebration at his Romuva grounds on the shores of Lake Sartai. The celebrants gathered at up to twelve different bonfires, all of which were visible from the highest hill in the area. Since 1979, students from the University of Vilnius have celebrated Rasa on the shores of the same lake. In the sixties, the founders of Ramuva revived Rasa in Kernavė, the first capital of medieval Lithuania. During the end of Soviet occupation, Rasa began to assume national significance. Since the

PARTICIPANTS ASSEMBLING AT THE RITUAL ENTRANCE
GATES FOR THE RASA (SUMMER SOLSTICE) CELEBRATION, 1998.
(PHOTO COURTESY OF THE AUTHOR)

restoration of Lithuanian independence, every city has a public celebration, and most regional centers have communal ones. The urban versions generally omit the traditions, focusing on commercialism and partying. Traveling by night, one will see bonfires spreading like a sea of stars across the Lithuanian (and Latvian) countryside on this night. Some Lithuanians, Latvians, and Baltic Byelorussians try to celebrate Rasa annually at the ancient Prussian sanctuary Romovė, by the city of Chernachovski in the Kaliningrad region, which once was Baltic Prussia. The Byelorussian and Lithuanian traditions are remarkably similar and share some *dainos*, indicating the antiquity of the holiday rites and traditions.

The Rugių *šventė* is the harvest and thanksgiving festival of the rye, held around 1 August. Rye is the single most important cultivated grain in Lithuania. It is a divine grain; its fields are sacred. Of the holidays described in this article, only farmers celebrate it: urban civilization has not adopted it. Maintaining the connection to the earth, grain, and harvest, Romuva practices it in rural areas.

Women and men wear their finest white linen for the ritual, and begin the harvest in these fine clothes. A procession to the rye fields assembles the family, their hired hands, and neighbors. The female head of the household greets the rye field with bread and salt, a traditional Lithuanian rite of homage to guests. She cuts the first sheaves of rye with one swing of a sickle. This is equal to about three handfuls of grain. She ties the sheaves together, brings them home, and places them in the most honored place in the home: the *krikštas* chair, located in the corner of the house above the foundation stone. In places, wreaths were woven instead to be worn as crowns. These first sheaves have a magical power, protect the home, and grant people health and well being.

The fresh rye grain is called by a variety of names in different parts of the country: Jievaras, Javinis ("wheat being"), Dirvolika ("remnant of the harvest"), Nuogalius ("naked one"), Plonis ("thin one," very rarely in the feminine: Plonė), and Rugelis ("dear rye"). These names identify the god of the final rye sheaf to be harvested. Once the sheaves arrive at the home, the oration "The Guest Named Rugys ("Rye") Has Arrived" is proclaimed:

> The guest named Rugys has arrived. He suffered hardship, cold, and rain all year. No one consoled him, no one cared for him. Only snowdrifts covered him in the winter. In the spring, heat and storms rose to revive the rye. The rye grew like rue. During the dear summer, the heavenly sun matured the grain, delighted children and the old ones. They all were waiting for young bread. The animals and birds also know that they will not die of hunger. When the yellow ears heavily dropped to the earth, young men and women cut and tied them. Now this guest is asking you to be received happily and pleasantly. He wants the houses to be swept, cleaned, and aired since he will rest here.[109]

The speech anthropomorphizes the rye grain and traces his life cycle through the year. He is compared to the rue, the flower that represents youth, purity, and virginity. The greeting reverences the rye and underscores its importance as a Lithuanian staple food.

Another set of rituals concludes the harvest. Saulė, the sun goddess, is thanked for the harvest. The eldest woman of the household would cut a few sickles of rye, turn to the sun, and bow several times. Everyone else would watch her in silence, facing the sun. In the evening, sunset is marked solemnly. The *daina* about the world tree, "Šaly kelio," discussed earlier, actually comes from the rye harvest. A rye crown is woven from some of the ears from the last sheaf. A procession brings the crown home, accompanied by ritual *dainos* about the rye. It is given to the heads of the household. They invite Jievaras into the home as a guest who will return to the fields. During the winter, the crown is hung above the grain bin. Jievaras is considered a newborn baby, one who is born annually. A variant of the wreath comes in the form of a rye sash, similar to a braided ponytail. After the harvest, the first loaf of rye bread is baked and eaten reverently. Romualdas Granauskas has memorialized this ritual in his novella *Duonos valgytojai* (Bread Eaters). In it, he eulogizes the loss of respect for bread baking in modern culture.

Vėlinės is the ancient Lithuanian holiday to commemorate the dead.[110] Traditionally, it began after completion of all the fall harvest celebrations and used to last for four weeks in October, culminating on the first weekend in November. Under Christian influence, the festival was reduced to a single day, 2 November, but the popular celebrations still last for several weeks. The name Vėlinės literally means the festival of *vėlės*, that is, of the "shades of the dead."

At home, memorial meals used to be held to commemorate the dead of the family or of the village. One meal is still celebrated. As mentioned, most Lithuanian farmers used to live on the same homesteads as their ancestors. Their ancestral *vėlės* protect and help them and bless their lands. Therefore, with candles in hand the head of the household circles the family lands—or at least the family house—in preparation for Vėlinės. As with all holidays, everyone must first bathe in the *pirtis*. For Vėlinės, the *pirtis* sauna was reheated after everyone had finished; everything was left for the *vėlės* to wash after the men, women, and children had done so.

The guests gather at the table in silence. The meal always begins with invitations of the ancestor *vėlės* into the home and prayers to them, requesting health for the people and animals, and blessing for the fields. In some places, this ritual took place in total darkness, in other places by candlelight. A door or a window to the outdoors would be left open in order to give the *vėlės* entrance to the home. In ancient times, the *žynys* (a semi-prophetic pagan priest in charge of funerals and Vėlinės celebrations) led this part of the ritual. The following prayer begins the meal, inviting the *vėlės*:

> *Vėlės* of the dead, whom we still remember in this home; respected ancestors of our family; honored women and men worthy of eternal remembrance; especially my grand-

mother and grandfather, mother and father [naming specific names as appropriate]; also relatives, children and all, whom death took from this home, we invite to our annual feast. May it be as pleasant for you as your memory is for us.[111]

In some places, those present named all the dead whom they wished to remember.

The invocations include beer libations. In Baltic Lithuanian religion, beer was the ritual sacrificial drink. At Vėlinės everybody—rich and poor—acquired beer, even if they could normally not afford it. A prayer would be said and *dainos* for Vėlinės would be sung. Then some of the beer would be sacrificed by pouring it on the ground. The libation included the words "This is for you, *vėlės*," or something to this effect.[112] After that, everybody present drank from the special cup, used only for commemorations of the dead. In some parts of Lithuania, this ritual was very complex.

The meals normally contain no meat or fish, although some parts of Lithuania include blood sausage. Dark and red dishes (symbolizing blood) made with beets would be served, along with grain, legume, cheese dishes, and the *kūčia* (also served at Kūčios). This is the traditional dish for feeding *vėlės*. In some locations, twelve or thirteen dishes would be served, symbolizing the solar or lunar year (another echo of Kūčios). Pancakes and small jelly-filled rolls—one for each living and dead family member—are popular in some parts of Lithuania.

The dead would be called to eat, as follows: "Sit and eat as the gods allow."[113] After some silent time, the living would sit down at the table to eat. The first morsel from every dish would be sacrificed to the *vėlės*. In some places, this meant "pouring" it as a libation on the floor. In other places, the food was placed on a special dish, placed at the corner of the table or on a table in the shrine corner of the home. Food would also be given to the dead by offering it in the hearth. In Vilnius, the following prayer was recited: "Remember the ones who burned to death, who drowned, who died from falling trees or from lightning bolts. Remember those exiled to foreign lands, the exhausted, and those who died in accidents. Come, *vėlės*, drink and eat with us."[114] Aromatic grasses would also be smoldered.

Single persons, the old and unmarried, widows and widowers, other lonely persons and *elgetas* (beggars) would be invited to the meal. The *elgetas* survived by living off alms, wandering from village to village. They were once viewed as religious hermits who could easily contact the *vėlės* and the gods. An *elgeta* did not have to be poor. In ancient times, even rich people took up being an *elgeta* for periods, during which they survived by begging. Other *elgetas* were the wandering poor and homeless. Food for the *elgetas* as well as for wandering *vėlės* would be placed on the house porch or outdoors underneath the kitchen window. Folk wisdom says, "What you do for an *elgeta*, you do for a *vėlė*."

In older times during the meal the *žynys* would watch for signs from the *vėlės* in attendance. One could see *vėlės* in the steam rising from food, in the reflection on the window, on the inside of rings, and in dreams. The meal concluded with Vėlinės *dainos* and folk dances, in which the *vėlės* participated.

After the meal, the dead would be asked to return whence they came with the following or similar words: "Be bountiful to us *vėlės*; be healthy, Godspeed, bless our relatives, peace to this home! Return to where destiny leads you, and remember not to do any harm to our yard, garden, grove, and fields." Then everyone would repeat: "There is, there is not, even a spirit here."[115]

During Vėlinės, people would also visit the graves of the dead. This is the national, popular rite of modern Vėlinės. Cemeteries used to be located in villages or just outside them in groves, indicating a close relation between the living and the dead. Numerous candles would be lit at the graves of the dead, as is still done today. At this time of year, Lithuanian cemeteries blaze in evening candle light. Food from the Vėlinės meals would be placed on the graves of the dead, again to feed the *vėlės*.

The following is a translation of a *daina* sung at Vėlinės and funerals:

> I went through a field—green rye; I went through another—a green grove. The birds of the grove chirp, they calm my heart. Birds of the grove whether you chirp or not, you will not calm my heart. I do not have a father; I do not have my heart. Oh, far, far away is my father. Oh, far, far away is my old one: on a high hill, beneath the grey earth. For nine days, I did not fall asleep, for nine days I burned lamps, while waiting for my father, while waiting for my heart.[116]

The *daina* is then repeated, replacing "mother" for "father." Further repetitions include "son," "daughter," "brother," or "sister." The *daina* moves from the world of the living rye field to the forest in search of a beloved person who has died. Even nature, via the birds, cannot console a person in grief. The dead person has already traveled to the afterlife, represented by the high hill. It is both the heavens as well as the path to the world of the dead. The lot of the dead is now the grey earth, in other words, burial. The intense mourning period after death lasts nine days. This equates to the time it takes the *vėlės* to travel to Dausos, the world of the dead.[117] The first ritual commemoration of the dead after the funeral happens on the tenth day.

Lithuanians celebrate a second series of rituals that follows the human life cycle.[118] These accompany pregnancy, births, rites-of-passage, weddings, and funerals. A progression of rituals invokes protection for the mother and child during pregnancy and prepares them both for birth. Name-giving is the main ritual after birth. Various rites-of-passage guide the child through maturity and adolescence. These culminate with the wedding when an adolescent becomes a man or a woman. It is probably the most complex Lithuanian rite. The parents repeat the ritual cycle first for their children, then again as grandparents for their grandchildren. In each cycle, the individuals perform different roles. The life cycle concludes when children perform the last rites for their parents in a funeral. This article will highlight the main ceremonies: the name-giving, the wedding, and the funeral.

Vardynos, the name-giving ceremony, celebrates the birth of a child.[119] It is called *vardynos* or *krikštynos*, but Christians have adopted the later term for baptism. This particular rite had a great variety of local variants. The ritual takes place a week after birth. It transitions the newborn child from the supernatural world into the family and human community. At the same time, it invests the family members assigned for the care of the child with new roles. The ritual takes place at the home hearth. The main participants are the child, its parents, the midwife (called *pribuvėja*), the name-giving parents (godparents), and other relatives. The archaic terms *kumas* and *kuma* for the name-giving parents have almost disappeared. In older times, the family selected more than one pair of *kumas* and *kuma* for the child. The family chose them according to their traits because the child was expected to inherit their personality characteristics. The child wears a festive linen shirt with a woven ethnic sash as a belt.[120]

The *pribuvėja* cares for the child and leads the ritual. She invites the parents and the *kumas* and *kuma* with the following oration: "An unseen, unheard, unknown guest has arrived from distant and unknown lands. He/she is said to be your relative. Mother Laima has sent you a helper: a tiller of the soil (for boys)/weaver (for girls). Do you want to accept him/her and give your son/daughter a name?" Prefiguring the adult life of a child, the folkloric formula calls children either tillers or weavers. These are the idealized roles of a man and woman in agrarian society. The parents take the child and thank the *pribuvėja*. They give the child to the *kumas* and *kuma*. The father gives the *pribuvėja* a drinking ladle with a ritual drink—usually beer—in it. She pours libations on the earth with the words: "Žemyna, keep the child in health and goodness. Be graceful to the baby." The *kumas* and *kuma* place the baby on the earth: this is a blessing and a communion with the earth goddess. The *pribuvėja* passes the ladle to the father, mother, *kumas*, *kuma*, and the guests. Everyone greets each other, sips and offers libation, and passes the ladle to the next person.

The *pribuvėja* addresses the gathered guests: "Dear *kumas* and *kuma*, honored family! We celebrate a holiday that is as old as our family and nation. This is a family celebration. If you accept this guest, you will have to take care that the child grows up according to our best traditions and virtues. Teach the child to respect and love his/her parents, his/her elders, and his/her family."

The *pribuvėja* and *kuma* wash or even bathe the child. The mother makes an offering of grains into the hearth fire and pours some of the grains on the assembled guests. The *kumas* circles the hearth fire clockwise with the child. The *pribuvėja* asks for the name of the child, and the *kumas* answers. She then addresses the child: "(name of child), this is how we will call you from now on. Your name is beautiful and meaningful. You have arrived in your family." The father wraps his child with an ethnic sash and blesses his child with a kiss. The mother does the same. The *pribuvėja* then prays to the goddess: "Laima determined the fortune for our ancestors. May Laima also protect our (name of child). Dearest Laima, give this baby a good fate. Be gracious to him/her." In older times, the *pribuvėja* and the mother went to the *pirtis* to make this prayer, since children were born in the *pirtis*. The ritual included sacrificing black hens.

The parents place the child in the *krikštas* chair that stands in the corner of the house with the home shrine. The word *"krikštas"* forms the basis for the alternative name of the ritual, *krikštynos*. A *"krikštas"* is also the name for a gravestone in Lithuania Minor. The chair is reserved for the rites of passage. The child symbolically leaves the world of the womb behind and enters the world of the living through this chair. After the child, the parents, *kumas, kuma*, and grandparents sit in the chair, accepting their new roles. The *kumas* and *kuma* take responsibility for raising the child in case something happens to the parents. Other guests sit in the chair, assuming their new roles: aunts, uncles, and so on. Each of the relatives holds the child in her or his hands, even children. They can dance with the child by twirling with him or her. The meal follows. The traditional foods are eggs, bread, cheese, and beer. The *kumas* and *kuma* bring a cake. The family discusses its ancestors and history during the meal and sings *dainos*. The guests bring gifts for the child and the mother.

Church officials staunchly opposed the Lithuanian name-giving ceremony because it interfered with baptisms. In spite of opposition from the church, parts of the ceremony survived into the twentieth century. At times, the church also forced Lithuanians to baptize their children. In response, the Lithuanians invented a rite to wash off the baptism by bathing in a spring, river, or lake on the way home from baptism. A Lithuanian name replaced the Christian name.[121] Romuva revived this rite in the twentieth century.

Vestuvės, the wedding, is probably the most complicated Lithuanian ritual.[122] It is a series of well-documented rites. The ethnographer Jonas Balys has published a 75-page summary article that organizes all the extant material on Lithuanian weddings.[123] The entire cycle of rituals contains twenty-nine separate parts, twelve of which have Indo-European origins and correspond to analogous practices in Hinduism.[124] There are countless local variations of the wedding customs. Each act in the wedding has symbolic, mythological, or magical significance. Lithuanians currently celebrate selections from the traditional wedding ritual cycle, mostly in abbreviated form.

Balys has identified two themes woven through the wedding rites. The first one emphasizes the separation of the bride from her home and family in preparation for a new life with her husband. This is an overwhelmingly sad experience, in spite of the anticipated joy of marriage. The second one transitions the couple from asexuality to wedded life. The accompanying rituals invoked various blessings upon the couple: success, happiness, love, prosperity, children, and protection. The important individuals in the wedding rituals were the matchmaker, the best man, the matron of honor, and the wedding couple.[125] The following summarizes the wedding traditions that are commonly celebrated today.

The evening before the wedding is the *mergvakaris*, "girl's evening." The bride and groom separately take leave of their homes, families, and friends. Both houses would be decorated with flowers, wreaths, and a *sodas*, or hanging straw garden. The *sodas* is the most important of the wedding decorations. It is a ritual, mythological object representing a symbolic home and a miniature model of the cosmos. The bride and her women sing sad *dainos*. The fear was that the bride would not be happy in her new house or with her new family. The bride takes leave of the home hearth and shrine. According to Trinkūnas, the bride and groom are orphans during the night, from a mythological perspective.[126] The groom and his men visit the bride and her women to serenade her with *dainos* that are tearjerkers. Some of the *dainos* invoke the goddess Laima, who promises to accompany the bride through her travel to her new home. The rue wreath, symbol of the girl's chastity, will also accompany her.

The morning of the wedding, the families would lead the bride and groom around the hearth of their respective homes. This was a blessing and a farewell, especially for the bride leaving the home. The groom and his men would ride to the bride's house on horseback, where they were greeted with hostility for stealing the bride. They would offer gifts and alcohol before they were invited in as members of the family. The steps leading to the wedding become a series of obstacles that the groom has to overcome. Next, the bride and groom exchange gifts. The bride then says her final farewell to her family and receives her parent's blessing. She would also kiss the ground. Orphans would travel to their parents' graves for this part of the ritual.

For Christians, the church ceremony follows, but many Lithuanians incorporate ethnic elements in their church weddings. Romuva uses the following marriage rite that was reconstructed from historical records. Most of the rite depends on symbolic actions, not words. The wedding takes place outdoors, preferably in a sacred location. The bride and groom, wedding party, and guests wash their hands and faces with fresh well water and dry them with a linen towel. This is a ritual purification. *Kanklės* music plays. Everyone encircles the *aukuras*, the fire altar. The following deities are invoked while the fire is lit: the fire goddess Gabija, the earth goddess Žemyna, the earth god Žemėpatis, and the life goddess Laima. The chief bridesmaid cuts a lock of hair from the bride and groom, passes the locks through the rings, and burns the locks in the fire. This begins the process of uniting the couple. It also blesses the rings. The matchmaker gives the couple the rings. The bride and groom exchange rings, the physical symbols of their commitment. Then they exchange rue wreaths, the symbols of their purity and innocence. These virtues are precious. With this act, the two quite literally give themselves to each other. The officiant ties their hands with a Lithuanian ethnic sash. The couple circles the fire and says the wedding prayer to the fire. This repeats the blessing undertaken at home by circling the hearth. In this case, the ritual action sanctifies the wedding oath. The couple offers greenery into the fire in an act of thankfulness and supplication. The chief bridesmaid and groomsman cover the lips of the newlyweds with honey: the couple takes its first kiss. The honey represents the sweetness of married life. The officiant blesses and greets the couple.[127] In an older version, the bride and the groom hold right hands with their right feet on a stone or boulder to exchange their vows. Latvian Dievturi use this rite today.

After the marriage ceremony, the newlyweds travel first to the bride's house. En route, they encounter obstacles set up by their friends. They need to negotiate and navigate through the unexpected difficulties of married life. At home, the bride's parents greet the couple with bread, salt, and wine. This is a traditional Lithuanian greeting and blessing (a fourth element of honey is often added because honey is not used in the church service). The couple traditionally circles the house before entering it. Inside, they are sprinkled with rye, barley, and wheat grains. These are symbols of agrarian prosperity. Sometimes, furs might be thrown on the newlyweds or laid at their feet: this is a blessing for wealth. The newlyweds encounter a ridiculous, cross-dressed wedding party at the family table. The imposters have stolen the wedding *sodas* that the newlyweds need to bring to their home. The wedding couple "bribes" the pretenders with sweets and alcohol. The wedding meal follows. Traditionally, the newlyweds eat from the same plate or bowl, indicating their new union.

The newlyweds then travel to the groom's home (the bride moves to his house). They bring a new, freshly kindled fire into the home hearth. It becomes the fire of the new family. The bride greets the hearth. The couple and their family pray to the gods and venerate the ancestors. They also bring their wedding *sodas*, a symbol of their new life together, into their home. The newlyweds sit in the *krikštas* chair assuming their new roles of husband and wife; the wife also becomes the daughter-in-law. The parents become in-laws.

The head bridesmaid or matron of honor organizes the *marčpietis*, "the dinner of the daughter-in-law," that is, the newlywed bride. Traditionally, the essential item of this meal is the wedding cake or sweet bread called a *karvojus*. It is richly covered with wedding symbols made of baked dough: birds, holding hands, garter snakes, suns, moons, rue flowers, etc. Snakes represent the renewal of life, while the cosmological symbols refer to the universe. Everyone has to eat a piece of the cake. Today, the wedding meal and the *marčpietis* are often combined.

Unmarried women in Lithuania did not wear any head covering or only a small scarf. Married women covered their heads, usually with a scarf. The last solemn act of the wedding removes the rue wreath from the bride's head and replaces it with a *nuometas*, the married woman's head covering. The bride and her bridesmaids resist, defending the rue wreath and the honor of the bride. In older days, women would wear the *nuometas* only after giving birth.

Weddings contain many humorous acts, some of which were noted above. The last one puts the matchmaker on trial for lying about the greatness of the groom and his exaggerated wealth. He is sentenced to death by hanging, but a life-size puppet takes his place on the gallows (tree branch). This jest frightens the children. The matchmaker had a serious role to play during the wedding, but he was also a prankster who injected all sorts of practical jokes and merriment into the festivities.

"Kur kukuoj gegelė," (Where the Cuckoo Cries), is a popular *daina* sung at weddings:

> Where does the cuckoo cry? Where does the nightingale warble? On the branch of a snow-ball tree. Where does the boy stand, my clover? On a silver bridge. Hey, why are you standing, why are you not riding (your horse)? Your father is waiting for you. He is feeding the dear steed, and doing business with the other one. My dear son will ride back. Let him feed, let him do business, for he knows that I will not

return. Seas, dear bays, green groves, the nights have not been experienced.[128]

The sea refers to the Baltic Sea, the bay is the Curonian Bay, and green groves grow all over Lithuania. The references indicate the *daina* originated along the shores of the bay. In the second repetition, the boy is mounted on a bay horse. His mother is waiting for him, sewing and mending his shirts. In the third repetition, he is standing in a silver stirrup. His sister is waiting for him, sewing and mending a scarf. In the fourth repetition, he is standing on a ferry bridge. His beloved is waiting for him, picking one wheat shaft and protecting another one. He responds, "For she knows that I will return ... the nights have been experienced," or in other words, filled with sexual activity.

In the *daina*, the family expresses sadness at the departure of the boy. At the same time, life and its chores continue without the son. He will not return as a son. He has a new, married life to lead. As a husband, he has a new role in the family. The boy travels closer to the girl with each repetition in the song. The mention of silver denotes a mythological connection to the moon, the archetype for a young male. His ride across a metaphorical silver bridge represents a multifaceted mythological transition from childhood to adulthood, from asexuality to sexuality, and from bachelorhood to married life. His symbolic developmental travels culminate with a real ferry crossing that physically brings him to his bride. The last line of each repetition also refers to licit sexuality: the boy did not have experiences in the night, but the man has these unnamed experiences. The first three repetitions of the *daina* fail in their aims of return, completing a full circle according to Lithuanian numerology. The fourth one, the one beyond the holy and magical three, succeeds: he will return to his new wife, who supplants his mother, and sister. Their chores will become her chores. His father's work will become his work.

The funeral concludes the life-cycle rituals, although various memorial rites follow the funeral.[129] The funeral is a series of rituals and the most somber of rites. Dundulienė maintains that Lithuanian funeral rites exhibit two general concerns. First, the *vėlė* or shade of the dead needs to travel to the next world, called Dausos. It is located on a high hill beyond the human realm. Second, agrarian Lithuanians believe that ancestral *vėlės* can help them and their fields.[130] Funerals usually take place two to three days after death.

THE KULGRINDA ENSEMBLE AT THE BALTICA FOLKLORE FESTIVAL, 2005, PERFORMING A WEDDING RITUAL DESIGNED TO ELEVATE THE BRIDE TO THE STATUS OF A MARRIED WOMAN. (PHOTO COURTESY OF JONAS TRINKŪNAS)

The preparation of the body, the wake, the burial, and the funeral dinner (called *šermenys*) are the most important parts of the rites.

The traditional preparation of the body is very simple. Family members wash the body and dress it in a white, linen shirt, with an ethnic sash tied around the waist. In past times the body used to be laid out on boards, but today coffins are used. In some places and at some times, the body used to be seated in the *krikštas* chair. This symbolized the transition from one life stage to another: from life to death. Items that were important to the deceased would be included with the apparel: jewelry, amber, and so forth. At times, beer and bread were included with the deceased so the *vėlė* would have food for the journey. Smokers, in particular, received tobacco or pipes. Coins might be added for the *vėlė* to pay for its grave that it shared with the others buried in it (the same grave would be reused each generation for new burials) and to have money for the trip to the afterlife. Religious items (both Lithuanian and Christian) would be added as amulets of protection. Too much should not be included with the deceased. One woman placed her daughter's entire dowry in the coffin. She later saw her daughter's *vėlė* dragging her dowry with her. She was suffering from the burden.[131] The church, as could be expected, opposed such practices. In its opposition, it left records documenting the burial traditions. Sometimes the dying left instructions regarding their funeral wardrobe: wedding dresses and ethnic outfits were typical requests. Modern dark outfits replaced the traditional burial garb in the twentieth century. Six candles would surround the deceased to accompany and protect the *vėlė:* two each at the head, waist, and feet. Originally, the candles were made of beeswax, but any type of candle has become acceptable. The candles cannot be extinguished, not even for the night, and need to be replaced when they burn out.

A wake, called a *budynės*, would take place before the funeral. This happened at the home of the deceased, in the living room, beside the open coffin. During the wake, people would sing a special type of funeral *daina* called a *rauda*, a mourning song. Wailing accompanied the *raudos*. Sometimes professional mourners would be hired to sing the *raudos*.[132] *Raudos* are very sad and slow. They ask the deceased why he/she died, why he/she left his/her family, if he/she did not like living with his/her family, did he/she not have a good lot in life, and so on. Some very unusual *raudos* refer to the "gates of the *vėlė*," meaning doors and gates through which the deceased will pass on the way to the burial and the afterlife. Another interesting concept is the "bride (or groom) of the *vėlė*," referring to the deceased. Such terms equate funerals with weddings. The *raudos* and wailing can become quite dramatic. However, people avoid crying for the deceased because it hurts the *vėlė* and causes it sorrow in the afterlife, especially if the parent cries for the child: the *vėlė* has to carry the tears of grief. On the other hand, children crying for their parents is acceptable. People should be happy for the *vėlė*, for it has entered into the afterlife. His or her fate is, after all, the unavoidable human fate.

The family and village participated in the funeral cortege, except for pregnant women who needed to protect their fetuses. The family would say its final farewell to the deceased and the coffin would be closed. The deceased used to be removed from the house in such a way that the *vėlė* could not return to haunt the home: the body was brought out through a window or carried feet first through the door. The door and gates that the body would pass through were immediately closed and locked behind the coffin. In some areas, a loaf of bread would replace the coffin without delay, so that the deceased could not take the bread (food) from the home. Grains would be poured on the deceased: it was food for the dead. In order to protect the harvest, the procession would not pass by planted fields. Funeral *dainos* (not *raudos*), bugling horns, and ringing bells accompanied the procession. Honorary knights would periodically swing their swords in the air to ward off evil spirits. The procession stopped at intersections, roadside shrines, the edges of fields, and other places where *vėlės* were thought to dwell.

Lithuanians dispose of their dead in two ways: burial and cremation. Burials used either shallow graves, similar to modern graves, or burial mounds that were six to twenty meters in diameter and one to three meters high. The wealthy and powerful were interred in the mounds, sometimes with their horses. At times, coffins were made from hollowed tree trunks, but most often came from planks that were hammered together. Coffins used to be brightly painted and decorated with birds, flowers, and trees of life. These were symbols of regeneration. Burials happened early in the day, at dawn or as close to dawn as possible. After a cremation, the remaining bones[133] and ashes were buried in a coffin. Modern cremations use urns that are made from natural materials such as pottery or wood. Urns are buried with the cremated remains. Prayers and funeral *dainos* accompany the burial. In ancient times, a fire ritual also took place. Romuva has revived this rite. After the coffin has been lowered into the grave, the final blessing has the mourners pour three palmfuls of soil on the coffin with the words, "May the earth be gentle to you."[134] This is a universal Lithuanian rite. The coffin is then covered with dirt. Cement boxes are not used. The goal is for the earthly remains to decompose and return to Mother Earth as quickly as possible.

The funeral concludes with the ritual funeral meal, called *šermenys*.[135] The participants return home. They wash with fresh well water and dry with linen towels, even though the individual might not have touched the deceased, the coffin, or the earth. The washing is a ritual purification. The table has food, drink, and drinking ladles, but no tablecloth or individual dishes. The eldest son or closest relative to the deceased invokes Dievas to be good to the deceased and to grant the living a good life. A series of libations are then poured on the earth. The ladle is refilled after each libation. Everyone participates. The libations are sacrifices to Žemyna for the *vėlė*. People also talk to the *vėlė*. Toasting has generally replaced the libations in urban settings (except, of course, for

Romuva). After the libations, another close relative says the prayer remembering the deceased and blessing the food. Everybody can then eat, but everyone must first offer three morsels of bread, meat, and three spoonfuls of other food to Žemyna by placing them on the earth. The invocation of the goddess asks her to be gracious to the *vėlė*, to protect it, and to provide for it in the other world.

Dainos for funerals and Vėlinės are interchangeable. The *daina* that opened this article is technically listed as a "war *daina*," but it often accompanies the untimely funerals of male children and adolescents. It is, after all, about preparation for death and the end of the world. The following is another variant of the *daina* in its entirety:

> Oh, on the hill, on the tall one, there stands a white crown. Underneath the white crown lies a grey stone. On the grey stone sits a mother and a father. There sits a father and a mother, sitting they weep sorrowfully. Sitting they weep sorrowfully, preparing their son for war. Oh son, oh child, who will be your dear father? Who will be your dear father and your real mother? And your real mother, your real brothers? Your real brothers, and your loving sisters? Oh, the moon in the sky is my real father. Oh, the sun in the sky is my real mother. Oh, the constellations in the sky are my real brothers. Oh, the stars in the sky are my dear sisters. Oh son, oh child, what will you put down for a bed, what will you use for a cover? Oh mother, oh dear heart, the green wind will be my bed; the sorrowful dew will be my cover. [136]

This *daina* contains numerous mythological motifs. The son prepares to accept the heavenly gods and goddesses in place of his human family; he faces and prepares for death. He also prepares to accept the cosmos for his new relatives and the wind and dew become his bed, that is, his grave. Lithuanians view death as a return to nature with which humans share a kinship. The anticipated transformation of the boy hints at metempsychosis: the boy's *vėlė* will migrate into another natural being such as a star in the sky, although typically it would be an oak tree for a knight, as this boy appears to be. In the variant of this *daina* at the start of the article, the fatherly god and motherly goddess instruct the young man to blow three horns. The first one makes his mother and father cry, the second one awakens Vilnius, and the third one shakes the entire world. The three horns are a doomsday motif in Indo-European mythology. In the *daina*, they signify not the end of the world, but the end of life for the young man and his family. Note how the city of Vilnius has become a sacred, mythological city in the *daina*: echoing medieval Arthurian tradition, Gediminas—himself a medieval king—waits there to return from the dust of the dead, in case he is needed to save the city (this is most likely a modern addition to the medieval myth).

Fire is one of the most important symbols of Lithuanian culture and the fire ritual is a central Lithuanian rite. This article has discussed fire many times. Some chronicles labeled Lithuanians as fire worshipers, probably because Lithuanian places of worship were fire temples with open roofs. Most holidays include fire in some form. The name of the fire goddess is Gabija. People would treat fire with sacred respect through a series of taboos: one cannot insult the fire, harm it, pollute it, spit or urinate into it, and kick or stomp it. These prohibitions still exist today.[137]

The home hearth was a household fire shrine that housed an "eternal" fire. People would feed it daily by giving it a morsel from every meal cooked on the stove: "Holy Gabija, protected, stay whole; ignited, stay bright" or "Gabija, be nourished." The "protection" refers to the head of the household "putting the fire to bed" every night by circling and covering it with coals and ash in such a way that the embers would kindle all night long. The fire would be reverently extinguished during certain holidays with fresh, cold, clean water. The family would later use embers from the communal holiday fire to reignite the household fire.

The Lithuanian communal fire ritual is as simple as igniting the fire, saying a prayer, and maintaining a moment of silence, as happens during Lithuanian national holidays. Fire often replaces Christian symbols and rituals in public Lithuanian and Latvian ceremonies. For example, both countries have fire altars with eternal flames in front of their respective statues of liberty and at their national cemeteries. The typical fire altar is a waist-high quadrangular pyramid made of unhewn stones. The top has a hole in it for the kindling and fire (modern versions have gas fixtures). Several Lithuanian churches also have open-air fire altars for national rites in their courtyards.

A complex fire ritual has the participants wash their hands and face with fresh well water, and dry themselves with a linen towel as they enter the area of the fire altar. The leaders ignite the fire in silence. On behalf of the assembled community, they then make various sacrifices to the flames, such as bread, beer, grain, and flowers. Everyone sings various *dainos* to the fire. Participants also circle the altar. Various Lithuanian ideological organizations have developed their own fire ritual traditions. For example, scouts carry embers from one camp to another, igniting bonfires from the embers of a previous camping experience. This reflects the Lithuanian belief that an extinguished, burnt stick bears the essence of the fire.

Romuva's Beliefs

Romuva differs very significantly from neopaganism and ceremonial magic. It does not even use the word "pagan," for a number of reasons. It rejected the label because of its potential negative connotations. The term has also been forced on Romuva with disparaging nuances. Moreover, Romuva in North America has had several negative experiences with certain Western pagan groups. Nevertheless, Michael York, who is of Lithuanian ancestry and a scholar of comparative religion with specialization in paganism, would classify Romuva as "recopaganism" because of its deliberate reconstruction of a past pagan religion.[138] Romuva revives the inherent spirituality and religiosity of Baltic Lithuanian religion that Lithuanian ethnic culture has preserved. No creation, re-creation, or anachronism is involved because it relies on the vast Lithuanian heritage and wellspring of sources, influencing folklore and traditions. Romuva also consciously avoids organizing synthetic pan-Lithuanian rituals. Instead, it reflects the local or regional custom with authenticity. For example, Kūčios in different parts of Lithuania will have varying practices. Most Lithuanians celebrate the same holiday, but everyone does it somewhat differently, including Romuva. Ultimately, Romuva seeks to foster a way of life and not merely celebrate ritual or sing *dainos*.

The premises of Romuva reflect common Lithuanian cultural values and traditions. Romuva professes Baltic Lithuanian religion based on the religious and spiritual elements present in Lithuanian folklore. It seeks universal harmony, reveres nature as divine, and follows Baltic morality.[139] It commemorates the ancestors; the living and dead share a communion. Death is an expected and natural part of the life cycle. When a body dies, the soul continues

LITHUANIAN PAGANS AT WORSHIP NEAR A SNAKE-ALTAR, SACRED TREE, AND FIRE-ALTAR. SIXTEENTH-CENTURY WOODCUT BY OLAUS MAGNUS.

to live, traveling to another existence. In accordance with the Lithuanian tradition, Romuva regards life, the world, the earth, water, fire, and bread as holy. It believes in justice and cooperation. It celebrates the annual solar holidays, and those connected to the human life cycle.[140]

The Lithuanian word for "harmony" is *darna*. Romuva claims the Lithuanian idea of *darna* is similar to the Hindu concept of *dharma*.[141] However, the two words are not related, and the concept of *dharma* has undergone significant historical development. Romuva presents *darna* as developing in stages. First, *darna* seeks inner harmony: people at peace with themselves. Second, it endeavors for harmony at home and in the community. Third, it pursues harmony with the ancestors. Finally, it seeks harmony with the universe—in other words, with life and with the divinities.[142]

Conclusion

This article has surveyed aspects of Baltic Lithuanian religion and summarized the salient features for popular understanding. It focused on the history, sources, deities, holidays, ceremonies, and beliefs. Much of the material that composes Baltic Lithuanian religion comes from a living folkloric tradition, parts of which have been revived over the last hundred or so years. The customs receive popular expression in Lithuanian culture, while Romuva professes and practices them as a religion.

To close the article, I would like to offer a traditional

Lithuanian prayer. The elderly sisters Elžbieta and Marijona Palubenskaitės recited this prayer publicly in 1938. The informants had smuggled books into Lithuania during the Czarist prohibition of Lithuanian publications in the latter half of the nineteenth century. The following prayer stems from those times:

> That I may love and respect my mother, father, and the elderly; that I may protect their graves from rending and destruction; that I may plant oaks, junipers, wormwoods, and silverweed for their rest in cemeteries. Those who do not love and respect their bearers will await hardship in their old age or will not grow old at all. That my hands may never become bloody from human blood. That the blood of animals, fish, or birds may not soil my hands, if I might kill them satiated and not hungry. Those who today kill animals with delight will tomorrow drink human blood. The more hunters live in Lithuania, the further fortune and a happy life escapes us. That I may not fell a single tree without holy need; that I may not step on a blooming field; that I may always plant trees. That I may love and respect bread. If a crumb should accidentally fall, I will lift it, kiss it, and apologize. If we all respect bread, there will be no starvation or hardship. That I may never hurt anyone; that I may always give the correct change; that I may not mistakenly steal even the smallest coin. The gods punish for offenses. That I may not denigrate foreign beliefs and may not poke fun at my own faith. The gods look with grace upon those who plant trees along roads, in homesteads, at holy places, at cross roads, and by houses. If you wed, plant a wedding tree. If a child is born, plant a tree. If someone beloved dies, plant a tree for the *vėlės* of the deceased. At all holidays, during all important events, visit trees. Prayers will attain holiness through trees of thanks.[143]

Notes:

1. Rytis Ambrazevičius, *Skamba skamba kankliai* (Vilnius: n.p., 1989), p. 2. Reprinted from: G. Četkauskaitė, *Dzūkų dainos, Lietuvių liaudies muzika*, vol. I (Vilnius: n.p. 1974).
2. The sections of this article on the history of the religion and the deities are a synopsis of material that I researched for my doctoral dissertation in Comparative Literature and German. The focus of the dissertation was on mythology. Audrius Vilius Dundzila, *Maiden, Mother, Crone: Goddesses From Prehistory to European Mythology and Their Reemergence in German, Lithuanian, and Latvian Romantic Dramas*, dissertation, University of Wisconsin at Madison, 1991. The remaining sections summarize relevant current research.
3. Elena Grigalavičienė, *Žalvario ir ankstyvasis geležies amžius Lietuvoje* (Vilnius: Mokslas, 1985), pp. 196–202; Laima Nakaitė, *Žalvariniai senolių laiškai* (Vilnius: Vyturys, 1991), pp. 45–46; Rimutė Rimantienė, *Akmens amžius Lietuvoje*, 2nd ed. (Vilnius: Žiburys, 1996), pp. 52, 105–06, 200–03; Rimutė Rimantienė, *Lietuva iki Kristaus* (Vilnius: Vilniaus Dailės akademijos leidinys, 1995), pp. 160–68.
4. Marija Gimbutienė (Gimbutas), *Baltai priešistoriniais laikais: Etnogezė materialinė kultūra ir mitologija* (Vilnius: Mokslas, 1985), pp. 28–39; Rimantienė, *Lietuva iki Kristaus*, pp. 168–77.
5. Gintaras Beresnevičius, *Baltų religinės reformos* (n.p.: Taura, 1995), p. 61; Gimbutienė, *Baltai priešistoriniais laikais*, pp. 46–56; Rimantienė, *Lietuva iki Kristaus*, p. 177.
6. Rimantienė, *Lietuva iki Kristaus*, pp. 153–60; Rimantienė, *Akmens amžius Lietuvoje*, pp. 52–53, 105–06, 200–03.
7. Gimbutienė, *Baltai priešistoriniais laikais*, pp. 25–31; Marija Gimbutas, *The Prehistory of Eastern Europe: Mesolithic, Neolithic, and Copper Age Cultures in Russian and the Baltic Area* (Boston: Harvard University Peabody Museum, 1956), pp. 29–30.
8. Marija Gimbutas, *The Goddesses and Gods of Old Europe: 6500 to 3500 B.C.: Myths and Cult Images* (Berkeley: University of California Press, 1982), p. 17; Colin Renfrew, *Archeology and Language: The Puzzle of Indo-European Origins* (London: Jonathan Cape, 1987), p. 30. For a comprehensive study of Old Europe, see: Marija Gimbutienė (Gimbutas), *Senoji Europa* (Vilnius: Mokslo ir enciklopedijų leidykla, 1996); Marija Gimbutas, *The Living Goddesses*, ed. Miriam Robbins Dexter (Berkeley: University of

California Press, 1999).

9. Gimbutas, *Goddesses and Gods of Old Europe*, p. 18; Marija Gimbutas, *The Language of the Goddess: Unearthing the Hidden Symbols of Western Civilization* (San Francisco: Harper, 1989), p. xx.

10. Gimbutas, *Goddesses and Gods of Old Europe*, pp. 11–12; Gimbutas, *The Language of the Goddess: Unearthing the Hidden Symbols of Western Civilization*, p. 175. For a philosophical interpretation of the Old European Goddess in Baltic thought, see: Vincent Vycinas, *The Great Goddess and the Aistian Mythical World*, American University Studies Series V Philosophy, vol. 9 (New York: Peter Lang, 1990).

11. Gimbutienė, *Baltai priešistoriniais laikais*, pp. 28–33, 46; Marija Gimbutienė (Gimbutas), "Matristinė Europos kultūra prieš siaubingų karų laikus," *Metmenys* 53 (1987), p. 10.

12. Cynthia Eller, *The Myth of Matriarchal Prehistory: Why an Invented Past Won't Give Women a Future* (Boston: Beacon, 2000). For another critical view see Lotte Motz, *The Faces of the Goddess* (New York: Oxford University Press, 1997).

13. Renfrew, *Archeology and Language*.

14. Gimbutienė, *Baltai priešistoriniais laikais*, p. 39.

15. Gimbutas, *Prehistory of Eastern Europe*, p. 168; Gimbutienė, "Matristinė Europos kultūra prieš siaubingų karų laikus," pp. 9–12; Marija Gimbutas, *The Balts, Ancient Peoples and Places*, ed. Glyn Daniel, vol. 33 (New York: Praeger, 1963), p. 38; Gimbutas, *Prehistory of Eastern Europe*, p. 140; Renfrew, *Archeology and Language*, p. 32.

16. Gimbutas, *Prehistory of Eastern Europe*, p. 146; Marija Gimbutienė (Gimbutas), "Indoeuropiečių protėvynė kurganų (pilkapių) kultūra penktame, ketvirtame ir trečiame tūkstantmetyje pr. Kr.," *Metmenys* 22 (1971), pp. 69, 86; Jaan Puhvel, *Comparative Mythology* (Baltimore: Johns Hopkins, 1987), pp. 36–37.

17. Gimbutienė, "Indoeuropiečių protėvynė kurganų," pp. 78, 80, 93.

18. Gimbutas, *Prehistory of Eastern Europe*, pp. 166, 189, 190, 192, 203; Gimbutienė, "Indoeuropiečių protėvynė kurganų," p. 93.

19. Mircea Eliade, *A History of Religious Ideas: From the Stone Age to the Eleusinian Mysteries*, trans. Willard R. Trask, (Chicago: University of Chicago, 1978), vol. 1, p. 189.

20. Georges Dumézil, *Mitra-Varuna: An Essay on Two Indo-European Representations of Sovereignty*, trans. Derek Coltman (New York: Zone, 1988), pp. 22, 67–68.

21. Eliade, *History of Religious Ideas*, vol. 1, p. 189.
22. Eliade, *History of Religious Ideas*, vol. 1, p. 190.
23. Miriam Robbins Dexter, *Whence the Goddess: A Source Book* (New York: Pergamon, 1990), p. 157.
24. Renfrew, *Archeology and Language*, pp. 253, 257.
25. Beresnevičius, *Baltų religinės reformos*, pp. 11–75.
26. Beresnevičius, *Baltų religinės reformos*, pp. 135–81.
27. Beresnevičius, *Baltų religinės reformos*, pp. 77–133.
28. Pranė Dundulienė, *Lietuvių etnologija*, 2nd ed. (Vilnius: Mokslas, 1991), p. 374.
29. Adolfas Tautavičius, *Vidurinis Geležies amžius Lietuvoje (V–IX a.)* (Vilnius: Pilių tyrimų centras, 1996), pp. 280–89.
30. Vladimir Terentevich Pashuto and I. V. Shtal, eds., *Gedimino laiškai* (Vilnius: Mintis, 1966).
31. Stasys Lipskis, *Vilniaus legendos* (Vilnius: Žuvėdra, 2003), pp. 5–9.
32. Jonas Balys, *Lietuvių liaudies pasaulėjauta: Tikėjimų ir papročių šviesoje* (Chicago: Pedagoginis lituanistikos institutas, 1966), p. 10.
33. Balys, *Lietuvių liaudies pasaulėjauta*, p. 10.
34. Jonas Trinkūnas, *Baltų tikėjimas: Lietuvių pasaulėjauta, papročiai, apeigos, ženklai* (Vilnius: Diemedžio leidykla, 2000), p. 31.
35. I interviewed a member of this group in the Garliava suburb of Kaunas in 1991.
36. I was the first *seniūnas* (the term for elder) in Kaunas, and faced a single act of discrimination for my activities: my landlord kicked me out of my apartment because she claimed I was corrupting the youth.
37. I was one of its faculty advisors in 1991–92.
38. Suniti Kumar Chatterji, *Balts and Aryans In Their Indo-European Background* (Simla, India: Indian Institute of Advanced Study, 1968), pp. 118–29.
39. Chatterji, *Balts and Aryans*, p. 69.
40. The following are the primary sources for the supplemental Latvian material: Haralds Biezais, *Die Gottesgestalt der lettischen Volksreligion* (Stockholm: Almqvist & Wiksell, 1961); Haralds Biezais, *Die himmlische Götterfamilie der alten Letten* (Uppsala: Almqvist & Wiksells [*sic*], 1972); and Haralds Biezais, "Baltische Religion," in *Germanische und Baltische Religion*, eds. Åke V Ström and Haralds Biezais, vol. 19.1 of *Die Religionen der Menschheit* (Stuttgart: Kohlhammer, 1975). The latter article covers both

Lithuanian and Latvian material.

41. Reprinted in: Trinkūnas, *Baltų tikėjimas*, p. 10. For the second printing the title was changed to Jonas Trinkūnas, *Lietuvių pasaulėjauta: Papročiai, apeigos, ženklai* (Vilnius: Diemedžio leidykla, 2003). The book is non-academic and lacks a critical apparatus. The *daina* was originally published in: *Lietuvių liaudies melodijos*, Tautosakos darbai, vol. V (Kaunas: 1938).

42. For a comprehensive discussion of the Lithuanian worldview, see: Balys, *Lietuvių liaudies pasaulėjauta*; Norbertas Vėlius, *Senovės baltų pasaulėžiūra* (Vilnius: Mintis, 1983).

43. Joseph Campbell, *Occidental Mythology*, The Masks of God, vol. 3 (New York: Penguin, 1976), p. 475.

44. Algirdas Julius Greimas, "Dievai viešpačiai" Metmenys 38–58 (1983), p. 57. The same author provides an in-depth study of select Lithuanian deities in the following: Algirdas Julius Greimas, *Tautos atminties beieškant: Apie dievus ir žmones* (Vilnius: Mokslas, 1990). The first half of the book was originally published as a separate volume and translated as: Algirdas J. Greimas, *Of Gods and Men: Studies in Lithuanian Mythology*, trans. Milda Newman (Bloomington: Indiana University Press, 1992). The following books provide comprehensive surveys of the Lithuanian deities: Pranė Dundulienė, *Pagonybė Lietuvoje: Moteriškos dievybės* (Vilnius: Mintis, 1989); Pranė Dundulienė, *Senovės lietuvių mitologija ir religija* (Vilnius: Mokslas, 1990), pp. 14–148; Marija Gimbutienė (Gimbutas), *Senovės lietuvių deivės ir dievai: Baltų mitologija* (Vilnius: Lietuvos rašytojų sąjungos leidykla, 2002); Jonas Balys, *Lietuvių tautosakos skaitymai*, vol. 2 (Tübingen: Patria, 1948), pp. 5–96. The following reviews the Lithuanian deities from a phenomenological perspective: Gintaras Beresnevičius, *Lietuvių religja ir mitologija* (Vilnius: Tyto alba, 2004).

45. Gimbutienė, *Baltai priešistoriniais laikais*, pp. 151–70.

46. Chatterji, *Balts and Aryans*, p. 117.

47. Dundulienė, *Senovės lietuvių mitologija ir religija*, pp. 14–15; Greimas, "Dievai viešpačiai," p. 56. The main sources concerning Dievas and the heavenly family in general appear in Pranė Dundulienė, *Lietuvių liaudies kosmologija* (Vilnius: Mokslas, 1988), pp. 70–89.

48. Biezais, "Baltische Religion," p. 324; Gimbutienė, *Baltai priešistoriniais laikais*, p. 162; Dundulienė, *Senovės lietuvių mitologija ir religija*, p. 22.

49. Biezais, "Baltische Religion," p. 324; Biezais, *Die*

Gottesgestalt der lettischen Volksreligion, pp. 42, 90, 136–40; Gimbutienė, *Baltai priešistoriniais laikais*, pp. 162–63; Dundulienė, *Senovės lietuvių mitologija ir religija*, p. 14.

50. Gimbutienė, *Baltai priešistoriniais laikais*, p. 163.
51. Biezais, "Baltische Religion," p. 324–26.
52. Gimbutienė, *Baltai priešistoriniais laikais*, p. 162; Dundulienė, *Senovės lietuvių mitologija ir religija*, p. 14.
53. Biezais, "Baltische Religion," pp. 327–28; Gimbutienė, *Baltai priešistoriniais laikais*, p. 162.
54. Blezdinga, *Parlėk blezdinga: Lithuanian Folk Songs*, CD, Maksima, Vilnius, 2001.
55. Biezais, "Baltische Religion," p. 363.
56. Dundulienė, *Pagonybė Lietuvoje*, pp. 42–45; Gimbutienė, *Baltai priešistoriniais laikais*, p. 156.
57. Biezais, "Baltische Religion," pp. 357–64; Dundulienė, *Pagonybė Lietuvoje*, pp. 42–44; Gimbutienė, *Baltai priešistoriniais laikais*, p. 155; Dundulienė, *Senovės lietuvių mitologija ir religija*, p. 63.
58. Biezais, "Baltische Religion," pp. 358–60; Dundulienė, *Pagonybė Lietuvoje*, pp. 47–54; Dundulienė, *Senovės lietuvių mitologija ir religija*, p. 63.
59. Dundulienė, *Senovės lietuvių mitologija ir religija*, p. 15; Gimbutienė, *Baltai priešistoriniais laikais*, p. 163; Dundulienė, *Pagonybė Lietuvoje*, p. 44.
60. Biezais, "Baltische Religion," pp. 361–62.
61. Biezais, "Baltische Religion," pp. 364–65.
62. Dundulienė, *Pagonybė Lietuvoje*, p. 55.
63. Dundulienė, *Pagonybė Lietuvoje*, pp. 56–57; Jonas Balys, "Die Sagen von den litauischen Feen (Deivės, Laumės)," *Die Nachbarn: Jahrbuch für vergleichende Volkskunde* (1948), p. 48; Gimbutienė, *Baltai priešistoriniais laikais*, p. 157.
64. For a study on Perkūnas, see: Nijolė Laurinkienė, *Senovės lietuvių dievas Perkūnas: Kalboje, tautosakoje, istoriniuose šaltiniuose* (Vilnius: Lietuvių literatūros tautosakos institutas, 1996).
65. Balys, *Lietuvių liaudies pasaulėjauta*, p. 42; Gimbutienė, *Baltai priešistoriniais laikais*, p. 167; Vincent Vycinas, *Search for Gods* (Hague: Martinus Nijhoff, 1972), p. 35.
66. Biezais, "Baltische Religion," pp. 341–42; Gimbutienė, *Baltai priešistoriniais laikais*, p. 167; Dundulienė, *Senovės lietuvių mitologija ir religija*, pp. 30–35; Balys, *Lietuvių liaudies pasaulėjauta*, pp. 42–44.

67. Dundulienė, *Senovės lietuvių mitologija ir religija*, p. 37.
68. Biezais, "Baltische Religion," p. 345; Dundulienė, *Senovės lietuvių mitologija ir religija*, p. 29; Gimbutienė, *Baltai priešistoriniais laikais*, p. 167.
69. Mindaugas Bartninkas, "Legends of Kaunas," *Vakarinės Naujienos*, 18–19 December 1991.
70. Greimas, *Tautos atminties beieškant*, p. 419.
71. For a compendium of folk customs dealing with the earth, see: Jonas Balys, *Lietuvių žemdirbystės papročiai ir tikėjimai*, vol 10 of *Lietuvių tautosakos lobynas* (Silver Spring, Maryland: Lietuvių tautosakos leidykla, 1986), especially pp. 201–41.
72. Dundulienė, *Pagonybė Lietuvoje*, pp. 87–97; Balys, *Lietuvių žemdirbystės papročiai ir tikėjimai*, p. 242; Dundulienė, *Senovės lietuvių mitologija ir religija*, p. 106; Gimbutienė, *Baltai priešistoriniais laikais*, p. 151.
73. Dundulienė, *Pagonybė Lietuvoje*, p. 89.
74. Dundulienė, *Pagonybė Lietuvoje*, p. 89; Gimbutienė, *Baltai priešistoriniais laikais*, pp. 152–53; Pranė Dundulienė, *Medžiai senovės lietuvių tikėjimuose* (Vilnius: Mintis, 1979), pp. 99–100; Algirdas Julius Greimas, "Apie folklorą, religiją ir istoriją," *Metmenys* 19 (1970), pp. 43–54.
75. Dundulienė, *Pagonybė Lietuvoje*, pp. 87–88; Dundulienė, *Senovės lietuvių mitologija ir religija*, p. 106.
76. Balys, *Lietuvių žemdirbystės papročiai ir tikėjimai*, pp. 236–47.
77. For a comprehensive study of Velnias, see: Norbertas Vėlius, *Chtoniškasis lietuvių mitologijos pasaulis: Folklorinio velnio analizė* (Vilnius: Vaga, 1987).
78. Norbertas Vėlius, *Lithuanian Mythological Tales*, trans. Birtuė Kiškytė (Vilnius: Vaga, 2002), p. 54.
79. Norbertas Vėlius, *Lithuanian Etiological Tales and Legends*, trans. Rita Dapkutė (Vilnius: Vaga, 1998), pp. 18–19.
80. For a study of Laumės, see: Vytautas Bagdanavičius, *Laumės: Jų religija ir kultūra* (Chicago: Pedagoginis lituanistikos institutas, 1982) and Balys, "Die Sagen von den litauischen Feen (Deivės, Laumės)."
81. Gimbutienė, *Baltai priešistoriniais laikais*, p. 159; Dundulienė, *Pagonybė Lietuvoje*, p. 13; Bagdanavičius, *Laumės*, pp. 250–271.
82. Bagdanavičius, *Laumės*, p. 259; Dundulienė, *Pagonybė Lietuvoje*, pp. 15, 21, 23–24; Gimbutienė, *Baltai priešistoriniais laikais*, p. 160; Balys, "Die Sagen von den litauischen Feen (Deivės, Laumės)," p. 57.

83. Dundulienė, *Pagonybė Lietuvoje*, pp. 21–22, 25.
84. Dundulienė, *Pagonybė Lietuvoje*, pp. 16, 18.
85. Vėlius, *Lithuanian Mythological Tales*, p. 21.
86. Dundulienė, *Pagonybė Lietuvoje*, p. 20.
87. The principle academic sources about Saulė appear in Dundulienė, *Lietuvių liaudies kosmologija*, pp. 13–25, 44–47.
88. Trinkūnas, *Baltų tikėjimas*, p. 71.
89. For a study of *sutartinės*, read: Daiva Račiūnaitė-Vyčinienė, *Sutartinės: Lithuanian Polypohonic Songs*, trans. Vijolė Arbas (Vilnius: Vaga, 2002).
90. The main sources concerning Mėnulis are provided in Dundulienė, *Lietuvių liaudies kosmologija*, pp. 25–47.
91. Amb. Jonynas, ed., *Dainos*, in *Lietuvių tautosaka*, ed. K. Korsakas (Vilnius: Valstybinė politinės ir mokslinės literatūros leidykla, 1962), vol.1, p. 175.
92. For a comprehensive study about Žaltys, see: Pranė Dundulienė, *Žalčiai lietuvių pasaulėjautoje ir dailėje* (Vilnius: Mintis, 1996).
93. Gimbutienė, *Baltai priešistoriniais laikais*, pp. 157–58; Dexter, *Whence the Goddess*, p. 58.
94. Dundulienė, *Senovės lietuvių mitologija ir religija*, pp. 118–19.
95. Bartninkas, "Legends of Kaunas."
96. Ibid.
97. The following authors provide thorough surveys of the major Lithuanian holidays: Dundulienė, *Lietuvių etnologija*, pp. 228–314, 345–80; Pranė Dundulienė, *Lietuvių šventės: Tradicijos, papročiai, apeigos* (Vilnius: Mintis, 1991); Stasys Gutautas, *Lietuvių liaudies kalendorius* (Vilnius: Vyturys, 1991); Gražina Veronika Germanienė, *Senovinis kalendorius* (Vilnius: Leidybos centras, 1997); Jonas Balys, *Lietuvių kalendorinės šventės: Tautosakinė medžiaga ir aiškinimai*, vol. VII of *Lietuvių tautosakos lobynas*, (Silver Spring, Maryland: Lietuvių tautosakos leidykla, 1978); Juozas Kudirka, *The Lithuanians: An Ethnic Portrait* (Vilnius: Lithuanian Folk Culture Center, 1991); Balys, *Lietuvių tautosakos skaitymai*, pp. 99–200. The following focuses on the mythological content of the *dainos* associated with solar holidays: Nijolė Laurinkienė, *Mito atšvaiutai lietuvių kalendorinėse dainuose* (Vilnius: Vaga, 1990). The following bilingual book surveys the Lithuanian holidays from a Catholic perspective: Dauntė Brazytė Bindokienė, *Lietuvių papročiai ir tradicijos išeivijoje: Lithuanian Customs and Traditions* (Chicago: Pasaulio lietuvių bendruomenė, 1989), pp. 139–362.

98. For a study about the traditional Lithuanian home, see: Angeleė Vyšniauskaitė, *Lietuvio namai* (Vilnius: Lietuvių liaudies kultrūros centras, 1999).

99. A. J. Greimas, *Tautos atminties beieškant* (Vilnius: Mokslas, 1990); J. Balys, *Lietuvių liaudies pasaulėjauta*.

100. For an ethnographic survey of current holiday practices, see: Skirmantė Valiulytė et al., *Atvažiuoja Kalėdos: Advento-Kalėdų papročiai ir tautosaka* (Vilnius: Lietuvos liaudies kultūros centras, 2000).

101. For an ethnographic survey of current holiday practices, see: Juozas Kudirka, *Kūčių naktis* (Vilnius: Lietuvos liaudies kultūros centras, 1990); Juozas Kudirka, *Kūčių stalas* (Panevėžys: Viktoras Bartkus, 1990).

102. Trinkūnas, *Baltų tikėjimas*, p. 49.

103. Ibid., p. 51.

104. For an ethnographic survey of current holiday practices, see: Juozas Kudirka, *Užgavėnės* (Vilnius: Mokslas, 1992) and Inga Kriščiūnienė, *Užgavėnės* (Vilnius: Techlab, 1992).

105. Dundulienė, *Lietuvių šventės*, p. 69.

106. For an ethnographic survey of current holiday practices, see: Juozas Kudrika, *Velykos* (Vilnius: Mokslas, 1992).

107. For an ethnographic survey of current holiday practices, see: Juozas Kudirka, *Joninės* (Vilnius: Vizija, 1991) and Nijolė Marcinkevičienė, *Rasos, Joninės, Kupolinės* (Vilnius: Lietuvos liaudies kultūros centras, 1991).

108. In comparison, it is almost nine hours long where I live, in Chicago, and twelve hours long at the equator.

109. Dundulienė, *Lietuvių šventės*, p. 229.

110. For an ethnographic survey of current holiday practices, see: Juozas Kudirka, *Vėlinės* (Vilnius: Mokslas, 1991).

111. Trinkūnas, *Baltų tikėjimas*, p. 82.

112. Ibid.

113. Ibid.

114. Ibid.

115. Ibid.

116. Ibid., p. 40. He quotes the song from Antanas Juška's collection of Lithuanian *dainos*.

117. For a detailed study of Dausos, see: Gintaras Beresnevičius, *Dausos: Pomirtinio gyvenimo samprata senojoje lietuvių pasaulėžiūroje* (Klaipėda: Tauras, 1990).

118. For a comprehensive overview of the major Lithuanian

rites-of-passage, see Stasys Yla, *Lietuvių šeimos tradicijos: Šeimos kūrimo vyksmai* (Chicago: Lithuanian Library Press, 1978).

119. For a descriptive collection of childhood rites-of-passage, see: Jonas Balys, *Vaikystė ir vedybos: Lietuvių liaudies tradicijos*, in *Lietuvių tautosakos lobynas*, (Silver Spring, Maryland: Lietuvių tautosakos leidykla, 1979), vol. VIII, pp. 1–63.

120. Dundulienė, *Lietuvių etnologija*, pp. 351–55; Trinkūnas, *Baltų tikėjimas*, pp. 28–31.

121. Dundulienė, *Lietuvių etnologija*, p. 353.

122. For a survey of the rites-of-maturation from 1800 to 1950, see: Žilvintas Bernardas Šaknys, *Jaunimo brandos apeigos Lietuvoje: XIX a. pabaigoje—XX a. pirmojoje pusėje*, Lietuvos etnologija, vol. 1 (Vilnius: Pradai, 1996).

123. Balys, *Vaikystė ir vedybos: Lietuvių liaudies tradicijos*, pp. 65–142.

124. Uršulė Žemaitienė, *Suvalkiečių vestuvės*, Lietuvių tautosakos lobynas, ed. Jonas Balys, vol. II (Cleveland: [Lietuvių tautosakos leidykla], 1953).

125. Balys, *Vaikystė ir vedybos*, p. 25.

126. Ibid., p. 33.

127. Trinkūnas, *Baltų tikėjimas*, p. 35.

128. Antanas Juška, *Lietuviškos dainos*, 3 vols. (Vilnius: Valstybinė grožinės literatūros leidykla, 1954), p. 266.

129. For a descriptive collection of funerary traditions, see: Jonas Balys, *Mirtis ir laidotuvės: Lietuvių liaudies tradicijos*, Lietuvių tautosakos lobynas, vol. IX (Silver Spring, Maryland: Lietuvių tautosakos leidykla, 1981).

130. Dundulienė, *Lietuvių etnologija*, p. 370. The material about funerals comes from the following sources: Dundulienė, *Lietuvių etnologija*, pp. 370–81; Balys, *Mirtis ir laidotuvės*, pp. 55–97; Trinkūnas, *Baltų tikėjimas*, pp. 37–39.

131. Trinkūnas, *Baltų tikėjimas*, pp. 77.

132. One of my grandmothers was a professional mourner for part of her life.

133. A wood-stoked cremation fire is not very hot. Only the small bones "burn" or incinerate in the flames. The large bones are not destroyed. These require burial. In contrast, modern cremations use a super-heated fire and crush the remaining bones into a powder.

134. After the death of Pope John Paul II, the media reported that, in his will, he wanted soil from his native Poland poured on

his coffin, but the church officials denied him this request. Since the Pope had a Lithuanian grandmother, I assume this must have been a family tradition or one that Poles share with Lithuanians (the two countries were a united kingdom). The Pope would also kiss the earth whenever he disembarked from a plane: the Lithuanian ethnic tradition calls for greeting the earth by kissing her on a daily basis.

135. In North America, Lithuanian communities incorrectly apply this term to the wake.

136. J. Čiurlionytė, ed., *Lietuvių liaudies dainos* (Vilnius: Valstybinė grožinės literatūros leidykla, 1955), *daina* no. 253.

137. Jonas Balys, *Lietuvių tautosakos lobynas* (Bloomington, Indiana: n.p., 1951), p. 39; Trinkūnas, *Baltų tikėjimas*, pp. 84–86. For studies of fire in Baltic and Lithuanian mythology, see: Daiva Vaitkevičienė, *Ugnies metaforos: Lietuvių ir latvių mitologinos studija* (Vilnius: Lietuvių literatūros ir tautosakos institutas, 2001) and Pranė Dundulienė, *Ugnis lietuvių liaudies pasaulėjautoje* (Vilnius: LTSR aukštojo ir specialiojo vidurinio mokslo ministerija, 1985).

138. Michael York, *Pagan Theology: Paganism as World Religion* (New York: New York University Press, 2003), p. 61.

139. Jonas Trinkūnas, ed. *Of Gods and Holidays: The Baltic Tradition* (Vilnius: Tvermė, 1999), pp. 149–58.

140. Jaunius [Jonas Trinkūnas], "Senoji baltų religija šiandien," *Romuva* 2004, p. 2.

141. Jonas Trinkūnas, "Baltų civilizacija šiandien," *Romuva* 2004, p. 6. This type of Hindu influence may come from the senior members of the Romuva movement who studied the writings of Swami Vivekananda in the 1960s (during the "Ramuva" period).

142. Trinkūnas, *Of Gods and Holidays*, pp. 158–59.

143. Adapted from Trinkūnas, *Baltų tikėjimas*, p. 93.

The End Times According to the Indo-European Worldview: Textual Selections From Four Traditions with Commentary

James Reagan

Introduction

The myth of progress and the linear view of history has become the official belief of modern, secular society. Conversely, the concept of decline and the cyclical understanding of time characterized the religious beliefs of Indo-European antiquity. Four traditions—Indo-Aryan, Greek, Celtic, and Norse—are considered in this brief study. The remarkable similarities in their respective eschatologies indicates a high degree of spiritual cohesion, rooted in a common Indo-European origin.

The Kali Yuga

The *Vedas* and *Purāṇas* represent the scriptural legacy of Indo-Aryan civilization. The doctrine of the four ages, or *yugas*, is articulated in these texts—the Kṛta Yuga, the Tretā Yuga, the Dvāpara Yuga, and the Kali Yuga, the latter of which is the focus of our attention here. The following excerpts from the *Viṣṇu Purāṇa*[1] contain a description of society and the conduct of man during the Kali Yuga:

> All kings occupying the earth in the Kali Age will be wanting in tranquility, strong in anger, taking pleasure at all times in lying and dishonesty, inflicting death on women, children and cows, prone to take the paltry possessions of others, with character that is mostly *tamas*, rising to power and soon falling. They will be short-lived, ambitious, of little virtue and greedy.

In the Kali Yuga, the traditional virtues attributed to the sovereign are inverted—he is greedy, without principle, and spiritually destitute, acquiring illegitimate and merely ephemeral authority. His lack of principles and manic instabilities result in terrible atrocities.

> They will follow the customs of others and be adulterated with them; peculiar, undisciplined barbarians will be vigorously supported by the rulers.

The rejection of tradition and the destruction of indigenous peoples is the inevitable byproduct of globalization. Multiculturalism reduces cultures to caricatures, coexisting in a compromised and confused state of identity.

> Because they go on living with perversion, they will be ruined. The destruction of the world will occur because of the departure from virtue and profit, little by little, day by day. Money alone will confer nobility. Power will be the sole definition of virtue.

Capital becomes the sole criterion of authority. Natural hierarchy, the basis of an organic society, is replaced by the artificial heirarchy of economic man—the predominant modern type.

The text continues:

> Pleasure will be the only reason for marriage. Lust will be the only reason for womanhood. Falsehood will win out in disputes. Being dry of water will be the only definition of land. The sacred thread alone will distinguish brahmins. Praiseworthiness will be measured by accumulated wealth. Wearing the *linga* will be sufficient cause for religious retreat. Impropriety will be considered good conduct, and only feebleness will be the reason for unemployment. Boldness and arrogance will become equivalent to scholarship. Only those without wealth will show honesty. Just a bath will amount to purification and charity will be the only virtue. Abduction will be marriage. Simply to be well-dressed will signify propriety. And any water hard to reach will be deemed a pilgrimage site. The pretense of greatness will be the proof of it, and powerful men with many severe faults will rule over all the classes on earth.

The text concludes with a final, apocalyptic prediction:

> Oppressed by their excessively greedy rulers, people will hide in valleys between mountains where they will gather honey, vegetables, roots, fruits, birds, flowers and so forth. Suffering from cold, wind, heat and rain, they will put on clothes made of tree-bark and leaves. And no one will live as long as twenty-three years. Thus in the Kali Age humankind will be utterly destroyed.

Further significant details are provided by the *Kūrma Purāṇa*:

> In the Kali there is fatal disease, continuous hunger and fear, awful dread of drought and revolution in the lands. Evil creatures born in the Tiṣya—wicked, unprincipled, weak in wit and strong in anger—speak lies. Fear arises among people because of brahmin errors in behavior: crimes, lack of knowledge, evil conduct and ill-gotten gains. In the Kali the twice-born are ignorant of the *Vedas*. Nor do they perform sacrifice; others of inferior intellect do the sacrifice, and they recite the *Vedas* incorrectly. In this Kali age there will occur the association of śūdras with brahmins through *mantras*, marriages and the practice of sleeping and sitting together. Kings who are mostly śūdras will have brahmins killed; abortion and hero-murder will prevail in this age, O king!¹²

The absence of men capable of grasping authentic traditional principles causes the instability leading to collapse. The fading inner qualities of the Brahmin, in this example, elevates those of lesser status to positions of power.³ This leads to the inverted and demonic conditions requisite for the end of a cycle.

The Iron Age

The Greek poet Hesiod is the author of the didactic piece *Works and Days*, described by Robert Lamberton as "a collection of agricultural wisdom poetry."⁴ Hesiod's description of the four ages bears striking similarities to the description we find in the Indo-Aryan tradition. The Golden, Silver, Bronze, and Iron Age are equivalent to the four Indo-Aryan *yugas*. The Iron Age, then, is analogous to the Kali Yuga. Hesiod provides a description of the Iron Age:

Thereafter, would that I were not among the men of the fifth generation, but either had died before or been born afterwards. For now truly is a race of iron, and men never rest from labour and sorrow by day, and from perishing by night; and the gods shall lay sore trouble upon them. But, notwithstanding, even these shall have some good mingled with their evils. And Zeus will destroy this race of mortal men also when they come to have grey hair on the temples at their birth. The father will not agree with his children, nor the children with their father, nor guest with his host, nor comrade with comrade; nor will brother be dear to brother as aforetime. Men will dishonour their parents as they grow quickly old, and will carp at them, chiding them with bitter words, hard-hearted they, not knowing the fear of the gods. They will not repay their aged parents the cost their nurture, for might shall be their right: and one man will sack another's city. There will be no favour for the man who keeps his oath or for the just or for the good; but rather men will praise the evil-doer and his violent dealing. Strength will be right and reverence will cease to be; and the wicked will hurt the worthy man, speaking false words against him, and will swear an oath upon them. Envy, foul-mouthed, delighting in evil, with scowling face, will go along with wretched men one and all. And then Aidos and Nemesis, with their sweet forms wrapped in white robes, will go from the wide-pathed earth and forsake mankind to join the company of the deathless gods: and bitter sorrows will be left for mortal men, and there will be no help against evil.[5]

For the Ancient Greeks, as in all Indo-European cultures, the concept of family and kinship held a high symbolic as well as practical significance. Family was an integral component of the organic hierarchy that organized a normal society. Intergenerational strife, and particularly the hostility of the young directed at the old, can more directly be understood as the rejection or even hatred of knowledge (γνώσις), such as is indicated in the *Viṣṇu Purāṇa*.

We also observe the same inversion of virtue foretold in the *Purāṇas*—particularly regarding the inadequacy of the rulers and the eagerness of the masses to support demagogues. Power is derived from force, devoid of any spiritual quality. Ineptitude and barbarism are the obvious consequences. The greatly feared deterioration, anarchy, and violence in society is an effect, not a cause, of the root source of this chaos: spiritual decadence.

The Age of the Wolf and the Morrígan Prophecy

The same doctrine of cycles was present in the cultures of northern Europe. However, the doctrinal tradition of the northern European peoples is received under entirely different circumstances than the Indo-Aryan or ancient Greek traditions. The textual evidence of the Norse and Irish traditions was recorded by Christian monks who brought their form of writing along with the new religion. The elder tradition was treated with varying concern by these scribes: they could be hostile, seemingly objective, or curiously interested. As a result, a regrettably incomplete body of work remains that is not always entirely reliable. In the Celtic tradition, for example, no substantial explanation of cosmic birth has survived, although this was most likely a part of Druidic lore. The lacuna seems rather significant.

Nevertheless, a number of highly relevant texts remain from both cultures, revealing a great deal about the pagan tradition of northern Europe. The Norse equivalent to the Kali Yuga is the Wolf Age. The *Völuspá*, among the more important poetic sources of Norse mythology, contains an account of Ragnarok, or the twilight of the gods. The final stages of the end times are described:

> Brothers shall fight   and fell each other,
> And sister's sons   shall kinship stain;
> Hard it is on earth,   with mighty whoredom;
> Axe-time, sword-time,   shields are sundered,
> Wind-time, wolf-time,   ere the world falls;
> Nor ever shall men   each other spare.[6]

The Irish text *Cath Maige Tuired*, or *The Second Battle of Mag Tuired*, tells of the famous mythological battle between the Túatha Dé Danann and Fomoire in pagan Ireland. This highly relevant cosmological battle is present in Vedic lore as the struggle between the Devas and Asuras, or in the Norse tradition as the conflict between the Æsir and the Vanir. *Cath Maige Tuired* is probably an eleventh– or twelfth–century retelling of a much older tale. Important scholars of Indo-European studies, such as Dumézil, Benveniste, and de Vries, have examined the tale for its comparative aspects. The final two stanzas contain the victory speech and prophecy of the goddess

Morrígan:

> Then after the battle was won and the slaughter had been cleaned away, the Morrígan, the daughter of Ernmas, proceeded to announce the battle and the great victory which had occurred there to the royal heights of Ireland and to its *síd*-hosts, to its chief waters and to its rivermouths. And that is the reason Badb still relates great deeds. "Have you any news?" everyone asked her then.

> "Peace up to heaven.
> Heaven down to earth.
> Earth beneath heaven,
> Strength in each,
> A cup very full,
> Full of honey;
> Mead in adundance.
> Summer in winter. ...
> Peace up to heaven..."

> She also prophesied the end of the world, foretelling every evil that would occur then, and every disease and every vengeance; and she chanted the following poem:

> "I shall not see a world
> Which will be dear to me:
> Summer without blossoms,
> Cattle will be without milk,
> Women without modesty,
> Men without valor.
> Conquests without a king. ...
> Woods without mast.
> Sea without produce. ...
> False judgements of old men.
> False precedents of lawyers,
> Every man a betrayer.
> Every son a reaver.
> The son will go to the bed of his father,
> The father will go to the bed of his son.
> Each his brother's brother-in-law.
> He will not seek any woman outside the house. ...
> An evil time,

> Son will deceive his father,
> Daughter will deceive. ..."⁷

A number of common themes in this incomplete text should be obvious by now. Unprincipled men seek conquest without guidance, crooked and deceitful behavior becomes the norm, loyalty vanishes, and the elders are mistreated or terrorized. The failure of the land, as predicted here, is the consequence of a society that has fallen out of harmony with nature. This is of course grotesquely obvious in modern Western society, at least since the Industrial Revolution, which by no coincidence is contemporaneous with the rise of revolutionary and counter-Traditional forces. For the ancient Irish, the land was perceived as a goddess, and had to be married by the king for normal, prosperous conditions to continue—without authentic leadership, there is famine and suffering. We live in kingless days; the land and the people will continue to flounder without sacred leadership.

The "mighty whoredom" mentioned in the Norse poem is here given several lines to impress the point. "Women without modesty" recalls "Lust will be the only reason for womanhood," already quoted from the *Viṣṇu Purāṇa*.

The End of an Illusion

The end times according to the Indo-European worldview presents a stark contrast to the biblical Apocalypse. The Indo-European eschatology has no millenarian overtones, but instead represents the beginning of a new cycle. Guénon also reminds us, "If one does not stop short of the most profound order of reality, it can be said in all truth the 'end of a world' never is and never can be anything but the end of an illusion."⁸ According to the Norse tradition, the world will be repopulated by two survivors who remain hidden during Ragnarok: Líf ("life") and Lífþrasir ("desire of life"). Man is again reinvigorated with the active element, the "desire," and another cycle is manifest.

Notes:

1. *Viṣṇu Purāṇa*, 4.24.70–97, in *Classical Hindu Mythology: A Reader in the Sanskrit Purāṇas*, ed. and trans. Cornelia Dimmitt and J. A. B. van Buitenen (Philadelphia: Temple University Press, 1978), p. 41.
2. *Kūrma Purāṇa*, 1.28.1–7, in ibid., p. 40.
3. See ch. 35 of Julius Evola, *Revolt Against the Modern World* (Rochester, Vermont: Inner Traditions, 1995) for an excellent description of "the regression of the castes"; cf. René Guénon, *Spiritual Authority and Temporal Power* (Hillsdale, N.Y., Sophia Perennis, 2001).
4. See his Introduction to Stanley Lombardo's translation of Hesiod's *Works and Day and Theogony* (Indianapolis: Hackett, 1993).
5. *Hesiod, the Homeric Hymns and Homerica*, trans. Hugh G. Evelyn-White (Cambridge, Mass.: Harvard University Press, 1914), ll. pp. 170–201.
6. *The Poetic Edda*, trans. by Henry Adams Bellows (New York: American-Scandinavian Foundation, 1968), st. 45.
7. *Cath Maige Tuired: The Second Battle of Mag Tuired*, trans. Elizabeth A. Gray (Dublin: Irish Texts Society, 1982), pp. 70–73.
8. René Guénon, *The Reign of Quantity & the Signs of the Times* (Hillsdale, N.Y.: Sophia Perennis, 2001), p. 275.

A Modern Minnesänger:
An Interview with Roland Kroell

Michael Moynihan

In the twelfth century at a southern German court, entertainment would have often been provided by a *Minnesänger*, a "singer of *Minne*": a troubadour and performing poet. So named for their most frequent theme, the word *Minne* could be translated as "love," keeping well in mind all the ambiguity of meaning that the latter term holds. For *Minne* was an elusive prize, one that could be earthly and physical, or transcendentally mystical—and many a shade in between—depending on which poet you heard speak and sing. Over the centuries the *Minne*-tradition faded away, later to be preserved only piecemeal in various manuscripts which are now the pride of a handful of European libraries.

While we are lucky to possess a considerable number of shorter courtly lyrical pieces in these collections—not to mention longer epics such as the anonymous *Nibelungenlied*, Wolfram von Eschenbach's *Parzival*, and Gottfried von Straßburg's *Tristan*—the music that would have accompanied the live performances of these texts is largely lost. In recent decades a number of scholars and early music exponents have attempted to recreate how such works might have originally sounded, though the results often seem as fragile and tentative as the dusty manuscripts that spawned them. Such musical endeavors are focussed on the problematic idea of replicating something ostensibly lost to the past.

But did the *Minne*-tradition really disappear? What if it simply retreated from the daylight, concealing itself as a hidden spark in the hearts of the initiates who would keep it alive over the centuries? Such a theory might be born out by the work of Roland Kroell, an extraordinary composer and multi-instrumentalist from the Alemannic area of southwest Germany. For him this past is very much alive, and not merely the object of scholarly curiosity. Over the last decade Kroell has dedicated most of his artistic energies to creating new musical adaptations of twelfth-century epic poems such as *Parzival* and *Tristan*, using the original Middle High German texts as his lyrical source. Kroell's music is firmly rooted in various European folk traditions: Irish and Scottish traditional music and balladry, his native Alemannic dialect and folklore, and

ROLAND KROELL WITH NORTHUMBRIAN SMALL PIPES, FREIBURG-GUNDELFINGEN, 2004. (PHOTO BY ASTRID BREINLINGER)

nature mysticism. He only employs acoustic instruments but does not restrict himself to any single style, instead forging his own variety of "Celtic-archaic song."

Roland Kroell was born in 1954 in Waldshut-Tiengen, in the German federal state of Baden-Württemberg, near the Swiss border. His homeland has exerted a strong influence upon his work and provides a deep well of inspiration. Over the years through performances and recordings Kroell has musically conveyed his interpretations of ancient Celtic music, Peasant War resistance anthems, songs from the revolutions of 1848, and Middle High German masterworks. In all of them a rebellious spirit comes through—sometimes overtly, like a clarion call, and sometimes subtly, like an initiatory key. In every case he feels the material as intrinsically connected to his local region, known as Dreiland or Dreyeckland: the "triangle-land" where France, Germany, and Switzerland meet.

Kroell's most readily available work, *Parzival*, a seventy-four-minute, sixteen-song adaptation of Wolfram von Eschenbach's epic work of the same name, obliterates over eight hundred years of distance between us and the original poem in a matter of seconds.

ROLAND KROELL PERFORMING THE PREMIERE OF HIS PARZIVAL ADAPTATION AT SCHLOSS BÜRGELN, BADEN, GERMANY, 1995. (PHOTO BY MARIA SPEIDEL)

Middle High German as sung by Kroell is a living language, crystal clear yet still possessed of great mystery. Musically, Kroell is a virtuoso on the *"Hexenschit"* (literally a "witch's wood," a local variant of the dulcimer found in the Vogesen region), bouzouki, guitar, zither, harp, glass harp, various bagpipes, whistles and flutes, and other instruments. The emotions he brings to the Middle High German poetic material, as well as those which he perceives within it and perceptively gives voice and melody to, do not allow for passive listening. The messages of these ancient poems are there for us to actively engage with and draw wisdom from, when we open ourselves to them. This is made all the easier when the words are carried on the wings of Kroell's passionate melodies.

Most recently, Kroell unveiled *Tantris und Isôt*, an adaptation of Gottfried von Straßburg's epic *Tristan* poem based on the old Celtic legend of the lovers Tristan and Isolde. The composition consists of thirty-two parts: twenty-four *Lieder* or songs, and eight spoken recitations—uttered in a strange but comprehensible "fantasy language" based on the Alemannic and Plaatdeutsch (Low German) dialects—that serve to contextualize the songs within the overall narrative. The sold-out concert premiere took place on 5 May 2007 as part of the eight-hundred-year jubilee for the town of

Laufenburg, which sits directly on the fabled Rhine river. This performance, divided into three acts, lasted over three hours and took place in an old theater on the Swiss side of the river. Kroell lives and works just across the bridge, on the German side.

In addition to his musical performances and recordings, Kroell is an expert on the geography and lore of the Black Forest region and its Vogesen mountain range. He is the author of seven books which detail the myths, legends, and older Celtic substratum of the region, along with its later Germanic, Christian, and other historical overlays. He has also produced and composed dozens of *Hörspiele*, or documentary radio plays, on these and related subjects.

Originally named "Heinz Roland" by his parents, Kroell has now taken to calling himself Heinrich Roland von Louffenburg after the fifteenth-century *Minnesänger* Heinrich von Loufenberg, who died in 1460 in Straßburg. Kroell, however, is not one to adopt false airs—he sincerely sees himself as the latest representative of a meaningful living tradition with spiritual roots that reach deep into the physical and cultural landscape of ancient Europe.

The following interview was originally conducted in German, and is compiled from correspondence with Roland Kroell over a year-long period from 2006–2007.

Please tell us a bit about your musical background. Did you formally study certain instruments and composition, or are you self-taught in some areas? When and how did you begin to first use medieval Celto-Germanic themes in your work?

My career in music is rather unusual. I come from a family that played a lot of classical music, but I was regarded as unmusical. It was only when I turned sixteen that I discovered my own love of music. I began playing guitar and singing protest songs, like those of Bob Dylan. It was in 1970 that I spent my summer vacation in Scotland and this was my first encounter with Celtic music. It really fascinated me—there were instruments that I'd never seen or heard before in my life like the uillean bagpipes, tin whistle, and the Irish *bodhrán* drum. Then in 1974 I spent three months in Ireland and studied with some well-known traditional musicians there like Micho Russell, the legendary flute player from Doolin on the West Coast. It was from Dan O'Dowd, one of the few pipe makers in Dublin, that I got my first set of uillean pipes. When I returned home, I began researching folksongs in Germany. My interest was primarily for songs of resistance. I didn't find much to speak of, so

I started composing rebel songs of my own based on historical events like the famous Peasant War of 1524–25, or about a resistance group called the "Salpeterer" that had existed in the Black Forest.

I brought this material to a German radio station and they ended up producing my songs. This resulted in my first recording, *Salpetererlieder und Balladen* (Songs and Ballads of the Salpeterer), which was made in 1976. I performed these songs more in the style of the Celtic music that I had learned over in Ireland. It was on account of my work with songs of rebellion that I decided to travel to France to discover more about the heretical medieval Cathar sect in southern France. It was this that first got me thinking in a mystical sense about the Holy Grail. That was in 1977. As a result, my music began to evolve in a more mystical direction. A girlfriend of mine played dulcimer, and I started playing this instrument as well. On most instruments, I am self-taught.

I then began working as composer of radio plays. This was a great opportunity for me to develop my musical talents. For these radio plays we created mystical, historical stories based on figures like Paracelsus, Kaspar Hauser, and the Cathars ... and for the past twenty-five years I have continued to work as a composer.

From this I developed my own repertoire of "Celtic-archaic" songs. I learned overtone singing, and since 1982 I have taken my music in a more meditative direction. In the beginning I was more political, and then I shifted toward a more inward process. This opened up a new world to me. I studied Celtic mythic material like the songs of the old Celtic bard Taliesin. I developed this new musical style over the course of more than nine years, and during this time I traveled to France many times and visited the holy sites of the Cathar sect. I began playing bagpipes in large caves like Lombrives in the Pyrenees. Then I read Wolfram von Eschenbach's *Parzival* and I was absolutely fascinated by his poetry. It seemed reminiscent to me of the poems of Taliesin. This was 1985, when I was trying to stake out a new direction for interpreting Celtic music. It was like finding an inner key of reflection into this material. At the time I was simultaneously studying the different spiritual movements that increasingly spread throughout Germany and Europe since the early 1980s. The more I heard about Buddhism, Sufism, shamanism, and so on, the more I felt that my own spiritual roots lay with the Celts and in the history of the early Middle Ages. So I began by translating the Middle Welsh texts of Taliesin and setting them to music. That was a unique experience;

LEFT: ROLAND KROELL PERFORMING AT A RALLY AGAINST A NUCLEAR POWER PLANT PLANNED FOR WHYL, NEAR FREIBURG, GERMANY, 1977. (PHOTO BY THOMAS LEHNER) RIGHT: ROLAND KROELL PLAYING SCHWARZWALD BAGPIPES IN THE HOTZENWALD COUNTRYSIDE NEAR GROSSHERRISCHWAND, SOUTHERN BLACK FOREST REGION OF GERMANY, 1980. (PHOTO BY TONIO PASSLICK)

I suddenly sensed the energy which spoke to me from the texts. I was always glad to be outdoors and liked visiting old Celtic cult sites, which are recognized as sacred places, in my home region.

Our ancestors knew that there are certain places that possess more energy than others. So they also immediately sensed the energetic difference of such a place and correspondingly built shrines at these geomagnetic points. Often such holy sites have not lost any of their power to this day. It is only that a modern person no longer has the fine "antennae" of perception which are necessary to sense such a distinction.

If we step into a location of this kind, our sense of time, for example, immediately starts to change and we begin to time-travel, becoming linked to a sacred space with its own sacred time. For any experienced shaman this is not a difficult thing. We should make ourselves conscious that here we have entered a transcendent world, one that the Celts called the "Otherworld." Whoever is able to sense this transition will also have already experienced how they can instantly think in a foreign language, or how a strange, unfamiliar melody can flow through them.

I had an experience of this sort for the first time in 1986 when I was staying in a garden at the Münsterhügel in Basel and suddenly a Celtic melody arose within me. I was raking leaves. I journeyed into a sort of trance and was swinging the rake over the ground in a repetitive, identical rhythm which produced something like a music of the spheres. The rhythm and the sound of the swinging rake functioned like a witch's broom, and words came forth. I suddenly began to sing to myself:

Monachen nada in, naada in
Sachenachen tre fa gem
Ogam ehu in

I believe I subconsciously picked up on something from the place itself. It was at the time when my daughter Verena was born and I was also very preoccupied with Celtic mythology. For a fleeting moment I had something of an extraordinary experience, a stark entry into that Otherworld, which in Alemannic is called *àhnedra* (the "other side"). Two thousand years ago the Münsterhügel was a Celtic settlement. It was the center of the Dreiland region. Looking out from this spot one can experience a fantastic sunset on the twenty-first of June. With a ten-hour hike you can reach the Belchen mountain in Baden—I have made this trek and describe it in one of my books. These ancient sacred sites have a healing effect on us, because they came into existence at a time when humans still lived in harmony with nature.

In 1988 I traveled frequently to southern France and played music in the giant caves with my bagpipes and flutes. Out of this came my CD *Höhlenmusik* (Music of the Caves). These were all preparations for when I eventually dared to start the large work based on *Parzival* in 1994. It develops new realms of sound that call forth authentic images of the soul (*Seelenbilder*). So it was not my intention to proceed in a strictly historical way. A single musical passage has come down from Wolfram von Eschenbach himself, the "Titurel melody," and these few notes inspired me, too. It was my task to create a special atmosphere.

Do the type of Bauernkrieg (Peasant War) resistance songs you were hoping to discover in historical sources simply not exist?

I did research in the Folk Song Archive in Freiburg, looking for these kinds of Bauernkrieg songs. There is a book by Wolfgang Steinitz, published in East Germany, which is an exceptional collection of German democratic folk songs. The exact title is *Deutsche Volkslieder demokratischen Characters aus sechs Jahrhunderten* (Six Centuries of German Folksongs of a Democratic Character). It was issued in two volumes by the Akademie-Verlag in 1954.

Which particular elements in Wolfram von Eschenbach's *Parzival* inspired you to undertake creating an epic musical version of this legendary tale?

The mystical words themselves provided me with a deep inspiration, and I also reflected on the poetry of old Celtic myths, such as the legends of King Arthur or Peredure of Wales. In 1994 I began actually composing it.

My search was for a hidden thread in the story. In line with this, I looked for passages in the text that were more like sacral speech. It was not easy to cull these words from the epic as a whole—you have to realize, it consists of more than 20,000 lines. There are sixteen books in Wolfram von Eschenbach's *Parzival*. Each one is like a chapter. Therefore I decided to create sixteen compositions for it, one for each of these chapters, and through them I wanted to illustrate the spiritual thread of the story.

Your approach is quite different from that of an early music purist. You have employed instruments from different time periods and geographical areas, and the musical motifs you have created are diverse in sound. How would you describe your method of working and the final results that you achieve?

I try to do it the same way as I did with the "Celtic-archaic" songs. My basis for the songs was dulcimer and singing. The dulcimer is an instrument that was used by minstrels in the Middle Ages in Germany, France, Italy, and Spain. My intention was to create a composition that reflects more the mood of the story. To this end I also employed a glass harp, and a large Balinese gong. The tones from the glass harp are like something from heaven. I then added some drums and flutes to the songs. Most of the compositions are based on the sun-tone CIS. The Balinese gong has a cosmic sun-tone. It symbolizes the sun-city of Kanvoleis in the Parzival saga.

Through my work with overtones, I was prompted in this direction in 1984 by the well-known German music journalist and historian of jazz, Joachim-Ernst Berendt. I then began working with planetary tones, following the calculations of the Swiss musicologist and mathematician Hans Cousto. Through some mysterious circumstances in 1993 I was able to acquire a Balinese gong with the sun-tone CIS. To me, this shimmering golden metal disc symbolizes the sun itself. The sun was reflected in the figure of the Celtic sun god Belen (Greek Belenos). The Celts, who were renowned as magicians of the metallurgical arts, also made use of gongs, among other things. This has recently been proven by archeological finds discovered in Italy that date to the La Tène period (ca. 300 B.C.E.–100 C.E.).

The way in which you perform certain parts, especially on the dulcimer, can be quite driving and rhythmically aggressive. Do you feel you have incorporated influences from outside the realm of folk music in how you play these parts?

Yes. In order to produce this "sound portrait of the soul" I do also make use of folk-rock elements. For me, musical tones correspond to a color palette—shrill rock sounds correspond to a gaudy red, and the soft pastel sound colors of the flute, dulcimer, and glass harp correspond to blue, green, violet, yellow, and white.

With the exception of Günter Buchwald's lively violin parts, for the *Parzival* recording you play nearly every other instrument.

Yes, except for the fiddle, I played all the instruments on this recording myself. Günther Buchwald played with me on the earlier album *Songs and Ballads of the Salpeterer* as well, and we once did a concert tour together through Brittany in France. Like myself, he is also a composer of radio plays. So he and I are quite familiar with one another, and we work very well together.

Have you performed *Parzival* in a live context before?

I performed about fifty concerts of the *Parzival* material in Germany and Switzerland between 1996 and 1998. We played in old castles and old churches in a group of three musicians. This was made up of Günter Buchwald on fiddle and drums, Ursula Kroell playing glass harp and making recitations, and myself singing and playing dulcimer, gong, and flutes. One concert we did was in a town called Wolfram Eschenbach, near the city of Nuremberg. The famous minstrel is buried there, and the town has a museum dedicated to *Parzival* and Wolfram von Eschenbach. The newspaper wrote: "Forget Richard Wagner—listen to the old version of *Parzival*!"

How do you feel about Wagner's adaptations and interpretations of this old material, or of something like the Nibelungen legend? Did he also manage to capture a certain spirit that you are able to appreciate?

After I had finished composing my work, I listened to Wagner's *Parsifal* in a relaxed state, playing it on LP records. My first impression was that I found the music to be very depressing. Wagner had based his adaptation of the material on the version by Chrétien de Troyes. He rejected the version by Wolfram von Eschenbach because it was too heathen. I think this was something that he couldn't completely understand, because of the era in which he lived. In the nineteenth century, absolutist beliefs concerning Christianity were still very strong. Wagner also somewhat softened the story. Even in the title, for example, he made the strong knight Parzival into the weaker "Parsifal"—the strong "z" became a soft "s," just as the "v" was made into an "f."

What sort of reception has the *Parzival* CD had in Germany and Europe? Has your work reached a large or widespread audience?

It's certainly not part of the mainstream. It is something for special people, those who appreciate old music from the Middle Ages and who like mystical tales. So, no, I do not have a large audience for this music. Nevertheless, it was a central event for me as a human being and as a musician. Therefore it was a great source of pleasure that I could make this record. It changed my life and it allowed me to really open my heart.

Do you have any new projects in the works?

ROLAND KROELL AT HAUS MARIAGRÜN, LAUFENBURG, 2006.
(PHOTO BY MARITA HÖCKENDORFF)

Yes—maybe you can already guess what it is? For me, *Parzival* was a source for spirituality and love. In Wolfram von Eschenbach's story there is a knight called Gawain. He is the embodiment of love, since he is the liberator of four hundred women who were kept prisoner in the castle of the evil king, Clinschor. So when I had finished my *Parzival* composition I started working with the story of Tristan and Isolde by Gottfried von Straßburg. He was a minstrel who lived at the same period as Wolfram von Eschenbach, although he is a little bit younger. Gottfried von Straßburg tried to continue the story of the Holy Grail, and his poetry was written in honor of love. I believe that if God exists, he must be love. And so for the past nine years I've been working on this story.

What else can you tell us about Gottfried and his version of the Tristan legend?

We know only a little bit about this renowned *Minnesänger*. The single testament that he has left to us is the *Minnelied* (love song) of Tristan and Isolde. Gottfried von Straßburg was occupied with this theme up until his death.

Presumably he studied theology, philosophy, jurisprudence, and the courtly arts of hunting, and later was active as a teacher and itinerant preacher. In his work he states that he based his poem upon the version by one Thomas of Britain. Only recently an old manuscript was discovered in Carlisle, England which confirms the existence of this version.

In the foreground of his poem we no longer find the figures of heroic knights who gain honor and glory in foreign lands by fighting victorious battles for their lords. No, Tristan was a fine tradesman who had developed the feminine side of his being and whose adventure consists in a deep encounter with love itself. Although he was not a member of the nobility, through a long period of study he acquired a strong sense of self-consciousness. And while he adapted his story from Thomas of Britain, Gottfried has given us the most elaborate of all the versions of the Tristan and Isolde legend. He expanded the epic, combined the story together with his personal experiences, and competed with the best of the minnesingers, such as Wolfram von Eschenbach who had already created an epic of comparable length with his treatment of the Parzival legend. Anyone who attentively looks at both of these works will get the impression that Gottfried, with his *Tristan*, has further developed the epic of Wolfram's *Parzival*.

With Wolfram von Eschenbach the theme of love receives somewhat less attention. It is not Parzival, but rather the fearless knight Gawain, who has to free the women from the magic castle of the evil sorcerer Klinschor by battling with a giant lion.

For Gottfried, love stood in the foreground as the highest form of human initiation into the mysteries. In his poem he professes a secret religion of love. It is Tantris—as the wounded

Tristan calls himself when he travels to Dublin in a tiny boat in order to be healed by Queen Isolde—who becomes a singer of love, a devotee of love. With the arrival of a new era in which the aristocrats began their building boom of new castles, the old heathen and heretical Christian currents in society were strongly curtailed. These groups had already been a thorn in the side of the Church for a long time. One could no longer experience free love, without conventions, and so life became more sorrowful for the free-spirited person. Out of Tantris, the singer of love, comes Tristan, whose name means "sorrow."

The tradition of the Tristan and Isolde legend from Wales is interesting. In it there are two knights who are courting Esyllt (Isolde): Trystan on the one hand, and on the other the knight March (Mark). King Arthur has to mediate between the two opposing parties. In the end a compromise is reached that Trystan be allowed to live with and love Esyllt during the short nights when there are leaves on the trees, and March in the long nights when there are no leaves on the trees. Esyllt comes up with a trick and points to the holly tree. This keeps its leaves even in winter, and thus Trystan is able to stay with her all year long.

Gottfried von Straßburg died before he could complete his epic poem. How do you bring your adaptation to its conclusion?

I let the story end as Tristan und Isolde, the pair of lovers, escape to *la foissure* (the Grotto of Love). In this way I followed the earlier Celtic version, in which the two lovers find one another in spite of all obstacles.

Why have you titled your composition *Tantris und Isôt* rather than "Tristan" or "Tristan und Isôt"?

With the title *Tantris und Isôt* I wanted to disassociate myself from the opera by Richard Wagner. In the creation of the work I was stimulated to sense the path of *Minne*. "Tantris" is the man of *Minne*, who takes up the old Celtic ritual of free love, outside of societal conventions. "Tristan," on the other hand, is the sorrowful singer who must obey the new order. In Ireland these old Celtic love customs were still dominant then. The three women themselves, Queen Isolde, Brangäne, and Princess Isolde are reminiscent

ROLAND KROELL AT HAUS MARIAGRÜN, LAUFENBURG, 2006.
(PHOTO BY MARITA HÖCKENDORFF)

of the three Beths, the three *Matronae*, the three Marys…

Were you assisted by other musicians for the premiere performance of *Tantris und Isôt*?

It was a solo performance. At the end, the final song "Driu fensterlîn" (Three Little Windows) was left open-ended. At that point a friend, Lucien Mayrich, played singing bowls. I also picked up a singing bowl and while playing it walked silently off the stage. I wanted no applause at the end of the final act. So I stepped out onto the street with my friend Miroslav and we went through the city on foot and back to my house. My friend Lucien continued to play in the theater. In this way the people in the audience could leave the hall slowly, whenever they felt like it. I had long pondered how I should handle the end of the performance, and then arrived at a decision based on my feelings. Since Gottfried von Straßburg did not leave us with an ending to the story, I also wanted to convey something open-ended.

It seems to me that your engagement with the Tristan material is even more personal and passionate than with the Parzival legend.

In my view the Tristan and Isolde material is a Celtic didactic paradigm. It introduces the initiate to the mystery of love. Gottfried's version is fantastic to me because he probably related it with his own lovelife, yet without betraying the true content of the story. In the strict sense it is not Christian, but rather goes against the convention of marriage and emphasizes pure love.

Why are these legends from so many centuries ago still relevant to you as an artist? What relevance do they have to human beings in the twenty-first century?

Well, I think this depends on a few things. There is something of an old spiritual message in these stories. They contain ancient wisdom that connects us with a much earlier period on earth. It's part of our spiritual history in Europe, but also part of the spiritual history for those who left Old Europe over the past two centuries and went to North America or to other places around the world. People today often seek out different religions, shamanism, Buddhism, and so on, looking for something for their soul. I think that in *Parzival* and *Tristan* I find a direct connection to my ancient spirituality. Because many aspects of old mystical things came together in these stories, and this provides a strength that gives you power for your heart and soul. Through it you can feel that you are grounded, with a set of roots as it were, despite being in a new, modern age where you are surrounded by technological things.

Discography/Bibliography

Albums by or featuring Roland Kroell:

Roland Kroell und D'Salpeterer, *Salpetererlieder und Balladen* (Trikont, 1977)
Roland Kroell und D'Salpeterer, *Scho sit duusig Joohr: Alemannische Lieder* (Werkstatt-Edition, 1983)
Roland Kroell und D'Salpeterer, *Live 1984: Unveröffentlichte Lieder* (Glasmann-Records, 2007)
Höhlenmusik: Symphonie für Tropfstein, Flöte und Dudelsack, (Glasmann-Records, 1992)
Archaische & Celtische Gesänge (Pan Tao, 1995)
Parzival (Erdenklang, 1996)
"Viel Tausend sich erheben...": Lieder zur Badischen Revolution 1848/49 (Glasmann/Südwest Rundfunk, 1998)
Keltische Klangwelten (Glasmann, 2004)
Tantris und Isôt (in preparation, 2007)

Books by Roland Kroell:

Mythologisch Reisen: Südschwarzwald/Kaiserstuhl. Lahr: Schauenburg-Verlag, 1997.
Das Geheimnis der Schwarzen Madonnen. Stuttgart, Kreuz-Verlag, 1998 (with Ursula Kröll).
Mythologisch Reisen: Mittel- und Nordschwarzwald. Lahr: Schauenburg- Verlag, 1999.
Sagen, Mythen und Legenden: Wandern im Dreiland. Basel: Reinhardt-Verlag, 2000.
Magischer Schwarzwald und Vogesen. Baden: AT-Verlag, 2005.
Magische Nordvogesen: Wanderungen durch altes Keltenland. Saarbrücken: Neue Erde-Verlag, 2006.
Magischer Südschwarzwald. Freiburg: Badische Zeitung-Verlag, 2007.

Selected *Hörspiele* (documentary radio plays) with contributions from Roland Kroell for the Southwest Regional Broadcasting and Saarland Broadcasting:

Die abenteuerliche Simplicissimus—Grimmelshausen, 1975
Die Salpeterer—keine Obrigkeit Untertane Leut, 1977

Die Sympathiedoktoren (Bauernschamanen) im Schwarzwald, 1979
Der Wunderdoktor mit dem Henkersschwert—Paracelsus, 1980
Kaspar Hauser, 1982
Geister und Hexensagen aus dem Schwarzwald und Kaiserstuhl, 1983
Lochheiri, eine Wilderergeschichte, 1991
Wie die Schwarzwälder Kuckucksuhr zu den Muselmanen kam, 1992
Das Glas so rein und klar wie Kristall, 1994
Rebellion an der Eisenbahnbrücke, 1996

Selected television programs produced in collaboration with Roland Kroell (all for Channel 3, Southwest Regional Broadcasting):

Die Ballade von Lochheiri, 1985
Glas aus dunklen Waldhütten, 1994
Das Belchenprojekt, 1993

For the music and books of Roland Kroell, and information on mystical-magical guided tours in the Dreiland region, visit: <www.schwarzwaldmagie.de>

Beta-lactam Ring Records
blrrecords.com

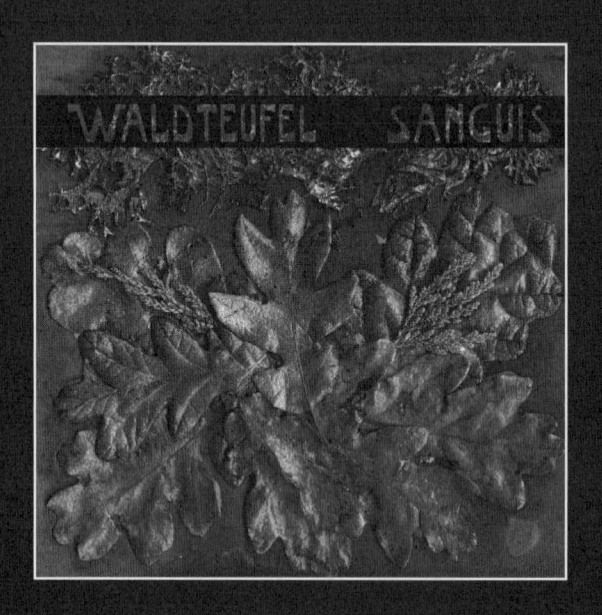

Waldteufel
"Sanguis"
CD/LP+7"/LP+7"+Artwork Sculpture/Download

It was weird enough when Markus first donned his Waldteufel hides in '9[?] after the sub-tribal thud of Crash Worship. 12 years on and he continues [to] crack open die Erde, and houses her escaping spirits and demons in Lieder for [?] Vreaky Volk to sing. "Musically, it runs the gamut from dense hypnot[ic] atmospheres, ritual passages to metallic chants and triumphant percussion-hea[vy] hymns."

Project of Markus Wolff — Crash Worship, Soriah, In Gowan Ring, Blood Ax[e], Witch-Hunt, Allerseelen, L'Acephale and Changes.

In ages past, Tyrsson Sinclair commandeered the extreme metal entity Warhate. His curre[nt] solo-project is Northman and he is also developing a new project called Hamramr.

Bitter Troubadour:
An Interview with Andrew King

Andreas Diesel and Marco Deplano

"Neofolk" music is the product of seemingly disparate origins, a hybrid genre created by post-industrial and electronic musicians who have rediscovered the evocative power of acoustic music. This has been accompanied by an interest in various arcane and *outré* themes, from paganism and the occult, to deviant sexuality and—more troublingly for critics—European ethnocentrism. Most neofolk musicians are at least superficially interested in European folk music and culture, and utilize traditional imagery on their albums and as part of their personas. Not surprisingly, this is often a case of style over substance. For Andrew Stewart King, however, an abiding dedication to *true* folk culture, and especially folk music, is the rationale behind each of his recordings and public performances.

King has worked with a number of neofolk artists, and albums like *The Bitter Harvest* and *The Amfortas Wound* have appeared on labels associated with the genre. But he is also a tireless laborer in the field of English traditional music. As a former project worker with the British Libraries' *Traditional Music in England Project*, King strove to catalog and preserve aging reel-to-reel acetate and cassette tape recordings from the fieldwork of collectors like Steve Gardham, Keith Summers, and Bob and Jacqueline Patten, as well as studying the cylinder recordings of English, Welsh, and Scots Gaelic singers made by the folk song collectors of the early twentieth century. These archives include shanties, dance tunes, ballads, children's music, customs, and stories. King's own tastes range even further afield, encompassing everything from Western classical music to descriptive ballads, hunting calls, military music, and the troubadours and minnesingers. As a traditional performer, King puts in regular appearances at venues such as the Musical Traditions Club, where other guests might include "source singers" like Fred Jordan, Ray Driscoll, Sheila Stewart, Bob Copper, or Oliver Mulligan.

On his own albums, King draws on his background as a traditional performer while incorporating electronic and experimental elements more familiar to his neofolk audience. His first album showcased his unaccompanied singing, while *The Amfortas Wound* features droning backing music arranged by King and performed with assistance from members of the group KnifeLadder (who describe their own music as "primal techno organic soundscapes"). This has been compared to the sound achieved by Shirley Collins (who King admires), although King has an edge that puts him more in line with the brooding minimalism of Nico, or at least the downward-spiraling Nico of the *Desert Shore* period.

In addition to the music, King's records feature his distinctive Symbolist artwork. He has also provided illustrations for the now-defunct Ghost Story Press, a publisher known for its sumptuous and much-sought-after editions by M. R. James, Dermot Chesson Spence, and Frederick Cowles. Recent music releases include a split-CD with the American group Changes, commemorating a concert in Sintra, Portugal, and a split-CD with Sol Invictus and Rose Rovine e Amanti. King also appears on a CD by the French group Les Sentiers Conflictuels, who recognized the depth, range, (and sheer Britishness) of his voice. This particular project, which was released as the album *1888*, conjures up an English ghost unlike the ones found in the pages of James or Spence: Jack the Ripper.

(*Introduction by Joshua Buckley*)

Tell us about your interest in European traditional music.

I have a deep and abiding interest in Western culture, but have always been aware that the "art culture" of the West is only a part of our story, and that for every movement or genre that can be found within it there exist numerous vernacular traditions that have been either neglected, ignored, or marginalized. This is partly due to the vulnerability inherent within what is a predominantly oral culture, but it is also due to the fact that the media, cultural, and educational establishments have unequivocally abandoned their cultural heritage in favor of postmodern irony and rootless cosmopolitanism. It is in opposition to this cultural shift that I have felt compelled to concentrate most of my energies for the last eight years or so. For while certain hateful ideologies, attitudes, and assumptions might have a stranglehold on the contemporary art scene, this doesn't actually endanger the creativity of myself and those other artists who exist independently of it. On the other hand,

ANDREW KING IN VIENNA, AUSTRIA.
(PHOTO BY ANNE SCHLIEPHAKE)

the attention and respect given to traditional (or vernacular) culture is at such a low ebb that I truly feel that any of my work, whether in the form of academic writings, archival research, field recordings, or even my own recordings, can quite tangibly aid the ancestral culture of my people. There will always be artists to fight against the decadence of the present dominant ethos. But the very nature of true vernacular culture puts it at a greater disadvantage. It therefore has all the more need for assistance and thus must be given priority in one's creative endeavors.

In your case, this has also been a professional endeavor. We understand that you worked in the archives at the British Library.

I was employed by the (as then) National Sound Archive of the British Library to digitise and catalogue English traditional music from unpublished field recordings as part of their *Traditional Music in England Project* [see: http://www.bl.uk/collections/sound-archive/traditional_music.html]. For those interested, the work that I have been responsible for (over twelve thousand entries) can be found online on the British Library Sound Archive web [url: http://www.bl.uk/collections/sound-archive/cat.html] under the Collection numbers C1002 (my friend, the late Keith Summers's Collection, mainly Suffolk), C1009 (the Steve Gardham Collection, mainly Kingston-upon-Hull and the East Riding of Yorkshire,), C1012 (The Nick and Mally Dow Collection, mainly Dorset), C1033 (The Bob and Jacqueline Patten Collection, mainly Somerset and performances from the West Gallery Music revival) and parts of C903 (The Reg Hall Archive). Unfortunately, though there is a considerable need for a full-time curatorial position devoted to British vernacular culture within the British Library—one would have thought this obvious given that it is supposed to be a national institution—the powers that be, for reasons obviously related to those that I just referred to, will only consider such work if it is externally funded. This has meant that at the project's end I was shunted from one humiliating and degrading position to the next, and was only occasionally permitted to utilize my expertise for the library's good. I have now been made redundant, which means that there is no longer even one member of the staff at that institute with a specialist's knowledge of British vernacular culture. During the appeal procedure a petition was organised on my behalf (signed by nearly every source performer and academic of consequence) to which the only reaction from the Head of British Collections was to insist upon a verbal disciplinary for having brought the library into disrepute—a reaction that to my mind still beggars belief! Furthermore, it was made very clear to me that this area was "not a priority" to the library. Coming from our National Institute, this is frankly shocking, and amounts to nothing less than a betrayal of the British people.

Work of consequence that I managed to do before leaving consisted of C1128 (Vic Ellis Collection, County Durham and Surrey), C1133 (Christopher Chaundy Collection; an important source for recordings of William Kimber) and—of greatest interest to myself—the re-cataloguing of the English Folk-Dance and Song Society section of C37, which consists of 106 pre–Great War wax cylinders of traditional singers from the British Isles. These cylinders are arguably the most important recordings of British traditional music in the world, and I find it staggering that so little has been done to make them better known. Certainly, had they been recordings of classical music (or of jazz or blues) they would have been exhaustively catalogued and published years ago. Unfortunately, until there is a permanent curatorial position within the British Library devoted to British vernacular culture, such omissions are always going to happen.

A growing number of people involved in the post-industrial/ experimental music scene are drawing influences from traditionally oriented music and themes. Where do you think this is leading?

Ideally, I would like to see it as the vanguard of a general cultural shift towards those historic virtues of integrity, continuity, and awareness of place and nation that one finds embodied in the traditional culture of the West. But I realize that this is at the moment highly unlikely to happen. Not only do we have the damage of modernism to deal with, but also that of its descendants, a plethora of vested interests whose ideologies (relativism, multiculturalism, rights-issues, and cosmopolitanism) are deeply inimical to the central historic virtues of our culture. The most brazen and shameful manifestation of this is the total abdication by the postwar liberal elite of the West's claim to moral and cultural superiority. It also manifests itself in the more banal forms of popular media entertainment, where the bottom line is now so obviously just that of the lowest common denominator. So to repeat my answer, I would like to see this scene acting as a harbinger of moral cultural change, but I realize that there is a lot to be overcome.

Is there a danger that the artists who embark on this course will simply lapse into a reactionary form of nostalgia?

"LIX NON TIMEBRIS A TIMORE NOCTURNO" BY ANDREW KING.
(COURTESY OF ANDREW KING)

With regards to nostalgia and its attendant risks, well, I think this depends very much on a group's sources, and their attitudes towards those sources. For example, the risk of creative atrophy is far less with those groups that ignore the postwar commercial folk revival and instead concentrate on early music and the more overtly obvious aspects of their own country's "*Volks*-culture." Good creative examples of this would be Ain Soph's version of "Retrowange novelle," Camerata Mediolanense's version of "L'Homme Armé," and Hekate's "Die Gedanken sind frei." For me, the question only becomes problematic with those neofolk (or for that matter, folk groups) that only base themselves on the published commercial repertoire of the stars of the postwar second revival, and the later "folk-rock" scene. Then we are encountering a form of thoughtless nostalgia. The irony in this is that regardless of the neofolk group's own ideology or politics they will (if British/European) be borrowing the mannerisms and baggage of a scene that was itself not only contrived, but also based on alien sources. Even if they go back to the "father figures" of the postwar revival—A. L. Lloyd and Ewan MacColl—it is without realizing that these men, though historically important, were Marxists who had their own baggage and political agenda for folk song. With a few notable and laudable exceptions, none of the postwar revival

"LXVII WE MUST OVERRULE OUR STARS" BY ANDREW KING.
(COURTESY OF ANDREW KING)

acts were what I would define as "source" performers. They were commercial popular musicians who came to traditional music second hand, and (to make matters worse) usually via American models. To illustrate this point, a neofolk group might cover a song that they initially heard on—to take a famous revival folk-rock example—a Fairport Convention album. Now, while Fairport Convention are certainly an influential and important group in the development of late sixties and early seventies popular music, they have absolutely nothing to do with traditional music in the sense that I would define it (which means singers such as Cyril Poacher, Harry Cox, Joseph Taylor, Esther Smith, Mrs. Overd, etc.). What we are getting in the interpretations of this hypothetical neofolk group isn't based on traditional music, but rather Anglo/American pop music from the early 1970s.

I don't mind people experimenting with traditional music—after all, I do that myself—but they should only do so from an informed position. They should know the importance of what they are working with, and most important of all, they should go back to the sources. This cannot be emphasized enough. It marks the difference between someone whose work should be respected, and those who are mere dilettantes, or, worse still, dabblers who think it might be cool to stick some "folksy" mannerisms in their work, or maybe cross them with some "ethnic" rhythms.

Your own music is conservative in the best sense of the word, as it removes the dust from something valuable from the past and preserves it for the future. But, as you just alluded to, you also embrace elements of innovation.

I thank you for your positive description of conservatism, which of course is its true meaning anyway. For what is a conservative other than one who wishes to "conserve" something that they consider of importance, whether that thing is their vernacular heritage, art culture, or racial identity?

Now fundamentally I have nothing against experimentation, but over the years I have come to realize that experimentation on its own rarely creates anything of consequence. There are a few doughty individuals or groups who, by constantly pushing the boundaries, achieve something of worth. Morton Feldman is one, Hermann Nitsch is another, Throbbing Gristle also comes to mind. But many in the various disciplines of postwar modernism and its attendant movements fail (and in this I would reluctantly include both John Cage and Pierre Boulez) in that their compositions might be fine things to read, consider, or write about, but they are rarely worth the trouble of listening to or looking at. The composition has become a poor second to the intellectual baggage that goes with it. This, to me, is a problem that needs to be addressed. Furthermore, for every one who succeeds in their experiments (or fails honorably) there are numerous third-rate talents who use "experimentation" or the latest conceptual fads as a convenient cover for having nothing of consequence to say. In fact, they would probably find the whole idea that one *could* have "something of consequence to say" laughable in the first place. Certainly, the present strangle hold that "Britart" has on the visual arts is only the most obvious example of the cultural cul-de-sac that modernism has led us to.

I am always reminded of how the great Danish composer Carl Nielsen's opinion of Béla Bartók was somewhat reduced when Bartók asked him "Mr. Nielsen, do you think my music is modern enough?" Now Nielsen's late symphonies and concertos are amongst the most challenging of the first half of the last century. But the point was never to be "modern" or "experimental." It was simply the logical organic development of Nielsen's creativity, which devised new ways of finding solutions to the complex symphonic questions that his character and creative development posed for him. It is worth remembering here that Nielsen was of peasant stock, and was deeply rooted in folk culture. It is thus of little wonder that though his work is challenging and difficult, it is never trivial, mannered, or soulless—traits that one finds in abundance in the "experimental" and "conceptual" scenes of today.

Why do you think that many English folk songs address morbid subjects, but often do it with a certain sense of humor? Is this a typical British trait?

The repertoire of the traditional singer can be quite far ranging, with the same performer often being acquainted with the earliest ballads, later glee songs, broadsheet ballads, and the popular compositions of the parlor ballads and music hall periods. Besides social and family background, a singer's repertoire is dictated by their temperament. This is probably why I sing a disproportionately high selection of morbid pieces. Speaking more generally, a song will usually only survive in the oral tradition if it is popular. When looking at the earliest surviving ballads it is not surprising that amongst those carols and semi-ritual songs that have come down to us is to be found a high percentage of an unusual, dramatic, or grotesque nature, such as "The Bitter Withy," "Dives and Lazarus," "Corpus Christi," and "Sir Hugh." This principle holds true with the slightly later great secular ballads (often called "Border Ballads") which in reflecting the values of their time—albeit in a form

ANDREW KING AT THE IMPERIAL WAR MUSEUM, LONDON, ENGLAND.
(PHOTO BY ELIZABETTA BARBAZZA)

refracted through the songs hypothetical context—tend to represent a world in which life truly was nasty, brutish and short, hence their tendency towards melodrama and violence. "Lady Maisry," "Andrew Lammie," and "Young Andrew" are all examples of this form. Along with these "Border Ballads" there are also the possibly earlier, and very nearly ritualistic question-and-answer ballads like "Lord Randal" and "Edward," as well as those songs that while obviously originally full narrative ballads, have only come down to us in truncated and garbled form. This is a process that actually increases their mystery and power. Good examples are "George Collins" and some versions of "Lamkin." The rise of the glee song in the seventeenth century and the Ballad Opera in the eighteenth century created forms of "art" song that—while influenced by the traditional idiom—were predominantly more lighthearted. The social tension generated by the agricultural enclosure movement and the rise of the "bloody code" in the latter half of the eighteenth century, when the legal code was extended so that the most negligible misdemeanor became punishable by death, contributed to the growth of the already existent genre of the gallows confession song. This gave rise to such songs as "The Prentice Boy," "The Captain's Apprentice," and (by the mid–nineteenth century) such "penny-dreadful" numbers as "The Folkestone Murder" and "Maria Martin." With regards to the humor inherent in some of these songs, certainly with regards to the later "confession" songs, this can be put down to "gallows humor."

What is the "Amfortas Wound"?

It is the wound that will not heal. It is utilized by Wagner in *Parsifal* when the Grail guardian Amfortas, due to his own errors, is wounded by Longinus's spear (the "Spear of Destiny"—which, incidentally, I finally got to see in Vienna last month), thus condemning himself to a life of continual physical and existential agony. This is of course an elaboration on Wolfram von Eschenbach's version of the tale (where the spear is descended from the bleeding lance to be found in Chrétien and the earlier Celtic myths), and previous commentators have identified it as being a symbolic representation of Schopenhauer's concept of *"die ewige Gerechtigkeit"*—eternal justice. Not only does this seem to me to be a remarkably accurate realization of the human condition. It mirrored my own mental and physical condition at the time the album was recorded.

What made you choose the songs featured on *The Amfortas Wound*? Why did it take so long to be released?

Unlike *The Bitter Harvest*, which to be honest I now realize was a prentice work, and where the songs were to a large extent dictated by the process of stylistic self-discovery that the eighteen months that I spent on recording that album brought about (we all have to start somewhere), *The Amfortas Wound* was the product of eight months of intensive sessions at KnifeLadder member Hunter Barr's studio in Camden, in which I stripped the album down to only those songs that I felt in some way or other reflected its title and my then aims and objectives. *The Bitter Harvest* was intended as a manifesto (my 95 Theses, or 39 Articles if you prefer) in which I nailed my colors to the mast. I wanted to present the world with a contemporary collection of traditional songs directly based on source singers and stylistically in complete opposition to the ethno-fusion and world music genres that at that time had a stranglehold on the folk scene. In the end it became a learning experience, in that I realised that I wasn't yet a singer of the caliber to carry such a purist vision successfully to fruition—not yet anyway. By the time of *The Amfortas Wound* I knew exactly what I wanted to say, and how I would say it. Unfortunately, the physical and emotional cost of working at this degree of white heat on the project, coupled with my then deeply problematic personal life, left me a complete wreck. (Listening back to "Sweet Williams Ghost" or "The Prentice Boy," it is quite obvious that this is the work of someone whose mind was at the end of its tether. In fact, with regards to the latter, I hadn't had any sleep in the previous twenty-four hours and one of my ribs was cracked. That said, some of the outtakes are quite amusing, or rather fascinating, in the way that a terrible accident can be fascinating.)

With the album completed, I promptly had a complete physical and mental collapse, ending up bedridden for most of the next three months. World Serpent deciding not to issue the album didn't help the situation. This was very dispiriting at the time, but in the long term it turned out for the best, as Athanor has proved an infinitely better company to work with. Not only do they respect their artists, they are not willing to cut corners in presentation (allowing me a large enough booklet to include not just full notes but also lyrics), and have consistently good access to European distribution. A final complication that added to the record's delay was the decision for there to be a limited version of the album with a lenticular print based on the alchemical imagery to be found in my paintings. This meant doing four paintings (the three in the print plus the cover) rather than just one, not to mention the whole procedure of having the prints manufactured and mounted on lead. The latter was a time-consuming process that only cheered me up with the knowledge that by working without gloves I was actually poisoning myself—hoorah!

On *The Bitter Harvest* and *The Amfortas Wound*, you worked with John Murphy, who is known for his work with the early industrial group S.P.K., as well as other heavily experimental projects.

I got to know John when I first moved to London, via my then flatmate Andrew Trail (formerly of Ministry of Love, Band of Pain, Autogeddon, etc.) who had known John in Sydney. John was based in London at the time, and when he and Andrew embarked on their KnifeLadder project the logical solution was for him to move in with us. Working together followed on from this, and John was happy to help with my first tentative steps at performing live (which started only as recently as 1999, and which I treat as something very separate from my "resident" spots at traditional music clubs). I am glad to say that this process of working together has continued through all his more recent stays in England, though the responsibility of being in the constant presence of a self-styled God-King-Emperor (in the Ancient Egyptian mold) is a heavy one, and it has sometimes led to lamentable confusion in the media. Once an Italian distributor described me as "percusionista de Death in June" and "ex-DIJ," which unfortunately upset a few people. I thought it rather funny, though, as the idea of my being a trained drummer, let alone a drummer for Death In June, is about as probable as my rapping on a dance record! Nevertheless, I have recently joined Sol Invictus; performing percussion, backing vocals, and lead vocals for the more traditional songs.

You have participated in a number of tribute albums, covering songs by groups like Kirlian Camera, Laibach, Ain Soph, and Sol Invictus. Is this an attempt to capture the same sort of continuity you have tried to establish with vernacular singers?

It's something that I go out of my way to do, and enjoy doing, as it gives me an opportunity to work outside the framework of traditional music with a clean conscience. Apart from these recordings, I have little interest in creating my own songs, or of covering non-traditional songs, unless they are obviously influenced by the vernacular idiom (that said, I am currently working on an album of

A. E. Housman settings). So working on these compilations is a wonderful way of experimenting without having to worry about how the experiments will work within the context of an album. Having known Tony Wakeford for many years, I was eager to contribute to *Sol Lucet Omnibus* (a Sol Invictus tribute album). I sent off my preferred choices to Cynfeirdd, only to discover that not only had no one else asked to do what I had put forward as my first choice, but that there had been no claims on my second option either! This seemed too good an opportunity to miss, and I went ahead and recorded both pieces. I gave them an introduction, basing "The Three Ravens" on Thomas Ravenscroft's setting rather than the traditional melodies. I consider "The Raven Banner" one of my finest moments, but still can't believe my luck that no one else wanted to cover "Raven Chorus." It's one of the great songs of all time. The Ain Soph, Laibach, and Kirlian Camera covers were a different matter, as I don't personally know the groups. I do take great pride in having been associated with each of those projects. This was especially so with "Tutti a casa!" as I have been championing Ain Soph over here since the mid-1980s. When *Aurora* was first issued I realized—after getting over my initial shock—that here was something of great consequence from which we could all learn. So I had always had the idea of doing an Ain Soph cover in the back of my mind anyway, the options (for me) being either "Retrowange novelle," "Légionnaire en Algiers," or "Datemi Pace." On reflection, I felt that any version that I did of the first of these wouldn't be sufficiently different from Ain Soph's to warrant doing, but with the other two the problem was that I am so poor at foreign languages (Latin excepted) that I knew that the final result would have been laughable. That left only "Legionnaire in Algiers." It saddened me that I had to do this in English, but in retrospect, I think my version works well, even though, as with the Laibach cover, I had to take a few liberties with the translation.

As a point of interest, one knock-on effect of this compilation work has been the desire to accommodate this same degree of experimentation within a full album, by which I mean an album that would still consist predominantly of traditional songs, but would also include other traditionally oriented, but not strictly traditional, compositions. I have slowly been recording these pieces since 2001, and hopefully they will appear as my next album, which goes under the provisional working title of *Deus Ignotus*. Along with the traditional songs there will be a remix of "The Three Ravens," an

"LXXXIII MERCURIUS SPIRITUS" BY ANDREW KING.
(COURTESY OF ANDREW KING)

extended thirteenth-century Middle English ballad called "Judas," as well as "Sic mea fata" from the *Carmina Burana* and Wolkenstein's "Fröleichen so well wir." The former of these is in Latin, and yes, I will be singing the latter in *Altdeutsch*, having had a series of intensive pronunciation lessons while visiting friends in Vienna earlier this year. You have been warned.

Earlier, you mentioned your gigs at traditional music clubs.

Although I take my recordings very seriously, I know that for any of it to "ring true" or be of consequence then I must do this work with constant reference to the tradition from which it sprang, and which is my heritage. As I have said, one must always return to the *sources*, to learn from older singers and to find one's own voice. The reason why so much contemporary folk music is so redundant (or simply embarrassing) is that nearly all the commercial folk groups of the revival failed to follow this simple rule. As my health hasn't been too good for the last few years I have cut down on my live appearances, but I have maintained "resident" spots at two London clubs, The Cellar Upstairs and The Musical Traditions Club. The former of these is a long-established folk club—in fact it's just had its thirtieth anniversary—that operates every week and (to be honest) has a much more open repertoire than I tend to like (singer-songwriters, folk groups, etc.). But because it is on every week, the main act will occasionally be a traditional performer. This is usually when I have been asked to be the resident, which means that I had a warming-up slot in supporting the main act and usually got to sing three or four songs over the course of an evening. Unfortunately, due to work pressures, I have had to curtail my appearances. The Musical Traditions Club is rather more select in that it concentrates specifically on source singers and musicians, but as there aren't so many of them around (and sadly, with each year their numbers become less) the club only operates once a month. Being a resident there simply means that you can always be relied upon to sing a song at short notice if needed. But such is the wealth of talent that they attract that you typically only get one song each. Several months ago I was asked to sing twice in one evening for the first time. In my book, this was a very great honor!

You have contributed cover art to albums by Current 93 (*Of Ruine or Some Blazing Starre*), Tony Wakeford (*Cupid and Death*), and L'Orchestre Noir (*Cantos*). You also did a number of illustrations for the Ghost Story Press.

During the last year of my art degree (in 1988) my work (which until then had mainly consisted of rather elaborate installation and performance pieces) became increasingly text oriented, to the degree that what had started as a concern for text compositions developed into a preference for writing academic papers. Thus, I put my artwork on hold and devoted two years to post-graduate studies. To a large extent I felt that I had said all that I wanted to say in the visual arts. But having abandoned art for academia, I found that certain themes, concepts, and ideas, usually of an archetypal nature, were now demanding attention and would not let me alone. In an effort to address this dilemma I turned to what struck me as the quickest medium at hand. This turned out to be painting, a genre that I hadn't previously concentrated on, as my background was firmly in conceptual art. Text played a role in these early paintings, and in one I had included a Current 93/Death In June "floating verse" from "Fall Apart." I thought it was only right that I should get in touch and ask permission to use the line and things developed from there. At roughly the same time I had also sent Sol Invictus the lyrics to the ballad "Sheath and Knife" because of its recurring solar imagery, though it wasn't until late 1996 with my contributions to *On* (a magazine published by Sol Invictus frontman Tony Wakeford) and *Cupid and Death* that I worked on any of Tony's projects.

In retrospect, I realize that my artistic development and background in conceptual art left me ill prepared for work as a jobbing illustrator. While I applied myself with great diligence to the Ghost Story Press volumes I worked on, the results were rarely better than adequate. Two or three of the pictures for the Harvey Peter Sucksmith volume stand up well on their own, but the majority of them are quite mediocre. I now only do "illustrative" work if it ties in with an idea that I am going to work with anyway, and even then only on the condition that I can guarantee that the final work will be able to stand on its on as a fully formed composition. It's ironic that I turned to painting as a quick solution to the problem of presenting ideas that didn't lend themselves to other mediums, only to find that many of my paintings take even longer to produce than my installation projects. It is also ironic that, as a conceptual artist, I turned to painting at the very moment that Britart took off, thus condemning myself to a life of ignominious penury—ha! Still, we must all follow our demons.

Your style is highly allegorical. Are you trying to appeal more to the mind or to the feelings of the viewer?

With regards to my utilization of allegory; just before my move towards text composition, I made a series of large triptych collages about that cusp in the development of Western civilization in the seventeenth century when the tail end of medieval faith, the last exponents of Renaissance occultism, and the beginnings of modern science coexisted at one and the same time. I was interested in the tensions that this generated, and the parallels that one could draw with our own time. The visual conceit that I used to personify these ideas I took from that famous scene in chapter 13 of book 2 of Bede's *Ecclesiastical History of England*, in which one of King Edwin's men describes the human condition as being like "the swift flight of a sparrow through the house wherein you sit at supper in winter ... the sparrow, flying in at one door and immediately out at another, whilst he is within, is safe from the wintry tempest; but after a short space of fair weather, he immediately vanishes out of your sight, passing from winter into winter again. So this life of man appears for a little while, but of what is to follow or what went before we know nothing at all."

I realised that the collages I was using had served their purpose for those compositions, in that they were quickly produced, and that the images directly related to the periods that I was concerned with, but I had a nagging suspicion that the works might have been superior if they had actually been painted rather than cobbled together from found sources. And so I found myself in my late twenties having to learn anew the whole process of painting, very much from scratch, in order to put my ideas into practice in a way that I hoped would remove as much as possible the influences of my previous art training. As already stated, I have little technical aptitude as a jobbing illustrator, nor am I one of those conceptual artists who can be a naturally brilliant draftsman when he wants to be (unlike, say, Makoto Aida, one of the very, very few contemporary artists that I admire). Poussin, Cranach, and Blake could all be phenomenally clumsy at times, but the shortcomings in their techniques actually work in their favor. The viewer is constantly being brought up short against any idea of correct classical representation (in a photographically accurate sense), and thus finds himself asking not "what is this of?" but "what does this symbolically represent, what does it stand for?" Such are the questions that underpin the formal aspects of my art practice.

Inevitably, my art is concerned with those aspects of Western high and folk culture that I consider to be of importance, and which I wish to see brought into new forms of existence. With regards to the question of whether my work is designed to appeal to the mind or the feelings of the viewer, I think it is obvious that while the historical and cultural references can be very cerebral, it is also obvious that the truly emblematic imagery comes from, inhabits, and returns to, the nether regions of the subconscious as well as the race memory of the West.

A number of your paintings feature female themes, for example "Cybele," "Diana and Actaeon," or "How the Great Satanic Glory Faded." Does this reflect a preoccupation with the "Eternal Feminine," or simply with specific female archetypes and mythical figures?

It is a bit of both really. As I mentioned before, my return to art practice was very much forced upon me by the images that had been dammed up within my subconscious during my sojourn in academia. This is very much how things have continued, and it probably comes with the territory that some of these images are going to be sexual, obsessive, or unhealthy. I would only start to worry if they were politically correct. Then something would definitely be wrong.

We were particularly interested in your painting of Judith above the ruins of Dresden. What is your intention in combining this motif from the Old Testament with the destruction of Dresden during World War II?

That was part of a series in which a number of themes came together. The first of the paintings was a recreation of the Cranach that was lost in the bombing (one of my favorite paintings). The second was a more overt commentary, utilizing Judith as a Morrighan figure to represent the wholesale destruction that happens "when a culture forgets itself." By allowing itself to succumb to the bloodletting exercise of the two world wars (which I think can be viewed not as two separate conflicts, but as a pan-European civil war that happened to have a twenty-year pause within it) the West tragically abdicated its position of political, moral, and cultural superiority. This has given rise to the world as we know it today.

Discography

Albums:

Andrew King, *The Bitter Harvest* (Epiphany, 1998)
Andrew King, *The Amfortas Wound* (Athanor, 2003)
Andrew King, *The Harbinger of the Decaying Mind* (Old Europa Café, 2004)
Changes/Andrew King, [untitled split-CD] (Terra Fria, 2005)
Les Sentiers Conflictuels and Andrew King, *1888* (Athanor, 2006)
Sol Invictus/Rose Rovine e Amanti/Andrew King, *A Mythological Prospect Of The Citie Of Londinium* (Cold Spring, 2006)
Tony Wakeford, *Into the Woods* (Tursa, 2007)
Sol Invictus, *London* (Tursa, forthcoming, 2007)
Andrew King and Brownsierra, *Thalassocracy* (National Express, forthcoming, 2007)
Andrew King, *Deus Ignotus* (forthcoming, 2007)

Compilations:

"The Bitter Withy," on *On—The World And Everything In It* (Tursa, 1996)
"Ninety and Nine," on *Variations 3* (Paradigm, 1998)
"War Poem," on *Schlecht und Ironisch* (Radio Luxor/SPV, 1999)
"George Collins II" and "Henry, My Son," on *Ostia* (Topi, 2000)
"Outside," on *Der Blaue Container* [from the *Kälte Container Boxset*] (Radio Luxor/SPV, 2000)
"Azazel," on *First* (Operative, 2001) [as Emblem]
"The Raven Banner (Corvus Terrae Terror/The Three Ravens/Raven Chorus)," on *Sol Lucet Omnibus* (Cynfeirdd, 2002)
"Little Boy Blue," on *Songs for Landeric* (Cynfeirdd, 2002)
"Legionary in Algiers," on *Tutti a Casa!* (Hau Ruck!, 2003)
"Turtle Dove," on *Songs for Aliénor* (Cynfeirdd, 2005)
"Have You News of My Boy Jack?," on *Looking For Europe* (Auerbach Tonträger, 2005)

Guest Appearances:

"Feline," on *Organic Traces* by KnifeLadder (Operative, 2002)
"The Captain's Apprentice," on *My Long Accumulating Discontent* by Andrew Liles (Nextera, 2004)

"Aeroplane," on *3 Ton Edition* by Leisur::hive (Actual Size, 2004) [glass sounds]
Harmonium on the forthcoming Foresta di Ferro album, 2007

Solo Art Exhibitions:

"The Image of Melancholy," Gwent College, Caerleon, performance and installation, 1988
Gregynog Hall, Powys, University of Wales Colloquium, video and presentation, 1989
Gregynog Hall, Powys, University of Wales Colloquium, video and presentation, 1990
"The Return To Image," Bury Museum & Art Gallery, Manchester, paintings, 1994
Meadow Street Gallery, Weston-Super-Mare, paintings, 1995
"How to Placate Spirits: Alchemical and Emblematic Paintings," Germ Books + Gallery, Philadelphia, Pennsylvania, paintings and music performance, 2005
"False True Lovers," Counter Media, Portland, Oregon, paintings and music performance, 2006

Group Exhibitions:

Toulouse Bienniale of Media and Telematics (video), 1986
Sheffield Media Show, Sheffield University (video and presentation), 1987
The Slade Media Show (video), 1987
Queens Arcade Gallery, Cardiff (video), 1988
BP Expo, Riverside Studios (video and film), 1988
"Passionage," Tobacco Docks Arcade, London (paintings), 1991
Coopers Gallery, Bristol (paintings), 1992
Coopers Gallery, Bristol (paintings), 1993
Kensington and Chelsea Artists Exhibition (paintings), 1996
Hoxton Distillery, London (paintings, texts, and music performance), 2002

Waldteufel - Rauhnacht CD/LP
Pagan folk and native Alpine ritual music.

ALLERSEELEN - Hallstatt
CD in digipack with sixteen-page booklet
The first new Allerseelen full-length album in four years.
Inspired by the beautiful Austrian village Hallstatt,
with its remarkable tombs and charnel house.

SVARROGH - Balkan Renaissance CD
A mystic journey to the ancient heart of the Balkan
mountains, caves, villages and people,
with their deep mythological roots.

AHNSTERN

Coming in Autumn 2007:
Werkraum - Early Love Music CD
Sangre Cavallum - Veleno de Teixo CD

SOULSEARCH - Liedersammlung CD
Pagan doom folkmetal featuring
German lyrics and Medieval influences.

Sturmpercht - Geister im Waldgebirg
CD in six-page digipack / double-LP in wooden packaging
Alpine folk songs about deep forests and the strange
creatures, that dwell therein. Featuring contributions
from Allerseelen, Sangre Cavallum and Waldteufel.

In Gowan Ring - Exists & Entrances Double-CD
A retrospective of this important and influential artist,
featuring rarities and unreleased tracks from 1995 to 2003.
Fourty songs and a running time of 157 minutes

Ahnstern is distributed by Steinklang Industries. We are your online-shop for industrial, folk, martial and neoclassical music.
www.steinklang-records.at

Reviews: Music

Sol Invictus—*Sol Veritas Lux* (Tursa/Strange Fortune)

It has now been nearly twenty years since the formation of Sol Invictus and as might be expected, the group has evolved considerably. Recent releases have benefited from elaborate orchestration, neo-classical and even jazz arrangements, coupled with neo-Romantic lyrics and imagery typical of the genre frontman Tony Wakeford helped to create. I admit to being only vaguely familiar with the "new" Sol Invictus, however. Although their musicianship is undeniable, and marked by a sophistication completely lacking from their first few releases, much of the group's force and passion seems to have been lost in the bargain. Chalk it up to youthful naiveté, but Tony Wakeford had a clear and powerful vision on *Against the Modern World* and *In the Jaws of the Serpent*—one which the mature aesthete has seemingly discarded.

Sol Veritas Lux contains both the aforementioned albums and is being re-released for the benefit of newer fans who might have trouble finding a copy, thanks to the fold-up of the British World Serpent label. This is by far the band's rawest expression, both musically and lyrically, an incongruous but somehow appropriate melding of traditional English folk music with post-punk adrenaline and angst. Following close on the heels of his work as Above the Ruins (a short-lived group Wakeford formed after his departure from Death In June), Sol Invictus at this stage still held closely to many of the themes that had characterized that abortive project (and which were merely implied in the more ambiguous Death In June). Backed by heavy percussion and pulsing bass-lines (contributed by long-time member Karl Blake on *In the Jaws of the Serpent*), Wakeford's vocals are driving and emphatic. Spewing invective against the stupidity of the masses, the ubiquity of American consumer culture, and the spiritual impoverishment of modern society, Wakeford invokes the heroic ethos of pagan Europe as an antidote, or at least a source of personal sustenance. Many of the album's finest moments are provided by Ian Read (who would later release his own music as Fire + Ice), a singer of considerably more natural ability than Wakeford. It is Read's contribution in particular that lends these albums an air of folksy credibility. This is rarer today than ever. While countless neofolk bands have taken what groups like Sol Invictus started and turned it into yet another clichéd subculture, few (if any) of them have managed to surpass the original. Even with two decades of hindsight, *Sol Veritas Lux* is richly deserving of another listen.

Joshua Buckley

Various Artists—*The Kalevala Heritage: Archive Recordings of Ancient Finnish Songs* (Ondine)

Rune songs are the last remnants of Balto-Finnic oral culture and feature an alliterative structure that differs considerably from the metrical scheme of most western European poetry. Rune singing was an integral part of communal life until the 1500s, when Lutheran reformers like Mikael Agricola began working to eradicate it. Nevertheless, the tradition persisted in eastern Finland, Karelia, and Ingria, and was famously documented by Elias Lönnrot, who cobbled together many of the folk stories contained in the songs to form the basis of Finland's national epic, the *Kalevala*. In the early 1900s, Armas Launis and other archivists recorded authentic rune songs under the auspices of the Finnish Literary Society (SKS). Rune songs have undergone a miniature renaissance in recent years thanks to the popularity of Scandinavian performers like Sinikka Langeland, Värttinä, Myllärit, Sattuma, and Hedningarna, who have reinterpreted the tradition in exciting and innovative ways.

This collection features original rune songs captured on wax cylinders by Launis, as well as scholars like A. O. Väisänen and Wilhelm Doegen, then the head of the Berlin State Library's recording department. The sound quality varies considerably due to the primitive recording conditions and—because of the limitations of the technology—most of these pieces are mere fragments. The oldest songs are those collected by Launis. These include a fire charm sung by Petri Shemeikka, and the opening of the Finnish god Lemminkäinen's epic (which also forms the basis of a suite by the Finnish composer Jean Sibelius) performed by Iivänä Harkonen. Another important mythologically themed piece is "The Kantele," which describes the instrument's role in the Finnish cosmogony. This was recorded by Doegen in 1922 and sung by Anni Kiriloff. The Ingrian region of Estonia inspired the collection of field recordings made in 1937 by folk music scholars Aili and Lauri

Laiho. The Ingrian songs were typically performed at weddings and other festive events, and have more domestic than mythological themes. Some contain practical advice, such as this "Counselling Song" from Valpuri Vohta: "Oh, son-in-law, since you've taken a bride, be careful to keep her too. Don't let her go bareshod on the road. Don't beat her so that the village can see, nor on account of only one reason."

This is unaccompanied singing in a style that will probably sound strange to modern ears; it is interesting to contrast with "updated" versions of the rune songs like those by the contemporary artists associated with the NorthSide label. Bear in mind that all epic poetry, from the Homeric epics to *Beowulf*, was once transmitted in a similar manner. As a historical snapshot of a culture where this oral transmission survived down into the modern period, *The Kalevala Heritage* provides a unique listening experience.

(As a final remark, it should be noted that Finnish rune songs have nothing to do with the runic alphabet. A quick Internet search will reveal that this is nevertheless a tremendous source of confusion, and I have found at least one "world music" site which lists the Norse pagan writer Freya Aswynn's CDs as examples of the style.)

Joshua Buckley

Kūlgrinda—*Perkūno Giesmės* (Dangus Records)

For most readers, Lithuanian culture and music probably represents unknown territory. The Baltic country's only musical giant, Mikalojus K. Ciurlionis (1875–1911), an impressionist composer and painter of strange, alternately cosmic and folkloric works, is still a relatively obscure figure in European musical history and Lithuanian folk music remains largely shrouded in mystery. Hopefully the engaging works of the veterans of the Lithuanian folk revival, Kūlgrinda, will remedy the situation.

This album, the title of which can be translated as "Hymns to Perkunas the Thundergod," is the group's fourth release and representative of its seventeen-year existence. The ensemble is led by the high priest of Romuva, Jonas Trinkūnas, and his wife Inia, who are both deeply involved in the pagan cultural renaissance in Lithuania. The performers are mostly young men and women. Kūlgrinda's musical focus is undoubtedly on its choral vocals; the accompaniment by *kanklės* (a type of psaltery), drums, bagpipes, and fiddle is minimal. Their chosen form of song, *sutartinės* (from *sutarti*—to harmonize) originated in the northwestern region of Lithuania and is an ancient example of polyphony, typically consisting of symmetrical melodies. Women traditionally sang folksongs in this style with instrumental versions performed by men. On the fifteen pieces presented on *Perkūno giesmės*, Kūlgrinda manages to integrate these traditions and reinvigorate them, breathing new life into this most archaic layer of their folk culture.

The simple call-and-response vocals combined with heartbeat drumming might remind some of certain Native American chanting; in fact, they have an essential shamanic character in common with much of ethnic music. The goal is to reach an "altered state" of union with the divine. While this goal has been lost in European folk cultures for centuries, its hypnotic, repetitive vestiges remain in folk music and dances. Many of the songs presented here also exhibit some of the deeply emotional, melancholic *Weltschmerz* characteristic of the music of neighboring Russia, likely because of their close cultural proximity.

The members of Kūlgrinda have become cultural ambassadors of sorts, having performed at a neofolk festival in Spain, in Poland, and in Germany, as well as at numerous festivals in their own country. Their specialty is the "Rite of Fire," an ancient ceremony accompanied by song and dance which was documented on a previous album, *Ugnies Apeigos*. The visual presence of the young performers dressed in their distinctive medieval costumes is particularly striking. All of Kūlgrinda's six releases (the others being *Old Lithuanian Secret Path*, 1994; *Žalvarinis*, a collaboration with heavy metal band Ugnėlakis, 2001; *Ugnies Apeigos*, 2002; *Sotvaras*, with experimental folk project Donis; and *Prūsų giesmės*, 2005) come highly recommended as authentic and powerful expressions of the Lithuanian folk soul.

Markus Wolff

Various Artists—*Wir Rufen Deine Wölfe* (Aorta)

Compiled by Gerhard of the Austrian group Allerseelen, this is an anthology that could have easily fallen flat. Each artist was asked to contribute a song based on the same poem by Friedrich Hielscher and the result might well have been repetitious and uninspiring. The finished product, however, is neither. Hielscher is a figure of considerable interest to those intrigued by the "secret history" of modern Germany. He was the subject of a substantial article in the second issue of *TYR* and the poem that forms the *raison d'être* of this compilation was translated as "We Call Your Wolves" in the same issue.

The music here ranges from folk to pieces with an almost pop sensibility to the martial atmospherics of Turbund Sturmwerk and Der Feuerkreiner, whose contributions provide some of the album's more intense moments. Werkraum's recent music tends toward folk and even early music but songwriter Axel Frank's Hielscher rendition is polished and catchy with a thumping, rock-inspired bass line. Allerseelen are in typically fine form, and Blood Axis supplies a piece with dual vocals, drums, violin, and a backdrop of howling wolves. As usual the group's work has an air of authenticity and sincerity, and is anything but contrived. The same can be said of Riharc Smiles, an Austrian group composed of musicians who moonlight in an early music ensemble, and whose use of bagpipes, hurdy gurdies, and nyckelharpas (a traditional Swedish instrument) gives their heavily percussive sound a welcome added dimension. As if to complement the international flavor, Spain is represented by Ô Paradis while Portuguese outfit Sangre Cavallum continue their hallmark fusion of traditional elements and modern innovation.

Although most of this collection is surprisingly impressive there are occasional lapses—the continual reliance on synthesizers, drum machines, and canned samples drags a few of the tracks down almost into the realm of self-parody. But all in all this is an eminently worthwhile release, and considering its arcane point of reference, a unique artifact of the esoteric underground.

Joshua Buckley

Amazing Blondel—*Evensong/Fantasia Lindum* (Beat Goes On)

The Amazing Blondel was a true anomaly, a group with affinities in the British folk revival who toured largely with prog-rock bands like Genesis and Procul Harem. Nevertheless, they never fit in with any existing "scene"—past or present. Emerging from the ashes of conventional hard rock band Methuselah in 1969 and consisting of John Gladwin, Terry Wincott, and later Eddie Baird, the Amazing Blondel borrowed their name from the court musician of Richard

I. Their music is exasperatingly difficult to categorize, a strange hybrid of Elizabethan/English baroque music and folk rock with psychedelic undertones. This trio of extremely competent musicians utilized every period instrument they could get their hands on, often playing dozens of different instruments in a single show. These included lutes, harmoniums, ocarinas, crumhorns, pipe organs, glockenspiels, citterns, dulcimers, and twelve-string guitars. As live musicians they established a reputation for never missing a note, and attracted a cult following who would watch their performances in a virtual state of awe.

Despite a reliance on traditional instruments and an entirely acoustic sound, the Amazing Blondel recorded mainly original songs. The band's lyrics were written in deliberately archaic language that would sound unbelievably pretentious were it not served up with a knowing wink. Like their prog-rock allies, their songs could take any number of twists, turns, and instrumental diversions. A case in point is the title track on *Fantasia Lindum*, which takes up an entire side of the original LP. *Fantasia Lindum*, along with the slightly less avant-garde *Evensong*, are both featured on this 2004 CD reissue. These are the classic Blondel releases from their heyday on Island, a label that never lost faith in the band despite its relatively small audience. The music still sounds remarkably innovative. While the idea of three seemingly stoned hippies done up in Robin Hood tights, playing recorders, and singing lyrics like "Lambs are playing/Sherwood's arraying/Her leafy splendour for to show" may not seem like such an appealing proposition, this is nonetheless one of the more interesting British experiments of the time.

Joshua Buckley

Sangre Cavallum—*Patria Granitica* (Ahnstern)

The members of Sangre Cavallum are from northern Portugal, and their music is very much rooted in the land and its history. In interviews and other texts the group identifies itself strongly with Gallaecia, a region now represented by modern Galicia and the Portuguese north. This was the area settled by the Gauls or Celts (as evidenced by the name *Gall*aecia) who merged with the Atlantic Bronze and eastern Mediterranean peoples to form the Castro culture. Castros were large stone hillforts, the inhabitants of which

HYMNS OF THE HORDES: SANGRE CAVALLUM.
(PHOTO BY LINO VILLAPOUCA)

are known to us from the colorful descriptions of the Romans, who saw them as fierce barbarians given to feasting and wild pagan rites.

It is this shadowy pre-Christian culture that Sangre Cavallum seeks to invoke and their music and attendant imagery and writings are filled with allusions to their Gallaecian ancestry, pagan survivals in medieval witchcraft, peasant superstitions, and the "magical landscape" of the northwestern Iberian Peninsula. They have also been known to pay homage to Portugal's rich heritage as a wine producer (the country has over five hundred indigenous grape varieties, and its *adegas* [wineries] are known for their madeiras and ports). *Patria Granitica* means roughly "granite fatherland," an obvious reference to the aforementioned castros and other prehistoric monuments. On the album, the group uses a wealth of traditional instruments, but is not averse to modern implements like synthesizers, electric guitars, and Ebows. Sangre Cavallum's sound is definitely more acoustic than electronic, however, and characterized by the presence of Portuguese guitars, mandolins, melodicas, flutes, Galician bagpipes, and tin-whistles. Another unique dynamic is added by the inclusion of found sounds and field recordings, mostly of natural phenomena. Although this latest offering is in many ways more produced than the group's earlier *Barbara Carmina* (Barbarian Songs) these elements still give the overall impression of something stark and primitive, and this is no doubt the intent. Graced with moments of considerable beauty, this is ultimately a rough and hard-edged music with a driving, unrelenting quality. While the average "world music" fan would probably find Sangre Cavallum conceptually interesting, the liner notes' references to "a lineage of fierce warriors ... ruled by the war Gods" and "hymns of the hordes" should serve as fair warning that this is hardly a quaint detour into Portuguese wine country. Sangre Cavallum have picked up the pieces of their native tradition, but they wield them like a heavy wooden club.

Joshua Buckley

Simon O'Dwyer—*Coirn na hÉireann: Horns of Ancient Ireland* (National Museum of Ireland)

I have had the opportunity to view some of the horns featured on this CD displayed in The National Museum of Ireland, where many of them are housed and where this recording took place. Cast in bronze, the instruments date from 1100 B.C.E. to 700 B.C.E, although it has been speculated that some examples may be as old as 3,500 years. Ireland is of course known for its diverse musical traditions and it seems appropriate that these horns comprise the largest collection of prehistoric musical instruments found anywhere. Those that I have seen first-hand are indeed a true marvel of art and engineering, a testament to the legendary metallurgical skills of ancient Celtic craftsmen.

Since scholars began cataloging the horns almost three hundred years ago people have wondered how they might have been played, yet no convincing explanation had ever been proposed. That is, not until the pioneering work of Dr. Peter Holmes. Holmes compared the horns to instruments played by surviving traditional peoples in the hopes that this would yield clues (Iron Age Celtic *trumpas*, for example, are almost identical to types of horns still played in Nepal). It did. While other musicologists had tried unsuccessfully to play the horns in the manner of modern, Western variants, Holmes discovered that they could be played like Australian didgeridoos. Spurred on by his discoveries, Prehistoric Music

Ireland was founded in the 1980s to construct historically accurate reproductions of ancient instruments. Simon O'Dwyer has been at the forefront of these efforts and has developed considerable proficiency in performing with the horns and other archaic instruments. His most recent work has been with the Wicklow Pipes, which are over four thousand years old. In 2004 he authored the book *Prehistoric Music Ireland* (Tempus Publishing) to chronicle his career.

What you will hear on this CD, however, is not O'Dwyer playing reproductions but O'Dwyer playing the actual ancient horns themselves. It is an incredible experience to hear this music after a silence of three thousand years. Eight horns are featured on the album and each is sampled playing a variety of notes, tones, and calls. Not surprisingly, the sound is very much like that produced by a didgeridoo. It is a deep, resonant music, well suited for the *nemeton* or the battlefield, although we can only guess at how and why these horns were originally utilized. On the last few tracks, O'Dwyer does attempt to recreate what the music might have sounded like when the instruments were played in tandem. This was accomplished by layering the sound of different horns in the studio. The effect is mesmerizing.

For listeners who wish to pursue these explorations further, O'Dwyer has released a companion CD to his book, and another of him playing Prehistoric Music Ireland's reconstructed instruments. He also appears on the compilation *The Kilmartin Sessions: The Sounds of Ancient Scotland*.

Joshua Buckley

Various Artists—*Gather in the Mushrooms: The British Acid Folk Underground 1968–1974* (Castle Music)

Appropriately enough, this recent compilation begins with Magnet's "Corn Rigs" which is immediately recognizable from Paul Giovanni's *Wicker Man* soundtrack (which, incidentally, has finally been released in proper form by Silva Screen Records). As Bob Highgate points out in his liner notes, the film is in many ways a visual embodiment of the kind of music you will find on *Gather in the Mushrooms*. Most acid-folk or psych-folk bands were trying to evoke the "atmosphere" of traditional music without actually playing it, or utilizing traditional structures despite foregoing traditional tunes and lyrics. Purists who dispute the value of the better known folk-revival bands from the late sixties and early seventies will denounce this approach as complete and utter kitsch. In many respects they are correct. This, however, should in no way diminish your enjoyment of the eighteen tracks collected here. These groups made no pretense of authenticity and much of what they created is, on the contrary, strikingly original.

While the majority of this music can be easily pigeonholed as part of the hippie subculture of the time, it differs from most comparable American fare in certain important respects. First, these groups were inspired by English traditional music even if their own creations were not traditional in any way. Second, most of these songs have a dark or at least melancholic quality. Coupled with their occasional neo-medievalism, references to English folklore, mystery, and apparent reverence for both the benevolent as well as the darker aspects of nature, they anticipate much later gothic and especially neofolk music. Forest in particular has a particularly foreboding edge, described elsewhere as "a surreal invocation of the hidden parts of a lost pagan existence." Their music featured traditional instruments as well as pipe and reed organs. Pipes and tin whistle are prominent components on the track "Graveyard," presented here from their *Nothing Else Will Matter* LP. The song "Rosemary Hill" by Fresh Maggots evokes a similar atmosphere. While the group's only album featured electric guitar from time to time, this particular track is an acoustic-based number that is haunting and ethereal. Compared to these largely unknown contributions, pieces by Sandy Denny and Pentangle will be familiar to most listeners, and seem more representative of the broader folk revival. Far more unexpected (at least if you haven't heard them before) is Comus, whose track "The Herald" weighs in at just over twelve minutes. The playing time alone would place the group more in line with the prog-rock acts that were then just taking hold, although their classic *First Utterance* album still has more acoustic than "plugged-in" elements. Named for a Greek Satyr god, Comus's music is unbelievably grim for the period with lyrics that hint at violence and the occult. Songwriter Roger Wooten allegedly spent time in a mental hospital and at least one contemporary heavy metal outfit consistently cites the band as an influence. At the opposite end of the spectrum is Vashti Bunyan, another artist who made only one album before vanishing into the shadows (at least until a few years ago). Written during her travels in a horse-drawn caravan, she later recorded her highly personal songs with help from Dave Swarbrick and Robin Williamson (of Fairport Convention and the Incredible String Band, respectively). "Winter is Blue" provides a nice introduction and, compared with the aforementioned Comus, demonstrates the incredible range represented on this compilation. Bunyan has reappeared of late with her first new album in thirty-five years, joined by musicians like Devendra Banhart and Joanna Newsome. The popularity of these latter two acts, which surpasses anything a singer like Bunyan was able to achieve in her own day, suggests that "acid folk"—or whatever you choose to label it—was more relevant than the short lifespan and relative obscurity of its chief proponents would seem to suggest.

Joshua Buckley

Sequentia—*Lost Songs of a Rhineland Harper* (Deutsche Harmonia Mundi)

Founded in 1979 by Benjamin Bagby and the late Barbara Thornton, Sequentia is undoubtedly the most popular early music ensemble in the world. They have produced over sixty-five concert programs and recorded albums that represent the entire spectrum of medieval music. Sequentia's *Canticles of Ecstasy* CD, which was based on the works of Hildegard von Bingen, was an international bestseller and even sparked an unexpected popular enthusiasm for period choral music.

Bagby remains the driving force behind the group, conducting most of the scholarly research that informs its various projects. In addition to multiple music-related degrees he studied German literature at Oberlin College, and he is known outside of Sequentia for his solo performances of Anglo-Saxon poetry. This resulted in the 2006 release of his tour-de-force bardic *Beowulf* performance on DVD, filmed in Sweden by Stellan Olsson. Under Bagby's lead, Sequentia has also released two CD's of musical reconstructions from Old Icelandic mythological texts: *Edda: Myths from Medieval Iceland* and *The Rheingold Curse*. This particular project involved the kind of intensive research Bagby is known for. He found examples of strophes from the Eddic poems set to musical accompaniment in the collections of the Danish court musician Johann Ernst Hartmann, and closely examined *rímur* and other Icelandic tradi-

BENJAMIN BAGBY IN PERFORMANCE.
(PHOTO BY OLGA GEORGE, COURTESY OF JON AARON)

tional music, as well as Faroese dance songs and Baltic folk music. Moreover, Bagby studied with the Icelandic philologist Heimir Pálsson and reconstructed a harp based on the remains of instruments found in a seventh-century Germanic gravesite. The *Edda* project eventually inspired a performance piece directed by Bagby and Ping Chong, and sponsored in part by the Lincoln Center Festival.

Lost Songs of a Rhineland Harper features songs culled from a manuscript preserved by Anglo-Saxon monks in the Abbey of St. Augustine nearly a thousand years ago, and represents Sequentia's attempt to recreate as authentically as possible the secular music of the period. The instrumentation is sparse and similar to that used on the *Edda* recordings. A six-string Germanic lyre based on an original found near Oberflacht, a fourteen-string harp, wooden flutes, and a swan-bone flute provide these songs with most of their substance. Bagby and Eric Mentzel handle the vocals, although the presence of Agnethe Christensen (of the Danish medieval music group ALBA) gives many of these pieces a simmering, sensual quality. This is entirely appropriate on tracks like "*O admirabile Veneris idolum*" or "*Veni, dilectissime*," with its explicitly erotic lyrics: "How I long for love … If you come with the key, with ah! and oh!

... You will soon be able to enter, with ah! and oh! and ah! and oh!" Love songs predominate on this collection, although there are a number of pieces which celebrate music itself, such as "*Magnus cesar Otto*," about Otto I "The Great's" harper, who purportedly used his playing to save the Kaiser's life. The most striking thing about these songs is the extent to which they anticipate themes from much later secular folk music. Bagby and company have managed to transfuse some of this earthiness into the texture of the sound itself, setting *Lost Songs of a Rhineland Harper* apart from the more conventional ecclesiastical music of the Middle Ages.

Joshua Buckley

Benjamin Bagby—*Beowulf* DVD (Charles Morrow Productions)

Hwæt!

Many a radical traditionalist has cursed the present American state for its trampling down of all things sacred. But the dollar stills reigns supreme and here its power is used for a truly worthwhile purpose for, although this performance was recorded live at Dunkers Kulturhus, Helsingborg, Sweden in January 2006, this DVD has been produced in New York and, furthermore, Mr. Bagby was born in Illinois.

Benjamin Bagby sings, chants and relates the great epic for ninety-eight minutes in Old English up to the *symbel* that follows Beowulf's heroic slaying of Grendel. Optional subtitles are included. Mr. Bagby accompanies himself with considerable skill throughout most of the performance on an Anglo-Saxon harp and this, as well as the range of his magnificent trained voice, makes for something which no superlative known to modern English can do justice. The sheer depth of emotion, so fully expressed by Mr. Bagby here, fair took my breath away; and there is humour too. The DVD has a further thirty-four minutes consisting of a roundtable discussion with Benjamin Bagby and three *Beowulf* scholars, and also a talk by Mr. Bagby on the music and instrument he uses here.

This performance belongs in the collection of all who value good art—Benjamin Bagby has done the English-speaking world a great service, and I salute him for it.

More information on Benjamin Bagby's *Beowulf* performance

can be found at the website: <www.bagbybeowulf.com>

Ian Read

Korpiklaani—*Tales Along This Road* (Napalm Records)

As a genre, heavy metal has evolved considerably in the last decade or so, to the point where many acts are now barely recognizable as "metal" bands at all. Particularly in Europe, the hokey Satanic aesthetic that has long characterized the movement has in many cases given way to an interest in home-grown forms of paganism. Of course, this often bears the mark of mere faddishness. Runes, viking ships, and Thor's hammers are now almost as much a part of heavy metal artwork as pentagrams and demonic imagery used to be (and still are, if to a lesser extent). However, in some cases the sentiment behind the style is genuine and those expressing it can marshal some measure of intelligence to back it up. More intriguingly, perhaps, is the influence this has had on the actual music. Many European metal bands now routinely incorporate aspects of traditional music into their repertoire, and reference elements of folk and traditional culture that run far deeper than their predictable rejection of Christianity. In the best instances, these groups might be seen as the true successors to the folk rockers of an earlier generation.

Korpiklaani is one "folk-metal" group that more than deserve this comparison. While their music is unquestionably "heavy," and will no doubt irritate listeners unaccustomed to loud, aggressive music, it is also strongly influenced by Finnish traditional music. One facet of the group I find particularly appealing is their unexpected sense of fun. Unlike metal bands who cultivate an image of perpetual glumness, Korpiklaani's music might almost be described as upbeat, with raucous singalong choruses that are more like speeded-up drinking songs than anything else. In fact, *Tales Along This Road* opens with "Happy Little Boozer," an English-language homage to Korpiklaani's prowess at imbibing. The Finnish lyrics on the album, contributed by Virva Holtiton, take a more serious turn with their allusions to the *Kalevala* and other elements of Finno-Ugric ethnic culture. Holtiton's background is obviously in heavy metal, although his own band, Poropetra, has made the switch to playing almost exclusively Finnish and Estonian folk music. In addition to the lyrics, Holtiton plays *kantele* with

KORPIKLAANI. (PHOTO BY TONI HÄRKÖNEN)

Korpiklaani, as well as demonstrating his abilities as a throat singer. Other traditional elements here include violin, mandolin, mouth harp, *torupill* (Estonian bagpipe), and *jouhikko* (three-stringed Finnish bowed lyre). Electric guitar and bass still predominate, although Korpiklaani has added a full-time accordion player, and this is a further driving force behind the music. It has led some reviewers to describe Korpiklaani (disparagingly, I am sure) as "polka metal" and I admit that, on first listen anyway, their sound can be somewhat incongruous. If you give this a chance, however, you might find that it is melodic, nuanced, and downright catchy—an experiment that is nearly as interesting as when the Pogues first fused Irish traditional music and punk rock almost twenty-five years ago.

Joshua Buckley

Waldteufel—*Rauhnacht* (Percht)

Rauhnacht is the latest release from *TYR* contributor Markus Wolff's music project Waldteufel and consists of a six-song mini-CD. Four of the featured tracks were previously released on the Portuguese label Terra Fria. However, this updated edition features considerably improved packaging and production in addition to the extra playing-time.

Before striking out on his own to form Waldteufel, Wolff spent a decade touring and recording with the "atavistic percussion" group Crash Worship. Although exploring markedly different themes, Waldteufel's music is also constructed around a foundation of thumping percussion. This fits nicely with the deep bass of Wolff's heavily intoned vocals, which he delivers entirely in German. On previous releases, the use of sparing acoustic instrumentation, including strings, led reviewers to describe Waldteufel as a "folk" project—although this hardly conveys the strangeness of Wolff's creation. Waldteufel's music might be inspired by any number of older European styles but, in the end, it embodies an idiosyncratically personal vision. Nevertheless, the group's plodding, shamanic rhythms conjure up a sense of undeniable archaicism. Wolff himself is a student of the ancient past, but his music is downright *prehistoric*.

Taken as a whole, *Rauhnacht* is considerably less structured than earlier releases, opting instead for multi-layered soundscapes rife with atmospheric intensity. The calls of hunting horns and cacophonous marching bands fade in and out of the mix, and the opening track, "Allerseelengebet" (All Souls' Prayer) sounds as if it was recorded in a migration-era Germanic village. "Hexe Hild" ("Hild the Witch") is perhaps the album's biggest surprise, featuring a completely unexpected heavy metal riff provided by Waldteufel member Tyrsson Sinclair. Conceptually, each piece presented deals with different aspects of Wotan's Wild Hunt. The lyrics (English translations of which are provided in the liner notes) are selected from the works of nineteenth- and early twentieth-century *völkisch* and Romantic writers. These include Friedrich Hielscher (1902–1990) and Ludwig Bechstein (1801–1860), a poet and librarian whose folk- and fairy-tale collections were more popular during his lifetime than those of the Brothers Grimm. The final track, a nearly twelve-minute, ritualized magic extravaganza entitled "Ur-Odin," consists of lyrics by Karl Wolfskehl (1869–1948). An enthusiastic member of the Stefan George Circle, Wolfskehl later became an equally committed Zionist. Interestingly, he never fully abandoned his identification with German culture.

Along with a handful of other (primarily European) music groups, Waldteufel make it feasible to speak of a new heathen aesthetic, manifested in sound.

Joshua Buckley

Halo Manash—*r.A.S.H.n.k.a.-RA* LP and DVD (Kaosthetik Konspiration)

Two young men stand on a lonely lakeshore, their faces and bodies stained with mud or ashes. Between them is a makeshift altar, lit by small torches. Some kind of religious rite is taking place: they are robed in red cloth, but the origins of the ceremony are indistinct. At first glance, they appear to be Tibetan Buddhist monks, but their clothing is more primitive and their ritualistic motions devoid of meditative chanting. There are no references to any textually based organized religion here. The musical accompaniment to their actions is full of equally ambiguous sounds. Horns manifest as if they were voices, or vice-versa; metal bells and bowls resound; sticks and bones make impact with skin and leather. The borderline between acoustic and electronic sound blurs.

In the course of *In4Elements*, a thirty-minute film on DVD, the sun repeatedly passes overhead and clouds shimmer by in time-lapse segments, yet the two men seem to enact their rites in a perpetual dawn or twilight. The four elements—of water, fire, earth, and air—intersect at this primordial crossroads, but they also dissipate into other forms. Mist rises from the water, trails of smoke spiral into the sky. The camera cuts to other locations: a birch forest where a makeshift structure, built from branches of deadfall, sits hidden

HALO MANASH AT WORK.
(PHOTO COURTESY OF HALO MANASH)

among the trees and adorned with large, dangling bones; an empty mossy clearing surrounded by tall evergreens. These arboreal clues indicate that we are somewhere in the Far North, a fact also hinted at by the occasional subtle runic imagery in the forms of tree branch shapes and tattoos. The structure in the woods is reminiscent of a *kota*, a traditional Sámi construction, but in this case was built from the limbs of fallen *kelo* trees, animal bones found in the wild, pieces of wood that had been struck by lightning, and heavy slabs of stone.

The enigmatically named Halo Manash is the sound and performance project of two young Finns, Antti Haapapuro and filmmaker Aki Cederberg (who perform under the names Anti Ittna H. and Akiz, respectively), occasionally abetted by others. In its approach to both sound and visual expression, Halo Manash can be viewed in terms of a now well-established tradition of "new ritual music" that has primary roots in industrial and ethnic musics. The industrial antecedent includes groups such as Throbbing Gristle, SPK, and 23 Skidoo, all of whom incorporated ritualistic elements into their work, especially in live performance. After Throbbing Gristle broke up in 1981 and "terminated its mission," an even more quasi-religious project rose from its ashes. This was Psychic Television, or PTV for short, which drew much inspiration from the theories of occultists such as Aleister Crowley and Austin Osman Spare. In the early days of PTV, its main protagonists Genesis P-Orridge and Peter Christopherson looked like apostles from a heretical sect of grey-clad Tibetan Jesuits. They encouraged their collaborators and fans to cultivate a similar appearance, taking on the trappings of a worldwide religious sect. Lesser-known music groups that trod on similar ideological ground in the early 1980s included Ain Soph, Lashtal, and Zero Kama (the latter recorded an entire album on instruments made from human bones). A parallel and overlapping genre of non-commercial atmospheric music, also emerging in many ways from a common industrial background, is evident in the work of mysterious collectives such as Germany's Cranioclast and England's Zoviet France.

Labeling this type of ritualistic music is difficult, and probably a pointless exercise. It is deliberate in its refusal to provide easy reference points. The blanket term which the art world might refer to it with, "experimental music," has always seemed unfortunate to me, since experimentation implies a sense of randomness and uncertainty. All of the aforementioned projects—Halo Manash included—tend to exhibit a sense of purpose that goes far beyond simply making sound "for its own sake." Their spiritual intentions may not always be clear, but they are undeniable. As a member of the group recently said to me: "Instead of merely using pre-existing symbols, languages, and maps of 'the sacred,' we intend to form our own, to circumvent the shrouds and go to the primal sources. It is about re-integration, primal returnings and awakenings."

In the case of Halo Manash's *r.A.S.H.n.k.a.-RA*, which also includes the full-length vinyl LP *InPolarDual*, the result is music that has little—if anything—in common with typical pop or even avant-garde classical compositions. These soundscapes occasionally possess a dreamlike and meditative quality, but more often they provoke the listener's active mental—and possibly spiritual—engagement. Watching Halo Manash on film in particular gives the impression of renunciates from modern civilization retreating to the wilderness, where they attempt to communicate with the spirits of the natural, elemental world. They seem to be seeking the source of a new (old) mode of religious experience. It is one almost entirely forgotten by the major religions of the West—and of much of the world, in fact—but this is in no way lessens its importance or alluring power.

More information on Halo Manash can be found at the group's website: <www.helixes.org/halomanash>

Michael Moynihan

Review Essay:
Paganism Without Gods

Collin Cleary

On Being a Pagan by Alain de Benoist. Softbound, 240 pages with index. Atlanta: Ultra, 2004. ISBN 0-9720292-2-2.

Introduction

Alain de Benoist's *On Being a Pagan*, as its title suggests, is a call for a return to paganism. Much more accurately, it is a call for a *new* paganism. There are a great many others on the contemporary scene, of course, who have issued such a call, and they range from prominent intellectuals like Benoist (who is the leading figure of the French "New Right") to the "New Agers." "Neopaganism" is a modern, Western phenomenon, now found in all the areas in which Christianity took root. Essentially, it calls for the rejection of Christianity and the return to something along the lines of the polytheism of our pre-Christian ancestors. However, anyone who spends some time delving into neopaganism will discover that it is a cacophony of differing voices, many of them speaking with little or no knowledge of the actual pagan traditions of the West. What neopaganism seems desperately to need, therefore, is something like a theology of paganism, which would address the following sort of basic philosophical questions: What does it mean to believe in gods? Is it even possible to recover the sort of belief our ancestors had? What are the fundamental differences between monotheism and polytheism? In what ways do modern neopagans unwittingly buy into monotheistic, and even specifically Judeo-Christian paradigms in attempting to reconstitute paganism? In what ways, if any, has the encounter with the Judeo-Christian tradition been positive, and what might neopagans want to preserve from this encounter, even as they seek to go beyond it?

On Being a Pagan addresses these and other questions and is the closest thing that has yet been written to a pagan theology. Inevitably, while its virtues are great, so too are its shortcomings. But the book is so filled with brilliant insights that one is inclined to overlook its flaws. It should be noted that Benoist's philosophy has evolved since *On Being a Pagan* was originally published. I shall discuss some of the ways in which he has altered his position in my conclusion. However, for the bulk of this review I intend to deal with *On Being a Pagan* on its own, as a self-contained work.

Benoist develops his account of paganism by systematically contrasting it with Judeo-Christian monotheism.

> Whatever some may maintain, it is not polytheism that is "old hat," but Judeo-Christian monotheism that now finds itself questioned and creaking all over, while paganism is again manifesting its attraction, although it may appear in forms that are often clumsy and sometimes aberrant.[1]

Much of the book consists in a polemic against Judeo-Christian monotheism. Indeed, so penetrating is this polemic that *On Being a Pagan* would be valuable on account of it alone, independent of the positive points Benoist makes concerning paganism.

Benoist sees Judeo-Christian monotheism as inherently dualistic, in the sense that it makes a sharp division between God and the world. According to orthodox (i.e., non-mystical) Christian theology, God entirely transcends the world, and in no way depends upon His creation. By contrast, paganism holds that the divine is present in the world, though not immanent in all things, as pantheists would maintain. Pagans find the sacred on earth, but as a result of its rigid separation of God and world, monotheism renders the entire world profane. God has given man dominion over the earth, the monotheists claim, and man may do with it as he pleases.

Dualism, however, proves to be the seed of destruction at the core of monotheism. Since the transcendent God is beyond experience, His existence must somehow be inferred logically. But the arguments for God's existence can all be refuted using the same logic: more than two thousand years of philosophical theology have not produced a single sound argument proving the existence of the one God. Recognizing this, atheists reject God and, in effect, elevate logic itself to the throne of heaven (Freud's "our God *Logos*"). Then they turn to the world. Do they question monotheism's profanation of the earth, or the idea that the earth is man's to do with as he likes? No. Instead, they accept these tenets and then get to work on the world using logic, in the form of scientific rationalism, to remake it according to their designs. From

Judeo-Christian monotheism they also typically adopt a linear view of history, which sees time as moving toward some final state of perfection. Thus is born the secular humanist ideal of "progress," including all the horrors of social engineering that have plagued much of the world since the Enlightenment.

Some of these points have been made by other authors, but I know of no better synthesis and elaboration of them than what we have in Benoist's book. To the foregoing criticisms of monotheism I would add the following: along with this ideal of progress usually goes a Promethean image of man as a godlike being. Atheistic humanism, the bastard child of monotheism, exalts man as the measure of all things and glories in his ability to transcend nature, even his own nature, and impose his ideal upon all. I would argue that this tenet is central to modernism and that it stands fundamentally at odds with the worldview of our pre-monotheist, pagan ancestors. Surprisingly, however, Benoist strongly endorses this radical humanism and, indeed, argues that it is of the essence of being a pagan. Here lies the grave problem with his account of paganism.

A Nietzschean Paganism?

Benoist's approach in *On Being a Pagan* is, from start to finish, Nietzschean. He makes no attempt to conceal this: Nietzsche is quoted again and again throughout the book. Indeed, an uncharitable gloss on Benoist's standpoint in this work would be to say that it is a Nietzschean humanism masquerading as paganism. This would indeed be uncharitable, given the book's wealth of insights, but it is not altogether inaccurate.

Benoist quotes at length a passage from Nietzsche's *Gay Science* entitled "The greatest advantage of polytheism":

> There was only one norm, *man*, and every people thought that it possessed this one ultimate norm. But above and outside, in some distant overworld, one was permitted to behold a plurality of norms; one god was not considered a denial of another god nor a blasphemy against him. It was here that the luxury of individuals was first permitted; it was here that one first honored the rights of individuals. The invention of gods, heroes, and super-humans of all kinds, as well as near-humans and sub-humans, dwarfs, fairies,

centaurs, satyrs, demons, and devils was the inestimable preliminary exercise for the justification of the egoism and sovereignty of the individual: the freedom that one conceded to a god in his relation to other gods—one eventually also granted to oneself in relation to laws, customs, and neighbors. Monotheism on the other hand, this rigid consequence of the doctrine of one human type—the faith in one normal god beside whom there are only pseudo-gods—was perhaps the greatest danger that has yet confronted humanity.[2]

This passage contains much of the inspiration for *On Being a Pagan*. First, there is the thesis that paganism is radically *man-centered*. By this I do not mean the claim that paganism is somehow especially conducive to human flourishing, a proposition for which good arguments have been offered elsewhere. Instead I mean something much more radical: the idea that the human serves as a supreme standard in terms of which the world is measured and the gods *created*. This last is the second major point in the passage which seems to have influenced Benoist: the claim that the gods and other beings of pagan myth are an invention. Further, the only justification for believing in these inventions is a kind of utility: belief in them leads to the "justification of the egoism and sovereignty of the individual."

The influence of Nietzsche on Benoist is, I believe, both positive and negative. Benoist is rightly critical of contemporary neopagans who believe naively that we can simply jump over more than a thousand years of Christianity and "go back" to believing as our ancestors did. He writes: "Post-Christianity cannot be an *ad integrum* return; it cannot be the simple 'restoration' of what once was. ... A new paganism must be truly new. To *surpass* Christianity demands both the reactualization of its 'before' and the appropriation of its 'after.'" In other words, today's would-be pagans must hold their noses and ask whether anything about humanity and the world may have been *learned* through the encounter with Christianity. He continues: "It is [on the occasion of their conversion to Christianity] that Europeans were able to acquire a clear awareness that they did not specifically belong to 'nature'—that they possessed a constitutive 'super-nature' and could acquire another by making the transition from human to superhuman." In short, if I understand him correctly, Benoist claims that through Christianity it was revealed to men that their being transcends the merely natural, and that it was possible for human nature to become, as it were, "divinized." I take it that this latter message was imparted to them through the figure of Christ. Certainly, the German mystics are full of the idea that the Incarnation is not a once-only event, but something that may come to pass in every human soul. However, Benoist notes, the Church erected terrific barriers to prevent individuals from realizing this "inner truth" of Christianity. The new paganism, Benoist insists, must be a paganism that has appropriated the truths about man that were won through the encounter with Christianity: specifically, the thesis that man is a super-natural being whose dignity consists in his autonomy and capacity for self-creation. Benoist concludes this passage by claiming, dramatically, that "The paganism of the future will be a Faustian paganism."[3]

In the foregoing, Benoist is very much in line with Nietzsche. In *Twilight of the Idols*, in a passage entitled "Whispered to the Conservatives," Nietzsche writes, "What was not known formerly, what is known, or might be known, today: a reversion, a return in any sense or degree is simply not possible."[4] It is impossible to "go back." In the *Genealogy of Morals*, Nietzsche presents a portrait of our pre-Christian ancestors, whom he refers to as the "master" types. Theirs is a natural system of values: strength, health, and courage are celebrated, whereas weakness, debility, and cowardice are scorned. While Nietzsche clearly admires the masters, he does not believe that we can go back to being them. The original masters were naïve, easy prey to the purveyors of the "slave morality" that inverted their values and turned them into guilt-ridden champions of the weak. Through this encounter with slave morals, terrible though it may have been, the human race emerged from its childhood and at least some of its members are now able to look without illusion upon the phenomenon of values as such, and to know the true sources from which values spring. These are, of course, the *Übermenschen* or overmen. Nietzsche bars us from going back, and exhorts us to go forward and to clear the way for the coming into being of humans who are actually, to use Benoist's term, superhumans.

So far as I can see, the only significant difference between Benoist's views and Nietzsche's is that Benoist chooses to call the overmen "the new pagans." But to designate them as such seems, at best, a half truth. Nietzsche's overmen do have some characteristics in common with their pagan, "master" ancestors (such as an heroic attitude toward life). But in Nietzsche's dialectic, the overman represents a stage in human evolution *qualitatively different* from that of the masters. This qualitative difference centers on the overman's abandonment of illusions of any sort, including religious illusions (and Nietzsche takes all religion to be illusory). If Benoist's "pagans" are essentially identical to Nietzsche's overmen then what Benoist offers us is a non-religious paganism, a paganism without gods. And this invites the obvious question, why does Benoist use the term "paganism" at all? Essentially, what Benoist presents us with is an atheistic humanism which re-appropriates some of the attitudes and values of ancient pagans, but eschews their religion. I think that there are many things to recommend this humanism, and in expounding it Benoist makes many points which are genuinely brilliant. But I cannot call this paganism.

The Gods and the Good

Let us take a closer look at Benoist's treatment of the religious aspects of paganism, specifically his treatment of the gods. Incidentally, I feel odd using such a term as the "religious aspect" of paganism, for I believe that pagan man's orientation toward the divine structured all aspects of his life, his worldview, and the makeup of his society. One of the difficulties with Benoist's account of paganism—perhaps the major difficulty—is his tacit claim that we can have the virtues and the "ideology" of paganism without the gods.

Benoist writes at one point that "while there is a difference of level between gods and men, there is no radical difference of nature. Gods are made in the image of men."[5] Now, it is certainly true to say that as a general rule the Indo-European pagans imagined their gods in the form of men, with human emotions, but it is not so clear that this means they *made* their gods. The experience of gods in polytheism was universally concretized in the form of human or animal characteristics, which made the gods accessible to all. But there are levels within any religion, and reaching the higher levels usually involves a realization that the iconography of the gods and descriptions of their actions are not always meant to be taken literally. That we have anthropomorphized our gods does not mean that we have invented them.

One might be justified in thinking that I may have read Benoist (or this translation of Benoist) too literally, but elsewhere he makes it very clear that he believes the gods to be a human invention: "'Creator' of nature, man is also the creator of the gods. He shares in God every time he surpasses himself, every time he attains the boundaries of his best and strongest aspects."[6] This is "paganism" by way of the idealism of Fichte, Hegel, or Feuerbach, take your pick: there is no divine independent of man; man "actualizes" the divine in the world each time he overcomes himself.

Just as Hegelians insisted (rather unconvincingly) that their master did not mean to make man God, Benoist insists that "it is not a question in paganism of putting man 'in God's place.' ... Man is not God, but he can share in God, just as God can share in him."[7] But given that "God" has the status in Benoist's philosophy of a kind of regulative ideal, not an objective reality, such language is misleading. Much earlier in the book, he writes that

> there is no need to 'believe' in Jupiter or Wotan—something that is no more ridiculous than believing in Yahweh however—to be a pagan. Contemporary paganism does not consist in erecting altars to Apollo or reviving the worship of Odin. Instead it implies looking behind religion and, according to a now classic itinerary, seeking for the 'mental equipment' that produced it, the *inner world* it reflects, and how the world it depicts is apprehended. In short it consists of viewing the gods as 'centers of values' (H. Richard Niebuhr) and the beliefs they generate as value systems: gods and beliefs may pass away, but the *values* remain.[8]

What Benoist seems to be saying here is that the gods represent fundamental values: to believe in the gods is to "enshrine" those values. Benoist seeks to revive these pagan values, but their embodiment as "gods" is not something we need necessarily believe in.

Setting aside the issue of whether this is a correct understanding of the pagan divinities, Benoist's discussion of pagan values is problematic given his Nietzschean treatment of values as such. Benoist several times sets forth the typically Nietzschean opposition to the idea of "objective" value. He writes, "Ethics is a fundamental given in paganism, but there is no universal moralization. This amounts to saying that there are no values in the world other than those resulting from our initiatives and interpretations." He then immediately follows this up with a line from Nietzsche: "There are no moral phenomena; there are only moral interpretations of phenomena."[9]

But Benoist's assertion of moral relativism (or what appears to be moral relativism) is just as problematic as Nietzsche's. The idea that belief in objective moral truth necessarily commits one to believing in moral "objects" (such as Plato's forms) is a straw man. Granted that there are no moral things, only moral "interpretations" of things, might there be grounds to prefer some interpretations to others? Benoist certainly writes as if he thinks paganism is *objectively better* than monotheism. He presents some two-hundred pages of arguments in support of this value judgment in order (apparently) to convince us that it is true. Doesn't this constitute a kind of universal moralizing? One encounters the same difficulty in Nietzsche: he asserts a "perspectivist" position with respect to values, but then writes as if master morality *really is* superior to slave morality. Elsewhere, he establishes "will to power" as an absolute standard of value: all that which enhances will to power is good, and so forth.

Again, just as in Nietzsche, Benoist's commitment to moral relativism flows from his commitment to a general relativism about truth as such. At the end of the book he writes that reclaiming paganism "involves no longer seeking an objective 'truth' outside the world, but intentionally creating one out of a new system of values."[10] But what can this mean? I understand what it means to *discover* truth. For instance, reading Benoist's book I discovered that the Greeks had set up a temple to the "Unknown God." I had no idea that this was true. Shortly after reading that, I opened an email which appeared to be a personal communication, only to discover that, in truth, it was spam. I confess, however, that I have no idea at all what it means to *create* truth. Again, one encounters the same problem in Nietzsche. Do Benoist and Nietzsche mean that we get to simply "make up" the truth, and then decide to believe in it? I cannot quite believe that this is what is meant.

Both men are entirely right in rejecting the idea that there is a truth to be had "outside" the world. However, to infer from this that truth is entirely subjective, and left up to the whim of individuals or groups, is a huge *non sequitur*. Here is the key problem with Benoist's approach to truth and values: he has simply accepted monotheism's premise that the only standard of objectivity would have to lie outside the world. Rejecting the idea that there is such a transcendent standard, he leaps to the conclusion that objectivity is therefore impossible. This is a recurrent pattern among French intellectuals; one finds it, for example, in Jean-Paul Sartre.

Years ago I remember hearing a lecture by a distinguished historian, who spoke about the problem of interpretation in history. Specifically, he was speaking against the subjectivist claim that there is no truth in history, only interpretation, and that different interpretations are equally valid. He said, "Years from now historians will still be arguing about Germany's motivations in invading Poland. Conflicting interpretations will abound. But I know one that will never be offered: no one will ever say that Poland invaded Germany." There are limits to "interpretation." All theories and interpretations stand or fall on the basis of evidence, and on the basis of such considerations as consistency, comprehensiveness, and explanatory power. These standards are not the property of any particular culture or historical period; no transcendent deity has decreed them, nor has any man, but they bind us nonetheless. We know this because all attempts to dispute them wind up covertly appealing to them.

It will be objected, however, that the truth about who invaded whom is quite different from the truth about moral or religious values. The former can be evaluated on the basis of evidence, the latter cannot. But such an attitude again buys into one of the most pernicious products of monotheism: the idea that all standards of value lay outside the world, and that the knowledge we have of this world is therefore value-free. Since many modern, Western people no longer believe in sources of value outside the world, all value claims are therefore declared to be "unscientific" and subjective. But might there be sources of objective value within the world? And wouldn't *that* be a truly pagan way to approach the question of value?

In formulating his theory of pagan values, Benoist should have looked not to Nietzsche but to Aristotle, who was a real pagan. In Aristotle, the objective basis for values is human flourishing (*eudaimonia*). Aristotelian ethics makes the simple, unchallengeable assertion that over time we have found that certain behaviors and ways of life tend to be conducive to human survival and happiness, whereas others tend not to be. The basis for some of these claims can be purely biological and psychological, whereas the basis for others has to do with the dynamics of interpersonal relationships. For example, Aristotle suggests in Book I of the *Nicomachean Ethics* that it is a risky thing to center one's life on seeking the approbation of others, as it makes us too dependent upon them and too vulnerable to being hurt, should those others withdraw their approval from us. In short, independence is desirable. In general, Aristotle makes claims about what is good for human beings that are universally valid—but at no point does he appeal to the sort of transcendent standard that Benoist believes must be appealed to if value claims are to be rendered objective.

Benoist's relativism is not just a feature of his new, Nietzschean paganism: he argues that it was the standpoint of the ancient pagans as well. Benoist quotes Ernest Renan: "The Indo-European peoples, before their conversion to Semitic ideas, never regarded their religion as an absolute truth. Rather they viewed it as a kind of family or caste heritage, and for this reason intolerance and proselytizing remained foreign to them."[11]

Setting aside what is meant by "absolute truth," a discussion of which could only bog us down uselessly, what does Benoist make of the phenomenon of syncretism as practiced by the Indo-Europeans? Caesar in his *Gallic Wars* identifies the German deities with his own Roman gods (e.g., Odin or Wotan is dubbed Mercury). The Greeks saw their gods in the Hindu pantheon when, led by Alexander the Great, they entered India in 327 BCE. Nor did the Indo-Europeans confine this procedure to their own peoples. In Egypt, the Greeks identified Thoth with Hermes, Imhotep with Asclepius, and Amon with Zeus. What does this reveal about the attitude of the Indo-European peoples toward their religions, and the religions of others? I think it clearly shows that they believed all polytheistic religions to be drawing on a mysterious, common source. Different peoples have given different names to their divinities, emphasized certain deities, and certain aspects of deities, over others. But underlying these surface differences there is a fundamental identity. Where the Indo-Europeans could not find an analogue for a god in their own tradition, they would often add that deity to their own catalogue of gods (e.g., the Roman worship of Mithras). This indicates their openness to the idea that other peoples had seen aspects of divinity that they had missed. Behind this there is, again, an assumption that there is a common religious truth, and that all are in some way groping toward it.

In sum, Benoist's relativism about truth and value seems to be quite un-pagan. Nor can he escape this problem by insisting that relativism, while not a feature of old paganism, is a desirable component of the new paganism. The philosophical difficulties with this position are very serious ones, and probably insuperable.

Conclusion

Having now written so much that is critical of Benoist's Nietzschean approach, I know I will surprise readers by saying that I sympathize with it in many ways. I have to agree with Benoist and Nietzsche that we cannot go back.

I am writing these words in a Starbucks coffee shop. The front of the store consists in one large window, and through it I can take in, at a glance, a CVS Pharmacy, a Burger King, a Sizzler, a GNC, and a sea of cars parked in the lot, my own among them. In this setting, it seems absurd to think about such things as gods and dwarves, land wights, giants, rainbow bridges, and rings of power. It also seems absurd to think about such things as heroes, and the virtues of honor, nobility, and purity of heart. When I am out in nature and away from modern civilization, all of this, even rainbow bridges, seems a lot less absurd, and I feel as if I understand—if only a little—why my ancestors believed as they did. But like most people I am seldom out in nature, and I am thoroughly attached to the comforts of modern civilization.

I have begun to think, with Benoist, that if Christianity is to be replaced with something else, it cannot be a straightforward return to the old religion. In fact, I believe something stronger than this: I believe that there must be, in a way, a kind of break with the past. Both the polytheism and monotheism of our past are moribund, and have little to say to life in the present. And we can only live in the present. I am not saying that we should become ignorant of the past. I agree with Benoist that we must understand our historical situation, and I also derive a great deal of pleasure, and guidance, from studying what was believed in the past.

If something has indeed been lost through the Christian experience—some truth our ancestors possessed—I believe that the only way to recover it is to make ourselves open, in a very special way, to what might come forth to fill the religious void that is in us. We do not know what this will be, and it is better to have as few presuppositions about it as possible. For my part, I believe that the paganism of the past was founded on a genuine religious experience of a reality that exists "in the world," but is not of human invention. Call it the supernatural, call it the *numinous*, call it the gods, whatever. This is the fundamental difference between my idea of paganism and Benoist's. Benoist has said elsewhere, "I have not personally had any experience of the divine (I am the opposite of a mystic). ... I have no connection to any religion nor do I feel the need to connect to one. ... In the world of paganism I am not a believer but a guest. I find pleasure and comfort there, not revelation."[12] He believes, if I understand him, that there is nothing "out there" to encounter should we open ourselves, whereas I do believe. His position is fundamentally atheistic; mine theistic.

How do we achieve this openness? Let me answer this, initially, by indicating what thwarts openness or makes it impossible. The death of openness is the Promethean anthropocentrism that characterizes modern man, and that, unfortunately, Benoist makes the essence of his new paganism. To raise man up as the highest thing in the universe, to declare that man is the measure of all things, to maintain that the gods, the truth, the good, and indeed reality itself are his to invent, is to effectively close ourselves to the vast, non-human cosmos which gave birth to us and shelters us and is there to instruct us if only we can swallow our pride and listen.

The position I am advocating involves a certain type of faith and expectation. Faith that there is something "out there" that corresponds, in some way, to what our ancestors called the experience of the gods, and expectation that should we succeed in altering our way of being this something will again enter our lives. But how do we alter our way of being? And what is the openness I referred to earlier? First, the alteration I speak of *does* consist in a going back to an earlier way. While I am skeptical that we can revive ancient traditions, I am hopeful that we can revive or recover the way of being that gave rise to them. Benoist is getting at this when he insists that contemporary paganism need not involve, for example, the worship of Odin, but does involve "looking behind religion and ... seeking for the 'mental equipment' that produced it, the *inner world* it reflects, and how the world it depicts is apprehended."

In what I have said so far, some readers may have detected the influence of Heidegger. If the neopagan movement is to ally itself with any philosopher, I believe that it is with Heidegger that it must ally itself, not Nietzsche. Heidegger characterizes the standpoint of modernity as *das Gestell*. This is usually translated, inadequately, as "enframing." What it means is that modern people essentially regard the earth and everything on it as raw material to be transformed in order to satisfy human desires and to conform to human ideals. The result of this, according to Heidegger, is that, "on the earth, all over it, a darkening of the world is happening. The essential happenings in this darkening are: the flight of the gods, the destruction of the earth, the reduction of human beings to a mass, the preeminence of the mediocre."[13]

To the modern attitude, Heidegger contrasts an older way of, to use his language, "comporting" ourselves toward Being: *Gelassenheit*. Translating literally, one could render this as leaving-ness, letting-alone-ness, allowing-ness, or letting-be-ness. Translators of Heidegger usually render it "letting beings be." *Gelassenheit* is a term Heidegger appropriates from German mysticism, where it is used to convey an attitude of surrender to the world and to God, so that God can come to be in the soul. It is the negation of egoism, which involves an aggressive and manipulative attitude toward the world: insisting that things must serve our interests, conform to our desires, and in general be only what we make of them. In his ethics, Kant proclaims that we must "act so that we treat humanity, whether in ourselves or in another, always as an end-in-itself and never as a means only."[14] *Gelassenheit* can be seen as extending this to all beings: in some sense we must regard all (natural) beings as ends-in-themselves, and never treat them *merely* as means.

The meaning of *Gelassenheit* is difficult to convey. Perhaps the best expression of what Heidegger means by this term is actually to be had in Lao-Tzu's *Tao Te Ching*, which is not a conventional philosophical work.[15] If one has read this text and feels that one has understood it and the central concept of *wu wei*, then I believe that one has understood *Gelassenheit*. *Wu wei* is often translated "non-action." Lao-Tzu writes, "the sage is devoted to non-action."[16] But this does not literally mean doing nothing. It means an approach to living in the world that is not grasping or controlling. It means learning the things of this world, in order to use without destroying. It means going with the grain, rather than against it. It means openness to the things themselves, rather than seeing things merely in terms of our own wishes or theories. Consider the following two passages from the *Tao Te Ching*:

> Trying to control the world?
> I see you won't succeed.
>
> The world is a spiritual vessel
> And cannot be controlled.
>
> Those who control, fail.

Those who grasp, lose.[17]

And:

> Act and you ruin it.
> Grasp and you lose it.
> Therefore the Sage
> Does not act
> [*Wu Wei*]
> And so does not ruin
> Does not grasp
> And so does not lose.[18]

Throughout his book, Benoist challenges the popular, Rousseauean conception of paganism, which sees a return to paganism as "getting back to nature." Benoist asserts, correctly, that human being is more than merely natural being, that man in some sense stands outside nature. Referring to Dumezil's three Indo-European "functions," he remarks astutely that the "naturalistic" idea of paganism is, at best, a "third-function" paganism seen through the lens of eighteenth- and nineteenth-century Romanticism. But when he attempts to formulate what the supernatural dimension of human being is, Benoist falls back on his Faustianism: man is the being who strives to impress his will on all of nature! He cites the ideas of Nietzsche and remarks, approvingly, that Nietzsche tells us that "man can only fully dominate the earth provided he can fully dominate himself."[19] Heidegger also believed that man has one foot outside nature. He believed, however, that this consists not in our ability to *negate* nature and refashion it, but rather in our ability to let beings be, and let truth be. The truth, for Heidegger, is not something written down, but rather an event: a *disclosure* of how things are (not, contra Nietzsche and Benoist, a "creation"). Human nature consists in being this being that discloses the truth.

In an interview with Benoist published a decade after the appearance of the original French edition of *On Being a Pagan*, the interviewer, Charles Champetier, says "The tone of *On Being a Pagan* was rather Nietzschean. But since then, your writings on the sacred ... appear to be more inspired by Heidegger."[20] In addressing this, Benoist acknowledges the influence of Heidegger on his thinking, and states "I think that paganism finds its own source in a sense of wonder, in the wondering gaze cast upon the world and [in] pondering the fundamental question: how is it that there is something, instead of nothing?"[21]

Earlier in the same interview Champetier remarks, "One sometimes has the impression that God is absent from neopaganism," and points out that some have suggested that neopaganism is a form of atheism. He then asks, "does paganism presuppose a faith or a belief?" In his answer, Benoist challenges (correctly) the idea that pagans "worshiped" their gods in the way that Christians worship God, but he appears to have moved away from asserting, as he does in *On Being a Pagan*, that the gods are simply a human invention. He goes on to say, "I believe ... that paganism is incompatible with atheism, if we define the latter as the radical denial of any form of the divine or the absolute that cannot be boiled down to man. And I would add that paganism is not 'Promethean': on the contrary, it implies a rejection of this Titan's hubris which led him to rob the gods of their duties in the vain hope of taking them on himself."[22]

In a later work, Benoist says of the pagan gods, "It is not a question of believing in their existence but of awakening to their presence."[23] This is exactly right. The only way to truly revive pre-Christian paganism would be to revive the attitude toward the world that allowed "the gods" to become present to human beings in the first place. Minimally, we would have to come back to the earth and to the present and become *mortals* again, beings that recognize their limitations, and recognize that those limitations define them and mark out their good.

> Look at plain silk; hold uncarved wood.
> The self dwindles; desires fade.[24]

We must make a space within ourselves and within our world in which numinous and uncanny things may again show themselves.

I suppose that many readers will react to these prescriptions by saying that they seem extremely vague, that it is not clear how to implement them, and that they are, perhaps, Romantic. Ultimately, from a Heideggerean perspective (and that is all I am attempting to lay out here), little more can be said. Indeed, some Heideggereans would object that I have already said too much. Heidegger makes it quite clear that there is nothing we can "do" to usher in a new age and cause the gods to return.[25] To assume that we can "do" something, that we can devise a plan or a method for returning to some pre-modern way of being *is itself a type of thinking that is wholly modern in nature.* The chief characteristic of modernity is the idea that everything—nature, human nature, history, consciousness, even the supernatural—is manipulable; we have only to find the right technique, and the world is ours to control.

For Heidegger, the most un-modern thing we can do, the only thing we can do to fight modernity, is to give up the idea that we can "do" anything. This type of thinking is typical of Taoism:

Best to be like water,
Which benefits the ten thousand things
And does not contend.
It pools where humans disdain to dwell,
Close to the Tao.[26]

The most powerful thing one can do, sometimes, is to surrender the attempt to do anything at all. Perhaps it is in this surrender, that that space I referred to earlier will open up, allowing the gods to re-enter the spiritual lives of Westerners. Then again, perhaps not.

Notes:

1. Alain de Benoist, *On Being a Pagan*, trans. Jon Graham (Atlanta: Ultra, 2004), p. 5.
2. Quoted in Benoist, p. 114.
3. Ibid., p. 168.
4. Friedrich Nietzsche, *Twilight of the Idols*, in *The Portable Nietzsche*, ed. and trans. Walter Kaufmann (New York: Penguin, 1982), p. 546. Later in the passage, Nietzsche states, "Nothing avails: one *must* go forward—step by step further into decadence (that is *my* definition of modern progress). One can *check* this development and thus dam up degeneration, gather it and make it more vehement and *sudden*: one can do no more."
5. *On Being a Pagan*, p. 33.
6. Ibid., p. 156.
7. Ibid., pp. 177–78.
8. Ibid., pp. 15–16.
9. Ibid., p. 186.
10. Ibid., pp. 199–200.
11. Quoted in Ibid., p. 115.
12. Alain de Benoist, "Thoughts on God," trans. Jon Graham, *TYR* 2 (2003–2004), pp. 74–75.
13. Martin Heidegger, *Introduction to Metaphysics*, trans. Gregory Fried and Richard Polt (New Haven: Yale University Press, 2000), p. 47. I am cheating a bit here, as this quote comes from the "early Heidegger," whereas *das Gestell* is a term out of the "later" Heidegger. But I am skeptical about treatments of philosophers that divide their ideas into "early" and "late" periods.
14. Immanuel Kant, *Grounding for the Metaphysics of Morals*, trans. James W. Ellington (Indianapolis: Hackett, 1993), p. 36.
15. Quite a bit has been written about the similarity between Heidegger's thought and Asian philosophy, and even about Asian influences on his thinking. See, for example, Reinhard May, *Heidegger's Hidden Sources*, trans. Graham Parks (London: Routledge, 1996). The author includes a chapter entitled "Dao: Way and Seeing."
16. Lao-Tzu, *Tao Te Ching*, trans. Burton Watson (Indianapolis: Hackett, 1993), p. 3.
17. Ibid., p. 29.
18. Ibid., p. 64.
19. *On Being a Pagan*, p. 200.

20. Charles Champetier, "On Being a Pagan, Ten Years Later: An Interview with Alain de Benoist," trans. Elizabeth Griffin, *TYR* 2, op. cit., p. 102.

21. Ibid., p. 103.

22. Ibid., p. 93.

23. Benoist, "Thoughts on God," op. cit., p. 65.

24. *Tao Te Ching*, op. cit., p. 19.

25. I should point out, lest I confuse readers unfamiliar with Heidegger, that Heidegger did not call himself a pagan and was not preoccupied with the idea of a return to the gods. Heidegger does use phrases like the "flight of the gods" to describe modernity, and he did famously state in an interview published after his death that "only a god can save us now." However, he seems to have used terms like "gods" and "God" in a largely figurative sense. My belief is that if we deliberately take such usages literally, then Heidegger can be read as saying something vitally relevant to neopaganism. (However, even if he had never referred to "the gods," I would still argue for the relevance of his thought.)

26. *Tao Te Ching*, op. cit., p. 8.

"Of what are those figures in the paintings of Botticelli and Casper David Friedrich dreaming?"

ON BEING A PAGAN
BY ALAIN DE BENOIST

In this concise yet far-ranging essay, Alain de Benoist offers a powerful rejoinder to the idea that the European tradition and the Christian tradition are somehow inseparable. Drawing on the deep wellsprings of pagan antiquity, he articulates a Nietzschean alternative that is life-affirming, creative, and heroic. Benoist's devastating critique of monotheist universalism has broad implications for European art, culture, and politics.

Originally published in Paris in 1981, *On Being a Pagan* is the first full-length book by Alain de Benoist to be translated into English. It remains the most comprehensive attempt to articulate a pagan theology ever written. This is neither a neopagan "how-to" book nor a speculative New Age grimoire. It is a philosophical exposition of the highest order. *On Being a Pagan* re-establishes paganism to its rightful place—as an intellectual and ethical force to be reckoned with.

Attractively presented and produced, *On Being a Pagan* features a preface by Stephen Edred Flowers and original cover art by Madeline von Foerster.

Mention this advertisement to receive a copy at the discounted rate of $18.00 postpaid in the U.S.A., or $28.00 postpaid to the rest of the world. Georgia residents please include 7% sales tax. To order, send a check or money order payable to:

Ultra
PO Box 11736
Atlanta, GA 30355

PayPal payments are also accepted at:
elecampane@bellsouth.net

Translated by Jon Graham and edited by Greg Johnson, with a preface by Stephen Edred Flowers. 6" x 9", 240 + iii pages with index, trade paperback, ISBN 0-9720292-2-2.

"The guilt, the fear, the narrow petty-bourgeois obsession with well-being, and the self-loathing love of the Other that has left Western man defenseless before the destructive behaviors of our nihilist age derive from the alien belief system that Christianity introduced to the West. They are not part of the pagan spirit that lives still in the *Rig Veda*, the *Illiad*, or the *Edda*. Benoist helps us rediscover these ancient wellsprings and the fonts from which future greatnesses may again flow."

—Michael O'Meara,
author of *New Culture, New Right*

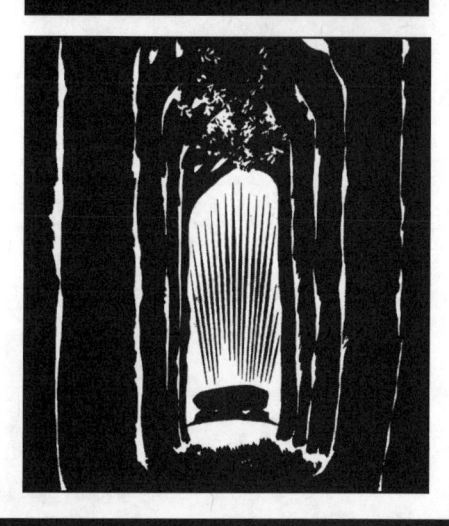

Odinn Exchanging His Eye for Wisdom

Fine Art Prints of the Painting by Madeline von Foerst[...]

These signed, limited edition Iris prints are printed with archival inks [...] 30 lb Somerset watercolor paper for an effect that is rich, soft, a[...] perfect in every detail. Prints measure 16 x 20" and are unframed. $1[...]

To Order, call (917)378-0057
or buy via Paypal at www.madelinevonfoerster.co[...]

Review Essay:
A Critique of Against the Modern World by Mark Sedgwick

Róbert Horváth

Against the Modern World: Traditionalism and the Secret Intellectual History of the Twentieth Century by Mark Sedgwick. Hardcover, 370 pages with glossary, bibliography, and index. New York: Oxford University Press, 2004. ISBN 0-19-515297-2.

Editors Note: As we have explained in the "Editorial Preface" to *TYR* 2, the editors of *TYR* are not Traditionalists in the strict sense defined by writers like René Guénon and Frithjof Schuon. We have described ourselves as "radical traditionalists," and so feel it necessary to make this distinction. The author of the review that follows *is* a Traditionalist, and his critical reactions to the work of Mark Sedgwick clearly reflect this position. He would undoubtedly find much to criticize in the pages of *TYR*, as well. However, we find his perspective intriguing, and trust our readers will appreciate it. A second review of Sedgwick's book appears in the "Book Review" section of this issue.

This book—whose curious cover is more reminiscent of a spy novel than an academic work—declares itself to be "a biography of René Guénon and a history of the Traditionalist movement that he founded" (p. vii). This is rather a strange objective on the part of an author who hardly makes any reference to the works of the most important authors of the spiritual current at issue, and who either fails to refer to its numerous representatives or just lightly touches upon some of their names.[1] Furthermore, he appears to know little about the periodicals of this current and mainly refers to those accessible through the Internet. In our view it is too ambitious to characterize a book as "a history of René Guénon and the Traditionalists" (ibid.) when the author is in the dark about certain important historical sources of the theme.[2] In addition to all this, he does not manage to give the precise date of birth of Julius Evola (p. 363), although he devotes nearly two chapters to him.[3] It is difficult for us to find a work reliable when, for example, of the twenty-one pieces of information that relate to Hungary, thirteen are false (pp. 186–87).[4] We do not intend, however, to dwell upon these mistakes too long, since the work of an assistant professor at the American University in Cairo includes much graver errors than these.

The author ultimately traces this extended and vast spiritual current back to only one single person: René Guénon—and to his works and influence. We certainly do not desire to belittle the significance of Guénon, but we consider this conception mistaken both historically and phenomenologically. How can one imagine that the influence of a single person—or of even a few—might be as great as that? The conceptions, ideas, and truths appearing (in a concentrated and clarified form) in the life-work of Guénon were once the guiding directives and principles of whole cultures; they cannot be seen as the creation of certain individuals. Their *reappearance* is a fact even if the written teachings in Guénon's works refer to generalities rather than practical details. Referring to the equivalents of the spiritual current long before Guénon, Mr. Sedgwick simply lists the names of a few individuals while arbitrarily distinguishing between Traditionalism and Perennialism. It must be emphasised that Ficino and Agostino Steuco are but two names in a long chain of representatives of a universal, strictly traditional spirituality and intellectuality.[5] It is also ridiculous to speak about "Vedanta-Perennialism" (pp. 24, 40), since *every* real tradition is a representation of spiritual Perennialism. In addition, the author mingles these "origins" with individuals and schools that—not only on the surface, but also in their very nature—show modern, and not at all traditional characteristics. Who was Reuben Burrow and who were all the nineteenth- and twentieth-century theosophists—we might ask—compared to those ancient people who believed in a perennial wisdom both in the East and in the West?

Mr. Sedgwick seems to be uninformed about the difference between *philosophia* and wisdom (*sophia*), and also about the fact that the Scholastic term *philosophia perennis* was also used in the academic circles of philosophers until the mid-twentieth century.[6] He does not seem to know that Plato was interested in the primordial wisdom of the Greeks and of Atlantis, or about Plutarch, one of the priests of the Shrine of Delphi, who was also versed in the Egyptian traditions. He seems to forget about Plotinus, who had his eastern connections, and whose influence upon Neo-Platonic European spiritual culture cannot be denied. Not a word is uttered about Ibn Sīnā (Avicenna), who first attempted to unify the Platonic and Aristotelian philosophies, nor about the outstanding role of Ādi Śaṅkarācārya who aimed at the unity of Hindu tradition. We could continue to list those ancient authors whose spirituality is either closely related to or analogous—if not identical—with the most recent traditional authors of our age. It naturally follows then that the author also fails to mention that the concept of the transcendent unity of the great spiritual traditions and world religions, or the idea of the primordial Tradition, are not new at all. That is to say, they are neither the creations of Guénon, nor Schuon, nor Matgoi, nor anybody else. The validity and reality of an idea do not depend on the fact that the religious tradition practised by the majority is silent about it. The Tibetan *ris-med* current and the following extracts from the Indian-Hindu sacred texts show the primordiality of the idea of a universal and integral Tradition:

> For whatever path men choose, they all come to me [the Godhead] in the end...
> ...that man sees the truth who sees *saṅkhya* and *yoga* as one.
> ...whatever form any devotee worships with true faith, I give them this unshakable faith.
> Even those who worship other gods and offer their sacrifice to them with faith, they, too, sacrifice to Me alone...
>
> "The ordinary man, who draws a [final] distinction among the divinities of the Trinity [Brahmā, Viṣṇu, and Śiva], surely will stay in hell as long as the Moon and the stars are glittering in the sky. My follower is allowed to venerate any gods, for by ascending towards them he can reach the knowledge leading to the ultimate liberation. Without rendering homage to Brahmā one cannot venerate Viṣṇu; without rendering homage to Viṣṇu one will not venerate me either." Having said that, Śiva, the Lord Supreme, the Merciful God uttered the following words in everyone's hearing: "If a follower of Viṣṇu hates me, or a follower of Śiva hates Viṣṇu, both draw curses upon their heads, and they will never realise Reality."[7]

The spiritual current at issue and the spirituality of the ancient authors are basically identical. This is only distorted by the fact that contemporary authors take modern circumstances into consideration while writing. This characteristic, however, makes them different only on the surface: in their approach to the topic, in their style, in their external starting point, and in their lives. They remain *essentially* identical. The numerous historical correspondences or, at least, the spiritual relationship also suggest that the most eminent representatives of this current must be called *contemporary traditional authors*, and not "Traditionalists." We are in complete agreement with Professor András László, who first applied this term to them. It also evidently follows that not every thinker connected to this current can be considered a traditional author. As we expressed in a previous article,[8] those "Traditionalists" to whom the worthy title of "traditional author" cannot yet be applied, might—by virtue of proper efforts and achievements—become traditional authors *one day*.

As we can see, in Mr. Sedgwick's book even the terms "Traditionalism" and "Traditionalists" are open to debate. If the author had taken seriously his aim of writing about René Guénon and the history of the spiritual current "he founded," he should have jettisoned the idea of using the expressions "Traditionalism" and "Traditionalists," as Guénon himself did.[9] Considering the events which have transpired since Guénon's death, our emphatic advice is not to separate Traditionalism from Tradition,[10] but to see "Traditionalism" as a strictly transitional and intermediary term.[11] This applies so much the more in the case of the term "movement." What might be politically acceptable, and in certain cases even desirable, is not always valid when referring to a higher order. Guénon himself was opposed to using such a fundamentally leftist label as "movement."[12] He and all the representatives of the spirituality re-embodied in his life-work have always represented spiritual aristocracy, the true spiritual elitism which has never allowed itself to have any of the characteristics of a "movement."[13] As to politics and the collective nature of influences, the characteristics of a movement might appear occasionally, although they are by no means essential. They are not something to which the true representatives of this current would pay much attention, nor the basis on which anything could be defined.

After all that has been said, the following question arises: has the author chosen his *ab ovo* erroneous starting points accidentally or intentionally? Immediately on the second page of the Preface one finds such unsavoury expressions as "anti-Semitism, terrorism, and fascism," while in the next sentence—as if that weren't enough—the terms "SS" and "Nazi Germany" catch one's eye (p. vii). What original impressions these words convey! Under their influence the average reader of the book will certainly turn with great interest and an open heart towards the spiritual current and look forward to learning more objective details about it! The Prologue begins by painting a similarly "winning" picture of the Russian intellectual state of affairs, from which we can learn—among other things—that an alleged representative of "Traditionalism" worked as a street-sweeper during the Soviet era (pp. 3–5). The basic tone of the book is set by many such allusions, which the Western readers will without doubt "profoundly understand," and which—right from the beginning—will surely illuminate the whole current in the "most favourable" light. Likewise, "a biography of René Guénon" also wishes to introduce the "founder" in the most bizarre environment possible: it names all the well-known scholars and artists who are the least significant from the spiritual current's point of view (pp. 22f, 29f, 36f, etc.), reports on the Theosophical Society (pp. 40–44, etc.), Isabelle Eberhardt (pp. 63–65), or Adam Alfred Rudolf Glauer *alias* Rudolf von Sebottendorff (p. 65f), most of whom had nothing or hardly anything in common with Guénon (who, it might be added, attacked their mentality at length in his writings). Mr. Sedgwick goes into full particulars about Guénon's "foolish youth" (p. 12), and to muddle things more, he also includes in Guénon's life-work those ideas which he later outgrew and criticised. For example, the author seems to know not only that Guénon occasionally smoked opium before he was twenty-six, but also that Albert Puyou (Matgioi), the Count of Pouvourville, had introduced him to it. He seems to have iron-clad proof: Matgioi has written a book on opium (pp. 58, 283). Mark Sedgwick also wonders—in the manner of a "good," modern historian—whether Guénon would have moved to Egypt had it not been for his new lover, Mary (Dina) Shillito (p. 74). Despite the fact that in Cairo many Muslims took Guénon to be a saint (or even more than that), it turns out that during Ramadan he did not refrain from "smoking a cigarette and drinking a coffee," and he did not go on a pilgrimage to Mecca (pp. 75–76). How terrible! By these criteria, then, are all the Muslims who do not smoke and drink coffee, but go to Mecca, much more eminent and considerable persons than Guénon? By this time we have reached the second part of the book, entitled "Traditionalism in Practice." Here we learn about Frithjof Schuon, in whose case the motif of love and psychology also appears (pp. 85–86, 90–91), and immediately after him comes chapter 5 entitled "Fascism," which, to say the least, is only loosely connected to the previous topics. Here, at least, it comes to light why von Sebottendorff had to be drawn into the story, although Mr. Sedgwick is careful not to mention that Evola wrote a work entitled *The Right-Wing Critique of Fascism*.[14] This hardly fits the conception of "Practice," and is therefore ignored. Regarding Romanian "Fascism," it is necessary to make some corrections: Mircea Eliade was not a "follower" of Evola (p. 109), nor was the Legion of the Archangel Michael identical with the Iron Guard (p. 113), and it was not Vasile Lovinescu who "introduced" Evola to Corneliu Codreanu (p. 114). As is evident, we are able to quote many examples of the author's lack of information. Indeed, on the basis of his standpoints, the given information, and the structure of the whole book, we cannot assume a *bona fide* ignorance on his part, but rather we can find traces of certain manipulations.

The spiritual current's influence upon academic life and its cultural and social impact seem to be sore points for the author. The way he treats Ananda Kentish Coomaraswamy is truly astounding (perhaps only Evola, Schuon, and Nasr are treated worse). We are informed that the reason why this prince among scholars, this "50-year-old museum curator from Boston," became more receptive to Guénon's Traditionalism was—in part—because Coomaraswamy's second wife had "become pregnant by [Aleister] Crowley in 1916. […] This incident presumably helped to diminish Coomaraswamy's enthusiasm for occultism" (p. 53), and in this he was supported by Guénon's critiques of occultism. The author is also able to reconstruct in which occult bookstore in New York Coomaraswamy might "possibly" have met with Guénon's works (p. 34). It reminds one too much of the psychologising methods of the numerous historians who inform us, for instance, about the *thoughts* of Adolf Hitler. Certainly such commentators sometimes delineate their ideas as mere hypotheses, but they are also fully aware that their readers soon forget the conditional structure.

As mentioned, the impact of the spiritual current at issue upon scientific-academic circles seems really disturbing to Mr. Sedgwick. He names many individuals whom he believes to be connected to the spiritual current (e.g., pp. xiii–xiv). On the one hand, this clearly reveals his ignorance about the latter, and on the other, confuses things even more. Thus he is able to get as far as stating his theory of "dangerous" "soft Traditionalism" which exercises significant influence in the cultural and social spheres, but this only results in his mixing even more names (Gérard Encausse [Papus], Jacques Maritain, Oswald Wirth, Mircea Eliade, Louis Dumont, Paul de Séligny, Alan Watts, Louis Pauwels, Ernst Friedrich Schumacher, the Aristasia, Edvard Limonov, etc.) with the true representatives of the current. His irritation is obvious with respect to the spiritual current's influence upon scholarship and academia in the U.S.A. (Huston Smith, Thomas Merton, World Wisdom Books, Fons Vitae [pp. 162–70, 190–93], etc.), upon culture and politics in Great Britain (Temenos Academy, John Tavener, Prince Charles of Wales [pp. 213–16], etc.), and he shows effective paranoia towards its general socio-political impact (Italy, Central-Eastern Europe, Neo-Eurasianism, Islamic countries, etc.). He is too eager to emphasise Evola's alleged influence on Italian terrorism in the 1960s, skilfully referring to the work of Gianfranco de Turris (pp. 179ff. and 319). He does not happen to mention that the work entitled *Elegy and Defence for Julius Evola; The Baron and the Terrorists* actually acquits Evola of the charges brought against him. It is even stranger that pages 222–40 and 257–60 of the book deal with the persons, schools, and parties that are admittedly "post-Traditionalists" at best (cf. p. 260), that is to say, who distanced themselves from Traditionalism over the course of time.[15] Naturally, the author feels compelled to operate in such a fashion. Otherwise his book would not raise enough interest: he could not toll the storm-bell of a "school" or "movement" which is so dangerous in its influence.

To those who still have their doubts about the negative manipulations of the author, suffice it to say that the book was written in such a way that it will appeal to sympathisers of the "Traditionalist movement" while judging them at the same time. One of the nadirs of this work is the introduction of the term "Traditional*ist* Sufism," by which the author suggests that it is an essentially modern current, which merely alludes to the Tradition, the various traditions, and Sufism. At this point he wants to be more Catholic than the Pope, similar to his Hungarian colleagues who—either as laymen or biased devotees—feel entitled to tell one what true Christianity, Gnosis, true Orthodoxy, and true Islam are, without heartfelt and unifying reference to the Godhead. In like manner, he attempts to point out why Sufis are not Sufis, and why traditional people are not traditional. His answers and arguments in most respects lack deep insight and profundity, and stand on the ground of formalism, dogmatism, and pharisee-ism. He seems to only know and acknowledge the conventional and rustic form of Sufism. Yet he keeps silent about the Sufi characteristics—of mostly Persian origin—of the eastern part of the Muslim world, those super-religious manifestations which were occasionally rejected by official Islam (and whose representatives were once burnt at the stake), but without whom Islamic metaphysics, esoterism, gnosis, and initiation would hardly exist today. The author is not—or at least appears not to be—conversant with the principle according to which the validity and reality of an idea are not negated by the fact that the religious tradition practised by the majority might keep silent about it.

> There is no doubt that the Lord of the inhabitants of Heaven and Earth, our Master, God's Messenger (may God bless him and give him peace) was openly manifested, like a sun on a standard, and in spite of that was not seen by all, but only by some. God veiled him from others, just as He veiled the Prophets (on them be peace) from certain men, and just as He veils the Saints from the men of their time, so much so that they slander the Saints and do not believe them. God's Book testify to this: "Thou shalt see them looking toward thee and they see not" (VII, 197) and they said: "What kind of a messenger is this, who eats food and walks in the markets" (XXV, 7) and so on, in all the other analogous passages. Two thirds or more of the divine Book tells how Prophets (on them be peace) were slandered by the men of their time. Among those who did not see God's Messenger (may God bless him and give him peace) was Abū Jahl [Ibn Hisham] (God's curse be upon him); he saw in the Messenger only the orphan who had been adopted by Abū Ṭālib. The same applies to the spiritual Master who is simultaneously ecstatic (*majdhūb*) and methodical (*sālik*), who is at the same time both drunk and sober; only a few find him.[16]

It is well known in traditional circles that spiritual Tradition is beyond conventions and religious forms. Mr. Sedgwick, however, noticeably blames Schuon for permitting the members of his community to drink beer (p. 126), and in one of the footnotes he draws a parallel with the hijackers of the 11 September 2001 attack in New York, who "had been seen drinking vodka" (p. 305).[17] After this, the author's negative bias and manipulations of the facts should be self-evident.

In Hungary, different assumptions have arisen about the author of this book. Some presume that he is a kind of Euro-Atlantic spy, whose official task is to hunt for anti-modern ideas that have fertilised the contemporary Islamic world.[18] According to others he was denied entry to an initiatory order with "Traditionalist" connections, and has written this book as revenge. Some hold the opinion that certain "Traditionalists" mistakenly chose him to write the history of the "movement" (cf. pp. 347–49). Whatever the case, the Oxford University Press should have been more cautious about whose book they were going to publish, since the scholarly value of this work is, to say the least, minimal. We do concede that—apart from everything mentioned above—the author successfully collected the secondary and tertiary historical sources of the spiritual current, and that he occasionally makes a proper distinction regarding certain authors. However, the primary sources of a work concerning the history of ideas should be the works of the significant representatives of those ideas, whom Mr. Sedgwick, unfortunately, hardly knows about. He refers to five books from Coomaraswamy; four books, two articles, and two letters from Schuon; only one book from Titus Burckhardt; and four books and two articles from Nasr (pp. 34, 316–18, 351–59). He also entirely ignores such works as *A Treasury of Traditional Wisdom* by Whitall Perry. These references, moreover, do not presume a thorough knowledge of the books, since the long—although partial—list of the works of Guénon and Evola (pp. 353–54) seems to be merely a nominal enumeration. With respect to this current's history of ideas, the *books* should be taken as primary sources—not websites, subsequently written analytical articles, or telephone, fax, and e-mail interviews. As for the personal interviews made with witnesses, these can only be seen as secondary sources, since, on the one hand, it is unascertainable who said what, and on the other—and this is the most decisive factor—the personal interests of the subjects of an interview should always be transparent and clear, since their memory and words show events in a personal light, emphasising only the idiosyncratic aspects or parts of history.[19] As proof of the author's familiarity with the basic works, periodicals, and articles, we would gladly have read about how and to what extent a topic, an idea, or a certain conception of the spiritual traditions were presented in the contemporary authors' thoughts and lives according to the evidence of their writings. We would have appreciated reading about the works of the significant authors, such as Vasile Lovinescu, the eminent writer and great authority on mythology and literature; Leo Schaya, the outstanding representative of theistic metaphysics; John Levy, the expert on Advaita Vedanta and non-theistic metaphysics; and others. We would happily have heard where, how, and in whose writing a traditional conception has appeared; who has taken up the thread again and how it has been expounded in more detail; and finally, which elements have persisted or disappeared in their works. Had the author written about such things, he would have presented a true history. We would also have been pleased to read about the theoretical debates (in the hope of understanding their different viewpoints, and not in terms of demonstrating "dissension" among them) between Evola and Guénon, Michel Vâlsan and Marco Pallis, Claudio Mutti and Antonio Medrano, instead of descriptions of the environment of Mutti's publishing office and the "appetizing smells of Italian cooking" which pervaded it (p. 11).

Taking all of this into consideration, we have practically read a *gossip book*, nothing more than a new false history. "But I say to you that for every idle word men may speak, they will give account of it in the day of judgement."[20]

(*Translated from Hungarian by Andrea Gál*)

Notes:

1. Thus, the related German thinkers such as Leopold Ziegler, Othmar Spann, Taras von Borodajkewycz, Walter Heinrich, and others, as well as André Préau, Arthur Osborne, Elie Lebasquais (Luc Benoist), Kurt Almqvist, Charles Le Gai Eaton, Lord Northbourne, William Stoddart, Rama Coomaraswamy, Gaston Georgel, Bruno Hapel, etc., are not mentioned at all, while John Levy, Leo Schaya, Whitall Nicholson Perry, Franco Musso (Giovanni Ponte), Renato del Ponte, and others receive only nominal mention.

2. The author is uninformed about sources of historical importance, such as the two unpublished letters of Michel Vâlsan to Frithjof Schuon dated 17 September 1950 and November of 1950; Florin Mihăescu's article entitled "Mircea Eliade e René Guénon" in the Eliade special issue of *Origini*, March 1997 (Milan), pp.

15–18; the volume with the title of *Eliade, Vâlsan, Geticus e gli altri* by Claudio Mutti (Parma: Edizioni all'insegna del Veltro, 1999); the book with the title of *Traditionalism: Religion in the Light of Perennial Philosophy* by Kenneth Oldmeadow (Colombo: Sri Lanka Institute of Traditional Studies, 2000); etc. He confesses in a footnote that he has not read the letters of Vâlsan, but in spite of this, he refers to one of them on more than one page (pp. 304–06). Had he known about the relevant article from Mihăescu, he could not have called Eliade even a "soft traditionalist." Some of his basic conceptions—in terms of the "Fragmentation" and the "Dissension" (pp. 123–31)—would similarly have been dashed had he informed the reader that Vâlsan in the above-mentioned farewell letters addressed Schuon as his "Most dear and honoured Master."

3. None of the listed mistakes had been corrected until the appearance of the book's Errata on the Internet: <http://www.aucegypt.edu/faculty/sedgwick/trad/book/errata.html> (8 August 2005). Incidentally, we find it strange that a non-Traditionalist has been occupying the following Internet address for years for his own purposes: <www.traditionalists.org>.

4. It is impossible to indicate each and every mistake here, but it is highly bizarre that Hungary—and therefore Béla Hamvas, for instance—is mentioned in a chapter called "Terror in Italy." A historian ought to have known that being "near the Romanian border" (p. 186) has never meant anything in terms of spirituality for the Hungarians.

5. The reference to Steuco originates from one of the Gifford lectures of Seyyed Hossein Nasr, but the author forgets to give his source. Cf. "What is Tradition?" in S. H. Nasr, *Knowledge and the Sacred* (New York: Crossroad, 1981), p. 69. (The author misstates the date of birth, as did Mr. Nasr: he writes 1497 instead of 1496.)

6. See, e.g., *Athenaeum*, vol. XXVIII (Budapest, 1941) pp. 136ff.

7. *Bhagavad-gītā*, IV, 11; V, 5; VII, 21; IX, 23; *Śiva-purāṇa*, Rudrasaṅhitā II, 43.17–21.

8. "A 'tradicionális szerzők' kifejezésről" (About the Term "Traditional Authors"), *Axis Polaris*, No. 5 (Budapest, 2003) pp. 5–9. Revised version: *Tradíció* year-book (Debrecen, 2004), pp. 19–24. Revised and expanded version: <http://www.cakravartin.com/archives/about-the-term-traditional-authors-by-robert-horvath>.

9. In Guénon's life-work the terms "Traditionalism" and "Traditionalists" never occur in a positive or approved sense.

10. See, e.g., René Guénon, *Le règne de la quantité et les signes des*

temps (Paris: Gallimard, 1995), pp. 203–09.

11. Cf. footnote 8.

12. Guénon rejected not only the principles of equality, democracy, and liberalism, but also socialism. See René Guénon, *Precisazioni necessaire: I saggi di diorama—Regime Fascista* (Padua: Il cavallo alato, 1988), p. 26. And cf. René Guénon, *Le règne de la quantité*, pp. 53–58; René Guénon, *La crise du monde moderne* (Paris: Gallimard, 1995), pp. 68–112.

13. We have no knowledge of anyone among the representatives of the spiritual current that would have belonged to the left wing. The "anarchism" of John Gustaf Agélii (Ivan Aguéli) was an exception, Henri Hartung had a positive attitude to Evola, and Tage Lindbom amended his early leftist attitude in no less than four volumes. Evola was the one who systematically expressed the political application of internal traditional spirituality, but the other outstanding representatives of the current also showed innumerable characteristics of a rightist attitude in the classical and traditional sense. See, e.g., Henri Hartung, "Rencontres Romaines au milieu des ruines," *L'Age d'Or*, No. 4 (Puiseaux, 1985) pp. 26–38; Tage Lindbom, *Omprövning* (Borås: Norma, 1983); Tage Lindbom, *Roosevelt och det andra världskriget* (Borås: Norma, 1985); Tage Lindbom, *Fallet Tyskland* (Borås: Norma, 1988); Tage Lindbom, *The Myth of Democracy* (Grand Rapids: Eerdmans, 1996); Ananda K. Coomaraswamy, "The Bugbear of Democracy, Freedom and Equality," in his *The Bugbear of Literacy* (Bedfont: Perennial Books, 1979), pp. 125–50; Titus Burckhardt, "A konzervatív ember," *Arkhé*, No. 1 (Budapest, 1996) pp. 27–33; Marco Pallis, "Do Clothes Make the Man?" in his *The Way and the Mountain* (London: Peter Owen, 1991), pp. 141–159; Martin Lings, "The Political Extreme," in his *The Eleventh Hour: The Spiritual Crisis of the Modern World in the Light of Tradition and Prophecy* (Cambridge: Quinta Essentia, 1987), pp. 45–59.

Under the influence of Alexander Dugin on one side, certain Islamic movements on another, and various representatives from the U.S.A. on a third, today many people are unfortunately toying with leftism, although—to our knowledge—none of them may be properly called a leftist.

Along with his partial cooperation with German National Socialism and Italian Fascism, Evola can be considered the most important twentieth-century theoretician of the right-wing attitude in the classical, traditional, and European sense.

14. First edition: *Il Fascismo: Saggio di una analisi critica dal punto di vista della Destra* (Rome: Volpe, 1964). Second and third editions: *Il Fascismo visto dalla Destra. Note sul Terzo Reich* (Rome: Volpe, 1970 and 1974). The latest edition is titled *Fascismo e Terzo Reich*.

15. Sedgwick puts too much emphasis on politics, even more than on psychology or sociology, although he noticeably disguises it. It is as if the whole book were centred around Alexander Dugin. Might it be possible that the author suffers from a well-developed phobia of Eastern Europeans and anti-modern ideas? Cf. note 4. Not incidentally do we remark that Dugin's political activity can be seen as modern in many respects. Cf. note 13.

16. Al-'Arabī ad-Darqāwī, "Letter 14" [at-Tarjumana] (English translation by Titus Burckhardt).

17. After this parallel, the author adds a disingenuous disclaimer that "these reports must be treated with extreme caution" (p. 305).

18. He gave a lecture on Islam to a Danish commando group. See <http://aucegypt.edu/faculty/sedgwick/lectures.html> (7 August 2005).

19. Mark Koslow, the later denouncer of Schuon, for instance, was obviously motivated by jealousy (cf. p. 174f). Even such an important historical source as the *Document confidentiel inédit* by Marcel Clavelle (Jean Reyor) cannot be viewed uncritically.

20. Matthew 12:36

from BOYDELL & BREWER

Runic Amulets
— and —
Magic Objects

Mindy MacLeod and Bernard Mees

The runic alphabet, in use for well over a thousand years, was employed by various Germanic groups in a variety of ways, including, inevitably, for superstitious and magical rites. Formulaic runic words were inscribed onto small items that could be carried for good luck; runic charms were carved on metal or wooden amulets to ensure peace or prosperity. There are invocations and allusions to pagan and Christian gods and heroes, to spirits of disease, and even to potential lovers. Few such texts are completely unique to Germanic society, and in fact, most of the runic amulets considered in this book show wide-ranging parallels from a variety of European cultures.

The question of whether runes were magical or not has divided scholarship in the area. Early criticism embraced fantastic notions of runic magic—leading not just to a healthy scepticism, but in some cases to a complete denial of any magical element whatsoever in the runic inscriptions. This book seeks to re-evaluate the whole question of runic sorcery, attested to not only in the medieval Norse literature dealing with runes but primarily in the fascinating magical texts of the runic inscriptions themselves.

List price $65 (discount price $48.75); 288 pp.; 16 line illus.; hardcover
ISBN-10: 1-84383-205-4; ISBN-13: 978-1-84383-205-8

CONTACT US AT

Boydell & Brewer • 668 Mt. Hope Ave., Rochester, NY 14620 • www.boydellandbrewer.com
(ph) 585-275-0419 • (fax) 585-271-8778 • boydell@boydellusa.net
Please quote the reference code $07149 when ordering to receive your discount.

Reviews: Books

New Culture, New Right: Anti-Liberalism in Postmodern Europe by Michael O'Meara. Softbound, 228 pages. Bloomington: 1st Books, 2004. ISBN 1-4107-6461-3.

Freedom, scientific objectivity, and the belief in "progress" as a historical inevitability have characterized classical liberalism since the Enlightenment. For philosophers like Lyotard, Derrida, and Foucault, however, the postmodern condition is one in which these grand narratives have collapsed, revealing a reality that is polyvalent and multidimensional. Whereas liberalism looked to a world in which reason would eventually overcome the differences between human beings, separated only by irrational prejudices, postmodernism recognizes that there may be no single overarching criterion of truth and that the differing perspectives of different human beings may be "true enough" in a relative sense—despite their mutual exclusivity. But rather than championing the historically rooted traditions and cultures which liberal progressivists had sought to overcome, postmodernists tend to privilege the identities and perspectives typical of late capitalist subcultures. That is, identities and perspectives that are entirely arbitrary, amorphous, and in a continual state of flux. Ironically, this means that postmodernism has simply exchanged one form of universalism for another. While liberal universalism was predicated on *one* criterion of truth, postmodernism's hyper-individualism is predicated on the idea that there is *no* criterion of truth. This is a philosophy ideally suited for the cultural anarchy of modern, market-driven societies. It is in these societies that identities are reduced to little more than fashions that can be bought, sold, and discarded as soon as they become passé. Where everybody is somebody—an atomized individual with no deeper frame of reference—nobody is anybody. Except, of course, a good consumer.

The New Right shares postmodernism's belief that the "grand narratives" have crumbled. This is, after all, borne out by simply observing the fragmented nature of the modern West, with its plethora of competing viewpoints, its lack of any common culture, and its endless variety of "lifestyle choices." But rather than embracing the transitory subcultures subscribed to by modern individuals, New Rightists argue for a return to the historically rooted traditions and cultures that liberal universalism originally worked to supplant. To this end, New Rightists invoke Heidegger's insight that Being and time are fundamentally inseparable. For this reason, the specific traditions of specific peoples remain relevant (although they have no monopoly on universal truth), since the past is continually reappropriated by the present. "Identity," Heidegger writes, "is the actualization of a heritage." Against postmodernism's extreme individualism and transitory subcultures, New Rightists propose replacing the grand narratives of liberalism with a "heterogeneous world of homogenous peoples." That is to say, peoples who have reclaimed their traditional and originary identities.

The New Right's appropriation and redirection of postmodernism's critique of liberalism represents but one component of a project begun in reaction to the "May Events" of 1968, when student rebellions brought French society to the brink of revolution—or at least so it seemed at the time. For Alain de Benoist, a young French intellectual, this was merely the culmination of a de-Europeanizing process that had begun with the Allied victory in World War II and the subsequent partition of Europe between the forces of American capitalism and Soviet communism—each, in its own way, the product of liberalism.

One of the strengths of Benoist's GRECE and of the New Right in general is that it has never developed a static ideology. Rather, its critique of liberalism is ongoing and constantly evolving. Nevertheless, O'Meara identifies several distinct tendencies that have fed into the New Right milieu, although none can be said to dominate its discourse, and all are susceptible to its criticisms. The first of these is postmodernism, which I have already discussed. In delineating several more of these "tendencies," in no particular order, the New Right's orientation will become clearer.

Scientism: The development of liberalism during the Enlightenment looked to deductive science to bolster its arguments, and put tremendous faith in the notion that rational enquiry would eventually vindicate its positions. Of course, this has hardly been the case. Genetic research, for example, has demonstrated time and again that human beings do not enter the world as "blank slates," but are endowed from birth with differing abilities that render all notions of "equality" meaningless. Biological differences between men and women indicate that gender may be anything but a "social construct." Growing evidence suggests that territoriality, ethnic solidarity, and various forms of aggression are evolutionary mechanisms that cannot be dismissed as mere "prejudice." Even the seemingly universal need for religion, the bane of atheist humanists, may be hard-wired into our neurological structure.

Nevertheless, the New Right has de-emphasized its attempts to undermine liberalism's sacred cows by invoking the hard sciences, although this was of central importance during the GRECE's formative years. Perhaps this is because this type of argument often proves ineffectual. Although human beings are quick to justify their deeply held beliefs in terms of "science," they are seldom inclined to change them based solely on the results of new research. Furthermore, dissenting opinions can always be found. No matter the general consensus, there will always be scientists who will argue that global warming does not exist, that there is no biological basis for the concept of race, or that creationism is the most plausible model to explain human origins—just to mention a few examples.

Traditionalism: The influence of Traditionalism on the post-war Right is somewhat questionable, although much has been made of Julius Evola's alleged influence on neo-fascist circles in Italy. Philosophically, the New Right's qualified relativism precludes it from sympathizing with Traditionalism's belief in "Tradition" as a metaphysical absolute. Nevertheless, there is still considerable room for dialogue between New Rightists and Traditionalists.

In *The Reign of Quantity and the Sign of the Times*, René Guénon described the decline of the West in terms of Cartesian rationalism's new criterion of knowledge. Whereas traditional societies had sought to understand their world in terms of higher referents (i.e., myths), Descartes and his successors countered that "real" (that is, practical) knowledge could only be had of quantifiable substances. This has meant that even human beings are now thought of in strictly rationalist terms, as clockwork mechanisms that can be subsumed into managerial political systems. Both capitalism and communism, for example, conceive of human beings in strictly economic terms. Against modernity's "reign of quantity," so aptly diagnosed by Guénon and the Traditionalists, the New Right seeks to restore to the political a "destining vision" beyond purely material concerns.

Neopaganism: In the second volume of *TYR*, considerable space was given to examining Benoist's paganism, therefore a great deal more need not be said here. Important to keep in mind is that the paganism embraced by the New Right has little in common with the New Age paganism embraced by American Wiccans, which is itself typical of the postmodern subcultures thinkers like Benoist condemn. Like proponents of more historically based reconstructionist religions, New Rightists see the return to paganism as the return to Europe's indigenous origins, a source from which a new, "destining" power might yet be claimed.

This paganism is also largely reactionary, and sets itself up as a foil to Europe's supposedly Christian heritage. Benoist rearticulates much of Nietzsche's assessment of Christianity as a "slave morality," which elevates the weak at the expense of all that is healthy, beautiful, or strong. More importantly, however, Christianity might be said to embody all that is worst in postmodernism, while paganism embodies its more beneficial aspects. Paganism makes no claims to absolute truth, and acknowledges its own perspectival nature. Pagan religions are the provenance of specific peoples; as such, they act as a force of cultural conservatism, without threatening the distinct cultures of others. Christianity, on the other hand, launches a dual attack on the very notion of community. It exalts the individual by making salvation an entirely personal concern, while devaluing culture in favor of its own universal ethic. In this sense, it is also the precursor of liberalism, in that it was the first creed to divorce itself from any one specific people or place, and to declare itself the absolute arbiter of truth for all peoples in all places. It is this homogenizing tendency that the New Right opposes in liberalism and Christianity alike.

One practical problem with New Right paganism is its almost wholly intellectual nature, not to mention the fact that it defines itself primarily in terms of *what it is not*. Of course, the question as to whether or not paganism could really be revived in the modern world is still an open one—and attempts in this direction have often resulted in the worst absurdities. (Just this morning, I read a news story about a British neo-Druid arrested for carrying his ritual sword into a hardware store.) But if Europeans are to re-engage with their pagan origins, as a means towards "actualizing their heritage," this will have to take place in something more than a purely abstract and theoretical sense.

Völkisch Communitarianism: Just as the New Right identifies Christianity as "the first assault on European identity," and thus on the very notion of community, so too does it reject the modern nation state. This may come as a surprise, since the "Right" has typically been defined in terms of its nationalism, as much as by its radical critique of liberalism. But the New Right is quick to point out that the state is inorganic, based only on contractual obligations, while a true community must be bound by ties of blood and culture, and would resemble, in some respects, an extended family. As such, it could never attain the scale of modern nations which are far too vast and encompassing to ever represent the individual interests of their constituent parts.

While groups like the GRECE would like to see far more regional and local autonomy they also envision a situation in which these regional units would come together to provide for each other's defense. This could take the form of a federated Europe. Nevertheless, the New Right rejects the direction European Union has taken, since it subjugates the political to the economic. What is needed is a new *imperium*, a Europe united around a common spiritual vision. This would be distinct from imperialism, in which geographic expansion is merely a tool for opening up new markets.

Perhaps the most difficult (or at least the most sobering) chapter in O'Meara's book is the one in which he examines the New Right's chief nemesis: America. Long before the collapse of the Soviet Union, Benoist and his associates recognized that the United States posed a far greater threat to the world's indigenous cultures than the Soviet East. America was founded in opposition to Old Europe, and the New Right sees its entire subsequent history unfolding as the direct antithesis of everything the traditional world represents. Of course, this critique is by necessity overly simplistic, since it must ignore many divergent trends within American society itself. But insofar as America can be treated as an idea, it must be admitted that the New Right's analysis is largely correct.

For writers like Benoist, America can be understood in terms of its rationalism and its Protestant religious heritage. Although both originated in a European context, they were allowed to develop unchecked in the New World, where ties of blood and history were more easily discarded. Despite the country's Anglo-Saxon origins, "Americans" are not a people but a conglomeration of peoples with little or nothing in common (a situation that has become particularly acute in recent years, as immigration has turned the U.S. into a veritable refugee camp). What makes one an American is adherence to the creed embodied in the Constitution and other rationalist political documents; each citizen is afforded the same rights, being equal in the eyes of the law. Of course, this precludes any form of natural hierarchy, and makes industriousness (and the acquisition of money) the sole determiner of worth. Protestantism evinces a similar disregard for caste or culture and celebrates the "self-made man" whose success in business becomes a sign of heavenly distinction. It is no coincidence that Americans have created comparably little of lasting cultural value. (There are exceptional American writers and artists, but they have often been rejected by their countrymen, or migrated overseas where they were better appreciated. The expatriate American littérateur is a well-worn cliché.) In the long run, the American model—in which everyone is reduced to an "individual" with no past or communal attachments, and wholly absorbed by the marketplace—represents the most damaging course for Europe, but the one down which it seems to be inevitably heading.

Being an American himself, O'Meara qualifies this damning analysis by pointing out that the Old South never conformed to this vision (it had to be militarily defeated before it was brought to heel) or that the scores of Irish Catholics who settled here had a very different sensibility from that of their Protestant cousins. Books like David Hackett Fischer's *Albion's Seed* have amply demonstrated that European folkways have survived in the U.S., particularly among the working classes, and despite the hostility of the dominant political culture. Nevertheless, any casual observer of America's vast suburban sprawl, with its endless assemblages of mini malls, fast food restaurants, and tract homes, must admit that there is something nightmarish in all that this country has become. The hatred much of the world feels for the U.S. is understandable enough, considering the sheer arrogance and self-righteousness inherent in America's perverse desire to export American "freedom" (the freedom to shop, the freedom to indulge in degenerate behavior—but not necessarily the freedom to think) to the rest of the world. Still, O'Meara would prefer to see the New Right's unilateral disdain for America mitigated by the recognition that the majority of Americans *are* at root Europeans, even if they have done their best to reject Europe itself. But the New Right has little patience for appeals to "white unity" (something which has never existed anyway), and has often sought alliances with Muslims and other Third World elements whose resistance to American globalization mirrors its own.

This is typical of O'Meara's criticisms, generally, as his own position is clearly more entrenched in the politics of race than is Benoist's. This is not to diminish the tremendous value of his scholarship and erudition. O'Meara's grasp of history, philosophy, and even contemporary pop culture gives his treatment of the New Right a far broader scope and depth than, say, the one presented in Tomislav Sunic's *Against Democracy and Equality* (a fine book in its own right, and as far as I'm aware, the only other English-language treatment of the GRECE and their allies). Furthermore, many of O'Meara's criticisms are valid regardless of his orientation. Most of these stem from the New Right's flirtation with postmodernism and thus with relativism. While this initially legitimated the New Right's defense of European culture (If it's okay to defend the indigenous cultures of others, then why is it not okay to defend our own?), it has ultimately divested this defense of much of its force. New Rightists are in practice true multiculturalists, whose recognition of the right of other cultures to exist now extends even to immigrant communities within Europe itself. This has led former GRECEists like Guillaume Faye to break with Benoist entirely, for betraying his original vision. But while O'Meara obviously sympathizes with Faye's contention that the immediate survival of European culture trumps any concerns over the rights of others, at least when these peoples encroach on the interests of Europeans, Benoist's acknowledgment of globalization as a *fact* which must be dealt with seems far more realistic. While the most desirable situation might be one in which the world's peoples are left to pursue their destinies within their own lands, rooted within the continuity of their own history, it seems inconceivable how this could come about now.

It is highly unfortunate that this groundbreaking study will never see print via a more reputable academic press—although this is in no way surprising. The New Right has long recognized liberalism's totalitarian aspirations, and its inability to accommodate dissent. Still, questions must be asked. Modernity is largely the actualization of the liberal ideology. Has it made the world a better place? Has it made us better people? Even if these questions are relegated to the fringes of acceptable discourse, they demand answers.

Joshua Buckley

The Longing for Myth in Germany: Religion and Aesthetic Culture from Romanticism to Nietzsche by George S. Williamson. Hardbound, 428 pages with bibliography and index. Chicago: University of Chicago Press, 2004. ISBN 0-226-89945-4.

In the inaugural issue of *TYR*, an article was devoted to the concept of "integral culture." Of course, the desire for cultural holism is nothing new. As George Williamson demonstrates, it was a significant component of the Romantic movement in Germany, fueled largely by the popular discovery of classical Greece. The Ancient Greek language became part of the German educational curriculum in the 1700s, inspiring a generation of neo-humanist scholars who saw the classical world as an organic and sensual whole, where the deep divisions characteristic of Western politics, religion, and art had not yet occurred. This would lead to the rediscovery of Germany's own mythic and cultural heritage and ignited in many the desire to formulate a new myth that could reconstitute German culture as an aesthetic and spiritual totality. This vision took many forms, and was set largely against the ongoing *Kulturkampf* between Protestantism and Catholicism. Williamson proves adept at maneuvering his way through the many groups and individuals involved in this discourse, providing both substantive background for, and detailed expositions of, their ideas. Many of these ideas have shaped the sense in which we understand myth today. Furthermore, Williamson has provided unparalleled access to a fundamental phase of the Germanic Revival seldom examined in such depth.

Johann Gottfried von Herder was a key figure in this revival, articulating ideas that would spur interest in Germany's mythic heritage for several generations to come. He was the first to describe the concept of the *Volk*, and highlighted the importance of myth as a "distinctive fusion of poetry and religion that expressed the essential spirit of a nation." Thus, it might be concluded, Christianity was unsuited for the Germanic people since it was an expression of the Jewish *Volk*. This idea fit well with recent biblical scholarship which, following Spinoza, had begun to question the literal truth of the Bible and to see the biblical narrative in its historical and cultural context—and as myth. Herder would even debate the merits of reviving the Eddic mythology as a more authentic expression of the German spirit, although ultimately he rejected this as prohibitively problematic. Later neopagan movements would show fewer reservations. Herder's real interest lay in creating a Germanic Protestantism cut loose from its moorings in the Old Testament, and displaying a continuity instead with the world of pagan antiquity.

The first calls for a "new mythology" among Romantics like Schelling and Schlegel were not based in a desire to resurrect paganism. Rather, it was the impetus provided by the French Revolution that resulted in calls for a religious melding of art and science that would give Europe a new galvanizing vision. Schelling, for instance, suggested that the gods of a new pan-European religion would arrive via the deification of history. But Herder's belief in the innate connection between a people and its myths lead instead to a growing fascination with the *Vorzeit* (roughly, prehistory). If Christianity had fragmented the integral culture of the ancient world—as Schlegel had declared—then perhaps a re-engagement with Germany's pre-Christian origins could help restore it.

Herder saw Christianity through the lens of contemporary European imperialism, as an occupying power. "Even Christianity," he wrote, "insofar as it works as the state machine of foreign peoples, oppresses them terribly. Among some it mutilates their unique character, so that even one-and-a-half millennia cannot make it right. Don't we wish that the spirit of Nordic peoples, the Germans, Gauls, the Celts, the Slavs, etc. had been able to spring forth pure and undisturbed out of themselves?" Jacob Grimm echoed this sentiment. His *Deutsche Mythologie* was the most groundbreaking study of its time and Grimm can largely be credited with the creation of Germanic philology as an academic discipline. He stressed the continuity between pagan and modern times and was one of the first to speculate on the connections between surviving folklore and customs and pre-Christian religion. He was also one of the first to identify the many pagan elements that Christianity had absorbed. But Grimm, like many of his contemporaries, also projected his own Protestant values onto the ancient Germans. Like the largely forgotten Franz Josef Mone, who had attempted to unravel the mythology of the *Edda* in terms of its supposed neo-Platonic symbolism, Grimm attempted to find traces of monotheism in the ancient Germanic worldview, making Wotan the center of the pantheon and describing the other gods as his lesser emanations. Grimm also anticipated modern advocates of "Goddess spirituality" by describing Nerthus as but one manifestation of a universal Great Goddess. But if Grimm believed that "monotheism is something so necessary and essential" other writers were not so sure—already, the values of polytheism were being reconsidered. Feuerbach, who would have considerable influence on the composer Richard Wagner, wrote that "science, like art, arises only out of polytheism, for polytheism is the frank, open, unenvying sense of all that is beautiful and good without distinction, the sense of the world, of the universe."

Wagner, of course, was more successful than any of his contemporaries in formulating a new mythology, while simultaneously popularizing the gods of Germanic antiquity. Upon discovering Grimm's *Deutsche Mythologie* he gushed "there rose up in my soul a whole world of figures ... the effect they produced upon my innermost being I can only describe as a complete rebirth." The early Wagner, like Herder and Grimm, saw the introduction of Christianity as an event that had devastated the ancient world, bringing about the "political, social, and sexual alienation caused by the collapse of pagan mythology." Nevertheless, Wagner did not advocate neopaganism. Like the Romantics, he hoped for a rapprochement between nature and human culture that would overcome these rifts. This would not be a solution for Germans alone. Wagner envisioned a revolution suitable for a new universal *Volk*, consisting of all mankind (a position seemingly at odds with the composer's infamous anti-Semitism). The unifying catalyst for such a dramatic world-revolution would be the *Gesamtkunstwerk* ("total work of art"), of which Wagner, in his guise as prophet, would be the creator. The later Wagner would amend these views significantly, due largely to the influence of Schopenhauer. He would even reconcile himself with Christianity, which he reinterpreted as consonant with Schopenhauerian pessimism. This was of course what led to the final break with Nietzsche, who would himself write extensively on myth, famously delineating the divide between the Apollonian and the Dionysian. But while Nietzsche lamented the fact that the departure of Apollo and Dionysus had consigned subsequent generations to a "mythless existence," he rejected all received metaphysical systems. The *Übermensch* of the future, though thoroughly pagan in spirit, would rely only on the myths that he himself created, while recognizing their fundamental subjectivity and untruth.

Inevitably, perhaps, Williamson sees the *völkisch* movement as it emerged between 1890–1920 as the logical successor to these first serious forays into Germany's pre-Christian past. Neopaganism would develop as an outright rejection of Christianity, although Houston Stewart Chamberlain's efforts to "Aryanize" Christ's teachings were far more representative. Williamson also sheds light on developments during this period that would have more resonant echoes in the present. Comparative mythology appeared as a viable discipline thanks to scholars like Adalbert Kuhn and Friedrich Max Müller. Debates about the historicity of the Bible (such as the one between the "right" and "left" Hegelians) would ultimately lead writers like David Friedrich Strauss to begin the work of serious biblical criticism, virtually unheard of before. And Herder's insight that the myths of specific peoples were representative of their "folk psychology," can probably be credited with the now largely accepted connection between myth and psychology, generally. It was also during this period that the innate value of polytheism, as a worldview of equal or greater worth than monotheism, began to be considered. All of this makes *The Longing for Myth in Germany* a valuable piece of intellectual history—particularly as it represents a facet of European cultural development that has not been so fully examined in the English language before.

Joshua Buckley

Against the Modern World: Traditionalism and the Secret Intellectual History of the Twentieth Century by Mark Sedgwick. Hardcover, 370 pages with glossary, bibliography, and index. New York: Oxford University Press, 2004. ISBN 0-19-515297-2.

You might wonder why we have decided to review Mark Sedgwick's 2004 history of Traditionalism twice—the first review appears as an essay earlier in this issue, and was written by the Hungarian Traditionalist Róbert Horváth. Horváth's critique is informed by his own position *vis-à-vis* the movement (a term to which he objects, at least insofar as Traditionalism is concerned) and is therefore the product of a very specific perspective. In this review, I hope to address some of Horváth's criticisms, to offer a few of my own, and to examine elements of Sedgwick's work that Horváth has only touched on or, in certain cases, ignored altogether. Hopefully, I can avoid too much repetition. Even if you find Sedgwick's work objectionable, it is a testament to his book that it demands this much attention. *Against the Modern World* is groundbreaking and controversial, detailed and thought-provoking—yet not without flaws.

To begin with, it should be pointed out that Sedgwick's research has been savaged by a number of Traditionalist reviewers: Horváth is not alone. While some of these writers have valid grievances, their criticisms often reveal more about Traditionalism than they do about Sedgwick's book. First and foremost, while his critics see "Tradition" as a set of unbending metaphysical principles—transcending time and space and informing the world's great religions—Sedgwick treats Traditionalism as an all-too-human phenomenon, with roots that can be traced to other ideologies, books, and occult organizations. This is his main affront. The second is dwelling on the (at times unflattering) biographical details of the lives of Tradition's leading proponents. From a Traditionalist viewpoint, these details are inconsequential; furthermore (these critics will argue), René Guénon was not an original thinker or the founder of a "movement." He was merely a vessel who allowed Tradition's perennial truths to speak through him. This is the view taken in *The Simple Life of René Guénon*, an "approved" biography by Guénon's lifelong collaborator, Paul Chacornac.

Of course, Sedgwick is *not* a Traditionalist, and there is something vaguely ridiculous about demanding that he write from a Traditionalist perspective. Moreover, Sedgwick is writing a history, and not an inventory of Traditionalist ideas—although the latter is obviously what his critics would have preferred. In a history it is perfectly reasonable to provide details about the personal lives of one's subjects, or to consider how their philosophy was formulated. Sedgwick's readers seem mortified to think that Guénon "got" his ideas from anywhere. Yet pointing out that a thinker had certain philosophical precedents hardly serves to discredit him. The same is true of his personal life. Sedgwick may demonstrate that Guénon or (especially) Frithjof Schuon could engage in unsavory personal behavior, but here again, this tells us almost nothing about the truth of their ideas. On this point, especially, Sedgwick seems to give Traditionalism the benefit of the doubt. One wonders why his Traditionalist readers are so adamantly unwilling to do the same for him.

That said, I have my own criticisms of Sedgwick's work—though my views are considerably more charitable than Horváth's. Mainly, I think Sedgwick is overly ambitious in trying to demonstrate Traditionalism's influence on "the secret intellectual history of the twentieth century." He sees evidence of Traditionalism almost everywhere, although this often amounts to little more than the fact that a given author has read Guénon's books. After drawing so many disparate elements into the "Traditionalist" orbit, Sedgwick tries to make sense of the whole muddle by creating categories such as "hard Traditionalism," "soft Traditionalism," and "political Traditionalism." On his website he has even spoken of "scene Traditionalism." This is connected with the neofolk and post-industrial music genres; in its more "serious" manifestations, it is represented by the journal *TYR!*

Contra Sedgwick, I would contend that the only "real" Traditionalists are the so-called "hard Traditionalists." These are writers like Guénon, Schuon, Ananda Coomaraswamy, and Julius Evola (despite the attempt of some present-day Traditionalists to excise him from their ranks, largely for political reasons) who openly declared themselves representatives of the current, and promoted its ideas in nearly all of their books, articles, and lectures. Traditionalism represents an absolute set of principles, and for this reason it seems strained to ascribe a Traditionalist viewpoint to writers who were merely influenced by Tradition. The same goes for those who accept certain Traditionalist postulates while openly rejecting others (I would probably place myself in this category). The influence of Traditionalism on the popular writer E. F. Schumacher, for example, seems rather negligible, and the fact that he—in turn—was widely read by members of the environmentalist movement tells us almost nothing about Traditionalism itself. The same goes for Sedgwick's chapter on Russia. He shows that writers like Alexander Dugin have read Guénon with approval, and have espoused Traditionalist ideas in the past. Their most formidable creation, however, is Eurasianism, a geopolitical philosophy with no appreciable connection to Traditionalism at all. By the chapter's end, Sedgwick is tracing the reception of Dugin's political ideology amongst certain radical Right groups in Israel—although even he admits that he has wandered woefully off topic. Lastly, there seems to be little reason for the inclusion of Rudolf von Sebottendorf in a book about Traditionalism, except for the fact that he was a European who experimented with Sufism. Horváth may be right that Sedgwick's real reason for invoking Sebottendorf is the "scandal" of his subsequent involvement with "occult Nazism."

Which, finally, brings us to the very strange case of Aristasia. Sedgwick spends several pages discussing "Aristasian Traditionalism," although he cites only one Aristasian book in which Guénon is mentioned (Nietzsche, Sedgwick admits, figures much more prominently). A cursory perusal of Aristasia's voluminous website reveals no mention of any major Traditionalist author and I can find no instance of any Aristasian referring to herself as a "Traditionalist"—although it is certainly possible that this has happened. It appears that most of Sedgwick's information about Aristasia is gleaned from the aforementioned website, and I am somewhat suspicious that his account of the group's origins in the

1960s is simply an Internet-generated myth. So what, exactly, *is* Aristasia? It is difficult to say. Aristasians characterize their activities as "life theatre." At their gatherings, members dress in pre-1950s costumes and attempt to recreate the "Aristasian" world (alternately described as a sort of mindset or, more recently, another planet) through role-playing. This is a world in which men do not exist, women are divided into "blondes" and "brunettes" (blondes are essentially *femmes*, while brunettes assume more masculine—though certainly not "butch"—roles), and hierarchy is enforced through a strict regimen of corporal punishment. Aristasians *are* anti-modern—they reject the workaday reality outside "Aristasia" (which they call "The Pit") for many of the same reasons Traditionalists reject modernity. They also profess certain religious convictions, although their Goddess-worship and matriarchal beliefs are in fact an inversion of Traditionalist doctrines. A far more significant impetus behind the group seems to be their obsessive sexual fetishism (though, I should point out, they vehemently deny this). The fact that this fetishism appears more indicative of masculine than feminine psychology raises yet another disturbing question about who, exactly, is behind the "feminine universe."

The Aristasian episode is interesting on a number of levels. First, it shows just how far Sedgwick is willing to go in his efforts to ferret out Traditionalist "influence." Second, it demonstrates how academic research can become distorted when representations made on the Internet are taken at face value. Amusingly, this has now come full circle. Obviously inspired by Sedgwick's book (and probably his blog, where he continues to provide updates about Aristasia) Troy Southgate's Synthesis website now lists Aristasia as a Traditionalist group, run by "neo-Evolian disciplinarians." An obscure Maltese nationalist organization also categorizes Aristasia as part of the European "New Right." Is it possible that they have never followed their own link, and actually *looked* at Aristasia's website? We will probably never know, since on the Internet, all reality is merely *virtual*.

Although Aristasia proves to be something of a dead end for Sedgwick, he succeeds rather brilliantly in delineating the influence of Traditionalism in two other important areas. The first concerns the famous scholar of comparative religion, Mircea Eliade. There has been an academic reappraisal of Eliade under way for some time now, although this often focuses on his youthful involvement with the Romanian Iron Guard while ignoring his actual work. Many of these *ad hominem* attacks can be quite nasty, and it is unfortunate that Sedgwick has chosen to situate his discussion in a chapter on "Fascism." Nevertheless, he makes a very convincing argument that in the case of Eliade, Traditionalism was an overwhelmingly significant—yet largely unacknowledged (and therefore "secret")—influence. There are several reasons for Eliade's reticence about his debt to Traditionalism. When challenged about this by Julius Evola, he explained: "the books I write are for today's audience, and not for initiates." More importantly, Eliade was writing for an academic readership, and he recognized the fact that the "Traditionalists sometimes denied the evidence of history and completely ignored the factual data gathered by researchers." (Ironically, Eliade himself has been accused of "uncritical universal generalization.") Eliade also felt that Guénon went too far in rejecting almost every facet of modern civilization. Nevertheless, Eliade's attempt to construct a cross-cultural model of human religiosity, his belief in the power of "archaic religion," and his focus on "primordialism" (for which "perennialism" could just as easily be substituted) are *essentially* Traditionalist. Earlier, I questioned whether the fact that a given author had encountered certain Traditionalist ideas was enough to make him one of Sedgwick's "soft Traditionalists." Eliade's repackaging of Traditionalist themes for a popular and scholarly audience, and the continuing resonance that this project has had with the educated public, would seem to justify precisely this conclusion.

The second area where Sedgwick convincingly shows the impact of the Traditionalist movement concerns the Western reception of Islam. This is especially pertinent in the last decade or so, as Europe has experienced a massive influx of Muslim immigration. The September 11 attacks, the ongoing wars in Iraq and Afghanistan, and the volatile issues of oil and Israel make Samuel Huntington's by now clichéd thesis about a "clash of civilizations" seem more and more prophetic. Traditionalists like Guénon and Schuon were some of the first modern Europeans to convert to Islam, and it remains the case that many Westerners who do the same today (excluding Black Muslims, who are another matter altogether), do so under the banner of Tradition. But Sedgwick shows that the form of Islam promoted in Traditionalist orders like Schuon's Maryamiyya is anything but orthodox. This is especially true when it comes to their *laissez-faire* attitude about Sharia law— a crucial point, since the very word *Islam* means "submission." Furthermore, Traditionalists liberally conflate Islam and Sufism in their books and articles, although the two are relatively distinct (most Sufis are Muslims, but most Muslims are *not* Sufis). Sedgwick makes the very useful observation that the widely read books on Islam by Schuon and Seyyed Hossein Nasr are actually espousing ideas that are peculiar to Sufism. In the Muslim world, they represent a minority viewpoint at best. Nevertheless, the Traditionalist take on Islam has now seeped into the Western popular consciousness. When HRH Prince Charles (who reads many Traditionalist authors) or President George W. Bush (who may not read anything at all) inform us that "Islam is a religion of peace"—in spite of the overwhelming evidence to the contrary—they may simply be repeating a notion indirectly popularized by the Traditionalists.

Sedgwick's work clearly suffers from certain methodological problems, and he often emphasizes material of questionable significance while downplaying what might have been more fruitful avenues of research. Another reason he has irritated Traditionalists is that he seems to delight in revealing every prurient detail of his subject's lives. While this might indicate a certain lapse in good taste, it does give *Against the Modern World* the quality of a real page-turner (despite being published by Oxford University Press, Sedgwick's style is at least one part Colin Wilson). To his tremendous credit, Sedgwick has used his website to correct many of his book's mistakes, and to engage in a dialogue with his detractors. He also addresses some of the issues I have raised in this review. It should also be added that while Sedgwick's stance is hardly uncritical, he obviously finds many Traditionalist concepts to be of philosophical and spiritual value. This makes some of the suggestions mentioned by Horváth—such as the idea that Sedgwick may be a "Euro-Atlantic spy" sent to hunt for "anti-modern ideas"—all the more absurd. On the other hand, these insinuations illustrate an unfortunate feature of Traditionalism which can be traced all the way back to René Guénon himself: paranoia.

Joshua Buckley

Confessions of a Radical Traditionalist: Essays by John Michell. Selected and Introduced by Joscelyn Godwin. Hardbound, 352 pages. Waterbury Center, Vermont: Dominion Press, 2005. ISBN 0-9712044-4-6.

Many readers will probably be familiar with John Michell's writings on a diverse array of esoteric topics. His career began with *The Flying Saucer Vision* (1967) and *The View Over Atlantis* (1969), both of which propelled him to vaunted status within the more mystically inclined outposts of the counterculture. Michell continues to occupy a rather strange niche. A true bohemian and eccentric, he is at the same time a genuine conservative—if the word is divested of its unfortunate political connotations. What Michell is trying to "conserve" are the timeless principles he finds embodied in Plato, hands down the master to whom he feels most indebted. He even puts in a kind word for the Victorians, whose chivalrous ideals and good manners stand out against the cynicism and vulgarity of us moderns. In an essay on William Cobbett, another prominent figure in the Michell canon, Michell describes pre-Reformation England as a society very close to the kind he himself clearly favors, "when a smiling countryside, replete with ancestral manors and farmsteads, was tended by skilled craftsmen and nurtured its large, native population in happiness and prosperity under the spell of religion." But Michell avoids the pitfalls of reactionary politicking such nostalgias might suggest. (For one thing, he is anything but a carping bore.) He knows full well that "piety and common sense, twin pillars of the old order, are today's lost causes."

Lost causes or not, Michell never descends into hopelessness or misanthropy, and seems to write with the conviction that people of good conscience can be made to see that there may be more to life than the powers-that-be (whoever they are) would like us to think. Even the progressivists, the natural enemies of tradition, are not personally to blame. "These people are everywhere," Michell writes, "setting up progress and novelty as the first principle in art, religion, philosophy and other inappropriate fields—not with evil intent, but because they recognize no higher values." These higher values have been subverted by a host of modern "isms," all of which Michell duly snubs: materialism, scientism, atheism, Marxism (and economism in general), and Darwinism. While each might describe certain facets of reality, they close us off to the sacred qualities of life, the intangible values that cannot be quantified, bought, sold, or downloaded on a computer. Michell rejects metrication because the meter is arbitrary while the foot relates the human body to the dimensions of the earth and is the basis of sacred geometry. He pleads for the restoration of the fireplace to the center of the home, as this kept our forefathers "centered"—literally. When he writes of strange phenomena, in the spirit of Charles Fort, it is largely to restore a sense of wonder the puffed-up experts have denied us. These are baby steps to be sure, but the Path has long been obscured and littered with all manner of detritus.

In many instances, Michell's observations are wholly (and pleasantly) unexpected. On the question of drug legalization, he suggests that the status quo might be perfectly adequate despite the absurdities of prohibition. After all, the underground networks necessitated by the trade's illicit nature have been the seedbed for most of the truly vital art and culture to appear in the last thirty years. On compulsory education, he bucks the virtually universal view that it is an unmitigated good. Perhaps, Michell opines, the world was a better place when the vast majority could not read or write and education (at least in the liberal arts) was the province of those (like himself) with a particular aptitude and inclination. Michell was perhaps the only British writer not to embrace Salman Rushdie when an Islamic *fatwa* was infamously issued against him, and elsewhere he speaks sympathetically of a religion that may be the "one formidable source of opposition … against the spread of secularism, usury and the spread of materialism." I am not so sure I agree with Michell, however, that Islam's extremes will eventually be tempered—they seem too much a component of its central doctrines. Whereas Christianity has always had its fanatics, their behavior cannot be attributed to Christ himself. The same cannot be said of the Prophet.

Joscelyn Godwin has done a masterful job of compiling the essays represented here and his introduction is entirely worthy of the work itself. Michell is a fabulous stylist, whose charm and sincerity virtually radiate from the page. He has all the wit of a sagely curmudgeon, albeit without the mean-spiritedness, and is simultaneously quirky and levelheaded, idealistic and down-to-earth.

And his is a profoundly religious vision. While he is all too aware of the ugliness and depravity of the modern world, he is also open to its beauty. Like the good Platonist that he is, he submits to the idea that even modernity's worst excesses may simply be part of God's (or the gods') plan, transcending mere human understanding, but necessary nonetheless. This is the traditionalist's "long view," however irritating those with more activist leanings may find it. We do what little we can.

The Apocalypse may be upon us, but it is no excuse for bad manners—or bad writing.

(*A slightly different version of the above review appeared in* Rûna, *Issue 17.*)

Joshua Buckley

New Religions and the Nazis by Karla Poewe. Softcover, 218 pages with bibliography and index. New York: Routledge, 2006. ISBN 0-415-29025-2.

This is but the latest in an ever-expanding genre of books about Nazism's alleged occult or pagan origins; were one to compile a bibliography of similar titles it would no doubt fill several pages. This literature ranges from absurd historical fantasy to more reputable academic research. In both instances (and perhaps inevitably, considering the volatile nature of the topic), it is useful to ask why "occult Nazism" still exerts such fascination. Of course, the answer is often sheer sensationalism and the public's insatiable need for titillation. Indeed, it would not be unfair to characterize much of this material as pure political pornography. More importantly, the act of ascribing "occult" or "Satanic" motives to one's adversaries neatly dispenses with the need to deal with their ideas in any remotely productive way. One can simply label them "evil," and that is the end of that.

Discerning the motives behind Karla Poewe's research is easy enough: she belabors her point on virtually every page of the present volume. That point is two-fold. First, Poewe (the wife of evangelical Anglican Irving Hexham) wants to exonerate the Church from any complicity in the Third Reich. Second, she hopes to draw parallels between the *völkisch* subculture in pre-Nazi and Nazi Germany and the "cultic milieu" of the postmodern West. The intent is to construct a highly questionable slippery slope. Today: Goddess worship, crystals, Tibetan singing bowls, and handfasting ceremonies. Tomorrow: gas chambers and secret police. This may sound a bit far-fetched to the average reader, but it is apparently the sort of logic that keeps Christians—even highly educated Christians like Poewe—awake at night.

The star of Poewe's narrative is Jakob Wilhelm Hauer, a professor of religious studies and Indology, and the founder of the German Faith Movement. Hauer's story is reconstructed through the author's extensive research in German archives where she combed through stacks of government documents, *völkisch* periodicals, and personal correspondence. Unfortunately, this story is not presented as a straightforward biography (so far as I know, no such biography of Hauer exists in the English language), and Hauer's ideas are never systematically explained. Instead, what we get is a fragmented account of the German Faith Movement's development and an almost mind-numbing inventory of the doctrinal and organizational controversies within it. This is arranged so as to make Poewe's point, alluded to above: Hauer was not a Christian, *ergo* Nazism was not Christian. While the first statement is undoubtedly true, the second can hardly be said to follow. Like many misguided intellectuals of the time (the philosopher Martin Heidegger being a much more prominent example), Hauer believed he could personally influence the Nazi movement, and Poewe takes him at his word when he declares that German Faith is the "essence of National Socialism." The problem is, she fails to make a case that practically anyone in the Party leadership agreed with him.

In fact, Poewe's thesis is contradicted on page after page of her own book. She tells us about Hauer's forced resignation from the SS and relates that his followers within the organization were subjected to "harsh and critical observation." She claims that many leading Nazis were "influenced" by Hauer, but can substantiate this only by saying that the admittedly eccentric Rudolf Hess was "inclined" toward German Faith. Many "important leaders" were members of Hauer's group. Yet here again, the most notable example given is Professor Herman Wirth, another eccentric (even by Third Reich–standards) who was removed from the Ahnenerbe and forbidden to publish. The fact of the matter is that the Nazis declared their commitment to "positive Christianity" time and time again, and actively persecuted those *völkisch* groups that actually were followers of alternative religions. Even Poewe concedes that 75 percent of the SS described themselves as adherents of Christianity, although they "expressed their hatred of it in letters." One wonders what Poewe could be referring to. Has she read every letter written by every active member of the SS? Hitler himself was probably insincere in his own professions of belief, but this hardly means that he was a follower of Hauer. The only evidence Poewe gives for Hitler's hostility toward the churches is a statement allegedly uttered in the presence of Hermann Rauschning. As to the reliability of Rauschning, Hitler biographer Ian Kershaw has written: "I have on no single occasion cited Hermann Rauschning's *Hitler Speaks*, a work now regarded to have so little authenticity that it is best to disregard it altogether." Poewe, apparently, feels differently.

Hauer's movement was influential but it was hardly "the essence of National Socialism." And while Hauer was definitely not a Christian, it is somewhat questionable whether or not he was a "pagan"—a term Poewe uses rather loosely. In fact (if we take Poewe's analysis at face value), "German Faith" seems to have been a fairly vague and indistinct set of ideas. Part of the reason it was successful was that it could encompass virtually anyone within the *völkisch* movement. Actual pagans like Ludwig Fahrenkrog were members, as were German Protestants who rejected Catholic universalism and the (Jewish) Old Testament. Even the Zionist philosopher Martin Buber was a personal friend of Hauer's, and engaged in a mutual ongoing dialogue with German Faith.

So what, exactly, did the "Faithlers" believe? Hauer himself was essentially a perennialist. He taught that there was one universal truth, manifested to different peoples through different—and mutually exclusive—cultural frameworks. The first issue of Hauer's journal announced that his followers, unlike literalist Christians, "do not believe the eternal ground of things was only revealed to Israel ... but that it is revealed in a special way to each *Volk*." He traced the "Indo-Germanic" revelation of this "eternal ground of things" through his idiosyncratic readings of the *Bhagavad-Gîtâ*, the *Eddas* and Icelandic sagas, and the writings of German Christian mystics like Meister Eckhart. Even the German Idealist tradition could be viewed as part of this unfolding. Like his friend Rudolf Otto, Hauer eschewed religious dogmatism in favor of religious experience. His ethical system was a fairly typical (for the time, anyway) blend of popular Nietzscheanism and the peculiarly masculine values of the war generation. Nevertheless, Hauer's movement (and Hauer himself) attracted a large female following, another reason—Poewe informs us—that he was regarded with suspicion by the Nazis.

Poewe does succeed in demonstrating Hauer's influence on the post-war Right, although she casually lumps together radical-conservative political parties, New Right groups like the GRECE and the Thule Seminar, and outright neo-Nazis. Most notable is Hauer's influence on Heidegger's former student, the best-selling author Sigrid Hunke. Hunke has been a key figure in the German Unitarians (not to be confused with the Unitarian Universalist Association), who profess a monism similar to Hauer's. Like Hauer, Hunke argues in her 1969 book *Europe's Other Religion* that there is a hidden, European (or, in Hauer's terminology, Indo-Germanic) tradition, traceable from pre-Christian times down through ostensibly Christian thinkers like Johannes Scotus Eriugena, Jacob Böhme, and Eckhart. This argument figures prominently in Alain de Benoist's 1981 book *On Being a Pagan*. All of this is well and good, until we reach the crux of Poewe's argument. She seems to suggest that the "paganism" of the New Right (which can hardly be equated with Nazism, anyway) is somehow indistinguishable from more popular New Age and neopagan New Religious Movements. These movements, she warns at the book's conclusion, may not be compatible with "western liberal democracies." This poorly reasoned alarmism seems unworthy of Powe's intelligence. It is, however, fully consistent with her Christian apologist agenda.

Unfortunately, that agenda seems to override Poewe's better judgment at almost every turn. She implicates much of Eastern philosophy in the crimes of the SS, pointing out that Himmler (like Hauer) was interested in the *Bhagavad-Gîtâ*. Thus, Poewe sees Nazi ruthlessness as an extension of the philosophy of detachment one finds in, say, Buddhism. The entire Indo-European worldview (unlike the obviously superior Judeo-Christian one) is characterized by Poewe in terms of its "lack of ethics." Contradicting virtually every Nietzsche scholar (including Nietzsche's famous Jewish translator, Walter Kaufman), Poewe inform us that Nietzsche was, in fact, an anti-Semite (although this view is "usually blamed on his sister"). The proof? His opposition to Christianity. In one of the book's strangest and most seemingly irrelevant digressions, Poewe explains that the emphasis on male bonding, "male force," and "male bias" within Nazi military organizations was not surprising, since "homoeroticism was rampant and homosexuality practiced." Does Poewe draw the same conclusions about the United States Marine Corps, another organization that relies primarily on "male force" and male bonding? Furthermore, one wonders how she has established the extent to which homosexuality was "practiced." While there were undoubtedly homosexual men in groups like the SS and SA, it is doubtful that they discussed their trysts in their archived correspondence. Of course, if one is particularly concerned with carnal sins, the suggestion that the entire Nazi Party was "gay" serves as further proof that it was not Christian. And that is precisely the point.

New Religions and the Nazis is not without value; unlike most books about *völkisch* religion, it is based on genuine historical sources. Nevertheless, if anything at all is to be gained from Poewe's not inconsiderable scholarship, the reader must be prepared to see beyond her distorting ideological lens.

Joshua Buckley

The Last Pagan: Julian the Apostate and the Death of the Ancient World by **Adrian Murdoch.** Hardbound, 255 pages with bibliography and index. Gloucestershire: Sutton Publishing, 2003. ISBN 0-7509-3295-3.

The Emperor Julian, more popularly known as Julian the Apostate (the name his enemies bestowed on him), may be the closest thing neopaganism has to a saint. He was the last pagan emperor of a Roman Empire that had been Christianized in 313 by his uncle Constantine, and his attempts at a pagan counter-reformation were guided by an idealism that persisted despite his failure to turn back the tide. He was, in the end, one of history's "beautiful losers."

Julian's early life was marred by conflict. Upon the death of Constantine in 337, almost his entire family was put to death in the inevitable battle for succession, in which Constantine's son Constantius would ultimately prevail. Murdoch suggests that part of Julian's antipathy for Christianity may have been guided by the fact that it was the religion of his family's murderers. But his affinity for paganism was also a reflection of his active intellect. Julian was an ardent student of the classics, and therefore of the pagan philosophers. When the opportunity arose to complete his education in Greece he leapt at the chance. While there, he was initiated into the Eleusinian Mysteries and, as ruler, he modeled himself after Plato's benevolent despot and the Stoic model provided by Marcus Aurelius. He was an ardent disciple of Cybele and sacrificed to the goddess Bilbona before battles. Yet while

Julian made no secret of his sympathies, he waited until his rise to power and the death of his rival Constantius before announcing them.

It was Constantius's wife Eusebia who promoted Julian to Caesar, and many have speculated that their relationship may not have been strictly platonic—although Julian's relations with his wife Helena appear to have been remarkably chaste. As Caesar, Julian quickly turned himself from bookish intellectual into hardened warrior. He put himself through boot camp, lived and fought with his troops, and drank beer instead of wine as a show of solidarity with the soldiery. He fought rigorously against the Alemanni and other barbarians, and his victory at the battle of Strasbourg is typically considered his greatest military achievement. It was in fact his popularity with the military that most facilitated his rise to emperor after the decisive split with Constantius in 359. He marched against his cousin, who (providentially, it seems) died of fever before Julian could formally unseat him. As emperor, Julian was a remarkably enlightened leader. He worked to undo the obsequiousness of the imperial court and was surprisingly approachable. He despised bureaucracy and favored a decentralized administration with increased autonomy being granted to the provinces. Most progressively of all, he was a genuine believer in the rule of law, even when it contradicted his personal whims. But it is of course in his role as religious reformer that Julian is primarily known to history.

Julian attended Constantius's funeral shortly after taking power; it was the last time he would set foot in a church. In a pragmatic sense, he despised Christianity's intolerance and refusal to acknowledge the gods of the Roman state. But unlike Diocletian and Nero, Julian never actively persecuted the faithful. His harshest act consisted of banning believers from teaching the classics, which essentially cut them off from potential converts. This did not stop them from claiming martyrdom at his hands. Among other things, one particularly salacious writer accused him of condemning naked nuns to be eaten by pigs. Julian did manage to destabilize the church with his "edict of religious tolerance." This legalized most Christian heresies, and immediately plunged the church into schisms and petty bickering. Julian also threw his support behind the Jews, long the target of Christian anti-Semitism. Despite their monotheism, he admired the fact that Judaism was a tribal religion (like paganism) that did not proselytize and that held its ancestors in high regard. He promised to rebuild Jerusalem, both out of respect for the Jewish people and to prove Christ a liar. Ultimately, Julian aimed to beat the church at its own game by creating a sort of loosely centralized pagan federation, with local pagan priests serving as bishops.

In the end, of course, it was a plan that was doomed to fail. Paganism's strengths—its tolerance as well as its diversity and local character—are also its primary weaknesses. Christianity's successes can be largely ascribed to its universal ethic, its relatively uniform creed, and its basis in a single book. Monotheist fanaticism has further ensured its triumph against a paganism that does not seek to impose its will on others, but simply accepts them as they are. The situation in Julian's time was not unlike the conflict in the West between secular liberal societies and Islam. Western "tolerance" for Islam appears to be based on the idea that religious fanaticism can be moderated by assimilation, and seems to me a gross underestimation of how tenacious and intractable this fanaticism might be. We should remember that Christianity, after routing paganism throughout western and northern Europe, persisted for two thousand years, and has only recently given way to secularism—which would itself have been unthinkable had it not grown out of the bedrock of Christianity. This is not to say that paganism should ape Christianity's totalitarian aspirations. It is, however, simply realistic to acknowledge why paganism has often proven a lost cause historically.

Julian's short-lived reign ended with his death during a campaign against Shapur II. Ironically, this was a fight that had been brewing since Constantine's plans to Christianize the Zoroastrian Persians. The only certain fact is that Julian's fatal wound came from a spear. Virtually every other aspect of his death is shrouded in mystery, including the identity of his slayer. The most favorable account has him dying like Socrates, philosophically rhapsodizing about the nature of the soul. The most popular Christian version records his final words as "thou hast won, O Galilean!" Although street parties broke out in the heavily Christian city of Antioch (where Julian had always been hated), most Romans were saddened by the news of his death. Posterity would not be so kind and Julian would be memorialized time and again as one of the church's favorite bogeymen. One popular tale from the Middle Ages has him dying at the hands of Saint Mercurius, his assassination having been ordered by no less a figure than Jesus Christ himself. Julian would be invoked as a symbol of evil in Snorri's *Heimskringla*, and even

Milton found it necessary to condemn him.

Not surprisingly, later generations would temper these harsh assessments. Montaigne was one of the first to begin rehabilitating Julian's image, while, during the Age of Reason, writers like Voltaire claimed him as a predecessor, a leader who had shunned despotism and tried to rule like a true Philosopher King. The Swedish writer Viktor Rydberg wrote a sympathetic novel about Julian, and Nikos Kazantzakis composed a play entitled *Julian the Apostate*. Gore Vidal's novel *Julian*, perhaps the most accessible modern literary treatment, presents Julian not as the villain he has long been thought to be, but as a hero. Modern pagans, Julius Evola among them, have taken a similarly favorable view and I know of at least one neopagan organization that bears the emperor's name.

But while Julian would no doubt smile on the waning power of the "Galileans" it should be remembered that he saw paganism primarily as a force for social cohesion. It was the gods who sanctified the Empire, making Christianity's aggressive rejection of them tantamount to treason. The modern world is indeed drifting towards some form of paganism, if only in the sense that modern Western societies can now encompass any number of divergent belief systems and the citizenry serve a multitude of "gods." But these are the gods of solitary individuals, and their rise signifies the *dissolution* of the social body. As in the last days of Rome, it is questionable whether any antidote—whether spiritual, social, or political—can restore it.

Joshua Buckley

Our Troth Volume 1: History and Lore **compiled by Kveldúlf Hagan Gundarsson. Softcover, 576 pages with bibliography. Book Surge Publishing: North Charleston, South Carolina, 2006. ISBN 1-4196-3598-0.**

In the last few years, "print-on-demand" handbooks on Ásatrú and other variants of Germanic neopaganism have proliferated at an unprecedented rate. Bypassing even the most rudimentary quality controls exercised by real publishers (even New Age publishers!), these books are often poorly conceived, poorly written, and poorly edited. Few, if any, have ever superseded germinal texts like Edred Thorsson's *Book of Troth*—which begs the question why they are even necessary. Here, refreshingly, is a welcome exception.

I have my share of reservations about the Ring of Troth (whose members wrote and compiled *Our Troth*) as an organization—for one thing, I see Ásatrú as an ethnic religion (not unlike American Indian spirituality) best suited to those of Northern European descent. Gamlinginn sums up the Troth's very different position with his exhaustive declaration that "Ásatrú is freely open to anyone who wants to accept it, regardless of gender, race, colour, ethnicity, national origin, language, sexual orientation, or other divisive criteria." Besides reading like a civil service application, one wonders if he would demand that the Sioux, or other indigenous peoples, adopt a similar policy in regards to *their* religious organizations? That said, there is little other evidence here of the ongoing factionalism between "folkish" and "universalist" Ásatrú. Both camps are presented fairly and accurately, something for which I commend both the authors and editors. In fact, *Our Troth* is characterized throughout by a remarkably balanced tone, presenting scholarly arguments and background alongside the more speculative material one must expect from any reconstructionist religion. Academic debates, such as that between proponents and critics of Georges Dumézil's theory of tripartition, are given a full yet concise airing. Chapter Seven, "The Rebirth," is one of the best treatments of the modern resurgence of Germanic paganism I have seen, surpassing by far the work of academic outsiders like Jeffrey Kaplan or Mattias Gardell (the authors of *Radical Religion in America* and *Gods of the Blood*, respectively).

This second edition of *Our Troth* (the original was published privately in 1993 and quickly sold out) has been significantly reworked, although it still sticks to its original purpose of acting as a sort of textbook on Germanic paganism (a second volume, focusing on Troth practice, has also just been released). Despite representing the efforts of numerous contributors the finished product reads as a cohesive whole, and is remarkably well organized. The first section covers history, with chapters on the Stone Age, the Indo-Europeans, the Bronze Age, the Iron Age, the Migration and Vendel Ages, and the Viking Age. This is to-the-point and highly readable. The next section covers the Germanic gods and cosmology. Here, as throughout the text, scholarly research and subjective speculations are presented side-by-side—but are seldom confused. A brief discussion of pagan or heathen ethics follows, along with a truly exemplary guide to further reading.

Adding to the overall accessibility of the writing is the contributors' consistent use of foreign and archaic language, which is both appropriate and sparing. All too often this is a major flaw of similar works, where Old Norse or Old English terminology is used (often incorrectly) simply to create an aura of profundity. It is this kind of undeniable common sense on the part of the editors that will long distinguish *Our Troth* as one of the best books of its kind.

Joshua Buckley

Witches, Druids, and King Arthur by Ronald Hutton. Hardbound, 365 pages with notes and index. New York and London: Humbledon and London, 2003. ISBN 1-85285-397-2.

I have written of my admiration for Ronald Hutton before; his books are filled with fascinating information and I find his perspective both challenging and appealing. A professor of history at the University of Bristol, Hutton has written extensively on the English Reformation and the Stuart period. However, it was the publication of two books on the ritual year in Britain and one on indigenous, pre-Christian religion that launched him into debates ranging well beyond the walls of the Academy. Hutton has delved deep into the supposedly "pagan" origins of British folklore and he is unique in addressing both the available scholarly literature, as well as the immense store of popular writings on the subject. At times, this has led to wild denunciations. The feminist lecturer Max Dashu opined that she was "staggered by the intense anti-feminism" of *The Pagan Religions of the Ancient British Isles*, her histrionics apparently brought on by the fact that Hutton finds little evidence for Neolithic Goddess worship in the actual historical record. Still, Hutton's commanding study of modern pagan witchcraft, *The Triumph of the Moon*, has led to a fruitful mutual dialogue with the neopagan community. He has consistently maintained that while he questions Wicca's claims about its own history, he finds much to sympathize with in neopaganism itself. He has emerged as something of a scholar of this and other New Religious Movements.

Witches, Druids, and King Arthur consists of a series of essays conceived largely as addenda to Hutton's last few books, and follows very loosely the themes alluded to in the title. I have heard Hutton's writing described as "dry," but to the contrary, I have found him engaging, witty, and keenly perceptive. "How Myths are Made" confronts the historical falsifications often underlying national identity (the modern nation-state itself is a very recent creation, after all), from the "myth" of the Scottish kilt, to the process by which Augusta Hall and Lady Charlotte Guest helped create a self-consciously Welsh identity. Hutton is not trying to demolish the idea of nationhood, however, and his observations regarding the psychology inherent in nation building are typified by the insight that "people caught in a struggle to fashion themselves will commonly fashion nations in the process." The popular and academic reception of Arthur is examined as a reflection of the Zeitgeist. While Geoffrey Ashe's books were embraced by the counterculture of the late 1960s, Hutton draws an interesting parallel between the rough-and-tumble spirit of John Boorman's *Excalibur* and the anarchic ethos of punk. He qualifies his skepticism about "pagan survivals" with an examination of "Paganism in the Lost Centuries," and looks for historical precedents for ritual nudity in Wicca—and finds them, at least to some extent.

I found Hutton's brief history of modern Druidry to be of particular interest. Another utterly compelling piece concerns the influence of paganism on J. R. R. Tolkien and C. S. Lewis. This has been well documented in the case of Tolkien, of course, and Lewis's Narnia is liberally populated with figures from classical mythology. However, I was unaware of the extent to which the young Lewis was bedazzled by Norse mythology, and his own youthful identification with a Romantic paganism. In spite of his famous conversion to Christianity, Lewis maintained the (rather heretical) notion that there was some continuity between the old gods and the new, and this perhaps explains the many pagan allusions in his oeuvre. Even as a committed Christian apologist Lewis would make the startling admission that Germanic heathenry "contained elements which my religion ought to have contained and did not," and that he felt more attraction toward Norse gods "whom I disbelieved in than I had ever done (for) the true God while I believed."

Underlying his considerable abilities as a scholar, it is probably safe to say that Ronald Hutton feels something of this attraction as well.

Joshua Buckley

The Cross Goes North: Processes of Conversion in Northern Europe, AD 300–1300 edited by Martin Carver. Softcover, 588 pages with index. Rochester and Suffolk: Boydell/York Medieval Press, 2003. ISBN 1-84383-125-2.

This hefty anthology consists of thirty-seven papers, all of which were presented in the Viking city of York at a conference commemorating two millennia of Christianity. The articles are ordered both in terms of geography and chronology and roughly follow the trajectory of conversion alluded to in the volume's title. Thus we begin in the Celtic territories and end far afield in the Baltic, where Christianity arrived very late indeed.

The focus here is partially on written evidence but is mainly concerned with material culture and the "conversion" of the landscape—that is, the appropriation of pagan sites as Christian holy places, the erection of rune stones and other markers, and the placement and style of burials. Another theme is the role of women in the conversion process as well as the role of women in religion generally, both Christian and pre-Christian. Most of these essays deal with the inherent problems of gauging belief from material evidence. The period in question is one in which both pagan and Christian artifacts are found side by side, raising all sorts of questions for the archaeologist or historian. Are we dealing with incidences of dual faith, syncretism, or simply religious confusion? Nineteenth-century folklorists were perhaps overly enthusiastic in seeing pagan elements in every fairy tale and rural custom they examined, and the prevailing tone here is considerably more circumspect.

The Cross Goes North concludes with Heiki Valk's "Christianisation in Estonia: A Process of Dual Faith and Syncretism." Due to its placement on the geographic periphery and the fact that the Eastern Baltic was the last part of Europe to be converted, Estonia is part of a region where we can quite confidently speak of pagan survivals. Sacred groves, or *hiis*-sites, as well as many sacred stones and springs, were venerated well into the nineteenth and early twentieth century. Burial customs have persisted from the pre-Christian period, in which participants celebrate feasts on the graves of their ancestors. Most striking are the survivals of actual gods. Reports of a priest dedicated to a thunder god similar to Thor are related as late as 1644 and a fertility god named Peko was still being worshiped in the Orthodox Setomaa region in the early 1930s.

Other equally enticing articles in this collection include: "The Politics of Conversion in North Central Europe" by Przemstaw Urbanczyk, "Christian and Pagan Practice during the Conversion of Viking Age Orkney and Shetland" by James H. Barrett, "Pagans and Christians at a Frontier: Viking Burial in the Danelaw" by Julian D. Richards, and "Runestones and the Conversion of Sweden" by Linn Lager.

Joshua Buckley

Witches, Werewolves and Fairies: Shapeshifters and Astral Doubles in the Middle Ages by Claude Lecouteux. Softcover, 200 pages with bibliography and index. Rochester, Vermont: Inner Traditions, 2003. ISBN 0-89281-096-3.

Although published by an imprint known for works of speculative metaphysics, this is a scholarly work of extraordinary scope and erudition. The author, Claude Lecouteux, is a professor of medieval literature at the Sorbonne and his work here draws on source material ranging from classical and early Christian writings to Icelandic sagas and the records of the Inquisition. In this highly original book, he traces the many strange and contradictory notions about the human soul in early and medieval Christianity to pagan beliefs, shedding valuable light on neglected aspects of European folklore along the way.

Lecouteux takes as his starting point the Norse conception of the soul as triple in nature. He describes at length the *fylga* (female follower), the *hamr* (physical Double), and the *hugr* (active spirit), and spends considerable space discussing the manifestation of these concepts in Norse mythology and the sagas. However, Lecouteux does not see the triple soul as unique to the Germanic peoples: it is, rather, representative of pre-Christian cultures generally. Conversely, it is the much narrower Christian notion of soul (articulated most clearly by St. Augustine) that was an innovation and, in the opinion of Lecouteux, an aberration. Ecstatic experiences, including Christian visions, are understandable only in terms of the triple soul, which leaves the body as Double to travel in other realms. Belief in the Double is typical of the shaman (or professional ecstatic), and is found amongst the Sámi as well as the lesser-known Hungarian Taltós.

Most intriguing is Lecouteux's assertion that the Double lays at the root of popular stories of lycanthropy and that many other aspects of medieval folklore can be explained in terms of the triple soul. Fairies, for example, carry out the same function in the Celtic cosmology that the *fylga* does in Germanic thought. While most academics now dispute the idea of a historical witch-cult, Lecouteux does not reject every story of witchery out of hand—particularly those concerning astral travel and out-of-body experiences. He relates these to doubling, and spends some time considering "witches salves"—herbal, and very possibly psychotropic, preparations like those used by shamans in most traditional cultures.

Surprisingly, and despite the consistently scholarly tone, Lecouteux treats his subject with unmistakable sympathy and enthusiasm. He contrasts traditional beliefs about the soul with those imposed by Christianity and clearly favors the former. *Witches, Werewolves, and Fairies* represents a substantial riposte to the idea that Europe's conversion to Christianity was an unmitigated advance, or that pre-Christian pagan cosmologies ever lacked for nuance, subtlety, or metaphysical depth.

Joshua Buckley

Sengoídelc: Old Irish for Beginners by David Stifter. Syracuse: Syracuse University Press, 2006. Softbound, 384 pages, with illustrations, tables, bibliography, and index. ISBN 978-0815630722.

The value of learning a language other than one's mother tongue cannot be overestimated. This applies on various levels. The commonly held notion among many modern English monoglots that "everything of importance gets translated sooner or later" is not only demonstrably false—it is arrogantly stupid. And the benefits of language study do not just come in the form of access to a greatly increased pool of literature, history, scholarship, and information. Learning a new language also forces the brain to make use of different—and often untapped—neurological channels than it had commonly done before. Even though this process is much more difficult for an adult than a child, the result is an ability to see and understand the world in new ways.

These "new ways" are actually very ancient, for they derive from the inherent structure and historical development of a language, along with the incomprehensibly vast and largely anonymous contributions of all those who have ever spoken it. In the face of the factors which serve to make up a specific linguistic tradition, one must be both bold and humble at the same time. To gain some facility in the new language requires a strong will, abundant energy, and dogged perseverance, not to mention an ongoing commitment of time. But it also requires a certain degree of humility and resilience, for there is always a potential for misunderstanding and misuse. No matter how much *"Sprachgefühl"* one is able to acquire second hand, this will never match what a native speaker effortlessly possesses by simply having been immersed in the language as a child. Rather than a deterrent, a realization like this should be a stimulant toward the endlessly edifying rewards that come with the challenge of language study.

All of the foregoing applies equally well to ancient languages, which brings us to another common notion: that these languages are "dead" and therefore useless. This is pure modernist bunk. Language is by nature a living thing, and not a very easy one to kill. A famously "dead" language like Latin lives on with vigor in Italian, French, Spanish, Portuguese, Rumanian, and various other Romance dialects. Ancient Greek has its modern counterpart, as do medieval Old Norse (in modern Icelandic) and Old Irish (in modern Irish and Scots Gaelic). Not only are these languages themselves very much alive, but so too are the invigorating insights—psychological, historical, and spiritual—that they offer to those who would step within their structures and pry open their wordhoards. Multilingual ability is not just an ideal of higher education in the liberal arts, but was also traditionally recognized as a necessary step on the initiate's path to wisdom. This is part of Sigurd's training in the *Volsungasaga*, and figures in the biographies of other medieval heroes.

Old Irish was spoken in Ireland, Scotland, and the Isle of Man in the period spanning from the sixth to the tenth centuries of the common era, and a significant body of vernacular manuscripts exists which dates from the latter end of this period. (The language then evolves into the so-called Middle Irish of the tenth to twelfth centuries, which is preserved in a considerably larger literary record.) Even among trained philologists, Old Irish is seen as a particularly difficult Indo-European language to master. While it certainly exhibits its share of phonological and other peculiarities, it is not intrinsically any harder to learn than Sanskrit, Greek,

Latin, or Old Norse—although in the case of the latter three a student is admittedly assisted by the large number of borrowed or cognate words that are part of English. Let's be cynical but honest: the underlying reason why the study of an old language is dismissed as "useless" is really because it entails a lot of hard work. The fact that older instructional manuals tended to be rather dry affairs didn't help to encourage any but the most dedicated to pursue the esoteric rewards that lay within them.

German scholars have been diligent in many disciplines over the centuries, with philology and linguistics ranking high among them. The great scholar of Old Irish in the early twentieth century, Rudolf Thurneysen (1857–1940), wrote among other things a grammar and reader in the language that have remained in widespread use for more than half a century, both in their original German versions and in English translation. These will continue to be essential reference works, but I think it safe to predict that *Sengoídelc*, a new beginning workbook in Old Irish, will replace them as a practical textbook.

The book's title—which is how the phrase "Old Irish" is rendered in the language itself—is more familiar than it might at first seem. The prefix *sen-*, meaning "old," goes all way back to Indo-European. Like many I-E roots, it still finds its way into everyday English speech untold millennia later. It is cognate, for example, with the first part of our word "senior" which derives from the comparative form of Latin *senex*. *Goídelc*, meaning "Gaelish," can be compared with the modern linguistic term Goidelic, which refers to one major sub-branch of historical Insular Celtic.

David Stifter, the author of *Sengoídelc*, is a young but experienced lecturer in Old Irish at the University of Vienna's Institute for Linguistics. He has created a work that will be welcomed by modern readers, and not just in the English-speaking world. It is detailed and rigorous, but it is also warmly enthusiastic. To guide the student Stifter uses the time-tested method of step-by-step lessons and graded exercises, together with extremely helpful, up-to-date phonological transcriptions. The translation exercises are to be done not only from Old Irish into English, but also vice-versa. In many ways, Stifter's approach reminds me of James Cathey's and Sigrid Valfells's *Old Icelandic: An Introductory Course*, which made use of similar techniques to great effect nearly a quarter-century ago. Like this predecessor, Stifter's book includes keys to the answers at the back, which means it can be employed for self-study.

The limitations of self-study are many, but to be able to make use of a book that allows and even encourages this is no small thing. Despite what seems to be an increasing interest in older languages and cultures, courses in subjects like Old Irish are seldom found even at larger universities. If they *are* to be found, by all means praise your good fortune and take advantage of them. But if you must march off into the archaic linguistic wilderness alone, you could not be better armed than with a book like *Sengoídelc*. It will serve you well as you begin to unlock some of the stories that this old-growth forest—otherwise known as the Old Irish language—has to tell.

Michael Moynihan

Modern Paganism in World Cultures: Comparative Perspectives edited by Michael F. Strmiska. Hardbound, 382 + ix pages, with illustrations, glossary, and index. Santa Barbara: ABC-CLIO, 2005. ISBN 1-85109-608-6.

In contemporary America and England, neopaganism is often immediately associated with loosely knit movements such as Wicca or "Celtic Druidism." The former is an eclectic and quite recent concoction, while the latter owes much of its pedigree to fanciful late nineteenth-century Romanticism. Any resemblances these might have to genuine ancient practices are practically coincidental, and despite their considerable number of adherents and domination of the pulp paperback racks in New Age bookshops, they are certainly not the end of the story.

A widespread "pagan revival" with much more solid footings has in fact been going on in various regions of the Western world for over a century. Depending on how one measures such things, evidence could be put forth for an even longer period of development. Until quite recently, however, the leaders and practitioners of this revival existed in relative isolation from others with similar goals. It is only since the late 1990s that an initiative called the World Congress of Ethnic Religions arose to formally cultivate dialogue between various indigenous traditional religions, both in Europe and elsewhere. The organization held its first conference in 1998 in Vilnius, Lithuania—a fitting location since the Baltic populations were the last in Europe to officially convert to Christianity. These areas remained pagan into the late Middle

Ages, and to this day have maintained a strong connection to their ancient history and traditions despite periods of political instability and the ravages of communism.

Modern Paganism in World Cultures is part of a growing scholarly literature that attempts to analyze and study various forms of neopaganism in a sympathetic but serious way. The book, which is ably edited by a professor of religious history, also redresses some of the imbalance in favor of Wicca—understandable, due to its popularity—that characterizes most comparable academic books.

Editor Michael Strmiska's substantial introduction serves as both a description of and an apologia for reconstructionist religions. It aims at clearing away many of the common misconceptions that often cloud similar discussions. The main text of the book is comprised of eight chapters, most of which treat specific individual branches of neopaganism (although one anomalous chapter deals with paganism in the U.S. military). These include Italian-American Stragheria, Irish Druidry, Icelandic and American variants of Ásatrú, Ukrainian "native faith," and Lithuania's Romuva movement. The most valuable of the articles are by far the last three mentioned.

Germanic heathenry is discussed in two different chapters, the first of which is Jenny Blain's "Heathenry, the Past, and Sacred Sites in Today's Britain." This title is somewhat misleading, as Blain fails to provide much more than a basic introduction to Germanic neopaganism. As with some of her other writings, it is noticeably skewed toward the practice of *seiðr* (cf. her book *Nine Worlds of Seid-Magic*, which was reviewed in *TYR* 2). Blain herself is a *seiðr* practitioner, and this surely accounts for her focus. The article on modern Ásatrú is written by Michael Strmiska and Baldur A. Sigurvinsson, an Icelander involved with the Asastruarfelagið (see the articles on Iceland in this issue of *TYR*). No doubt thanks in part to the contributions of a native practitioner, the information on Iceland is fairly detailed and provides a useful history of the pagan revival there. Unfortunately, the material on American Ásatrú leaves more to be desired, consisting largely of profiles of several rather arbitrarily chosen individuals.

The pieces on traditionally based neopaganism in the Ukraine and Lithuania are extensive and exemplary, offering much information that is otherwise unavailable in English. As a result, they make for fascinating reading. Adrian Ivakhiv's "The Revival of Ukrainian Native Faith" briefly discusses the reconstruction of ancient Slavic religious traditions by modern scholars and the contributions made by archeologists, linguists, and philologists to this endeavor. Ivakhiv then provides a detailed but little-known history of revivals and reconstructions by organized groups in the nineteenth and twentieth centuries. His analysis is not limited strictly to the Ukraine but also concerns the activities of immigrants to North America. Pagan Ukrainian revivalist efforts have often been influenced by controversial sources such as the *Book of Veles*, which purports to be a thousand-year-old collection of pagan Slavic texts. It is almost surely a modern forgery, not unlike the Frisian *Oera-Linda Book*. The article concludes with a survey of modern Ukrainian neopagan groups that looks toward the future. "Romuva: Lithuanian Paganism in Lithuania and America" takes a similar approach, while providing more information on specific pagan practices. It is co-authored by Michael Strmiska and Vilius Rudra Dundzila. The latter author has contributed an even lengthier piece to the current volume of *TYR*.

Modern Paganism in World Cultures, despite some weaker contributions (and not surprisingly these concern groups or movements that are associated with Wicca and neo-Druidry), is a welcome volume and an overall useful work. It is a book primarily aimed at institutions, so interested readers might encourage their local libraries to add this to their reference shelves. Hopefully it will enlighten some of those who encounter it, disabusing them of shortsighted or historically engendered prejudices.

Michael Moynihan

***Runes and Their Secrets: Studies in Runology* edited by Marie Stoklund, Michael Lerche Nielsen, Bente Holmberg, and Gillian Fellows-Jensen. Hardbound, 461 pages, with illustrations. Copenhagen: Museum Tusculanum Press, 2006. ISBN 87-635-0428-6.**

This volume collects twenty-two articles which were originally presented at the Fifth International Symposium on Runes and Runic Inscriptions held in Jelling, Denmark, in August 2000. At the conference more than a dozen further papers were delivered, some of which sadly did not make it into the anthology (they have likely now been published elsewhere). Two that stand out among this list are Merill Kaplan's "Legends and runestones: A folklorist reads the runic corpus editions" and Svante Fischer's "Runes, Latin & Christianity in Merovingian Gaul." That being said, the present volume is substantial, well edited, and produced to high standards typical of the Museum Tusculanum Press. It exhibits a wide range of approaches to a highly specialized and erudite subject. Rather than attempt to describe all of the book's contents in detail, the following comments will point to some of the highlights which stood out for this reviewer, particular those which might speak provocatively to a broader audience.

In the first article, "Standardised *fuþarks:* A useful tool or a delusion?" Michael P. Barnes admonishes against placing too much weight on the various *fuþark* rows (older, long branch, short twig, staveless, etc.) as they appear in the scholarly handbooks. For the student of runology, these tidy arrangements should, "much as cigarettes, be accompanied by an appropriate health warning" (p. 14). Barnes enumerates a number of problems that arise when one tries to categorize runestaves according to such retroactively applied standards. While the original carvers clearly followed certain models, we do not know exactly what these were. They were furthermore subject to variation across time and space. Barnes's article contains a great deal of sharp, analytical wisdom, and its premise could be fruitfully pondered by scholars in other disciplines having nothing to do with runology. One of the most frustrating characteristics of modern scholarship is the tendency to apply overly restrictive models—often cooked up in the mind of a single individual largely disconnected and unsympathetic to his or her subject matter—to historical persons, artistic developments, cultural expressions, and the like. Such tendencies regularly result in absurd interpretations of the past, but have equally inadequate and appalling results when they attempt to grapple with contemporary, living phenomena.

"On Öpir's Pictures" by Lise Gjedssø Bertelsen offers an art-historical and symbolic analysis of the dynamic picture stones signed by a certain "Öpir," a prolific rune-carver of the Late Viking Age. Just as runestones were typically raised up to ensure the lasting renown of those they commemorate, it was not uncommon for the runecarvers to identify themselves so that they, too, might gain a similar share of immortality. Öpir's stones feature both pagan and Christian motifs, many of which (serpents, for example) could fall into both categories simultaneously. This overlapping and blending of traditions is a consistent feature of medieval Germanic art and literature, whether in Scandinavia, the Continent, or the British Isles. Such cross-fertilizations were also geographical, and artistic influences from insular British and Irish traditions are taken into account here. Bertelsen's examinations are detailed but occasionally lopsided when she turns to interpretation. An example would be her tendency to ascribe any numerological features to Christian influence, when many of these (such as the number three) have much deeper roots in the native tradition. Nevertheless, the article offers an unusual opportunity to consider the work of Öpir as a singular but masterful emanation from a larger tradition.

Stephen E. Flowers contributes "How to Do Things with Runes: A Semiotic Approach to Operative Communication." Here he applies the semiotic/communicative theory of magic, first explicated in his 1986 study *Runes and Magic*, to the inscription on the so-called Lindholm amulet, a small carved piece of animal bone. He treats the subject of "runic magic" in a serious and analytical way, attempting to clearly define what types of processes may be at work. This is exactly the sort of intellectual rigor that typically goes out the window, even among scholars, as soon as the word "magic" is invoked. All too often, commentators are content to throw the word around in a vague and undefined way rather than tackle its implications head-on in any given situation. Flowers draws some useful parallels to Mediterranean traditions such as those of the Greek magical papyri. These help to illuminate the underlying principles that may have been at work in a literate magical "speech act" as exemplified in the Lindholm inscription.

A number of the articles here concern specific historical or technical aspects of the runic tradition. Enumerating some of them will help give an idea of the scope of inquiries and varied issues that are intertwined with this scholarly discipline. They include: Anne-Sofie Gräslund's "Dating the Swedish Viking-Age rune stones on stylistic grounds," Jan Ragnar Hagland's "Runic writing and Latin literacy at the end of the Middle Ages: A case study," Jørgen Steen Jensen's "The Introduction and use of runic letters on Danish coins around the year 1065," Katrin Lühti's "South Germanic runic inscriptions as testimonies of early literacy," Mindy MacLeod's "Ligatures in Early Runic and Roman Inscriptions," Bernard Mees's "Runes in the First Century," Hans Frede Nielsen's "The Early Runic Inscriptions and Germanic Historical Linguistics," R. I. Page's "Anglo-Saxon Runes: some statistical problems," Terje Spurkland's "From Tune to Eggja—the ontology of language change," Marie Stoklund's "Chronology and Typology of the Danish Runic Inscriptions," Gaby Waxenberger's historical linguistic assessment of certain phonological issues (centering on the *yew*-rune) in the Old English corpus, Nancy L. Wicker's "Bracteate Inscriptions through the Looking Glass: A Microscopic View of Manufacturing Techniques," and Kristel Zilmer's "Christian Runic Inscriptions in a Dynamic Context."

For those who can read German there are two very different but equally thought-provoking articles: "Das Norwegische Runengedicht—was sich hinter den zweiten Zeilen verbirgt" (The Norwegian Rune Rhyme—What Lies Hidden Behind the Second Lines) by Bernd Neuner and "Zur Runeninschrift auf dem Schemel von Wremen" (On the Runic Inscription on the Benchseat from Wremen) by Mattias D. Schön, Klaus Düwel, Rolf Heine, and Edith Marold. Neuner's article is a discussion and reassessment of certain aspects of one of the more enigmatic of the medieval Scandinavian *fuþark* poems. The poem has long vexed its readers due to its unusual form and the apparent semantic disconnection it exhibits between the first and second lines of each couplet. Neuner looks at six of these couplets specifically, and points out some interesting ideographic connections between the form of the rune itself (not actually pictured in the original poem, although the first line of each couplet begins with the rune-name) and the second line of its couplet. The second German article details a relatively recent (mid-1990s) runic find from a fourth- to fifth-century C.E. boat grave in Lower Saxony. The inscription under discussion appears on the edge of a rustic but quite beautifully carved *Schemel* (a loan word from Latin *skamella*; a variant of this word also seems to appear in the inscription itself), or "bench seat." The article's authors each deal with different aspects of how the new find can be reported upon and analyzed. The result is a fast-paced glimpse into the multifaceted—indeed interdisciplinary—"field work" of modern runologists.

As if all this were not wide ranging enough, the collection is rounded out by a few further contributions. Alan Griffiths looks at some of the traditional Germanic rune-names and their possible parallels in kennings for Irish ogam letter names that appear in various medieval manuscripts. Per Stille's article in Swedish, "Johan Bure och hans *Runaräfst*" (Johan Bure and his *Runaräfst* [Rune Inquiry]), discusses a particular work by the Swedish Gothicist and royal antiquarian Bure (1568–1652). More commonly known by his

Latinized name Johannes Bureus, the latter's role as an esoteric figure in the northern Rosicrucian tradition is matched by his importance as one of the forefathers of modern runology. Anne Pedersen's "The Jelling Monuments—Ancient royal memorial and modern world heritage site" offers a very readable history of the discovery, excavations, and changing interpretations of the massive royal mounds at Jelling (since the time Pedersen's article was written, these have also been reassessed with comparative analysis in a fascinating way by Charles Doherty of Trinity College, Dublin). The volume concludes with the text of the witty speech given to the symposium dinner by Raymond I. Page, the doyen of the runologists present. He concludes the more serious side of his talk with this advice (p. 461): "If we are going to ensure that there is no general farewell to runes, we must continue with our rigorous and far-reaching study of the script. But we would do well to remember that we must also strive to make our material more generally accessible, both to scholars in other fields and to the world at large. Runic study cannot survive as the preserve of professional runologists alone, however bustling their departments."

Mr. Page need not worry too much. If *Runes and Their Secrets* is any indication, there is ample evidence for the vitality of the scholarly study of runes among the pages of this impressive collection of papers. I suspect it will gain a large share of enthusiastic readers.

Michael Moynihan

Encyclopaedia of Uralic Mythologies. **Volume 1:** *Komi Mythology* **(hardbound, 436 pages, with illustrations and index, 2003, ISBN 963 05 7885 9). Volume 2:** *Khanty Mythology* **(hardbound, 241 pages, with illustrations and index, 2006, ISBN 963 05 8284 8). Budapest: Akadémiai Kiado and Helsinki: Finnish Literature Society.**

Long before the dawn of the historical era, nearly all of Europe (and various areas outside of it) came to be dominated by the presence of the speakers of Indo-European languages. There are, however, a few non-Indo-European languages and cultures which have survived into the modern age within Europe despite—or maybe on account of—their marginal, isolated status. On the western edge of Spain and France, for example, there are pockets where Basque is still spoken. This probably represents a remnant of an indigenous pre-Indo-European culture that was already active for millennia before the arrival of waves of Indo-European speakers from the east. Another distinct language family is Uralic, which includes Finno-Ugric and Samoyedic branches. The Finno-Ugric in turn comprises the Finnish and Hungarian languages (disconnected geographically but clearly related to one another) as well as a number of other languages which are spoken in areas of the Baltic (e.g., Estonian) and northwestern Russia, or maybe better put, "the Eurasiatic North." It is the numerous tribal groups which have traditionally lived in the latter territory that are the subject of the *Encyclopaedia of Uralic Mythologies*.

This ongoing work of scholarly research and documentation is simply remarkable. The books are translations from Russian, but co-edited by an international team of scholars and co-published by Finnish and Hungarian academic societies. Each individual volume documents a specific ethnic group and their mythology. The first volumes have appeared on the Komi and Khanty (or Ostyak) peoples, and further volumes will document the Mansi (or Volgul) and Selkup, among others. The Komi peoples (an umbrella term for various subgroups) have a present-day population of less than five hundred thousand and live primarily in the Republic of Komi, the Perm Krai, and other areas of northwestern Russia. The Khanty indigenous group is considerably smaller with less than thirty thousand speakers of the language; its members are inhabitants of the Khanty-Mansi Autonomous Okrug and surrounding areas in the Urals district of Russia. Since each volume in the *Encyclopaedia of Uralic Mythologies* is prepared by a particular group of experts, they vary slightly in their approach to content. For example, the Komi volume includes a large amount of linguistic detail, comparative and otherwise, which is not present in the Khanty volume. The editors remark concerning the series: "All the volumes ... are different in size, in the amount of entries, and in the way mythology is viewed and interpreted by the authors. This is due not only to the research tradition and ideas represented by the writers but also to the differences in the mythologies themselves" (vol. 2, pp. 9f). Nevertheless, both volumes succeed admirably in their goal of illuminating the essential features of these mythologies, which are to be understood "in an exceptionally broad sense, including not only myths proper but also information about religious beliefs, connected rituals, the sphere of magic and its specialists" (vol. 1, p. 10).

Each volume typically begins with an introduction to the history, cultural background, traditional economy, spiritual beliefs, artistic practices, and current status of the group. Information is then provided on the written sources for the foregoing, as well as the history of scholarly study. The earliest written sources are usually Old Russian chronicles from the High to Late Middle Ages. Accounts from scientific expeditions begin to surface in the early eighteenth century, and there is often a surge in the gathering of traditional lore and linguistic information which coincides with the early nineteenth-century influence of Romanticism. The latter impulse fueled widespread interest in the deep past of national cultures. Most famously exemplified in the work of the Brothers Grimm in Germany, this was truly a pan-European phenomenon. It is usually only at the end of the twentieth century that members of these indigenous groups begin to study their own cultures in a formal, academic way. There are, however, some noteworthy exceptions. These include G. S. Lytkin, a university-educated Komi-Zyryan who in 1899 published a monograph on the Zyryan region which remains an invaluable source of folkloric material, and A. V. Krasov who a few years earlier in 1896 published a work entitled "The Zyryans and St. Stephan, the Bishop of Perm" which among other things examined the pre-Christian pantheon and beliefs of the Komi in detail. Given the turbulent history of the last century, I would assume the recent rise of indigenous scholarship to be driven largely by a desire to preserve aspects of the cultural and religious traditions that are increasingly under threat of disappearing.

Each volume contains two sections of central importance. The first of these is the "encyclopedia," or explanatory and etymological dictionary, of the relevant mythological and religious vocabulary. This is also illustrated by a small section of photographs and images. The detail and amount of information contained in these encyclopedic entries makes for utterly fascinating reading. Here we are offered a glimpse into the extensive folklore, traditional shamanistic practices, and often syncretistic beliefs (coming from various sources such as older Indo-European influences or those of the Eastern Orthodox Church) that contribute to the worldview of each group. The encyclopedia also serves as both a primer and point of reference for better comprehending the section that follows it, namely a collection of actual folklore in the form of tales, songs, poems, and charms.

The modern encyclopedist tradition goes back to the Age of the

Enlightenment, but its roots have precedence over a millennium earlier in early medieval glosses and works such as Isidore of Seville's massive seventh-century *Etymologiae*. The best of these works are those which open up new and previously unseen worlds for their readers. *The Encyclopaedia of Uralic Mythologies* does exactly this in the most distinguished way, and the generations of scholars whose work it is built upon are all to be commended, not least of all those who have put such painstaking work into realizing this complicated, long-term project. One can only hope that the cultures under discussion here are able to maintain this lore as part of a living cultural matrix, rather than see it reduced to a curiosity preserved only on paper.

Michael Moynihan

***The Warwolf: A Peasant Chronicle of the Thirty Years War* by Hermann Löns. Translated and introduced by Robert Kvinnesland. Hardbound, 198 pages. Yardley, Pennsylvania: Westholme, 2006. ISBN 10: 1-59416-026-0.**

This is the second translation of the Hermann Löns historical novel *Der Wehrwolf* into English, following Marion Saunders' *Harm Wulf: A Peasant Chronicle*, which was issued in London and New York in 1931. The work has also been translated into Dutch, French, and Italian. The original was published in 1910 and sold half a million copies by the mid–1930s, making it one of most popular German novels of its time. Löns's tale is one of the more important examples of the late 1800s and early 1900s *Heimatkunst* movement, which is generally marked by anti-modern, anti-clerical, and regionalist as well as nationalist sentiments.

The setting is a Lower Saxon community of peasants who band together against invaders during the Thirty Years War. The main character, Harm Wulf, reluctantly transforms into the "Wehr-Wulf" after losing his family to these marauders. He forms a secret band of men and begins to fight violence with violence. The "Warwolves'" guiding motto is "Help yourself, and Our Lord God will help you." Much of *Der Wehrwolf*'s immediacy is the result of the author's in-depth studies of historical sources, including Grimmelshausen's famous novel *Der Abenteuerliche Simplicissimus Teutsch*, which appeared only twenty years after the end of the war. It also contains autobiographical strains, as Dr. Widar Lehneman has noted: "And yet something else had to be present to make his novel into the unique work that it became: the poet's own character and soul. This is above all present in the main character."

In order to convey the regional qualities of the novel, Löns used many words and expressions culled from Lower Saxon dialects. For the sake of his "east and south German readers" he added a glossary at the end of the book. In it, he explained archaic terms such as "Ulenflucht" (lit. "flight of the owls" = dawn) and "Wolfsangel" (translated as "wolf-hook" by Saunders and "Wolf-rune" by Kvinnesland).

The translator of the present edition, Robert Kvinnesland, had not seen the prior translation when he undertook the project. This makes his effort all the more impressive. His language is at once more immediate and more archaic. Saunders' work has its charms, but overall Kvinnesland's version is more precise as well as more poetic. The translator's short preface—as well as his copious footnotes in the first part of the novel—help to immerse the reader in the historical period that Löns is trying to evoke.

Another notable achievement of the new translation is the rendering of all the rhymed songs and speeches into English equivalents. Löns concluded eleven of the novel's thirteen chapters with rhymed verse; this is essential to the continuity and poetic structure of the work. There are several rhymed speeches as well. Combined with the generally austere style of the prose, they give the impression that Löns was at least partially inspired by the Norse sagas.

Saunders also evaded translating the double-entendre of the novel's title by simply using the protagonist's full name. In contrast, Kvinnesland has conceived the brilliantly simple *The Warwolf*. "Wehrwolf" itself is a word invented by Löns and combines the German *Werwolf* = werewolf and *wehren* = to defend. Löns once denied any supernatural aspects of the book's title but was most likely aware that the period in which the novel takes place was marked by a widespread belief in werewolves, and that such a name for a band of vigilantes would have struck fear into the minds of their foes.

This highly recommended volume is hardbound and comes in a handsome dust jacket featuring F. H. Ernst Schneidler's drawing from the original frontispiece. [For a more thorough biography of Hermann Löns, see Markus Wolff, "Hermann Löns: An Introduction to his Life and Work," in *TYR* 1, pp. 143–57.]

Markus Wolff

Ludwig Fahrenkrog: Das goldene Tor. Ein deutscher Maler zwischen Jugendstil und Germanenglaube by Claus Wolfschlag. Softbound, 86 pages, 9 color and 43 b&w illustrations, bibliography, no index. Dresden: Verlag Zeitenwende, 2006. ISBN 3-934291-39-2.

After Daniel Junker's *Deine Tat Bist Du*, an excellent study of the Germanische Glaubensgemeinschaft (GGG), the religious organization founded by Ludwig Fahrenkrog, now comes a book that examines Fahrenkrog's important artistic career.

The author Claus Wolfschlag has borrowed the title of the book—which translates to "The Golden Gate"—from a 1927 publication of the same name that was subtitled "Poetic Creations in Word and Image." The original 150-page volume collected seventy-five of Fahrenkrog's paintings and drawings as well as accompanying poems, and was published on the occasion of the artist's sixtieth birthday. The "new" Golden Gate is certainly of more modest dimensions, but manages to pack in substantial information as well as excellent reproductions of Fahrenkrog's drawings, paintings, and rarely seen sketches. Only the wonderful "Allvater" drawing is sadly cropped, without mentioning that it represents only a partial view.

After introducing Fahrenkrog as an advocate of the reform movements, as well as a proponent of Symbolism and Art Nouveau in *fin-de-siècle* Germany, Wolfschlag goes on to analyze his German Faith worldview, which sought to strike a balance between pantheism and pre-Christian Germanic beliefs in cyclical time and the sun. As a free spirit, Fahrenkrog stressed a non-dogmatic approach and was a moderate voice within the *völkisch* spectrum. His books about religious matters emphasize the quest of the soul towards light and transcendence.

In the main section of the book, Wolfschlag explores Fahrenkrog's pictorial themes by placing them in groups, such as "Creation," "Sky and Sun," and "Urges and Demons." By doing so, he leads the reader through Fahrenkrog's work thematically instead of chronologically. This is a refreshing approach that is often lacking in works on art history.

Sadly, the book includes only three of Fahrenkrog's poems. Although by no means a major poet, the original *Das goldene Tor* includes numerous examples of his Symbolist verse. Still, this is a very commendable effort, and will hopefully serve as a point of entry for further, more detailed studies.

Markus Wolff

Gardens of the Gods: Myth, Magic and Meaning by Christopher McIntosh. Softbound, 203 + xviii pages, indexed. London: I. B. Tauris, 2005. ISBN 1-86064-740-5.

Gardens are a perfect place to ponder one's existence and the ways in which man might make his way through the tumult of the world outside the garden gates. Some gardens are specifically designed for such reflections and some as an initiation into the profound secrets of life. In the garden, the otherwise hidden world of the wild comes shimmering into view. The pagan past, which lives on in the wilderness, mixes with the mundane contemporary world. Behind the garden wall, where Pan still plays his pipes, a wood nymph might let herself be seen and the center of the world—or paradise itself—might still be found. Christopher McIntosh explains at the outset (p. xv): "This book is an invitation to look at the garden in a new way. ... My theme is the garden as a sacred space, an outdoor temple carrying an intentional transformative message, religious, mystical or philosophical in meaning."

A garden's design, plants, and the architectural and sculptural objects within it comprise a garden's language. The author sets out to read gardens as if they were poems, establishing first a vocabulary of symbols generally found in the purposefully cultivated landscape. Although many objects such as fountains, trees, and crosses turn up in gardens throughout the world, cultural differences often give them different meanings. "Woods, for example, are traditionally sacred in northern Europe but grim and perilous places in the south" (p. 2). Throughout different times and places, the balance between wilderness and cultivation leans heavily to one side or the other, depending on how nature is viewed—whether it is seen as something to cultivate, to tame, to exaggerate, or to imitate.

McIntosh has traveled for decades visiting some of the world's most famous and unusual gardens, and writes of his personal experiences as well as the historical and cultural contexts of the gardens, making his book an enjoyable travelogue as well. Most of the photos are from his personal archives.

The journey begins in Asia. Taoism and *feng shui* are the pervasive influence in Chinese gardens, and later in Japan. *Chi*, the vital spirit of existence, is found in all things—man and nature, trees, flowers, rocks, and water. A garden designer must consider how to best enhance its movement through everything. The Taoist garden seeks to replicate the wilderness using the principles of *feng shui* in order that man may "glimpse, within a confined space the oneness of all things and the mysterious workings of the Tao" (p. 20). The Japanese garden is strongly influenced by Chinese philosophy, but obtains its own delicate design. Once the bustle of Tokyo is left behind "it is easy to imagine that the whole Japanese landscape is a garden—where the gods are never far away." The Japanese garden reserves a special place for stones and a complete garden was meant to contain a representative of all 130 categories. In both countries the mountains, water, and the forces of nature are significant elements of garden design.

The Islamic garden is a creation of paradise on earth. Even the word "paradise" itself comes from old Persian *pairidaeza* "meaning a walled garden, that is to say what we would today understand as a garden or park" (p. 36). The tomb-garden of the Taj Mahal is one of the greatest examples of this type of garden, and the author spends a good number of pages on it.

The enclosed monastery gardens of medieval Europe served the community as a space for growing medicinal and culinary herbs and plants. During the same period, the courtly poets used garden symbolism to convey ideas about love, femininity, and alchemy. "The courtly love tradition, which in many ways ran counter to the mainstream of Christian orthodoxy, is one example of how gardens and garden symbolism were often the vehicle for unorthodox or even subversive currents" (p. 49). McIntosh even dwells for a moment on the connection between gardening and alchemy: "in both activities nature is brought from its raw state into a condition of greater refinement" (pp. 49f.).

Myth, magic, and meaning collide spectacularly in Italian Renaissance gardens. The classical era was rediscovered, the gardens of Arcadia were tilled, Pan awakened from his slumbers, and nature was welcomed back into civilization. There was a playful order in the Renaissance gardens where a "topiary was moulded to resemble sculpture and architecture, while other features, such as grottoes, were natural in appearance, but could serve for human activities" (pp. 51f.). A good example is the Villa d'Este gardens in Tivoli with its famous gods, fountains, and stairs. McIntosh was first impressed by the garden in his youth, sensing that some great message or meaning lay beneath the incredible design. He returned to this garden years later to unlock its mysteries. Figures from Ovid's *Metamorphoses* mingle with motifs from the *Hypnerotomachia Poliphili* (The Strife of Love in a Dream). The latter, a strange story first published in 1499 (and translated into English by Joscelyn Godwin five hundred years later), was very influential in Renaissance garden design.

The most famous garden influenced by the *Hypnerotomachia Poliphili* is Versailles, built by Louis XIV. It is a Baroque masterpiece and, like many artifacts from that era (including the Sun King himself), both magnificent and absurd. The sun is the dominant motif, beginning "with the palace itself, which was intended to be compared with the palace of the sun as described in the *Metamorphoses*" (p. 78). Louis XIV authored a guide to his gardens, recommending the route the visitor should take to experience initiation.

England is well known for its soft stance on eccentrics, and famous for the extravagant, symbolic, and allegorical gardens that they build. English garden designers turned their backs on the formal grandeur of Versaille, and looked instead toward Arcadia. They cultivated dramatic landscapes with a "gothic" atmosphere of gloom and mystery. "Gardens began to be filled with follies and artificial ruins ... and were reshaped to create rugged or dramatic features rivaling the wild landscapes that were now admired, whereas before they had often been shunned as rude and primitive" (p. 85). The gardens at Stowe and Stourhead are excellent examples of eighteenth-century English gardens.

The chapter "The Symbol-strewn Landscape" begins (p. 91): "An orangery in Potsdam built to look like an Egyptian Temple; a serpent curled around a pillar near Goethe's Garden House in Weimar; Osiris peering from the foliage of a Florentine garden; sphinxes guarding the approaches to terraces; pentagrams set into paving stones, pyramids, labyrinths, obelisks and more obelisks— are these mere follies and antiquarian whimsies, or do they hold a deeper meaning? We are in the era when the English style of gardening spread to the continent of Europe along with another phenomenon of British origin, namely Freemasonry." Theatrical elements such as a hermit's grotto complete with hermit could be found along with "a continual alteration between light and darkness, the airy heights and underground passages" (p. 99), leading the visitor through an initiatory journey toward enlightenment.

As the tour of gardens proceeds through history, the gardeners themselves become more visible. Eclectic and unusual gardens, many built by artists, dominate the second half of the book. A garden of particular interest is the Bossard Temple in the Lüneburg Heath, described (p. 110) as "a garden of the Nordic gods" and a *Gesamtkunstwerk*, or total work of art. The garden included as many of the arts as it could and encompassed a private home, art gallery, and temple. The temple is called the "Edda Hall" and is "richly ornamented with murals, reliefs and sculptures and motifs from Nordic mythology. A prominent figure is that of the one-eyed Odin ... Bossard, who had lost an eye ... identified himself with Odin and never tired of painting or sculpting his image" (p. 111). There is also a semi-circle of stones, a "tree temple," and many more motifs from the northern world.

The twentieth century bring us an explosion of gardens, many informed by superficial fancies and tastes. Nevertheless, one can still find gardens built with meaning and an underlying philosophy. The first one described is the the poet Ian Hamilton Finlay's "Little Sparta" in Scotland, another *Gesamtkunstwerk* garden which strives to combine poetry and plants under an umbrella of "spiritual vision."

The author is clearly moved by "the potently magical gardens" of Dumbarton Oaks in Washington, D.C. After entering, the path leads east "to a little Pan figure ... holding a pipe in his left hand and pointing the way south with his right." The path continues down a hill to a pond, the other way leads to "an enticing complex of terraces, arbours, fountains, enclosed gardens..." (pp. 123f.). McIntosh's favorite spot is the "Star Garden," with a ten-pointed star set into the stone and a fountain and Aquarius figure, representative of the garden's "vision of civilization, beauty and divine order" (p. 126).

There is a chapter on the spiritual aspect of gardening and horticulture. In discussing how to approach and communicate with the green world, McIntosh introduces ideas ranging from Rudolf Steiner to the Findhorn community in the chapter "Creating a Garden of Meaning." Because the author has built and tended his own garden, he can speak with first-hand knowledge about plants and how to grow them. But interestingly, much of *Gardens of the Gods* is devoted to the architecture of the garden—sculptures, fountains, entrances, and so on. Some space is given to trees, but very little is devoted to plants. Of course, these are the shortest lived and most changeable things in the garden, but they are obviously a vital part. That said, the book's themes of history, art, and initiation would make it of interest to readers who might not otherwise consider the design of gardens. It is a compelling discussion of how gardens can be used for secret ways of communicating to one's contemporaries, and to the visitors of the future as well.

Annabel Lee

The Counsels of Cormac: An Ancient Irish Guide to Leadership translated by Thomas Cleary. New York: Doubleday, 2004. Hardbound, 64 pages. ISBN 0-385-51313-5.

The noted scholar of Eastern philosophy and religion, Thomas Cleary, has turned his attention to the Far West with the publication of this volume. The text is a translation of *Tecosca Cormaic*, an Old Irish text ascribed to Cormac mac Airt, high king of Ireland, who reigned from 227 to 260 C.E. Cormac was recognized by many of his contemporaries as the ideal ruler, a patron of the arts and culture who won the admiration of the powerful *filidh* (poet, seer). During his flourishing reign, he established institutions of learning, renewed the strength of the traditional Irish (Brehon) law, and authored works on an impressive variety of topics. The *Counsels*, one among these works, is a collection of advice regarding the proper conduct of leadership, revealed in dialogue between Cormac and his son, Carbre.

The qualities of a king consist of clarity, stillness of mind, and generosity. Cormac's opening response sets this precedent: "Composure rather than wrath, / Patience rather than contention, / Geniality rather than arrogance." The authority of a king is "gained by his excellence," or *areté* as Plato might describe it, an innate quality found in an extraordinarily rare number of individuals. He becomes the "sun of the banquet hall" by merit of his inner virtues, his "legitimate claim to truth," and "with the dignity of a king." Considerable emphasis is also given to openness and "an inquiring mind"; a leader must hold counsels, assemblies, and a regular court—he must be open to his people and to the wise. He supports "every branch of learning," fosters the "Study of each art, / Knowledge of each technical vocabulary, / Diversified skills in craft." It is also said, "Let him be a lover of knowledge and wisdom."

He must be not only fair and just, but "Let him love justice."

An orderly society, or "stable land," and the upholding of tradition were of critical importance to the ancient Irish. A strict hierarchy was observed, based not upon the purely economic pseudo-hierarchy that defines our present society, but on an organic system that allowed people to follow their true nature, based on their natural abilities and affinities, "according to his skill." On the back cover of this edition, a certain *Wall Street Access* CEO praises the book as relevant to other "corporate leaders" in this "age of business gurus." But this book has nothing authentic to offer the world of business, having been conceived by a man who operated on a much higher plane. Nevertheless, one is likely to find this book at a bookstore in the same section with titles like *Sun Tzu and the Art of Business* or *The Tao of Management*. This is characteristic of a society that has replaced the sacred, a concept central to Cormac and his age, with materialism and the rule of economics. Wisdom and knowledge become distorted, quantified, and commercialized.

This text may only be comprehended by those who think outside this trap and other confusions of our times. The *Counsels* was intended for kings and the sons of kings, and as such is suitable only for leaders or, we might say, the "differentiated man" by Evola's reckoning. The availability of this work in such an accessible translation should serve as a welcome reminder of the wisdom and great learning of our ancestors in the westernmost corner of Europe.

James Reagan

"A tour de force of historical investigation and cogent analysis....As timely as it is sharp." —*Choice*

MAGIA SEXUALIS
Sex, Magic, and Liberation in Modern Western Esotericism
HUGH B. URBAN

"A fascinating account of the development of Western sexual magic through the nineteenth and twentieth centuries. Urban focuses on an extraordinary set of historical figures, and his rich analysis illuminates the sexual—and supernatural—undercurrents that have shaped modernity."
—Randall Styers, author of *Making Magic*

$55.00 hardcover

Also by Hugh B. Urban
Tantra
Sex, Secrecy, Politics, and Power in the Study of Religion
$24.95 paperback

At bookstores or www.ucpress.edu

UNIVERSITY OF CALIFORNIA PRESS

About the Editors

Joshua Buckley was born in 1974 in Sharon, Connecticut. He is a voracious reader and an occasional writer. His publishing efforts include the 2004 translation of *On Being a Pagan* (Ultra) by Alain de Benoist. He has also released music by Markus Wolff's heathen percussion group Waldteufel. He lives in Atlanta, Georgia, with his wife, three children, cats, an Australian cattle dog, and a fish. He is quite fond of them all, and must be persuaded to leave the house.
Email: <elecampane@bellsouth.net>

PHOTO: LIBERTY BUCKLEY

Michael Moynihan was born in 1969 in New England. He is an artist, musician, author, editor, and occasional winemaker and bookbinder. He has traveled and performed music throughout Europe, as well as in Japan. The latest release of his and Annabel Lee's music project Blood Axis is *Anthology* (Storm/Tesco), a collection of rare tracks spanning the fifteen-year existence of the group. His book *Lords of Chaos* (revised edition: Feral House, 2003), co-written with Didrik Søderlind, has been published in French and German editions to widespread interest. He has written and edited numerous articles and has contributed to scholarly encyclopedias and topical anthologies. With Annabel Lee he also runs Dominion Press, whose most recent publication is a limited, clothbound edition of Joscelyn Godwin's *The Golden Thread: The Ageless Wisdom of the Western Mystery Traditions.* Together with Stephen Flowers he has revised and expanded *The Secret King: The Myth and Reality of Nazi Occultism* (Dominion/Feral House, 2007). Forthcoming Dominion books include a translation of a major new biography of the *fin-de-siècle* Austrian rune mystic Guido von List. In addition to his work for *TYR*, he is a co-editor of *Rûna*.
Email: <dominion@pshift.com>

PHOTO: CARL ABRAHAMSSON

About the Contributors

Alain de Benoist was born on 11 December 1943. He is married and has two children. He has studied law, philosophy, sociology, and the history of religions in Paris, France. A journalist and a writer, he is the editor of two journals: *Nouvelle Ecole* (since 1968) and *Krisis* (since 1988). His main fields of interest include the history of ideas, political philosophy, classical philosophy, and archaeology. He has published more than fifty books and three thousand articles. He is also a regular contributor to many French and European publications, journals, and papers (including *Valeurs actuelles, Le Spectacle du monde, Magazine-Hebdo, Le Figaro-Magazine*, in France, *Telos* in the United States, and *Junge Freiheit* in Germany). In 1978 he received the Grand Prix de l'Essai from the Academie Francaise for his book *Vu de droite: Anthologie critique des idees contemporaines* (Copernic, 1977). He has also been a regular contributor to the radio program *France-Culture* and has appeared in numerous television debates.

Jónína K. Berg was born in Akranes, West Iceland in 1962. Until the age of sixteen, she spent her childhood at the farm Giljahlíð, which lies close to Reykholt in Borgarfjörður, the one-time home of Snorri Sturluson. Her ongoing interests include theosophy, occultism, philosophy, religion, and the forces of nature. She has been educated as an art teacher, aromatherapist, healer, and iridologist, and is the mother of two children. In 1996 she became a *goði* of West Iceland, and served as the Allsherjargoði of the Ásatrúarfélagið between 2002 and 2003.

Collin Cleary, Ph.D., is an independent scholar living in Sandpoint, Idaho. He is a Fellow in the Rune-Gild and a contributor to *Rûna*.

Marco Deplano is a freelance researcher, scriptwriter, and translator. He contributes to articles and translations regarding countercultural trends and subcultures, the media, true crime, comics, and esotericism. He also assembles sounds and visuals for the music projects Foresto di Ferro and Wertham.
Email: <wertham@gmail.com>

Andreas Diesel was born in 1976 in Saarbrücken, Germany and works as a translator and author. His poems and short stories have been published in magazines and anthologies, and he has conducted interviews and reviewed records and books for several music journals. Together with Dieter Gerten, he has written the book *Looking for Europe: Neofolk und Hintergründe* (Prophecy, 2005; forthcoming French edition from Camion Blanc), which chronicles the works, ideas, and influences of various apocalyptic folk and post-industrial artists worldwide.

Vilius Rudra Dundzila, Ph.D., D.Min., is a Professor of Humanities and Comparative Religion at Harry S Truman College (City Colleges of Chicago). He has graduate degrees in Lithuanian Studies, Comparative Literature, Spirituality, and Ministry. He has published a number of academic articles on Baltic religion and mythology. He served as *seniūnas* (Elder, i.e., minister) of the Lithuanian Ethnic Church Romuva for twelve years in Kaunas, Lithuania, and Chicago.

Stephen Edred Flowers, Ph.D., is the world's leading expert on esoteric, or "radical," runology. He has published over twenty books on this and related subjects. In 1980 he founded the Rune-Gild, the world's largest and most influential initiatory organization dedicated to Rune-Work and the Odian path. His work in runology extends into academic pursuits and in 1984 he received a Ph.D. from the University of Texas at Austin with a dissertation entitled *Runes and Magic* (Peter Lang, 1987). Dr. Flowers is also the founder of the Woodharrow Institute for general studies in the culture and arts of the Germanic and Indo-European peoples. He and his wife, Crystal, are also the owners of Runa-Raven Press. His work is devoted to seeking the principle of RUNA—the Mystery—as understood in the mythic idiom of the Germanic peoples.

Joscelyn Godwin, Ph.D., was born in Oxfordshire in 1945 and educated at Radley College, Magdalene College, Cambridge, and Cornell University (Ph. D. in Musicology). As a writer, editor, and translator he has specialized in the philosophical and occult aspects of music, and in the Western esoteric tradition. His musical publications include *Music, Mysticism and Magic* (Arkana, 1987) and *Harmony of the Spheres* (Inner Traditions, 1993). In the esoteric field, *Arktos: the Polar Myth in Science, Symbolism, and Nazi Survival*

(Phanes Press, 1993) has appeared in French, Italian, Greek, Japanese, and two German editions. He has translated many books including the erotic-architectural epic *Hypnerotomachia Poliphili* of 1499 (Thames & Hudson, 1999). His latest works are Athanasius Kircher's *Theatre of the World* (forthcoming from Thames & Hudson), and two mystery novels with occult themes, written in collaboration with Guido Mina di Sospiro: *The Forbidden Book* and *The Forbidden Fruit*. Since 1971 he has taught at Colgate University in Hamilton, NY 13346.

Jon Graham is a translator, writer, and editor who was born in 1954. His recent translations include *On Being a Pagan* by Alain de Benoist (Ultra, 2004), *Little Anatomy of the Physical Unconscious, or the Anatomy of the Image* by Hans Bellmer (Dominion, 2004), and the Inner Traditions titles *Christianity: The Origins of a Pagan Religion* by Philippe Walter (2006), *The Secret Message of Jules Verne* by Michael Lamy (2007), and *Books on Fire* by Lucien X. Polastron (2007). He has also translated the forthcoming Inner Traditions titles *Eleanor of Acquitaine: Queen of the Troubadours* by Jean Markale (2008), *The Reality Excess* by Annie Le Brun (2008), and *The Underground Realm of Agartha* by Christiama Nimosus (2008).

Elizabeth Griffin is a translator of Romance languages with over twenty years of professional experience. She has worked for Naval intelligence and the Smithsonian, and as an artist has had her work published in national magazines. She has three children and lives in New Zealand.

Carlos F. W. B. von Hagen-Lautrup III was born in Chile of exile parents with strong European roots. His academic studies and teaching career began at the University of Chile, and continued in America at the University of Texas at Austin, University of Washington, UCLA, and Santa Monica College. His principle areas of work have been Psychotherapy, Geography, History, Anthropology, Linguistics, and Theater. He maintains one of the largest sound archives in the world, and for many decades was highly active in educational radio and television, producing over seven hundred one-hour documentaries on a vast range of musical and cultural topics. His interests in European literature and the art of translation have resulted in his translating hundreds of poems from various languages, mainly into English and Spanish. He has long maintained a deep sympathy for Icelandic culture and older religious traditions, and since 1999 has lived in Iceland.

Róbert Horváth (b. 9 March 1971, Veszprém) is a Hungarian philosopher. He has been granted a doctorate *honoris causa* in theology and is the author of more than 150 studies, essays, and reviews in different areas. His main field of research is Oriental metaphysics, particularly Advaita Vedanta and Hindu Tantrism. He is also known as an admirer of René Guénon, Julius Evola, and the so-called Perennialist School. He is the co-editor of the annual journal *Tradíció* (Tradition) and chief editor of the political bi-monthly *Északi Korona* (Northern Crown). Some of his early lyrical-metaphysical texts are used on the CDs of the Hungarian music groups Actus (*Das Unbennenbare, Sacro Sanctum*) and Scivias ("*...and you will fear death not*"). He lives in Budapest and works at the Hungarian National Library.

Thierry Jolif was born in 1972 in Brittany, France. A musician since the age of fifteen, he is also a writer on cultural and spiritual topics. After studying orthodox theology, Breton and Irish languages, and Celtic civilization at the University of Rennes, he has published four monographs with the French publisher Pardès: *Mythologie celtique* (2000), *Tradition celtique* (2001), *Symboles celtiques* (2004), and *Druides* (2006). He has also published articles on traditional matters in diverse journals including *Rûna*, *Contrelittérature*, *La Règle d'Abraham*, and *Sophia*. He is currently working on two books; one on esotericism (forthcoming from Pardès) and the other a study of the British composer Sir John Tavener.

Gordon Kennedy was born in California in 1956 and grew up in Anaheim. With close proximity to mountains, deserts, and beaches, he developed a strong love of the natural world and a keen appreciation for music and fitness. The youngest of four children, he had a front row seat to the sixties, and spent several days in San Francisco during the "Summer of Love" in 1967. By 1969, at age thirteen, he had taken up backpacking, hitchhiking, and eventually, surfing. After high school he moved to the San Jacinto Mountains where he lived in a cave for a year on an Indian Reservation, and had an epiphany after reading a ten-cent copy of *Kon Tiki* by Thor Heyerdahl. The following year he began a career as an orchardist, and an avocation as a serious student of Guanche studies as well as the cultural influence of German immigrants upon varied aspects of California subcultures. The research is ongoing. Mr. Kennedy still resides in the California desert, where he is active in backpacking, yoga, orcharding, meditation, self-publishing, and troglodism.

Annie Le Brun was born in Rennes, France in 1942. In 1963 she became a member of the surrealist group in Paris. After the group's dissolution in 1969, she and her partner Radovan Ivsic formed Editions Maintenant with several of their former surrealist colleagues, including the Czech painter Toyen. Annie Le Brun's poetic work is complemented by her critical activity in which she has undertaken radical examinations of feminism, the Gothic novel, Sade, and the rising tide of conformity. One of her works has already been translated into English as *Sade: A Sudden Abyss* (City Lights, 1991), while a translation of her recent work *The Reality Excess* is planned for 2008. Annie Le Brun lives in Paris.

Annabel Lee, M.A., M.F.A., is an herbalist musician, and translator. She has translated *Witchcraft Medicine: Healing Arts, Shamanic Practices, and Forbidden Plants* by Claudia Müller-Ebeling, Christian Rätsch, and Wolf-Dieter Storl (Inner Traditions, 2003); *Shamanism and Tantra in the Himalayas* by Müller-Ebeling, Rätsch, and Surendra Bahadur Shahi (Inner Traditions, 2002); and sections of *The Encyclopedia of Psychoactive Plants* by Rätsch (Inner Traditions, 2004), *The Encyclopedia of Aphrodisiacs* by Rätsch (Inner Traditions, 2008), and *Plants of the Gods* by Albert Hofmann and Richard Schultes (Inner Traditions, 2000). She is currently working on the translation of a forthcoming biography of Guido von List. She is the co-director of the independent publishing company Dominion Press. Her violin and compositions can be heard on over fifteen recordings, including those of Alraune, Blood Axis, Fire + Ice, In Gowan Ring, and Waldteufel. Email: <alraune@pshift.com>

Pentti Linkola is an influential Finnish field ornithologist, and served as an editor of the standard Finnish ornithological handbook *Pohjolan linnut* (Otava, 1963–67). In more recent years, he has established himself as a "militant green fundamentalist." Since 1959, he has lived outside Saaksmaki in a two-room cabin with no running water, where he works as a fisherman. He is a popular university lecturer, a regular guest on Finnish television, and a best-selling author. Linkola is known for his colorful and controversial pronouncements. He has estimated that the earth's population is now 2.5 times greater than it should be, that this situation might be remedied by war or famine, and that "green police" might be empowered to keep "progress at bay." "Everything we have developed over the last hundred years," he writes, "should be destroyed." Despite his status as one of Finland's leading intellectuals, "Linkolaism" is virtually unknown in the United States. This is probably not surprising to the fisherman philosopher, since "the U.S. symbolizes the worst ideologies in the world: growth and freedom."

Christopher McIntosh, Ph.D., was born in England in 1943 and grew up in Edinburgh, Scotland. He studied philosophy, politics, and economics at Oxford and German at London University, later returning to Oxford to take a doctorate in history with a dissertation on the Rosicrucian revival in the context of the German Enlightenment and Counter-Enlightenment. After working in London in journalism and publishing he spent four years in New York as an information officer with the United Nations Development Programme, then moved to Germany to work for UNESCO. In parallel he has pursued a career as a writer and researcher specialising in the esoteric traditions. His books include *The Astrologers and their Creed* (Praeger, 1969); *Eliphas Lévi and the French Occult Revival* (Weiser, 1972); *The Rosicrucians* (latest edition Weiser, 1997); *The Rose Cross and the Age of Reason* (E. J. Brill, 1992), based on his D.Phil. dissertation; *The Swan King: Ludwig II of Bavaria* (latest edition Tauris Parke, 2003); and *Gardens of the Gods* (I. B. Tauris, 2005). His fictional work includes the occult novel *Return of the Tetrad* published in Czech as *Navrat Tetradi* (1998). He also has a long-standing interest in paganism and nature-oriented belief systems. He has lectured widely and is on the faculty of the distance M.A. programme in Western Esotericism at the University of Exeter, England. His home is in Bremen, North Germany.

Thomas Naylor, Ph.D., born in 1936, is Professor Emeritus of Economics at Duke University and founder of Vermont's independence movement, the Second Vermont Republic. The most recent of his thirty books are *Downsizing the U.S.A.* (Wm. B. Eerdmans, 1997), *Affluenza* (Berrett-Koehler, 2001), and *The Vermont Manifesto* (Xlibris, 2003). He is currently completing a book entitled *Rebél*.

Géza von Neményi was born in 1958, and is a prominent and often controversial figure in the German heathen revival. Von Nemenyi found his calling in the pursuit of spiritual endeavors at an early age. This initially led him to the study of magic and esotericism, and later to the study of Germanic languages and prehistory. In 1985, he helped found the Germanic heathen association Heidnische Gemeinschaft in Berlin, and he soon became its main priest, or Gothi. In 1991, von Nemenyi decided to revive the Germanische Glaubens-Gemeinschaft (GGG) and gained the support of its last chairman, Ludwig Dessel. The GGG was one of the earliest neo-Germanic religious groups, and was established by Ludwig Fahrenkrog in 1907 (see "Ludwig Fahrenkrog and the Germanic Faith Community: Wodan Triumphant" in *TYR* 2 [2003]). Within the GGG, von Nemenyi holds the title of Allsherjagode. Since the late 1980s, he has been increasingly active as an author. This has included editing the GGG magazine *Germanen=Glaube* and publishing forty-eight issues of the "Germanic Series" on various topics relating to the Germanic religious revival. His recent work *Götter, Mythen, Jahresfeste* (Gods, Myths, Annual Feasts [Kersken-Canbaz-Verlag, 2004]; a revision of a 1988 book) is conceived as a comprehensive introduction to the traditional Germanic worldview and ritual cycle. A newly revised edition of his rune book *Heilige Runen* (Ullstein) appeared in 2004.

Michael O'Meara, Ph.D., studied social theory at the Ecole des Hautes Etudes and modern European history at the University of California. He is the author of *New Culture, New Right: Anti-Liberalism in Postmodern Europe* (1st Books, 2004).

Nigel Pennick was born in Guildford, Surrey in southern England in 1946. Trained in biology, for fifteen years he was a researcher in algal taxonomy for a government institute. During this time, he published twenty-nine scientific research papers including descriptions of eight new species of marine algae and protozoa before moving on to become a writer and illustrator. He is the author of over forty books on European folk arts, landscape, customs, games, magical alphabets, and spiritual traditions.

Ian Read writes, composes, and sings with his band Fire + Ice. He also edits and produces *Rûna*, a magazine "Exploring Northern European Myth, Mystery, and Magic." As Drighten of the Rune-

Gild in Europe, Ian teaches runes (mysteries) in the hope that something of the old knowledge will remain when this modern world finally collapses, and a new world is built on its ruins.

James Reagan was born in 1980 in Arkansas. He moved to North Carolina at an early age, and still spends part of the year in Asheville. He received his undergraduate education at Appalachian State University and University College Cork, acquiring a B.S. in Anthropology in 2003. He has worked as a professional archaeologist throughout the United States and Ireland. In 2006, he completed an M.A. in Landscape Archaeology from the National University of Ireland, Galway. He is currently employed as a seasonal park ranger. His interests include environmental sustainability, organic farming, philosophy, literature, poetry, traditional music, indigenous cultures, firearms, wilderness survival, hunting, fishing, theology, and prehistoric religion.

Ike Vil (b. 1970 in Helsinki, Finland) is a Finnish musician, writer, and translator. He has studied Cultural Anthropology at the University of Helsinki, Field Artillery doctrine at the Reserve Officers' School in Hamina, and the human condition on tour with various musical (and some not so musical) groups around the world. His interests include rejected knowledge, military history, and Hal Foster's *Prince Valiant*.

Markus Wolff is an artist and musician residing in Cascadia. His current musical projects are Waldteufel, L'Acephale, and A Minority Of One. He is also working on a cycle of paintings entitled *Ragnarok*. Email: <dagaz@spiritone.com>

About the Cover Artist

The painter Odd Nerdrum was born on 8 April 1944 in Sweden. He studied at the Art Academy in Oslo, Norway, and later with Joseph Beuys in Düsseldorf, Germany. While his contemporaries were championing abstract and conceptual art, Nerdrum taught himself to paint in the demanding style of the seventeenth-century Dutch Masters. Although his technique is profoundly conservative, he remains engaged with modernist themes—most fundamentally, perhaps, as a critic of modernity. Nerdrum is both a traditionalist, and a radical.

Nerdrum's early work contained elements of social realism, while anticipating the archetypal and broadly humanist concerns of his later style. A typical example is *The Murder of Andreas Baader* (1977–78), in which the "extrajudicial" assassination of Baader at the hands of the German authorities becomes an unmistakable allusion to Christ's crucifixion.

By the early 1980s, Nerdrum had begun to develop the jarring alternate universe that is the setting for most of his mature work. These paintings allow fleeting access to a stark, apocalyptic world populated by the likes of "Seed Protectors," "Namegivers," and "Water Protectors"—recurring characters whose very names convey something of the primordial dramas they enact. Nerdrum has said that these works represent "modern man having returned to primeval society in his flight from civilization. He no longer has any roots in our time. He is back in a prehistoric existence." Nerdrum himself clearly sympathizes with the "flight from civilization"—he is a student of both Max Horkheimer and Oswald Spengler. Yet while his subjects have left the modern world behind, theirs is no Edenic utopia. The figures in Nerdrum's paintings bear the existential scars of modernity on their anguished, contorted faces. They reflect the paradox that man can find contentment neither within civilization, nor without it.

Despite their horrific dimension, Nerdrum's paintings are imbued with an almost heart-rending spiritual pathos. Ensconced in their mythic, ahistorical otherworld, and bathed in the lustrous glow of transcendental Spirit, his subjects betray that pained longing for eternity—Nietzsche's *"alle Lust will Ewigkeit"*—which once characterized the Western tradition. In our modern, deconstructed world, such longings are barely comprehensible, at least to

About the Cover Artist

THE PAINTER WITH A SELF-PORTRAIT, LATE 1990S.
(PHOTO COURTESY OF ODD NERDRUM)

the jaded intelligentsia. So disgusted is Nerdrum with the cynical intellectualism of his art world colleagues, that he regularly denies he is an artist at all. He has ceremoniously crowned himself the "King of Kitsch"—if "kitsch" is defined as representational art, aimed at man's profoundest emotional, religious, and even erotic feelings.

In his writings and speeches, Nerdrum has explored the historical processes that led to this distinction: "In the same way Christianity demonized its competitors, so too did Modernism. And the ruler of Modernism's hell was christened 'kitsch'..." In Nerdrum's contrarian appropriation of the term, kitsch "serves life and therefore seeks the individual, in contradiction to art's irony and dispassion." The intractable conflict to which Nerdrum bears witness can be summed up in one of the painter's pithy aphorisms: "Art is a car. Kitsch is a horse."

Nerdrum recently relocated his family to Iceland, having severed all ties with the despised Norwegian media and modern art mafia. The backgrounds in many of his paintings are modeled after his new homeland's bleak but dramatic lunar landscape, and he is an enthusiastic student of the *Eddas* and sagas. In addition to painting, Nerdrum has served as artistic director for a number of films. These include Hrafn Gunnlaugsson's *Myrkrahöfðinginn* (Witchcraft/Flames of Paradise, 1999), which chronicles the confrontation between Christianity and renascent pagan witchcraft in a seventeenth-century Icelandic rural outpost.

The painting which graces the cover of this issue of *TYR* is Odd Nerdrum's 1992 work, *Five People Around a Waterhole*. We extend our gratitude to the King of Kitsch for his kind permission to reproduce it here.

(*Joshua Buckley and Michael Moynihan*)

Sources:

Castor, Paul A. "The Importance of Being Odd: Odd Nerdrum's Challenge to Modernism," *Artcyclopedia*, 2004. <http://www.artcyclopedia.com/feature-2004-02.html>

Nerdrum, Odd. *Themes.* Oslo: Press Publishing, 2007.

Nerdrum, Odd, et al. *On Kitsch.* Oslo: Kagge Forlag, 2001.

Tisdall, Jonathan. "Odd Nerdrum Near Icelandic Citizenship," *Aftenposten*, 12 December 2003. <www.aftenposten.no/english/local/article690154.ece>

Vine, Richard. *Odd Nerdrum: Paintings, Sketches, and Drawings.* Oslo: Gyldendal Norsk Forlag, 2001.

ROBERT WARD (LEFT) PERFORMING A BLÓT, 1997.
(PHOTO BY JUSTIN FOTION)

Dedication

This issue of *TYR* is respectfully dedicated to the memory of Robert Martin Ward (10 December 1968–17 September 2004).

Robert was a writer, editor, and graphic designer, best known for his work on the pioneering underground culture magazine *The Fifth Path* (1990–94). What set *The Fifth Path* apart from other periodicals of the time was its unique content and perspective. Marshalling together seemingly unrelated elements of avant-garde youth culture, the occult, and neopaganism, the magazine helped create a niche that Robert's many imitators and successors continue to inhabit. The fact that *The Fifth Path* boldly defied virtually every shibboleth held dear by the alternative culture mandarins only added to its appeal.

After *The Fifth Path* ceased publication, Robert assumed the editorship of the Northern European pagan magazine *Vor Tru*. He brought with him his considerable abilities as an artist and designer. He also expanded the magazine's scope beyond its organizational and antiquarian focus, to include the sort of broader underground cultural concerns that had characterized *The Fifth Path*. Once again, this elicited both praise and consternation. It also increased *Vor Tru's* circulation exponentially.

During his lifetime, Robert was involved with numerous artistic initiatives, local musical and cultural events, and publishing ventures. He also dedicated considerable energy to various

Germanic reconstructionist religious groups in northern California, where he resided for all of his life.

Robert lives on in the hearts and minds of those who drew inspiration from his friendship and work. The editors of *TYR* partake of that fount of inspiration, and dedicate this issue of *TYR* to his legacy.

(Joshua Buckley and Michael Moynihan)